Pittsburgh Series in Composition,
Literacy, and Culture

David Bartholomae and
Jean Ferguson Carr,
Editors

THE ORIGINS OF COMPOSITION STUDIES IN THE AMERICAN COLLEGE, 1875–1925

A DOCUMENTARY HISTORY

John C. Brereton, Editor

University of Pittsburgh Press
Pittsburgh and London

Published by the University of Pittsburgh Press,
Pittsburgh, Pa. 15260

Copyright © 1995, University of Pittsburgh Press

Manufactured in the United States of America

Printed on acid-free paper

Library of Congress Cataloging-in-Publication Data
The origins of composition studies in the American college,
1875–1925: a documentary history / John C. Brereton,
editor.
p. cm.—(Pittsburgh series in composition, literacy, and
culture)
Includes bibliographical references (p.).
ISBN 0-8229-3783-2 (acid-free paper).—ISBN 0-8229-5535-0
(pbk.: acid-free paper)
1. English language—Rhetoric—Study and teaching—
United States—History—19th century.   2. English
language—Rhetoric—Study and teaching—United States—
History—20th century.   3. Education, Higher—United
States—History.   I. Brereton, John C.   II. Series.
PE1405.U6075   1994
808'.042'071173—dc20   94-19483
                                                   CIP

A CIP catalogue record for this book is available from the
British Library.

Eurospan, London

Acknowledgments
For permission to reprint materials I wish to thank the
following: Harper Collins Publishers for Rollo Walter Brown,
Dean Briggs; Purdue University for Herbert LeSourd Creek
and James Hugh McKee, "The Preparation in English of
Purdue Freshmen," from *Purdue Studies in Higher Education* 5;
the University of California for Howard Eugene Potter,
*Abilities and Disabilities in the Use of English Found in the
Written Compositions of Entering Freshmen at the University of
California;* and the University of Wisconsin for Warner
Taylor, *A National Survey of Conditions in Freshman English.*

To the memory of
Mina P. Shaughnessy

Contents

6. Writing the Essay   437

Preface

RECENT YEARS HAVE WITNESSED A RESURGENCE OF interest in the history of English studies, part of an attempt to understand how the present got to be the way it is. In composition studies this work has taken many forms: the two-volume history by James Berlin; monographs on a single aspect of rhetoric's history like those by Anne Ruggles Gere, Nan Johnson, and Sharon Crowley; historical articles by Robert Connors and Donald Stewart; and book-length analyses relying on history, like those by Susan Miller. These and other scholars and critics have different purposes and subject matter, but they all seem to gravitate toward the formative years of English as a discipline, during the last third of the nineteenth century. Their constant return to beginnings recalls the way French historians are continually reinterpreting the French Revolution. They do it not in order to achieve any kind of "fixed" understanding of the historical circumstances, but because the events of 1789 are the site of the French citizens' sense of what France is all about; as France changes, so does the French historian's search for a usable past. It may be that scholars of English studies in general and composition in particular, in their modest way, share this characteristic with the French; they will always be defining themselves by their relationship to their origins. (I am also aware that some regard the French fascination with their revolution as little short of an obsession.)

To aid this ongoing reexamination of origins, this book gathers together in one place some of the major documents in the establishment of composition studies. Many scholars have used some of these documents in research libraries and university archives; now a wider audience can have easy access to original sources. For literature, Gerald Graff and Michael Warner have led the way in producing *The Origins of Literary*

Studies in America: A Documentary Anthology. I hope this collection can serve the same purpose as theirs, to supply researchers, students, and all those interested in the history of English composition with some of the most significant documents in readily accessible form. A good many of these original documents are hard to find. Some exist only in a few large research libraries; many are old and crumbling books printed on acid paper. Even the best research libraries do not have them all.

Now is a particularly appropriate time for such a collection. The past fifteen or twenty years have witnessed what seems to be a distinct stage in the recovery of the history of the discipline. In 1991 Robert Connors and Nan Johnson each mapped out two distinct phases of historical research: an early period, dating roughly from 1935 to 1955, which included historical research mainly conducted by members of speech departments, and the current one, beginning in about 1970, which has been dominated by composition scholars (Connors, "Writing" 55; Johnson 7–14; North, using different criteria, also discerns two "generations" of historians, 66–68). The 1970–90 research into the origins of college composition is rooted in the dramatic changes that occurred within composition studies during the 1970s, when the field first began to cohere as a distinct academic discipline. New thinking about the composing process, about teaching writing to entirely different groups of students, and about the purview of composition research reinvigorated the field and gave it a renewed sense of professional standing. Composition specialists of the 1970s and 1980s, eager to distinguish what was best about their field, quite naturally emphasized the change from poor composition teaching to good. In some cases they frankly acknowledged a "propagandistic agenda" to become "reformers as well as scholars" (Connors, cited in North 87; Vitanza 79–83). In an attempt to separate the good from the bad, and to disown what they saw as generations of unproductive teaching and textbook writing, some condemned the great mass of composition work between 1875 and 1960 with the derogatory term "current-traditional rhetoric."

In both eras, 1935–55 and 1970–90, most historians have lamented the transition from traditional rhetoric to modern composition that took place in the late nineteenth century. To them it represented a significant decline, a loss of rhetoric's ancient place as a master discipline of the humanities. One reason for such a view is that most of these historians have been genuine rhetoricians, steeped in the classical tradition or at least impressed enough by it to give it great respect. Naturally, their vantage point encouraged them to see the greatness of rhetoric, its decline in the nineteenth century, and its potential for revival. No one embodies the feeling of decline more than Albert Kitzhaber, whose brilliant 1953 dissertation on nineteenth-century college rhetoric was for so long a prime source for composition's early history. Because of Kitzhaber's great influence, most historians have regarded rhetoric as the ideal, composition as a fall from grace, and the last two decades as the beginnings of a great recovery.

While this perspective has helped colleges to regard composition as a distinct discipline, by letting some insights in it has had to exclude some others. A term like "current-traditional" by its very nature lumps together a vast array of practices in the interest of making a larger point. And it discourages us from looking at a whole range of educational practices that were occurring in those supposedly weak composition courses that proliferated for nearly a century. In other words, interpreting the history of composition as a loss and then a revival of rhetoric has given a partial view, a view that explicitly devalues almost a century of teaching and learning. And an unwieldy name like current-traditional, one that almost scorns precision, is about on a par with "Dark Ages" as a satisfactory investigative or taxonomic tool.

The 1970–90 stage of historical research devoted much more concentrated attention to theory than to practice. One reason for this disparity, no doubt, lies in the fact that theory is easier to get at. Many books and articles embody it, while few tell of practice, especially of what actually happened in the classroom. Another reason lies in a genuine interest in the philosophical underpinnings of nineteenth-century rhetoric, as evidenced by Nan Johnson's and Sharon Crowley's important books on the subject. Still another reason stems from a desire to return to a time when rhetoric was a fully theorized discipline rather than an eclectic assemblage of lore and experimentation. Finally, the interest in theory connects to the way American English departments grew fascinated with literary theory during the 1970s and 1980s. Whatever the source, a good many historians have tended to intellectualize; eager to establish the field as a worthwhile enterprise, we gravitated toward theories, philosophies, and ideologies. We looked for psychologies buried in theories of rhetoric; we pieced out intellectual stances from textbooks; we inferred philosophies from teaching materials. Over and over again we probed, interrogated, and erected theories, trying to determine an underlying philosophy. This yielded excellent results; we now know a good deal more about composition instruction than, say, instruction in English literature. In fact, without quite setting out to do so, historians of composition have created the single most impressive body of knowledge about any discipline in higher education, a fact that seems to surprise historians of other fields (Turner 94–95). Still, in searching for the ideologies, historians sometimes ignored the actuality of the experience of students and teachers, curriculum planners and administrators. Indeed, we rarely looked at the writing itself. Many took textbooks as the embodiments of courses, rather than as necessary props, and looked on administrative plans as the curricular structures. In short, what often got left out was the detail, the everyday fabric of history as lived by the student, the teacher, and the general public. Some historians seemed unconcerned with this loss of detail, while others saw its absence as only temporary, until "after the major currents of the age—important figures and theories—have been mapped out" (Connors, cited in North 73). Now, after so much good work has been done and so much territory has been mapped, may be the time to begin another phase.

This book sets out to supply some—but by no means all—of the connections between theory and practice. The documents reprinted here reveal a number of hitherto hidden points: most of them were excellent examples of rhetoric themselves, attempts at persuasion rather than transparent statements of fact to be taken at face value. (It's a nice irony that historians have sometimes underestimated the rhetorical stance of early textbooks, journal articles, statements of purpose, and manifestos. [For examples of some who *are* aware of the rhetoric, see Berlin, "Revisionary History" 48–50; Schilb 30–31; and Vitanza 83–84.]) The documents also reveal a startling degree of self-consciousness, which has often gone unremarked; early composition theorists and practitioners were very aware of what they were doing, and often made quite conscious choices. Many early-twentieth-century practitioners knew their history. The professional literature abounds with references to progenitors like Alexander Bain, to the inauguration of the Harvard writing program, and to the fading influence of traditional rhetoric. And the documents display a great deal of diversity, which may belie the notion that things were so uniform—or so uniformly bad. Within late-nineteenth- and early-twentieth-century professional discourse one may observe different schools form, join forces, and split apart. As those who have looked closely at the sources know well, it's possible to see a diversity of voices and a conflict of different theories and practices. Also, this volume prints some of the papers themselves, to get at least some idea of what the discussion was about. The lack of these papers in the histories is something of a scandal; even though any piece of student writing cannot fully be understood outside of its context, it seems crucial to know what students were writing, what examples of student prose nineteenth-century scholars and administrators were discussing, and how the writing itself was represented to contemporary eyes.

This book presents the printed record, the key documents known to practitioners at the time. It is not intended to be a "secret history" of composition instruction. University archives have large quantities of student essays, course syllabi, lecture notes, and teaching materials. Though to teachers nothing seems more ephemeral than student papers, students did save them and eventually donate them to university archives. (That a large number of students thought their themes were worth preserving should be a sobering thought to today's teachers penning comments in the margins.) Untold numbers of student papers sit in American college and university archives. These repositories vary widely, from the superb facilities at Harvard's Pusey Library, to a section of the library at Wellesley, to a dreary basement at the University of Minnesota, to a back room full of uncatalogued boxes at New York Theological Seminary. It is in these archives, with their unfailingly helpful staffs, that we will find a fuller selection of student voices, of class notes, of the real record of what the compositions looked like. I have been in archives and found and read many papers, but though this volume prints a range of compositions, I have deliberately taken them from printed rather than manuscript sources; I wanted to publish the public record, what composition specialists said to each other, to their students, and to concerned citizens. Most of the documents here were *not* obscure at the time; the majority were part of the common knowledge of composition teachers and administrators. They were once available for many to read; now they are again.

One limitation that stems from my choice of the public record is that some important kinds of writing get less emphasis. For instance, the most widely circulated professional documents of the time ignore important trends in writing instruction by women: the writing groups chronicled so well by Ann Ruggles Gere, for instance ("Kitchen"). And a great deal of what we would now regard as postsecondary writing was done by immigrants in settlement houses, by men and women in Bible colleges and normal schools, and at historically black institutions. It is clear that many of these groups took goals and methods from white, mainstream universities, but we are learning that some students and some teachers asserted themselves in new and important ways. So my decision to include the major texts of the time, the pieces that aroused the most debate and response, should in no way suggest that I have presented the whole story. The documents I reprint were the ones most fully discussed by the profession at large; scholars are beginning to uncover new and different documents that paint a fuller, more varied picture (Hollis, "Liberating Voices"). There is lots of exciting work ahead in this field.

I am all too aware of the other limitations of this book. The selection is inevitably partial; I have had to be content with portions of key books, all the while knowing that nothing can replace the entire text (and the look and feel) of the original. I am comforted by knowing that many of the major texts of the period are still available at research libraries. The selection is partial in another way too: I concentrate on the first-year composition course, the centerpiece of writing instruction for well over a century. But one could easily print student writing done outside the standard composition class: lab reports, research papers, class notes, remedial writing exercises, advanced composition themes, technical reports, forensics, journalism, diary entries, college magazine pieces, letters home. That anthology would be as thick as anything collected from beginning composition and a good bit more varied. First-year composition came to dominate teaching and professional discourse about college writing instruction, but it in no way dominated writing.

Principles of Selection and Editing

I CHOSE WHAT I considered representative texts from the era, but since I deliberately printed somewhat larger selections from the least accessible documents, length of excerpt does not always correlate to its absolute importance. I have tried to reproduce the original documents precisely, even when this led to certain inconsistencies. For instance, I have retained the original punctuation, spelling, and methods of citation, which changed considerably between 1875 and 1925 and are not always in accordance with modern practices. In a very few cases I have silently corrected obvious typographical errors.

When possible, complete sections have been reprinted. Minor omissions as well as longer omissions are marked with ellipses. All notes appear in the original except for those marked [ED.], but in accordance with modern practice the notes are numbered consecutively and placed at the end of the excerpted section.

In determining the most useful sections of early readers, I decided not to reprint entire essays, since they are usually readily available. Prefatory materials and/or tables of contents have been reprinted, keeping the page numbers in order to indicate the original length of each essay or section.

Throughout the book I have taken care to distinguish between the authors' citations and my own cross references. Within the selections themselves, all page citations are as in the original. Whenever the citation refers to a selection that appears elsewhere in this book, I add the relevant page number in brackets. Outside of the selections (i.e., in introductory material), I have referenced selections that appear elsewhere in this book by citing chapter as well as page.

Acknowledgments

THIS BOOK GREW OUT OF MY LONG-STANDING INTEREST in the history of writing instruction, an interest that led to my 1985 collection, *Traditions of Inquiry*. Over the past fifteen years I have spent more time than I can count in college archives, in periodical rooms, or in tracking down old textbooks. Often it has seemed a solitary occupation, but I've been happy with the knowledge that a good many others have seen fit to engage themselves in this vocation as well. Their work has given me encouragement as well as a good sense of what needed to be done.

The model for this collection of documents is Gerald Graff and Michael Warner's 1989 collection *The Origins of Literary Studies in America*. And over the years my conversations with Gerald Graff about the history of English studies have been enjoyable and helpful. He has been a strong supporter of this project from the very beginning.

Plenty of friends have helped and encouraged me, some I'm sure in ways they didn't even suspect. I simply list their names in thanks: Lynn Z. Bloom, Barbara Couture, Carol Hartzog, Winifred Horner, Nan Johnson, Erika Lindemann, Richard Lloyd-Jones, Donald McQuade, Sharon Quiroz, Hephzibah Roskelly, Mariolina Salvatori, Nancy Sommers, and Edward White. Scholars of composition studies have built a rich body of knowledge that I have drawn upon in ways that go beyond mere citations in the body of the text. In particular, this book is indebted to the work of the late James Berlin, Susan Miller, and the late Donald Stewart. And most of all, Robert J. Connors, both in person and in his many superb articles, has pointed to key issues in composition's historiography.

David Bartholomae first put the idea for this book in my head, and he and Jean Ferguson Carr have helped every step of the way, from cloudy idea to rough proposal to early drafts to final copy. A writer could not ask for smarter, more supportive editors. At the University of Pittsburgh Press, Elizabeth Detwiler provided exemplary guidance through a difficult and lengthy editorial and production process.

This book has benefitted from close readings by friends who devoted time and energy to helping me get the history right. I particularly want to thank John Burt, Neal Bruss, Richard Marius, Linda Peterson, and David Russell for being willing to read the whole manuscript and give me their reactions. My best critic, as always, has been Virginia Lieson Brereton, a writing teacher, a writer, and a historian of education whose questions and close readings have improved this book immeasurably. I hope I have incorporated all my readers' best suggestions, but of course I take full responsibility for any failings the finished book may have.

At the University of Massachusetts at Boston I have been surrounded by some of the best (and nicest) writing scholars in the country, and lunches, coffee breaks, and hallway conversations with Pamela Annas, Elsa Auerbach, Ann E. Berthoff,[1] Neal Bruss, Judith Goleman, Susan Horton, Eleanor Kutz, Donaldo Macedo, Margaret Mansfield, Louise Smith, and Vivian Zamel have been a source of support and enlightenment. Parts of this book were presented, in different form, at the UMass/Boston graduate colloquium series, and the responses of colleagues and students have made it stronger.

At UMass my research assistants have made my task much easier. For one semester Anya Bonduransky and Sandra Howland helped gather information. For three semesters Coleen O'Hanley and Helen Price have provided superb assistance with everything from fact checking to copyediting to proofreading. Hundreds of places throughout the book are better because they cared.

A book like this also depends on great libraries and their staffs. I first started work at the University of Michigan's superb libraries. Most of the additional work took place at the Boston Public Library, the New York Public Library, the archives of the Universities of Minnesota and Wisconsin, Boston University's Mugar Library, the Library of Congress, the libraries at the University of Massachusetts at Amherst and at Boston, and most of all, the Pusey and Widener Libraries of Harvard University.[2]

Finally, it is a pleasure to acknowledge the National Endowment for the Humanities for an award that provided much-needed time and the University of Massachusetts at Boston for a sabbatical leave in 1991.

NOTES

1. Ann E. Berthoff also gave me the copy of Woolley's *Handbook of Composition* her father used as a student at Cornell College in 1915.

2. Part of my enjoyment in working in the Widener Library is that so many of its books were once owned by the very people I am writing about. Thus the copy of Adams Sherman Hill's *Principles of Rhetoric* I used had been President Charles W. Eliot's own, with Hill's compliments written on the flyleaf.

The Origins of
Composition Studies in
the American College,
1875–1925

I

Introduction

THE COMPOSITION COURSE AS WE KNOW IT TODAY, like the university that teaches it, is a product of late-nineteenth-century America. Both began life in the 1870s, in the age of invention that saw the birth of the hydraulic elevator, the electric light, the telephone, and the phonograph, and both were shaped by the reform impulses that pervaded late-nineteenth- and early-twentieth-century America during the Progressive Era.

Right after the Civil War the American college (there were no universities) was an institution in danger of becoming irrelevant to a rapidly changing nation. The small number of students who attended college were drawn mostly from a fairly narrow range of society, and the collegiate curriculum did not do much to broaden their horizons. Almost all colleges put their students through a four-year program of required courses. There were no majors, hardly any electives, no sections, and precious little course work outside of classics, mathematics, and some science. It was hard to find a course in English literature, history, or a modern language. Classes were conducted by the recitation method, with students mastering a text for homework and "reciting" it, upon the teacher's demand, in class. There was no discussion, no question period, and lectures were reserved mostly for seniors. The professors were rarely professional educators or scholars. Faculty were often Protestant clergymen; the college was dominated by the president, who customarily taught the seniors a course in "moral philosophy," a mix of religion and ethics. The purpose of the college was to build character, not to supply useful knowledge. This school, dominant in 1860, would be swept away by 1900.

The rise of the university took place very rapidly; in a single generation, from 1870 to 1900, the American college moved from a unified small, elite school to a diverse, large, fragmented university organized by academic disciplines. In the field of writing instruction, it is tempting to make a neat distinction between the old college and the new university on the basis of orality versus literacy. The evidence shows that orality was highly regarded in the pre-1860 college, while literacy became increasingly important from 1860 on. Oral examinations in the college were replaced by written ones in the university; public oral discourse gave way to written compositions. A curriculum that honored speech by providing opportunities for declamations, disputations, and debates became heavily weighted toward writing, toward the page of text. But such a distinction overlooks how large a role literacy played in the old college; it seems more accurate to say that the nineteenth-century college had a more balanced mix of oral and written work, and that the new university dropped much of the oral emphasis and consequently valued the written word much more. Plenty of writing took place in eighteenth- and nineteenth-century colleges. At Yale in 1766, "compositions" were handed in to the instructor before they were delivered orally (Wozniak 8). And the University of North Carolina's archives contain many early nineteenth-century compositions (Lindemann, "Student Writing"). Lab notes and lecture notes were rigorously kept. Attention to grammar, spelling, and punctuation were handled every day through work in Latin and Greek. In fact, the old college was much more language-based than the new university; classics masters taught grammar thoroughly and exactly, paying meticulous attention to detail through class exercises, recitations, and written compositions in Greek and Latin and in written translations into English. Proponents claimed that the ancient languages provided mental discipline and trained the powers of the mind, pointing to the extremely close attention to the details of language, both oral and written, that characterized college Greek and Latin classes.

Though the old college stressed language study, English rarely had an official presence in the curriculum. A few institutions made provision for a professor of English or belles lettres, and most colleges fostered speech making, essay writing, and literary readings in a host of extracurricular student-run clubs, but most colleges in 1860 had no course in composition or in English literature. By 1900, on the other hand, every college had an array of composition and English literature courses. What happened? The creation of the modern university transformed writing instruction. Composition rose as an academic subject with the new university, and it took on the special characteristics it did because of the way the new university was formed. Of all the complex factors that influenced the university's formation, four stand out: the influence of the German university model, the changing nature of knowledge, the dramatic expansion of higher education, and the efforts of a few visionaries to update the university's purview. All of these factors were to shatter traditional rhetoric and to aid in the emergence of modern composition.

The German Model

BEGINNING IN THE EARLY nineteenth century, Americans in search of advanced degrees went to Germany and returned imbued with the university ideal. The German universities they studied at stressed research, the creation rather than the transmission of knowledge. In 1876 Johns Hopkins University was founded on the German model and overnight became the single most potent force for upgrading the educational standards of American scholarship.

The ten thousand or so Americans who studied in Germany between 1815 and 1915 (Diehl 1) quite naturally imported key parts of the German university when they could: lectures rather than recitations (lectures in American colleges had been mostly reserved for seniors); seminars for truly advanced work, including graduate instruction; and a model of conceptualizing academic subject matter that emphasized freedom of inquiry, fostered a high degree of specialization, and stressed the links between research and teaching. This German influence helped shape the American graduate schools, but it had a whole series of side effects on undergraduate rhetoric and composition programs. First of all, it encouraged specialization in place of breadth. The old liberal arts ideal stressed the essential unity of knowledge, a common set of courses, and a reliance on the tried-and-true classics of antiquity. The German model stressed innovation, electives, and specialization. Following this German ideal (if not the exact model, which was altered as it crossed the Atlantic), professors immersed themselves in their studies or laboratories to produce research, the disciplines organized themselves on scholarly rather than pedagogical lines, and universities slowly abandoned much low-level teaching to an underclass of instructors and graduate student assistants. Finally, the German model did not include rhetoric; Americans interested in English studies came home with a German doctorate in philology, not rhetoric. And writing instruction was missing too; German (as well as most other European) universities simply did not teach composition. Students learned writing in lower schools; all who earned the coveted secondary school diploma passed a stringent series of written tests, and the tiny percentage who went on to university were usually quite competent writers. University professors did not study the process of composition, student writing style, topic selection, or audience. Germany, source of so much American scholarship, simply had no models for rhetoric and composition on the university level. Thus the adoption of the German model meant the breakup of old arrangements, and among those arrangements was the very prominent scheme of rhetorical education that would not survive the century.

Expansion of Knowledge

THE SECOND ENGINE behind the growth of the new university was the dramatic expansion of knowledge, particularly in the sciences. American ingenuity and the native intelligence of people like Thomas A. Edison (who attended school for all of three months) produced a stream of wonderful inventions, while universities were producing theoretical advances at an astounding rate in biology, geology, physics, and chemistry. Specialized training in these fields required specialized knowledge, and the nineteenth century saw a protracted struggle between the proponents of a classical education (codified by the Yale report of 1828, in Hofstadter and Smith I: 275–91) and those who favored the new science-based learning. Already by 1803 the new military academy at West Point trained engineers, and the founding of Rensselaer Polytechnic Institute in 1824 and the inauguration of a new scientific curriculum at Union College in 1828 had pointed the way to the future (Rudolph, *Curriculum* 141). The forces of this expanded knowledge led to the founding in the 1840s of the Sheffield Scientific School at Yale and the Lawrence Scientific School at Harvard; both offered three-year practical programs that had lower admissions standards and omitted the specialized Latin and Greek curriculum. At Lawrence the presiding genius was the great zoologist Louis Agassiz; but one of the junior faculty was

German-trained Charles William Eliot, later to be Harvard's president. On the staff at Sheffield was Daniel Coit Gilman, also German-trained, who would become the first president of Johns Hopkins. These two scientists, soon to head major universities, believed strongly in specialization, in allowing students to concentrate their studies in electives rather than forcing them to take required courses. Until the Civil War the American college had succeeded in channeling the demand for scientific training and specialization into second-class academic institutions, but the dominance of the classical curriculum would not last much longer. As Richard Ohmann claimed in "Writing and Reading, Work and Leisure," the emergence of the new university would make a traditional, unified subject like rhetoric obsolete and replace it with a new, utilitarian writing course, more attuned to the times (see also Douglas, "Rhetoric for the Meritocracy").

Increase in Students

COLLEGES IN 1865 were small, hardly an important part of the American prospect. They did not play a large role in American intellectual life; that was the province of general circulation magazines, newspapers, lyceums, and theaters. Neither was culture dominated by colleges; many an eminent writer (Walt Whitman, Harriet Beecher Stowe, Mark Twain, William Dean Howells) had never studied in one. The three traditional fields that colleges prepared for, the ministry, the bar, and medicine, all offered alternative means of certification, though naturally the college-educated still dominated. Americans were well aware that the president who saw the North through the Civil War, Abraham Lincoln, an acknowledged master of eloquence, was not a college graduate.

College enrollments were relatively static in the years 1850–80, growing much less than the population. Then came the boom. Between 1890 and 1910 enrollments practically doubled, and by 1920 almost doubled again (see Veysey 4; Cremin 545; Connors, "Modern University" 80–81). This explosion of students called for a vast increase in faculty members (with a huge rise in graduate enrollments to train them). College became a much larger part of the American scene by the turn of the century; college was important and exciting, even if it still enrolled a small percentage of the population.

Individuals with a Vision

THE FINAL INGREDIENT in the change stemmed from the determined efforts of many individuals to change American higher education. Laurence Veysey's *The Emergence of the American University* chronicles the efforts of the men who in the space of thirty years led their universities into a new era: Andrew White of Cornell, James Angell of Michigan, Daniel Coit Gilman of Johns Hopkins, David Starr Jordan of Stanford, and many others. Already in 1862, at the height of the Civil War, farsighted congressmen had passed the Morrill Act, which provided for the establishment of land-grant universities, with special attention to agriculture and technology. (Mining, engineering, and even farming were themselves becoming complex enough that trained expertise was seen as necessary.) The 1865 founding of Cornell University, a school which promised that anyone could learn anything there, was a sign that a determined philanthropist with enough money could influence the course of education. And the individual who seems to symbolize the change the most is Charles W. Eliot, Harvard's president from 1869 to 1909, the man who transformed Harvard into a modern university. Eliot had graduated from Harvard, studied in Germany, taught chemistry at Harvard's Lawrence Scientific School, then moved to the newly founded MIT. He had outlined a model of a modern university in two *Atlantic Monthly* articles (February and March 1869; excerpted in Hofstadter and Smith II: 624–41). His accession to the Harvard presidency was regarded at the time as a sign of dramatic change at America's most prestigious university.

By 1869, when Charles W. Eliot was inaugurated as Harvard's president, all the conditions were ripe for a transformation of the American college into a modern university. And with Eliot's accession came what we now know as English composition.

The Birth of the Modern Composition Program

THE FIRST MODERN composition program was begun at Harvard, with President Charles W. Eliot as its sponsor and his classmate Adams Sherman Hill as its creator. Other colleges quickly followed Harvard's lead, but it is to Harvard that we must look for the rationale behind the rise of composition. Eliot's Harvard did not introduce English composition or English literature to the American college; as documents in chapter 2 show, there was extensive instruction in rhetoric and writing at Harvard and elsewhere well before 1869. What Eliot did was to ally the modern university with a new emphasis on English and to raise writing and English literature to the level of more hallowed studies like mathematics and classics. English for Eliot was to be the modern, up-to-date equivalent of the ancient subjects, a preparation for citizenship and productive work in the modern American democracy (Douglas, "Rhetoric for the Meritocracy").

To carry out his new emphasis on English, Eliot in 1872 appointed Adams Sherman Hill, a lawyer turned newspaperman, as assistant to Harvard's Boylston Professor of Rhetoric, Francis James Child, a German-trained Ph.D. who preferred collecting ballads and researching literature to reading student themes. Hill quickly set up the first change, a placement examination in English composition, based on literary topics, with writing linked to literature. (A description of that first examination appears in chap. 2, p. 34.) In this manner English entered Harvard's extensive entrance examination schedule, and all preparatory schools had to change their curriculum to accommodate Harvard. (The documents in chap. 2 link the new placement examination with Harvard's attempt to upgrade secondary school education.)

The traditional, pre-Eliot Harvard writing program, like that at most colleges, required a mix of oral and written composition throughout all four years of college, with a single rhetoric course to provide a theoretical grounding in the principles of effective prose, usually by way of brief examples from the English classics. Students did not learn to write in a single course, but got instruction at all stages of their academic careers. As David Russell has shown, this system was at risk with the rise of the disciplines and especially with Eliot's great innovation, the elective system. When students had a set curriculum for four years, a college could build in additional help or add on workshops, confident that the assistance would reach all students at the same stage in their studies. But when electives took a larger and larger share of a student's time, a workshop here or a required course there would intersect each student's career differently. What worked well in the old curriculum—small amounts of writing instruction strategically placed throughout a common curriculum—did not fit in with the new. Soon writing, like everything else, was confined to well-defined courses, and at Harvard after the turn of the century, required composition dwindled to the first-year course and some very limited upper-level requirements that were soon to disappear entirely (Russell 51–56). A small number of elective writing courses would remain at Harvard and elsewhere, but they would have nothing like the enrollment of first-year composition and very little impact on the intellectual life of the English department.

If the elective system cordoned off writing instruction into single courses and inexorably did away with upper-level writing requirements, an even larger change loomed ahead. At Harvard and elsewhere, knowledge was being partitioned into departments; English organized itself as a distinct discipline, slowly but surely imbued itself with the research ideal (not without battles, as Graff's *Professing Literature* makes clear), and began to grow. Yet the single largest part of English studies in the 1880s, composition, did not have a research agenda of its own; the principles of teaching writing were not in question, so what was there for a scholar to study? Adams Sherman Hill's *Principles of Rhetoric* (1878), like most other nineteenth-century rhetoric texts, argued that rhetoric was an art, not a science (Kitzhaber 76–81; Hill, chap. 5, p. 321). Over time, this was to be a devastating stance, for the art/science divide was what separated the old knowledge from the new; art was often related to skills that could be inculcated, while science was connected to knowledge, to research, in short, to the new disciplines that were embarked on expansion. To argue that rhetoric was not a science, not a way of knowing, was to consign it to training, to an introductory level of college, to pedagogy. If it was art, its instruction depended upon the skill of the teacher, not on a knowledge base built up by concentrated study, by research. There was nothing to discover, only some pedagogical arrangements to be worked out, some teaching methods to be made more efficient. And that is where the energy went, into teaching, correcting countless themes, and writing textbooks. Over the next twenty or so years, Harvard's English staff threw itself into the work of teaching writing, publishing widely in composition, and developing an ambitious and successful program. But the writing faculty did little rhetorical research, produced no advancement in knowledge, and earned themselves a reputation as teachers, not scholars, a serious handicap in the new university.

Over a relatively short time Harvard created a genuine composition program, a system of instruction that stood out as an example to imitate or avoid. At that time Harvard was one of the largest and certainly the most respected of American colleges; in 1909 its enrollment of 5,558 was second only to Columbia's (Slosson 475). Its football team was dominant, its professors were eminent, its president was the most famous educational leader in the nation. It cast a shadow over the college scene as no American university ever has, before or since. And Harvard went about composition, like everything else, in a big way. At its height in 1880–1910, the Harvard system included three elements: a particular kind of writing; a wide array of course work; and an eminent, highly visible composition staff. Some colleges had one or two of these elements; no place had them all, or in anything approaching the depth of Harvard. The Harvard program marks the only time a major university made such a total commitment to student writing. For thirty years the United States' oldest and most prestigious college devoted the majority of its English teaching resources to composition from the first year to senior level, from entrance examinations to senior forensics, from advanced composition to writing across the curriculum. Some of the most famous scholars and critics in America devoted the best part of their intellectual energy to student writing. There has never been anything like it.

Harvard's standard, required composition course was English A, first given in sophomore year and then, after 1885, moved to the first year. In 1899–1900 its enrollment of 620 to 630 students and staff of eleven instructors made it one of the largest college courses of any type in the country (Copeland and Rideout 1). English A was a two-semester course in rhetoric and writing almost totally based on Adams Sherman Hill's *Principles of Rhetoric;* though plenty of literary topics were covered, there were no outside readings. In 1900–01 writing assignments included a mix of daily themes, which were brief two or three paragraph sketches, and more extended fortnightly themes; topics were up to the student and thus varied widely, but the dailies usually asked for personal experience while the longer ones covered a mix of general knowledge. Two characteristics marked English A and most other writing courses at Harvard: the insistence that students develop their own topics, and the absence of extended readings outside the textbook; hardly any teachers assigned essays or poems or plays for reactions. In fact, in contrast to other contemporary rhetoric programs (e.g., Genung's at Amherst, or Gayley's at Berkeley) there was hardly any emphasis upon reading at all. (Chapter 6, p. 439, presents the examination required in Hill's English A for the 1887–88 academic year.)

The writing course that Harvard is most famous for is daily themes, English 12 (see chap. 2, pp. 32 and 107), which was an elective course originated in 1884 by the young Barrett Wendell; elements of it were later transferred to the first year (Copeland and Rideout). In 1905 Charles T. Copeland took over English 12 and kept it famous until the late 1920s.

Upper-level writing courses played a major role at Harvard. In 1896 sophomores were required to take one of three one-semester courses, depending on their grades in first-year English: English B for the weakest or English 22 and English 31 for the strongest writers. Another writing course, English 5, was aimed at graduate students. Other important writing courses included senior forensics, which taught argumentative writing through the subject matter of the students' own upper-level work in other courses. Forensics were in many ways holdovers from the old era of rhetorical education and were a constant source of English department tinkering. David Russell's *Writing in the Academic Disciplines, 1870–1990* gives an excellent overview of Harvard's advanced writing instruction at every stage in a student's career (see especially 51–61); at first it was much like the built-in writing instruction that characterized the old pre-1860 college. But in an environment increasingly hostile to writing instruction, Harvard's upper-level writing courses virtually disappeared after 1910.

Besides its distinctive writing course work, Harvard boasted the most famous array of rhetoricians in the nation. The Boylston Professorship of Rhetoric and Oratory, founded in the eighteenth century, had been filled by eminent professors from the very beginning, when John Quincy Adams, its first occupant, published his lectures. Edward Tyrrell Channing, occupant from 1819 to 1851 and the rhetoric teacher of Emerson, Thoreau, Motley, Prescott, and Parkman, also published his lectures (see Scott, chap. 3, p. 179). Francis Child, occupant from 1851 to 1876, published in literature and philology, not in rhetoric, and when almost lured away by a job offer from Johns Hopkins, was persuaded to become Harvard's first professor of English with the understanding that he would no longer have to read student themes (Kitzhaber 33). He was replaced in the Boylston chair by Hill from 1876 to 1904. The next two occupants were also extremely visible figures in the field: Le Baron Russell Briggs from 1904 to 1925 and Charles T. Copeland from 1925 to 1937, both revered men on campus, dedicated to undergraduates, eminent teachers (they were not Ph.D.'s and did not conduct scholarly research), and strong believers in the composition program. In addition to this string of Boylston professors, Harvard had Barrett Wendell, whose *English Composition* (1891) was by far the most elegant and urbane treatment of rhetoric and composition to date. These were true academic stars, known across the country in the profession, a formidable array of talent unmatched elsewhere. And besides those stars were others who worked in the Harvard program like Byron Hurlbut, who later served as dean, George Pierce Baker, who wrote *Specimens of Argumentation* before moving in 1925 to begin the drama program at Yale, and George Rice Carpenter, who wrote on composition at Harvard and later was a professor of rhetoric at Columbia. And of course there were many instructors and lecturers who taught composition while working toward a doctoral or a law degree, men who left Harvard with strong impressions of the writing program (see Phelps and Aydelotte, chap. 4; Manly, chap. 5; Valentine, chap. 6). The presence of eminent figures like Briggs and Copeland meant that by 1900, when composition was losing its luster elsewhere and men like Wendell were confessing that theme writing didn't seem to train students well enough, the Harvard program remained vital, perhaps past its time. Composition had more prestige at Harvard than elsewhere, and its prominence lasted longer. But when Copeland retired in 1937, Harvard marked a definite break in the tradition by appointing the poet Robert Hillyer, not a rhetorician, to the Boylston professorship. For half a century Harvard's program depended on powerful teachers, not scholars; it never developed a graduate research program in rhetoric that might have given undergraduate instruction the needed stability or theoretical sophistication.

Most colleges followed Harvard in replacing the traditional required rhetorical work spread over four years with a single year-long required first-year course; this is the freshman composition course that by 1900 had taken hold almost everywhere. (Other colleges also attempted to offer upper-level writing courses, mostly as electives.) The rapid spread of the freshman composition course has been described by John Michael Wozniak, who traces the transformation of traditional rhetoric into modern composition by following textbook adoptions at Eastern colleges.

Harvard's Critics

THE HARVARD CURRICULUM from 1875 to 1910 had its critics at the time and has had them ever since. Perhaps because it represented such a commitment to writing instead of to literature, the Harvard system gave rise to much dissent, both at home and at rival colleges. Essentially it was attacked for three reasons: for not making a difference in student writing, for being expensive in terms of a teacher's time and energy, and for distracting faculty efforts from more important things (i.e., literature). Chapter 4 contains some of the many attacks on the Harvard curriculum.

From the outset there was a traditional alternative to the Harvard program that persisted relatively unchanged for many years in smaller colleges. This was an old-fashioned rhetoric course that set an eighteenth- or early-nineteenth-century textbook by Blair, Campbell, or Whately to be mastered by students and tested in recitations and examinations. By the mid-1890s, fully twenty years after Harvard's program began, a few colleges in the East were using one of the traditional texts (Wozniak 145). Such an approach lasted because faculty members were wedded to it, or because a college prided itself on its traditionalism, or because the college was simply bypassed by intellectual currents. Significantly, the very traditional approaches survived at colleges, not universities, in the East and South.

Chapter 4 concentrates on a number of alternatives to the Harvard system, alternatives that would eventually overwhelm Harvard's method and in turn remain dominant for more than half a century. The first alternative to the Harvard method, as outlined by two strong articles in the popular press ("Two Ways of Teaching English," chap. 4, p. 238 and Lounsbury, chap. 4, p. 261), was to require no writing at all. Students would arrive in college with good writing abilities and would pick up additional writing practice as a function of their work in other courses. To operate this way a college would have to have extremely high entrance requirements and a reliable supply of good students from feeder schools. A few colleges could make this alternative work successfully for a long time (Princeton was one), and over the years some colleges, thinking their entering students good enough to survive without direct writing instruction, abolished required composition and assumed that students would improve their writing through course work in what were called the "content areas." This somewhat haphazard approach to writing instruction was understandably implemented at relatively few colleges, and only sporadically. The no-writing alternative was not what eventually displaced the Harvard system. What eventually prevailed was an eclectic mix of three other approaches: personal writing, writing about literature, and writing about ideas.

The personal writing course is often thought of as "pure" composition; it consists of just students and teacher, with no rhetoric textbook, no anthology of readings, maybe just a handbook for reference. This course's roots lie in the quite personal topics students wrote about in Harvard's writing courses, descriptive sketches that captured a moment or a mood (for samples see chap. 6, p. 514). At Harvard such themes were not meant to explore the inner self or to be regarded as truly expressive pieces of writing; rather they were to represent an individual perspective on experience, and so topics were never assigned. They are remarkably close to some forms of creative writing and also have affinities with an artist's sketchbook. In the late nineteenth century everyday experience was proving rich material for a new generation of American painters and writers, so it is no surprise that some influence shows up in theme writing, particularly in a program run by a former journalist like Hill and in the classes of a sometime novelist like Wendell; and they even show up in Genung's aims for his students' themes at Amherst. (See chap. 3, p. 133; Miller, *Textual Carnivals* 58–59, critiques this new type of theme topic.)

At the University of Michigan in the 1890s Fred Newton Scott argued for using such personal themes to connect writing to real experience. To be sure, this same rationale was used for the Harvard program; in fact, throughout this period it is fairly easy to find statements about how writing is best when it springs from real experience. Such statements, unfortunately, are not evidence that much raw, unfiltered experience was permitted in the classroom or in papers. The true test of whether student experience was valued comes not from statements of high purpose but from actual practice in the classroom and the writing itself. Scott's argument for a genuinely personal approach to writing has had a good many adherents over the years, but during the period 1875–1925 it was never close to dominant. At Vassar, Scott's student Gertrude Buck wrote articles that provided some of the most sensible rationale for this kind of writing (see chap. 4, p. 241) and wrote a text embodying it.

The modern composition course devoted to writing about English literature predated the Harvard composition program; it was invented and popularized by one of the most prominent linguists of the late nineteenth century, Thomas Lounsbury at Yale, a man who had long experience reading student themes during his teaching career. Yale, which did not require composition, was in 1870 the site of Lounsbury's most innovative course, a literature elective requiring plenty of student writing. This in embryonic form was the kind of course that would be widely adopted throughout the country by 1900 and has persisted to this day, at Yale and elsewhere, a sort of introduction to literature which required writing about the literary points of the reading. This approach assumed that writing worked best when students had something substantial to write about, and that the most substantial thing an English department could provide was English literature. Cornell operated under this belief (see James Morgan Hart, "Cornell Course" 183), as did many liberal arts colleges. The literature course grew so common that there were any number of variations upon it, all of which contained some elements of the old rhetoric course's emphasis on belles lettres, style, and examples drawn from English literature. In the most common type of literature-based course students read a wide variety of English (and later, American) works: poems, some plays, plus a novel or two, and wrote critical essays about them. Indeed, it was often in such composition courses that students got their first English department exposure to current American authors, most of whom were excluded from literature course work.

By the time the literature-based composition course became popular a hierarchy began to develop: the better the student, the more literature in the composition course. We can see this operating at Yale at the beginning of our era, and at Wisconsin at the end. Throughout the era 1875–1925, literary works prevailed in elite colleges (with the exception of Harvard), while the least prestigious colleges concentrated more on grammar and mechanics drills. At Wisconsin in the 1920s, 65 percent of first-year students had some literature in their composition course, and the best students had all literature (Taylor, chap. 7, p. 555).

The third alternative, the idea course, became popular after the turn of the century and won many influential adherents; it consisted of close analysis of important essays, a sort of literary nonfiction course with the emphasis upon the structure of the ideas, definitely not the style, and rarely the effect. The first such course was introduced at Indiana in the 1890s by Frank Aydelotte; by 1915 it had spread to Columbia, Wisconsin, and to many other schools that employed one of the popular anthologies stressing this approach, Foerster, Manchester, and Young's *Essays for College Men* or Steeves and Ristine's *Representative Essays* (Berlin, *Rhetoric* 51–53). One strain of the idea course would later imperceptibly slip into a course in "great ideas" or "great books" and become a key component of general education programs. After a time such programs stopped devoting much attention to direct writing instruction at all. But the other, more popular side of this course developed into the most common of all early-twentieth-century composition courses, the expository writing course stressing certain key works of serious nonfiction (there soon grew a sort of unacknowledged composition canon, with Arnold, Newman, Huxley, Ruskin, and Woodrow Wilson most common early on). Students would analyze the prose and sometimes react to its ideas, at other times imitate its structure or style, following the example of Robert Louis Stevenson's "sedulous ape" (Berkeley, chap. 5, p. 383). This canon was often embodied in a common textbook of the time, a rhetoric/reader like Fulton's *Expository Writing* (1912), which contained instructions on writing along with copious selections to read, imitate, and discuss. Other exposition courses assigned a separate reading text, which was often accompanied by a rhetoric textbook; sometimes a handbook was used as a reference, at other times the rhetoric contained a handbook section. (See chapter 5 for readers, handbooks, and rhetorics.)

From Rhetoric to Composition

THIS BOOK CHRONICLES the move from composition at every stage of a student's college career to composition confined to the first year, and from a saturation in a rhetorical tradition of some two thousand years to its replacement with a new, streamlined curriculum which, as later chapters demonstrate, emphasized error correction and the five modes of discourse. These were simplifications perfectly suited for the mass-production education carried out in so many universities after 1900. How did the rich and complex world of rhetoric get replaced so quickly with composition?

The first way to answer that question is to look at the relegation of writing instruction to the first year, something Adams Sherman Hill worked hard for at Harvard; it took him from 1872 until 1885, because the classicists didn't want to give up their control of first-year course work. Putting composition at the beginning of a student's career earned it the right to be a "foundation" for all that followed. But along with the foundation came its reputation as a transition from high school to college, connected with introductory work, with bringing students up to the required level. In fact, putting composition into the first year was a recognition of its newly developed remedial overtones: freshman year was to make up for what preparatory schools had failed to teach. That goes a long way to explain composition's lowly status. Furthermore, colleges have long had an unspoken rule, "You are what you teach." Working with first-year students is a job for a teacher, not a scholar. And of course since even its proponents argued it was an art, not a science, the notion grew that just about anyone could teach it, and before long just about anyone did. Even before teaching assistants were common, teaching composition was an entry level job, one to leave behind after acquiring seniority.

Even worse, the composition course came to stand for a kind of teacher slavery—relentless correction and strict supervision of writing. The literature is full of complaints about the paper load (see chap. 4, p. 288, and Connors, "Overwork/Underpay"). Why did colleges pile the writing on, even when alternatives were available? Why process every single essay? (Some teachers did devise peer grading; see chap. 6, p. 458.) Could some writing tasks carry their own justification, be worth doing, and teach writing in the act of writing itself, yet not need to be read by the teacher? Why weren't such assignments even imagined in nineteenth- and early-twentieth-century instruction? To address that question requires some understanding of how the relationship between teacher and student made the first year of college very much resemble high school. For years the gap between college student and professor was maintained rigidly, with strict rules of behavior, tight regulations for dormitory life, and distinct expectations of courtesy. All students were expected to listen, to be kept under control, and to be passive learners. Nowhere did these expectations come out more forcefully than in composition, which imposed incredibly strict rules and enforced them thoroughly. The composition teacher was, willingly or not, the accomplice of the authorities, or in fact the enforcer. The rules about plagiarism were a perfect example of this authoritarian system; chapter 6 contains the composition rules pamphlet from the University of Minnesota in 1913; its tone and contents display some of the strictness imposed at the time. At its worst there is a sense that in composition, students are on trial, that they are not really a part of things until they get through their ordeal. As Susan Miller's *Textual Carnivals* depicts the difference, composition was "low," while literature was "high."

And what was the actual classroom teaching like? A remarkably large amount of it seems to have been adversarial, with the teacher as a stern taskmaster skilled in rooting out falsehood and cant and the student in fear of the teacher's scorn. Accounts of the recitation system and paper evaluation sessions conducted by Hill and Channing (Briggs, cited in Kitzhaber 61; Scott, chap. 3, p. 179) at Harvard or Northup at Yale (Cross), and a host of others (see Simmons 106–29) suggest that students spent much of their time in fear of being called on in class and found wanting. On the other hand, personal accounts of the Berkeley program (Frank Norris in Graff and Warner 133–35) or of Fred Newton Scott's Michigan program (Theodore Roethke's experience as described in Seager 116–17) speak of teachers' blandness and students' lack of interest in theme writing.

Feminist Rhetoric

THE COLLEGE WRITING and reading curriculum depicted in these documents was overwhelmingly male. (Only 15 percent of college students in 1900 were female, though the percentage was growing throughout this period.) The early twentieth century was the site of a specifically female rhetoric, of course; the two great successes of the women's movement, temperance and suffrage, were achieved through old-fashioned oratory, brilliant pamphleteering, and highly sophisticated manipulation of public opinion. In short, they were triumphs of rhetoric. A whole generation of women participated in massive efforts to transform public opinion, and in the process developed a wide range of rhetorical skills. During these struggles there were distinctly different audiences involved. Since in most cases the electorate was male, a male-targeted rhetoric prevailed.

At the same time, since much work needed to be done to convince other women to join these causes, signs of a specifically female-targeted public rhetoric were also emerging.

We still do not know enough about the connections between college course work and the public and private examples of female rhetoric. We do know that the women's colleges were the scene of a continuing debate over whether they should offer the same subjects as the men's colleges or whether they should offer subjects specifically tailored for women. M. Carey Thomas, for instance, argued that the subject matter of a woman's education should be the same as a man's; in keeping with this general idea, Harvard professors gave the same courses at Radcliffe as they did in their own departments. At some other colleges the stress for women was on a preparation in home economics and child-rearing. And we also know that the women's colleges did not always mirror the rapid rise of women's rhetorical skills. Controlled as they often were by male presidents (and overwhelmingly male trustees), many women's colleges had official policies against demonstrating, leafleting, or even speaking on behalf of suffrage. Even so, it is possible to detect the emergence of a distinctly feminist rhetoric among women professors at this time. Gertrude Buck's emphasis on personal writing (chap. 4, p. 241) helps to separate her from the mainstream of male rhetoric. Recent dissertations on Buck (Campbell; Weir) tend to emphasize her differences from her teacher Fred Newton Scott and stress her search for a distinct, specifically feminine community.

In the era 1875–1925 there were hundreds of women teaching composition and thousands of women students learning to write in college. But not surprisingly, the most widely circulated documents of the time, with very few exceptions, do not reveal very many distinct signs of a specifically feminist rhetoric, or even a feminist slant on writing. The male model dominated the national discourse about writing and the writer. This is true despite the fact that women professors produced some of the era's path-breaking textbooks—the first reader to use student papers, by Wisconsin's Frances Campbell Berkeley (see chap. 5, p. 378), and one of the first handbooks, by Oregon's Luella Clay Carson (see chap. 5, p. 353). These books reveal little of a distinctive female rhetoric, reminding us of the existence of a narrow range of attitudes among women writing college textbooks and of the continuing dominance of male discourse.

We need to ask many questions: To what extent did timorous publishing houses suppress signs of an identifiable feminist rhetoric in textbooks? Did feminists, eager to mount the platform and debate suffrage and temperance, avail themselves of the characteristically male oral rhetoric of the time straightforwardly, or did they give it their own personal dimension? Just what was the range of attitude and instruction among women rhetoricians? Answers to these and other questions will no doubt shed light not just on women's education but on the flexibility and adaptability of the whole educational enterprise to particular student populations.

Similarly, African-American writers were forging a distinctive voice (or series of voices) in nineteenth-century America, but any concerns black educators had about college writing instruction were not at all part of the general discourse. In writing, black college faculty and students were forced to assume the white world's styles and standards, as Fisk University graduate W.E.B. DuBois did when he elected Barrett Wendell's writing course at Harvard (DuBois 123). Arnold Rampersad (124) claims to discern some signs of the Harvard program on DuBois's prose style, but it is hard to find the opposite, a trace of a black writer or orator in composition's professional literature. Black or Latino or Native American concerns seem invisible in the professional literature of writing instruction between 1875 and 1925, while most black colleges seem to have taught writing in strict accord with the standards of white America.

Transition

AS COMPOSITION ENTERED the twentieth century, common patterns of professional work emerged, patterns that would remain until the 1970s and even beyond. Composition moved away from the Harvard model (which lost much of its credibility with Harvard's own faculty; see Perry, chap. 4, p. 311) and became the recognizably modern system that still prevails: professors teaching advanced literature courses, and instructors, part timers, and graduate students teaching composition. By 1910, composition had become almost totally apprentice work, and responsibility for its oversight became the province not of a scholar or curriculum expert but an administrator. Despite some well-known exceptions like Michigan and Wisconsin until the late 1920s, and some liberal arts colleges which preserved a respect for teaching, English departments decreed that literature teaching—the serious intellectual occupation of the discipline—would get the rewards. In fact, literature itself came to *be* the reward; a long apprenticeship in composition would be rewarded with literature teaching once promotion came.

This hierarchy was practically inevitable given the fact that university English departments organized themselves on the German academic model, rewarding research and privileging the doctorate, the learned article, and the monograph. Textbooks, curriculum materials, and teaching had their place in this system, but ranked significantly lower. And, with the single exception of Fred Newton Scott's Michigan program, there was no doctorate in composition, no research, no learned journal, no research seminars. Some professional discussion about composition took place, of course, but it was mainly about pedagogical goals and administrative matters (see chap. 3, p. 233). The major professional organization, the Modern Language Association (MLA), long confined talk of composition to its pedagogical section, and abolished even that from its convention in 1903. It is tempting to think that the disappearance of this section in 1903 marked the decline of composition's professional place, but I would argue that the real damage occurred in the relegation of composition to pedagogy in the first place. Once it was determined that composition work was to be considered pedagogical, not the product of research or a province of the aesthetic imagination, writing instruction's place at the bottom was sealed. (While composition was being marginalized, many other topics in English studies were departing: speech, journalism, theater arts, and linguistics. The splits were often done on research verses nonresearch lines: those who researched the history of the Globe Theatre found a welcome in the higher ranks of the English department; those who actually directed plays were encouraged to take their business elsewhere. Those who published on language development and variation were grudgingly accepted; those who taught students how to give speeches were relegated to the lower ranks.)

Still, despite the imposition of a rigid hierarchy, some faculty remained interested in composition and rhetoric. What options did they have? In a department organized as English was on a research model, composition specialists faced three choices: (1) join the small but influential band of academics who attacked the research model as inadequate, (2) initiate what their peers would recognize as high-quality research, or

(3) break away from the English department. At this time, roughly from 1905 to 1920, some influential academics were mounting attacks on the research model, what William James had called "the Ph.D. Octopus." In modern language studies the most prominent critic was Irving Babbitt, a classicist with a position in Harvard's French department, whose *Literature and the American College* (1908) is a strong attack on doctoral studies in English and a plea for a genuine, humanistic understanding of "ideas." Babbitt had followers among intellectual conservatives who knew the current composition scene firsthand and who published significant writing textbooks: Norman Foerster of Wisconsin, North Carolina, and Iowa (see chap. 5, p. 390); Frank Aydelotte of Indiana, MIT, and Swarthmore (see chap. 4, p. 300), and John Erskine of Columbia. These men were not sympathetic to traditional rhetoric, and they certainly were not inclined to equate composition with personal expression. Instead they wanted their students to write about ideas, and all three tried to transform composition into courses in liberal culture or great books, an influence that would live on in many composition readers for over half a century. All three would found programs to infuse the undergraduate years with required humanistic training and counter what they regarded as the diluting effect of electives and premature specialization. At first Foerster and Aydelotte took the composition course seriously, putting first-rate teaching into it and giving entering students some meaty books to read. Soon, however, their courses crowded writing instruction out in favor of concentrating on the reading. Over time, someone interested in new thinking about writing instruction and rhetoric would find little of interest in their course work. Still, they displayed confidence in their students, and from our vantage point they look much more intellectually respectable than their English department mandarin counterparts who were happy shunting first-year students off to untrained teaching assistants.

The second option available to a composition specialist, to carry on high quality writing research, was taken by Fred Newton Scott, chair of the rhetoric department at Michigan and a tireless worker for composition's status. He ran a successful and highly popular doctoral program in rhetoric, began a scholarly series to publish promising dissertations, headed the MLA and its pedagogical section, edited works on rhetoric, literature, and criticism, and published articles and textbooks on rhetoric and composition. Scott had a department of his own, excellent graduate students, first-rate research, and the respect of his professional peers. But his program was essentially a one-man show; the people he appointed to teach in his program were not influential in the field, and he himself was stretched very thin, running composition, journalism, the MLA (president, 1907), and the National Council of Teachers of English (NCTE; founding president, 1911–13). And Scott also lacked successors; his program did not survive him. Upon Scott's retirement, Michigan's English department absorbed the rhetoric program, succeeded in reducing composition work to pedagogy, and relegated teaching to a minor role (Stewart, "Two Model Teachers" 128).

Little evidence shows that composition specialists besides Scott willingly followed the third alternative—independence from the English department. This was the route taken successfully by speech, which English had also reduced to the status of a support course. At the 1913 NCTE convention speech teachers voted to break free of English department domination and found their own association; their earliest manifestos speak eloquently of the need to conduct research, to be scientific, in a word, to compete in the university world on an equal footing with other academic disciplines (O'Neill 56–57).

Composition failed to take any of these routes; instead, it made its alliances across the gap between college and high school, casting itself as an ally of school teachers in the NCTE, an organization with distinctly pedagogic aims that fostered a Midwestern, egalitarian attitude toward education rather than the Eastern elitist approach. Such an attitude pervaded the newly formed *English Journal* (established 1912), where composition articles would appear for the next eighty years. (*English Journal* branched off into a college edition and later split into *College English,* which still publishes composition articles: *PMLA* hasn't published an article by a composition scholar in eighty years.)

It was no crime to select teaching over scholarship; in fact, it may have been the better choice. But given the way higher education worked, such a choice had severe consequences. It meant one was removed from the sources of professional glory: grants, released time, graduate students, the very things that conferred status and sustained research. It meant relegation to a service role, while the profession moved on to new frontiers of scholarship. It meant that administrative work became necessary for advancement. To be sure, there were notable exceptions. Hoyt Hudson published widely in rhetoric and moved from Cornell to Princeton, while Charles Sears Baldwin had a distinguished career in rhetoric at Columbia. Many others made their mark in administration, including Porter Perrin at Washington and Frank Aydelotte at Swarthmore. But most promising rhetoricians' careers would resemble those of the many scholars who taught and published in rhetoric while young and migrated to literature when older. That was true of Barrett Wendell at Harvard, John Genung at Amherst, Gertrude Buck at Vassar, Norman Foerster and Karl Young at Wisconsin, Hyder Rollins at Texas, Stith Thompson at Indiana, and many more who published early work in composition and then moved on to more "important" work within English departments or in administration. And common too was the path taken by many women who did not establish names for themselves or become well known: Maria Louisa Sanford (1836–1920) of Swarthmore and Minnesota published articles on suffrage, religion, and public speaking but made her main contribution through years of teaching; Luella Clay Carson of the University of Oregon published composition texts but little else during a long career (chap. 5, p. 353); Frances Campbell Berkeley (later Young) left the profession when she married (chap. 5, p. 378). The early twentieth century offers very few examples of well-known professionals, male or female, who staked out composition as their field, published primarily in it, and persevered in it for their entire careers.

By 1920 composition had assumed the shape it would retain for the next half century. Many changes would occur, changes which are well worth investigating (and which the emphasis on current-traditional almost precludes). But these changes would occur within a universe determined by composition's fixed place within the curriculum. The half century from 1875 to 1925 had witnessed an enormous revolution in the relation of composition to students and to other academic subjects, all within the context of a transformation of American higher education. It is not surprising that this period of ferment should have been followed by a period of stasis. Laurence Veysey argues that for all higher education the period 1910–45 "was largely a period of drift, characterized by a sense of letdown" and "the continuing divorce of the entire curriculum from the wellsprings of student energy" ("Stability and Experiment" 9–10). Composition, like much in the American curriculum, had become stable, at a point very far away from the rhetoric of the 1850s.

2

The First Composition Program: Harvard, 1870–1900

H ARVARD ESTABLISHED THE FIRST MODERN COMPOSI-
tion program, and for two decades its faculty wrote extensively about the
subject. This chapter contains articles and documents from the Harvard
program, including large sections from the Harvard reports which are
often cited in histories of composition. These reports were part of an
attempt to get the secondary schools to improve their writing instruction; in effect, though, they diminished the role of first-year composition
and expressed the hope of removing it entirely from the college curriculum and placing it in the schools. In order to understand the connection
between the Harvard reports and the growth of composition, one needs
to look at school-college relations in the 1870s.

Throughout most of the nineteenth century the great bulk of secondary education for the college bound took place at private academies and
preparatory schools. Colleges that wished to improve the quality of their
students had to raise admissions standards, yet colleges were totally
dependent upon preparatory schools. Charles W. Eliot saw matters
clearly in early 1869, just before he came to the Harvard presidency:

The higher and lower institutions are, indeed, mutually dependent; if the
admission examiners of the colleges and polytechnic schools seem, on the one
hand, to sharply define the studies of the preparatory schools; on the other hand,
it is quite as true that the colleges and advanced schools are practically controlled in their requisitions by the actual state of the preparatory schools. They
can only ask for what is to be had. They must accept such preparations as the
schools can give. ("The New Education" 204)

For over two centuries Harvard had demanded knowledge of Latin,
Greek, and mathematics from its entering students, and a group of

academies and preparatory schools had been set up to provide them to young scholars. Now, with Eliot's new emphasis on English, the preparatory schools were faced with another task: teach English, and particularly writing, to their charges. And for the first time the schools were to be judged by a public standard, by writing *everyone* could understand. They had had a monopoly on Latin and Greek instruction; they set the standards and colleges had to accept their students, since there was no other source of supply. But with English the field was suddenly open; here was an achievement practically everyone was qualified to judge, and not surprisingly the public (and Harvard too) would judge by obvious marks of error in spelling, punctuation, and grammar.

In the early 1870s, after Harvard set up a written examination in English composition, it began to prod its preparatory schools about improving their writing instruction, beginning a twenty-year-long acrimonious debate over composition in the schools. Faculty spoke to headmasters at professional meetings; professors wrote newspaper and magazine articles about the poor quality of writing; and finally Harvard published lengthy official reports pinpointing the problem and laying blame on the preparatory schools. (Midwestern colleges handled matters with less acrimony; colleges dominated their feeder schools by offering them official certification if they met certain standards. Students from certified schools were automatically eligible for admission to the local state university. See Gayley, chap. 3, p. 168, and Scott, "College-Entrance Requirements.") The shock expressed by Harvard faculty at the low quality of student writing on entrance examinations seems to have been mostly for effect. Everyone teaching English at Harvard had been an undergraduate there and was quite familiar with the quality of student English. And every year saw plenty of college writing assignments that demonstrated student abilities. The new examination in English did not reveal some long-hidden weakness so much as supply Harvard with new, objective evidence to use in the effort to improve the secondary schools, which was one of Eliot's lifelong ambitions.

Another part of Harvard's battles over writing instruction involved a long and ultimately successful fight with the classicists. Eliot's privileging of English and other modern languages was a direct attack on the hegemony of the classics at the college level, since English would thus be entitled to its own share of class time, time that had to be taken from classics. At the school level the battles involved a concerted attempt to break the power of the classics as well. One element of this battle was Harvard's claim that the classics simply weren't doing their job in producing entering students who could handle English well enough. The traditional claim of the classicists was that their subjects provided the mental discipline students needed to succeed in all their subjects. The Harvard reports questioned whether skill in Latin and Greek would indeed transfer to those other subjects like English. In particular, Harvard had two specific complaints about the classics: students produced atrocious examples of "translation English" instead of idiomatic, straightforward English; and students could not master simple grammatical English despite years of a language-based curriculum. So it was no accident that the person appointed from the Harvard Board of Overseers to head the Committee on Composition and Rhetoric was the nation's most outspoken enemy of mental discipline through classical instruction, Charles Francis Adams (*Three Addresses* 33–34). The documents in this chapter, then, depict the rise of Adams Sherman Hill's powerful program, and Charles Francis Adams's equally powerful indictment of secondary education, an indictment that undermines the Harvard writing program's very reason for existing.

Rollo Walter Brown
Dean Briggs (1926)

    ❧   *Brown (1880–1956) received his B.Litt. from Ohio Northern in 1903 and an M.A. from Harvard in 1905, where he was befriended by Le Baron Russell Briggs. He taught at Wabash College, 1905–20, and Carleton College, 1920–23. His publications included* How the French Boy Learns to Write *(1915) and a memoir,* Harvard Yard in the Golden Age *(1948).*

    In this affectionate portrait of one of Harvard's most revered figures from the turn of the century, Brown supplies a nice overview of Harvard's role in establishing composition. Brown also makes a claim for Briggs as the originator of freshman orientation. The fact that Briggs could add such orientation on to composition instruction illustrates the dual nature of the writing course: important enough to require of every student, but unstructured enough that a third of it can be taken over by a semiacademic orientation to college life.

As FAR BACK AS 1872, PROFESSOR ADAMS SHERMAN HILL HAD BEEN brought to Harvard to supplement the scholarly work already being done in the Department of English. President Eliot, then a young man of thirty-eight, foresaw a greatly increased attendance at the colleges and universities of the country. Not only that; he felt sure that this attendance would be made up in large part of men and women who would work in the sciences and other subjects not linguistic or literary. Anyhow, the older literary training was rigid and artificial, and altogether too exclusively designed for state occasions. He would have students forearmed with such a working acquaintance with their mother tongue as would serve them unaffectedly in their daily lives.

So Professor Hill was brought to the College Yard to see whether or not such an acquaintance was possible. He was a thin, cadaverous man who had received his bachelor's degree from Harvard in 1853—in President Eliot's class. He had subsequently studied law, and then had worked on the New York *Tribune* under Horace Greeley. When he came to the college he shared President Eliot's belief that students should write with direct clearness, and his experience in a newspaper office had led him to the somewhat unorthodox conviction that there were certain practicable means of approaching this end. At first he had no sense of discipline—as the word is used pedagogically—and the students, carrying on the easy traditions of a course that had been under the direction of young men who taught transiently, were not inclined to look upon his work with overmuch seriousness. In truth, they sometimes hummed pleasant academic melodies while he read a man's themes in the classroom. He encountered, in addition, no little unfriendliness in influential quarters. But despite his frail health and the uninviting atmosphere, he persisted. By the early 'eighties he had made such progress that both he and President Eliot believed the time had come when he should have associated with him more men than a mere young assistant or two. By 1883 he had gathered about him three young men who were to undertake the further development of his "idea." These were Barrett Wendell, W. B. Shubrick Clymer, and Le Baron Russell Briggs.

In 1883–84 the prescribed course in English, at that time required in the sophomore year, was officially in the hands of Professor Hill and Mr. Briggs; but on account of Professor Hill's poor health, he delegated most of his authority to his young associate. From Dean Briggs's boyhood to the day of his withdrawal from all university duties he always gave people the impression that he was timid; yet quite as consistently, whenever anyone came to him with a difficult task, he was always ready to undertake it. So when Professor Hill handed him classroom lectures and said, "I am too sick to meet the class, and you must lecture to them," he accepted the difficult commission and read valiantly. Students who were in the course at that time were so impressed by the pink-faced boy's efforts to fill the mature man's shoes, and by his deep, almost desperate earnestness, that they listened to him with more respect than they had supposed they could command.

At the end of that year he was to have the opportunity to show just how a new idea begins its earthly journey. He and Professor Hill believed that the prescribed English should come at the beginning of a student's course rather than in the second year. They proposed a change. If the course came in the freshman year, it would help the student when he most needed help, and it would not break into his other studies after he had taken them up. To a young man's unclouded vision, that was clear beyond question. But he had to encounter minds made heavy by too much wisdom. The older members of the faculty were engaged in a mad scramble to enlist recruits among the freshmen for their elective courses. They did not want Professor Hill and this young upstart to put a pre-scribed course back into the open field and hamper the early beginnings of a right pursuit of truth. And the young man had the audacity to ask for something more! He wished to make the prescribed English into a course that would meet three times a week instead of two. Some of the distinguished members of the faculty became savage. But Professor Hill and young Briggs promised that should the course be pushed back to the freshman year and made a three-hour course, they would see to it that no work outside the classroom was required for the third hour. Upon that basis the change was made.

Now how could this transaction, by any stretch of the imagination, become a matter of national significance? The answer is to be found in certain theories of democracy cherished by the American people. They wanted as much education as possible for everybody. They wanted their children well taught in the colleges and universities. Harvard, with an honorable past, attracted many men who expected to do college teach-ing. These men, when they went to their posts all over the country, carried with them, as every college graduate must, some memory of the way things were done by their Alma Mater. And when these newer institutions sought a means of preventing students from disgracing them-selves every time they put pen to paper, they almost invariably made use of Harvard's experience and established prescribed freshman courses in writing. A glance at the college and university catalogues of America will reveal how few of the institutions did not follow the precedent which young Briggs, after much opposition, was allowed to establish.

This simple change in the schedule of the university, moreover, enabled him to start another variation in college practice. He had agreed not to require outside work of students for the third hour of his course. He must, then, devise means of occupying this hour profitably. In casting about, he discovered, among other things, how little the freshmen knew about the college and the world in which they lived. They needed not merely courses in Greek and chemistry and German; they needed general information. They knew little about the social machine, and they did not feel their place in it with sufficient distinctness to give import to their college work. He would make use of this "third hour" by trying to give his freshmen some glimpses of the world in which they supposedly lived. And he called on others to assist him.

This practice likewise spread throughout the country. At first, many teachers in the colleges where young instructors in English attempted to carry out the practice declared vehemently that it was "unscholarly" and that it did not "fit into" any well-organized curriculum. In fact, it did fit into any curriculum that was not too well organized! And to-day, helping the freshman to orient himself is so generally regarded as a necessary part of a college education, that it is accepted as though colleges had always fostered the idea. The sequence is clear enough: first, occasional hours were devoted to what a freshman should know; then regular hours; then a separate one-hour course—in many colleges—with compiled volumes of liberalizing essays; then full-fledged courses in "orientation" in which freshmen are brought face to face not only with the world, but with the universe! Whatever else may be said about college freshmen to-day, they must be more alert than they were obliged to be thirty or forty years ago.

But see how Briggs and Wendell, working together, were able to enter still further into the educational life of America. The pushing of the prescribed course back to the freshman year inevitably left one sophomore class, that of the year 1884–85, without the customary instruction in English. So Barrett Wendell, under the direction of Professor Hill, undertook to give for the sophomores the identical course, so far as possible, that Le Baron R. Briggs, under the same direction, was giving for the freshmen. It was in that year also that Wendell first offered

English 12, an advanced course in writing that soon took a place next to Professor Hill's English 5 as a magnet for those who wished to learn whether they had any capacity as writers. While he was laboring with his classes that year he "invented" the daily theme. Although he was in his last years looked upon as something of a tory, he was as a youth and as a young teacher rebellious enough; and he rebelled against the incessant practice of imitating the stiff eloquence and, in some instances at least, the stiffer poetry of New England. He had kept a diary himself, and had profited by the daily writing. Why should not students write a little each day? From Briggs's practice of discussing many matters with the freshmen, he completed the idea: he would have his students look squarely at some little part of the world, try to catch the color or flavor of what they saw, and then write as significantly as possible. Longer themes of one kind or another were not to be given up, but if men were ever to write with any flexibility, they must have a certain amount of daily practice with a variety of manageable subjects.

Wendell's idea, which was closely akin to the entire conception of the freshman course as Briggs was developing it, likewise went to every part of the country. The idea had the good fortune, as Briggs's ideas had, of coming to birth at the time when institutions everywhere were drawing upon Harvard heavily in their efforts to establish adequate courses. Some years later, after the freshman course had been perfected by the touch of many skilled hands, the demand for information about it became so great that two of the men then teaching in it published a book in which the methods of the course were set forth in detail.[1] Teachers in hundreds of colleges wanted to know more about this method of helping men to see clearly and to write directly. Newspaper editors rejoiced that college men were learning to write straight sentences; and magazines and weeklies discussed the educational value of the "daily theme eye."

A "literary movement" is always too complex to be explained simply. Men, moreover, who find themselves better off as a result of any such movement, are pleased to feel that their increased well-being has emanated from their own virgin genius. Least of all are they willing to admit that men in an institution of learning have had anything to do with it. But when some one sits down to explain why in the early years of the twentieth century the younger readers and writers of America began to concern themselves with something less hollow, less conventionally formed than much of the literature conveniently styled "New England," he cannot leave Briggs and Wendell out of consideration. They trained men to look at the world with their own eyes, and to write directly and honestly about what they saw, without regard for the traditional ways of looking at things. The men thus trained went all over the country to teach in the colleges and universities, and they carried with them the gospel that the world right where one lives is interesting if one will only look and think. And the students whom these men in turn trained went away from college by the thousands—and later by the tens of thousands—to find joy in the same unaffected experience. Only the blind can say that this fact has had nothing to do with our attempt, more or less national, to develop a literary art directly from the soil.

NOTE

1. Copeland and Rideout, *Freshman English and Theme Correcting in Harvard College.* 1901. [See chap. 6, p. 514.—ED.]

Three Harvard Catalogue Course Descriptions from *Twenty Years of School and College English* (1896)

&⅃ *The following curriculum descriptions document the evolution of the Harvard English curriculum in 1874–75, 1879–80, and 1896–97. They show how the Harvard of 1896 depicted the changes that had taken place in its own composition program and demonstrate four key trends: the growth of composition course work, the movement away from traditional rhetoric and toward modern composition, the expansion of the undergraduate literature curriculum, and the growth of the graduate program in literature. A close look at the 1896–97 listing also reveals a luxuriant growth of courses in writing without much differentiation in subject matter, approach, or form. Harvard's extensive composition course work does not seem to make up a coherent, easily grasped sequence. (One could always say the same is true of Harvard's 1896–97 literature courses, yet they have a built-in order in that they cover authors or periods or genres.)*

HISTORY OF THE REQUIREMENT IN ENGLISH FOR ADMISSION TO HARVARD COLLEGE.

The first mention of anything approaching an examination in English as a requirement for admission to Harvard College appears in the Catalogue for 1865–66:

"Candidates will also be examined in reading English aloud."

For four years this sentence was, as Mr. Hurlbut says, "tacked to the end of the list" of prescribed subjects with nothing to call attention to it. In the Catalogue for 1869–70 we find for the first time the heading "English." The requirement for 1870 runs as follows:

"English."

"Students are also required to be examined, as early as possible after their admission, in reading English. Prizes will be awarded for excellence. For 1870 students may prepare themselves in Craik's English of Shakespeare (Julius Caesar) or in Milton's Comus. Attention to Derivations and Critical Analysis is recommended."

For the next three years this paragraph remains substantially unchanged except that Goldsmith's "Vicar of Wakefield" is substituted for Shakspere's "Julius Caesar." In the Catalogue for 1872–73 the candidate is for the first time informed that the quality of his written English will be taken into account:

☞   *Correct spelling, punctuation, and expression, as well as legible handwriting, are expected of all applicants for admission; and failure in any of these particulars will be taken into account at the examination.*"

In the following year an examination in English composition was for the first time imposed on every candidate for admission to Harvard College. The requirement for that year as printed in the Catalogue for 1873–74 is as follows:

"*English Composition.* Each candidate will be required to write a short English Composition, correct in spelling, punctuation, grammar, and expression, the subject to be taken from such works of standard authors as shall be announced from time to time. The subject for 1874 will be taken from one of the following works: Shakespeare's Tempest, Julius Caesar, and Merchant of Venice; Goldsmith's Vicar of Wakefield; Scott's Ivanhoe, and Lay of the Last Minstrel."

The requirement for 1878 says that the "short English Composition" must be correct not only "in spelling, punctuation, grammar, and expression," but also in "division by paragraphs;" the requirement for 1879 precludes a common kind of misunderstanding by making clear that "Every candidate is expected to be familiar with *all* the books in this list."

In the Catalogue for 1880–81 the following paragraph appears for the first time:

"In 1882, every candidate will also be required to correct specimens of bad English given him at the time of examination. For this purpose the time of the examination will be lengthened by half an hour."

Although the time for the examination was lengthened to an hour and a half, the examination continued to count as a one-hour examination.

The Catalogue for 1886–87 says:

"*English* (after 1887) must be reserved for the candidate's final examination for admission. With this exception, candidates may offer themselves for the preliminary examination in any studies, elementary or advanced, *in which their teachers certify that they are prepared.*"

The Catalogue for 1891–92 has the following addition:

"The English written by a candidate in any of his examination-books may be regarded as part of his examination in English, in case the evidence afforded by the examination-book in English is insufficient."

In the Catalogue for 1893–94 teachers are explicitly told how to deal with the prescribed reading:

"The candidate is expected to read intelligently *all* the books prescribed. He should read them as he reads other books; he will be expected not to know them minutely, but to have freshly in mind their most important parts. Whatever the subject of the composition, the examiner will regard knowledge of the book as less important than ability to write English."

In conformity with the recommendations made at a meeting of teachers held at Philadelphia in 1894, a change was made in the requirement. The new requirement was optional in 1895, but is prescribed for 1896 and subsequent years. As stated in the Catalogue for 1895–96 it is as follows:

"*English.*—English may be offered either as a Preliminary or as a Final subject. In 1896 and thereafter the examination will occupy two hours.

"The examination will consist of two parts, which, however, cannot be taken separately:—

"I. The candidate will be required to write a paragraph or two on each of several topics chosen by him from a considerable number—perhaps ten or fifteen—set before him on the examination paper. In 1896 the topics will be drawn from the following works:—

"Shakspere's Midsummer Night's Dream; Defoe's History of the Plague in London; Irving's Tale of a Traveller; Scott's Woodstock; Macaulay's Essay on Milton; Longfellow's Evangeline; George Eliot's Silas Marner.

"The candidate is expected to read intelligently *all* the books prescribed. He should read them as he reads other books; he is expected, not to know them minutely, but to have freshly in mind their most important parts. In every case the examiner will regard knowledge of the book as less important than ability to write English.

"As additional evidence of preparation, the candidate may present an exercise book, properly certified by his instructor, containing compositions or other written work.

"The works prescribed for this part of the examination in 1897, 1898, and 1899 are as follows:—

"In 1897: Shakspere's As You Like It; Defoe's History of the Plague in London; Irving's Tales of a Traveller; Hawthorne's Twice Told Tales; Longfellow's Evangeline; George Eliot's Silas Marner.

"In 1898: Milton's Paradise Lost, Books I and II; Pope's Iliad, Books I and XXII; the Sir Roger de Coverley Papers in the Spectator; Goldsmith's Vicar of Wakefield; Coleridge's Ancient Mariner; Southey's Life of Nelson; Carlyle's Essay on Burns; Lowell's Vision of Sir Launfal; Hawthorne's House of the Seven Gables.

"In 1899: Dryden's Palamon and Arcite; Pope's Iliad, Books I, VI, XXII, and XXIV; The Sir Roger de Coverley Papers in the Spectator; Goldsmith's Vicar of Wakefield; Coleridge's Ancient Mariner; De Quincey's Flight of a Tartar Tribe; Cooper's Last of the Mohicans; Lowell's Vision of Sir Launfal; Hawthorne's House of the Seven Gables.

"II. A certain number of books will be prescribed for careful study. This part of the examination will be upon subject-matter, literary form, and logical structure, and will also test the candidate's ability to express his knowledge with clearness and accuracy.

"The books prescribed for this part of the examination are:

"In 1896: Shakspere's Merchant of Venice; Milton's L'Allegro, Il Penseroso, Comus, and Lycidas; Webster's First Bunker Hill Oration.

"In 1897: Shakspere's Merchant of Venice; Burke's Speech on Conciliation with America; Scott's Marmion; Macaulay's Life of Samuel Johnson.

"In 1898: Shakspere's Macbeth; Burke's Speech on Conciliation with America; De Quincey's Flight of a Tartar Tribe; Tennyson's Princess.

"In 1899: Shakspere's Macbeth; Milton's Paradise Lost, Books I and II; Burke's Speech on Conciliation with America; Carlyle's Essay on Burns.

"No candidate will be accepted in English whose work is seriously defective in point of spelling, punctuation, grammar, or division into paragraphs.

"In connection with the reading and study of the prescribed books, parallel or subsidiary reading should be encouraged, and a considerable amount of English poetry should be committed to memory. The essentials of English grammar should not be neglected in preparatory study.

"The English written by a candidate in any of his examination-books may be regarded as part of his examination in English, in case the evidence afforded by the examination-book in English is insufficient.

"The attention of candidates who have passed in English at the Preliminary Examination is called to the subject of Optional Examinations for the Anticipation of College Studies (on pp. 210, 211*)."

*See the University Catalogue for 1895–96.

COURSES OF INSTRUCTION IN ENGLISH OFFERED BY HARVARD COLLEGE.

For 1874–75.

PRESCRIBED STUDIES.

Prescribed Rhetoric. —Asst. Professor A. S. Hill.

Sophomore Year.

Campbell's Philosophy of Rhetoric (Book 2, Chapters I–VI). — Whately's Rhetoric (Part 3). —Herbert Spencer's Philosophy of Style. — Written Exercises.

Two hours a week. First half-year.

Junior Year.

Whately's Rhetoric (to end of Part 2). —Lessing's Laocoon (Chapters 13–26).

Two hours a week. Second half-year.

Prescribed Themes and Forensics.

Sophomore Year.	Six Themes: Asst. Professor A. S. HILL.
Junior Year.	Six Themes: Professor CHILD.
	Four Forensics: Asst. Professor PALMER.
Senior Year.	Four Forensics.

Candidates for Honors may substitute for Forensics an equal number of Theses in their special departments, provided such substitution is permitted by the Instructors in those departments.

Electives.

English 1.—Professor CHILD.

English.—Hadley's History of the English Language.—The Elements of Anglo-Saxon.—Morris's Historical English Accidence.—Lectures.
Two hours a week. 1 Junior, 13 Sophomores, 1 Freshman.

English 2.—Professor CHILD.

Anglo-Saxon and Early English.—Beówulf.—Mätzner's Altenglishe Sprachproben.
Three hours a week. (Not given this year.)

English 3.—Professor CHILD.

English Literature. — Chaucer. — Shakspere. — Bacon. — Milton. — Dryden.
Three hours a week. 7 Seniors, 8 Juniors, 2 Sophomores, 2 Freshmen.

For 1879–80.

Prescribed Courses

Sophomore Year.

Rhetoric.—Hill's Principles of Rhetoric.—Abbott's How to Write Clearly.—Addison, Goldsmith, Irving, Macaulay, Scott.—Burke's Speech on Conciliation with America.—Exercises in Writing and Criticism. *Twice a week.* Mr. WARE.
Six Themes. Mr. PERRY.

Junior Year.

Six Themes. Professor HILL and Messrs. WARE and PERRY.
Four Forensics. Asst. Professor PALMER.

Senior Year.

Four Forensics. Professor PEABODY.

Elective Courses.

1. English Literature. — Chaucer. — Bacon. — Milton. — Dryden. *Three times a week.* Professor CHILD.

2. English Literature. — Shakspere. *Three times a week.* Professor CHILD.

3. Anglo-Saxon. — Sweet's Anglo-Saxon Reader. *Twice a week.* Professor CHILD.

4. Early English. — Mätzner's Altenglishe Sprachproben. *Twice a week.* Professor CHILD.

5. Rhetoric and Themes (Advanced Course). *Three times a week.* Professor A. S. HILL.

6. Oral Discussion. *Once a fortnight (three hours), to count as a one-hour course. Open to Seniors only.* Professor A. S. HILL.

7. Principles of Literary Criticism, in connection with English Literature of the Eighteenth and Nineteenth Centuries. *Once a week.* Professor A. S. HILL.

Students wishing to take Course 5 or 6 must consult the Instructor in advance.

One hour of Course 5 can be used as an equivalent for Junior Themes, in which case the course will count as two hours of elective work.

For 1896–97.*

Primarily for Undergraduates.

A. Rhetoric and English Composition. — A. S. Hill, *Principles of Rhetoric* (revised and enlarged edition). — Lectures, recitations, written exercises, and conferences. I. *Mon., Wed., Fri., at 10;* II. *Mon., Wed., Fri., at 11;* III. *Mon., Wed., Fri., at 12;* IV. *Tu., Th., Sat., at 10;* V. *Tu., Th., Sat., at 11;* VI. *Tu., Th., Sat., at 12.* Professors A. S. HILL and BRIGGS, and Messrs. HURLBUT, COPELAND, COBB, J. G. HART, LA ROSE, and ——. (X.)
Course A is prescribed for Freshmen and for first-year students in the Lawrence Scientific School.

*A detailed account of the instruction offered by the Department of English will be found in the pamphlet of that department. The University issues each year special pamphlets of the courses of instruction offered by the various divisions and departments. These pamphlets may be had on application to the *Corresponding Secretary.*

In the daily exercises the class will be divided into six sections as indicated above; but at the Mid-year and Final Examinations the whole class will be examined together. Since these examinations are held on the same days with the examinations in Elective Group X, no member of English A is allowed to elect any course in Group X.

Bhf. English Composition.—Twelve Themes.—Lectures and discussions of themes. *Half-course.* I. *Tu., Th., at 12;* II. *Tu., Th., at 1.30;* III. *Tu., Th., at 2.30.* Asst. Professor WENDELL, and Messrs. ABBOTT and ——.

Course B is prescribed for Sophomores who, having passed in Course A, take neither Course 31 nor Course 22. It is open to those students only who have passed in Course A.

Chf. English Composition.—Forensics.—A brief based on a masterpiece of argumentative composition. Three forensics, preceded by briefs. Lectures, class-work, and conferences. *Half-course.* I. *Tu., Th., at 10;* II. *Tu., Th., at 12;* III. *Tu., Th., at 1.30;* IV. *Tu., Th., at 3.30, and other hours to be appointed by the instructors.* Asst. Professor BAKER, and Messrs. T. HALL, PRESCOTT, and ——.

Course C is prescribed for Juniors who have passed in Course B, Course 31, or Course 22, and who do not take Course 30. It is open to those students only who have passed in Course B, Course 31, or Course 22.

BChf. English Composition.—Written exercises and conferences. *Half-course. Wed., at 1.30.* Messrs. HURLBUT, T. HALL, and J. G. HART. (XIII.)

This course, which corresponds in part to Course B and in part to Course C, is prescribed for students in the Lawrence Scientific School. It is open to those only who have passed in Course A.

Course B C cannot be counted towards the degree of A.B., except with the permission of the Deans of the College and the Scientific School.

31. English Composition. *Tu., Th., at 2.30, and conferences at hours to be announced.* Messrs. GARDINER and DUFFIELD. (XI.)

Course 31 is open to those who, having passed in Course A, prefer an elective course to Course B. It is counted as the equivalent of Course B and a half-course of elective study.

Students who signify their intention at the beginning of the year may take Course 31 for the first half-year as the equivalent of Course B.

22. English Composition. *Tu., Th., at 1.30, and conferences at hours to be announced.* Messrs. GATES, ABBOTT, and ——.   (XIV.)

Course 22 is similar to Course 31, except that it is open to those only who have attained Grade C in Course A. It is counted as the equivalent of Course B and a half-course of elective study.

28*hf.* English Literature.—History and Development of English Literature in outline. *Half-course. Tu., Th., at 10 (first half-year); Tu., (and at the pleasure of the instructor) Th., at 10 (second half-year).* Professors CHILD, A. S. HILL, BRIGGS, KITTREDGE, Asst. Professor WENDELL, and Messrs. J. G. HART and LA ROSE.   (VIII.)

This course is for Freshmen and first-year Special Students only. It is open to those only who have passed the admission examination in English.

*30. Forensics and Debating. *Mon., Wed., Fri., at 3.30.* Asst. Professor BAKER and Mr. HAYES.   (VI.)

Course 30 is counted as the equivalent of Course C and a half-course of elective study.

*6*hf.* Oral Discussion of Topics in History and Economics. *Half-course. Th., 3.30–5.30.* Professor TAUSSIG, Asst. Professors HART, E. CUMMINGS, and BAKER, and Mr. HAYES.   (XII.)

Course 6 is open to Seniors only.

*10*hf.* Elocution. *Half-course.* I. *Mon., Fri., at 10;* II. *Mon., Fri., at 12.* Mr. HAYES.

Course 10 is open to those only who are approved by the instructor as having already attained some proficiency in Elocution.

3^1*hf.* Anglo-Saxon.—Bright, *Anglo-Saxon Reader. Half-course. Mon., Wed., Fri., at 1.30 (first half-year).* Dr. GARRETT.   (XIII.)

Course 3^1 requires no previous knowledge of Anglo-Saxon.

For Graduates and Undergraduates.

1. English Literature.—Chaucer. *Mon., Wed., Fri., at 9.* Professor KITTREDGE and Dr. GARRETT.   (I.)

*A starred (*) course cannot be taken without the previous consent of the instructor.

2. English Literature.—Shakspere (six plays). *Mon., Wed., Fri., at 10.*
Professors CHILD and KITTREDGE.   (II.)
Course 2 may be taken in two successive years.

11¹*hf.* English Literature.—Bacon. *Half-course. Mon., Wed., Fri., at 10*
(first half-year). Dr. GARRETT.   (II.)

11²*hf.* English Literature.—Milton. *Half-course. Mon., Wed., Fri., at 10*
(second half-year). Dr. GARRETT.   (II.)

32¹*hf.* English Literature of the Elizabethan Period. From Tottell's Mis-
cellany to the Death of Spenser (1557–1599). *Half-course. Tu., Th.,*
at 12 (first half-year). Mr. GARDINER and an assistant.   (X.)

32²*hf.* English Literature.—From the Death of Spenser to the Closing of
the Theatres (1599–1642). *Half-course. Tu., Th., at 12 (second half-*
year). Asst. Professor BAKER and an assistant.   (X.)

[15²*hf.* English Literature.—From the Closing of the Theatres to the
Death of Dryden (1642–1700). *Half-course.*]
Omitted in 1896–97; to be given in 1897–98.

7¹*hf.* English Literature of the Period of Queen Anne. From the Death of
Dryden to the Death of Pope (1700–1744). *Half-course. Mon., Fri.,*
at 2.30 (first half-year). Mr. HURLBUT and an assistant.   (V.)

7²*hf.* English Literature.—From the Death of Pope to the publication of
the Lyrical Ballads (1744–1798). *Half-course. Mon., Fri., at 2.30*
(second half-year). Mr. COPELAND and an assistant.   (V.)

[8¹*hf.* English Literature.—From the publication of the Lyrical Ballads
to the Death of Scott (1798–1832). *Half-course. Tu., Th., at 11*
(first half-year). Professor A. S. HILL and an assistant.]   (IX.)
Omitted in 1896–97; to be given in 1897–98.

[8²*hf.* English Literature.—From the Death of Scott to the Death of
Tennyson (1832–1892). *Half-course. Tu., Th., at 11 (second half-*
year). Mr. GATES and an assistant.]   (IX.)
Omitted in 1896–97; to be given in 1897–98.

12. English Composition. *Tu., Th., at 2.30.* Asst. Professor WENDELL
and Mr. CORBIN.   (XI.)
Course 12 is open to those only who have attained Grade C in Course
B or in Course 22 or in Course 31 or in Course BC. With the

consent of the instructors, it may be taken as a half-course for the first half-year.

[*18*hf.* Argumentative Composition.—Eight forensics preceded by briefs.—Lectures and conferences. *Half-course. Fri., at* 9. Asst. Professor BAKER.]   (I.)
Omitted in 1896–97; to be given in 1897–98.
Course 18 is open to those only who have passed with credit in Course C.

Primarily for Graduates.

19²*hf.* Historical English Grammar. *Half-course. Three times a week (second half-year).* Professor KITTREDGE.

16*hf.* History and Principles of English Versification. *Half-course. Fri., at* 11. Mr. GATES.   (III.)

3²*hf.* Anglo-Saxon.—Béowulf.—*Half-course. Mon., Wed., Fri., at* 11 *(second half-year).* Professor KITTREDGE.   (III.)

[25²*hf.* Anglo-Saxon.—Caedmon.—Cynewulf. *Half-course. Three times a week (second half-year).* Professor KITTREDGE.]
Omitted in 1896–97; to be given in 1897–98.

4. Early English.—English Literature from 1200 to 1450.—Mätzner, *Altenglische Sprachproben. Mon., Wed., Fri., at* 11. Professor CHILD and Dr. GARRETT.   (III.)
Course 4 is open to those only who are acquainted with Anglo-Saxon.

21²*hf.* Early English.—The Metrical Romances.—Lectures and theses. *Half-course. Tu., 12–1, Th., 11–1, (second half-year).* Professor KITTREDGE.   (X.)
Course 21 is open to those only who are acquainted with Early English and Old French.

[26²*hf.* Langland and Gower. *Half-course. Three times a week (second half-year).* Dr. GARRETT.]
Omitted in 1896–97; to be given in 1897–98.

17¹*hf.* English Literature of the Fifteenth and Sixteenth Centuries in relation to Italian and Spanish Literature of the Fifteenth and Sixteenth Centuries. *Half-course. Tu., Th., Sat., at* 10 *(first half-year).* Mr. FLETCHER.   (VIII.)

*27¹*hf.* The English and Scottish Popular Ballads. *Half-course. Tu., Th., Sat., at 10 (first half-year).* Professor CHILD.   (VIII.)
This course is for Graduates only.

13*hf.* Literary Criticism in England since the Sixteenth Century. *Half-course. Mon., at 3.30.* Mr. GATES.   (VI.)

14*hf.* English Literature.—The Drama from the Miracle Plays to the Closing of the Theatres. *Half-course. Wed., at 11.* Asst. Professor WENDELL.   (III.)
Course 14 is open to those only who take or have taken Course 2.

9²*hf.* English Literature.—Spenser. *Half-course. Tu., Th., Sat., at 10 (second half-year).* Mr. FLETCHER.   (VIII.)

23*hf.* English Literature.—The works of Shakspere. *Half-course. Wed., at 2.30.* Asst. Professor BAKER.   (V.)
Course 23 is open to those only who have taken English 2.

29*hf.* The English Novel from Richardson to George Eliot. *Half-course. Wed., at 10.* Professor A. S. HILL.   (II.)

24¹*hf.* The Poetry of Wordsworth, Coleridge, Scott, Byron, Shelley, and Keats. *Half-course. Tu., Th., at 11 (first half-year).* Professor A. S. HILL.   (IX.)

*5. English Composition (advanced course). *Mon., Wed., Fri., at 12.* Professor A. S. HILL.   (IV.)
With the consent of the instructor, Course 5 may be taken in two successive years.
With the consent of the instructor, Course 5 may be taken as a half-course during the first half-year.

Courses of Research.

20. During the year 1896–97 the instructors in English will hold themselves ready to assist and advise competent graduates who may propose plans of special study which shall meet the approval of the Department.

20*a.* English Literature in its relation to German Literature, from 1790 to 1830. *Wed., at 4.30.* Mr. GATES.

[20*b.* English Literature in its relation to Italian Literature in the Sixteenth Century. Mr. FLETCHER.]
Omitted in 1896–97; to be given in 1897–98.

Adams Sherman Hill
"An Answer to the Cry for More English"
(1879)

&. *Hill (1833–1910) graduated from Harvard with Charles W. Eliot, went to law school, then worked on newspapers in New York. Eliot hired Hill in 1872 and made him Boylston Professor of Rhetoric in 1876. Hill was the author of an important textbook,* The Principles of Rhetoric and Their Application *(1878; 2nd ed., 1895; see chap. 5, p. 320). During his years at Harvard, Hill taught literary criticism, modern literature, and a variety of composition courses.*

Hill won a measure of fame not as a scholar but as a language critic, a proponent of good usage who could reach large numbers of educated people, much as his friend Charles W. Eliot did on educational matters. Hill's popular Chautauqua lectures, published as Our English *(1889), aligned him with those who examined usage from a critical rather than a scholarly stance. Hill's student and colleague Barrett Wendell also derived a writing book,* English Composition, *from a lecture series; so did Hill's student Arlo Bates, whose two popular volumes* Talks on Writing English *appeared in 1896 and 1901. Hill retired in 1904. (Kitzhaber 60–63, has a brief biography.)*

Addressing himself to secondary school teachers, Hill describes Harvard's experience with its new entrance examinations and complains of the low quality of writing among applicants. This strain of complaint was to increase over the next twenty years. In 1896 Harvard reprinted Hill's article along with similar complaints in Twenty Years of School and College English. *The Harvard teachers found little good about the preparatory school training in writing. Their definition of composition is quite narrow; if preparatory schools were to follow their advice, they would produce students who would write safe, dull essays without mistakes.*

W E CAN ALL REMEMBER A TIME WHEN OUR SCHOOLS AND COLLEGES gave even less instruction in the art of writing and speaking the English language correctly than is given at present, and that too without much complaint from any quarter. Children who learned their ABC's under the old system could call the letters in a word by name, but were often unable to pronounce the same word, or to understand its meaning. Boys and girls who were well on in their teens could talk glibly about "parts of speech," "analyze" sentences, and "parse" difficult lines in Young's

"Night Thoughts" or Pope's "Essay On Man," but could not explain the sentences they took to pieces, or write grammatical sentences of their own. Those of us who have been doomed to read manuscript written in an examination room—whether at a grammar school, a high school, or a college—have found the work of even good scholars disfigured by bad spelling, confusing punctuation, ungrammatical, obscure, ambiguous, or inelegant expressions. Every one who has had much to do with the graduating classes of our best colleges, has known men who could not write a letter describing their own Commencement without making blunders which would disgrace a boy twelve years old.

Common as such shames were, they went on, not indeed without protest, but without criticism loud enough to disturb those through whom reform, if reform was to be, must come. The overburdened and underpaid teacher had every inducement to cling to the prescribed routine; the superintendent of schools was too busy to listen, too busy with the machinery of "the marking system," with his pet theory of education, with the problem how to crowd a new study into "the curriculum," or how to secure his own re-election; the professor, absorbed in a specialty, contented himself with requiring at recitations and examinations knowledge of the subject-matter, however ill-digested and ill-expressed; journals of the better class affirmed that, though such a book was not written well, it was written well enough for its purpose, and sneered at those who took pains to correct gross errors in others, or to avoid them themselves; and even some acknowledged masters of English held, with Dogberry, that "to write and read comes by nature."

Within a short time, people have partially opened their eyes to the defects of a system which crams without training, which spends its strength on the petty or the useless, and neglects that without which knowledge is but sounding brass and a tinkling cymbal. Voices have been raised which command attention. At least one school-committee and one board of supervisors have moved in the right direction. At least one college has increased its force of instructors and its number of courses in English, and has done what it could to stimulate the schools; and one president of a university [Eliot—ED.] has gone so far as to say, in an oft-quoted sentence: "I may as well abruptly avow, as the result of my reading and observation in the matter of education, that I recognize but one mental acquisition as an essential part of the education of a lady or a gentleman,— namely, an accurate and refined use of the mother tongue."

We should, however, not blind ourselves to the fact that the reform has only begun. What a recent article in "The Saturday Review" says of England is at least equally true of America: "A large proportion of our fellow-creatures labour under the hallucination that they could write as well as Macaulay, Thackeray, or Dickens, if they chose to take the trouble." They are like the man who told Charles Lamb that he "could write like Shakspere if he only had a mind to." "All he wants, you see," said Lamb, "is the mind."

The scepticism on this point which used to pervade the high places of education still lingers on the low ground, and must be dispelled before a healthy state of feeling can exist. So long as people think literary skill easy of acquisition, they will be unwilling to have their children spend time in acquiring "an accurate and refined use of the mother tongue." If the movement in favor of those things which make for good English is to be of much practical utility, it must spread widely and penetrate deeply; every school-committee must insist that, whatever else is done or is left undone, a serious effort shall be made to teach boys and girls to use their native tongue correctly and intelligently; all our colleges must put English upon a par, at least, with Latin and Greek, and must provide their students with ample opportunities for practice in writing and speaking the language they will have to use all their lives. If the schools and the colleges do this work thoroughly, a short time will suffice to bring parents to a sense of the paramount importance to every one of knowing how to read and write, and to show them how much labor that knowledge costs.

The better to understand what has yet to be done in order to secure the desired end, let us first see what is now done in the schools, as tested by the examination in English which all applicants for admission to Harvard must pass, and what is now done at Harvard.

In 1874, for the first time, every applicant for admission to Harvard was required to present English composition. The requirement[1] was as follows:

English Composition. Each candidate will be required to write a short English composition, correct in spelling, punctuation, grammar, and expression, the subject to be taken from such standard authors as shall be announced from time to time. The subject for 1874 will be taken from one of the following works: Shakespeare's Tempest, Julius Caesar, and Merchant of Venice; Goldsmith's Vicar of Wakefield; Scott's Ivanhoe and Lay of the Last Minstrel.

It was hoped that this requirement would effect several desirable objects,—that the student, by becoming familiar with a few works holding a high place in English literature, would acquire a taste for good reading, and would insensibly adopt better methods of thought and better forms of expression; that teachers would be led to seek subjects for composition in the books named, subjects far preferable to the vague generalities too often selected, and that they would pay closer attention to errors in elementary matters; that, in short, this recognition by the College of the importance of English would lead both teachers and pupils to give more time to the mother tongue, and to employ the time thus given to better advantage.

Naturally enough, these ends were not reached at once. Some of the schools did not, at first, take the requirement in a serious light; others failed to comprehend its scope; others still deemed it a high crime and misdemeanor to take an hour for English from Latin, Greek, or mathematics. In applying the requirement, moreover, the examiners gave it a liberal construction—as was proper while it was new—and the Faculty of the College, posted on the heights of the classics and mathematics, descended with difficulty to petty questions of spelling, punctuation, and grammar. This laxity of construction, coupled with the belief that a good writer had no advantage over a poor one in the studies of the Freshman year, and but a slight advantage in the subsequent years of the course, confirmed the schools in their disposition to slight the new requirement.

Within the last two years there has been a marked change for the better. More work is done in the schools; a greater proficiency is demanded from the candidate for admission; the Faculty frankly accept the requirement in English as standing upon a par with the other requirements; and many of the college instructors take account of a student's ability or inability to express his ideas with precision and clearness.

As yet, however, the amount of improvement in the schools is slight, as is shown by the results of the examination for admission to Harvard last June. For that examination the requirement was as follows:—

English Composition. Each candidate will be required to write a short English composition, correct in spelling, punctuation, grammar, division by paragraphs, and expression, upon a subject announced at the time of examination. In 1879, the subject will be drawn from one of the following works:—

Shakspere's Macbeth, Richard II., and Midsummer Night's Dream; Scott's Guy Mannering; Byron's Prisoner of Chillon; Thackeray's Henry Esmond; Macaulay's Essay on Addison; the Sir Roger de Coverley Essays in the Spectator. Every candidate is expected to be familiar with *all* the books in this list.

The time allotted for the examination in this subject was an hour, and the paper set was as follows:—

ENGLISH COMPOSITION.

Write a short composition upon one of the subjects given below.

Before beginning to write, consider what you have to say on the subject selected, and arrange your thoughts in logical order.

Aim at quality rather than quantity of work.

Carefully revise your composition, correcting all errors in punctuation, spelling, grammar, division by paragraphs, and expression, and making each sentence as clear and forcible as possible. If time permits, make a clean copy of the revised work.

I. The Character of Sir Richard Steele.
II. The Duke of Marlborough as portrayed by Thackeray.
III. The Style of "Henry Esmond."
IV. Thackeray's account of the Pretender's visit to England.
V. Duelling in the Age of Queen Anne.

The whole manner of persons who presented themselves for examination in this paper was 316—including those applying for immediate admission and those taking the first, or "preliminary," half of the examination, the rest to be taken in some subsequent year. Of this number 157, almost exactly one half, failed to pass, the percentage of failure being but slightly larger among the applicants for a "preliminary certificate" than among the candidates for admission.

The causes of failure were diverse. Some of the unsuccessful, an eighth or a tenth of them perhaps, avowed or displayed utter ignorance of the subject-matter: several, for example, confounded Steele with Sir Roger de Coverley, others the period of Queen Anne with that of Richard Cœur de Lion, others the style of "Henry Esmond," the novel, with the manners of Henry Esmond, the hero of the novel. Some—a smaller number, however, than in previous years—showed such utter ignorance of punctuation as to put commas at the end of complete sentences, or between words that no rational being would separate from one another; and a few began sentences with small letters, or began every long word with a capital letter. Many, a larger number than usual, spelled as if starting a spelling reform, each for himself. Of these vagaries specimens are subjoined, including vain attempts to reproduce proper names that were printed on the examination paper itself:—*duells, jelosie, cheif, opposit, suprising, Collossus, compaired, repetedly, fourth* (for forth), *to* (for too), *thrown* (for throne), *ficle*, white-winged *angle, beaverage, broak, carrige, champaign* (for champagne), *insted, haled* (for hailed), *endevors, sucess, preasant* and *presance, widly, wating, differance, superceeded, prepaired, comand, conspiritors,* to *finnish, avaritious, undoubtibly, granfather, peice,* fashionable *bell, writen* and *writtings, maniger* (for manager), *untill, jovility* (for joviality), *ficticious, couard* and *couardise* (for coward), *exhisted, origen* and *origonal* (for origin and original), *kneeded* (for needed), *genious, marrid, mad* (for made), *wer* (for were), *cleaverly, differculty, existance, abscent, lolier, repare, ennoubling, agrieved, of* (for off), *susceptable, proclamed, loose* (for lose), *principle* (for principal), *lead* (for led), *Rip Van Rincle, Adison* and *Adderson, Queene Ann, Macauley, Thackery, Steel* (Sir Richard), *Henery, Harries* (for Harry's). Of these mistakes some are evidently much graver than others; but some of the worst were found in several books, and not a few are apparently due to an unconscious effort to represent to the eye a vicious pronunciation. Many books were deformed by grossly ungrammatical or profoundly obscure sentences, and some by absolute illiteracy.

To bring himself below the line between failure and success, a writer had to commit several serious faults; and even if he did commit such faults, he was allowed to pass if he offset them by tolerably good work in the rest of his book. Even apparent ignorance of the nature of a paragraph, or of the principle of sequence in thought or in language, did not of itself form an insurmountable obstacle to success. The books of many who managed to get above the line were, as regards all but the A B C of composition, discreditable to the teachers whose instruction they represented. If the examiner erred, it was in giving the candidate the benefit of too many doubts, in tempering justice with too much mercy. He meant to make the requirement more serious than in previous years, but he did not mean to demand as much as might reasonably be expected from boys between sixteen and twenty years of age.

The great majority of the compositions this year, as in previous years, were characterized by general defects, which, though not taken into account by the examiner, point to grave imperfections in the method (or want of method) of the preparatory schools. The suggestions at the head of the paper were often disregarded in the letter, and almost always in the spirit. The candidate, instead of considering what he had to say and arranging his thoughts before beginning to write, either wrote without thinking about the matter at all, or thought to no purpose. Instead of aiming at good work, and to that end subjecting his composition to careful revision, he either did not undertake to revise it at all, or did not know how to correct his errors. Evidently, he had never been taught the value of previous thought or of subsequent criticism.

To the rule there were, of course, exceptions. A few boys showed the results of excellent training; but out of the whole number only fourteen received a mark high enough to entitle them to the distinction of passing "with credit."

On the whole, the examination makes a poor showing for the schools that furnish the material whereof the university which professes to set up the highest standard in America, has to make educated men. If she does not succeed in giving to all her graduates the one mental acquisition deemed by her president the essential part of education, the fault is not altogether or mainly hers. For her to teach bearded men the rudiments of their native tongue would be almost as absurd as to teach them the alphabet or the multiplication table. Those who call for "more English" in the colleges should cry aloud and spare not till more and better English is taught in the schools.

In the schools the reform should start. From the beginning to the end of the pre-collegiate course, the one thing that should never be lost sight of is the mother tongue, the language which the boy uses all the time as a boy, and will use as a man. Till he knows how to write a simple English sentence, he should not be allowed to open a Latin grammar. Till he can speak and write his own language with tolerable correctness, he should not be set down before the words of another language. Whatever knowledge he acquires, he should be able to put into clear and intelligible English. Every new word he adds to his vocabulary, he should know in the spelling and with the meaning accepted by the rest of the world. Every stop he inserts in a sentence should serve a definite purpose.

The work begun in the primary school should be carried on by the grammar school, the high school, the private tutor. No translation from a foreign language, whether oral or written, no examination book, no recitation, should be deemed creditable unless made in good English. Gradually a boy should be led from the construction of a well-formed sentence to that of a well-formed paragraph, and from paragraph to essay. Gradually he should be led from the skillful use of materials for composition provided by others to the discovery and arrangement of materials for himself, from the practice of clothing another's thoughts in his own language to the presentation of his own thoughts or fancies in appropriate language,—care being taken, of course, to provide, at each stage in his education, subjects suited to his powers and attractive to his tastes.

The teacher of English should be equally quick to detect faults and to recognize merits of every description, and should know how to stimulate his pupils' minds till they are as fresh and alert at the desk as on the playground. He should possess special qualifications, for his task is at once difficult and important. The best talent in each school—it is not too much to say—cannot be better employed than in teaching the use of the great instrument of communication between man and man, between books and men, the possession without which learning is mere pedantry, and thought an aimless amusement.

When schools of all grades are provided with instructors in English who are neither above nor below their business, it will be possible to make the requirement in this subject for admission to college decidedly higher than it is at present, and the work after admission correspondingly better. When the schools shall be ready to teach the laws of good use in language and the elementary principles of rhetoric, a great point will be gained.

The next best step would be to give to English two hours or more a week during the Freshman year. Could the study be taken up at the threshold of college life, the schools would be made to feel that their labors in this direction were going to tell upon a pupil's standing in college as well as upon his admission. Unfortunately, however, it has not been found possible to make room in the Freshman year for English, no one of the departments which now occupy the year being willing to give up any of its time, and each supporting the others in opposition to change.

While things remain as they are, the only way in which progress can be made is by a disposition on the part of those who instruct Freshmen in other studies to insist upon the use of good English whenever, in oral or written work, any English is used; and this to a certain extent is done, some of those who are most unwilling to surrender a half hour of their own time to the instructor in English taking most pains to require good language from their pupils: but they have too many other things in hand to do this thoroughly, and there are obvious obstacles in the way of their achieving results that could easily be reached with younger boys in smaller classes.

At Harvard, then, a student receives no direct instruction in English till his Sophomore year. During that year two hours a week are given to the study of rhetoric. A text-book is used which aims at familiarizing the pupil with the principles that underlie all good composition, as deduced from the best authors and illustrated by examples or warnings from recent works; exercises are written and criticised; and writers noted for clearness, like Macaulay, or for strength of statement and logical coherence, like Burke or Webster, are studied to the extent that time permits. Every Sophomore, moreover, writes six themes on assigned subjects, which are corrected and criticised by the instructor, and are rewritten by the student to the end that he may seize the spirit as well as the letter of the suggestions he has received. The books studied ought to tell on the themes, and they do so tell with faithful students who assimilate what they learn.

Juniors are required to write six themes and four forensics. The themes are in the hands of three instructors. One has the A division, which is composed of the best writers in the class, and is small enough to enable the teacher to read each theme either with its author or aloud to a section of the division, and thus to make the criticism more searching and the revision more thorough than is possible under any system of notes on the margin. The B and C divisions, comprising the rest of the class, are so large that their themes for the most part have to be treated like those of the Sophomores.

The forensics, which, in theory at least, are execises in argumentative composition, are read and weighed, but not criticised. For them candidates for Honors are allowed to substitute theses in their several departments, that is, writings which call for learning rather than for argumentative power.

Seniors have to write four forensics, which are criticised from a rhetorical as well as from a logical point of view. For them, as for the Junior forensics, theses may in certain cases be substituted; and for two of them a Commencement Part is accepted as an equivalent.

Commencement Parts themselves (with the exception of one or two written in Latin) may be regarded as exercises in English composition. Early in November, the professor of rhetoric meets those whose rank at the end of the Junior year renders it probable that they will receive degrees "with distinction" at the end of the course. He tries to impress them with the importance of the academic festival in which they are to take part, and with their duty to do their best, both for their own credit and for that of the University. Each is left to choose his own topic, subject to the approval of a committee of professors representing all departments of the University, and to treat the topic chosen in the way that best suits his powers. The Parts must be written by the first of May. The best of them are read by their authors to the committee, who select from the whole number the five or six best adapted to the occasion,— subject, treatment, and delivery, being all taken into account. Every year the honor of speaking is more highly prized; every year the competitors show better work and more thorough comprehension of the essentials of a successful essay; every year the committee find more difficulty in deciding which among several productions to select—a difficulty which is likely to increase now that, in consequence of certain changes in the regulations concerning degrees, the number of competitors is more than doubled, over fifty being entitled to write this year, as against twenty-three or twenty-four last year. The testimony of those who are in the habit of attending Harvard Commencements (that of Rev. Dr. Bellows, for instance, as expressed in his enthusiastic speech last June) supports the opinion that there is, from year to year, a gradual improvement, sufficient to indicate that the labors of those who have helped the cause of good English have not been thrown away, that the ambition of the young men has not been appealed to in vain, and that the newly-awakened interest of the community in its own language has penetrated the academic shades.

In addition to the prescribed work in English, an advanced elective course was established two years ago. To this course none but Seniors or Juniors who have proved their ability as writers are admitted. Every member of the class is required to write a composition once a fortnight, sometimes on a subject of his own, sometimes on an assigned subject or on one of several assigned subjects. Occasionally the instructor calls for a written criticism of an author whose works he deems worthy of study, or for a critical estimate of the relative merits of two authors of the same general character. Three hours a week are spent in criticism of the themes in the presence of the class, criticism in which all take part and which now and then leads to animated discussion. Often the best themes present the most matter for comment; and some of the best as well as some of the worst writers make great improvement in recasting their essays after they have been criticised. Two examinations occur in the course of the year, at which the class write upon subjects announced at the time, subjects drawn from books that have been read in preparation, or from current questions or familiar topics.

Last year, a course in "Oral Discussion" was established. In order to give ample time for preparation, the class meets only once a fortnight; in order to give ample time for debate, each session lasts for three consecutive hours. A question—political, historical, or literary—which presents a fair field for argument, and demands both reading and thought, is announced a fortnight before the time fixed for its discussion; two members of the class are appointed to open the argument on each side, and one to close it, each of the opening speakers to have ten minutes and each of the closing ones fifteen minutes. Between the opening and the closing speeches nearly an hour is given to volunteers on either side, each being allowed five minutes only. The remaining hour is spent in comment by the instructor on the debate to which he has been listening, comment which extends to points of manner as well as of matter, to the way of putting things as much as to the things put, the general aim being to teach the young men how to make everything serve the main object— the object of convincing or persuading a hearer. Awkward attitudes, ungrammatical or obscure sentences, provincial or vulgar locutions, fanciful analogies, far-fetched illustrations, ingenious sophisms, pettifogging subtleties, ineffective arrangement—all come in for animadversion; and corresponding merits for praise. The debate is judged as an exercise in spoken English as well as in reasoning; and observation shows that, as might have been anticipated, a strong writer is usually a strong speaker also.

These two are the only elective courses which make the writing or the speaking of good English their principal aim; and since the efficiency of each requires that the class should be limited in number and that preference should be given to the most competent writers or speakers, it is not unlikely that some who become conscious, at the end of their Junior year, of deficiencies in their powers of expression, are unable to avail themselves of these opportunities to supply their deficiencies, and that many more do not open their eyes to their needs till after they have left college. If, however, the demand for elective work in English should greatly exceed the supply, the College will doubtless provide new courses sufficient to meet the demand. In establishing a course in composition in 1877, and one in oral discussion in 1878, the Faculty anticipated, rather than gratified, the wishes of the students; but both courses, as the event has proved, supply real wants.

Though the courses described are the only ones which aim, first and foremost, at good English, there are others which exercise a marked influence in the same direction. Prominent among these are the courses conducted by Professor Child, one of the most accomplished living English scholars,—those in philology making the student familiar with the sources of the existing language, and those in Shakspere, Bacon, Chaucer, Milton, and Dryden, bringing him into close contact with the greatest of our writers. There is also a course in the English literature of the last and the present century; there are readings and lectures in English, and literary courses in other languages, none of which can fail, in one way or another, in a greater or a less degree, to cultivate a faithful student's powers of expression. A similar influence may be traced to the courses in the fine arts, in mental and moral philosophy, in history, in political economy, and even to some of the scientific courses. Every instructor who himself speaks and writes good English, and who demands good English from his pupils, is of great service; and the number of those who keep this object in view is steadily increasing.

On the whole, it seems fair to conclude that Harvard College, if not doing as much for the English of her students as can reasonably be expected while the schools do so little, is yet doing more and more every year, and that the most serious shortcomings in this respect on the part of her recent graduates cannot justly be laid at her door. English composition is the only study that every student *must* pursue after the Freshman year, every other subject being now optional; in the elective courses in writing and speaking English, the best men have ample opportunities for practice; in other courses, the best influences are indirectly at work to cultivate the students' powers of expression; instruction in elocution is given to all who desire it; Commencement Parts and Bowdoin Prizes (for dissertations on stated subjects) offer rewards for excellence in writing, Lee and Boylston Prizes for excellence in reading aloud and in speaking;

and there is now no doubt that in all the governing bodies of the University the current of opinion sets strongly in favor of good English.

NOTE

[1]"Requisition" in the article as originally published, that being the word then used in the University Catalogue. "Requirement" is the proper word.

Le Baron Russell Briggs
"The Harvard Admission Examination in English"
The Academy (1888)

ટ**ે**   *Briggs (1855–1934) was a student of Adams Sherman Hill's and would succeed him as Boylston Professor of Rhetoric. As instructor in English, Briggs grew up teaching in the Harvard system and never knew anything else, since he spent his whole career there. When Briggs became dean of Harvard College in 1891 it marked the entrenchment of the composition system, despite the growing emphasis on literature in the English department. Briggs also served as president of Radcliffe College, 1903–23.*

This article, which first appeared in The Academy, *a journal for secondary school teachers and administrators, was reprinted in* Twenty Years of School and College English.

THE HARVARD ADMISSION EXAMINATION IN ENGLISH IS WIDELY discussed and little understood. It is worth while, therefore, to show what this examination is and what sort of work the candidates do in it.

Every candidate is expected to write off-hand a respectable little theme, and to correct specimens of bad English. Subjects for composition are drawn from a few English classics, which the association of New England colleges prescribes; specimens of bad English are taken from the examination books of earlier years, from students' themes, from newspapers, and from contemporary literature.

A scheme of examination must meet two tests: it must be rational on paper, and must be rationally administered. Whether the English examination at Harvard meets the first of these tests is still an open question. Substitutes for it and modifications of it are suggested on every hand. One teacher would try the candidate's knowledge of English by all his examination books, considered, whatever their subjects, as English Composition. This is an alluring plan, ideal in its excellence, and, alas, ideal in its impracticability. The books must be read under the lash: it is only by straining every nerve that the examiners can finish their work in time. If all the books of each candidate should be collected and should be examined as English Composition by some competent person, the delay would be unbearable. Moreover, such an examination would not touch English Literature; and in this "practical" age it is well to teach a boy that classics exist. The proposal to substitute for the present test an examination in English History, and to mark each book twice, once for History and once for English, is open to like objections: it would double the time needed for handling the books, and it would require no knowledge of literature. It would introduce, besides, the danger of fixing a boy's study of composition on what is known as "the historical style," which is often conventional and unlovely. Some teachers would prescribe Mr. Stopford Brooke's *Primer of English Literature;* but this plan, too, is objectionable. It would force the candidate to study not literature, but facts (and opinions) about literature—names of authors whose works he had never seen; dates, which, without a first-hand acquaintance with the books they represent, stare blankly at the mind, and at which the mind too often stares blankly in return. Other teachers would do away with the correction of bad English, and would fasten a boy's attention on good English only: yet up to this time no one has devised a better half-hour's test of acuteness and accuracy than the Bad English paper; and until the English of Freshmen becomes less slovenly than it now is—or until accuracy becomes a lost art—some test is essential. Others still, would have no English requirement. They would suffer boys to come to college without a sense of literary form, and to "dump" their knowledge promiscuously into their examination books. I am no admirer of the present requirement; I live in hope of something better: but I am as yet unable to see in any of the proposed substitutes a scheme at once superior and practicable. Besides, the present plan has passed, for a time at least, beyond the control of Harvard examiners and of Harvard University; it must stand for several years more whether we like it or not.

The second test that an examination is bound to meet is the test of rational administration: it is not enough that the scheme of requirements is defensible; the examiner must ask none but reasonable questions, and must mark the answers by a reasonable standard. Nobody who has inspected examination papers and the records of admission to colleges pretends that he can judge the severity of an examination by the printed scheme alone. Harvard College and other colleges print the same English requirement, but set different questions and mark by different standards. Acquaintance with the method of marking is clearly necessary to the understanding of an examination. I have in mind two questions from the Greek admission papers of minor colleges: one asked who Zeus was; the other called for an account of the uses of the genitive case. Either may have demanded enormous intelligence in the candidate, and may have demanded none whatever; neither, I must add, showed much in the examiner.

In such discussion of the English examination as I have heard, nothing has impressed me more than the ignorance of teachers about the real nature of the test. The College is quite as responsible for this ignorance as the teachers are, since it has not done much to enlighten them; but the teachers are responsible for irresponsibility, if for nothing more, when they publicly express such views as a thorough acquaintance with the subject would prove untenable.

The candidate, as I have said, is required to write a short composition on one of some half-dozen subjects from one or more of the prescribed English classics. It is possible, no doubt, to pick out from a collection of Harvard admission papers a few subjects unintelligently chosen; it is possible to pick out many that demand either a close acquaintance with the books from which they come or a touch of originality in the boy who treats them well: but it is, I believe impossible to find a paper that does not offer at least one subject of which no conscientious boy can complain. If one or two subjects are hard, candidates (and teachers) should remember that among the three hundred applicants of a single year there are a few whom individuality or literary instinct guides to the maturer subjects, and that these few may be worth a hundred of the others. Nevertheless the multitude has carried the day: the Commission of New England Colleges[1] has practically tabooed the more advanced subjects; and the paper for last June—as printed below—contains nothing that is abstruse, and little that even in appearance is minutely exacting:—

ENGLISH COMPOSITION I.

Write a composition—with special attention to clearness of arrangement, accuracy of expression, and quality rather than quantity of matter—on one of the following subjects:—

1. The Story of Viola.
2. Viola's Errand to Olivia.
3. How Malvolio was Tricked.
4. Sir Andrew Aguecheek's Challenge and What Came of it.
5. Mr. Darcy's Courtship.

Whatever the subjects offered, it is safe to say that no candidate ever failed through ignorance of the details of a prescribed book. Doubtless many candidates have believed, and asserted, that they failed for this reason; possibly their teachers have believed it, and have spread the report: but, as a matter of fact, the examiner's first question to himself is always, "Can the boy write English?" If he can, he may pass the examination, though, with Julius Caesar for his subject, he declares that Mark Antony loved Caesar less and Rome more. In June, 1887, two or three boys passed who acknowledged that they had never read the book from which the subjects were drawn, and who substituted subjects of their own choice from the other prescribed books. They would not have passed if their own English had not been good and their correction of bad English intelligent. When a boy takes his own subject, it is right to demand a better theme of him than of others; and since he may have come to the examination primed with a composition not his own, it is right to demand of him unusual skill in the correction of bad English— the only work that is beyond question his. This year a candidate passed with a disgracefully ignorant little theme, called "The Story of Viola" but really a feeble fiction of his own. He knew almost nothing of Viola except that she wore boy's clothes. He was saved because his work with the "specimens" was good, and the English of his composition bearable. Besides, he needed clemency in order to be admitted to college, and a condition in English would have turned the scale against him. Here is his theme:—

"The Story of Viola."

"As it happened, Viola went out in a ship in company with her brother. They had been gone some time and were far out at sea, when a storm arose and wrecked the ship. During the disaster Viola got separated from her brother, and each was obliged to look after himself. They succeeded in saving themselves, but each one thought that the other had been drown.

"Some while afterwards, Viola happened to wander to the town in which her brother at that time was staying. She saw him and recognized him, and so went and put on a boy's apparel and engaged herself into a family as a messenger boy to run on all errands that should come up. She kept her position for some time, continually making trouble for the people around her, and playing jokes on the lovers in the play.

"Finally she gave up and told her brother of her identity, which he would not believe at first, but finally accepted her as his sister with great joy."

I was ashamed to pass this theme, and am ashamed to print it as part of a successful examination; but I wish to show that Harvard does not insist upon that minute and diversified literary knowledge which strains a boy's head and baffles a teacher's imparting skill.

Leniently as the books are judged now, it might be well, as some one has suggested, to supplement the test of a theme written off-hand by that of one written at school and certified by the teacher as a fair specimen of the boy's work. The plan resembles that already adopted for the examination in Experimental Physics. The certified theme, if presented by a trustworthy teacher, might now and then offset in the examiner's judgment, the effect of nervous excitement or examination fright. So far Harvard might move toward the plan of admission by certificate, but no farther.

The master of a famous preparatory school makes two complaints which deserve special consideration: first, that his worst pupils always pass in English; and secondly, that his best pupils fail to get "credit" or "honors." Good and bad are lumped, he declares, so that he can rouse neither ambition nor fear.

It is easy to see why his poorer scholars pass. He has boys of more than average intelligence; he pays more attention to the English requirement than most teachers are as yet willing to do; he uses good English himself, whereas many teachers do not; and, above all, he gives admirable instruction in Greek and Latin. Thus his pupils have peculiar advantages; and even the weakest of them do as well at the English examination as better scholars from many other schools.

Some masters push English Composition into a corner, and a dark corner at that; others are guilty of sentences like "When *will we* be able to *really commence* work?" others, not so inaccurate, prefer oratorical or dressy English to the style of a straightforward gentleman, and vitiate a boy's writing with a vulgarity that it takes years to counteract; others still—to borrow Professor Hill's expression—praise the English that is "free from all faults except that of having no merits;" and many suffer their pupils to turn Greek and Latin into that lazy, mongrel dialect, "Translation English."

The Greek and Latin requirements tell for so much more than the English requirements that a boy spends at least three school hours in producing hybrid translation to one in producing English. Consequently, at the English examination he writes, *"One of the strangers having been informed of the youth's mission, set out to find the sought for uncle of the youth."* I condition him, but with pity rather than blame; for the teachers, too, are infected with the disease of construing. When a boy writes *"you was"* or *"a little ways,"* he may show the influence of an uneducated home—an influence that his teacher is perhaps powerless to offset. What gives a peculiarly melancholy aspect to *"He having been informed, set out to find the sought for uncle,"* is the fact that no illiterate boy could produce it; that it is the direct result of an educational process for which the teacher is beyond escape to blame. In a school where the teaching of Greek and Latin is, as it should be everywhere, the teaching of English also, no boy will have much trouble with the English requirements.

The complaint that boys of marked capacity in English fail to get "credit," is a serious one, and I am unable to meet it satisfactorily. Before this year the requirement for credit was too high. This year the college lowered it slightly; yet, even with an unusually easy paper in "Sentences," it was impossible to give "credit" to more than five books; and not one of the five showed remarkable promise. I print one as a specimen:—

"The Story of Viola."

"The story of 'The Twelfth Night,' in which Viola appears, opens with the landing of Viola, with her friend, the captain, upon the shores of Illyria. She is in quest of her brother, Sebastian, whom she has not seen since the time of the ship-wreck, a disaster which seperated [sic] them some time ago. She remembers having heard her father speak with the greatest admiration of the duke Orsino, who lives in a city near by, and determines to enter his service as his page.

"Now the duke is at this time violently in love with the Countess Olivia, a beautiful woman, who is in mourning for her brother and has vowed that man shall never look upon her face again. Every advance of the duke is rejected; his entreaties are in vain. When he sees Viola, Orsino at once employs her, thinking her to be a man, and sends her to press his suit with the countess. He sees that Viola is beautiful and thinks that she can more easily obtain an interview with Olivia.

"He is right; Viola not only gains access to the palace, but a private interview with the countess. She tells Olivia of the duke's insatiable love, but all her efforts come to naught; again and again, she tries to soften Olivia's heart, but always with the same result.

"Meanwhile, Olivia, also thinking Viola to be a man, has fallen in love with her, and Viola has grown to love the duke. These three are now entangled in a web from which time alone can extricate them. The duke is in love with the countess, the countess loves Viola, and Viola tells the duke that she will never love wife more than him.

"At the palace of Olivia, lives her cousin, Sir Toby, whom Sir Andrew Aguecheek is visiting. Sir Andrew is wooing the countess and, seeing that she looks with favor upon Viola, sends Viola a challenge for a duel.

"In the mean time Viola's brother, Sebastian, has arrived in the city. In walking about, he happens to enter the court-yard of of Olivia's palace. Sebastian looks exactly like his sister, and, when Sir Andrew sees him, he thinks it is Viola and attacks him. Being very skilled in the use of the sword, Sebastian easily overcomes Sir Andrew.

"Olivia, now meeting Sebastian and taking him to be Viola, tells him of her love for him and proposes that they be married. Sebastian, not disliking the looks of the countess, accepts, and the knot is tied.

"Viola now enters with the duke, and brother and sister meet for the first time since the ship-wreck. Everything is quickly explained, and Orsino, remembering Viola's professions of love, marries her.

"Thus happily ends 'The Twelfth Night' and the romantic experience of Viola."

This composition has none of a boy's freshness, no marked sign of literary taste, no peculiar vigor. Besides, there are taints of translation in it, such as "*being very skilled,*" and "*taking him to be Viola * * * proposes that they be married.*" Its English, however, is usually accurate and unpretending; and the boy, tame as he is, shows undeniable skill in marshalling his facts. He has constructed a clear and well-proportioned summary, has done a solid hour's work, and deserves praise. He makes some bad slips with the "specimens," but not many; and I give him the coveted "Good." Other boys show more cleverness and more imagination; but their English is slipshod, or grandiose, or miscellaneously exuberant. They may be brilliant writers by and by; but they lack those qualities without which no elementary work earns a high mark.

In three cases of failure to get "credit" complaint has reached the examiners. In two of these cases Professor Hill re-read the compositions and found plague-spots of "Translation English." Complaint in the third case came to me, nearly two years after the examination. I had then seen the young man's work in his Freshman and Sophomore years. He was interested in literature, and his mind was strong and fertile. At his best he wrote admirably; at other times he was diffuse and undisciplined— fond of tricks that seemed almost too vicious for his good sense to overcome or his vitality to struggle through. Nor was he even accurate. He wrote *"twighlight,"* for instance, with all dictionaries at his command and a fortnight for preparation. Such a young man might earn from sixty per cent to one hundred, according to his mood; and nobody could foresee whether he would or would not deserve "honors" in English.

It is almost inevitable that the extremes of marking should lie nearer together in the English examination than in any other. In mathematics and even in translation, total failure is possible; but every boy who thinks himself ready for Harvard College can produce a few English sentences, and correct some of the more glaring errors in the specimens of bad English. A book in mathematics may be perfect, and a book in translation accurate; but no one knows what perfect English is, and scarcely any one keeps clear of conspicuous inaccuracy. Again: the "sentence paper," though easy to do something with, is hard to treat perfectly in the time allowed by the Faculty. These causes narrow the range of marking.

I have tried to show what the English examination is; it remains to consider some characteristics of the examination books.

Spelling is bad, and probably always will be: *loose* for *lose* is so nearly universal that *lose* begins to look wrong; *sentance* prevails; *dissapointed* and *facinating* are not unusual; sporadic cases are *Sir Tobby* [Belch], *Sheassphere* [of Stratford], and *welthey aeris*[2] [Portia of Belmont]. Punctuation is frequently inaccurate—that is to say, unintelligent and misleading. The apostrophe is nearly as often a sign of the plural as of the possessive; the semicolon, if used at all, is a spasmodic ornament rather than a help to the understanding; and—worst of all—the comma does duty for the period, so that even interesting writers run sentence into sentence without the formality of full stop or of capital. To many candidates the principle that punctuation has no excuse for being, except so far as it guides the reader to the writer's meaning, seems never to have occurred. As for paragraphing, I am aware that it is a delicate art: yet that is no reason why some whole essays should be single paragraphs—solid, unindented blocks of conglomerate; or why in others nearly every sentence should make a paragraph by itself, so that a page, except for its untidiness, might be taken from a primer. Here is a composition of the former kind:—

"Viola, disguised as a boy, was sent by the Duke to see Olivia. Viola was sent with intention that she should try and persuade Olivia to love the Duke. Viola, however, instead of gaining the love of Olivia for the Duke, gained it for herself. At last, even, Olivia wanted to marry Viola, but Viola being a girl was forced to refuse her. It happened that Viola's brother passed there soon after this. Olivia taking him for his sister asked him to marry her, which he, after he was over his surprise, did. Olivia the next time she met Viola, taking her for her brother, was quite indignant because she did not recognise her as her wife. Shortly after this Viola's brother meeting Oliva and Viola together, is overjoyed to meet his sister, whom he thought dead. The Duke then also comes by and recognised Viola. After the Duke hears that Olivia is married he askes Viola to be his wife which she with great pleasure does. The Duke and Olivia therefore instead of becoming man and wife, become brother and sister."

I give two specimens of the minced themes, one narrative and one ethical:—

I.

"Mr Darcy was invited by Mr Bingley to make him a visit at his place.

"It happened that, early one morning, Elizabeth Bennet had taken a walk, and on her way had visited the Bingleys.

[3]"Here she met Mr Darcy, and at first sight took a dislike to him.

"She took cold on account of her walk and was not able to go home for two days; so her sister came and took care of her.

"The sister of Bingley wanted to marry Mr Darcy on account of his money, although she could not consider herself poor.

"It seems that Mr Darcy was struck at the first sight by the handsome face of Elizabeth and Mr Bingley also was not slow to acknowledge that he liked Jane, Elizabeth's sister,

"Soon after the malady was cured, the sisters returned home.

"In a few days Mr Bennet invited Mr Darcy and Bingly to a dinner.

"Here also Mr Darcy showed a desire for Elizabeths company.

"At this time there was quatred at Longbourn a regiment.

"This was a very pleasing addition to the pleasures of the Bennet's, for there was always some entertainiment going on, in which they generally took part.

"A Mr Wickham made his appearance here in order to join the regiment.

"He was very handsome, and could keep up a lively conversation so that he was liked by everyone, especially the Bennets.

"One day Mr Darcy with Mr Bingley were riding through Longbourn when they met the Bennets who were with Mr Wickham. As soon as Wickham saw Darcy he turned colour and passed on. Elizabeth noticed this and related it to her sister and they two had a great amount of gossip over the event.

"The next time Elizabeth met Wickham she enquired of him when he and Mr Darcy had met before.

"He told her a story that threw a dark light on Mr Darcy and made himself out as a very wronged man.

"This was believed by all who heard of it untill Wickham eloped with Lydia Bennet leaving great many debts behind him.

"These Mr Darcy paid and found out where the eloped couple were staying, and reported his find to Mr Bennet's brother.

"This transaction was found out by Elizabeth, who immediately had to admit to her sister that she liked Mr Darcy more than ever.

"This soon grew into love which finally resulted in her marriage."

II.
"Mr. Darcy's Courtship."

In the Courtship of Mr. Darcy we see one hand, much for lovers to copy after and desire, while on the other much that they should avoid.

"A warning should be taken from the despicable manner in which Jane is treated by Darcy's sister. It is unfair to say the least.

"Why should a respectable young man be prevented from courting a young lady even if she be not wealthy?

"The course of true love cannot be put to an end, no matter what is brought to bear upon it.

"If every lover would have the patience and faith of Jane in a man, especially when outward circumstances are very, very dark, we should have less divorce cases to-day in the courts.

"While Darcy is prevented from seeing his object of love no one can be lead to think that he has no thought of her.

"He appears to think of her all the time wishing to see her and to declare his love for her. Perhaps Darcy did not endeavor as much as he was able, to either find or write Jane.

"Some would censure him in this respect, but for my part, when a man is hindered from anything and when he knows that if he does that thing, it will be contrary to the best wishes of his own sister, I have not the courage to blame him.

"A lover should be carefull and not arose the passions of his or her love.

"It is not to be wondered at that Darcy's conduct should seem strange to Jane.

"This walking in the dark is not to be envied by any means.

"In spite of trial and difficulties Jane and Darcy meet again and renew their love.

"Soon Darcy's Courtship ceases for they are united in the happy bond of unity."

The "lukewarm moral atmosphere" of the last essay suggests a serious fault of many examination books, the fancied necessity of infusing morality somewhere. The favored spot is usually the end; and the moral peroration is so common that some teachers, as I fear, must encourage it. A few examples will do:—

1. "Many people can write a pretty frivollous story, but few is the number, of those, who can put into that story lessons that, if a reader learns them, he can follow all through life. This power has been given to Miss Austen."

2. "On the day when these two [Darcy and Elizabeth] were united, two hearts, properly adapted to each other but of different birth were made one, not for a few years nor for life but forever."

3. "Such is her [Viola's] story, and beautifully has the great Shakespeare told it. She leaves us all a wide field for thought and an almost perfect example of what true manhood should be. Character into which right principles have been implanted at its first forming is impressed indelibly. So Viola, beautiful in character, righteous in deed, and pure in heart lived every nobly and although her appearance was changed yet the heart was the same,

> 'Like the vase in which roses have once been distilled;
> You may break, you may shatter the vase if you will,
> But the scent of the roses will hang round it still.' "

4. "Miss Austen evidently intends to show that even our most powerful feelings of dislike can be overcome in time and that we should not judge that as we now feel we shall always feel."

"Everything is liable to change, and we ourselves are not excluded, it is wisely ordained thus, for terrible would be the results were all first impressions permanent."

The last passage recalls the schoolgirls' sentiments in *Elsie Venner*—"that beauty is subject to the accidents of time," and the like. The rest of the same theme, however, is neither oratorical nor flat; so that the work as a whole is far better than that of the following essay, where vicious morality and "fatal facility" blight every line:—

"Mr. Darcy's Courtship."

"What a strange paradox of character Darcy at first seems? You hardly can account for it. It may seem unnatural when first you think of it. But think. Know you not many of your friends whose actions seem to be inconsistent. Aye, look you at your own. Think how often you astonish yourself, as well as those who know you, by your various actions and then look at Darcy.

"Pride and Prejudice—Darcy's character alone would have given the first part of the title of the book. But what is pride? Does it not continually display itself? Does it not *consist* itself in display. How noticible then when it occurs. Surely pride in itself is no tremendous fault, but its disagreeableness lies in this very characteristic—display.

"But you wonder how this has anything to do with his *courtship*. Aye, in every way. Do you not remember his pride, the very first time you saw him there in the ball-room? how he was above dancing? Do you not remember seeing Bingley go up to him to beg of him to dance? and can you not remember his reply, remarking that Elizabeth was only tolerable? But that same Elizabeth in a few years is mistress of Pemberley. Mark how he only watches the second Miss Bennet, but he is too proud to court openly. Also, by way of remark, I think I remember hearing him speak to Bingley about the Bennets' vulgar relatives. Even his love breaks not through his pride; his Pride and Love go hand in hand, if Pride does not lead the way. But his love is safe, for that love's bitterest enemy, pride, is overthrown by Elizabeth's disdainful rejection. Could you not almost foresee this? Would any one have been a wonderful prophet to have told that he was in love with Elizabeth, nay even that he would propose, (and why should he not for he, through his pride, was confident of acceptance?) that Elizabeth would scornfully refuse, and that his pride would be broken? What could more surely break one's pride than have a proposal, in assurance given, cast back in one's face, as Darcy's was?

"There was something that made me love Darcy from the beginning. It shone through his pride, through his arrogance, and made me feel that, behind that unpleasant outside, there was a true man. I know not what it was, but it made me feel that I wished I had that man's character without his pride.

"With Elizabeth's refusal his true courtship really begins. Before, he was courting his own pride; now, he courts Miss Elizabeth Bennet. His love, no longer smothered under the wet blanket of his pride burns unhindered; and to have Darcy's unhindered love was to have a most precious, most priceless thing. It was not a mere passionate affection, that lived merely for the pleasure of its existence. It was a love of tender regard, that lived solely for the being to whom it was directed and because of whom it came into existence.

"Can it not be put this way? Darcy had pride. Love crept in. That love grew and grew. That love startled his pride. It was too late for the love to be stifled, it could only be restrained. His pride was broken, and his love unrestrained filled his life. Pride can no more enter that heart of which true Love has full possession."

None but a cynic can fail to sympathize with the writer of this theme for the agony that awaits him in Harvard College, the lashing that he must endure before he finds his true place in that hard-hearted little world. If there is one thing that Harvard College will not tolerate, it is "gush,"—"gush" in general, and moral or oratorical "gush" in particular. I may whisper parenthetically that some young men have gushed unseen, or seen and uncondemned, if they have chosen verse as the outlet of their feelings; that the "Harvard man," afraid of making a fool of himself, would rather accept nonsense as poetry than set up himself for a critic of poetry: but in prose detection is certain at Harvard if anywhere. Illiteracy a student will pardon (it is the weakness of a man and a brother, and no drawback to touchdowns or home runs); even immorality he will often overlook: but the blatant moral oratory of a man that he thinks no better than himself cannot be lived down in a four years' course. All this is not as it should be; but I am trying to state things as they are.

As a rival of the moralist, there is the interpreter of character:—

"Viola's Errand to Olivia."

"As there are a great many things which might be said concerning the errand of Viola we can only turn our attention to one of those thins.

"The most important thing connected with any action is usualy the result. This is what we will concider in the present essay. The result of the message was to arrouse in Oliva a most passionate feeling of love for Viola. One might criticize the suddenness of the act and condemn it as hasty and unadvised, but we must concider that where a man has to *think* to decide what he should do a woman *feels,* and when she feels she acts, and if she thinks at all it is after the thing is over.

"That this sudden love did not spring from any weekness of character may be seen from the persistancy with which she held the Duke at bay. If she had been week, the power and pomp, the grandure of the name, together with the fine personal appearance of the Duke, and the flattery of the love of such a man would long ago have won her. But she was not week. She was strong and being strong must love strongly when she loved at all; and who, we would ask, could love strongly and not show it."

One sentence, from a book written some years ago, combines the ethical and the analytic:—

"That Caesar was ambitious there is not a doubt in my mind, but that he ought to have been killed for his ambition there are a great many."

Humorists (conscious humorists, I mean) are scarce; but I have gathered a few specimens of their work:—

1. He [Mr. Darcy] has come at last! They have seen him! What do they think of him? They all without an exception think him 'just too horrid,' but any one of them would be willing to take him if they could."

2. "Sebastian consented; the priest of the house was called; the marriage ceremonies were performed. Sebastian stepped out to see some friends,⁴ when Cæssario, with the Duke, stepped into the palace."

3. "Now there were several families residing near Mr. Bingley's new home, and there were several mothers who were busily engaged husband hunting for their daughters. One family in particular had a full quota of fair ones who had not yet worn the orange blossom. So this was a dangerous region for two young knights to explore if they expected to retire with unbroken hearts."

4. "After Olivia's departure, she sent a ring claiming it to have been left, but though Olivia understood the action she did not wish to have a woman make love to her (it was not leap-year). The Lord sent her again and this time the lady asked her to marry her then, as a priest was below, but she left."

Queer figurative and half-figurative mixtures are common: Viola "fills her position, flitting about like a ray of sunshine;" Mr. Darcy "could not prevent an attachment for the charming girl from springing up in the seat of his affections, which by the way were not always easily observed;" Mr. Darcy, "having once broken through the ice, finds but little trouble in progressing in the paths of love." Again: "Love was brooding between them [Mr. Darcy and Elizabeth] but not as yet had the fire been burning, and as it seems, the match was lighted at this point."

Mixed figures, however, are so often the produce of a fertile, though unweeded, mind that in a boy of seventeen they are almost encouraging. "We mournfully contemplate the fate of that great poet soul [Burns], a jewel of nature, highly endowed, that perished in its bloom,"—these words were the end of a good theme, and the work, I suspect, of a boy who proved the best writer in his class. Nor am I discouraged by such blunders as, "Mr. Darcy was perfectly nonpulssed;" nor by the occasional use of a degraded phrase, like "don masculine habiliments" (of Viola). I am discouraged by pervading inaccuracy, by incontinent oratory, and by chronic morality.

More than all, I am discouraged by wooden unintelligence. Though the admission books in English are gradually improving, it is true now, as it was true some years ago, that "few are remarkably good, and few extraordinarily bad;" that "a tedious mediocrity is everywhere." Dulness is the substance of scores of themes, and inaccurate dulness at that: there is neither a boy's sprightliness, nor a man's maturity, nor a scholar's refinement, nor yet a reporter's smartness. The average theme seems the work of a rather vulgar youth with his light gone out; and this unillumined incompetency takes the place of characteristics in about three quarters of the books. To show what I mean, I take the first theme of average mark that I can lay my hands on, a theme clearly above the passing line. The subject is "Mr. Darcy's Courtship." The boy does not dream that the story is full of life; to him it is something to go through—like statistics. Accordingly he tabulates it, and appends a moral duller than his tables:—

"Mr. Darcy's Courtship."

"Mr. Darcy, a young man of distinguished birth and great wealth, with that peculiar pride in his character which young men of wealth generally acquire from the adulation paid to them by ignorant people, is surprised at and delighted with the independence and frankness of spirit with which a certain Miss Bennett receives him. This Miss Bennett he first saw at an evening party given by the sisters of a friend of his. He afterwards saw her at the home of his friend where, contrasting the sharp, witty conduct of Miss Bennett towards him with the ignorant adulation of his friend's sisters, he falls in love with her.

"Miss Bennett is so influenced by the insinuations of a renegade ward of Darcy's father that she despises him. When, by chance, they meet at the country house of Darcy's aunt, Darcy proposes and is rejected by Miss Bennett who flaunts in his face the wrongs charged to him by his father's ward. Darcy is so incensed that he says nothing and leaves. After some consideration, he concludes to explain away these falsehoods and does so to the entire satisfaction of Miss Bennett who now begins to see many noble traits in Darcy and, after a while, falls in love with him.

"Darcy, after he has done many favors for Miss Bennett's family, again proposes to Miss Bennett and is heartily accepted. Darcy, when asked by Miss Bennett why he fell in love with her, admits that it was principally on account of her humbling his spirit of pride and teaching him the pleasure of treating one's supposed inferiors well.

"Darcy finally marries Miss Bennett to the great chagrin of his friend's sisters (the Bingleys) who make great protestations that the match is pleasing to them.

"The moral of all this, I think, is that slavish flattery will never attract the attention either of those who may deserve our praise or of those who do not to any qualities, either of mind or body, which we may posess. While, on the other hand, frankness and independence of spirit will always obtain for us, even among the greatest of men due consideration and respect."

In the treatment of the Bad English paper I see the same decrepitude of the more active powers. The one notion that possesses a boy when he faces the sentences is that something must be changed. His mind saunters up to each sentence, looks at it vacantly, changes the first word that comes half-way to meet him, and moves languidly on. In *Neither she nor Tony entertain any thoughts of marriage,* he changes *nor* to *or,* and leaves the rest; in *If the tariff were taken off of wool, we would be obliged to close our mills,* he touches nothing but *were,* which he changes to *was;* in *It prevents him bending the elbow more than a little ways,* he corrects the second blunder with the genteel substitute, *beyond a certain degree.* Sometimes unintelligence goes farther yet. In *Turning into the square, the post hit him causing him to shy, causing him to shy* is emended to *which made him very shy.* The sentence, *I think the style bad, and that he has a good deal of the old woman in his way of thinking,* passes muster for its English but not for its etiquette. The bad construction is unchanged; but *a good deal of the old woman in his way* becomes *much of his mother's manner.* One might think this change humorous; but I am convinced that it is not. It is as unconscious as a sentence in an admission theme on *The Merchant of Venice*,—"Shylock departed with neither money nor flesh."

It is a mistake to suppose that any practicable change in the English requirement would do away with the evils that appear in the books. Many of these evils will remain so long as a single prominent teacher in a single large school suffers slipshod English to be used by his pupils or by himself. Preparation in English is a complex matter; and the "English teacher" is but one of a thousand influences that make or mar it every day. The difficulty lies deep, when every subject is taught in English, and when the English of so many learned men is radically bad. As a general thing the school gets out of the teacher all that it pays for: and until schools can afford to pay trained and polished men; to give those men such relief from routine and bread-winning as shall enable them to cultivate themselves; and to demand of them not the raw power of keeping fifty boys in order and hearing five recitations a day, but a spirit at once gentle and manly, and a culture that must reveal itself without pedantry in every recitation, whatever the subject—until this millennium arrives, we shall see in our English examination the results of weary or perfunctory or—worst of all—decorated teaching. Meantime we must thank the teachers of English for their up-hill work.

NOTES

1. "The Commission of Colleges in New England on Admission Examinations."
2. The reformed spelling of *heiress*.
3. There is some doubt whether the writer meant to begin a paragraph here.
4. I am not sure that the humor is conscious here.

Charles Francis Adams, Edwin Lawrence Godkin, and Josiah Quincy
Report of the Committee on Composition and Rhetoric (1892)

8** *Adams (1835–1915), who claims authorship of the reports in his autobiography, was a grandson of John Quincy Adams (Harvard's first Boylston Professor of Rhetoric) and brother of Henry Adams, who taught history at Harvard, 1870–77. Adams had reorganized the Quincy, Massachusetts, public schools, written an exposé of unsafe railroad practices, and served as* *president of the Union Pacific Railroad. He is famous for two extended discussions of the classics: the first attacking, the second defending. They are collected in* Three Phi Beta Kappa Addresses.

Godkin (1831–1902), born in Ireland and an 1851 graduate of Queens, College, Belfast, served as war correspondent in the Crimea for the London Daily News. *He moved to North America in 1856, became a lawyer and friend of powerful Boston aristocrats, who in 1865 made him the first editor of the* Nation; *from 1882 to 1900 he was an editor of the* New York Evening Post. *During the second half of the nineteenth century Godkin was one of the most influential journalists in America. In an 1875* Nation *article he attacked traditional rhetoric in language reminiscent of Plato's* Gorgias *because it promoted "glibness" ("Rhetorical Training").*

Quincy (1859–1919) was the great-grandson of a Harvard president and a mayor of Boston; the grandson of a mayor of Boston; and he himself served as mayor of Boston, 1895–99. He graduated from Harvard in 1880 and Harvard Law School in 1884. After he left the Board of Overseers to become mayor his appointed replacement, George R. Nutter (1863–1927), helped produce the next three reports. Nutter graduated from Harvard in 1885, Harvard Law School in 1889, and studied in Munich. He served as President Eliot's secretary, was a law partner of Louis Brandeis in Boston, and taught English 12 with Barrett Wendell.

Harvard's Board of Overseers, elected by alumni for five-year terms, stood between the faculty and the trustees. In the 1890s overseers were usually men of the world elected because they took an interest in the workings of the college. The board routinely formed visiting committees to evaluate departments, schools, and programs. Between 1892 and 1897 the Committee on Composition and Rhetoric, which had only one change in membership, published its four highly charged reports. Combining as it did some of the most eminent names in Harvard's and Boston's history with the prestige of highly influential journals and law firms, the Committee on Composition and Rhetoric was immensely powerful and well connected.

The first and most famous of the four Harvard reports written for the Board of Overseers, this is a lengthy survey of what is wrong with the writing of students entering Harvard. The report covers some 450 papers written by students on the subject of their secondary school education in English composition. It prints many student essays, including 77 in facsimile (some of these facsimiles appear in chap. 6, pp. 506–13), arranged by preparatory school, underlining the report's purpose—to condemn the way the schools taught writing. And the

report itself, written in Adams's idiosyncratic style, is a far cry from the bland
prose reports that would come to typify so much of higher education in the
twentieth century.

To the Board of Overseers of Harvard College:—

Few persons not intimately connected with the system of instruction
now pursued in the College, or, indeed, with the existing Department of
Rhetoric and English Composition, have any conception of either the
amount or the nature of the work now done by the instructors in that
department. In quantity this work is calculated to excite dismay; while
the performance of it involves not only unremitted industry, but mental
drudgery of the most exhausting nature.

The above language is undoubtedly strong; but, while it contains an
acknowledgement due to the instructors in the department under review,
a recital of the facts will justify it. Instruction in English Composition at
Harvard is now divided into prescribed and elective courses, the prescribed courses consisting of what are known as "English A," "English
B," and "English C." As the Committee has confined its investigations,
so far as the present report is concerned, to certain features in the
prescribed work, no further reference to the elective courses is necessary.

"English A,"—the course prescribed for the Freshman class—is designed to give (1) elementary instruction in the theory and practice of
English Composition, and (2) an introduction to the study of English
Literature. The theory is taught throughout the year by lectures; the
practice is obtained in short weekly themes, written in the class-room and
criticized by the instructors. One of the instructors in this course writes to
the Committee as follows in regard to it and those taking part in it:—

"English A is prescribed for all Freshmen; it has, therefore, been thought
unfair to exclude from the course Freshmen who have not passed the entrance
examination in English. The number of these men is not very large. Besides,
there are a good many special students in the College and the Scientific School
who wish to take English A in order to work into a class, or as a useful part of
their special course. There are about a hundred such men, and very few of them
have tried the entrance examination. About one half of these special students are
as well fitted for the course as the great majority of the Freshmen are—not very
well at the best. The conditional Freshman and the incompetent special students, constituting from one-seventh to one-fifth of the entire number of men
taking English A, have always made the task of the theme reader more severe

than it is naturally, so to speak. They drag down the grade of instruction in the class, and, at best, they simply scrape through the course, and go on to burden the other prescribed courses in English—B and C. In 1890–91, the lecture-room provided for the Freshmen was so crowded that a division of the class had to be made. It was thought that perhaps some relief from the burden of the unprepared might be obtained by sending them off to be lectured to separately. Accordingly I lectured to about a hundred men, including Freshmen who had been conditioned at entrance and all special students in all departments of the University who had not passed the entrance examination. The themes of these men were not separated from the themes of the rest of the class, and all took the same examination. The best of the special students did very well—quite as well as the best Freshmen—half of the division stood very low."

The theme writing in English A is of the most elementary description; but the compositions in this course, over 6000 in number during each half year, are carefully criticised by the proper instructor, and returned by him to the student. They are then rewritten, and often recast. Owing to the number of these exercises and the constant accumulation of fresh papers the rewritten themes are not read by the instructors, except to determine the final grade of a student whose mark is doubtful. The work of criticising and correcting the English A themes is not inaptly described by certain of the instructors engaged in it as of a "stupifying" character, to which it is difficult to give more than four hours of intelligent attention per day; and, judging by a single set of 450 papers, your Committee is disposed to consider the adjective "stupefying" as a mild term to apply to such work, while four hours per day would seem to be an excessive time to devote to it.[1]

In order to give some idea of what the necessary college work of composition reading now is, the Committee will merely say further that, outside of English A, in the prescribed course for Sophomores known as English B, it amounted during the current year to 20,000 pages of 150 words each; while in the higher course known as English 12, intended for students who have passed in English A and B and wish further to pursue the study of composition, it amounted to some 25,000 pages averaging 130 words each. The number of separate exercises annually handed in to all the instructors of the English Department is estimated at thirty-eight thousand (38,000).

A cursory examination of a fractional part of this immense mass of written matter led your Committee to entertain grave doubts whether the difficulty in the situation as it now exists, as apparent in the overtasked condition of the instructors in the Department of English Composition, was not largely due to defective and inadequate training in the preparatory schools. In other words, as the department is now organized, under the existing standards of admission, the College seemed to be compelled, during the Freshman year, to do a vast amount of elementary educational work which should be done in the preparatory schools.

It is unnecessary in this connection to remind the Board that the academic department of the College has changed greatly within the last twenty-five years. During that period, the age of admission has been gradually raised, until now the average student entering the Freshman class is nineteen years old, instead of seventeen years old, as formerly; and it would certainly seem not unreasonable to insist that young men nineteen years of age who present themselves for a college education should be able not only to speak, but to write their mother tongue with ease and correctness. It is obviously absurd that the College—the institution of higher education—should be called upon to turn aside from its proper functions, and devote its means and the time of its instructors to the task of imparting elementary instruction which should be given even in ordinary grammar schools, much more in those higher academic institutions intended to prepare select youth for a university course.

Nevertheless, the statement in the College Catalogue of the course of instruction prescribed during the Freshman year, and a slight examination of the papers handed in during that year satisfied the Committee that the students were in this respect imperfectly prepared, and that a large amount of work not properly belonging to it was consequently imposed on the College. The Committee, therefore, concluded to begin its work not with the methods of instruction pursued by the College, but with the methods apparently pursued in the preparatory schools which fit students for college. In order to ascertain what those methods really were, and what results were attained through them, the Committee requested the instructors in charge of the English Department to call upon all the students attending the English A course, including special students, to write papers in the lecture room, setting forth the methods of instruction in English composition pursued in the school in which the writer of each paper had been prepared for college. It must, of course, be borne in mind that where a paper of this sort is called for in a class the instruction of which takes place by divisions, those in the later divisions of the class will have knowledge of what is expected of them, and the papers handed in will to a certain extent have been prepared outside of the recitation-room. When, therefore, these papers, 450 in number, were sent to the Visiting Committee, Professor Hill, in forwarding them, notified the members of the Committee that, in the opinion of the instructors, the papers in question were calculated to give a more favorable view of the quality of the work done than was warranted by the facts. Three-fifths of those attending the course had already written about their preparation in English, their exercises had been criticised, and each of them had thus been shown how to make his production better in form and more interesting in substance. Accordingly, such of the papers as the instructors examined before sending them to the Committee, were found to be in their judgment decidedly above the general average of work done by those whose names were signed to them. The further examination of the Committee fully confirmed the opinion thus expressed by the instructors, and proper allowance on this account should accordingly be made in connection with such of these papers as are included, in facsimile or otherwise, in the present report.

As already stated, the Committee received in response to its call some 450 papers, the writers of which came from no less than 160 different preparatory schools; a certain additional number had been specially fitted for college by tutors or otherwise. As the present report is intended to operate directly on the preparatory schools, with a view to elevating the standard, and, if possible, changing radically the methods of instruction in English Composition pursued in them, and as this result can best be obtained by showing what is now actually done in each and all, thus bringing the systems in use, so far as they vary, into direct comparison, the Committee has decided to pass the schools referred to in review, so far as it may seem desirable so to do, by printing as part of this report certain of the papers handed in, and further by reproducing in facsimile a number of the papers in order thus to show beyond question what the elementary training in the preparatory schools now really is, and how low a standard, so far as English composition is concerned, is set for admission to Harvard College. Of the total number of schools the methods of which were set forth in these papers nearly 120, or three out of four, were represented by a fraction over one student each. In order to save space, therefore, no reference has, as a rule, been made by the Committee to schools represented by less than three students, unless something in the papers submitted seemed to indicate that the system of instruction in English pursued in schools represented by a less number was specially deserving of notice. Of necessity the selection had to be somewhat arbitrary; but it is believed that all the leading preparatory schools fitting boys for Harvard are included among those selected, which, again, fairly represent the whole number.

School I.

In this school, according to the papers submitted by the students admitted from it, the course of instruction is the usual one. The term is four years. During the first of these four years, three hours a week are devoted to reading prescribed English books, with one hour in two weeks spent in composition. During the second year, the time spent on English is reduced to two hours a week. During the third year, this time is further reduced to one hour a week, with about one hour in each two weeks passed in writing a composition, including the correction of sentences in bad English and the study of punctuation. Finally, one-eighth part of the whole school time, in round numbers, is devoted to the study of English.

It is proper to state that in this, as in all other courses, the poorest papers only of those handed in have been used for purposes of illustration. This was necessary to accomplish the object of the Committee; for, just as the strength of a chain is measured by the strength of the weakest link in it, so, as will be seen in the course of this report, the progress of a class admitted to college is regulated by the qualification of the least prepared element in the class. In other words, the course of instruction of the whole is mapped out in view of the presence in it of an element not properly there,—the element described by Mr. Lathrop in the extract from his letter quoted in the earlier part of this report,—an element which has not received the preparatory training enabling it to go forward with advantage in a college course, and for which special provision has to be made much in the nature of a grammar-school department.

. . . .

School II.

The following paper from one of the students admitted from this institution gives a fair idea of the course pursued in it:—

"Although I received no instruction for the entrance examination, at the school where I prepared for college, I nevertheless did considerable outside work, read the required books, and was fortunate enough to pass the English examination. The greater part of my time, however, was devoted to Latin and Greek and, as my reading and preparation for English was done wholly out of school hours, the time devoted to my other studies was ten times as much.

Occasional newspaper work and the editing of the school paper gave me some facility in writing and certainly increased my meagre vocabulary. I have a fair knowledge of dramatic literature. Judging from my work on the school paper and from essays submitted for prizes, that I was in tolerable shape to take English examination, the headmaster of the academy deemed it best for me to devote my time wholly, to the classics."

It will be noticed that the preparation of the student in this case was largely due to occasional newspaper work and the editing of a school paper. This is an experience not peculiar to the writer, but one to which the Committee desire to call attention, as emphasis will be laid upon it in another portion of this report.

Two students only presented themselves for admission from institution II., both of whom succeeded in passing the entrance examination in English composition.

School III.

In the case of this school, according to the papers submitted, the time given to instruction in English Composition, so far as theme writing is concerned, "varied from half an hour to an hour a week. The scholars wrote on an average one essay a week. Very often in addition to the regular work the teacher would give the scholars regular examinations, generally using the old examination papers of Harvard College. The time devoted to the study of English never fully equaled that devoted to any other study." Two candidates only presented themselves for admission to Harvard in 1891. One of these failed to pass in English Composition; the other succeeded in passing. . . .

School IV.

Two candidates only for admission presented themselves from this institution. The following paper submitted to the Committee by one of these students, who passed the examination, has seemed from its clearness and general excellence to merit publication in full:—

"My preparation for the English course in Harvard University naturally divides itself into two parts, viz.: first, the work done in a seminary, second, the work done in ———.

"The work done in the preparatory school was very limited. Indeed it was almost entirely neglected. I never wrote an essay until the time of my graduation, and even that was done without any aid from the faculty. We had no regular instructor in English. So that I can truly say that I never had any direct training in English composition. We studied rhetoric; but only as a theory. We were told what beauties of language lay buried in metaphors; but we never unearthed any to prove to ourselves what gems were there. The students, feeling greatly the lack of the English department, organized a literary society, and we met once a week for practice in extemporaneous speaking and in essay writing. Of course, we were our own critics. I never wrote more than six essays during a three years' membership in this society. However, I did much extemporaneous speaking.

"Whatever direct preparation I may have for the present work it really began when I entered ———. Three written exercises per term were required. The remainder of the work consisted in studying the principles of rhetoric. We spent much time in punctuating sentences and in correcting specimens of bad English. Then, too, we had a reading exercise. We read Christmas Carol and Cricket on the Hearth, paying especial attention to tone and inflection. We were allowed to choose our own subjects for themes.

"Last summer I read Webster's Bunker Hill Oration, Old Mortality, and another book. (I have forgotten the name.) I think the proportion of my English work to other studies is as one is to four."

In this case, it will be noticed, actual practice was limited to "three written exercises per term."

School V.

Eighteen papers were submitted by students prepared at this institution, one of those which send up the largest number of students for entrance to Harvard. A facsimile (No. 4 . . . [see chap. 6, p. 510—ED.]) is presented of the first of the papers submitted from these students. The writer passed the examination.

Another of the students, who also was successful in passing his examination, writes as follows:

"The class had instruction in this study (English composition) five times a week. In connection therewith we were required to hand in written exercises at stated intervals. What these intervals were I do not know; but I am sure they were no less than a week in length. It is more probable that their length was two weeks, or possibly even one month. This referred to what is called the Junior class. During the next year one hour a week was given to English exercises. Only once or twice, however, during the whole year was this hour given to practice in English composition. On those occasions we were required to write a short article on some school matter, such an article as might be published in the school paper. In our third, or middle year, we employed one hour out of sixteen recitation hours per week in correcting bad English. During the Senior year two essays had to be written, which was all that we had to do that year."

The following extract from the paper handed in by one of the students from this seminary has seemed to the Committee worthy of publication, as containing statements and suggestions which throw much light on the results obtained there:—

"The opportunities for correct thinking, declamation and power afforded by the debating society; and those offered for cultivation of a concise, simple, practical style, through the columns of the semi-weekly school paper. These incentives, although not offered by the school, are upheld by private munificence and school-boy enthusiasm. To my mind they are more efficacious in inspiring and cultivating a fluent and correct style in expression than the prescribed course. They afford an attractive, open, free field to the boys and they are not slow in entering it.

"Besides these should be mentioned the emphasis given by instructors to parallel readings with the studies, besides direction given to the best books and authors.

"The one weak feature of the work is, not that all the ground is not gone over, but that the actual practice in writing, correcting, and criticizing, is not sufficiently frequent and unremitting. The foundation is laid for the student, but he is not forced to actual, daily practice."

Another student in the course of his composition writes as follows:

"Professor ———, the head of the ——— department, has for several years been making every effort to have a chair of English established in the academy and he now seems in a fair way to succeed within the next year." The Committee will merely remark that, judging from the papers presented by those prepared in this school, it would seem to be most desirable that the efforts of Professor ——— —in the direction indicated should be crowned with early success.

Two other students write as follows:—

"My Preparation in English.

"I graduated from ———, but I cannot say that I had any preparation in English there, though of course I did in the other branches of learning. All that I had to do in English at ——— was to write two essays of about five hundred words each. These essays were to determine about the parts at graduation.

"Before going to ———, I graduated at the ——— High School. There I had English twice a week, and at each of these exercises I wrote a composition. These were given back, criticized and corrected, at the next exercise. Between the exercises, we had to rewrite the corrected compositions, and hand them in again. Besides these semi-weekly compositions we had to write essays every month, and they were criticized and corrected like the others. In the ——— High School, I think that the proportion of my English to all my other studies combined was about as one is to ten.

"I took the entrance examination in English to enter Harvard College and passed."

"Preparation in English.

"Perfection in systems of education seems yet an impossibility. Every school has its failings; so has ———. And its weakest point—to confess the truth—is English composition. No one realizes this more than the management itself. Accordingly they have this year engaged a graduate of ——— to direct the work in this branch alone. This ought to secure the necessary system in the study, which has before been lacking.

"All (I think) of the last class who tried the Harvard examination, passed it: but this can hardly be attributed to their preparation at ———. As far as composition itself is concerned, during three years at the academy, I had to compose six pieces of English. During my first year, one composition was required and during the last one, two were expected, in order to decide the choice of commencement speakers. At one time, Prof. ——— started the practice of once a week devoting fifteen minutes of the Latin hour to the writing of short exercises; but owing to the scarcity of time this was done only once. During the Junior middle year some of the books required for admission to Harvard were critically read, and in connection with two examinations upon them, descriptions of certain of the chracters had to be written. This is all of the work required in English composition itself, but I think we received much greater benefit indirectly from the careful choice of words which was expected in the translation of both of the classics."

The following composition is printed in full, for it seems to give a tolerably clear and comprehensive idea of the course pursued in two institutions prominent in preparing students for Harvard:—

"I began my preparation in English composition about six years ago at —————— School, Boston, at which school I attended for two years and a half. I have not a very high opinion of the methods employed there in many of the subjects, but I consider that English composition was given as much attention there and as thoroughly mastered as in any preparatory school in New England.

"A subject was given out every month on which we wrote a four or five page composition. These were corrected and handed back to us, then after we had looked them over, the instructor, a man who thoroughly understood the subject, went through them with each pupil individually, explaining the reasons for the corrections. The subjects were such as a boy of from fourteen to sixteen years of age could be expected to understand and write upon and covered as wide a range as possible. Two which I remember were, 'A Description of my Summer Vacation' and 'The —————— Exhibition' in Music Hall.

"In addition to this we read every two months (as I remember it) some such book as one of Scott's novels and wrote a short abstract of it from memory.

"After leaving —————— I went to ——————, where the nature of things seemed to be reversed. There a great deal of attention is paid to the classical studies and mathematics, for which the school is no doubt equal to any in the country, and almost none to English composition. Things may have changed now. (The step taken by the —————— Alumni offering a prize for work in English having started a very good course in that subject during my last year.) But in my three years in that school, I only wrote three compositions at the most, and at present I can only recollect two. I do not remember that these were handed back or corrected. We all felt that the subject of English composition was neglected, and were thankful when the —————— Alumni brought the matter to the Faculties' notice.

"In justice to —————— I must say that we had in our second year a very thorough course in Shakespeare's Julius Caesar, and in the middle year in preparation for the Harvard prize examination a lesson once a week in Hill's Rhetoric.

"I do not know the result of my English composition examination for admission to Harvard, for as I did not pass enough subjects to enter, that would not have been counted if I had passed it."

. . . .

School VI.

The following paper, though like the last, written by a special student who did not pass the entrance examination, is printed in full as setting forth an original condition of affairs altogether too common in the preparatory schools, together with an example of improvement which might profitably be imitated elsewhere:—

"My School work in English Composition.

"I was a student for four years in the ——— High School. During those four years I was a witness to many changes in the mode of instruction in composition.

"I remember distinctly my first year's work in English. I look upon it now as a distinct failure. 'Composition day' came once a week, and it was considered the most distasteful day of the whole week. On that day each of us had to hand in a composition on some simple subject of history or literature which we were expected to have written during the week previous. But most of us did the work the night previous to the day on which we had to hand it in. In what light the faculty held the composition work we never knew. But we knew that no one ever was 'dropped' in it, no matter how poor his work. And so it came to be considered as a course that had crept into the school work no one knew how, but it had to be done and we felt that the course counted little in the general averages.

"The next year matters improved a little. We had a new principal, also a new teacher in composition who demanded better work. The class was divided into several sections, and each section was expected to hand in compositions every two weeks. We wrote on many different lines, on matters pertaining to history, literature, nature, and ourselves. We were marked according to ability displayed. The course had a regular business standard in the school and the work had to be done.

"The next year brought a still greater change. Another new teacher of composition awaited us at the opening of the school in the fall. At the first meeting of the class we were informed that 'the work in composition must not be slighted. I have been engaged to teach the work, and I intend to teach it as it should be. If you don't do good work you'll have to take the work over again.' We looked at each other in dismay. She evidently meant business, and we soon found out such was the case. Our work was criticized in a manner wonderful to behold. Our papers were interlined and crossed with red ink to such an extent that sometimes we couldn't read the original. About every three weeks a composition from each of us was due. The line of work pursued was about the same as that of the previous year. We were marked according to our work, and our marks were always displayed in bold figures on the outside sheet where any one could read them, be they good or bad. I believe I passed with credit and was advanced to Senior work.

"In my Senior year we wrote several compositions, and then as I offered myself as a candidate for prize essay work, I was excused from the regular work. Mr. ——— each year offers prizes for historical work in essay writing. I went into the work earnestly and was fortunate enough to get second prize.

"The work in the last two years had vastly improved in the school. It had been put on a sounder basis of work. But the proportion of work done in that subject, compared to the other branches, was very small. However, the school has an excellent teacher of composition now, and the work grows better each year. It is a required study, and a student is expected to do good work or not pass."

. . . .

School XXXII.

More members by far of the Freshman class received their preparatory training in this institution than in any other of the 160 institutions represented, the papers received by the Committee from them being no less than forty-seven in number. For this reason special attention will be paid to the system pursued at ———. It is described in the following papers:—

"My School work in English Composition.

"I prepared at ——— Academy where the English course is the least important thing in the school work.

"During the Middle and Senior years we had two compositions to write, one of these was the Life of Lord Clive.

"Some times, perhaps once or twice a term, we had a written exercise in class, on the book we had been reading. Then we exchanged papers with our neighbors, and tried to find how many mistakes each made, without the least attempt to correct them.

"The criticise we got from our instructor was hardly worthy of the name, for whenever any one asked him to explain something that had been marked as wrong, he was told to 'look it up.'

"Two hours a week were devoted to English, but about two in two or three months to the composition.

"English was the course that had the least stress laid upon it. Mathematics, Greek, Latin, German, and French were held five hours every week, so the proportion is about ten hours of other work to one of English.

"I read the number of books prescribed for the Harvard examination, but I fear they did not aid my writing on account of having no opportunity for practicing.

"The result was that, after long hours of 'grinding' the night before, I 'flunked' or rather failed my examination in English."

"My Preparation in English.

"When I entered the ——— Academy two years ago, some of the books required had been already read and these I had to make up outside. In my first year the writing of themes was very scarce. Perhaps once a month we wrote compositions on the books we were reading in class, but the attention paid to rhetoric was very slight, almost nothing compared to the work in other departments. In the Senior year practice in theme writing was increased and about every two weeks we wrote on subjects taken from the books we were reading in class and those we were supposed to have read outside. These essays were corrected and sometimes were read before the class. The subjects we wrote on were varied. The different character, incidents, or scenes, or some time a summary of the whole work. In this particular we were allowed great latitude. I never found it necessary to devote any time to English composition outside of the class-room, nor, do I think, did the majority of the students. The relative time was very little, English being the 'snappiest' course in the Academy and one which we never prepared for or took much interest in. In the examination I did not experience much trouble with the theme or the sentences and was not much surprised at passing."

"My Preparation in English.

"As I was admitted on a certificate from ———, I have not taken the examination in English, although I was prepared to do so after graduating from ———.

"At ——— Academy, very little work in English composition is done for a student during the last two years; only one written exercise a month is required, and this is usually an outline or sketch of some book or play that the class may have read.

"The time devoted to English composition at both ——— and ——— cannot exceed one hour a week, or including the time spent in reading plays and books required for the college examinations, two hours a week at ———.

"The other subjects occupy from thirteen to sixteen hours a week at both of these schools; so it may be seen that English has but a fifth or sixth part of the student's time in class room work.

"At ——— University, there is no work at all in English during the Freshman year, and during the Sophomore year very little work is done, and the study of Greek, Latin, and Mathematics take most of the time. No preparation in English is required for the entrance examinations. During the Sophomore year some practice is gained in English by writing monthly themes, but these are very often written carelessly and no permanent good in many cases can result.

"It seems to me that more attention should be given to English composition in these two foremost preparatory schools of New England, and that stress should be laid on the quality of the work done, as well as on the relative amount of time given to the study of English, especially at ———, more at ——— and much more at ———."

"Preparation in Composition at ———.

"I think I can best explain the work in written exercises by answering directly the questions proposed by the Board of Overseers in English.

"First. What was the number and nature of written exercises? I do not believe that during my entire course the number of exercises, of whatever description, amounted to more than twelve or fifteen. In the preparatory year the written work consisted principally of paraphrasing, as laid down in Chittenden's Elements of English Composition. During the Junior and Middle years, there were a few written exercises required, generally the same in character as those of the preparatory year. During the Senior year we wrote synopses and summaries. For example, after reading Macaulay's Essay on Lord Clive, we were asked to write a brief summary of the most important incidents. When we had read Bacon's Essays, we were given several titles from the essays, and were expected to write in our own language the substance of the essay we selected. In the same manner, after reading Hawthorne's House of the Seven Gables, we were permitted to choose from several subjects, such as Clifford and Phoebe, The Old Puncheon House, Hepzibah, etc., and were then expected to write the story as it occurred in The House of the Seven Gables. One young man, who ventured to make the criticism that he thought Hawthorne's depiction of Hepzibah, as an old maid, was faulty from the fact that Hepzibah did not have a cat, was ridiculed by the instructor for mentioning something foreign to the character of the composition.

"There is really no original composition required at ———, and from such a preparation we enter English A at Harvard, where a great deal of original work is required.

"Second. What is the relative amount of time devoted to English composition? There are only two recitations in English literature per week, while the number of recitations in other branches will average five per week. I should say that the proportion of the number of written exercises to the recitations in English was about one to seventeen.

"Third. Did you pass entrance examination in English? I did."

"After graduating from the high school, I took a two years course at ——— and there I received an excellent fit for Harvard in everything but English. Our course in English there took but two hours a week, while Greek and Latin each occupied four hours, with a great deal of outside work. We never looked at our English books outside of the recitation room, unless we had some poetry given us to learn; and as for essays, they were almost unheard of. I say 'almost,' for about once in two months we were called upon to write an account of the plot of some book we had been reading. Our work in class amounted to little more than reading aloud either some of Scott's poems or of Emerson's essays, and a fellow with an ordinary reading-knowledge of the English language, or in other words less cumbersome, a fellow who knew how to read distinctly, could easily get a 'B' and a good recommendation for Harvard. We had a little work in rhetoric during our Senior year, but with a teacher who made the remark in class concerning a word of doubtful etymology. 'It isn't hardly necessarily a conjunction,' our instruction was of little avail. Doubtless, our instructor was teaching us as well as he knew how. . . .

"I was fortunate enough to pass my examination in English for Harvard. But I attribute this as much to my experience as associate editor on the literary monthly, during the latter half of my Senior year, as to my instruction in English received while there."

[See chap. 6, p. 508 for a composition by a student from this school.— Ed.]

. . . .

School XXXIV.

This is one of the institutions considered most successful in preparing for Harvard. The system pursued in it, so far as English education is concerned, is set forth in the following papers:—

"My Preparation for English Composition.

"We were obliged, at the ———— School, to write a composition regularly once a month. But we also had subjects given out to us in class, on which to write short themes. Our general preparation in English was as follows:—

"We would read the books, one after another, prescribed for College English, in class. Each student was called upon to criticise certain portions of the passages read. Sometimes, after having read a chapter, the class was told to write out during the remaining portion of the hour a summary, or more generally a criticism, on that chapter. Then again the students might be told to write a summary or criticism upon the next chapter, which was to be read at home, and brought in at the next English. These were not to be carefully written, but were to be read in class, and the class was to criticise these productions.

"Once a month, however, subjects were given out to us to write upon one week or more in advance of the time the composition should be due. The subjects were greatly varied, but they all had some bearing on the school work in English. Several subjects were given at a time for us to choose from. We might have to write an essay on the author whose books we were reading or a criticism on one of his works. There were many other subjects of a different character, which time does not allow me to enumerate.

"These compositions generally covered seven or eight pages. They were carefully criticised in red ink by the teacher, who used the Harvard abbreviations, were to be corrected and handed back to him. Our teacher taught nothing but English, and had our class in English three hours during the week. Latin and Greek occupied five hours a week, French, German, and Mathematics generally three.

"I passed the English examination at Harvard College."

"English Composition for College.

"My preparation for college was at the ———— School where there was a good deal of stress put upon English. We wrote compositions regularly, once a month, and when the compositions were corrected, they were rewritten and improved as much as possible. English, throughout the school course, came three times a week; of this about one hour a week was devoted to English composition, both to the writing of themes and to correcting and criticising them. In the other two hours there were usually rules and examples of rhetoric given.

"The subjects were varied: such as descriptions of places, incidents in your life, and subjects which required arguments. The aim seemed always to be to have the student use his own thoughts and expressions, and not give him subjects which he could copy from books. Of course, near the Harvard examinations, themes were written on the books and the principal characters, like the themes we would be called upon to write.

"The criticisms were very numerous and as thorough as could be, the same mode of marking being adopted as is used at Harvard.

"The proportion of English to the other studies was: Latin and Greek from four to five times a week and the other studies from two to three times. English composition, strictly speaking, came once a week. But in the other two hours of English during the week, matters were given and discussed in direct relation to English composition.

"I passed the entrance examination in English."

As a rule, so far as method is concerned, the papers presented by students who had received their preliminary education at this school are better than average. . . .

In order, if possible, to avoid reaching a wrong conclusion as to the courses of study in English and English Composition and the amount of time given thereto, both absolutely and relatively to other studies, the Committee endeavored to verify the statements made in many of the foregoing papers by reference to the printed programmes of studies in the schools or academies referred to. To a certain extent this was done; though, at the outset, serious doubt suggested itself as to how far the programmes were in practice regarded, and the possible extent to which, under pressure of time, etc., one study might be sacrified to another. Neither did such a process of verification seem likely to affect the results. These spoke for themselves in the form and substance of the papers examined; and, in the judgment of the Committee, it mattered little whether all the statements made in those papers were or were not correct, or in accord with the programmes of the institutions the systems of which were described. It is possible, also, and even probable, that in many of the papers presented, and in several of those printed or reproduced, injustice, intentionally or otherwise, may have been done to schools or individual teachers. All names, therefore, have been omitted, as the printing them seemed calculated to draw discussion away from facts to personal controversy.

Finally, it was possible that the papers handed in, especially those facsimiles of which are submitted with this report, might not fairly present the attainments of those whose names were attached to them. To assure themselves on this point, the Committee caused the original entrance examination-books of the writers of the letters in facsimile to be hunted up, and carefully examined them. These papers showed clearly that the instructors in the English department had good grounds for cautioning the Committee that the body of papers prepared for it, and on which this report is based, were for reasons they gave "decidedly above the general average of work done by those whose names were signed to them." The Committee do not consider it necessary to increase the bulk of this report by reprinting in connection with it any considerable number of these examination papers, much less by reproducing them in facsimile; but, in order to fortify the conclusions reached, they have selected a few of them at hap-hazard as specimens of the whole, and included them in the Appendix. . . . Those thus selected are written translations of passages from the Greek and Latin classics. They show both the educational system pursued in the schools, and the degree of mastery of their mother-tongue possessed by those responsible for the papers; and, did space admit of their reproduction in facsimile, it would further be apparent that they are no more creditable in form than they are in expression. This body of evidence, corroborative of the statements made and the conclusions reached in this report, is still in the hands of the Committee and open to examination.

The inferences drawn from the 450 papers specially prepared for the examination of the Committee by the 1891 students in English A have been further confirmed by the report of the results of the examination of candidates for admission to the Freshman class in June, 1892. English Composition papers were then prepared by 414 applicants. Of these no less than 47 per cent., or nearly one half of the whole, either passed unsatisfactorily or were conditioned. In other words, it may be said that one half of the total number of candidates for admission to the Harvard Freshman class who presented themselves in June of the current year were unprepared in the department of elementary English for admission to the College. They could not write their mother-tongue with ease or correctness. On the other hand, out of the 414 applicants, but nine, or 2 per cent., were marked as passing the examination "with credit," as against 20 per cent. who failed wholly.

Basing a judgment on the body of evidence thus presented, the conclusion which in the opinion of the Committee must be reached is that the system of instruction in written English now pursued in the preparatory schools is, almost without exception, limited to the requirements for admission to college. In that system, as developed in the material examined by the Committee, can be found only here and there the trace of an idea that the end of preparatory instruction in English Composition is to enable those taught to write the English language easily and well, so that the writer may be able to use it as a tool familiar to his hand, as speech to his tongue, in the further process of education and in the subsequent pursuits of life. The Committee cannot speak of other departments, but in the matter of English Composition the scholar in the preparatory school receives, indeed, nothing which can with any propriety be called an education: he is trained to pass a given examination; that and nothing more. The present system, therefore, is radically defective. The difficulty also, so far as your Committee is advised, is by no means confined to the advanced schools which fit for college. It permeates in another form the whole American grammar-school system.

Some years since, for instance, in the course of the examination of certain schools in the country towns of one of the counties in the immediate vicinity of Boston, the examiner, an official of the State Board of Education, made the usual inquiry of the scholars:—"What is the object of the study of English grammar?" The answer of the scholars was immediate, that it was "the art of reading and writing the English language correctly." The examiner thereupon told the members of the class in question that he wished them, having then studied grammar for several years, to show what the results of their instruction had been by at once sitting down and writing to him an ordinary letter asking for employment—such a letter as they might, and, indeed, certainly would, be called upon to write at some time in subsequent life. The teacher of the school promptly interfered, stating that the test was one of a most unheard-of character, and that, in justice to himself, he objected to having his scholars subjected to it,—"They had not been taught in that way!"[2] In other words, the children in this school had been taught to parse, as it is called, and to repeat after the manner of parrots certain rules as to gender, and subjects and predicates, and to distinguish orally parts of speech. They had never had any practice to enable them to make use of their knowledge; and so they could not compose a letter of the most ordinary character, or, indeed, express a thought in writing.

The course now pursued in the classical academies fitting for Harvard would seem to be defective in a way only slightly different from the foregoing. The theory is, and long has been, that the proper way to learn to write English is to translate orally Greek and Latin. One great object of the study of the classics undoubtedly is to perfect the student in the use of his native tongue. Meanwhile, in not more than two instances do the preparatory schools, the methods of which have been described in the papers submitted to the Committee, seem to have adopted the ordinary and apparently obvious practice of causing the students to do two things at once:—that is, to translate their Greek or Latin and learn to write English simultaneously. It goes without saying that the classic, as compared with modern languages, are in their modes of expression much the more concise. An obvious way of acquiring the familiar use of good concise written English would, therefore, seem to be to compel students, as a daily exercise, to make written translations of portions of those Greek or Latin authors in the study of which they are engaged; but, so far as the systems in vogue in the schools which prepare for Harvard College are concerned, the papers printed in the Appendix . . . while a sample only of the similar papers in the hands of the Committee, show conclusively that in America, under the educational systems prevailing in the preparatory schools, no attention whatever is paid to the rendering of Greek or Latin into concise written English. Now, as forty years ago, the reflex influence on the student's English of translating Latin or Greek into the mother tongue seems, when subjected to a practical test, to amount to nothing.

Accordingly, if the great mass of papers examined by the Committe can be accepted as evidence, the rule seems to be almost universal that the difficult work of writing the mother-tongue is to be taught to a sufficient degree by having an exercise of an hour each month, or possibly an hour in each fortnight, devoted to it.[3] So far as writing English is concerned, therefore, the grammar-school theory would still seem to be the one enunciated by Dogberry some centuries ago, that "to write and read comes by nature"; while, in the collegiate preparatory schools another, not very dissimilar theory obtains, under which the scholar who passes hours each day in the oral translation of Greek or Latin authors, is supposed, when a pen is put in his hand and a sheet of paper before him, through some mysterious mental sleight-of-hand, to apply without practice his familiarity with the classics to the work of English Composition,—an educational process which is in fact calculated to produce the desired result in much the same way and just about as rationally as that adopted by the gentleman who, proposing to discuss Chinese metaphysics, read up in the encyclopaedia under the two heads of China and Metaphysics, and combined his information.

Satisfactory results, except perhaps so far as getting boys through an examination and into college is concerned, cannot be expected from such a method. Its crudeness is apparent; it is in no sense education.[4] Indeed, there is not an instructor in any one of the academies, the systems of which have been described in the papers submitted to the Committee, who would not receive with derision the mere suggestion that the process through which instruction in English Composition is imparted should be used in the acquirement by a boy of a reasonable degree of facility in any outdoor game or form of amusement. To write English correctly and with ease is something not quickly or easily to be acquired. It is a good deal more difficult to acquire than, for instance, a fair degree of proficiency in the games of base-ball or lawn-tennis, or than riding on a bicycle or sailing a boat, or than skating or swimming. Yet nearly every boy from the academy can do some one at least of these things with ease, and a degree of skill calculated to excite admiration. How is this facility acquired? It certainly is not acquired by studying rules in treatises, or by listening to lectures on curves, equilibrium, buoyancy of bodies or science of pitching and batting. The study of underlying principles is here discarded in favor of practice; and the practice is not at the rate of an hour in a month, or even an hour in two weeks,—the mere suggestion of such a thing would excite derisive surprise,—but it is daily and incessant. It is only through similar daily and incessant practice that the degree of facility in writing the mother-tongue is acquired which alone enables student or adult to use it as a tool in his work,—the way in which it ought to be used in the course of a college career. It is there not an end; it is an instrument.

What is English Composition? It is the art of writing the mother-tongue. Not infrequently it is said that certain persons have a natural facility in composition, while others are unable to acquire it. Undoubtedly, the power of composing, like everything else, is acquired by some much more easily than by others. But it is, in the judgment of the Committee, little less than absurd to suggest that any human being who can be taught to talk cannot likewise be taught to compose. Writing is merely the habit of talking with the pen instead of with the tongue. People are apt to forget that facility in talking is acquired only by incessant practice,—practice daily and hourly pursued from infancy throughout life. If children were taught to talk as the scholars in our schools are taught to write, what facility of oral utterance would they ever attain? Sitting in dumb silence, with the exception of one hour a month, or, in the schools disposed to be more thorough, one hour in two weeks,—as is now the case with written utterance,—they would ultimately speak English with about as much fluency and about as correctly as the average American college graduate now speaks French or German. On the other hand, if, as part of the necessary school discipline, the scholar were compelled to use his pen instead of his tongue for one or two hours a day, what skill in composition would he not attain? What he wrote would, it is true, probably not repay reading, just as what he says is, as a rule, not worth listening to; but that, as a result of practice, any youth could be trained to express himself in writing with as perfect an ease and facility as he does in speaking, cannot well be gainsaid.

This would seem to be obvious; and yet, judging by the papers printed or quoted from in this report, such a method would seem in hardly a single case to enter into the recognized curriculum or system of any one of the scores of schools and academies which now undertake to prepare youths for entrance to Harvard College.

What is the result? That result can be studied in the papers and facsimiles submitted as part of this report. There are eight printed papers and forty-two facsimiles,—the facsimiles being nearly ten per cent. of the whole number of papers handed in. In the judgment of your Committee the writer of no one of those forty-two facsimiles had received adequate, or even respectable preparatory training in a branch of instruction undeniably elementary, and one accordingly in which a fair degree of excellence should be a necessary requisite for admission to a college course; for no young man who has not acquired a certain facility in writing his mother-tongue is in condition to derive advantage, such as he should derive, from such a course: that is, he cannot use a tool necessary to doing the work he has in hand to do.

The College, consequently, instead of being what its name implies,— a seminary of higher education,—becomes, in thus far, a mere academy, the instructors in which are subjected to the drudgery of teaching the elements. On the other hand, the remedy is within easy reach. At present a large corps of teachers have to be engaged and paid from the College treasury to do that which should have been done before the student presented himself for admission. While teaching these so-called students to write their mother-tongue, these instructors pass years correcting papers a mere glance at which shows that the present preparatory training is grossly inadequate.

As a result of its inquiries, therefore, and on the evidence set forth in this report, the recommendation of the Committee is distinct and emphatic,—it is that the College should forthwith, as regards English Composition, be put in its proper place as an institution of advanced education. The work of theme writing ought to be pronounced a part of the elementary training, and as such relegated to the preparatory schools. The student who presents himself for admission to the College, and who cannot write the English language with facility and correctness, should be sent back to the preparatory school to remain there until he can so write it. The College could then, as it should, relieve itself of one of the heaviest burdens now imposed upon it, while those admitted to College would be in position to enter immediately on the studies to which they propose to devote themselves; and if, during the College course, they take English Composition as an elective they should pursue it in its higher branches, and not, as now, in its most elementary form.

Presumably it may be urged by those in charge of the preparatory schools that the requisites for admission to the College have been now so raised that the schools cannot, with due regard to other and more necessary work to be done, devote more than an hour a month, or, at most, two hours a month, to a branch of instruction so crude, so unimportant, and so easily self-imparted as English Composition. The answer to this objection, if it is made, is obvious and conclusive: written English, like spoken English, must be taught as an incident, and not as an end, — collaterally. Exercises, especially in translating the classics or books in foreign tongues, should be in writing, as well as oral, and the student would thus acquire by daily practice a facility which he never can by any possibility acquire under the time-wasting systems now in general use. The Committee have called attention by the use of italics to the statement of one student that in the "small private school" in which he was fitted for College—"the preparation of English was carried out in every other subject; my translations from other languages were carefully criticised for their English; my geometry propositions I have rewritten many times on account of poor English." The Committee see no reason why this most rational system thus said to be applied in one school should not be applied in all; nor does it seem any act of hardship so to alter the present tests for admission as to compel the adoption of such a system.

The Committee recommend that a sufficient number of copies of this report be printed for the use not only of the Board of Overseers, but of the Faculty of the College, and the instructors in the preparatory schools. They would further recommend that steps be taken in relation to the standard of English Composition required for admission to our colleges which shall compel the preparatory schools to change their present systems, and raise the standard to the required point. While the Committee are confident that this result could easily be brought about, the only injury which, apparently, could ensue would be to keep out of college, possibly for one term, a certain percentage of young men whose presence there now acts as a mere drag or hindrance upon those more adequately prepared.

All of which is respectfully submitted.

Charles F. Adams,
E. L. Godkin,   } *Committee.*
Josiah Quincy.

Appendix.

Specimen examples of written translations in . . . Latin, from the examination papers of candidates for admission to the Freshman class, June, 1891. The passages translated are from Cicero's speech for Cornelius Balbus.

. . . .

Latin.

No. 1.

"Therefore, for these reasons he was given over from the state by Cnaius Pompey. The accuser does not deny this, but blames it. Thus they wish the fortunes of a perfectly innocent man, and the deed of a most excellent general to be condemned. Therefore the life of Cornelius, the deed of Pompey is brought (called) to trial. You grant that this man was born of a very honorable family in that state in which he was born, and from his youth up laying aside everything else, he spent his time in our wars, and with our commanders, and was absent from no task, no siege, and no battle. All these things are not only full of praise but also the peculiar traits of Cornelius, nor is there any blame in these things. Whence therefore is the charge? Because Pompey gave him over from the state. A charge against this man? Surely least of all, unless honor is to be considered a disgrace. Against whom therefore? In actual fact against no one, but in the argument of the accuser against him alone who did the giving. If he led on by influence had gained over by reward a less worthy man, nay even if a good man, but not so deserving: if, finally he said that something had been done not contrary to what was allowed, but contrary to what was fitting, nevertheless all blame of this kind, ought to be rejected by you, O judges. Now indeed, what is being said? What does the accuser say? That Pompey has done what was not allowed him? This is more weighty than if he said that that had been done by him which was not fitting. For there are some things which are not fitting, even if they are allowed. But whatever is not allowed, certainly is not fitting."

No. 2.

"Therefore, for those reasons, he has been given the citizenship by Cnaeus Pompey. The complainant does not deny that, but demands it back again; thus they wish the fortunes of a most innocent man and the deed of a most eminent commander to be condemned. Therefore the head of Cornelius and the deed of Pompeius are called to judgment. For you acknowledge that my client was born of most honorable rank in the city in which he was born; and that from his boyhood he has left all his own business and, with our commanders, has been engaged in our wars, and that he has been ignorant of no toil, no siege, and no battle. These things are all not only full of praise to Cornelius, but also due to him, and there is no accusation in them. Where, then, is the accusation? That Pompey gave him the citizenship? Pompey's accusation? Least of all, unless ignominy is to be considered an honor. Whose then? In truth no one's: it is at the instigation of the complainant, and of the man who gave it. But if he influenced less by favor, should bestow a reward upon a worthy man, nay even if upon a good man, but not so deserving a one; if, finally it should be said that something had been done not contrary to what is allowed, but contrary to what is right, nevertheless, Judges, all such taking back ought to be rejected by you. But now what is said? What says the complainant? That Pompey has done that which he was not allowed to do. And this is more serious than if he said that that had been done by Pompey which ought not to have been done. For it is something which ought not to be done even if it is allowed. But whatever is not allowed certainly ought not to be done."

NOTES

1. Mr. Lathrop writes on this subject: "This year I have read about eighty such exercises every week. At the beginning of the year I have found in my experience (of only two years) that the amount of correction necessary is so great, and the corrections have to be explained so much in writing, that I can read only eight an hour." To the same effect Mr. Hurlbut says: "At the beginning of the college year I read and corrected eight themes an hour, four hours a day. I could not, however, read for four hours in succession. At present I can read fifteen themes in one hour, twenty-five in two hours; a third hour at the same work is wasted. In one day I read carefully and corrected sixty Freshman themes; the next day, however, I could do no work well. On an average I devote a little over two hours a day to Freshman themes."

2. Report of Examination of Scholars in Norfolk County, in Forty-third Annual Report (1880) of the Massachusetts Board of Education (pp. 132, 146, 158).

3. "The work done in the preparatory school was very limited. Indeed it was almost entirely neglected. I never wrote an essay until the time of my graduation, and even that was done without any aid from the faculty. We had no regular instructor in English. So that I can truly say I never had any direct training in English composition."—[chap. 6, p. 510—ED.]

"During the Senior year two essays had to be written, which was all that we had to do that year."

"All I had to do in English at————was to write two essays of about five hundred words each."

" 'Composition day' came once a week."

"The amount of time taken by [themes] was perhaps an hour a month."

"The whole number [of compositions] for a year would amount to only four or five."

"A composition about once in two weeks."

"It would be safer to reckon [the written exercise] in months than in weeks."

"Twice a year we wrote compositions, . . . not more than five hours a year was given to actual English composition."

"One hour a week was supposed to be devoted to English, but it averaged nearer one a month . . . until the last year English was almost ignored."

"When I entered upon the work of the fourth year . . . the only hour which had been set apart for the study of English was now devoted to Algebra and Geometry."

"We had compositions every three weeks." [chap. 6, p. 507—ED.]

"One written composition was required from each student every four weeks."

"One written composition in four or five weeks."

"We wrote compositions once a week, the time for the composition was one hour."

"One written essay or composition every two weeks."

"It seems to me that much more was said that would be done, than was actually done. We were to write a theme every two weeks, but during the whole [four years] I handed in only two exercises."

"The English work of those preparing for college was done at odd moments."

"I considered English my easiest study, and the reason given by the instructor was that the requirements and examinations set by Harvard College in English were not as severe as those set for other studies."

"About one in two weeks, and sometimes not so often as that."

"During the Middle and Senior years we had two compositions to write. . . . Sometimes, perhaps once or twice a term, we had a written exercise in class."

"Perhaps once a month we wrote compositions."

"About once in two months we were called upon to write an account of the plot of some book we had been reading."

4. "This neglect of the fundamental principles . . . is in itself a disgrace to the name of education."

Charles Francis Adams, Edwin Lawrence Godkin,
and George R. Nutter
Report of the Committee on Composition and Rhetoric
(1897)

&�;&⋈;   *The fourth and last of the reports, based on an analysis of*
1,300 student themes illustrating the range of writing among Harvard and
Radcliffe students in 1896. It has a particularly interesting description of all the
Harvard writing courses and a thoughtful analysis of the change from an oral to
a literate college culture during the last quarter of the nineteenth century. This
report contains a rare effort, however incomplete, to examine women's writing.
The committee finds nothing but stereotypical differences: the women are neater
and more conscientious, the men more robust and self-assertive (below, p. 108).

The second report (April 1895) described a brief experiment testing the relation-
ship between skill at Greek and Latin translation and abilities in English composi-
tion; the third report (October 1896) printed a lengthy reply from schoolmasters
attacking the second report's conclusions about secondary preparation.

The fourth report was not meant only for the Harvard administration; on its
cover it bears the legend "[Price 25 cents]."

To the Board of Overseers of Harvard College:—

In dealing with the question of College English, or the advanced
education in writing, a serious difficulty is met with at the outset, from
the lack of an accepted basis of comparison between the present and the
past. The believers in the ancient methods and their results are always
numerous; nor is it easy to decide whether they are right or wrong in
their assertions, so long as the evidence of results actually achieved
through what are commonly described as "the good old ways," and of the
condition of affairs which really prevailed in past times, rests almost
wholly on memory and tradition. How deceptive impressions so based
are, is seen in the familiar instances of the weather and longevity. Exceptional storms or seasons, or cases of extreme old age, linger in the
popular memory, and, in the absence of the records of a weather bureau
or of statistics of vitality, are generalized into "old-fashioned winters"
and a patriarchal tenure of life wholly unlike the present. So as respects
the traditions of College English; individual instances in the past, which
examination would probably show to be quite exceptional, have left an
impression; and, in the absence of any record, or reliable basis of compari-

son, these exceptional cases are referred to in discussion as if they represented the average standard of their time.

In examining the written work now done, and the results attained, and pronouncing upon it and them, not only so far as the Academic Department of any University is concerned, but also in the institutions of Secondary Education, it would, therefore, be of the utmost assistance if visitor or instructor could turn from the papers of the present year to a collection of similar papers prepared under the methods in use in 1850, and again in 1800. Such a direct comparison, did the data exist, besides being of interest in itself, could hardly fail to set at rest several now much controverted questions.

Feeling at every step of their investigations the need of some such data of comparison the Committee on Composition and Rhetoric thought it would be wise in any event to make provision for the future in this respect. Accordingly, after consultation with the instructors of the Department, the following subject for a written composition was prepared, and given out to all the students in the several English courses. The preparation of the paper was necessarily optional with the students, as it could not be treated as a regular exercise, nor count in the prescribed college work. In calling for the paper, the instructors explained the object for which it was desired, and the students understood that they were to prepare it at such times and with such care as they saw fit.

The subject was as follows:—"Describe the training you received, or the experience you may have had, in writing English before entering College, giving the names of the schools in which, or the instructors from whom, you received it; and then, speaking in the light of your subsequent work and experience in College, point out wherein your preparatory training now seems to you to have been good and sufficient, and wherein it seems to have been defective and to admit of improvement."

This subject was given out in the latter part of November, 1896; and the papers upon it were handed in during December. They were, from the College proper, 1170 in number, the following table showing the courses, the full number of students in each course, and the number of those who actually filed papers:—

Name of Course.	Number of Students in Course.	Number who wrote.
English A	562	467
English B	91	64

English 22	312	278
English C	450	163
English 5	16	15
English 12	90	71
English 31	130	112
Total	1651	1170

Sixty-eight (68) students of the Lawrence Scientific School, and seventy (70) of Radcliffe College also handed in papers; making the aggregate number 1308. In the College proper, papers were received from 70 per cent. of the students in the several courses. All of the papers were, when received, at once packed up and forwarded to the Committee without examination, or with only a very cursory examination, on the part of the instructors.

Before considering these papers as a whole, or attempting to draw any general conclusions from them as a body of evidence, it is necessary as matter of record, and for the information of those unacquainted with the Harvard College system now in use, to explain briefly the scope of each course, and to summarize the papers filed by the students taking it.

Course A.

This course is prescribed for Freshmen, and for first-year students in the Lawrence Scientific School. Being an elementary course, it may be, and not infrequently is, anticipated by the more intelligent students or those from the better preparatory schools. Papers were handed in by eighty-three (83) per cent. of the total number of those taking the course. These papers may, therefore, as a whole be taken as a sufficient representation of it; though it would not be unfair to assume that the seventeen (17) per cent. who failed to hand in statements were probably not among the best equipped. Taking the students who enter college annually as a whole, it might, therefore, be not unreasonable to consider those in the course thus unrepresented by papers as an offset to those who had anticipated the course. The papers filed would in this way constitute a fair average Freshman showing.

The most noticeable feature in these papers, taken as a whole, is their extreme crudeness both of thought and execution. Indeed, the first impression derived from a cursory examination of the two large volumes (I and II) of the originals would probably be one of surprise that such a degree of immaturity should exist in a body of young men averaging nineteen years of age, coming from the best preparatory schools in America, and belonging to the most well-to-do and highly educated families. Some 60 out of the 467 papers showed clearly that the writers, from deficiency in purely elementary training, were not prepared to go on profitably in a college course. They might be able to read; they certainly could not write. The remainder were, so far as the faculty of written expression was concerned, fitted to pursue a college course advantageously; but, as a rule, their papers revealed other defects in the systems in use in the schools from which they came, which will be hereafter more particularly referred to.

Course B.

This course is prescribed for Sophomores who, having passed in Course A, take neither Course 31 nor Course 22. It is open to those students only who have passed in Course A. Courses B, 31 and 22 are on the same footing, but those take B who do not care to follow English composition or wish to do no more in it than is prescribed.

Of the 91 students taking this course, 64, or 70 per cent. of the whole, a fairly representative number handed in papers. These papers show in a marked way the effect on the writers of the work done in Course A, though the deficiency in earlier elementary training is still apparent in the unduly numerous examples of bad penmanship and incorrect spelling. The average attained is about that which under other and more intelligent systems might reasonably be looked for from scholars of eighteen years. In other respects the papers in this course (Vol. III) afford merely cumulative evidence as to the preparatory school methods indicated by the papers in Course A.

Course C.

This Course is prescribed for Juniors who, having passed in Courses B, 31 or 22, do not take Course 30. It is open to those students only who have passed in Course B, 31 or 22.

Of the students taking this course, practically one for the Junior year,

163 out of a total number of 450 filed papers, or only 36 per cent. of the whole. Not improbably this deficiency was in large degree due to the fact that a subject almost exactly similar had already been assigned for a paper to be prepared in the regular course; and, naturally, a large proportion of the students did not care to prepare two papers at the same time on one subject. Meanwhile the papers filed (Vol. VII), while, perhaps, not to be accepted as a fair example of the whole, were most noticeable for their improvement over those of the earlier courses, and, indeed, for their general intrinsic excellence. Not over one in twenty certainly, or less than five (5) per cent. of the whole, were open to criticism on grounds of bad penmanship, defective punctuation, or lack of good grammatical expression. The average age of the writers was about 21 years, and the work is satisfactory as indicating a sufficient proficiency in written English for every practical purpose in life. The papers speak for themselves, and reflect credit on the excellent work done in the English department of the College. Moreover many of them are highly suggestive, coming as they do from young men of more mature mind and larger experience. The writers almost uniformily express a decided judgment that the instruction given in the preparatory schools in written English is inadequate, and that Course A belongs properly to the Secondary Education. It may indeed be said that not one of these papers which shows any degree of capacity in the writer, fails to express this opinion.

These papers also reveal in a striking, because almost always unconscious, way, what has heretofore been the great defect in the methods of instruction in written English in vogue in the common preparatory schools. It has been taught almost wholly objectively, or as an end; almost never incidentally, and as a means. This will be referred to more fully later on in this report, and is merely alluded to now in connection with these papers from Course C. In the great majority of the preparatory schools, English is still taught, it would seem, not as a mother tongue, but as a foreign literature. The reason is obvious. Formerly English was not taught in these schools at all. It was supposed to be picked up incidentally, as it were, and by the wayside, in pursuing the beaten path of classical drill. Then it was by degrees introduced as a new college requirement; and, almost as a matter of course, the masters, following the instincts of analogy, taught the new language required as they were in the custom of teaching the old,—English was taught not incidentally and in connection with other studies, but independently, and as Latin and Greek were taught, through the analytical reading, or perhaps rather the spelling out, of writings of certain specified authors, and by exercises in so-called "composition," at stated times. The results of this method are pointed out in the papers of Course C, and can be studied in those of Course A.

Courses 22 and 31.

These two courses should properly be considered together, as Course 31 is practically but the second division of Course 22.

Course 22 is counted as the equivalent of Course B, but as an elective it is open only to those who in Course A have attained the Grade C; while Course 31 is open to all who, having passed Course A with any sufficient grade, prefer an elective to Course B. Courses 22 and 31, while in some respects equivalent to Course B, are intermediate between Courses A and C and are to a large extent Sophomore courses.

From Course 22, ninety (90) per cent. of the students handed in papers, and eighty-six (86) per cent. from Course 31. They may probably be taken as fairly representative. Of these papers about ten (10) per cent. in Course 22, and fifteen (15) per cent. in Course 31 are below the proper standard both in thought and in mechanical execution. They show that in these respects, and to this degree, the college instruction had not yet made good the deficiency in the elementary drill in the preparatory schools. If examples of slovenly school-boy scrawls, which would disqualify the writer for employment in any counting-house or office, were needed, they could easily be furnished in fac-simile from the papers on file (Vols. IV, V, VI) in these two courses.

Certain of these papers are suggestive in one important respect. They were written by graduates of Normal Schools. Teachers from those schools should appreciate the necessity of early training in written English, for it is their especial mission to impart it to others at the most impressionable period of life. They should, therefore, in their work give evidence of severe, mechanical, elementary drill, received in the Normal Schools. They ought themselves to be writing-masters. The indications are, however, that the Normal school standard is in this respect unduly low, and that our teachers need themselves to be taught. (Appendix Nos. 1 and 2.)

Course 12.

This Course is open to those only who have attained Grade C in Course B, 22 or 31, already referred to. Those composing it are chiefly Juniors or Seniors, though among them are some Sophomores and a few students from the Lawrence Scientific School, Special Students and Resident Graduates. Of the 90 taking the Course, 71, or eighty (80) per cent. submitted papers (Vol. VIII).

The papers from Course 12, while noticeably better and, in all mechanical respects, more workmanlike than the papers from the earlier courses, are especially suggestive as coming from scholars who had left the preparatory schools several years ago, and before the effects of the recent agitation on the subject of written English had made themselves felt to the extent they since have. In these papers, therefore, the old system is described in a number of schools which have since introduced improved methods. The several steps in the process of change can thus be studied by comparing the statements of students in this course with the statements made by students from the same schools included in the earlier courses. In this respect many of these papers are of value.

Course 5.

This is an advanced course. Fifteen out of the sixteen students taking it handed in papers, and they are of interest, first, because of the conclusions and suggestions to be found in them, and, secondly, because they show the degree of workmanlike capacity acquired by the most mature and highly trained of all those among the Harvard students taking written English instruction. As a rule these papers bear closely on the questions fundamental to this discussion.

Lawrence Scientific School.

The papers in Course BC, sixty-eight (68) in number, were handed in later than the others, and are bound by themselves in Vol. IX. This course corresponds in part to Course B and in part to Course C, and is prescribed for students in the Lawrence Scientific School. It is open to those only who have passed in Course A.

The papers filed in this course were noticeably inferior in nearly all respects,—thought, neatness of execution, spelling, penmanship and observation,—to the papers in the other courses. They contributed nothing to the general result, and no extracts from them are included in the Appendix. Taken as a whole they were the least creditable, as well as least suggestive, part of the exhibit.

Radcliffe College.

This cannot be said of the seventy (70) papers from the Radcliffe College students (female) which are included in the collection. (Vol. VIII.) These have an interest and value of their own, and will repay examination. Nearly all the English courses are represented in them. In mechanical execution,—neatness, penmanship, punctuation and orthography,— they show a marked superiority in standard over the papers from the courses of the College proper,—perhaps three (3) only of the whole failing to reach the proper level. In their contents also they reveal unmistakably a greater degree of conscientious, painstaking effort,—the desire to perform faithfully and well the allotted task. On the other hand, in thought and in form, they are less robust and less self-assertive. A few are sprightly; none of them indicate any especial capacity for observing, or attempt, in pointing out defects and difficulties, anything which might be termed a thoughtful solution of them.

The 1,308 papers handed in as above from the students in the seven specified Harvard courses, the Lawrence Scientific School, and from Radcliffe, have all been read by the Committee, and upon them the present report is based. They have also been carefully gone over and indexed under the heads of the writers' names, and the names of the schools mentioned. The whole collection, together with the index, has then been bound in nine (9) large volumes, which have been deposited in the College Library for the information of all who may now be interested in the subject of this report, and also as a starting point, as well as basis of future comparison.

As a body of evidence bearing on the present condition of the Secondary Education, and the methods of instruction in written English there in use, these papers have seemed to the Committee both of direct and indirect value. Their direct value is found in the statements made in them concerning the systems now or recently pursued in some four hundred and seventy-five (475) different schools in all parts of the United States, together with a few in Europe. These statements are entitled to various degrees of weight, depending on the intelligence, the correctness of recollection, and the power of observation of those making them; and these qualities of the writers, it is proper to say, vary in such a marked degree that it is at times difficult to reconcile the accounts of a school given by several scholars coming from that school at the same time. In such cases, however, the intrinsic evidence in certain papers of care, accuracy and intelligent insight almost invariably suffices to enable a reader to select such as most nearly present the real state of facts.

In this connection reference may also perhaps best be made to another point. It has sometimes been urged that putting this evidence of past scholars as to the schools in which they had been taught on the shelves of a library for public inspection is open to grave criticism, inasmuch as opportunity and even temptation is thus held out for false and possibly malicious ex parte statements, through which, so to speak, old scores might be wiped out, often in an unjustifiable way; while the master, from the very nature of the case, is cut off from any defence either of his system of instruction, or of himself. He might thus find himself held suddenly up to lasting ridicule or opprobrium, without remedy, or even the possibility of answer. This objection the Committee wishes once and for all, to say has been kept steadily in mind. The papers have been carefully read with a view to excluding any statements which were unfair, harsh or indicative of malice. They proved, however, noticeably free from everything of the sort. In most cases both schools and teachers are spoken of in a kindly, and often even an affectionate, tone; and, while, as would naturally be the case, the systems in use are frequently criticized, and, in the light of fresh college experience, pronounced wrong or inadequate, in no single instance was this done in an unworthy spirit or abusive tone. Indeed, it has seemed to the Committee that the masters of the preparatory schools named,—and there are few of the better equipped schools of the country which are not named,—could hardly pass a day more profitably than by turning in these volumes to the papers now written by their former pupils, and reading there fresh criticisms of themselves and their methods. They would find much that is dull, commonplace, unintelligent and unappreciative; much, also, the reverse of this: but they would see themselves and their methods as, in the light of subsequent experience, others see them, and might derive therefrom profit always and encouragement sometimes.

But, as a body of evidence on the present condition of the Secondary Education as respects instruction in written English, the chief value of these papers lies in the indirect, or unconscious light they throw upon a curiously heterogeneous system of almost undirected, natural growth. In this respect they are not open to question. Their mechanical execution, their admissions and their omissions, their forms of expression, and efforts at observation and criticism speak for themselves. They reflect, and reflect accurately, because unconsciously, a transitional phase in education. Their future value from this point of view can hardly fail to be considerable, and ever increasing.

An examination of them reveals also the reason of the break, or perhaps lack of perfect connection, which at present seems to exist between the Preparatory Schools and the College; it also reveals the tendency of development which has already in great degree brought the two into a more perfect connection; and, finally, it indicates in a manner not easily to be mistaken the process now going on, and through which the desired result will, in the opinion of the Committee, at no remote day be brought about. These several deductions it is proposed to develop in the present report. In so doing use will be freely made of the various papers as evidence, or for purposes of illustration. No fac-similes seem to be required. A sufficiency of such have been furnished in the previous reports of the Committee; and, though many more could be furnished from the body of papers now under consideration, were more needed or called for, it seems, for present purposes, merely necessary to quote in print from certain of them. These papers, whether reproduced in whole or in part, have in every case been selected because they contain some peculiarly clear and simple statement; or because they vividly illustrate some phase of development or point in controversy; or, finally, because they indicate on the part of the writer a grasp of the subject, or a special literary aptitude. For, while the mass of the papers are, as was of course to be expected, commonplace and monotonous, a few of them contain matter bright, observant, reflective, and at times humorous; and from such the Committee has endeavored to make selection.

———————

In the first place, the Committee desires to premise that, taken as a whole, the conclusions and inferences to be drawn from these papers are distinctly and unmistakably encouraging. That much room still exists for improvement and an elevation of standard, is apparent, when it is said that the papers from English A show conclusively that about 25 per cent. of the students now admitted to Harvard are unable to write their mother tongue with the ease and freedom absolutely necessary to enable them to proceed advantageously in any college course. In other words, one in every four of the papers filed in English A is in a mechanical way so badly done,—so ill-written, incorrectly spelled, ungrammatically expressed, and generally unworkmanlike,—that it clearly shows the writer out of place in college, and material proper for the Grammar even, rather than for the Secondary school. This is made apparent even by a cursory examination. And yet, none the less, these very papers have their value, inasmuch as they reveal through the statements they contain wherein is to be found the root of the trouble; and, moreover, they further indicate the steps now being taken to remove that trouble. In this connection it is difficult to over-estimate the importance of the work done by the English Department of the College. It has been described in the document recently published entitled "Twenty Years of School and College English;"[1] and it affords the Committee no little satisfaction to say that the papers under consideration furnish evidence, both abundant and incontrovertible, of the far-reaching and beneficent influence of the policy and efforts therein referred to.

To appreciate, however, the necessity as well as the nature and scope of this recent work of the English Department, it is necessary to understand its connection with what has gone before,—the situation must be considered from the historical point of view; for, only when so considered, can the process of gradual and necessary development which has been going on for a score of years, and will probably continue for an equal time to come, be intelligently comprehended. That it should be intelligently comprehended, especially by those engaged in the work of secondary instruction is most desirable; for it seems to be altogether too frequently supposed that the increased English requirements for college admission have no other object than the development of a new and somewhat superfluous branch of general education, in no way necessarily connected with the other and traditional branches; and, moreover, one which is handled in a somewhat vexatious and incomprehensible fashion.

Yet that this has not really been the case becomes apparent the moment the situation is looked at in its antecedent connection.

Speaking generally, and in the absence of any accepted basis of evidence, it may be said that forty years ago Harvard College, and the schools which prepared for admission to it, were in close touch with each other; or, in other words, the systems of instruction pursued in the two were much the same. In each, it was in largest part oral; that is, in the college as in the school, the scholar prepared his lesson, and, when called upon, stood up in class and recited to the instructor, answering questions and otherwise indicating orally his familiarity with the subject. Themes and forensics were prepared and handed in at certain stages of the college course and at stated intervals,—once a month or twice a term, as the case might be. The college classes, also, were then comparatively small, and the work imposed on the instructors correspondingly light, and limited to the recitation room.

About the year 1870 a change began to make itself felt, first in numbers and then in the methods of the college, which gradually brought about what amounted to a revolution. The classes increased in size nearly fourfold, so as to become wholly unmanageable for oral recitation, and the elective system was greatly enlarged; step by step, the oral method of instruction was then abandoned, and a system of lectures, with periodic written examinations, took its place; so that at last the whole college work was practically done in writing. The need of facility in written expression was, of course, correspondingly increased. Without the power of writing his mother tongue readily and legibly a college student was not equipped for the work he had to do, inasmuch as he did not have at his control an implement essential in doing that work. Writing English had thus become a mere incident, and no longer an end, in the student's college processes. This was so from the day he presented himself for the entrance examination forward to his graduation; and, probably, at no time in his whole course did he feel the need of the tool so acutely as on the day when he sat down, a candidate for admission, with the dreaded examination papers before him.

Meanwhile, naturally enough, no similar or corresponding change took place in the system of instruction in vogue in the preparatory schools. They went on in the traditional oral methods. The scholars continued to stand up in class as their fathers had done before them, and what written work they did was almost never incidental, but by and for itself. Confined to stated exercises in penmanship or, so called, composition, at given intervals of time, it was not sufficient in amount to give the scholar a sense of familiarity or ease. It was as if a boy had been taught to skate, to ride a bicycle or to play ball, through oral and theoretical instruction in the principles of lines, curves and balancing, with one hour of practice once a month, or even twice in three weeks. Of course, through such a method of instruction, without daily practice, he would never learn to play ball or skate familiarly or well.

Thus the schools by degrees ceased to prepare for the college. Scholars accustomed to oral work presented themselves for a written examination, with practical results which have been set forth in the facsimiles submitted in previous reports of this Committee. The College Faculty, perplexed at the unprepared condition of those they were practically compelled to admit, went on raising the requirements in written English, while the schools still continued their English instruction in the old-fashioned objective way,—more "themes," "compositions," "essays," were exacted, but the oral class instruction was adhered to. The friction, for such it amounted to, between the school and the college thus steadily increased.

The Freshman course known as English A was accordingly introduced, representing what might be called the intermediate stage,—that between school and college. The scholar trained in the oral system, with English simply used objectively, or as an exercise by itself and for itself, was compelled to take this course in order that he might learn to use English incidentally, or as a necessary medium in other courses. The papers forwarded to the Committee from the students taking this course, and now placed on the shelves of the Library, were not only in number more than those from any other course, constituting indeed 40 per cent. of all sent in, but, taken as a whole, they were the most interesting and suggestive; though to a very large extent unconsciously so.

The problem presented is obvious to any one who will take the trouble to read these papers in English A; while the difficulty in the way of its solution at once suggests itself. At the same time, in theory at least, the way to overcome that difficulty is not far to seek. The problem is to increase to a very great extent the work in written English now done in the preparatory schools, and at the same time largely to change its character. More practice, more daily drill and severe discipline are required. The difficulty is to find time for this practice, drill and discipline. The contention is that the requirements already made occupy all the time available; and the daily theme or essay or composition, however desirable, can only be got from the scholar by sacrificing some other, and more necessary, study. The solution seems to be simple;—English should be taught in the preparatory schools not, as now, altogether objectively, but incidentally, and in connection with other studies,—mathematics, geography, history and, especially, foreign languages and the Classics.

Take the Classics as an example of what is proposed. The theory upon which the study of the Classics, both Greek and Latin, has always been, and still is, insisted upon as the best introduction to a college course, is that in no other way can a knowledge of construction, grammar and vocabulary be so well acquired. It is the most thorough possible grounding in written expression. However true this may be in theory, it is in practice, under the oral methods now pursued, to a very large extent fallacious. The two things are taught separately, and, as the previous reports of the Committee demonstrate, the candidates for admission to Harvard can neither write English, nor translate into English the classic authors. Yet few who look into the subject carefully will, it is probable, feel disposed to deny that the rendering of passages from the classic authors into written English is on the whole the most severe discipline possible both in the study of Greek and Latin, and in writing English. The candidate for admission to college who is able to meet that test, need feel no apprehension as respects the other branches of English. Here then is a place where time can be saved, and the necessary discipline given in clearly written English. The present slovenly, inexact oral method of rendering the Classics "into that lazy, mongrel dialect, 'Translation English,'" can, and, as the examination papers show, should give way, at least in part, to daily written work.

The practical objection made to this method of instruction is obvious. It is supposed to involve great additional outside labor on the part of the masters of the preparatory schools. The written translations, it is assumed, must be examined, out of school hours, by the instructors, corrected and returned to the scholars. If this were indeed the case the objection to the method proposed would be final. School-masters are mortal; and, being mortal, they must have rest from their labors. They cannot work out of hours, as well as in hours. But is this process necessary? It would not so seem. The course here suggested is not proposed as a substitute for the present English and classical instruction, but as incidental to it. Every other day, for instance, the recitation from the Classics would be, not oral, but, as in the college, written. The scholars when they came into the class, would appear with a written translation in their hands. Instead then of rendering the lesson of the day orally, as now, such of them as were called on would read from the papers they had prepared. These papers the instructor could take, in the class, glance over them, and satisfy himself as to the execution; the papers of such as were not called upon at that recitation would then be handed to the master for such further examination as he might wish to give to them, or consigned directly to the waste-paper basket,—in either case the scholars would have had their drill in preparing the lesson, and their turn to be called upon would come some other day. The whole class is not necessarily called on for oral recitation now; it would not be called on for written recitation then. The severe, constant, daily discipline and practice would, all the same, have been undergone; and the master would have disposed of his work during school-hours.

The system would, too, admit of alternation, and a consequent variety of exercise, which would afford a much needed relief to both instructor and scholar, by breaking up that tedious monotony of method, the bane of the average school. The written exercise in the Classics of one day, could the next be followed by one in mathematics, or history, or French, or German, or geography. But every day some recitation, now conducted orally, should be conducted in writing. In this way the scholars would be accustomed before entering college to use written English as a means, and not merely as an end. They would then write as they now speak;—in other words they would in their preparatory training be taught to talk with the pen.

It is, indeed, not unsafe to say that the schools and the college will not be brought into close sympathy and complete touch until this incidental method is introduced into the Secondary Education. But, on the other hand, there should be no misunderstanding as to the extent of the change in method proposed, or the way in which it should be introduced. The incidental method of instruction is not intended to supplant either the old oral method, or the present training in English composition, but merely to take their place to a limited but an ever increasing extent. The oral method has its distinct educational value, for the ability to express oneself in speech is of even more importance than the ability to express oneself on paper; and, in this respect, the present college system may, perhaps, be open to criticism. But, this apart, as between the preparatory schools and the college, the two methods should not be distinct; they should, on the contrary, insensibly merge into each other. It might be well for the college to recur in some degree to oral methods; but, whether it does or does not, it is obvious that during the last two years of every preparatory course it should be the practice to have more and more of each day's work done in writing. But again this incidental class-writing must not be made a substitute for the formal written work now done. It must be in addition thereto; and regular written compositions, periodically called for, should, as now, be subjected to severe, out-of-school, correction, and equally severe, in-school, revision.

Such is the problem; and such the theoretical solution of it. As is usual, however, the solution proposed fails to commend itself to the judgment of a large portion, perhaps much the larger portion, of those engaged in the work of secondary education. It is, when not character-ized as absurd, pronounced not practical as an every day, working, school-system. Wedded to the accustomed methods and the ancient ways, neither teacher nor pupil take kindly and at once to innovations, and especially to innovations which involve more severe mental effort and more exacting drill,—in a word, more drudgery. There is, among the extracts from the papers submitted in the Appendix to this report one (No. 90) both interesting and suggestive on this point, the introduc-tion of the method proposed having led to "a storm of angry criticism"; yet, afterwards, its efficiency was recognized. As a system it is, perhaps, open to the objection that it involves drudgery; indeed, effective systems of discipline, intellectual or physical, educational or military, are usually open to that objection. The traditional oral method in school-teaching may be slip-shod and slovenly; undeniably—for the college papers prove it—it does lead directly "into that lazy, mongrel dialect 'Translation English'" already referred to; but, none the less, it has the advantage of being easy. The written method, on the contrary, is crucial. It brings ignorance and carelessness at once to the surface, and compels their correction. This commends itself neither to the average teacher nor to the average scholar; and they become at once fertile in objections.

It is in their bearing on this phase of the problem that the papers herewith submitted are most valuable. They constitute in themselves, as the extracts from them show, not only an unconscious debate, but a debate that is, on the issue presented, final and conclusive. There is in them a general and decisive agreement that English A as now conducted is not a proper college course, but should be relegated to the preparatory schools. On this point there is practically no division of opinion. But here the agreement ceases, and the writers divide themselves into two classes. The first, and by far the larger class, representing, indeed, the great bulk of the schools, raise the objection of time; they describe how the methods in use in the schools from which they came,—the occasional theme, composition or essay,—the reading and analysis of authors and the consequent discussions of "style,"—consumed the school hours. They then declare that the daily theme, however desirable, could not have been introduced without a displacement of some other indispensable study. . . . This conclusion, and the thoroughly practical considerations on which it is based, could not well be expressed more concisely than in the following extract, typical of many, from one of the papers handed in to the Committee:—"I believe that I received far too little training in writing English, for my own good; but I feel sure that I could not have given up a part of any other subject to make more time for writing English, without greatly lessening my chances of passing all my examinations for Harvard College."

Such is the contention on one side. On the other side a much smaller body of writers describe a different system as already prevailing in the schools from which they came,—the incidental system,—the exact system which suggests itself in theory, and which is so frequently, and somewhat contemptuously, dismissed, as being excellent in theory, but in working not practical. Though all indications of the sources from which they came are for obvious reasons suppressed in the papers and extracts from papers herewith submitted as bearing on this subject, it is noticeable also that the schools which are described as rapidly drifting into the incidental methods and accommodating themselves to the new conditions, are almost invariably those generally recognized as the more intelligent and progressive, and those, also, the students from which present the most creditable and observant papers. From these papers . . . it will be seen that a number of schools have brought themselves already into touch and sympathy with the college, assuming English A as a part of the preparatory course, and thus sending up their graduates equipped at the outset to go forward in advanced work.

For this reason the Committee has referred to the discussion to be found in these papers as final on the point at issue. It is difficult to persist in declaring a system of training absurd, or even not practical, which is found to be both in actual use, and in a use which is both increasing and successful; and that, too, in the most approved schools. Whatever may be said to the contrary, its general adoption becomes then a question only of time. The evidence contained in the body of papers and extracts herewith submitted is in the judgment of the Committee so conclusive on this point, as to obviate the necessity of further discussion; and for this reason, as a mere unsupported assertion in regard to its existence and character would not probably be accepted as sufficient, it has seemed to the Committee expedient to spread that evidence upon the record to an extent which, under other circumstances, might be thought unnecessary. Moreover, the debate itself, conducted as it was by those looking at the issue from no mere abstract or theoretical point of view but in the light of fresh personal experience, is in a marked degree graphic and instructive. It is not the evidence of one witness or of several, speaking of a local and exceptional experiment and its results, nor is it testimony slowly elicited in response to leading interrogatories. On the contrary, as will be seen from an examination of these extracts, at once many and copious, they are the spontaneous expression of a large number of students, fresh from many schools, bearing, always directly, often unconsciously, on a phase of educational development. As such they, in the judgment of the Committee, constitute the one portion of this report likely to prove of permanent value. Hence the space allotted to them.

The Committee have thus endeavored to set forth (1) the historical origin of the unsatisfactory state of affairs as respects "College English," now existing, and of which so much has of late been heard; (2) the steps which have, more or less intelligently, been taken in consequence thereof; (3) the gradual remedial process now going on: while the large body of papers placed in the College Library in connection with this report throw, as the Committee has already said, a light both interesting and valuable on the different phases and the ultimate tendency of that process. As regards the last, also, the rate of progress indicated in these papers, while seeming slow to some, can hardly be considered otherwise than satisfactory, considering the size and wholly unorganized character of the body to be influenced,—hundreds of schools, public and private, general and specialized, planted amid surroundings which vary greatly in character, preparing thousands annually for admission into scores of institutions of the advanced education. A few of the numerous passages to be found in the papers submitted, bearing on the great number and varied character of the schools, have been selected, and can be found in the Appendix. . . . They will suffice for purpose of illustration. But where a body of institutions so heterogeneous, so widely scattered, and of such varied environment are to be influenced and brought into line, progress must necessarily be slow, and cannot but be attended with friction and loss of power, inevitable, but not the less on that account to be regretted.

But, while all this is true, it should also be added that the lamentable waste of time and expenditure of misdirected effort revealed throughout these papers, is largely due to a misunderstanding among those engaged in the work of the proper functions or province, as respects English education, of the college and the secondary schools. The two, it is apparent, have not yet assumed their recognized relations to each other; and, in consequence, while the college is today forced to do much work of a purely elementary character which properly should be done in the secondary schools, those schools on the other hand are in many cases endeavoring to do the work which properly belongs to the college.

The course known as English A is the debatable ground, and to that course it is always necessary to recur in carrying on the discussion. The scope and character of Course A have already been referred to. The instruction given in it is purely elementary,—teaching boys the rudiments of English composition; to which, as the evidence herewith put on record altogether too clearly proves, penmanship ought by good rights to be added: for, if the University undertakes to do Grammar school work, it should at least do it thoroughly, and not, as now, in a half-hearted way. Accordingly, if it means to continue what is known as "English A" as part of the college course, it should, under existing conditions of the primary and secondary education, proceed forthwith to create chairs of Chirography, Orthography, and Punctuation to supplement the existing chairs of Rhetoric and Belles-Lettres, and to relieve their now sadly overworked occupants. In other words the students when sent up for admission lack elementary training; and, in subsequently giving that training to them, the University has to do the work of both the Grammar and the Preparatory schools. In this respect, and it is a very important respect, the present requirements for college admission seem to the

Committee decidedly too lax. They should be raised at least to the point of compelling candidates to prepare their examination papers neatly, legibly and with a certain amount of mechanical facility, including a decent regard for penmanship, grammar and spelling. As the papers herewith deposited in the Library conclusively prove, these are not now requirements for admission to Harvard.

On the other hand these papers show an equally strange confusion in the minds of a large proportion of the teachers concerning the province of the secondary schools in the matter of English composition. Because the college requirements call for a certain amount of written English, including papers in the nature of abstracts of a number of specified books, it seems to be altogether too frequently assumed that the institutions of secondary education are expected annually to send up for admission to college solid phalanxes of potential authors, essayists, and litterateurs. The evidence of this delusion is to be found almost everywhere in the nine volumes of papers under consideration,—evidence incontrovertible, because wholly unconscious, and some of it comical, did it not, from its revelation of misdirected effort and unintelligent zeal, verge on the pathetic.

Take, for example, the matter of reading standard authors. It is, of course, most desirable to set good literary models before children in the preparatory schools, and to familiarize them as early as possible with the names and works of the great English writers; and the college, therefore, very properly demands on the part of candidates for admission a certain familiarity with our better literature[2] and with the masters of what is known as "style." From the educational point of view, and as an element in learning how to write, the reading the works of these writers is just as important as, reverting to the comparison already used, it is for a boy eager to excel in skating, in playing base-ball, or in riding a bicycle to watch experts or professionals as they perform their feats upon the ice, in the rink, or on the ballground. Provided he is observing and interested, the boy, while thus looking on, learns to distinguish really good skating, good ball-playing, and skilful bicycling from the work of bunglers; and this helps him greatly in his own daily practice. It is well, however, that both instructor and scholar should realize that the mere reading of books, though good so far as it goes, will no more of itself make a writer than the looking at masterpieces will make an artist, or listening to music a composer.[3] There is no easy road, any more than there is a royal road, to excellence in any of these fields. In all of them, on the contrary, not excellence, but only proficiency, is the ordinary result of long-sustained, strenuous labor under careful instruction; and mere proficiency even will not come through parrot-like imitation.

The instructor, too, must not only appreciate this somewhat important fact, but he must have a clear understanding of his own part in the work. Unfortunately, as the evidence herewith submitted only too plainly shows, this is at present not always the case. The instructor, in altogether too many instances, does not know how to do his part in the work, and consequently the study of literary models as now carried on in our schools of secondary education not infrequently does more harm than good. Not only, as the papers show, is it marked by a pitiful waste of valuable time, but it leaves behind it a sense of weariness and disgust rather than mind hunger. For instance what possible benefit can immature boys derive from devoting a large portion of a whole school term to the analysis of a single oration of Webster's by paragraphs, sentences and clauses; or what but a sense of repulsion can result, if children, needing assimilative nutriment and craving the stimulant of interest, are daily dosed with long and to them nauseous, because unintelligible, drafts from Emerson, Ruskin, Cardinal Manning, Matthew Arnold and Walter Pater? Upon this point the papers which accompany the present report are curiously suggestive.

Indeed, such educational performances as are again and again described in them with perfect simplicity and obvious truthfulness would be reckoned impossible in anything but what is known as "English composition,"—something obviously supposed to be quite other than plain written English. "Composition," it is apparent, is assumed to be high art in writing,—what is somewhat ambitiously known as Rhetoric and Belles-Lettres. Accordingly, educational eccentricities are sometimes revealed in the preparatory schools which would scarcely be thought credible but for the evidence now placed on record. For instance, taking once more other branches of development, for purposes of illustration, the great masters of written expression are no less rare than the great masters of painting or of music,—a Milton, an Addison, a Burke or an Emerson would rank in the individuality or choiceness of his work with a Rembrandt, a Titian or a Millet in painting, or a Mozart, a Beethoven or a Wagner in music. A school-master, whose business it was to instruct children of from 15 to 18 years of age in the elements of drawing, painting or music, with a view to passing an examination for admittance into some Academy, would naturally devote his time and that of his classes, to a severe discipline in the first rudiments of music and draughtsmanship,—the practice of the scales and the drawing of straight lines, the flexibility of the muscles, the facility of the fingers and the correctness of ear and eye. But what would be thought of a master who, instead of this, exhibited a copy,—a good copy, perhaps,—of a portrait by Titian or Velasquez, Rubens or Reynolds, or played to his pupils, or took them to hear, a composition of Wagner, Mozart or Beethoven,—analyzing according to his lights and after his own fashion the master-pieces under consideration, pointing out differences of method and manner, and then, after thus directing the budding intelligence of those who did not yet know really how to draw a line or strike a note, and who were not mature enough to have any correct appreciation of what they had seen or heard, should tell them to sit down at their desks and paint a portrait after the manner first of Rembrandt and then of Velasquez, or compose a symphony in the style of Mozart as distinguished from that of Beethoven? Yet, incredible as it seems, this is now done in some of the preparatory schools.

The papers, especially those of English A, afford many examples and instances, a few of which are reproduced and herewith submitted in evidence of the defects and absurdities of instruction just referred to. (Appendix. . . .) Indeed, as a whole, these 1300 papers may be said to be full of loose, meaningless talk,—perhaps cant would not be too strong a descriptive word,—about "style," "mass," "individuality," "rhetoric," "originality," "expression," "technique," "barbarisms," "sole-cisms," etc., etc., indicating an utter lack on the part of those who had instructed the writers of the proper limits of the work assigned them to do;—that is, of the true province of the schools of secondary education as respects written English as opposed to the province of the college.[4] No satisfactory result can be hoped for until these limits are not only de-fined, but generally understood and accepted.

The province of the secondary education is, then, not to train up and develop whole classes of potential Miltons, Defoes, Addisons, Macaulays and Hawthornes,—it has, on the contrary nothing whatever to do with such processes, and whatever mistakenly, or from excess of zeal, it may do in that direction will probably be ill done, and have of necessity, with much vexation of spirit, to be wholly undone and painfully redone. . . . It is the University, not the Preparatory School, which has to do with "style" and "individuality," "Mass, Coherence and Form," with, in a word, that much abused and misused branch of study known in educational parlance as "Rhetoric." The province of the preparatory schools is to train the scholar, boy or girl, and train him or her thoroughly, in what can only be described as the elements and rudiments of written expression,—they should teach facile, clear penmanship, correct spelling, simple grammatical construction, and neat, workmanlike, mechanical execution. And this is no slight or simple task. It certainly, as these papers show, is not generally accomplished now. Nor will the desired result ever be brought about by occasional or spasmodic exercises of a half hour or one hour now and again, at intervals of three days, a week or a fortnight, throughout the school course,—it demands steady, daily drill, and drudgery of a kind most wearisome. Its purpose and aim are not ambitious,—its work is not inspiring;—no more ambitious and no more inspiring than the similar elementary drill in the musical scales, or the mixing of colors and drawing of straight lines. Its end is to so train the child, muscularly and mentally, from its earliest years, that when it completes its school education he or she may be able on occasion to talk with the pen as well as with the tongue,— in other words to make a plain, clear, simple statement of any matter under consideration, neatly written, correctly spelled, grammatically expressed:—And this is English A.

The scholar, when this result is accomplished, and not before, is prepared for admission to college. The preparatory school has then, in so far, done its work, and done it well. It remains afterwards for the student, guided by his necessities or following his aptitudes, to decide what use he will make of his elementary training. In nineteen cases out of twenty, it will be found to suffice for his future needs. He has all the power and facility of written expression he requires to enable him, whether in college or in practical life, to do his work or accomplish his aims. He may feel no call, and have no wish, to become an essayist, an author, or a litterateur,—but in his business or vocation he can express himself indifferently with the tongue or with the pen. Fortunately our college classes are not wholly composed of would-be or even nascent Macaulays, Carlyles and Ruskins, Walter Paters or Stevensons; but when the one man in twenty presents himself, who, after full and sufficient drill and drudgery in the rudiments, elects to go forward to a more advanced literary education, it then becomes the province of the University to take him in hand, and afford him every facility for so doing.

Both the secondary and the advanced education will, in the judgment of the Committee, continue in the present transitional, and somewhat confused transitional, phase, until these distinct provinces are recognized, and each confines itself to, or is left free to fulfil, its proper functions. For a considerable time yet to come, it is to be feared, the preparatory schools will continue worse than wasting much valuable time, under the erroneous idea that through attempts, at once futile and ludicrous, to make crude boys bear a remote resemblance to certain great authors, they are merely meeting college requirements; on the other hand, they will also go on sending up a large proportion of those who annually present themselves for admission to the colleges untrained in the rudiments of written English, for the very obvious reason that those thus sent up have never been subjected to that monotonous daily practice without which case in the use of the pen can no more be obtained than could excellence in foot-ball, rowing, or tennis. Meanwhile the college must continue to accept this unprepared material, and practically devote a very considerable part of one of the four years of its course to teaching those who now should be students, but are in fact still school-boys, how to use the necessary tools. Having taught them this, it is next necessary to disabuse them of the notions about "style" and "rhetoric" which have been laboriously instilled into them.

The 1300 papers, part of this report, show clearly enough the degree of progress made up to the present time in this process of separation,— delimitation it perhaps might be called. That it has not been more rapid is greatly to be regretted; but, none the less, the indications are distinct that the system is steadily tending towards the desired results, and that its attainment is a mere question of years. In fact, as the body of evidence now placed on file shows, in this, as in all cases of radical change, a new generation of instructors had both to be brought up and allowed time in which to make their influence felt. The old generation,—the masters of the old school,—as their criticisms on the changes introduced into the system to which they were accustomed, clearly showed, could only in rare individual instances adapt themselves to the new order of things, or appreciate either its significance or its necessity. It has devolved on Harvard to lead in this great change, the far-reaching educational consequences of which cannot yet be measured. It is enough for the present to say that it manifestly aims at nothing less than elevating the study of English to the same plane of dignity which has for centuries been the peculiar attribute of the classic tongues.[5] Their exclusiveness in the domain of the advanced education is challenged; and a race of young instructors is now at work, and is going out from the University in yearly increasing numbers, whose influence has only begun to make itself felt, but will in the end be little less than revolutionary.

Under these circumstances, the Committee believes that the present report, with the documentary matter placed in the College Library in connection with it, will be the last of the series it has felt called upon to make. Those reports have been four in number and consecutive, in each case the evidence upon which the Committee based its conclusions being made part of the permanent record. As such this evidence will hereafter speak for itself, either in justification of the conclusions drawn, or otherwise. A basis for future comparison is thus at least provided; and it will remain for the Committee which in 1920, or thereabouts, may then have imposed upon it the duty of examining into the Department of English Composition and Rhetoric to report, after comparing the results at that time attained with those now placed on record, whether the present Committee is correct in its judgment as respects the tendency and force of the influences now at work. To the Committee the trend of development as seen in the papers prepared for it seems so pronounced and so strong, that the attainment of the end it has all along had in view may be assumed. Correct, elementary, written English will in the near future be scientifically taught as part of the primary and secondary education. The complete relegation of the course known as English A from the college to the preparatory schools will be the first manifest result of this more intelligent elementary training, and will be sufficient evidence that the change has taken place. That result the Committee does not believe is remote; but it is not likely to be hastened by further action on its part. When, however, it is attained,—be that time five yeras hence, as the Committee hopes, or fifty, as may prove to be the case,—then, and not until then, will the preparatory schools perform their work in elementary English instruction efficiently, and without encroaching on the work appropriate to the University; while the University, relieved of rudimentary drill, will be able thenceforth to devote its means and energy to its proper function, that of the Advanced Education.

Charles Francis Adams,
E. L. Godkin,   } *Committee.*
George R. Nutter

APPENDIX.

Normal Schools.

No. 1.

At the Normal School [Massachusetts] we were given no training in English as English. In connection with the various studies we were told to write essays on the different phases of the work, but the work was criticized only in reference to the knowledge contained; the English being made of little account. I think any work in English would be a most beneficial addition to the Normal training. A course in theme writing might well be introduced. Power to use English correctly should be most thoroughly drilled into persons intending to be teachers, and yet there is no such training given in any Normal School in the state.

I should therefore recommend at least a one year course in English writing for the Normal School. Daily themes—describing matters of present interest— together with fortnightly themes would afford an excellent course to round out the otherwise excellent training which the Normal School affords.

No. 2.

The defects in my preparatory training are very evident. My compositions never underwent severe and careful criticism. In the High School I had practically no training in writing English; merit, it had none, its defects were due to negligence. The time that should be given to composition was devoted to the study of grammar. The same is true of the Normal School. The writing of compositions was delayed too long. We were supposed to write a good thesis without any training. The system can easily be improved by giving much less time to the formal study of grammar and much more time to the writing of regular and careful compositions.

NOTES

1. Four papers prepared by Professors Hill and Briggs and Mr. Hurlbut between 1879 and 1892, and republished with an "Introductory Note" and Appendix among

the Harvard University Publications, in 1896. An acquaintance with this document is necessary to any correct understanding of the present phase of the "College English" discussion. [See chap. 2, pp. 45 and 57 for Hill and Briggs.—ED.]

2. The nomenclature is sometimes a little startling, if it assumed to indicate familiarity with the works of great English writers; as, for instance, the following in one paper, "certain books, such as Scott's 'Old Immortality and Lady of the Lake,' and Longfellow's 'Evangeline.' "

3. "I do not wish to say a word against the particular school which I attended, nor against the schools of the West. From all I can hear this lamentable state of things exists in nearly all the high schools of our country, East or West. This system of teaching English,—of pounding very abstract principles into very concrete heads is one of the subjects of my complaint. A person may know every note of a piece of music, he may know and feel every mark of expression, on the mental instrument he may execute the composition with wonderful skill,—but, seated before the real piano, his untrained fingers will wander helpless in the confusion of keys. A person may have read every book written on the life, language and customs of Homer and his time, but the only way to know Homer is to read Homer himself. So it is I think the only way to learn to write English, is to practice writing English." Extract from an English A paper, by a student from Montana.

4. "I think, too, that my style of writing was never paid enough attention to. One teacher told us that, unless we were geniuses, we probably had no style of our own. I was no genius, but I had a style, and a very poor one it was. The form of my work was criticised, grammatical and rhetorical errors were pointed out, but no one was good enough to tell me to get back to simplicity and leave off trying to make an impression. That I have had to learn myself." The foregoing extract from one of the papers submitted by the Radcliffe College students is, in several respects, suggestive. The writer was a graduate of a Massachusetts city High School and Normal School.

5. "The Greeks would not have obtained so perfect a literary expression if they had devoted less attention to their own language than to Assyrian or Egyptian; but that is practically, in principle, what we are doing." Appendix, No. 61. Extract from a paper in Course 12.

Barrett Wendell
"English at Harvard University"
in *English in American Universities*
Edited by William Morton Payne (1895)

ᨧ *Wendell (1855–1921) was one of Harvard's most distinctive personalities. He graduated from Harvard in 1877, spent a year in law school, then taught English at Harvard, becoming professor in 1898 and retiring in 1917. He began by teaching composition and ended with literature, having decided that composition teaching was futile. He was famous for English 12:*

daily themes, and for his popular text, English Composition, Eight Lectures Given at the Lowell Institute. *(See chap. 5, p. 332, for excerpts, chap. 6, p. 446, for course description.) A biographical sketch of Wendell appears in Kitzhaber 66–69; see also Wallace Douglas, "Barrett Wendell."*

Wendell's brief overview of the entire English curriculum is by someone whose teaching and publishing spanned both composition and literature.

DURING THE PRESENT YEAR (1893–94) THE TEACHERS OF ENGLISH at Harvard are three professors, two assistant professors, three instructors appointed for terms of more than one year, three instructors appointed for one year, and seven assistants,—a total of twenty. During the present year these teachers have in charge nine courses and seventeen half-courses. A whole course at Harvard meets three hours a week throughout the year; and a half-course either three (in some cases two) hours a week for half the year, or once a week for the whole. In addition to the courses actually in progress, one course and seven half-courses announced by the department of English are not given this year, but have been given in the past, and will be given in the future, alternating with some of those now in hand.

The report of the Dean of the Faculty of Arts and Sciences for the preceding year (1892–93) shows that the state of affairs that year, which may be taken as typical, was as follows: In nine full courses,—including the course in English composition prescribed for Freshmen, which numbered 499,—there were 52 graduate students, 113 Seniors, 119 Juniors, 136 Sophomores, 377 Freshmen, 88 special students, 62 scientific students, 1 divinity student, and 3 law students,—a total of 952 enrolments. In thirteen half-courses,—including the courses in English composition prescribed for Sophomores and for Juniors, which together numbered 648,—there were 58 graduate students, 188 Seniors, 382 Juniors, 281 Sophomores, 12 Freshmen, 51 special students, 25 scientific students, 1 divinity student, 3 law students, and 1 student of agriculture—a total of 998 enrolments. No statistics are available as to how many of these students were enrolled in more than one of the courses under consideration. These figures, then, are valuable chiefly in showing the amount of teaching, in terms of courses and half-courses, actually demanded from the teachers. It may be added, however, that, as a rule, no Freshman is admitted to an elective course in English, while for the regular half-course in English composition prescribed for Sophomores there is an alternative elective full course in the same subject, in which last year 122 Sophomores were enrolled. The full course in English composition prescribed for Freshmen and the half-courses in the same subject prescribed for the two years following comprise all the required work in English at Harvard.

In the course prescribed for Freshmen, Professor A. S. Hill's *Principles of Rhetoric* is used as a text-book. Lectures based thereon are given, and also lectures dealing with some aspects of English literature. Of these lectures students are required to write summaries. Besides this written work, every member of the class writes a composition in the class-room once a week; and these compositions are carefully criticised by the teachers. In the half-course prescribed for Sophomores, lectures are given on exposition, argument, description, and narration; and during the year the students write twelve themes of from five hundred to a thousand words. These are carefully criticised by teachers, and generally rewritten by the students with this criticism in mind. In the half-course prescribed for Juniors, lectures are given on argument; and the students make one formal analysis of a masterpiece of argumentative composition, and write four arguments—known as "forensics"—of from a thousand to fifteen hundred words. Each of these is preceded by a brief, which is criticised by a teacher before the forensic is written. The forensics themselves are also carefully criticised and usually rewritten. All teachers engaged in these courses keep frequent office hours for personal conference with their pupils.

Apart from these courses, all the work in English at Harvard is elective. Of the elective courses, only one—an elementary half-course in Anglo-Saxon—can be called purely linguistic. Three courses and five half-courses may be described as both linguistic and literary. These deal with various specimens of English literature from *Béowulf* to Milton, in each case attending both to the literary meaning of the matter in hand and to grammatical details in the broadest sense of the term. One full course and five half-courses may be described as literary, demanding a great amount of reading and critical work but paying no attention to linguistic detail. These deal with various periods of English literature, from the sixteenth century to the present time. In the broader sense of the term, all these courses—linguistic and literary alike—may be called philological. Of the remaining work, two courses and two half-courses are in English composition; one half-course is in elocution; and one consists of oral discussion of topics in history and economics.

There is no sharp distinction, then, between literary courses and linguistic. The single full course given this year in literature apart from linguistics is a very advanced one in special research. Of the teachers, one professor, one assistant professor, and one instructor concern themselves wholly with the work classified as both literary and linguistic. All the remaining teachers concern themselves more or less with composition, either prescribed or elective. The courses in literature apart from linguistics are this year in charge of four of these teachers—one professor, one assistant professor, and two instructors.

Last year the largest elective courses were in composition, when the most elementary numbered 154, and the next 148. The largest course among those both linguistic and literary was one in Shakespeare, which numbered 111; the largest half-course in literature, which dealt with the Eighteenth century, numbered 122. In general, the courses dealing either linguistically or otherwise with the earlier periods of English literature were small and mature. One, of the nature of a "seminary," so called [seminar—Ed.], which dealt with Early English metrical romances, numbered only six, all graduate students.

In the courses in composition, prescribed and elective alike, little importance is attached to theoretical knowledge of rhetoric as distinguished from constant practice in writing under the most minute practicable criticism. In the two full elective courses given this year, the students write both daily themes of about a hundred words and fortnightly themes of from five hundred to a thousand words. This work is frequently discussed in person with the teachers, who for this purpose keep office hours—quite distinct from regular classroom appointments—averaging five hours a week. It will be seen, then, that the use of text-books, as distinguished from personal instruction, is reduced to a minimum. The text-books actually in use have been written for the purposes in hand by the teachers who use them.

Of the courses in linguistics and in literature alike it may be said that no text-books are generally used. In linguistics the student must naturally provide himself with a good standard copy of the text under consideration; but the better part of the comments on these texts is supplied by the actual teachers. In literature the student is always sent directly to the works of the writers under consideration. Of these he is often required to read so much as to make the purchase of the works in question impracticable. In such event students commonly read in the college library, where as many copies as possible of the works under consideration are reserved for their use. In no course in literature is any regular text-book employed.

In the matter of methods, it has long been held by the teachers of English at Harvard that each teacher's best method is his own. When a course is given into a man's charge, then, he is absolutely free to conduct it in any way he chooses. The natural result is such wide divergence of method in detail that no valuable generalization concerning such detail can be made. One man finds recitations useful, generally interspersed with frequent comment; another gives lectures; a third prefers personal conference; a fourth finds the best results coming from properly directed discussions of special topics by his class,—and so on. Furthermore, in certain cases the methods of the same teacher greatly vary with different classes and at different times. On only two points, perhaps, may definite agreement among the teachers be asserted: the first is that a candidate for honors in English, in addition to very high proficiency in six elective courses, ought to know at least the elements of Anglo-Saxon, ought to have made some study of pure literature, and ought to write respectably; the second is that the best educational results are attainable by such free and mutually cordial efforts of teachers differing widely in temperament and special interests as we at present enjoy.

It may be added that the Secretary of Harvard University will gladly send to any applicant a pamphlet describing in detail our courses in English; and that any teacher of English at Harvard will gladly explain his actual methods to any properly accredited inquirer. Persons seriously interested in these methods, then, will probably find a visit to Harvard instructive.

3

The New Writing Curriculum, 1895–1915

Harvard's establishment of a large composition program had inaugurated the start of similar, though less ambitious, programs nationwide. Meanwhile traditional rhetoric had continued its steep decline, to be replaced by a different model of composition. But not all colleges had the resources to mount a program as powerful as Harvard's, and in fact not all colleges wanted to. Many, no doubt influenced by the 1892 Harvard report's conclusion that composition belonged in the secondary schools, felt they could avoid the "problem" altogether. William Morton Payne's *English in American Universities* depicts the diversity of writing programs in 1895.

By the turn of the century members of the Modern Language Association began a careful look at composition courses in a series of remarkable reports published in 1901, 1902, and 1903. The reports, based on surveys sent mostly to members of the profession, testify to the desire to improve the intellectual quality of the college curriculum and to the glaring lack of consensus about how composition courses should function. This chapter includes reports of these MLA convention debates, the last time for over half a century that composition became a topic for the major professional organization in language and literature. By 1900, as Payne and the MLA documents suggest, the balance had shifted toward literary studies all across the nation. English departments would gain their renown from scholarly work in literature, not work in composition.

No English departments ever established their national reputations for work in writing, except for Harvard between 1875 and 1900. But some other writing programs did become quite prominent for their concentration of faculty in the field: Columbia, between 1900 and 1915, saw composition texts by Charles Sears Baldwin, George Rice Carpenter,

John Erskine, and the team of H. R. Steeves and F. H. Ristine; Michigan's rhetoric program, headed by Fred Newton Scott, awarded 140 master's degrees and 23 doctorates between 1904 and 1930, while English awarded 25 doctorates (Kitzhaber 72). Between 1907 and 1915 Wisconsin produced eight composition books (seven of them texts) by seven separate faculty members. Between 1898 and 1915 three members of a very small Vassar faculty published five writing textbooks and a number of journal articles. Between 1895 and 1920 Cornell's literature-based composition program produced significant texts and journal articles from four senior English faculty members as well as important contributions in rhetoric from other faculty (Corbett, "Cornell School of Rhetoric"). These represent significant concentrations of talent, yet they mostly represent a particular kind of publication, the textbook, and a particular kind of writing, collaboration. Hardly any scholarly monographs appeared. Then as now, composition textbooks represented the single most widely studied product of English departments; after all, *everybody* takes first-year composition. The composition programs established at colleges and universities across the country produced texts, articles, curriculum plans, and untold student papers. What they did not produce was a disciplinary field that could gain the admiration of their fellow faculty.

John Franklin Genung
The Study of Rhetoric in the College Course (1887)

    ❧ *Genung (1850–1919) attended Union College (B.A., 1870) and after graduating from Rochester Theological Seminary in 1875 was ordained a Baptist minister. He studied in Germany (Ph.D., Leipzig, 1881, with a dissertation on a living writer, Tennyson). During most of his long career at Amherst he taught both composition and literature, with the latter gaining ground as he aged. Genung is the perfect transitional figure: a minister and a German Ph.D., a trained scholar of English literature and a teacher devoted to undergraduate instruction. (There is a brief portrait of Genung in Kitzhaber 63–66; see also the memorial tributes in* Amherst Graduates' Quarterly 9 *[1920]; for a less flattering account, see the memoir of Genung's successor, John Erskine,* My Life as a Teacher.*)*

This is the most thorough contemporary description of the changes that had overtaken rhetoric in the late nineteenth century by one of the most prominent thinkers about composition. Genung spent his entire career at Amherst and wrote best-selling texts in the new "practical" style he champions here. Genung demonstrates an enlightened attitude for the time, warning against minute criticism of student papers and arguing for simple, "common" paper topics. His generous, appreciative attitude toward his students contrasts with the impersonal atmosphere at huge universities like Harvard and Columbia.

THERE ARE ENCOURAGING SIGNS THAT THE SOMEWHAT CONTEMP-tuous toleration which for many years has been the prevailing attitude toward the systematic study of rhetoric, is near its end. Educators and educated alike are coming to recognize in the art a practical value, immediate and universal, which calls for a treatment heartier than toleration. They see in it, or at least in its aim, something that works in not only with the studies of the college course, but with all after studies as well, supplementing them with just what is needed to give them practical efficiency; for it is the art wherein if anywhere is to be found the power and skill to communicate properly what is known and thought. To seek the mastery of such an art is certainly a worthy aim, and large enough for any elaborateness of discipline. If a study so purposed has earned contempt, the blame must evidently lie with defective methods, not with wrong principles; for surely, rightly interpreted and rightly conducted, the study of rhetoric has a justification for existing, second to no other.

And indeed I think much is chargeable to defective methods, and, beginning more deeply than methods, to very vague conceptions of the fundamental aim of the study. The scope of rhetoric has been left so ill-defined, at least as a working idea, that other things have been mixed with it as essential, or substituted for it as equally good, which yet have impeded it; while at the same time results have been looked for with which its alloy or substitute was inconsistent. Then further, as to its progress and ordered sequence in the college course, and still more as to uniformity of procedure between colleges, anything like a developed system in rhetorical study has hitherto been almost entirely lacking. Compare the course, for instance, as it ordinarily exists, with the consistent progression of the Latin and Greek departments. It must be confessed, the facilities for studying how to use our mother-tongue make a rather poor showing. The language that the student uses every day and for every purpose is so left to take care of itself that frequently when he gets his diploma the very weakest point in his education is that which in common sense ought to be strongest.

It is not the present purpose, however, to rail at existing defects in the study of English, real and rife though they are. The constructive problem before us is too important to let fault-finding detain us. We are setting out to consider the study of rhetoric as conditioned by the time and opportunities open to it in the undergraduate course. What may be done, and what ought to be done, under existing facilities and limitations?

I.

First of all, in order to lay a proper foundation for the discussion, let us inquire what should be presupposed as the direction and scope of the study.

Its direction needs to be defined, because in one sense, and that the most fundamental, rhetoric stands in contrast, not merely with other studies, but with other English literary studies. It requires a different attitude, faces toward an opposite goal. The others all contemplate acquisition: in pursuing them the mind gains possession of certain facts and principles, and achieves a certain discipline as the result; but from beginning to end its attitude is mainly receptive. The study of rhetoric contemplates presentation: in pursuing it the student's mind, though equally occupied with facts, principles, discipline, is set predominantly in the attitude of construction, creation. Other studies are something to know; this is something to do. The facts and principles comprised in rhetoric represent what the writer must have in mind in the actual production of literature; guides they are for his mind's acting, not incomes of knowledge whereby his mind is merely acted upon. This character of the study puts rhetoric into a class by itself; it stands alone in presupposing the student an originator, not a mere absorber, of thought and impulse.

Now the rhetorical course should labor to be throughout the exponent and inspirer of this creative attitude. It misses its grand opportunity if it is not. As mere knowledge indeed rhetoric is worth little; it is as skill and power that its true worth becomes manifest. Nor does its value end with the college course. Herein, in truth, lies in great part our encouragement, that long after college days are over, when in meeting the real tasks of life the man has forever shelved his Latin and Greek and mathematics, he begins to inquire anew into the principles of expression. He has thoughts, and wants to impart them. He sets himself to recollect or discover the procedures that once, perhaps, he little esteemed; they are very real and important to him now. Thus this undergraduate study of rhetoric is the initial stage of a discipline that must last the student through life, must be his resource whenever he has occasion to write. Some day the ability to express himself through literature may be bread and butter to him,—an art that he *must* be master of. If when that day comes he is so situated that he must do much in limited time, he will be tempted to do ill-considered and slipshod work; and especially if he discovers, so late, that he has neglected principles that constitute the ABC of his art. It is irksome to learn a new alphabet in middle age. It is humiliating to be tantalized with rebellious pronouns, mixed metaphors, and absurdly collocated clauses, when the writer's whole energy should flow unvexed and unimpeded in the current of a powerfully conceived thought. The study of rhetoric in college aims to forestall that coming time of need, aims to get the tools ready and sharpen them, to show how they are wielded, and to point out the unhappy results of unskilful use. It is preparing in secret for that future when the student shall begin to think for himself. And most of all, it seeks to induce that attitude of watchfulness, carefulness, contrivance, creativeness, which must be his when he has done with merely taking in knowledge, and addresses himself to giving it out again, newly minted and stamped with his individuality.

All this is obvious enough, and old enough; it is no discovery of mine. I think it needs to be said anew, however, because some other tendencies in English study have obscured the true conception of the aim and direction of rhetorical training.

A few years ago a demand arose for more study of English. The plea was right and timely; more English was needed. Students were learning much of ancient languages, were devoting themselves to the minutiae of dead syntax and idioms; while the history and development of their own mother-tongue were things unknown. With the practical use of English it was faring little better,—certain antiquated philosophizings from Aristotle and Quintilian, and the lengthy discussions of Blair, Campbell, and Whately constituting for the most part the rhetorical stock-in-trade. Students were supposed to learn the composition of English by studying Latin grammar, while they conned their rhetoric in order to learn the mysteries of anacoluthon, aposiopesis, the Sublime, the Pathetic, and the Nature of the Nervous Style. ["Nervous": "Possessing or manifesting vigor of mind; characterized by strength of thought, feeling, or style; forcible; spirited (*Webster's New International Dictionary*)." The dictionary cites the nineteenth century Yale linguist William Dwight Whitney as a source: "*Nervous,* idiomatic English."—ED.]

It was obvious that something was wrong in a course that so loaded the student with useless names and distinctions and yet left him helpless in the presence of a real literary task. So in this state of things the call for an English revival, not nicely discriminating, took the shape of a reaction against the "prunes and prisms" ["Father is rather vulgar . . . Papa . . . gives a pretty form to the lips. Papa, potatoes, poultry, prunes, and prism, are all very good for the lips, especially prunes and prism." Dickens, *Little Dorrit*—ED.] of literary composition. A perfectly healthy plea it was,—for more simplicity and directness of expression, more of the natural spontaneousness that seems to disdain literary rules in the plain earnestness of practical issues, or in the sweeping tempest of enthusiasm and spirit.

> "Good sense and truth are good enough for men.
> Hast anything to say? Out with it, then!
> And the more natural the style, the better."

It became the fashion to say, Give us the strong sturdy Saxon; eschew hard words and labored constructions; make your language the people's everyday language. This was timely enough; it called for just what was needed. Only in the demanded return to nature the fact was forgotten that the art itself is nature, and that the ability to use sturdy Saxon, without labored constructions, is an acquired ability,—the result of discipline and training,—as truly as is the more artificial work. So under the emphasis and impatience of this reaction, writing was left mostly to each man's individual notion, and rhetoric as a study and discipline passed under the cloud of contemptuous toleration from which, we hope, it is just emerging.

While the public mind was thus calling vaguely for some English discipline that should yield practical help, it was met by an answer which seemed at first full of promise. From the philological side came a revival of English study which, in the hands of exceptionally able teachers, soon awakened a widespread interest in the history of the language.

But this very interest soon became, outside of the leading few, largely a conventionalism. Under the influence of such leaders as Mr. Sweet, Mr. Skeat, and the New Shakespeare Society, it speedily became "the thing" to dig for etymological roots and minute changes in verbal forms. Anglo-Saxon and various readings were going to bring the new era. Here indeed was the strong, sturdy Saxon pure and undiluted; here was all the material of a natural style. The study was tempting and full of novelty. Rhetoric, little conscious of its true significance, was becoming superannuated; and soon all distinction between art and science, between activity and passivity, was swallowed up in the overwhelming impulse to look for the spirit of the language in its bones. Seeking power to write, men were fed with philology. And thus the attitude of the student was determined in the contra-rhetorical direction. English was pursued as an acquisition, not as an art.

Now far be it from me to cast any shade of reproach on Anglo-Saxon and various readings. They have their important place in courses of philological and literary study. If any language in the world should be investigated in the minutiae of its etymology and syntax, surely as patriotic English speakers we should not neglect our own. And yet with the very highest respect for Mr. Sweet, Mr. Skeat, and the New Shakespeare Society, I must have the temerity to ask if the rhetorical value of such study may not be a good deal overrated. Is it not indeed more truly a matter for the specialist than for the general student? While the soul of historic ages is breathing through our noble literature, and students everywhere are hungering to have inner communion with it, may not a little philology go a good way in comparison with the boundless work of the higher kind that is clamoring to be done? Without insisting on an answer to this, however, I would emphasize the necessity of defining justly what philology may do and what it may not do. To look for results from it incongruous with its nature will not pay. Philology cannot be regarded as supplying every discipline needed for the making of literature. When it is valued as if the acquisition of so many early English words and familiarity with so many etymologies and old syntactical forms were to stand as the solver of the numberless problems of adaptation, accuracy, order, emphasis, which we know are the inevitable attendants of the careful writer, its sphere is wrongly estimated. As philology it is as good as any philology, with the added interest that it deals with our own heritage and birthright; as the working outfit of a literary art it is worth as little as any other merely receptive, acquisitive study.

The fact is, English instruction is groping to find a method. Instruction in Latin and Greek, to which it would naturally look for a model, bases method and training on the grammar and the lexicon, which furnish unfailing opportunity to keep students at work, and which, being capable of application quite apart from the interest or efficiency of the instruction, afford a most grateful refuge to dull and perfunctory teachers. It is mainly on account of this large capacity for systematized routine, I suppose, that educators are pleased to distinguish Latin and Greek, as "the disciplinary studies." But the grammar and the lexicon are just what fail in the study of English; the knowledge of them is taken for granted, as the student's natural heritage. The lack of these appliances raises a very serious problem,—how to make the study of the mother-tongue laborious enough, furnish it, as it were, with sufficient brimstone and treacle, for discipline. To solve this problem requires the adoption of an entirely new method. But methods of instruction do not spring full-armed from the pedagogic brain. They must submit to the tests and survivals of a slow evolution. And in the case before us the difficulty is increased by the demanded creative attitude; for to set the student in the originative vein makes great and constant demands on the enthusiasm and versatility of the teacher. Thus English instruction labors under a double difficulty: it cannot thrive under mediocre teachers, nor can it easily devise a routine that will run itself when dullness is in the chair. Meanwhile philology, with its glossaries and its historical grammar, which furnish a good substitute for the grammar and lexicon of the classics, affords an interesting study in the line of the old methods, and does not tax the teacher's ingenuity to devise daily new appeals to the student's interest. A useful study in its place, yet it has entered quite to the confusion, temporarily, of the rhetorical course.

Still it must be acknowledged that such philological study of English possesses one very great advantage. It is concrete, definite; it deals with the facts of the language. This quality it was, I think, that more than any other caused the popular mind to desert the old rhetorical methods for this new pursuit. Rhetoric had become mainly theory, philosophizing, speculation; it had gone on discriminating figures of speech with long Greek names and vaporing about the Nature of the Nervous Style, until there was very little juice left in it. In fact, it had lost its direction, and had come to be pursued as a mere acquisition; and it must be confessed that when the study was at such a pass, the concrete facts of philology were much more interesting and in no way less practical. There is neither blame nor surprise for those who left the old for the new under such conditions. But we have here the needed suggestion for the future of rhetorical study. That it must be an art more than a science, that it must foster the creative mood above the receptive, we have seen. But further, it must draw its new life from the concrete, must deal with facts more than theory. Its problem is, going straight to literature, to note the effects that have been wrought, and to trace the means that wrought them,—means that, having succeeded once, may succeed again. This is not a speculation out of some one's head; it is scientific method. Rhetoric is the constructive study of literature, as distinguished from the philological and the historical study. It is concerned with the same subject, only approaching it from another side and maintaining a different attitude. It properly includes, therefore, many facts of history and philology, so far as these give practical help toward the solution of its constructive problem. Nay, with this same constructive standard, its field is as broad as the field of literature; it draws suggestion from every department of nature and life. Boundless indeed the art is in its capabilities, so complex and diversified that the faithfullest devotee dies still learning. But it is no more subject to vagueness and mere theorizing than any other art. The means of making a description vivid, or of giving clearness and point to an exposition, depend on as definite principles as does the etymology of a word. Let but the creative mood, the impulse to express thought, be present, and all the question of ways and means becomes a luminous and engaging study. This attitude also dictates to a sound common sense what is practical and what is unpractical. The writer is spared the necessity of having his theorizing done for him, just in so far as he is set in the way of doing his own. He is moving among concrete, definite requirements, and his invention is quickened to meet them.

So far as to the direction and attitude of rhetorical study. A word now regarding the scope of rhetoric.

The great change that has taken place in the aim and inclusion of the college course, as well as in the lines of activity open to the graduate, makes it imperative that the study of rhetoric be correspondingly broadened. Years ago, when the great majority of college students had the Christian ministry in view, rhetoric very naturally had oratory for its almost exclusive goal, and the student was trained to compose orations. Other forms of literature were very crudely treated, hardly at all; and indeed the oration still holds its place in most text-books as the centre of rhetorical invention. It seems to me that now, however, when theological students are in a minority, and when the vast increase of popular and periodical literature has greatly multiplied the forms of literary production, the whole subject of invention needs to be re-studied and re-developed. It can no longer content itself with being a mere fore-school for homiletics. The writers who are studying in our colleges to-day must know the literary art for many purposes, of which oratory is only one. What these purposes must be is suggested by the kinds of reading-matter that come to our breakfast tables every morning. The editorial paragraph; the reporter's column; the story, short or continued; the essay on social, political, or scientific topics;—all these prevailing literary forms, which are exemplified in every daily newspaper, call for special developments of rhetorical skill, and for resources of style quite beyond the province of Latin grammar to teach. There is much grumbling over the careless and slovenly way in which such things are written, and much abuse of the vast loads of stuff that are daily dumped at the reader's feet; while the writers in turn say, "Your rhetorics never taught me better; I had to make my own way, and what wonder if it is a poor one?" The rhetorical course of the future must set itself to point out this way clearly, not only for the preacher but for the journalist. It must teach the student to write paragraphs as well as sermons, racy reports and descriptions as well as exordiums, scientific expositions as well as perorations. It must recognize as legitimate a form of prose that has not the orotundity and balance of pulpit and lyceum eloquence. And until it has thus provided for the broadening needs of literature, and indicated how writers should do what the day gives them most constant occasion to do, rhetoric itself must remain more or less under eclipse.

II.

But we are delaying too long on the preliminary question; let us inquire now more particularly concerning our practical task, its promise and its limitations. How much of literary training, then, can reasonably be expected from a college course?

It is no small achievement in any man's life to develop the style that fully and naturally represents himself. This is the universal testimony of those who have most to do with the matter. Men have awaked and found themselves famous; but never has any one had a style sent him in his sleep. It comes, in all but the very exceptional cases, only by long labor, only by absorbing study. When therefore we teachers of rhetoric set ourselves to train artists in literature, we are undertaking to conduct them to a very high goal, which only the few have fully reached. Can we do the whole work in the limits of the college course?

Yet the world expects it. Every year, about commencement time, we have to meet that well-seasoned newspaper joke, as perennially laugh-producing as the famous story of the grouse in the gun-room,—about the student with his diploma, who knows Latin and Greek and metaphysics and biblical politics, and yet has no really practical ability to give his thoughts expression, and who accordingly fares very hardly, with his sonorous but prolix periods, at the hands of the editor who contemplates giving him a job. The joke is ostensibly on the student, but its sharpest sting is directed against us teachers. Have we then failed in our duty because the student who came to us from preparatory school with scarcely the rudiments of an idea what style is, cannot face the world after four years, a finished man of letters and affairs? Can we in reason expect that he should?

Consider the case. Those authors who stand nearest the goal tell us that two things are mainly necessary to the formation of a pliant, individual style: absorbing study and faithful practice. Of course we cannot set the ideal lower than the highest; but yet these two things are just what most lack opportunity in the college course. It probably cannot be otherwise. The student, who must divide his time between rhetoric and several other pursuits, has at best only a small margin left for practice. To what does this margin serve? In the broad field covered by rhetoric, which field he must traverse in college or not at all, he can hardly do the same kind of work twice over: he can try each kind merely enough to catch the principle involved, and then must go on to something else. This is not practice, yet it is about the best he can do. Again, the student cannot well become absorbed in some line of original literary study; he cannot get down to that strong grasp and stern tenacity which are necessary to make a subject give up the heart of its secret and every word take its inevitable place as a vital part of the tissue. Such absorption is essential to the literary life. How can the college course permit it? The student, we will say, has secured a couple of hours for writing; but just as he has well overcome his pen's inertia he must break off and get a Greek lesson. Then come other duties; and his literary work must go until the next day or the next week. This distribution—shall I say dissipation?— of energy, necessary though it may be in college, is a most deplorable hindrance to the literary life at any time, and to its formative period a deadly foe.

It cannot really be expected, then, that during the undergraduate course the student should develop a full-formed style. We his teachers must be content with a result less than this, however we may long to turn out a finished writer. Our beginning must in most cases be too rudimentary and our opportunities too limited to ensure the perfected result. What then must we seek? Evidently, if such a source can be found, some line of discipline and study that shall give the impulse, open the way, set the student in the channel of such habits and standards as shall some time guide his active and earnest endeavor to the goal. We are laboring to impart something that shall be recalled by spontaneous association, and be found useful, when the student tastes the experiences of the world and faces real literary tasks. Thus we are sowing seed for future harvests, I had almost said for future germination. It is well-nigh all we can do.

But to have done thus much during a college course, and to be reasonably sure at the end that the soil is well charged with good seed and free from cockle, is something, is a great deal. And indeed, *could* more be done by a teacher? Must not the rest, which is the bulk of it, be *discovered*, be achieved, by the writer himself, when he goes forth to meet real issues, to learn the world not from tutors and governors but by grim experience? Style is so interwoven with thought that it must wait on the days of thought, which comes not in the cloister-world of college. The formation of a vigorous and individual style must, after all, be for the most part postponed to the time of actual contact with men and affairs; and what we do towards it must be present discipline with a future bearing.

An advantage we have, however, that should not be ignored or neglected,—the advantage of taking the student at the starting-point. There are literary ideas and habits, too often indeed developed late and hardly, but that cannot be implanted too early. To find these and give them firm lodgement in the student's mind at the outset is our worthy and sufficient task. Let me name two or three of these. First of all, we need to arouse the desire for sober accuracy in thought and expression,— the desire to see a thing truly, and to state it just as it is seen and felt. Nothing can be more indispensable to the callow writer than this. He needs to know that writing is not juggling with words, not making ideas show off, but expressing the truth, plainly, directly, completely. Such solid endowment outweighs all the "brilliancy" in the world without it. Very close to this, merely its ripened result, is literary conscientiousness and patience;—"strict literary conscience and long literary art," as an accomplished writer puts it. It is this which crosses the grain with the college student. He is ready enough to emulate the slashing style, which says saucy and glittering things, apparently without effort; but he can little realize that the way even to true spontaneity, if this is to be worth anything, is the way of toil. Yet he must learn this very disillusive fact in college course, or else unlearn a great deal afterwards. Another habit that we should work to implant now is the habit of seeing truth for one's self and forming independent conclusions. How little idea of this there is ordinarily in college, one can easily observe in the desperation with which, when a subject for discussion is assigned, the student will clutch at any old essay or periodical article, and, failing in this, in the timid and halting step with which, under querulous protest, he ventures on a line of thought where some one of authority has not done virtually all the thinking before. The student needs to learn that some day he must cast off leading-strings and stand alone: what time so fitting, then, to try his legs, as now, when if he stumbles the consequences are confined to this little cloister-world?

Such are some of the fundamental ideas and habits that we as teachers may labor to inculcate, quite apart from and anterior to our superintendence of the student's work in composition. Anterior, I say, logically first, is this general training, because it sets the student in the vein of calculating and correcting for himself. Good writing is taught fully as much by communicating an impulse, kindling a love for literature, inducing an author's attitude, as by teaching and criticizing details of composition. These latter of course may not be neglected; and yet the details of individual work are far too numerous to be imparted by any teacher. Besides, none of us become good writers merely by hanging on a teacher for minute suggestions of usage and grammar. It is only as such details *stand for something,* only as they may be made the starting-point of a broader principle or habit that shall regulate many such details, that we may with profit busy ourselves with them. From the minutiae we are ever to find a way to the workings and habits of the student's mind; and after all we are to keep the *man* above the individual composition. It is the permanent impulse communicated to him that counts. On this point I will quote from an esteemed friend and teacher a paragraph which, though perhaps a little extreme in some of its ideas, enforces well the vital requisite.

"It is a capital mistake," says Professor William Cleaver Wilkinson, "for boards of college oversight to suppose that they have done the best for the literary education of young men, when they have provided them with an instructor who is willing to go through unlimited drudgery, in the way of minute rudimentary criticism of their essays with the pencil or the pen. Infinitely better, in our judgment, it would be for college classes, if their rhetorical teacher should even, save in exceptional cases, never once *see* the essays of their pupils. This is no place for discussing a point of education, and we cannot pause to vindicate our opinion. We scarcely state it, indeed. We baldly suggest it. Stimulus, more than criticism, is what the forming literary mind requires. Vigorous growth can better be trusted than the most laborious pruning-knife, to give symmetry of form. Besides, only vigorous growth responds to the pruning-knife with desirable results. The criticism that is applied should be living criticism—by which we mean oral criticism, in which the criticized writer himself should share as respondent, while the writer's classmates, under stimulating and regulating direction from the head of the department, should take a principal part in it. It is in some such way that the voluntary societies of a college manipulate their members; and many a student will testify that he is more indebted to their influence than to the influence of the regular instruction for the forming of his literary habits. This colluctant play of mental faculties in generous social exercise, is worth, for literary discipline, all the dead pen-strokes that could be strewn on a manuscript essay by the most industrious grammarian in the world. A teacher who can do, has done, is doing literary work of acknowledged value himself, provided always that it be with art, and not wholly by instinct, is the man to teach literary workmanship to college students. Such a man will not be a drudge. And such a man need not be. An ounce of stimulus here outweighs a ton of drill."

Thus, when we come to take an inventory of resources, we find that the rhetorical teacher's sphere, which at the beginning of our inquiry seemed so limited, opens after all no narrow field of activity. We cannot hope, indeed, to make finished authors: time fails for requisite practice; so does occasion, which must be real, practical, present,—the occasion that only contact at first hand with the world can supply. Nor can we, to any great extent, invade the domain of individuality in style; we must leave the subject and the man to make the style humorous, or sublime, or satirical, or epigrammatic, while we seek to guide and criticize each man on his own personal standard. But we can hope to make students know what literature is, in the various problems of its construction, and to make them love it for its own sake; we can by our own enthusiasm and example teach them that literature is an art, the most delightful of arts, while also it is the most practical and honest. We can be living representatives of the literary stimulus and impulse, existing perpetually to guide and foster the upspringing thoughts of young men. Such a work is great enough, worthy enough, and faithful enough to employ the best energies of any teacher, and the wisest provisions of any course.

Nor should we forget that the most effective stimulus is the stimulus of generous interest and sympathy. We must subdue ourselves to look at things through a student's eyes, nay, and to take enjoyment from that limited vision. There will certainly be redeeming features in the student's view of things, if honestly taken; and for these he is entitled to the meed of sympathy. Imagine an English instructor in one of our foremost colleges saying, as reported, "I know of nothing more dreary than college men's intentional good writing." Indeed. And one is tempted to ask, What business has such a man in a chair of English instruction? Wearing out his valuable existence by conducting daily discipline in a work than which he "knows of nothing more dreary." Now of course it is useless to blink what is patent enough to the student himself, to say nothing of the matured writer. A carefully written, conscientious college essay *is* stiff and self-conscious; the thought is meagre and commonplace, the style is wooden. It is not apt to be absorbing reading for the world at large. But the real question is, what is to be done with it here in college? Two ways suggest themselves. One way, and it seems to me the reasonable one, is to treat its stiffness and self-consciousness as a matter of course, endeavoring all the while to supply such corrective, such education in taste, such encouragement to wiser effort, that these defects may in the natural course of things yield to that masterful art which conceals itself. After all, these are but the faults of an art on the way to mastery. They may ordinarily be trusted to disappear when the author finds himself; and even as faults they are more promising than the brilliantly crude and breathless instinctive writing. I believe there must be a more or less wooden period in all earnest authorship; and in all worthy thinking there must be a commonplace period, while the writer is thinking off his surface-thoughts and ridding himself of the echoes of others. It takes sometimes several years to get through those stratified accumulations down to the place where our innermost self begins to think. May not we teachers regard ourselves as taking students at the beginning of this period, just as they are first turned loose into the vast fields of thought; and, following them a little in their play-issues, in their callow mimicry of great mental achievements, may we not hope to give them a right helpful God-speed toward that time when they will begin to add original treasures to the world's acquisition? I confess I like to think so. A second way, however, has its votaries. That is, to deprecate anything that shows for *intentional* good writing, and, making a kind of "rattlin' roarin' Willie" of the student, to keep him slashing ahead, always fluent, if not always so cunning, until he happens to write something eminently racy and individual. The deadly sin of this procedure is dullness. By all means be readable and interesting; don't be exact, don't be formal, don't be careful and conscientious,—or at least don't get caught at it. Very good advice—for a matured writer. Readableness and interest are certainly indispensable. I am not so clear, however, that these are the supreme qualities of style, that, once secured, will ensure the rest. It seems to me they come more naturally afterward, when they can bring solid qualities with them; and that sober fidelity to the subject and to literary usage has rights that we are first bound to respect. This matter reminds me of the different ways I used to see students taking to learn the German language in Germany. There were two classes. The first would pay little attention to books, and attempt to pick up everything by way of conversation. Soon they would be able to rattle off German with the utmost assurance, but in such genderless and orderless style as would result from the mere commutation of German for English words. I once asked a German concerning a mutual acquaintance who had learned the language by this wholesale process: "Herr So-and-so speaks German quite readily, does he not?" "O ya, er spricht Deutsch,—aber, du lieber Himmel, wie!—O yes, he speaks German,—*but, good heavens, how!*" "But," said I, "he seems to speak very fluently." "Fliessend ist es, ya, freilich,—furchtbar fliessend.—Fluent it is, yes, indeed,—*fearfully* fluent." With such fearful fluency my acquaintance went on, his German increasingly voluble and increasingly bad. Another class of students did not try to make so immediate a conquest of the language. They were shamefast enough to burrow pretty diligently in the grammar and in sentence-writing until they had obtained an idea how the German language is built; and then when their halting tongue essayed to speak, they would think twice before they spoke once. It was slow work at first, and for a while they seemed quite at disadvantage by the side of their "fluent" brethren; but little by little they gained self-confidence; and when the fluency came, as come it did, it was fluency in real German.

These two methods of learning a foreign language are not without their analogy in the methods of learning the literary art. And if, like the old stories, we may draw a moral, let it be, not to despise the crude attempts, the wooden commonplaces, of beginners; they may be, after all, the beginnings of great things. Nor can we safely conform our standard only to those few students who from the exceptional influence of a cultured home have already become free and fluent with the pen. We must go lower than that, and be a guide to those honest country fellows who have read little and written not at all; who have it therefore all to learn. We must plod with them until under our direction they have shaped wings to fly. It is not always easy to give such men just the right impulse; but least of all, it seems to me, can we trust in the rattling roaring method. Rather let us begin with them on the plane where they are, and aim to make them useful, honest writers; and if the spirit of higher things is in them, it will move, some day.

III.

So much for our general object, and its limitations and encouragements in the actual possibilities of the case. The question of particulars is now inevitably suggested. How may these principles of instruction, so conditioned, shape themselves into a serviceable undergraduate course?

The answer to this question must of course be adapted, in any college, to the size of the classes, and to the amount of time that can be secured for rhetorical study. I speak for conditions as they essentially exist in Amherst College: for classes of from seventy to one hundred; and for a course of at least three terms of class-room work, besides the individual training in writing and revising essays. I leave unconsidered, on the one side, work in declamation and elocution, and on the other, the historical study of English Literature, both of which studies belong properly to other courses. Thus, by the rhetorical course, we are to understand the analytical study of the principles of literary art, and the application of them in practice, by written composition, criticism, and revision.

It is perhaps not superfluous to say here that I believe thoroughly in both practice and precept. To leave out the first, and study rhetoric only philosophically, is to lose the fundamental direction of the study, which, as we have seen, is towards construction, creation. To leave out the second, on the plea sometimes urged that writing is learned only by writing, is to submit the literary art to the rule of thumb. It is strange that in institutions where every other department represents the well-garnered scholarship of the ages, in this department alone it should so often be thought enough to put a pen into the student's hand and say, as the angel said to John, "Write." That is merely what the young man's parents bade him do, when he left home. It is strange indeed if we, as teachers of rhetoric, have nothing higher to do than to correct bad spelling and clean up slovenly sentences. But we need not multiply words; if art means anything, it means more than this. The problem that here rises, then, is, how to combine precept with practice in one course; and this, I take it, means ideally the interweaving of the two, so that, though in some part of the course one or the other may predominate, there shall be no part without some definite proportion of both. This ideal we will keep in view.

Of the three terms of rhetorical work in the class-room, the first is properly devoted to the study of literary style. Here, owing to the present unsatisfactory state of English study in preparatory schools, we have to begin with more rudimentary work than ought to be pursued in college: we ought to be able to take for granted that the grammatical and mechanical features of composition, those principles of language which it is not so much a credit to know as a shame not to know, are mastered by every student, beyond uncertainty. This would leave us freer to study the more artistic and literary qualities of style. We cannot count on this at present, however. Under style, then, as the existing state of English study limits us, we include diction, figures of speech, phraseology, sentence structure, and paragraph structure. Thus the beginning of the study is concerned with what is most constant and fundamental in writing,—with those practical details of contrivance and adaptation which must be present with the writer in the construction of every sentence and the choice of every word. Much depends on the thoroughness of this beginning. It is confessedly dry and strenuous work; for it does not yet contemplate the finished plan with its brilliant relations of thought, nor is it concerned to turn out compositions for exhibition, like the little pieces of music and paintings in oil that used to show off the pupil's first course of lessons in our fathers' days. The practice-work is as yet but exercises, which, if the student has becoming modesty, he will keep shut up in his note-book. And because the work is apt to be dry, a special duty lies on the teacher to make it interesting; for, as we have seen, the love of the work counts for much in composition. A text-book furnishes, of course, the basis of each hour's procedure; but in addition to the recitation much discussion should be encouraged on the part of the students; the aim being not merely to ensure the student's knowledge of the various principles, but also in each case to base that knowledge on a practical philosophy, to show its working in actual literature, and above all, to induce in his mind from the outset the habit of thinking for himself and applying his thoughts to such patient constructive and critical work with words and sentences as must be submitted to by every earnest writer.

Along with these recitations and discussions, in order that theory may not outrun practice, there is needed frequent drill. This, in classes so large, cannot well take as yet the form of original composition, nor is the course ripe for it. The best drill, perhaps, is found in the criticism and correction of supplied sentences and paragraphs, so constructed that the rewriting of them will necessarily apply the principles learned. For this part of the work existing text-books make rather unsatisfactory provision. A suggestion of the kind of exercises I mean may be seen in E. A. Abbott's little book "How to Write Clearly"; it is to be hoped that a more comprehensive exercise book may before long be supplied. These exercises should alternate at suitable times with the recitations. It should be remarked, too, that these sentences and paragraphs for drill should not be corrected *vivâ voce*, but carefully written out, every one. The fact needs to be impressed that this is the study not of puzzles but of composition; so each passage should be written out in full and made the student's own, because he cannot fully realize how a sentence ought to read until he sees it by itself, cleared from the rubbish and *débris* of mistaken or crude expression.

The work of the second term is devoted, by the same means of recitation and discussion, to the principles of literary invention. Under this head are properly included not only the general procedures involved in finding, planning, and amplifying the material of a work, but also the more particular applications of inventive skill to such work as description, narration, exposition, argument, and persuasion. It is, in effect, a study of the various literary forms; and is a subject wherein it is of much importance to keep theory in constant contact with actual literature. Precept alone has almost inevitably an unreal and arbitrary look; but there is no gainsaying when we can study what has really been done and note how the procedure resulted. In the matter of exercises, therefore, a change may now be profitably made. It is time to study models. In connection, therefore, with the various principles and forms, as the student meets them in theory, the study of the text-book should be supplemented by the analytical study of extended selections illustrative of each kind or process of composition. Here again I must remark that a systematic and progressive collection of such extracts for study is something much to be desired. These selections may either be recited upon or their points written out; and features of style may be noted incidently, by way of review.

The work of these two terms completes the student's theoretical study for the course. It consists, as is evident, merely of a compendious treatment of the whole ground to be traversed in making a literary work of each of the fundamental types, with barely enough work by way of exercises to make the principles familiar and definite. There is not sufficient time to make the observance of these principles second nature; they can only be inculcated, and their importance evinced by examples.

Further work in rhetoric must now be in the way of practice. Here, however, a difficulty has to be acknowledged. To prescribe exercise in composition for a class of from seventy to a hundred in such a way that each man shall have enough to do, yet so also that each man's work shall pass under the eye of the instructor, is confessedly no easy problem. And it must be premised that if the instructor is overmuch disposed to spare himself, he has missed his calling. The work should be copious, varied, progressive. The various kinds of composition, with their special procedures and cautions, should be discussed and explained, and the members of the class should have opportunity to estimate and criticise each other's work. As I interpret the matter, it is not for the sake of getting so much work done, though of course quantity is one consideration, but for the sake of learning to do work of certain determinate kinds, that classes in composition should be formed. The course should therefore be a systematically ordered, progressive series, not a mere demand for so many written productions.

As the present paper undertakes not to legislate but simply to suggest, it may be of interest, by way of illustration, to describe the attempt already made at Amherst to solve this problem of a class in composition. The experience of two years—during which time its pleasant daily working, a genuine interest on the part of the students, and gratifying progress in power and naturalness of style were abundantly evinced—justifies me, perhaps, in dwelling a little upon the subject.

We have at our disposal four hours a week. These it was thought wisest to arrange for each division (for of course a large class must be separated into manageable divisions) into two sessions of two hours each. Thus the student's preparation, which for each session consists of a written production on a subject previously assigned, involves, coming as it does twice a week, a reasonable amount of work,—such an amount also as may be looked over by the instructor without undue drudgery. Of course such a large number of papers cannot receive minute criticism; nor perhaps, on other grounds, should the little technicalities of style be the object of criticism at first. The interest should centre in the subject; and the predominating object at first should be to gain freedom with the pen and confidence in one's own powers of portrayal. Verbal criticism should not be undertaken to any great extent until the student has achieved something to criticise. In this respect it will be noticed that the practice is carried on in an order inverse to the study of theory. That began with questions of manner; but when it comes to originative work, the stimulus must come, as far as possible, from the intrinsic interest of the subject-matter.

It will readily be seen that the success of the class, both as to interest and progress, depends very largely, perhaps principally, on the nature of the subjects assigned. Let me therefore dwell a little on this matter. It is a very prevalent but very mistaken tendency among students to contemn or at least to ignore simple subjects. They think they must enlighten the world on The Tariff, International Law, and the Progress of Thought, when perhaps there would be much more real profit in trying faithfully to describe the view from their window. This tendency is not to be regarded as mere folly on the part of the student. He knows that he is tackling a ridiculously big subject; but his plea, that he wants to learn something of these important matters and takes this way of informing himself, is not without claim to consideration. However, he needs to be directed to simpler things. He needs to be shown, by the example of the great names of literature, that simple description and narration are forms of work that may employ a man's best powers. He needs also, and this I think first of all, to become aware that he has eyes and ears and a mind of his own, and that if ever he achieves success as a writer, he must rely on himself. To boil together an armful of books and articles on some big subject, and skim off the surface-ideas as a fifteen-hundred-word essay is, perhaps, a useful exercise for some point well along in the course; but much is to be learned first. The men who originally thought out those big subjects began with the vigorous use of eyes and ears. And the greatest works of the greatest men—of the Shakespeares and the Bacons and the Wordsworths and the Miltons—are full of the endeavors to impart a clear and moving idea of common things, common events, common thoughts. Nay, we can find in any of them masterly work devoted to subjects of which a college student is too apt to be ashamed.

Now in the composition class I am describing, the beginning is made by assigning subjects requiring simple observation or imagination; and afterwards the student is introduced to subjects requiring exercise of thought. He is not required to "read up" at all; nay, the subject often precludes reading. But he must use eyes and ears; he must endeavor vividly to realize facts; and he must lean wholly on his individual powers. The series of subjects follows the general course of literary forms, as he has studied them in the manual. Descriptions, to begin with, of such objects as may be studied from reality, or imagined from pictures and models. Then come narratives, constructed from outline data, or related from personal experience. These are followed by subjects requiring study and interpretation of general ideas, as embodied in terms, propositions, and extended passages. Finally comes work in argumentative composition, preparation and debating of questions, and the like. Such in brief is the character of the subjects assigned. It may be of interest here to give a list of the kinds of work done in one term.

1. Portrayal of Persons (historical personages generally, to be studied from portraits).
2. Description of Interiors (private rooms, halls, galleries, etc.).
3. Description of Exteriors (buildings, also streets, squares, etc.).
4. Description of Scenery (including also towns, etc.).
5. Description of Works of Art (pictures, statuary, machinery, etc.).
6. Portraiture of Character.
7. Account of Mental Impressions and Experiences.
8. Discursive Narration (excursions, games, etc.).
9. Historical Incident (central data, as personages, scraps of conversation, and action, given; the incident then to be clothed with accessories).
10. Plotted Story (illustrative of some given sentiment or character).
11. Interpretation of Passage (chosen for the condensed suggestiveness of its thought).
12. Analysis of Extended Passage.
13. Exposition by Comparison (terms nearly synonymous or contrasted given, to be defined by each other).
14. Exposition by Illustration and Analogy.
15. Exposition by Restriction (ideas in some particular application).
16. Preparation of Question for Debate (exposition of terms, fixing nature and extent, etc.).
17. Construction of Arguments (from principle, example, etc.).
18. Criticism of Fallacious Assertions and Arguments.

These subjects cover, it will be observed, just such simple literary work as lies close to us every day; but it is no mere boy's tinkering. It is such work, and involves such processes as demand the writer's highest powers; while also it is practical, involving such things as each man will have to write, if he writes at all, in after life.

A few words must now be devoted to describing the manner in which the work of the class-room is conducted.

For each session four or five subjects are assigned, all representing the particular kind of work allotted to the day. Of course these have to be announced two sessions beforehand, so that when the actual exercise comes the productions shall have been presented and looked over by the instructor. The several subjects obviate the monotony of reading several productions on the same theme before the class, and give the student also some freedom of choice.

The two-hour exercise, which fills up each session of the class, is conducted as follows. The first hour is taken up with the reading and criticism of four or five representative productions selected from those which the instructor has last looked over. These are not chosen for their special excellence, nor does the writer know beforehand that his production will be read; but each man's work is in turn subjected to criticism, being liable to be selected at any chance time. It is for various reasons better that the instructor read the productions; better reading is thus ordinarily ensured, and, being anonymous, the productions are more freely discussed by the class. The criticisms, in which class and instructor join, are on general points, such as faithfulness to fact, vividness, consistency, and such points of style as may be picked up by one hearing. An intermission of a few minutes follows this first hour's work, after which the work of the second hour is taken up. This consists first of a short lecture on the kind of work in hand, with discussion of procedure, problems, and cautions to be observed. Notes are taken by the class; and a periodical examination is held. This short lecture is followed by the reading and analysis of a series of passages, usually five or six, from standard authors who are confessedly eminent in the particular kind of literature under discussion; of which readings also the class take notes and references. Thus at each step the student's work is held up in comparison with the best, and subjected to the standard of literature. This is a great influence to give reality and stimulus to the student's work; while his constant walk in the company of renowned authors can hardly fail to increase his love of literature.

Let me pause here one moment to speak of the delightful interest of this last-named feature of the exercise, and of the surprising "finds" that are continually made in the rich storehouse of literature. Everything that the student is set to do finds some striking illustration. He is introduced, for instance, to Carlyle's magnificent study of Dante's portrait, in the "Hero-Worship," and to his matter-of-fact descriptions of Huntingdon and Naseby, drawn in a few simple words, in the "Cromwell"; he sees in Irving's sketch of The Stout Gentleman, in "Bracebridge Hall," how a living fancy glorifies the most commonplace theme imaginable; he compares with keen zest the very divergent accessories with which Hawthorne has twice clothed the same incident—the incident of Governor Endicott and the Flag—in his "Twice-Told Tales" and in his "Grandfather's Chair." Such examples conduct him into the very workshop of the world's literature; and the interest they arouse is the interest of genuine instruction.

The written productions of this term can hardly be called essays; they are merely extended exercises embodying the leading processes of discourse. The student is now ready to write more ambitious essays, wherein his ability to gather and sift material, to plan his thought, and to wield an adequate style, are alike tested. To this end, the succeeding term is devoted to the writing and private presentation of essays, on subjects chosen from a liberal list. The instructor holds himself in readiness to furnish suggestions as to finding material, determining the manner of treatment, and the like; and when the essay is handed in, and reviewed by the instructor, he appoints a private interview with the writer, in which any points of style or workmanship that need correction are discussed. The essay is then returned for rewriting. Two such essays are presented and reviewed in the course of the term.

The work I have thus described constitutes no inconsiderable course in rhetoric. Bounded, as it must be, by other demands on the student's time, it is still sufficient to open the way and impress the habits and principles of literary procedure, which is perhaps enough to hope for from the undergraduate course. Its systematized and progressive character also gives significance to each point, as an integral part of an ordered whole; and this is a great advantage. From the point to which I have traced it, the literary work of the student now passes into the care of the various teachers, who require essays, abstracts, criticisms, and the like, in the line of their individual studies. I need not specify these at length; but I ought not to leave unmentioned the work of the classes in English literature, which is carried on predominantly by essays and critical study, nor should I neglect to speak of the several terms of class debates and the classes in oratory. All these may be regarded as contributing largely to the rhetorical course.

Many observations rise to mind in thinking over the requirements and possibilities of a course in rhetoric. Two or three remarks on secondary and general points may perhaps be allowed in closing.

In all the student's work in composition the standards of judgment and criticism to be applied to him should be the standards that obtain in letters. His productions are to be treated not as school-boy task-work, but as earnestly meant literature. He means them so; and if they are so treated, he will endeavor to make them worthy by that standard.

In every class, especially if the work is required, there will be a certain proportion, generally a small one, of careless and slipshod work, such as does not represent the writer's true powers. The most effectual rebuke of such work is to treat it as if it were the best that the writer could do. Criticise him thoroughly on the low plane he has chosen, estimate his powers once by the hasty production he has let represent him, and he will not be likely to present such another.

The teacher must necessarily have much routine work in looking over and criticising the numerous productions of his class; but he should not let it become a drudgery,—above all he should not reveal that it is a drudgery. It will inevitably be a bore to the student to write if it is a bore to the teacher to examine his work. Nor need it be irksome to the teacher. Consider the golden opportunity he has, to study the writer's individual powers and aptitudes, to come through the writings, into friendly personal communion with the man, to share in his sympathies, feelings, views of things. A new standard of judgment will, in a sense, be adopted for each individual; and the less perfunctory the criticism, the more valuable to the student, and the more conscientious the work induced. Indeed the rhetorical teacher may well value his position; for it gives more favorable occasion than perhaps any other place in the faculty to lessen that distance between teacher and taught which, as all acknowledge, is the most deplorable feature of college life.

William Morton Payne, Editor
English in American Universities, by Professors in the English Departments of Twenty Representative Institutions (1895)

English was growing important enough for the literary and general-interest magazine The Dial *to commission the chairs of important English departments to describe their programs. Payne (1858–1919), a Chicago high school English teacher, literary editor at Chicago newspapers, and associate editor of* The Dial, *collected the articles as a book in 1895. Payne's book provides the most convenient place to see what English was like just before the turn of the century at a range of prominent American colleges and universities.*

The selections included here illustrate the dramatically different attitudes toward composition extant in 1895. Only Harvard, Amherst, and Michigan have genuine programs with a coherent intellectual focus. At almost all other universities composition has already become remedial work mostly confined to the first year and rarely taught by senior faculty. Most chairs express the hope that composition will soon be relegated to the schools.

It soon turned out that the schools were not capable of producing the kind of writers the colleges wanted, so composition instruction would struggle along, unwanted by chairs, scorned by most faculty, but absolutely necessary for the students and the university. Payne's introduction places college English studies in the context of the 1892 Harvard report (see chap. 2, p. 73) and the 1894 secondary school recommendations of the Committee of Ten, headed by Harvard's President Charles W. Eliot.

WHILE COLLEGE AND UNIVERSITY ENGLISH IS THE SPECIAL subject of the volume to which these pages serve as an introduction, it seems to me that the subject of elementary and secondary English cannot here be wholly ignored. The subject of the teaching of English is a unity, however varied the details at its successive stages, and it is truer of this subject than of most that mistakes made in the earlier years are difficult, if they are not impossible, of subsequent correction. The English Conference named by the famous Committee of Ten on Secondary Education soon came to realize these facts, and their report differed noticeably from those of the Conferences upon other subjects, by covering, not only the period of secondary education, but also the years that come before. The Report of that Conference, and the Harvard Report on Composition and Rhetoric, made public a year or so earlier, are responsible for much of the recent awakening of interest in the subject of English instruction. In fact, the Harvard Report may be said to have given to the reform movement its strongest impulse, and made a burning "question of the day" out of a matter previously little more than academic in its interest. The subject was made to reach a larger public than it had ever reached before, and this new and wider public was fairly startled out of its self-complacency by the exhibit made of the sort of English written by young men and women supposed to have enjoyed the best preparatory educational advantages, and to be fitted for entrance into the oldest and most dignified of our colleges. The report was more than a discussion of the evils of bad training; it was an object-lesson of the most effective sort, for it printed many specimen papers *literatim et verbatim,* and was even cruel enough to facsimile some of them by photographic process.

The seed of discontent having thus been sown broadcast, the field was in a measure prepared for the labors of the English Conference named by the Committee of Ten; and the Report of that Conference, made public early in 1894, has kept the question of English teaching as burning as ever, if, indeed, it has not fanned the flame into greater heat. Not only the educational periodicals, but also many published in the interests of general culture, and even some of the newspapers—in their blundering way—have kept the subject before the public. Educational gatherings have devoted to it much of their attention, and it has been largely taken up by writers for the magazines.

. . . .

Viewing this collection of reports as a whole, it is clear that they supply the material for a considerable number of fairly trustworthy inductions. A few of these I will endeavor briefly to set forth. The statistics given to show the numbers of students pursuing English courses at the respective colleges show that these courses are nearly everywhere very popular. They run the classical courses closely, and in some cases seem to attract a larger number of students, although the figures are lacking for any exact comparative statement on this subject. In a recent review article Professor Woodrow Wilson contends that the twin bases of the new liberal education ought to be the study of literature and the study of institutions. As far as the study of literature is concerned, it would seem that the contention is already justified, or nearly so, by the fact. The thousand odd students at Yale (and Sheffield), at Harvard, at the Universities of Michigan, and even of Nebraska, give eloquent testimony to the popularity of English teaching, to say nothing of the eight hundred and seventy-three reported by California, the six hundred and twenty-nine by Chicago, and the four hundred and fifty by Stanford. Equally eloquent, from another point of view, are such English faculties as that of Harvard, with twenty men, and of Chicago, with fifteen. Courses are reported in so many different ways that comparison is not easy; but Chicago, with upwards of sixty hours a week, seems to head the list, while Harvard, Stanford, and California are not far behind.

The important subject of entrance requirements is not discussed in the majority of our reports, but the few allusions made to it are of the greatest interest. During the past year, Yale has for the first time required an entrance qualification in English. From Pennsylvania comes the vague report that "English literature" is required for entrance. As we go West, we do better and better. Indiana has relegated the bugbear of "Freshman English" to the preparatory schools, and Nebraska has accomplished a similar reform. The most interesting reports upon this subject come from the Pacific Coast. The University of California requires "a high-school course of at least three years, at the rate of five hours a week; and it advocates, and from some schools secures, a four years' course." This requirement is further said to be fifty per cent more extensive and stringent than that made by the New England Association of Colleges. Stanford University started out with what was substantially the New England requirement, but has since raised that standard upon the side of composition. "This year," it is said, "we have absolutely refused to admit to our courses students unprepared to do real collegiate work. The Freshman English course in theme-writing has been eliminated from our programme, and has been turned over to approved teachers, and to the various secondary schools. Had this salutary innovation not been accomplished, all the literary courses would have been swept away by the rapidly growing inundation of Freshman themes, and all our strength and courage would have been dissipated in preparing our students to do respectable work at more happily equipped universities."

Yale University: Albert Stanburrough Cook

One of the most eminent early scholars of English, Cook (1853–1927) earned a B.S. at Rutgers in 1872 and studied in England and Germany (Ph.D., Jena, 1882). He taught at Johns Hopkins, Berkeley (1882–89), where he served as liaison with the secondary schools, and most notably at Yale (1889–1921), where he specialized in graduate work in Old English and the Bible. He served as MLA president in 1897. Cook published many scholarly works; his history of English studies in America, "The Teaching of English" (1901), shows him as acutely aware of the fragmentation of both literature and rhetoric and unusually sensitive to the problems of the secondary schools.

In 1895 Yale was in transition, and Cook's description reveals a changing set of requirements and electives. Yale had long held out against composition, but in 1895–96 would require composition course work for all sophomores. The description of English composition below on page 161 is from Yale's Sheffield Scientific School, which required juniors to take the literature-based writing course introduced by Thomas Lounsbury in 1870.

IT WILL BE OBSERVED THAT THERE IS AT PRESENT NO METHODICAL instruction in rhetoric in Yale University, and that in Yale College composition is systematically taught in but one course, and that an elective, though incidentally in connection with the preparation of papers in the literature classes. In the Sheffield Scientific School, Juniors receive instruction in composition for an hour a week throughout the year. In the College, provision has at length been made for the regular teaching of both rhetoric and composition in the future. Dr. Charles S. Baldwin, late of Columbia College, will have charge of this work. For next year he will give to the Sophomores a required course of an hour a week out of the three devoted to English, besides conducting the criticism of Sophomore essays. The subjoined announcement will indicate the nature of his proposed work with upper-class men:—

Competitors for the Porter, DeForest, Townsend, TenEyck, Betts, and McLaughlin prizes have the privilege of regular consultation with Dr. Baldwin in rhetoric at his office in 15 White Hall. The same privilege is offered to a limited number of competent Seniors and Juniors who wish to combine an optional course in composition with any elective course requiring essays, or who have shown special aptitude for some distinct kind of writing.

. . . .

English Composition.—This course, required of the entire Junior class, consists of weekly exercises based on selections from the writings of well-known authors, such as Irving, De Quincey, and Macaulay. While it intends in the first place to give freedom of expression and the correction of the most obvious faults by practice in writing rapidly the substance of a passage previously assigned, it also aims to direct the attention of the student to qualities of style and methods of composition, to arouse his appreciative interest in the works as literature, and to improve the quality of his writing by improving the quality of his thought. To this end occasional discussions of the selections read will occupy a part of the weekly hour.

Stanford University: Melville B. Anderson

According to Anderson (1851–1933), the newly founded Stanford University rejected what he calls the New England model, the attempt, best represented by Harvard, to teach writing directly to all first-year students. Yet Anderson allows that Stanford does teach plenty of writing, and will need to hire additional faculty to do so in the future. Thus Anderson dismisses the "drudgery of correcting Freshman themes" as being below the dignity of college faculty, yet plans to increase the work. (Anderson distinguishes between "approved teachers" and "professors." The former seem to be tutors or instructors hired to teach composition, while the latter are regular faculty members.)

BEFORE PROCEEDING TO DESCRIBE THE COURSES, IT MAY BE WELL to advert briefly to the English preparation exacted for admission to the University. The requirements for admission were at first modelled upon those of the University of California, which are similar to those of the New England Association of Colleges; namely, a play or two of Shakespeare, the *Sir Roger de Coverley Papers,* a story of Thackeray, and a few of the masterpieces of English and American poetry. Under this system the examination consists mainly in a test of the applicant's ability to quote readily, to explain allusions, to write outlines and abstracts, and in various ways to show upon paper that he has read and digested the work in question. While this system is a great advance upon the old practice of requiring an acquaintance with rhetoric and the formal side of grammar and composition, experience shows it to be not quite sufficient. The tendency is to encourage the "getting up" of a certain number of books, and the cramming of a modicum of information about words and etymologies, rather than the attainment of such a practical acquaintance with the vernacular as a student needs in order to take a college course successfully. We have therefore thought it wise to lay more stress upon the student's preparation in composition than has hitherto been customary in our secondary schools. While there has been no nominal increase in the requirements for admission in English, it has become, as a matter of fact, more difficult for the graduates of high schools and other secondary schools to satisfy our requirements. Thus, out of perhaps a hundred and fifty applicants for admission in English at the beginning of the present year, only some forty wrote satisfactory papers. It is hoped that our course in adhering rigidly to the relatively high, but really very moderate, standard of admission in English will have a salutary effect upon secondary instruction in California and elsewhere. All that we really ask on the side of style is that the student be pretty familiar with the mechanical details of composition,—spelling, punctuation, correct sentence structure, paragraphing, and the like,—and that he be able to express himself with some idiomatic fluency.

During the first two years of the short history of the English department here, the professors were worn out with the drudgery of correcting Freshman themes,—work really secondary and preparatory, and in no sense forming a proper subject of collegiate instruction. This year in accordance with the programme sketched above, we have absolutely refused to admit to our courses students unprepared to do real collegiate work. The Freshman English course in theme-writing has been eliminated from our programme, and has been turned over to approved teachers and to the various secondary schools. Had this salutary innovation not been accomplished, all the literary courses would have been swept away by the rapidly growing inundation of Freshman themes, and all our strength and courage would have been dissipated in preparing our students to do respectable work at more happily equipped Universities. As it is, no student is admitted to the course in English composition until he has acquired the proficiency above indicated. Instead, therefore, of requiring the undivided attention of a half-dozen professors, the work in English composition now occupies most of the time and strength of two. It is plain, however, that one or two additional instructors in this important division of the work will be necessary next year. It would be bad policy to allow any instructor to devote the whole of his attention to the work in English composition; for, however great a man's enthusiasm for such work may be, it is incident to human nature that no man can read themes efficiently for more than three hours at a stretch, and that the professor does his theme-reading more intelligently and more humanely when a portion of his time is spent in research preparatory to higher instruction.

At the outset of his university career, the student of English is advised to begin or continue an acquaintance with one or two, at least, of the chief foreign languages, ancient or modern. It is also suggested that he make himself proficient in some one of the natural or physical sciences, in order that he may not remain entirely a stranger to the great current of positive research and philosophy.

Apart from the advanced work in English composition and forensics, intended to qualify the student to express with idiomatic grace and logical cogency whatever he may have to say or to write, the first work which confronts the student of English at Stanford is a careful study of some of the prose writers of the nineteenth century: such as Macaulay, De Quincey, Carlyle, Savage Landor, Cardinal Newman, Matthew Arnold.

It is a fact that the majority of students enjoy good prose at an earlier stage of their culture than is requisite to the real appreciation of poetry. It is, moreover, observed that such a study of the best prose writers gives the instructor a fine opportunity to become acquainted with his students, and to throw out suggestions that may help them to correct or cure their illiteracy. Moreover, this course proves an invaluable adjunct to the course in composition, inasmuch as nothing conduces more to the mastery of a good style than an intimate acquaintance with the best models.

University of Iowa: Edward Everett Hale Jr.

Son of the famous Unitarian preacher and author, Hale (1863– 1932) took his B.A. at Harvard and Ph.D. at Halle. He taught at Cornell (1886–90), Iowa (1892–95), and beginning in 1895, at Union College. His books include Constructive Rhetoric *(1896), a biography of James Russell Lowell (1899), and an edition of ballads (1902).*

In his description of the small but growing Iowa program Hale distinguishes between modern English studies and the older forms, such as elocution and debate. Within composition he differentiates between the "formal rhetoric as the art is usually presented in the older text-books" and the newer, more "constructive" approach.

THE STATE UNIVERSITY OF IOWA HAS ONE PROFESSOR OF ENGLISH and one instructor, and offers during the present year eight courses. All but one of these are two-hour courses, making a total of seventeen hours, the actual teaching time being somewhat more, owing to division in classes. Of these eight courses, four are required. In the Freshman year a choice is given between courses I. and II.; in the Sophomore year, between III. and IV. There are about two hundred and fifty students registered in the various courses, counting perhaps twenty names twice. Besides these courses, the University offers two courses in elocution and a good deal of private work under a special instructor, and for next year it offers a course in debating under the joint supervision of the professors of political science, philosophy, and English. But these latter matters hardly come within the scope of the present series of articles.

In the required work of the English Department, there are two lines offered to the student. Courses I. and III. are strictly rhetorical in character, being the only courses in rhetoric that we give. In these courses our idea is not exactly to teach formal rhetoric as the art is usually presented in the older text-books, but rather to present the subject in a constructive way, according to the general line of recent thought on the subject. We try to habituate the student to writing (as well as possible, of course, but criticism is not our first aim), to give him practice in thinking over his material and putting it into good form, to give him exercise in the different modes of presentation. Such is the tendency of most of the handbooks on rhetoric, and of most of the discussions of the matter published in the last few years.

The alternative courses offered the Freshmen and Sophomores are literary with a rhetorical flavor. In the first year a number of prose authors are read, with comment on their style. In the second, the class uses Professor Minto's admirable *Manual*. It seems that there are always a number of students who make very little of rhetoric as usually taught; we want, in these courses, to see whether they can do as well by reading good authors as their classmates do by more direct practice in means and methods. In all four courses there is a good deal of essay writing. But, as far as we can see at present, the direct work will give the better results.[1]

In the elective courses, we draw the line sharply between linguistic work and literary. If it were practicable, I should like to divide further, giving courses devoted particularly to literary history and to the interpretation of literature. As it is, however, these last subjects are treated in the same courses. In linguistics we give this year a course in Old English and another on historical English grammar. But these courses (and a course in Middle English, as well, that has been given) are not favorites with the student body, and are only given in alternate years.

For courses in literature, besides the Freshman course (II.) described above, and the course in English prose (IV.) there is given this year a course of lectures on English poetry. The subject of this course is changed each year, so that the student who wishes may in three years get a fairly complete view of English poetry from Chaucer down, including a good deal of work on Shakespeare.

A seminary [seminar—ED.], in the stricter American sense of a research course, we do not have. We do, however, give a course for seniors and graduates, which bears a fairly close resemblance in character to the seminary of a smaller German university. The work of this course is generally concerned with some aspects of criticism, and we follow sometimes one method, sometimes another. I have gone over a text-book, or lectured, or given out topics for original work. The main idea is that by means of the closer personal relation possible through the informalities of the seminary, the spirit of self-reliance and independence shall be developed in the members.

It will easily be seen from this sketch of our work that the basis of our method is the cutting our coat somewhat according to our cloth. We have a good many students, and there are certain things that must be done. We try to compass the necessities first, and of the possibilities we grasp at as many as circumstances will permit. We have two main ideas: first, to give plenty of opportunity to those who wish to gain a good English style; and second, to encourage a feeling and taste for good literature. It is a pity that we cannot develop further than we do the more scientific aspects of linguistic study and of criticism and literary history. But these are matters which for the present we have to leave almost untouched.

NOTE

1. Our recent experience leads us to drop these courses as required work, leaving only the two courses in rhetoric. Course IV. will be retained as an elective.

Indiana University: Martin Wright Sampson

Sampson (1866–1930) studied at Cincinnati (B.A., 1888; M.A., 1890) under James Morgan Hart, and, along with William E. Strunk and Lane Cooper, contributed to the 1910 festschrift, Studies in Language and Literature in Celebration of the Seventieth Birthday of James Morgan Hart, November 2, 1909. *He continued his studies at Munich but did not take a Ph.D. Sampson taught at Iowa (1889–91), Stanford (1892–93), Indiana (chair from 1893 to 1906), and Cornell (1908–30) during the time of the Cornell rhetoricians. Sampson wrote a textbook,* Written and Oral Composition *(with E. O. Holland, 1907) and specialized in English drama and poetry.*

In SEPTEMBER, 1893, THE ENGLISH DEPARTMENT OF THE UNIVERsity of Indiana was completely reorganized. Six men—a professor, and five instructors—were appointed to carry on the work. The present course is our attempt to meet existing conditions. Each department must offer a full course of study leading to the bachelor's degree. Our students graduate in Greek, in mathematics, in sociology, in English, or in any one of the dozen other departments, with the uniform degree of A.B. About a third of the student's time is given to required studies, a third to the special work of the chosen department, and a third to elective studies. The department of English, then, is required to offer a four years' course of five hours a week; as a matter of fact, it offers considerably more.

The English courses fall into three distinct natural groups—language, composition, and literature,—in each of which work may be pursued for four or more years. One year of this work is required of all students; the rest is elective. With two exceptions, all our courses run throughout the year.

In composition, the work is as completely practical as we can make it. Writing is learned by writing papers, each one of which is corrected and rewritten. There are no recitations in "rhetoric." The bugbear known generally in our colleges as Freshman English is now a part of our entrance requirement, and university instruction in composition begins with those fortunate students who have some little control of their native language when a pen is between their fingers. We are still obliged, however, to supply instruction to students conditioned [accepted with conditions—Usually this meant making up a deficiency in a basic subject like composition.—ED.] in entrance English, and the conditioned classes make the heaviest drain upon the instructors' time. The first regular class receives students who write clearly and can compose good paragraphs. The subjects of the year's work are narration, description, exposition. In the next year's class, an attempt is made to stimulate original production in prose and verse. A certain amount of criticism upon contemporary writing enters into this course—the object being to point out what is good in (for example) current magazines and reviews, and thus to hold before the students an ideal not altogether impossible of attainment. A young writer confronted with the virtues and defects of Macaulay and De Quincey is likelier to be discouraged or made indifferent, than inspired, as far as his own style is concerned. If he is shown wherein a "Brief" in *The Dial* is better than his own review of the book, he is in a fair way to improve. And so with the sketches, stories, and even poems. Of course current magazine writing is not held up as ideal literature; nor, on the other hand, is the production of literature deemed a possible part of college study. The work in this branch of English is rounded off by a class for students who intend to teach composition. The theory of rhetoric is studied, and something of its history; school texts in rhetoric are examined; and finally the class learns the first steps in teaching by taking charge of elementary classes.

University of California: Charles Mills Gayley

Gayley (1858–1932) took his B.A. at Michigan in 1878 and continued his studies in Germany in 1886–87. He taught at Michigan, where he met Fred Newton Scott, and moved to Berkeley in 1889, where he served as chair and later dean. Gayley collaborated with Scott on A Guide to the Literature of Aesthetics *(1890) and* Methods and Materials of Literary Criticism *(1899). He was famous for a school text,* Classic Myths in English Literature *(1893; repr. 1911).*

Gayley reveals a high consciousness of the symbiotic relationship between high schools and colleges in California at the time. Charles William Eliot had referred to similar ties between Harvard and New England's preparatory schools in his 1869 Atlantic Monthly *article (see chap. 2, p. 26), but by the mid-1890s Harvard had clearly achieved independence from its feeder schools. California, as a public institution, was not in a position to assert itself as firmly as Harvard or even Stanford did, whether it wanted to or not.*

IN THE MATTER OF ENTRANCE REQUIREMENTS IN ENGLISH THE University has adopted an increasingly high standard. It calls for a high-school course of at least three years, at the rate of five hours a week; and it advocates, and from some schools secures, a four years' course. These requirements can scarcely be described, as in the fourth article of this series, as similar to those of the New England Association. [Gayley is referring to Anderson's description above, p. 162.—ED.] The requirements of that Association, so far as they go, are similar to those of California; but they do not go more than two-thirds of the way in extent or in stringency. There is nothing, to my knowledge, in the English requirements of other universities that is equivalent to our course in Greek, Norse, and German mythology as illustrated by English literature (required of all applicants for admission), or to the course in arguments and orations (hitherto, three of Burke's), or to the course in English poetry which covers some twenty-five of the longer masterpieces. These are additional to the usual requirements in essay, drama, and narrative. While the preparatory work in literature is generally well done, the work in rhetoric and composition is not yet up to the mark. Our system of examining and accrediting schools is, however, so strict, and the supervision of English teaching in the schools so minute, that we look for decided improvement, within a reasonable period, in the matter of composition. The Department does not content itself with requiring a satisfactory test-composition of students at matriculation; for, although that would be an easy way of shifting the burden from the University to the schools, it is but a poor substitute for the pedagogical assistance due to the schools. With the annual application for accrediting in English, each school is required to send for inspection samples of compositions and other exercises written by pupils of all classes. If these samples are satisfactory, the school is visited by one of the professors of English, who carefully scrutinizes the work of teachers and pupils. The Department is conservative in accrediting; and English is generally considered to be one of the most difficult studies in the curriculum of the schools of California. Non-accredited pupils are, of course, subjected to the usual entrance examination in literature, rhetoric, and composition. As supplementary to personal supervision, the professors of English have recently published for the guidance of teachers a pamphlet entitled *English in the Secondary Schools,* outlining the preparatory course, indicating the proper sequence of studies, and suggesting methods of instruction.[1]

With regard to the equipment and administration of the department, while the divisions of rhetoric, linguistics, and literature and criticism are severally represented by Professor Bradley, Professor Lange, and myself, and while each of the instructors is held responsible for a certain subject and certain sections of students, it is the policy of the department to observe a reasonable *Lehrfreiheit.* This it accomplishes, first, by maintaining a conservative rotation (say, once in three years) of the teachers in charge of courses involving drill and routine; and, secondly, by encouraging each teacher of preliminary courses, when once he has his prescribed work well in hand, to offer at least one elective higher course. Accordingly, of our instructors, Mr. Syle offers courses in the literature of the eighteenth century; and Mr. Sanford in Spenser, and in the romantic movement. That the same man should teach the elements of style, or of literary history, or should correct themes, year in and year out, is, even though texts and methods be varied, pedagogical suicide.

The plan here described does much to counteract the insensibility, or disgust, that frequently attends prolonged indulgence in the habit of theme-correcting. We find also that the occasional conduct of preliminary courses acts as a tonic upon teachers habituated to higher, and graduate, courses. While in all cases the specialty is still pursued, the field of information is widened, methods are liberalized, and the zest of teaching is enhanced by the adoption of the principle of *Lehrfreiheit*.

. . . .

The preliminary courses are announced as types of English prose style, supplementary reading, practical rhetoric, English masterpieces, general history of English literature, and argumentation. The first is required, at the rate of four hours a week through the year, of all Freshmen in the Academic Colleges; the second (one hour any two consecutive terms) of non-classical students in these Colleges. The third and the fourth are prescribed in the Colleges of Chemistry and Agriculture. All other English courses are elective; and in the Engineering Colleges English is altogether elective. Of prescribed preliminary courses, that in English prose style aims to acquaint the student, at first hand, with the features and elements of effective workmanship in prose-writing, and to train him to discern the salient qualities of any well-marked prose style presented for his consideration. The course is based upon the direct study of selected groups of authors. The course of supplementary reading extends, as far as time will permit, the acquaintance of the student with the Hellenic, Teutonic, or Romance epics, or other classics in translation. It serves as an introduction to the common and traditional store of literary reference, allusion, and imagery, and as a basis for paragraph-writing. The best translations of the *Iliad,* the *Odyssey,* the *Béowulf,* the *Jerusalem Delivered,* Morris's *Sigurd the Volsung,* etc., are studied. These courses, and the course in practical rhetoric for scientific students, in general serve to stimulate constructive effort and practical skill in writing *pari passu* with analytical effort and the acquisition of information. They accordingly include first the weekly exercise in paragraph-writing, written in the class-room upon some topic not previously announced, but involving acquaintance with the supplementary reading assigned for the week; and, secondly, a carefully supervised series of compositions. Three themes have been required each term. The supervision, which is personal, extends to methods of using the library, of securing material and of taking and arranging notes;

to limitation and definition of subject; to construction of a scheme of presentation in advance of the writing, as well as to careful criticism of the finished work. The organization and development of these courses is in large measure due to the exertions of Professor Bradley, to whom I am indebted for the details of this description. It should be added that essays are required in connection with all work in the English Department. The course in English masterpieces for scientific students, given by Mr. Armes, involves the careful reading in class of representative poems and essays of the foremost writers, and supplementary reading out of class.

. . . .

The advanced courses for undergraduates are grouped as (1) Rhetoric and the theory of criticism: four courses; (2) Linguistics: four courses, including, besides grammar, history, and criticism, the comparative study of the Germanic sources of English culture, and Germanic philology; (3) The historical and critical study of literature: eleven courses in chronological sequence, by (*a*) periods, (*b*) authors, (*c*) literary movements, (*d*) the evolution of types. The first of these groups is essential to the other two. It involves the differentiation, for advanced work, of rhetoric into its species (exposition, including methods of literary research and interpretation, argumentation, narration, etc.), and an introduction to the comparative and aesthetic methods. A course in poetics outlines the theory of art, the theory and development of literature, the relations of poetry and prose, the principles of versification, and the canons, inductive and deductive, of dramatic criticism. It is usually accompanied by lectures on the aesthetics of literature. This course is followed by the problems of literary criticism: a comparative inquiry into the growth, technique, and function of literary types other than the drama. The attempt is made to arrive by induction at the characteristics common to the national varieties of a type, and to formulate these in the light of aesthetic theory. The resulting laws are applied as canons of criticism to English masterpieces of that type. The method has been described by a former student in the *Century Magazine,* January 1891. The reading and discussions are guided by questions, suggestions, and reference lists—part of a manual of literary criticism now in press (Ginn & Co., Boston). For lack of space the courses in linguistics and literature cannot be enumerated. Students making English their principal study must include in their elections linguistics, poetics, criticism, and the intensive study of at least one literary master and of one literary type or movement. For the teacher's certificate linguistics is indispensable.

. . . .

With regard to methods of instruction no stereotyped habit obtains. In our lower classes the text-book is not always used. When used it is treated as a guide, not as a bible. In both lower and higher classes, recitations, reports on reading, discussion of topics, informal or formal lectures, interpretative reading, and personal conference prevail, in such combination or with such preference as the instructor may deem wise. Students, however, are always put to work on the masterpieces themselves.

With regard to methods of investigation, we believe that a certain catholicity of attitude—not inconsistent with alertness—should be observed. The present anarchy, sometimes tyranny, of method is due generally to a deficient organization of studies; and that, in turn, to an incomprehensive view of the field. Hence, the uncertainty of aim with which instruction in English is frequently reproached. This lack of system is, however, indicative only of the fact that literary science is in a transitional stage: no longer static, not yet organic, but genetic.

NOTE

1. Since the policy of issuing departmental monographs on methods of secondary instruction is perhaps novel, it may be well to say that teachers in the public schools may obtain copies of this pamphlet from the Recorder of the University, Berkeley, Cal. Postage, two cents.

Amherst College: John Franklin Genung

(See the biography above, p. 133.) Genung describes the integrated manner in which a leading New England college conducted English studies.

N0 STUDY IN OUR AMERICAN COLLEGES IS SO DIRECTLY AND PRACTI-cally important as the study of English; yet none is so beset with problems of administration and method. To detail all of these would take up too much space here; I will merely indicate some of the leading ones, to the solution of which the teachers of English at Amherst have been devoting their attention during the last dozen years. There is, first of all, the question what to do with it as a required study. For the old idea seems a sound one, that whatever the predominance of elective studies, English, at least English composition, should be required of all; that is, that no possibility should be opened for any student to gain his degree without some training in the practical use of his mother-tongue. Yet as a required study in the midst of electives, English is at a disadvantage; the very fact that it is compulsory weights it with an odium which in many colleges makes it the bugbear of the course. This ill repute was increased in the old-fashioned college course by the makeshift way in which time was grudged out to it in the curriculum. Under the name of "rhetori-cals," English declamations, orations, and essays used to be sandwiched in where some little crevice opened between other studies, once a week perhaps, or at some irregular hour supposably unavailable for anything else. Now every teacher knows that a once-a-week study cannot be carried on with much profit or interest; it cannot but be a weariness to student and instructor alike. It finds its way into the hands of incompe-tent and inexperienced teachers; it has to rank as the Ishmael among the studies.

It was the conviction of the teachers of English at Amherst that such ill repute was by no means a necessary accompaniment of their depart-ment. They believed that English, if granted a fair chance, could trust to its own intrinsic value and interest for survival, as confidently as could any other study. I need not here recount the history of their quiet and steady work, first to gain a fair meed of time for the various branches of their department, then to obtain recognition for it as an elective study by the side of other electives, finally to retain the proper relation and balance of elective and required study. All this came about so naturally as to seem a spontaneous evolution rather than what it actually was, a strenuous and determined working out of a plan.

Another problem, especially perplexing on the composition side of the study, is the problem what to do with English as a mother-tongue, with which the student has been conversant all his life, from which, therefore, the mystery and labor of grammar and lexicon are eliminated. The time devoted to grinding at these in the classics, or to puzzling over intricate mathematical problems, is time gained for study and hard drill. What shall be done with a subject that has no such study-compelling advantages, a subject, indeed, whose highest prizes of grace and sponta-neity seem perversely to refuse themselves to the student almost in proportion to the strenuousness of his labor? Drill must be furnished, but the drill must be wisely directed. And one thing can be done. It can be recognized that such seeming is not the whole truth; that beyond the stiff and labored stage in writing, as also beyond the dashing and accidentally brilliant stage, there is a calm permanence of assured mastery, corresponding to what the runner calls his second wind, wherein the writer can do his best and keep it up. Toward this goal of mastery the drill of writing and exercises in language should be directed; and this not only by setting the student working systematically *through* the crude and rudimentary stage, but by infusing into his task such interest as will give it vitality.

The best term, perhaps, by which to characterize the way in which the teachers of English at Amherst have met these problems is *laboratory work* [for "laboratory" see Scott below, p. 180—ED.]. Whatever the diversities of aim and method between the teachers, in this respect they are at one: each of these courses is a veritable workshop, wherein, by systematized daily drill, details are mastered one by one, and that unity of result is obtained which is more for practical use than for show.

The required work in English, which is all under the charge of Professor Henry A. Frink, has to do with the English of oral expression. It consists of two.terms of elocutionary drill, or declamation, in Freshman year, and one in Sophomore year; two terms of rhetoric, carried on by means of essays, exercises, and lectures, in Freshman year; and three terms of debates, both extemporaneous and prepared, in Senior year. This comprises in itself a body of work fully as large as obtained in the old days of "rhetoricals"; and when we consider the careful emphasis given to individual drill and criticism, in which work the services of five assistants are employed, we may well regard it as far beyond the average of the old courses in efficiency.

In the elective study of English, each college year has its course characteristic of the year. These courses, in the way in which they supplement each other, form a natural sequence; yet they are independent of each other, each professor being supreme in his sphere, to plan, carry out, and complete, according to his own ideas—a trio in which the members work side by side, in co-operation rather than in subordination.

The elective English of the Sophomore year, under the charge of the writer, centres in written expression, the study and practice of rhetoric. The rhetoric thus pursued—as the many users of the writer's text-books throughout the country need not be reminded—is not the mere broadened study of grammar; it is a study of the organizing of discourse, from the choice of words up, as a real author must seek to effect it; a determinate study, in however humble way, of literature in the making. Two terms of work, based on the text-book and on the *Handbook of Rhetorical Analysis,* are carried on by daily recitations and written exercises, these latter, invented to illustrate in succession the rhetorical principles under consideration, being progressive in character and requiring as they advance more originative work on the part of the student. The exercises thus become very nearly equivalent to what in other colleges has been successfully introduced under the name of "daily themes," with the advantage that these themes, while no less vital in subject matter, are progressive applications of literary procedures and rules. The course has too many interesting and novel features to detail here; one of these, which has proved very profitable and interesting, is the setting up in type of many of the students' written productions, and the reading and criticism of them in proof.

The third term is devoted to the writing of essays and careful individual criticism of each one in personal interviews. Each man in the class presents an essay about once a fortnight. By the side of this work there is carried on, as time and numbers permit, a course of reading and discussion of the leading prose writers. Throughout the year, in connection with the rhetorical department, is conducted a voluntary English seminary, after the manner of the German universities.

In the Junior year begin the elective classes of Professor Frink. Two hours a week in the first term are devoted to the study of logic, and two hours to a progressive and systematic course of public speaking. The work of this foundation term takes the form of debates, study and analysis of American and British orations, and Shakespearian readings. In a similar manner, public speaking is continued through the second term, the debates, discussions, and speeches of various kinds having to do with the rhetoric of oral expression. Much stimulus to these studies under Professor Frink is supplied by the numerous prizes offered for proficiency in the work of each term. Nor, though the number of men concerned and the extent and variety of the work would seem to necessitate much that is merely perfunctory, is this work anything like a mere routine. The industry and genius of Professor Frink in adapting his labors and interests to the personal peculiarities of each individual precludes that; and in the sunshine of such friendly relations many a man finds powers awakened that he had not suspected in himself, or powers that were running wild ordered and steadied.

With the third term of the Junior year begins, under Professor H. Humphrey Neill, the study of English literature. Here the aim is to do with a good degree of thoroughness whatever is done; hence familiarity with a limited number of the great writers is sought, rather than a smattering information about many. The method of work, as in the other English studies, is eminently the laboratory method; and this, while based in just proportion on facts and details, is so aimed as to get at the spirit of the literature. The opening term of the course is devoted, in part through text-books and in part through lectures and discussion of the principles of literary criticism, to the course of the literature down to the end of the sixteenth century; special attention being given to Chaucer, Spenser, Bacon, Milton, and Dryden. Shakespeare is reserved for a special term. In the study of these, dependence is placed not so much on reading *about* the author as on familiarity with the author himself.

With the beginning of the Senior year the students work more independently. The first term is devoted to the prose writers of the eighteenth and the early part of the nineteenth century; the second to the poets of the same period. Two weeks are given to the study of each author; and on each author certain members of the class read extended and carefully studied essays. These essays, in connection with the readings and topics prescribed, are made the basis of the class discussions and examinations. In this way men are taught to form and test their own opinions. In the third term of Senior year (the fourth of the course) the study is Shakespeare. A minute exegesis of one or two of the greatest plays is given by means of lectures and topics for reading. In addition to this, four other plays are studied as a collateral course by the class, and made the subject of written examinations. This Shakespearian course is open to all, whether they have elected the three preceding terms or not.

A special course is also given to a few who, in every class, having pursued the course of the three prescribed terms, wish to carry their literary studies further. It consists of special investigation under the direction of the professor, but with no stated recitations.

Such, in a very meagre outline, is the course of English study at Amherst. To pass judgment on it is for others, rather than for us who conduct it; but one remark by way of comparison ought perhaps to be made. It does not seem to make a great showing of names and subjects by the side of the minutely subdivided and specialized courses of some other colleges; but this fact, I am convinced, is no indication of its meagreness. The ground is not only broadly traversed, but thoroughly, as college courses go; and the stern weeding out of what is merely speculative and unpractical leaves so much the more time and energy to devote to the greater literary forms, and to learn how close they are to the requirements of daily life.

University of Michigan: Fred Newton Scott

Scott (1860–1931) spent his career at the University of Michigan (B.A., 1884; M.A., 1888; Ph.D., 1889; and faculty from 1889 on). He was president of the MLA (1907) and of the NCTE (1911–13). Beginning in 1903 Scott chaired his own Department of Rhetoric at Michigan, a department that was abolished following his retirement. Among his distinguished graduate students were Gertrude Buck, Charles Carpenter Fries, Sterling Leonard, and Ruth Mary Weeks. (For additional biography see Stewart in Brereton 26–49.)

Michigan's rhetoric program was to become the most comprehensive in the nation, exceeding even Harvard's through the diversity of its graduate component; in 1895, though, Scott was one of four full-time faculty in an English department responsible for teaching some 1,200 students a year. His description of the Michigan English program reveals him badly in need of additional faculty in order to give some personal attention to all those students.

For the collegiate year 1894–95, the University of Michigan announces twenty-one courses in English and rhetoric. Ten are courses in literature, historical or critical; five are in linguistics; and six are in rhetoric and composition. There is the usual division into courses which may and courses which must be taken by those who intend to graduate, but with us the requirements differ for the different degrees. Candidates for the engineering degrees, and for the degree of Bachelor of Science in chemistry or biology, are let off with a single course in composition. Candidates for the degree of Bachelor of Letters must take two courses in composition, besides one in literature and one in linguistics. All others are required to elect two courses in composition. The work is in charge of four men: a professor of English and rhetoric, who is head of the department; a junior professor of English, an assistant professor of rhetoric, and an instructor in English composition. In addition to this, the regular force, there are two graduate students who devote a part of their time to teaching composition or reading essays.

The number of students who elected courses in English the past year, not allowing for names counted twice, was 1,198. To this number should perhaps be added 110 applicants for work in composition for whom provision could not be made. The distribution of the elections was as follows: In modern literature, 225; in Old and Middle English literature, and linguistics, 252; in rhetoric and composition, 721.

. . . .

Of the six courses which fall under the division of rhetoric and composition, four, each for one semester, have for their main object the cultivation of good writing; though one of the four, known as the science of rhetoric, combines with a large amount of practice a small amount of instruction in theory. In addition to these, there are two, one for graduates and one for undergraduates, which deal with rhetoric in its scientific aspects. For the required Freshman work, there is provided this year a two-hour course in paragraph-writing under Mr. Dawson and an assistant. As in other large universities, this part of the work presents peculiar difficulties. The big classes are about as heterogeneous as they well can be, most of the students writing crudely, some execrably, and only a few as well as could be wished. These differences call for differences of treatment, yet it is impossible, with our present teaching force, to give adequate attention to individuals or to distinguish grades of proficiency. The most that can be done is to put in a section by themselves the engineering students, whose performances in prose are often at the outset of a quite distressing character.

The course in paragraph-writing is followed by a two-hour elective course in theme-writing under Mr. Dawson; and this by a three-hour course, conducted by myself. The latter is required of all except the engineers and candidates for the degree of B.S. in chemistry and biology. It must be preceded by a course in psychology or logic, and hence is usually taken in the second semester of the Sophomore year or the first semester of the Junior year. An advanced course in composition completes the list of practical courses. For those who wish to supplement practice by theory, there is a course in the principles of prose style, and a

graduate seminary course in which the evolution of rhetoric is traced
from Aristotle to the present time.

It will appear, I hope, from this outline, that the work in composition is intended, first and foremost, to be practical. The aim is not to
inspire students to produce pure literature, if there be any such thing, or
even to help them to acquire a beautiful style. If we can get them first to
think straight-forwardly about subjects in which they are genuinely
interested, and then, after such fashion as nature has fitted them for, to
express themselves clearly and connectedly, we have done about all we
can hope to do. Perhaps the other things will then come of themselves.
In trying to accomplish these ends, I have been accustomed in my own
work to aim at three essentials: first, continuity and regularity of written
exercises; second, much writing, much criticism, and much consultation; third, adaptation of method to the needs of the individual student.
To secure the first, the student is made to write frequently and at
regularly recurring periods, and is encouraged to write at set hours
regardless of mood or inspiration. The second point I may be permitted
to illustrate by saying that I have read and re-read this year something
over 3,000 essays, most of them written by a class of 216 students. The
third essential seems to me the most important of the three. That the
instructor should somehow lay hold of the student as an individual is, for
successful composition work, simply indispensable. This was the secret
of the older method of instruction, such as that of Edward Channing,
described by the Rev. E. E. Hale in *My College Days:*—

"You sat down in the recitation-room, and were called man by man, or boy
by boy, in the order in which you came into the room; you therefore heard his
criticism on each of your predecessors. 'Why do you write with blue ink on blue
paper? When I was young, we wrote with black ink on white paper; now you
write with blue ink on blue paper.' 'Hale, you do not mean to say that you think
a Grub Street hack is the superior of John Milton?'"

I think all teachers of composition will feel that Ned Channing's
method was good, and will understand very well how it happened that
Hale and his seatmates "came out with at least some mechanical knowledge of the mechanical method of handling the English language." But
it must be borne in mind that in the larger universities the day of small
and cosey classes is long past. Now the hungry generations tread us
down. We hardly learn the names and faces of our hundreds of students

before they break ranks and go their ways, and then we must resume our Sisyphaean labors. Is there no way in which we can return to the Arcadian methods of those early days? For my part, I think there is a way, and a very simple one: Increase the teaching force and the equipment to the point where the instructor can again meet his students as individuals, and can again have leisure for deliberate consultation and personal criticism. As Professor Genung has well said, the teaching of composition is properly *laboratory work*. If that is true, why should it not be placed on the same footing as other laboratory work as regards manning and equipment? I confess that I now and then cast envious eyes upon our laboratory of chemistry, with its ten instructors and its annual expenditure of ten thousand dollars, and try to imagine what might be done in a rhetorical laboratory with an equal force and a fraction of the expenditure. Nor is the comparison absurd. The amount of business which needs to be done in order to secure dexterity in the use of language is not less than that which is needed to secure dexterity in the manipulation of chemicals. The student in composition needs as much personal attention as the student in chemistry. The teacher of composition, if he is to do his work without loss of time and energy, and if he is to secure the benefit which comes from constant variation in methods of instruction, needs all the mechanical helps which he can devise. He needs, for example, conveniences for the collection, the distribution, and the preservation of the written work. He needs a set of Poole's *Index,* not in a far-off library, but at his elbow. He needs a card-catalogue, revised daily, with thousands of subjects of current interest especially adapted to the uses of his class. He needs a mimeograph and a typewriter; possibly he needs a compositor and a printing-press. Above all (and I do not mean to include these among the mechanical aids) he needs, not one or two, but a score, of bright, active, enthusiastic young assistants to share his arduous labors with him. Under these Utopian conditions—perhaps not wholly Utopian after all—the teacher of composition could no longer pose as a martyr, and so might miss the sympathy he has been so long accustomed to; but I believe that on the whole he would be a happier man, and I am certain that in the end he would do a vast deal more of good in the world.

In running over the list of courses offered, the reader will doubtless have noticed that the department does not announce many which are exclusively for graduate students. This must not be taken to imply that provision for such students is not made. As a fact, there is always a considerable body who are pursuing advanced work in English. Many go into undergraduate courses and there find what is suited to them. But for a large proportion special advanced courses are arranged, as they are needed, after consultation with the student. These are obviously too variable in character to be enumerated here.

University of Nebraska: Lucius Adelno Sherman

Sherman (1847–1933) studied at Yale (A.B., 1871) then taught grammar-school Greek while getting his Ph.D. (Yale, 1875). After Yale he moved to the English department at Nebraska, which he chaired from 1882 to 1902. He served as dean of arts and science from 1887 to 1901 and retired in 1929. His books include: The Analytics of Literature: A Manual for the Objective Study of English Prose and Poetry *(1893),* Elements of Literature and Composition, a Manual for Schools *(1908), and* How to Describe and Narrate Visually *(1925).*

In 1895 Nebraska, like a few other universities, had two separate departments, one called "English" (described below) and one called "English Literature."

THE STUDY OF ENGLISH AS RHETORIC AND COMPOSITION, AND AS English literature and philology, is completely differentiated in the University of Nebraska. Writing is taught on the theory that constant technical practice is necessary, but practice in the development and adjustment of meaning in the mind as well as in appropriate and effective statement. In other words, not facility with the *media* of expression, not automatism in phrasing merely, but organic, completed communication, in both matter and manner, is the aim of the study. As contributive to this end, work in oral composition or public speaking—not required, but elected very generally by the students at some period in their course—is arranged for and emphasized by the Department head. Of fourteen hundred students in attendance this year, almost the entire number, excepting specials, and including nearly nine hundred young men and women in college courses, are under rhetorical instruction of some kind. One professor, two instructors, and two assistants are exclusively responsible for this work. As a division of the general subject and of University instruction, this department is known as the Department of English.

University of Pennsylvania: Felix Emanuel Schelling

Schelling (1858–1945) spent his entire academic life at Penn (A.B., 1881; LL.B., 1883; A.M., 1886; English faculty, 1886–1934). He was the founder of the modern English department at Penn and instituted a doctoral program, a course in modern novelists, and studies in American literature. He published on Elizabethan literature and served as MLA president in 1914.

Schelling describes "forensics" in passing; like Harvard, Penn has upper-level courses in written and oral argumentation, usually relying on students' other courses for their subject matter. The regimen in first-year composition, "two or three themes a week," recalls the influence of Harvard's daily themes course. And like Harvard, Penn still requires some writing for sophomores and juniors ("except those hopelessly given over to technology"). Most of the work Schelling describes sounds like dull practice and drill, complete with vigilant surveillance and constant correcting.

THE DEPARTMENT OF ENGLISH AT THE UNIVERSITY OF PENNSYLVA-
nia, as at present constituted, is concerned with four subjects: (1) composition, (2) English literature, (3) English language and philology, and (4) forensics. Of these, (1) and (4) are confined to undergraduates, the others extend to graduate courses. Whether for good or bad, we make comparatively little of forensics, beyond care exercised incidentally in reading aloud, and in opportunities offered for declamation by students of the lower classes. Elective and voluntary courses in speaking and debate follow in Junior year; but the chief practice of our students in these subjects is derived from the exercises of their literary societies. There is an opinion prevalent at the University that it is perhaps well that "elocution" be not too professionally taught; but that the character of the individual should be developed in his utterance rather than overwhelmed with the oratorical mannerisms to which special teaching sometimes leads.

In composition work we set before the student one simple aim—the plain and unaffected use of his mother tongue; and we believe that the shortest way to facility of expression in writing is constant practice, and a practice unaffected and free from false conceptions of the purpose of such practice. With this in view, every Freshman in the University writes two or three themes a week; Sophomores and Juniors, except those hopelessly given over to technology, at least one a week; whilst in Senior year the subject—except as indirectly represented in the papers of the seminaries or study-classes in literature—remains optional. All of this work is carefully superintended by the instructors in charge; every composition is read,—occasionally before the class or a section of it,—corrected, annotated, if need be handed back to be rewritten, the faults explained with the principles involved, the personality of the writer studied as far as possible, his abilities trained and directed. In the assignment of themes there is an endeavor to avoid subjects which can be read up and crammed for the occasion, although the student is kept in continual touch with good English style by required collateral reading. The study of rhetoric is developed out of the reading and composition work: and, although systematized by reference to a text-book, is not studied as a thing apart from daily practice.

Wellesley College: Katherine Lee Bates

After taking her B.A. at Wellesley (1880) Bates (1859–1929) taught high school for five years and then served in Wellesley's English department from 1885 to 1925. She published verse, including the words to "America the Beautiful," and also wrote travel books and scholarly works on English and American literature.

Bates, like Sherman of Nebraska, speaks of separate departments for rhetoric and composition. She also laments the low level of entering students, especially all those who arrive "conditioned." An indication of the weak writing ability is her admission, "To have mastered the paragraph is to become, so far as the Rhetoric Department is concerned, a Sophomore." Argumentation and debate at Wellesley were taught by Harvard's George Pierce Baker, a sign that Wellesley's rhetoric teaching did not hew to a strong feminist line, despite the presence of many well-known feminists among the Wellesley faculty.

NOTHING, THEN, COULD BE MORE PRACTICALLY HELPFUL, AT THIS stage of the experiment, than these descriptions of English courses now pursued in American colleges, especially where the professors in charge are committed to the literary aim. [Bates refers to the serial publication of these descriptions.—ED.] Upon this accumulated material of experience, theory will soon be at work. *The Dial* has already given judgment in favor of dividing English, as a university subject, into the science of linguistics and the art of literature. From the various reports, however, it would appear that composition and rhetoric, elocution, and comparative literature, must also be taken into account as candidates for separate departments.

. . . .

The Professor of English Language and Rhetoric, Miss Margaret E. Stratton of Oberlin, finds time for some linguistic work, but the rhetorical side of her department secures the lion's share of attention. Professor Scott's longed-for Utopia is not located at Wellesley. Frequent themes are required of Freshmen, Sophomores, and Juniors, these classes numbering, in the aggregate, about six hundred. Moreover, here, as at Stanford and Indiana, classes of conditioned Freshmen are a conspicuous feature of the Rhetoric Department, the training of the secondary schools being grievously inadequate. Miss Hart of Radcliffe, and Miss Weaver, trained in England as well as in America, bend their united energies to developing in the Freshmen the ability to write clear, correct, well-constructed English sentences. To have mastered the paragraph is to become, so far as the Rhetoric Department is concerned, a Sophomore; and to proceed, under guidance of Miss Willcox, whose preparation was in part received in an editorial office, to the structure of the essay. This involves, together with the analysis of masterpieces and the making of outlines, various studies in the orderly and effective arrangement of material. Subjects may be drawn from any course of study in which the student is interested, and some slight opportunity is afforded for experiments in storytelling. With the second semester comes, to able students, the chance of electing, in place of the regular work, a course in journalism. This undertakes the gathering up and editing of news from far and near, the condensing and recasting of "copy," the writing of book reviews and editorials. A newspaper staff is organized, the members rotating in office, and from time to time the class is addressed by working journalists. The *Wellesley Magazine* furnishes an immediate field for such youthful activities; while, for better or worse, the calls from newspapers, the Union over, for student reporters of college life grow more numerous with every autumn.

The Junior year brings the course in argumentation, which, making as it does for logical thinking, is speedily felt in every line of college work. This course, conducted by Mr. George P. Baker of Harvard, and similar to the forensic course given by him in that university, is described in Professor Wendell's foregoing paper. [See chap. 2, p. 127.—ED.] Mr.

Baker offers, too, an elective course in debate. The crowded Senior elective, however, is the daily theme course, conducted by Miss Weaver. The purpose of this elective is to quicken observation and give as much practice as possible in the sifting and grouping facts of personal experience, and in the clear, concise, and cogent statement of whatever there may be under a Senior cap to state.

These various instructors are united in the persuasion that the laws of rhetoric should be assimilated, so far as may be, by an informal and almost unconscious process, and that there should be no unholy divorce between the English of the pen and the English of the lip. They stand for graded and orderly advance, for the development of the perceptive and inventive powers, as well as of taste and reason, and, in general, for a fuller experience and more accurate expression of life. It is unfortunate that they are themselves mortal, and have thus far been unable to accede to the desire of the other Departments that all students whose technical themes and examination papers, while good in substance are bad in statement, shall be conditioned in English and turned over to the Rhetoric Department for reformation.

University of Minnesota: George MacLean

MacLean (1850–1938) took his A.B. at Williams (1871) and a divinity degree at Yale (1874) before serving as minister in New York. He left the ministry to study Anglo-Saxon in Germany (Ph.D., Leipzig, 1883), taught English at Minnesota from 1883 to 1895, became chancellor at Nebraska (1895–99), president of Iowa (1899–1911), and in 1917 a federal government education expert, producing surveys of British education.

MacLean had Professor Maria Louisa Sanford (see chap. 1, p. 25) of the separate Department of Rhetoric and Elocution prepare the description of the composition program printed here. The description displays sympathy for problems confronting immigrants, but the program's emphasis remains firmly committed to drilling for correctness.

The work in rhetoric consists of the required course of the Freshman and Sophomore classes,—one hour a week for the two years; and elective courses of four hours a week throughout the Junior and Senior years.

In the Freshman class the work is largely technical and mechanical.

Many of our students, and often those who develope power and taste in English composition, are of foreign birth or ancestry, and come to the University well prepared in mental development, but ignorant, or at least unskilled, in the use of the English language. Constant practice in writing, constant attention to correct grammatical and rhetorical forms in speech, and thorough drill in the text-book, is the work of the Freshman year. It may be urged that the high schools should do this work. Very true, and some of them are doing it admirably; but where, as in Minnesota, so large a proportion of the population consists of foreigners who are ambitious and capable, the University must be content to do a part of this drill. A boy may lead his class in mathematics and Latin and chemistry, and still be unable to free his tongue from the Scandinavian accent, or his written page from foreign idioms. The high schools are year by year doing better work, but with a foreign population so intelligent as ours, and furnishing so many of our common school teachers, the fundamental work of the University must be a struggle for correctness.

Note: Many libraries have reprint editions of *PMLA* which include the scholarly articles but unfortunately exclude these reports of section meetings.

William Edward Mead
"Report of the Pedagogical Section: The Graduate Study of Rhetoric"
PMLA 16 (1901)

&▲ *Mead had taken his Ph.D. at Leipzig and was professor of English at Wesleyan. In 1894 he had published a writing text,* Elementary Composition and Rhetoric, *a book notable for its Scott-like insistence on making the subject of writing "a real thing," derived from a genuine question students need to answer.*

This and the following two reports represent the efforts of Fred Newton Scott, head of the MLA pedagogical section, to put a serious examination of composition research and teaching on the MLA's agenda. Scott was successful; these three reports are the fullest, frankest professional discussion of the role of composition within English departments ever published in PMLA. *They are also the last; in 1903 the pedagogical section was excluded from MLA annual meetings, and articles about teaching no longer appeared in* PMLA. *(Up until then roughly 10 percent of* PMLA *articles had been pedagogical, with a higher percentage in the beginning years and a much lower percentage by the turn of the century.) The 1900 meeting witnessed the MLA's first serious inquiry into the possibilities of advanced study in rhetoric. At that time no university offered a doctorate in rhetoric, and only a few places (notably Michigan and Harvard) offered much graduate course work in composition. This MLA report shows members as quite willing to see rhetoric established as a graduate study. (This report was most definitely not representative of the entire MLA membership, which was rapidly moving toward concentration upon literature.)*

In this first report Mead simply reprints selections from the answers of sixty-three "teachers of English and . . . others who might presumably have an opinion on the topic." We do not know how these respondents were chosen; Mead reports that most are college professors in the northern states. What is remarkable is the willingness of the majority to consider graduate course work in rhetoric; those in favor are not talking about writing instruction or a teaching methods program, but theoretical or "scientific" inquiry into discourse, including some of what now would be regarded as literary criticism. Here, in 1900, was a group well aware of what serious graduate work could be, though as Mead admits, the definition of "rhetoric" was deliberately left imprecise.

ABOUT TWO MONTHS AGO THE PEDAGOGICAL SECTION OF THE MODern Language Association suddenly developed a very unusual, if not alarming energy, the credit for which belongs entirely to Professor Scott, the President of the Section. As a result of this new activity, somewhat more than a hundred circulars containing the following questions were sent to teachers of English and to others who might presumably have an opinion on the topic under investigation:

1. Is Rhetoric, in your opinion, a proper subject for graduate work?
2. If so, what is the proper aim, what is the scope, and what are the leading problems of Rhetoric as a graduate study?
3. If Rhetoric, in your opinion, should not be admitted to the list of graduate studies, what do you regard as the strongest reasons for excluding it?

Of the sixty-three reports that were returned, all but seven attempted answers more or less detailed to the questions. Most of the colleges and universities represented in the reports are northern institutions, but they are situated in nearly all of the principal states from the Atlantic to the Pacific.[1]

The most striking fact that I have noted in reading the reports is that men of apparently equal ability and equal interest in the subject take diametrically opposite views of the fitness of Rhetoric as a graduate study. This may be due in part to the lack of agreement in the definition of the term Rhetoric, which was purposely left without interpretation or limitation in the questions, with a view to drawing out from various sources a statement as to the proper scope and aims of the subject. One thing, however, the investigation may fairly lay claim to have settled, and that is that the term Rhetoric should either be abandoned for one less equivocal, or that it should be more strictly defined. Owing to the prevalent vagueness of conception as to what Rhetoric really is and should cover, the various reports read a little like debates on a question in which the meaning of leading terms has not been agreed upon. Yet in this very fact there are some compensations; for there have been called out a variety of suggestions as to the possible extension of the field of Rhetoric, and the introduction into our graduate courses of an organized group of related subjects that have not hitherto been systematically combined.

With these few words of preface, I now turn to the actual reports. You would be interested, I am sure, to have a considerable number of the arguments on both sides of the main question, but the time allowed for this matter is so brief that I can do little more than outline the positions that have been taken, and read a few of the more detailed reports.[2] There is, as might be expected, more or less repetition.

I.

A decided majority of the writers hold that the subject, as they define it, has a legitimate place as a graduate study. To clear the ground, I therefore present the negative view first. It is only fair to say, however, that possibly some of those who most object to the inclusion of Rhetoric as a graduate study would heartily favor as graduate studies some of the subjects suggested below, only they might prefer not to regard them as branches of Rhetoric. The narrowness of meaning given to the term in some of the reports is as remarkable as the vast extension of its meaning in others.

The principal objection urged against Rhetoric, considered as a graduate study, is that it is primarily an art rather than a science; that mere knowledge of what has been the practice of great writers, what has been the history of the development of the theory, in short, mere knowledge of the subject as at present taught, or as it has been taught in the past, is a matter of comparatively small practical importance. The main thing is practical assimilation of a few fundamental principles. But all this and more is brought out in the reports, and I therefore present these without further delay, and let the advocates of either side speak for themselves[3]:—

(a) "I cannot conceive any form of rhetorical science or rhetorical art as having sufficient body; as having any interesting field for exploration and discovery; as having adequate interior organization; as being under the government of general laws; as being free from the tyranny of dogma and authority; I say I cannot imagine any single rhetorical entity which is not a mass or an assemblage of dicta in no way interdependent, and which may not at a thousand points be discussed as a matter of opinion, but never decided by any energy of investigation."

(b) "I think that Rhetoric is only useful in so far as it is practically helpful to the student in enabling him to write better; and further, it may, in *some small measure,* be useful in helping him to appreciate good literature.

"Unless the eye is kept fixed on these two aims, Rhetoric, it seems to me, may easily grow into a large scheme of divisions and definitions, which may give an impression that something is really being accomplished, but which is about as desirable for the student as a revival of the metaphysics and logic of the school men."

(c) "If by Rhetoric as graduate study we mean 'criticism,' 'philosophy,' 'logic,' or 'aesthetics' my answer is that we already recognize it under these several titles, and that the return to an antiquated use of a word will gain nothing. If by 'Rhetoric' we are to mean, as popularly, composition, I think that the place of that study is in the college, not in the university. I see no sphere for 'Rhetoric' as a graduate study except in a trespass upon literature, aesthetics, logic, or pedagogy—if it attempt the art of teaching how to teach composition."

(d) "The chief reason (for excluding Rhetoric) would be that Rhetoric, as a compendium of general principles, can be easily expounded in a single volume. If the study involves diction and style, it is usually included in the department of Literature."

(e) "My experience had tended to show that the personal element plays too large a part in rhetorical study for anything like accurate or scientific results to be obtained."

(*f*) "The object of teaching Rhetoric is, in my judgment, not theoretical but practical, as propaedeutic to composition and literature, and the undergraduate course should suffice for this. The graduate course should be literature itself, which has no limit."

(*g*) "I am sure that I do not believe in making Rhetoric a subject for graduate study, but I find some difficulty in expressing my reason. The practical part of Rhetoric ought surely to be studied before graduation; and what I may call the learned part of Rhetoric has always seemed to me to be a peculiarly unprofitable study with which I should not be inclined to do much, either after graduation, or before it."

(*h*) "Rhetoric seems to me wholly unprofitable, and therefore an improper subject for graduate investigation. On the other hand, a course in English composition, as training in thought and expression, may often be profitable to a graduate student; and such a course may be of much assistance to the study of English literature."

(*i*) "Rhetoric, as distinguished from criticism, is merely the formulation of certain principles of good writing. Since writing which produces literature is one of the fine arts these principles are of necessity few and very general. As soon as these principles are reduced to a rigid and scientific system they become misleading and mischievous, for the essence of every fine art is individuality of conception and of execution. Tabulation of facts and generalisation in such matters very rarely produce anything except results which were already obvious, or rules whose very rigidity condemns them."

"Regarding Rhetoric as the art of speaking and writing correctly, I am of the opinion that it is an unsuitable subject for graduate study. When a man has obtained his A.B. degree he ought to be able to write his language with sufficient correctness to be responsible in the future for his own style. If he has not thus learned to write reasonably well he probably never will learn.

"Regarding Rhetoric as a science, that is, an enquiry into the why and wherefore of the effect of words and the like, etc., or as a subject for historical treatment, I should think the material rather slight for graduate work, except as some individual might care to take it up. The materal furnished by the XYZ school, for example, which has gone as far as any into the science of the thing and is excellent in its way, if not very suggestive or exact, would furnish an intelligent student with material for only a fortnight of study, and is wholly worthless as a practical aid to an advanced and capable writer. From this so-called scientific point of view, Rhetoric ought to be regarded as a mere detail of psychology or linguistics and be treated as such. Historically, Rhetoric affords small material, and that of the most academic and arid kind; what has heretofore been said about the subject from Aristotle to Whately, should not occupy a serious man a great while. He would have to study it for his own curiosity rather than as an addition to his teaching equipment."

(*j*) "Though I should hesitate to say that any subject is not suitable for this purpose, Rhetoric strikes me as anything but particularly adapted to it. I should regard it as a better subject of study for a person interested in philosophy than for one interested in English. For such a one I should even consider it dangerous, one in which he was likely to become mazed—to the great disadvantage of the luckless freshmen he will later, probably, have to teach. Of men who fling Aristotle every few minutes at beardless youths, of men so infested with the aesthetic bee in their bonnets that they try to make dull undergraduates theorize instead of teaching them to write, I have seen enough to warrant this statement. For the teaching of English composition, I consider the advanced study of Rhetoric almost if not quite useless; I should regard it as suitable for study in the same spirit as Logic."

(*k*) "In my opinion, Rhetoric, in so far as it concerns itself with principles deduced from the practice of good writers and speakers and applied to a student's own composition,—useful though it is to everyone who would perfect himself in the art of expression,—is not a proper subject for graduate work leading to a degree.

"A graduate student should, of course, be able to present in appropriate literary form the results of labor in his chosen field; but he should have done preparatory work to that end before he became a graduate. If he has not mastered the general principles of Rhetoric and learned how to apply them to his own writing before he enters a graduate school, he should supply his deficiency as soon as he can,—should supply it as he would supply a deficiency in arithmetic or in any other subject that belongs in the school or the college curriculum; he should make Rhetoric a supplementary study. It is hardly necessary to add that a graduate student should use his knowledge of Rhetoric as an aid in all his written work. From Rhetoric thus used he will get far more advantage than could be obtained in any other way; for it will be to him not an end in itself but a means to a higher end, not a matter of knowledge but a source of power in the use of knowledge. He will thus avoid the danger which besets those who study Rhetoric by itself or who write essays on subjects in which they take a languid interest,—the danger of valuing style for style's sake, of setting form above substance, of treating good English as something apart from the daily work of life.

"In so far as Rhetoric may be regarded as a science, it does not seem to me of sufficient importance to be entitled to a place among studies leading to a graduate degree. Under this head, a possible subject is The History of Rhetoric, Ancient and Modern; but a graduate student would not be likely to discover anything new in a field which has been so thoroughly explored, nor would he probably put the old facts into better shape. The study of purely theoretical Rhetoric would, I fear, in the hands of a graduate student lead either to vague generalities or to pedantry in one form or another,—such as technical terms, confusing diagrams, statistics of words in sentences or of sentences in paragraphs. Between metaphysical subtleties on the one hand, and mechanical devices on the other, he would lose sight of those living and life-giving qualities in a great writer which make him great.

"If, however, Rhetoric be held to include the study of a great author or group of authors, with special reference to style as affected by subject matter, individuality, and contemporaneous influences, it may, under favorable conditions, be a subject leading to a graduate degree. Those conditions imply a student of exceptional literary taste and talent, a professor willing and competent to oversee and direct work of a very high grade, and a committee willing and competent to pass judgment on a thesis which embodies the results of such work.

"My conclusions are confirmed by the testimony of the members of a small class in English Composition, to whom I read without comment the questions under consideration, and who answered them in writing. Of the sixteen men who wrote, eleven are graduates, and several of them have taught English in secondary schools. The eleven graduates, taken together, hold diplomas from fourteen or fifteen colleges, three or four having received them from two or more institutions. Of the undergraduates, one was prepared for college at an English public school. All, undergraduates and graduates, are students well on in life and mature in mind. As a whole, the class may be fairly regarded as representing—to the extent that such a small class can represent—the opinions of advanced students in English on the questions in hand.

"Of these writers every one discussed the main question as if Rhetoric were to be understood to mean English Composition as a whole or in part. Not one seriously considered the possibility of making Rhetoric a study by itself. Those who answered the first question in the affirmative contended that a graduate who had had no instruction, or next to none, while in college, or who had failed to profit by the instruction provided, should be allowed to use a part of his work leading to a graduate degree as a means of making up for lost time. Some of these writers seemed to think that a graduate school might be made to serve as a school for critical or creative genius; but their plans for the conduct of such a school were not very definite. Those who answered the first question in the negative maintained that there is no more reason for putting Rhetoric among the studies leading to a graduate degree than for putting arithmetic, political geography, or table etiquette there; that Rhetoric, as even undergraduates discover early in the college course, ought to be studied not for itself primarily, but for its value to the student in all his other work in English, and that to give it 'the false dignity of isolation' would be to diminish rather than to increase its importance."

II.

In reply to all this the advocates of the subject maintain that there are many legitimate topics for graduate study within the field of Rhetoric. In general, they propose three or four main lines of inquiry—historical, psychological, or philosophical, and pedagogical.

On the historical side they suggest (1) the history of Rhetoric and the development of rhetorical theory, particularly in the writings of the great masters from Aristotle down to the present; (2) the historical study of English Syntax; (3) the history of usages and the study of the usage of given authors; (4) comparative historical study of forms of expression in kindred languages and exhaustive classification of the existing material; (5) the history of English literary criticism.

Philosophical or psychological study of the subject would involve an investigation of the problems of literary art, of the principles underlying expression, of the relation of logic to Rhetoric; a study of the theory of literary criticism, of aesthetics, the basis for niceties of style; and, in general, what may be included under the term philosophy of style.

On the pedagogical side some hold that the future instructor in Rhetoric should be trained in methods of teaching the subject. Some urge, too, that practical exercise in composition should be included in the graduate work, through several were careful to exclude that as counting for a degree.

I now take up as before the actual reports and will read as many as time permits:—

(*a*) "The only reason I can see for excluding Rhetoric is that it is not an individual subject, but a composite of parts of grammar, psychology, logic, literary criticism, and perhaps other studies. But though Rhetoric borrows its fundamentals, it applies them in a way that is its own. This fact, it seems to me, justifies its existence as a subject of higher study. I recall a thesis for the degree of Ph.D. on the development, philosophy, and use of the English paragraph. Every one will no doubt agree that this subject is well worthy of research, yet I doubt if any department of psychology or of English literature would encourage its students to choose it for a doctor's thesis. There are many similar subjects which will not receive the scholarly attention they deserve if Rhetoric is not recognized as a graduate study.

"Rhetoric is not, however, equal in importance to those subjects that have an independent existence, and if it is to be pursued as a graduate study its relation to other branches of knowledge must be fully realized. It would be nonsense to plan graduate work in Rhetoric which should simply continue the mixed lessons given under that name in elementary text-books."

(*b*) "I believe Rhetoric to be a proper subject for graduate work leading to a degree, if logic and literature and psychology are.

"I read Rhetoric as essentially a branch of psychology; it is the psychology of the creative activity applied to the processes and problems of literature. Its practical utility as a graduate study arises from the fact that it deals with the form of mental activity with which men have most to do in life, either as production or as appreciation; it introduces men to the true inwardness of literature with which, as matter of refining culture, they are to be conversant all their lives. As to scope, it covers all the field of literature in the making; and its problems are analogous to the problems that arise in learning the technique of any art.

"With this view of Rhetoric, I am inclined to put it later in the college course than is sometimes done; for fair appreciation of its significance I think we must go as late, at least, as Junior year.

"I give no reason for excluding it; but I think I know, in part, why the question of retaining it was raised at all. Rhetoric has been pursued merely as composition, that is, with the object of making writers; and now it is discovered that writers are not made either by going through certain paces in a strait-jacket of refined grammar, or by jotting down daily what the student saw on his walk to the post-office,—in fact it is beginning to be suspected that writers are not made at all. But in view of this discovery I should not advocate throwing the whole study overboard. I should interrogate the study more closely to see what it contains worth keeping, and revise my methods to correspond. For myself—after considerable study of Rhetoric, and experience in teaching it to undergraduates—I have much faith in the study and its capabilities, though these are not so exclusively utilitarian as they have been regarded; I believe it may be just as practical, just as interesting, just as profitable, just as liberally educative, to study literature constructively (in other words, rhetoric), as to study it historically."

(c) "Most certainly Rhetoric is a proper subject for gradute work leading to a degree.

"(1) Aim: investigation into the nature and functions of discourse, its proper conditions and results, definition of the various kinds of discourse in psychologic terms, determination of the aesthetic basis for certain rhetorical effects, etc. The historic development of rhetorical theory should also be traced.

"(2) The scope of graduate work in Rhetoric is bounded neither by present rhetorical dogma nor even by the developing history of rhetorical theory from the Sophists and Plato down. It touches for subject-matter both literature and linguistics; for method psychology, aesthetics, and sociology.

"(3) Problems: some suggested under (1). The nature and function of figures of speech in general, of specific figures. Prose rhythms. The relations of argument to formal and real logic. The psychologic basis for descriptive writing, narrative structure in its aesthetic bearings, etc.

"Ignorance on the part of its opponents, as to the real nature of the subject of Rhetoric and the meaning of its study, is the only reason for excluding it which can be offered.

"Note: My own experiences as graduate student and as director of graduate courses has convinced me that the field of rhetorical investigation is rich in opportunity for original, thorough, philosophic work. Without a fairly complete training, however, in modern psychology and aesthetics, as well as in literature and language, only dilettante work is possible, and that has long discredited the name Rhetoric in our colleges and universities."

(d) "Admitting that our current terms 'literature' and 'Rhetoric' overlap even to the extent of some confusion, I think that courses such as the following are both properly graduate and properly Rhetoric:

"(1) *Courses in the theory of criticism.*

"(2) *Courses in poetics* (though for practical reasons Rhetoric may well be confined to prose).

"(3) *Courses in a particular prose form* (e.g., the novel), where the aim is not so much to show the historical development as to expose the scope of the form and appreciate various treatments of it. The fundamental theory of narration, the fundamental classification by epic (or realistic) and romantic, the exploration of a distinct and widespread form such as the short story, and finally, the analysis of a particular method such as George Meredith's, seem theoretically to be matters of Rhetoric and practically not to be otherwise provided.

"(4) *Courses in verse-forms.* These are purely rhetorical, beginning and ending in form as such. (But cf. note on (2).)

"(5) *Courses to train teachers* in the presentation of theory, and especially in handling essays.

"(6) *Courses in research,* 'methodology.'

"So far for theory. In practice a given department is not to be divided *a priori,* with certain men strictly for 'literature' on one side of an imaginary line, and certain men for 'Rhetoric' on the other. This, being entirely a matter of organization, seems not to affect your question. Again, it is often unwise for a student that has pursued several undergraduate courses in writing to go on after graduation with further courses in writing. On the other hand, since every graduate school has students evidently in need of further practice, either special courses in writing should be provided for graduates alone, or undergraduate courses should be open to graduates. The latter being usually the more economical solution, I am doubtful whether there should be, at least in universities whose undergraduate courses in the practice of composition cover four years, strictly graduate courses to the same end. I am regularly called on for help in the ordering of doctoral dissertations; but that is usually because the candidates have had no adequate undergraduate instruction, and the difficulty would hardly be met by a separate course.

"In sum, then, I think the theory of Rhetoric is distinctly a subject proper for graduate work leading to a degree; the practice of composition not so distinctly, if at all. I should say not at all, if I did not bethink me of a year's work with a playwright, a year of hard practice, very profitable to me and, I venture to think, to him. Certainly, in spite of exceptions easily made, the proper field for the particular education that comes through systematic practice under systematic criticism is undergraduate.

"*Note.*—I have made no references to aesthetics; for in practice that seems more naturally to belong to the psychology-philosophy group. On the other hand, in certain universities, as Princeton and Michigan, I suppose Rhetoric has its foot firmly planted there. As to the correct theoretical division I am quite incapable of pronouncing judgment."

(*e*) "Rhetoric, in my opinion, is a proper subject for graduate work leading to a degree, but not in so far as it is composition, which should be an undergraduate study, or, if graduate, should not count toward a degree.

"In so far as it is theory, Rhetoric is as proper a study for graduate work, in my opinion, as any other art of the linguistic field. Not of course the elementary side of the theory, which is for undergraduates alone, but the history of Rhetoric, the fundamental principles, if there are any, tested by psychology, philosophy, etc. Now that our students and professors of Rhetoric are beginning to have a good philological training, I hope to see the form-side of English prose covered as well as the form-side of English poetry is being covered. But Rhetoric is a horrid name for the theory of word-usage and style, and I wish we could drop it, including the whole higher field under some such general term as linguistics or philology. I am giving, myself, a graduate course in the history of theories regarding word-usage. Students seem to like it, and it has at least the effect of giving them a new conception of the scholar's and the good citizen's attitude towards words and of knocking out of their heads the foolish dicta of the popular text-books on Rhetoric."

(*f*) "I believe that the strict aims of Rhetoric as a graduate study should be pedagogical in their nature. Paidology [child study—ED.], the aesthetics of prose, the history of language, and the history of Rhetoric, are proper fields of that research which shall discover a scientific basis for teaching an efficient use of the mother tongue. The psychology of childhood and youth as related to problems of language-teaching, and the history of language as throwing light upon those problems, are matters very imperfectly understood as yet. Even the dry history of Rhetoric, a subject closed to students who have small Latin and Greek, is profitable unto humility. It at least saves the student from some of the crude dogmatism of them who in each generation reinvent theories tried by Corax and Tisias, and by them found wanting."

(g) "If regarded as a science it would be conducted on the same lines as Grammar or Language. The History of Rhetoric—the History of Rhetorical Treatises—Comparative Rhetoric, etc., would be proper objects of research.

"If regarded as an art there would need to be a change in the interpretation of the advanced degrees. For the Oxford doctorate in music the candidate must present a musical composition as part evidence of proficiency. I do not see why a rhetorical composition, an essay, a novel, a poem, or other literary kind, should not count toward a degree in literature. In that case graduate Rhetoric would be simply an extension of the theme system now used with undergraduates."

(h) "I find there is as much ground for investigation in 'Rhetoric' as in any other branch of English work, and as, I believe, in any other subject pursued in universities. We have here considerable classes working upon problems connected with the evolution of present prose modes and styles, and also investigating experimentally into what may be done in characterization, nature-work, etc. I confess I do not see why a degree may not be earned by achieving knowledge of how present literary form has been evolved, or by acquiring the power to use the modes of the masters consciously and confidently and with scientific selection."

(i) "It seems to me the value of Rhetoric as a subject for graduate work depends upon whether it be regarded as an art or as a science, if these distinctions will be allowed. Rhetoric should be mastered in its practical aspects before the student completes his undergraduate study; but as a science I believe it is eminently suited for graduate work. It should be regarded in this latter sense as a phase of psychology; and its problems should be looked upon as psychological at bottom. In general the study should relate to the outcome of various modes of language-expression upon the behavior of men; the minor questions falling under this general problem would relate to the effects of particular qualities or characteristics of expression. I think the study should be on one side historical, aiming to discover what manner of discourse men have employed in the past to influence their hearers and readers, and if possible to trace the outcome; as a phase of the historical study, perhaps, students should analyze the the qualities of expression of great works which have endured for a long time and have exerted a marked influence on human conduct, as well on account of their style as of their content. I think there is a place too for the experimental study of rhetoric, the aim of which should be to determine by test the influence upon people of different modes of expression of the same idea. If we could get anything like an accurate account of the effect which various modes have upon men as they are subjected to them in their practical lives there would not be such need for accurate experiment, but thus far we have been unable to do this.

"I am convinced that not enough attention has been paid to the psychological aspects of rhetoric; the attention has been devoted too largely to treating the subject from the standpoint and according to the method of linguistics, which is all right as far as it goes, but it seems to me that finally all the principles of rhetoric rest upon principles of psychology of the individual and of the social mind. A graduate student ought to be led up to a way of looking at rhetoric from the psychological point of view, and subjecting all rhetorical principles to the psychological test. I think grammar can be treated by the linguistic method much more effectively than can rhetoric; the former is more or less arbitrary in respect of psychological law, while the latter is at every point vital and dependent upon psychological law. I should say that the undergraduate should be made familiar with rhetoric mainly on its art side, while the graduate should master it on its psychological and philosophical sides."

(j) "Mere Rhetoric, understood as the teachings of technical treatises called Rhetorics, is hardly in itself a subject for graduate study. The history of rhetorical theory, as a branch of the history of criticism, is a proper subject. Investigations into the psychology of rhetoric and style (e.g., Herbert Spencer's 'economy of attention') or scientific study of the history of style (whether as the rhetoric of prose or the rhetoric of poetry) are proper subjects. Rhetoric in this sense is a part of the study of the history of literary form. It should not be admitted, however, except in close and constant connection with the copious and extensive study and reading of the body of literature itself and with the study of literary history. There should be no separate curriculum of graduate study in Rhetoric.

"Mere theme-writing, however sublimated or raised even to the nth power, ought never to be a part of the credits for a higher degree. If this is understood to be a part of Rhetoric then Rhetoric, so far, should be excluded."

(*k*) "I know no field so unexplored and so profitable for graduate work as Rhetoric. The relation of Rhetoric to Psychology deserves exhaustive investigation; is full of problems of interest and practical significance. The relation of Rhetoric to Logic, the history of Logic and Rhetoric, the philosophical implications of Rhetoric, are all crying for treatment and discussion. A comparison of the methods of the new logic and rhetoric would be a most valuable study. I believe in formal Rhetoric *per se* there is a most spacious field for work. Our text-books have been confined to too practical ends and have obscured the larger issues involved in rhetoric as an art as well as a science.

"A study of Rhetoric on liberal lines I believe may have the highest disciplinary value for graduate learning and does offer problems of profound interest for research."

(*l*) "In the highest conception of the study Rhetoric is, in my opinion, a proper subject for graduate work leading to a degree.

"The proper aim, the scope, and the leading problems of Rhetoric as a graduate study are:—

"1st. The study of the historical grammar of the English language, so as to reveal to advanced students, especially from the literary side, the meaning and association of words and construction and elements of style.

"2d. The study of logic, both deductive and inductive, so as to reach the principles of composition; the methods of proof and the arrangement of topics and arguments.

"These are the two chief aims to be kept in mind in the intellectual training of the advanced students. Their thesis-work shows only too clearly how much they stand in need of these two special disciplines."

(*m*) "Rhetoric is or is not a proper subject (I should prefer the term 'field') for graduate study, according to the side approached. If Rhetoric be approached as a theory, a discussion of what ought to be a comparing of methods, an appreciation of forms, then it is, in my judgment, useless for graduate study. Perhaps even worse than useless. I doubt the value of rhetorical study even for undergraduates, beyond a certain point. What the young need is practice in actual composition, with a minimum of theory and a maximum of correction.

"What the graduate is going to do with the debatable questions of style, the so-called analytics of style, is to me a mystery.

"On the other hand I am always glad to see any one investigate the actual historical growth of forms. I have in mind such work as Lewis's *Growth of the English Paragraph*, an admirable bit of scholarship, and no less practical [a University of Chicago dissertation, published in 1901—ED.]. I hope that we may live to see similar attempts at elucidating the use of the relative pronouns (*who, which, vs. that*), the *shall—will* business thoroughly sifted, the growth of *dialogue* in prose story-telling, the vicissitudes of the *short story.* In truth, there are dozens of questions upon which we need the enlightenment of history. Why then waste time and brains in thrashing over again something which is after all only subjective opinion? Mere aesthetic theorizing should be left to the magazine writer or to the really gifted critic who feels himself competent to tread in the footsteps of Lessing.

"My view has always been that the college (university) is a place for research, for scholarship, for finding out something hitherto unsuspected. Such is the object of our libraries and our seminary methods. The outside world hasn't the time to investigate; *we* must do the investigating. For instance, is any one prepared off-hand to state accurately the growth of the ceremonial terms of address: Your Majesty, Your Grace, Your Holiness, etc.? The procedure is old; there are abundant traces of it in Bede. But where did it begin? With the Greeks? Or with the Romans! What are the steps in the fashion? Through what forms has it passed in English? Now that is what I should call rhetorical study fit for the ablest graduate. But for one may I be spared all doctrinal disquisitions upon style! I have had only one here, in ten years, and that one satisfied me of the uselessness of such work. Henceforth, I accept only research."

To the forgoing expressions of opinion there is little that I need add. A dogmatic decision by this Committee as to the merits of the main question would be unlikely to further any of the interests involved; and the divergence of opinion as to the proper field of Rhetoric is too wide to permit more than an impartial presentation of the arguments on either side. As a matter of personal opinion, however, the Committee may venture to suggest that the term Rhetoric as heretofore generally employed, may well be enlarged in meaning so as to include much more than practical composition and that the field thus opened will afford abundant opportunity for investigation by the serious student.

This report was discussed by Professors F. N. Scott, James W. Bright, Herbert E. Greene, E. H. Magill, and Calvin Thomas.

NOTES

1. About one hundred and fifty circulars have also been sent to representative European scholars and writers, but reports from them have not yet arrived in sufficient numbers to be included in this survey of opinion.

2. It has been thought desirable on various grounds to publish no names in connection with the reports, but the aim has been to make the presentation of opinion practically complete on both sides of the main question. Many excellent reports have been crowded out owing to lack of space, though the trend of the arguments has been carefully followed in the general statement.

3. For the sake of brevity I dispense with connective words, and arrange the individual reports under the letters (*a*), (*b*), (*c*), etc.

William Edward Mead
"Report of the Pedagogical Section:
The Undergraduate Study of English Composition"
PMLA 17 (1902)

  This is a continuation of Scott's efforts to invigorate composition studies. The report is quite remarkable for three different discussions: (1) a large group of English professors addressing themselves to the question of what was then called the "direct" teaching of composition (i.e., through composition courses) versus "indirect" teaching (i.e., through reading literature and writing about it); (2) the first extended discussion of empirical research in composition studies; (3) a superb closing analysis by Columbia's Charles Sears Baldwin, a scholar of rhetoric with an English department appointment and a writer of influential college composition textbooks.

A YEAR AGO THE PEDAGOGICAL SECTION OF THE MODERN LANGUAGE Association investigated the question as to the feasibility of making advanced work in rhetoric (using that term in the broadest sense) a part of graduate university work counting toward a degree. The report read at the December meeting of last year was printed in the *Proceedings*. This year the investigation has been carried a step lower down, and has endeavored to test the opinions of competent judges on the question whether the methods of teaching composition now so widely followed are beyond the reach of criticism.

With this in view the committee selected, from a brief article in the *Century Magazine*, a passage representing an attitude of extreme hostility to the plan of compelling students to write frequent themes which should be corrected and returned to the writers. [The complete article appears in chap. 4, p. 238.—ED.]

The passage runs as follows:

A wide reader is usually a correct writer; and he has reached the goal in the most delightful manner, without feeling the penalty of Adam. . . . We would not take the extreme position taken by some, that all practice in theme-writing is time thrown away; but after a costly experience of the drudgery that composition work forces on teacher and pupil, we would say emphatically that there is no educational method at present that involves so enormous an outlay of time, energy, and money, with so correspondingly small a result. . . . In order to support this with evidence, let us take the experience of a specialist who investigated the question by reading many hundred sophomore compositions in two of our leading colleges, where the natural capacity and previous training of the students were fairly equal. In one college every freshman wrote themes steadily through the year, with an accompaniment of sound instruction in rhetorical principles; *in the other college every freshman studied Shakspere, with absolutely no training in rhetoric and with no practice in composition. A comparison of the themes written in their sophomore year by these students showed that technically the two were fully on a par.* That is weighty and most significant testimony.—*The Century Magazine* (vol. LI, pp. 793, 794). [The original lacks italics.—ED.]

Comments were requested on the question raised by this quotation. Details of similar experiments, if known, were called for. And, finally, the question was raised as to the possibility of conducting an experiment, or a series of experiments, which should furnish conclusive proof of the value, or the futility, of requiring freshmen to write themes steadily through the year.[1]

The reports that came back in response to these inquiries varied in length from a line or less to elaborate discussions which filled several pages. Taken as a whole, they may be regarded as fairly representative of the present position of college and university teachers of English throughout the country as to the relative importance of reading and theme writing. Harvard University, Yale, Columbia, Cornell, the Universities of Michigan, Wisconsin, Minnesota, Chicago, Leland Stanford Jr., Johns Hopkins, Louisiana, and many other institutions have had a voice in the discussion.

Our report naturally divides itself into three parts: (1) A summary of opinions on the question raised by the quotation; (2) an account of experiments similar to that just outlined; (3) a discussion of methods for determining with some accuracy the relative value of reading and practical work in composition.

So much depends in this investigation upon the experiments that we are naturally most curious to learn whether this question has been very generally tested. I therefore take up the second division first. Unfortunately, most of those who answered the questions in the circular of inquiry knew of no other such experiments. Some teachers thought they had tested the matter by noting that students in their classes in composition wrote better at the end of a course than at the beginning, or by observing that the winners of prizes for literary work in the various college publications were almost without exception students who had had systematic training in composition.

One professor of rhetoric[2] holds that he has proved the falsity of the position taken in the quotation, and he sends on a printed collection of unedited college themes, which he offers to compare with a collection of articles written by college undergraduates who have not had drill in theme-writing. One instructor had been led to the conclusion in his own classes that the most omnivorous readers are often careless writers, because they write as they read, without much thought.

We have, however, a few accounts of positive experiments. One of our pedagogical psychologists writes:

I am getting short themes written in class from high schools in different parts of the country, with the intention of comparing the quality of the work with the nature of the instruction given. In some cases there is regular theme-writing, in others not. In some cases there is much required reading of English classics, in others little.

The results of his work are not yet tabulated, but they ought to be of considerable importance, if sufficient safeguards are employed.

The next witness has experimented only upon himself, but he has had "some convincing personal experience." He says:

I have published several books on the subject of rhetoric, and I considered myself fairly expert in the art of composition, besides trying to cultivate a sense of style. I never had instruction, but obtained whatever proficiency I had from reading and the teaching of composition. Last summer I was printing a book on a literary subject, and the proof-sheets passed through the hands of a friend who is also a teacher of rhetoric. Scarcely a paragraph or sentence was left as originally written. But now the book has been said, by several competent judges, to be written in a pleasing and unaffected style! I honestly believe that this practical instruction I obtained has yielded certain and important results which my reading never has yielded and never can yield. This case is not quite parallel to a student's case, but, as being in the nature of expert testimony, should be worth something.

The three following are the only reported experiments similar to the one mentioned in the quotation; and these must be confessed to be not altogether conclusive. Says one:

I have tried a similar experiment twice, for a period of three months. I found that the study of Shakspere influenced the vocabulary of many students the next quarter, but did not affect their prose style otherwise.

A Harvard instructor writes:

The only experiment of the kind I know of was in the comparison of a certain number of papers written in a course in literature at Yale College with a number of similar papers written in a similar course at Harvard. Of three or four of our men here who examined the papers, all but one agreed that the papers written at Harvard were better written, and showed the result of the time given to English composition.

This is presumably the experiment described in our quotation.
Lastly, we have the following:

In one of our eastern colleges, about two years ago, the course in rhetoric and theme-writing was transferred from the sophomore to the freshman year. As a consequence, the sophomores had no course in rhetoric and theme-writing during the first year of the new plan. Nevertheless their writing showed in the junior year no important difference from that of the succeeding junior class. Having myself read the essays of both classes, I may affirm that a slight improvement in sentence-structure, and a little more freedom from glaring faults of taste and method, were the only noticeable distinctions. I fail to see that the later class commanded a style a whit more resourceful or effective. In short, the result was negative, not positive. And I venture to say that this negative result—of mechanical correctness, not real correctness—is all that is obtained in teaching unread students in any college of the United States.

Some sympathy with the conclusions of the writer of the paper in the *Century* is expressed in several of the reports; but, taken as a whole, the reports reveal a pretty general skepticism concerning the conclusiveness of the experiment therein described. One experiment, it is urged, is not enough to establish a conclusion so far-reaching in its results.

Evidently, after this showing, anyone who is seeking an unclaimed subject for investigation has a well-nigh virgin field to work in. This leads us to a discussion of the possibility of settling the question by experiment. A considerable number of teachers hold that the matter lies outside the range of conclusive experiment, owing to the difficulty of taking all the factors into consideration, and one volunteers the opinion that pedagogy is running mad and needs an infusion of common-sense. Some think experiments to be possible, but very undesirable for the students.

We do not [says one] tie up a student's arm and then read him anatomy; we exercise the arm. We have no business to tie up his writing-hand for a year and expect him to absorb technique of any sort through the skin.

One suggests a test course, half of a large class doing writing, and the other half receiving instruction in literature, the experiment to be continued for two years. To another, such an experiment seems possible at a very large institution, but too risky for a small one. Some think the case for composition already made out, and the experiment therefore needless. "Experiments to determine whether freshmen should profit by practice in composition are futile, but experiments to ascertain suitable methods of instruction should prove of the highest value." "Results," however, "cannot be obtained by a condensed report of many opinions where all are at sea, but through an investigation of the essential principles and conditions of effective work."

Many of the suggestions go no further than to propose the division of a class into sections. One section of freshmen could be admitted immediately to a required course in English literature without a prerequisite course in composition. At the close of the year these freshmen could be tested and the results compared with the written work of the freshmen who had taken the prescribed course in composition. But this plan, it is urged, would interrupt the regular course of instruction and be unadvisable, because the results would necessarily be uncertain and unscientific.

A more elaborate scheme, but adopting essentially the same method, is the following:

Take a freshman class of a hundred or more students. Let this class be conducted for a few weeks as a class in English literature, and let the study be of poetry rather than of prose, which might serve as a model. Call for weekly short papers and for one or two essays in which emphasis is laid upon thought, not upon form. Upon the information thus obtained, divide the class as soon as possible (in two months at the outside, sooner if practicable) into four sections, A, B, C, and D. Let sections A and B contain the upper half of the class—better still, the upper third, or even the upper quarter—the grading to be based solely upon the work in this single subject up to the time of the division of the class.

Let Section A study English literature (prose and poetry) during the rest of the academic year; let Section B study rhetoric. At the end of the year it will probably be found that there is little difference between the members of the two sections as regards skill in writing. Each section will furnish some of the best writers in the class.

Let Sections C and D (the lower half, or, better still, the lower two-thirds or three-quarters of the class) be treated in the same way. Let Section C study English literature; let Section D study rhetoric. At the end of the year it will probably be found that there is a marked difference between the members of the two sections as regards skill in writing. A few members of Section C will write as well as those in Section D, perhaps, even, as well as the average members of Section A or Section B: there must inevitably be some mistakes in grading. The members of Section D (rhetoric) will, however, write with more accuracy, with more freedom from the faults that abound in the manuscript of nearly all students who have not received special instruction in English composition. Especially will this be true if the members of Section D have been required to do some reading of good prose in connection with their study of rhetoric. My own classes are required to make an analytic study of nineteenth-century prose in connection with their study of rhetoric.

A suggestion that might be adopted without too great an expenditure of time, and without interfering with the work of students, is the following:

It is proposed that a collation be made of the data to be found in the registrar's offices in our colleges and universities with reference to the influence of various lines of study upon the use of English. "I now have several people at work," says the writer, "upon the data in the office of the registrar in our own university, with the end in view to see if I can get any evidence relating to the effect of classical and other fields of special study upon the appreciation and writing of English. I am taking the records for a number of years of students in the different courses and comparing these with reference to their grades in English to see if the figures reveal anything. Of course there are difficulties of a serious character surrounding the investigation, since students come with different kinds and qualities of preparation, and those who elect science often do not have a chance to show the influence of their scientific training upon their English before they pass out of this study. But I still think something of value may be gained, and I wish the work could be repeated in the various universities, and taken up also in the high schools. I mean to examine the records in our registrar's office of pupils graduating out of different courses in the high schools and compare their standings in English. This may perhaps give us more satisfactory results than the examination of the records of the university students."

The most extensive outline of a proposed experiment is the following. It comes from a well-known investigator in the Teachers' College of Columbia University [E. L. Thorndike—ED.]. He criticises the experiment described in the quotation as "extraordinarily carelessly devised and lazily administered," and goes on to say:

Even conclusive proof can be obtained as to the exact amount of the value of composition work in improving the ability to write English, in case there is such.

If, for instance, five or six or more colleges would split the freshman class into two sections, dividing them at random (alphabetically), and would give one section theme-writing and the other a reading course, data could readily be obtained that would settle the question.

The data should be four or more themes written during the first two weeks of the year by all the students, and a similar number written during the last two weeks of the year.

To make the test valid requires (1) that the students be representative of the general class "college students," and not peculiar in any respect; (2) that there be enough of them to reduce to a negligible quantity the chance variation in quality of the work of individuals which occurs in theme-writing as in anything else; (3) that the instruction in theme-writing and in the reading course be of the same relative grade of efficiency (e.g., if the instructors in the theme courses are such that out of a hundred college instructors picked at random 27 per cent. would be superior to them, then the instructors in the reading courses must also average at the same percentile grade).

(1) Would be satisfied by picking students at random from colleges picked at random.

(2) Would be satisfied, I am fairly sure, by four hundred individuals in each of the two classes, "students with a year's theme work" and "students without that, but with a year's reading course in its place." Probably two hundred in each class would do to get a result accurate within 10 per cent."

(3) Would be satisfied by the random selection of pairs of instructors at approximately the same rate of salary in the case of each pair.

It would be possible to answer the question even without splitting classes into two sections, though less surely and less easily.

If eight or more colleges now giving regular theme courses would provide the data mentioned above, and eight or more colleges giving approximately the same quality of general work would do the same, but replace their theme courses by reading courses during the year, the data would serve.

The matter of gaining an exact measure of the results of the year's work in the case of both sorts of training, and of comparing these measures, is a very elementary problem in statistics. If ten fairly trustworthy critics of English writing, *e.g.*, assistants in rhetoric in colleges, and four experts, *e.g.*, editors or college professors, would each read 300 themes, or if twenty assistants and eight experts would each read 150 themes, and if the expenses of correspondence were defrayed, anyone skilled in handling educational statistics would probably be willing to work up a report on the data and risk his reputation upon its accuracy.

There are means of getting precise measures of the improvement of the ability to write good English; measures that will not be invalidated by personal bias, or be so vague as not to advance us beyond common-sense opinion.

It is impossible for me to take the time to describe in more detail how the test themes should be obtained, *e.g.*, whether all should write on the same subject in some cases or not; whether a time limit should be set in some cases or not; whether more than four themes are needed or not. If one knew just what opportunity could be granted by teachers of English in the colleges for any such experiment, one could plan its details with surety.

The only difficulty in the world is to get the data. If colleges would turn over to me the data I mention and money to hire men to read the themes, I could get the answer in a month. The exact statistical treatment is perfectly possible.

We are now prepared to take up the discussion of the question suggested by the quotation from the article in the *Century Magazine.* The comments upon the quotation are not easily summarized in a few words.

But they generally emphasize the fact that composition is an art rather than a science, and therefore can be mastered only by practice; and this preferably under competent instruction. They point out important aspects of work in composition that may or may not co-exist along with technical correctness, such as unity of conception, logical development of a theme, proportion of parts. These and many other matters that have to do with the work of the accomplished prose-writer are, they urge, the very things that trouble us most, even when we have read widely and carefully for years, and have given anxious thought to the task of expressing ourselves with clearness and precision.

I should, however, be very unfair to the contributors to this discussion were I to attempt in a word or two to summarize their arguments. I must therefore be content to indicate thus briefly their general drift, and allow as many as possible to speak for themselves.

As a matter of fairness I present first the views of those who are in general agreement with the position of the writer of the article in the *Century*. Says one:

> I hesitate to express an opinion which is still unsettled in my own mind. I am, however, somewhat strongly inclined to sympathize with the writer from whom you quote. Of the two, I feel sure that reading is better training than writing; but I do not believe that either will help a student to write well if he has to be driven to it. I think, therefore, that the first aim of the teacher of English to underclassmen in college should be to interest them in what they read. If he succeeds in this, they will perhaps afterward be ready to profit by instruction in the principles of rhetoric; if he does not succeed in the first task, I think the second is in most cases foredoomed. I have known of men who got little pleasure or profit from their instruction in English literature, yet learned a good deal from their later work in rhetoric; but in my experience such cases have been decidedly exceptional.

Of the same general tenor is the following:

> Wide reading is certainly, in my opinion, much more valuable than study of the text-book and practice in theme-writing—in the proportion of ten to one more valuable. For, by reading, the student attains a vocabulary, an array of phrases and idioms, and a notion of the qualities of style. Not one of these benefits, it strikes me, has ever been attained by the text-book and the required essay. Teaching English composition to a student who is unread is much like trying to make bricks without straw.

Says another:

The writer seems to me to have overstated his case. I should agree with him, however, that in many of our colleges there is too much theme-writing. For some years I have had a section of freshmen in English, and I feel strongly that the daily themes which by the custom of the institution I must require of them, are not only unproductive of good, but by their monotony they depress the student, and render him less capable of genuine pleasure in composition. I hope for a change, but I trust that it will not be quite so radical as that suggested by this quotation. My own plan would be to give two-thirds or three-fourths of the time to reading, and to require a few themes. These would give the student a chance to try his hand, and should be criticised with reference to matters in which reading is not a sure help.

Apart from some very brief expressions of opinion, on the whole favoring the extreme position taken in our quotation, this is nearly all I have to offer on the one side. On the other hand, the opponents of this position furnish an embarrassing mass of material, of which I can present but a small part. Says one:

Looked at theoretically, the proposition that a pupil can learn to write good English by reading Shakspere, with no practice in composition, is as absurd as to maintain that one may become a good pianist by listening systematically to good piano-playing; or that one may become a good skater or a good painter by watching the performances of those who excel in these arts. I believe that the great fundamental error which lies at the bottom of our prevalent unsuccessful teaching of English is that of considering English composition as a science, and not as an art. If it is a science, then the comparatively easy method of sound instruction in rhetorical principles will be successful. But if it is an art, then, like every other art, it can be mastered only by long and faithful practice.

Another says:

I do not think that there is any necessary connection between wide reading and good writing. I have myself known mature men, scholars of exceptionally wide reading in many languages, who wrote in a style not absolutely incorrect indeed, but exceedingly dull and difficult. Wide reading forms the style and enlarges the vocabulary of the born writer, the man who, like Stevenson, reads with an instinctive feeling for style, in its broad effects and its niceties of phrase. But such a reader turns naturally from reading to writing, using what he has gained from the style of others, unconsciously or (as in Stevenson's case again) by a deliberate reproduction.

Such cases manifestly give no support to the generalization in your quotation. The Stevensons hardly enter into the problem of the instructor in English. The fine appreciation of style in others is naturally and commonly associated with the power and probably with the desire to write, but this conscious and discriminating appreciation of style is rare. Thousands read widely who neither possess nor acquire it; reading for the matter and oblivious of the manner. In such cases wide reading has but little or no effect on style.

In general I should say, that the art of writing (so far as it can be learned at all) must be learned by writing, as the art of painting must be learned in the studio rather than by looking at pictures in a gallery. Practice in either art should begin early. As to the experiment cited, it seems permissible to ask, if the results claimed were gained by a study of Shakspere, why give up reading for writing in the sophomore year, or the junior year, or the senior? If the ability will come by reading, a very burdensome occupation will be gone.

It is important to note that, in the judgment of a Harvard instructor—

the opinion quoted from the *Century* is not borne out by the experience of the department of English at Harvard. We find a marked difference between the work of the freshman and sophomore classes in English composition, a difference which shows that the writing of the same man before the course in freshman composition and after it, is technically of very different quality. With one exception all the members of the department who teach English composition agree in this opinion.

Objection to the position taken by the writer of the article in the *Century* is raised in the following report on the ground of psychology:

There is a great difference between (1) interpreting visual forms to get their meaning-equivalents, and (2) employing these forms to express one's own thoughts. A simple illustration of this is found in the case of adults who read Shakspere and who enjoy him, but who could not possibly construct a half-dozen sentences on the Shaksperian plan, because their relations with their author have not involved this factor of reproduction of his phraseology and peculiar modes of expression. Then to proceed on the plan of having pupils read widely without the necessity of writing will not accomplish as much as the quotation claims for it. But if occasion be made for the pupil to convey his thoughts in the happiest and most effective manner, the best preparation therefore is unquestionably to have him brought into vital, sympathetic connection with models in which these qualities are embodied. An individual will grow in the power of literary expression mainly by the more or less close imitation of good models presented in his literary environment; just as in the formation of character in general it is far more effective to put one in the presence of a concrete, living personality exhibiting certain desirable qualities of conduct than to give him a program of formal rules setting forth how he should behave himself. One can imitate an act more easily than he can transform into execution a verbal description of the act. So the life, the spirit, the effectiveness at any rate of one's linguistic expression must come, it seems to me, from his reading rather than from his formal study.

But still formal, technical things must often be learned in a formal, technical way. A pupil may read ever so widely and still go on using the split infinitive in his own writing. Again, some of the larger characteristics of good expression will often be missed by even the widest reader if his attention has not been especially directed to such matters. For instance, I have in mind now a man who has pastured in all the richest literary fields, but who frequently presents an anti-climax in his written performances. The fact is that most readers are interested in the content of what they are reading, and not in the forms of expression, and so they never get hold of these latter so as to use them. Without doubt much experience will give a certain kind of consciousness of things technical, yet it is certain that in some cases, at any rate, this consciousness will not be vivid enough to have a controlling influence upon the individual's writing. It must be remembered that the processes involved in motor execution are not immediately connected with the processes of interpretation of visual symbols, so when a man takes a pencil in his hand it does not follow by any means that the experience gained through the eye will determine the activities of the fingers.

This connection is to be established by a certain amount of attention which will weld together the graphic and other language processes, and the initiative in turning the attention upon the proper things must often be taken by some one other than the learner himself.

Emphasizing the same general thought in a different fashion is the following:

Though the average student may be a wide reader, he is certainly a careless reader; he will never acquire a good style by unconscious imitation. In every college are to be found students who spell badly, who punctuate indifferently, whose diction is meager and inaccurate, who have little feeling for idiomatic phrasing or for sentence-structure, who will write an entire essay in one or two paragraphs, or who will make a paragraph of each sentence; so blind have they been to the examples of correct usage that have been before their eyes ever since they learned to read.

In the matter of form, of constructing an essay that shall have an organic relation of parts, even very good students may be deplorably weak; in fact, one may have a good command of language, yet fail entirely to write about his subject. I quote an instructive passage from the *Autobiography* of Philip Gilbert Hamerton: "I offered two or three papers to the 'Westminster,' which were declined, and then I wrote to the editor asking him if he would be so good as to explain, for my own benefit and guidance, what were the reasons for their rejection. His answer came, and was both kind and judicious. 'An article,' he told me, 'ought to be an organic whole, with a prearranged order and proportion amongst its parts. There ought to be a beginning, a middle, and an end.' This was a very good and much-needed lesson, for at that time I had no notion of a synthetic *ordonnance* of parts."

This lesson, I submit, might have been given by a college teacher; but a teacher of that kind Hamerton never had; and I admit that the lessons that are given by an editor—when he is willing to give them—are more deeply imprinted in the mind, and are more completely learned. Certainly this lesson was an important one for the youth, who—whatever his merit as a writer may be— eventually became a successful editor and the author of a dozen or more of interesting books.

If the college cannot help the student in the matter of English Composition, why expect the preparatory school to succeed? Or why stop there? Is it right to place so much drudgery upon the grammar and primary schools? Where is the line to be drawn? At spelling? or punctuation? or at the ability to construct sentences that are grammatical? Or shall we leave everything that comes under the head of English Composition to be learned by unconscious imitation, by absorption, and devote our energies to the teaching of Shakespere?

The question really resolves itself into this: Can instructors in English Composition accomplish anything with their students? I believe that even the dullest students can be taught enough to justify the time and the nervous energy that are expended by their instructors, that much can be done toward the correction of faults, something even in the direction of positive excellences.

I freely admit that this work involves a considerable outlay of time, energy, and money; but I doubt whether the result is correspondingly any smaller than is the case with certain other subjects. In colleges in which mathematics is required throughout the freshman year, can the instructors felicitate themselves upon the attainments of the lower half of the class, especially upon those of the lowest quarter of the class? And do not the members of this lowest quarter hold on to the little English that they have learned, and get more profit from it, than the members of the lowest quarter in mathematics get from their little learning?

The spirit of the large number of individual reports is, I think, substantially expressed in the foregoing extracts, though the limitations of space compel the omission of much material worthy of a place in this discussion.

So able and complete are the expressions of opinion already presented that it is quite unnecessary for this committee to add anything. The case for reading as a sufficient independent means of teaching composition has evidently, in the judgment of most college teachers, not yet been made out. The burden of proof, therefore, still rests upon the advocates of reading as against theme-writing. No one doubts the value of reading as an aid to composition, and most of us will probably agree that the constant endeavor to draw something out of nothing is as dismal a failure as the attempt to get up steam in an empty boiler. On the other hand, to rely wholly upon reading as a means of reaching the rhetorical goal is, to quote the picturesque phrase of one report, about as satisfactory as trying to walk on one leg instead of two.

The report was discussed by Professors C. S. Baldwin and F. N. Scott. Professor Baldwin spoke as follows:

My own comparison of two cases as nearly parallel to the one cited as may be led to an inference directly opposite. But I should not call either the one experience or the other an experiment. The principles involved in this question have an importance so general that I beg the privilege of the floor long enough to discuss the subject rather than the quotation, and to use these notes, prepared in reply to the circular.

Since the quotation seems to imply a confusing distinction between rhetoric and composition, let me say that I understand the topic for discussion to be the college study of prose composition and diction, both theory (as in manuals, lectures, and analysis of good prose) and practice (as by the writing of themes regularly for regular criticism). This study, by whatever name it be called, is not uniformly valuable in all its parts. For first, *diction* (*i.e.,* all that relates to words and phrases separately and to their harmony) cannot to any great degree be directly inculcated. The development of a man's vocabulary being largely the development of his experience, a theme-reader's criticism of it is limited usually to correction and general suggestion, *i.e.,* is largely negative. This is the less unfortunate since the best means towards range, precision, and force of phrase is reading. I should have thought this a truism, if it had not been so solemnly affirmed in the quotation. And I have to add only

(1) that "wide" reading is not so likely to be productive as deep reading; and

(2) that just here courses in rhetoric and courses in literature, instead of clashing, may complement each other.

Assuming, then, that in general (it would by no means always be true of a given case) diction may be improved as well by reading as by writing, we have still unanswered the whole question of composition in the literal sense; *i.e.*, of construction. But this is the proper domain of rhetoric. Therefore the fallacy in the inference quoted on the circular is in arguing mainly beside the point. The real question is in effect this: Can the average student learn as well how to make his own writing lucid and forcible in construction by reading the best poems, plays, and essays as by practice and criticism directed toward his specific ends? Remembering that the student may do both, and in fact often does both concurrently, observe that composition may be roughly divided into the *logical* sort, the sort that proceeds from proposition to proposition, and the *artistic* sort, the sort whose progress is not measured by propositions. The two sorts overlap, especially in what we call essays, but the distinction is real. Now the practice of the latter sort, the artistic or literary, is the affair of the few. The study of it in masterpieces covers almost the whole range of college courses in English literature, and I suppose we all agree to this as part of any scheme of liberal education; but the practice, the composing, for instance, of short stories is the affair of the few and these few precisely the ones to whom teaching, whether of rhetoric or of literature, is least important. That college courses in rhetoric are useful even to these is sufficiently established by experience; but the point is that such courses must be a small part numerically of college work in rhetoric.

We are brought, then, by exclusion to this important fact, important enough, it seems to me, to be called cardinal; *the main business of rhetoric with the undergraduate mass is to teach—by precept, by analysis of masterpieces, by example,— logical composition.*

To this I should add a corollary: It is also clearly within the province of rhetoric, as we now use the word, to teach artistic composition; but since this is the ground where courses called "rhetoric" and courses called "literature" over-lap, the time devoted to it by a given group of courses in rhetoric should depend upon the number and character of the courses in literature; should depend, that is, on the particular college. In this regard colleges vary, and will doubtless continue to vary widely, both in the extension given to the terms *rhetoric, English,* and *literature,* and in the actual proportion of hours given, on the one hand mainly to reading, and on the other hand mainly to writing. In short, the teaching of rhetoric may profitably spend on the artistic side so much time as seems wise in a given college to complement the teaching of literature; so much, furthermore, as will give to any student the opportunity for consecutive criticism of any artistic form he shows himself capable of pursuing; but in every college the teaching of rhetoric must devote its main time to the training of the average student on the logical side.

Finally, let me explain what I wish to include in that term logical. Argumentation, of course, debate and other kinds of speech-making. Persuasion must always remain for most men the main skill sought by rhetoric. Its importance is not in the least diminished by such changes in outward form as have ensued upon modern conditions. But the term logical is meant to include also what the books call exposition, either as subsidiary to persuasion or as independent and self-sufficing; in a word, to include essays as well as speeches. Either may or may not be literary in diction; both are logical in construction. Logical progress, in the whole and in every part, the lucid conduct of a theme to its conclusion, is attainable by every student through courses in rhetoric; it is attainable, without far greater labor, in no other way; and through courses in the history of literature or through "wide" reading without practice it is not attainable at all. "Reading" in the sense of logical analysis, the study of the whole framework and of each part, is of course directly contributory; but this kind of "reading" is confined practically to courses in rhetoric.

This logical group, this bringing of knowledge to bear, which is one of the most fundamentally valuable results of a college education, is subserved more directly, I believe, than in any other single way, by the teaching of rhetoric. Essentially different from all other courses in seeking directly a skill, an ability, rhetoric may thus be made to serve in particular each course on which it depends for material and in general the great object of all the courses together. Here, it seems to me, is its main claim to a place in any scheme of college education. Whatever was once meant to be included in the idea of logic as the "*organon*," our "*organon*" in college to-day is rhetoric.

NOTES

1. The circulars of inquiry were issued under the direction of Professor F. N. Scott, of Michigan University, the president of the Pedagogical Section.

2. For a variety of reasons it has been thought desirable to suppress the names of the writers of the individual reports and to allow the opinions and facts to speak for themselves. Much care has been taken to secure a really representative expression of opinion. Names will, however, be furnished on application.

William Edward Mead
"Report of the Pedagogical Section: Conflicting Ideals in the Teaching of English"
PMLA 18 (1903)

&⁊ *The last of a remarkable series of reports, this one concentrates upon the question of composition as practical study versus composition as a kind of creative writing. Opinion on the matter is heated; some think the simple opposition of those two "ideals" is inaccurate; others believe that so very few college students possess literary talent that to encourage it is unfair.*

Harvard always encouraged the "creative" side of composition, especially in advanced courses like English 12, which asked for a kind of impressionism; this side of composition instruction would slide more toward creative writing when Charles Townsend Copeland, the famous "Copey," flourished after 1900. (The first creative writing course began in 1920 when Robert Frost took up residence at the University of Michigan. Scott, then in charge of the rhetoric department, seems not to have had any contact with Frost. And when the rhetoric department was dismantled, Michigan's creative writing program inherited Scott's seminar table, still in use today in the Hopwood room.)

It requires but slight investigation in educational matters to discover that there is great difference of opinion on many questions of fundamental importance. With a view to determine in some measure how widely teachers of English composition are at variance in their theory and practice, two expressions of opinion, apparently as divergent as they could well be, were sent out by the Pedagogical Section in a recent circular of inquiry. The two quotations, with the appended questions, are as follows:

"English composition is already taught in the schools, but it connotes the art of writing clearly and correctly about ordinary matters and with such limitations as you expect in a good business letter; whereas, this book (Cornford's *English Composition*) is a manual of the art of writing as Stevenson understood it. Inspired by Continental practice, particularly the French, Mr. Cornford sets out to teach schoolboys to think literary thoughts and write them down with literary force and grace; . . . is it well to teach the literary art to English schoolboys? We do not think it is well; . . . it is alien to the genius of the nation."—*London Academy*, 24 Nov., 1900, p. 496.

"I have always regarded rhetoric as dealing, in all its parts and stages, with real literature in the making, and composition, however humble its tasks, as veritable authorship. . . . To put the student frankly on the basis of authorship, . . . is to impart immensely greater reality to his study of rhetoric."—Professor J. F. GENUNG.

Two distinct ideals of teaching composition seem to be suggested in the preceding extracts: (*a*) the art of writing clearly and correctly about ordinary matters; (*b*) the production of literature.

1. Which of these lights do you think the teacher of composition should chiefly follow?
2. Should there be any difference in the ideals of the teacher of composition (1) in the elementary school, (2) in the secondary school, (3) in the college? (In the college would you distinguish between (a) beginning classes, (b) advanced classes?)
3. In your opinion is it in any sense "alien to the genius" of this nation to teach schoolboys (as a class—the rank and file) to "think literary thoughts and write them down with literary force and grace," or to lead them to suppose that in their themes they are undertaking "veritable authorship"?

At the outset it should be emphasized that the Pedagogical Section as such has advocated neither side of the main question, and has not ventured to indicate whether there is necessarily any conflict in ideals or methods. In a purely objective way the attempt has been made to learn what are the actual opinions current on the fundamental questions of aim and method. We may regret as much as we please that other people do not think as we do; so much the worse for them. But surely the first step toward conversion is to discover how much we hold in common and how widely at certain points our opinions diverge.

The views about to be presented are taken from a mass of material that has poured in from a variety of sources, from college and secondary school teachers of English, from educational psychologists, from editors, and from professional men of letters. All, or nearly all, the great universities are represented, as well as many smaller institutions from Massachusetts to California. As was to be expected, there is considerable diversity of opinion, though some of the diversity is largely verbal. At all events, the investigation, imperfect and tentative as it is, seems to prove the desirability of coming to something like agreement on this fundamental part of our educational system. Until we do, we shall leave the problem chiefly to the publishers of educational novelties, or to the blundering ineptitude of teachers who drift along without aims or methods, and who, as in one case I recall, may be set to teaching English composition because they will probably do less harm there than elsewhere.

But I must not longer delay the presentation of the material which constitutes the real value of this report. In analyzing the opinions as to which of the two ideals the teacher of composition should chiefly follow,

I find that they can be divided into three tolerably well defined groups, the first two decidedly favoring one view or the other, and the third aiming at a harmony of the two views expressed in the quotations.

I first turn to those who practically agree with the writer in the *Academy*. The reasons given are not in all cases identical but they emphasize in general the fundamental necessity of clear thinking and habits of accurate expression as "the absolutely essential preparation" for success in literary efforts. I need cite but two or three typical opinions.

"My experience," says one, "has taught me that students are in the end best prepared to produce literature when their preliminary writing has been upon ordinary matters with the purpose of teaching clearness and correctness."

Of the same tenor are the two following:

"The boy is not to make literature in his theme, but his theme is to be judged by literary canons. Only one ideal can appear, therefore, and 'clearness and correctness' is a rung in the ladder to it."

"The majority of schoolboys are quite incapable of understanding literary ideas. Professor Genung's view may be well enough for exceptionally gifted students, not for the majority. The desideratum is the ability to write plain, straightforward English. Furthermore, I see no need of making composition, which, after all, is, for most people, a matter of plain common sense, the rather repellant but often fascinating thing which the terms 'real literature' and 'veritable authorship' imply."

A College teacher of long experience writes:

"My conclusion is so decided that I am tempted to be impatient with anybody on the other side. All that the school and the college can require or seriously attempt is 'writing clearly and correctly about ordinary matters.' We may be devoutly thankful if we succeed in getting that much. To attempt more is to me hallucination."

These positions are unmistakable. The advocates of a training which aims from the outset at "real literature in the making," are for the most part less emphatic, though some would lay the principal stress on that side, and, if they had to make a choice, would prefer to take their chances in attempts at producing real literature. But most of those whose leanings are towards an essentially literary training recognize the importance of the formal drill, if one is to be saved from slovenly habits of expression and from the flabbiness of languid aestheticism. In actual practice "an intelligent teacher will be governed somewhat by the nature and ability of his students." The majority, therefore, of those who advocate in a measure the development of the beginner into a real author frankly recognize the importance of both sides of the work.

Here as elsewhere I can present only typical opinions:

(*a*) "No man can draw the line between plain composition and literary art. Every advance in the former is an approach to the latter. Keep the emphasis on the former."

(*b*) "There is not so much difference between these 'ideals' as might appear from the rather unfortunate terms in which they are stated. If I am to agree with either, I agree with Genung; for I certainly would not restrict the student to such subject and manner as would be appropriate to a *business* letter. But then, on the other hand, 'ordinary matters' are the stuff out of which the best literature is made, though it never can be made by rhetorical rules. When Stevenson wrote letters on 'ordinary matters' he made literature out of them every time; if the boy is a Stevenson he will make literature. If he isn't, you can't teach him to make literature by 'putting him on the basis of authorship,' whatever that may mean. Teach the boy to express his own thoughts as best he can; never mind the literature."

(*c*) "I cannot see that the two methods are mutually exclusive, but if more weight must be given to one, I should say that the first should be emphasized in all earlier work, and that 'literary' writing should begin with the formal study of English literature."

(*d*) "The teacher of composition should keep both ideals clearly in mind. His first duty is perhaps to teach writing as a matter of business, but it is equally his duty to develop in every pupil such literary graces as he can, and where he finds special capacity to exist, to suggest its further development. Everybody can learn to write and speak in a practical, logical way, while only the few can become artists, and then only after long practice: but while the interests of the many demand the greater part of the teacher's time, the interests of the few must have their share of attention. I cannot believe that it is right to neglect either ideal for the other."

(*e*) "To write 'clearly and correctly' is in some measure to write in a 'literary' style. Mechanical, dead-level writing is never, in any worthy sense, correct. Let the student, then, by all means be taught to produce literature, if by literature we mean that work which possesses grace, power, and effectiveness."

(*f*) "To teach the art of literary expression, as a thing to be acquired apart from general culture and to be practiced apart from the writer's genuine personality, appears to me a vicious proceeding. Instead of a race of sincere and virile thinkers, this method tends to produce a class of superficial stylists, with whom a few rhetorical tricks count for more than solidity of thought."

(*g*) "The only thing the teacher of composition can do—that is, the only thing susceptible of being imparted by teaching—is what may be called the mechanics of literature, what is included for the most part in writing clearly, correctly, and perhaps strongly. Beyond these qualities the pupil must work out his own salvation, according to the mind he has. If he has a dry, contracted mind he will write baldly; if he has the touch of imagination it will show itself in the turn of his sentences. As to writing about ordinary matters,—well, it is out of ordinary matters that literature is produced, as well as out of extraordinary. I do not think the matter should be discriminated on the ground of ordinary and extraordinary; the teacher should try to *find* his pupil in the subjects he prescribes, and the pupil should be encouraged, as far as systematic discipline will allow, in working out his own bent, in subject as in style."

(*h*) "It seems to me that the first ideal stated, that of 'writing clearly and correctly about ordinary matters,' is fundamental, that it must come first in the order of time, and must for a time be the sole ideal. As soon as practicable, however, some glimpse of the higher ideal of Cornford and Genung should be set before the pupils. There should be a steady change in the point of view, as the students rise on the stepping stones of clearness and correctness to higher things."

(*i*) "Expression, oral and written, is the chief means for carrying on the process of education. That it should conform *gradation* to present fashion is an important but secondary consideration. The 'ideal of teaching composition' can, therefore, be neither 'the art of writing clearly and correctly about ordinary matters,' nor 'the production of literature.' Neither the professional artist nor the correct philistine constitutes the goal of teaching. The highest degree of varied self-expression in forms best suited to individual aptitudes and stages of growth—this seems to me to be the only ideal worth having or attainable."

The next extract is especially important as representing the aim and practice of the entire department of English composition at Harvard.

(*j*) "It is our practice in the composition classes at Harvard College to help the great body of students, so far as we can, in saying simply and directly what they have to say; thus a large part of our work lies in showing young men how to remove obstacles to the effective expression of their thought. It is our further practice to encourage, so far as we can, any sign of literary power, and to encourage it without tempting its possessor to feel past learning anything.

"From what I have written, you will see that we try to adapt our teaching to individual needs. Sometimes we succeed, and sometimes we fail; but we believe in the effort. Incidentally, every teacher here, so far as I know, connects English composition with English literature, wherever he can. I do not mean that he constantly asks students to write about books; I mean that he uses books as illustrations, not merely of bad qualities, but of good ones, and that he works hard to help students toward an appreciation of what is best."

(*k*) "The art of writing clearly and correctly about ordinary matters that would not be discussed in ordinary conversation, does not seem to me to lead to power, or even in any proportionate degree to correctness and clearness. If by 'ordinary matters' we are to understand glimpses of character, or minor manifestations of manliness or womanliness, such as fall within the range of the schoolboy's experiences, I should wish to count these as of the other and higher category of materials postulated under the division (*b*). I consider such things wholly literary, in kind, and often, as experience proves, not less than literary in degree. Putting pupils at the task of 'visualizing' any attractive or interesting object, or of developing the character of some person who has inspired such treatment, is literary work *to them*. It is found, in our five years' practice of it here, to be not only successful in itself, but very valuable in enabling the correctness and clearness that we have tried to secure without it. Writing, done with inspiration, begets momentum in expression, and this momentum brings with it better and more correct form than can be produced by dogged working at meaning that is uninspired and hence more or less inorganic."

(*l*) "The teacher (of elementary classes: 'in the schools') should first aim at 'writing clearly and correctly.' The reasons for this are easily understood by the beginner. But the teacher should also have in mind the ultimate cultivation of 'taste,' and therefore should aim to introduce the more advanced 'beginner' to notions of selection and preference in modes of expression and arrangement of sentences, etc. In this way 'the production of literature,' or 'veritable authorship' may, in some measure, come to be understood at an early age."

(*m*) "My tendency is, on the whole, to agree with Prof. Genung rather than with the London Academy. Yet I hardly know how to make practical use of so sharp a distinction as you draw under your (*a*) and (*b*). What do you oppose to 'ordinary matters'? You leave me uncertain what you mean by 'literature.' I am half inclined to oppose to your (*a*) such a (*b*) as this: the art of writing astonishingly and profusely, the subject being of no consequence. We are having a fad, a mania, for cleverness. The literary self-consciousness needs to be explored, that we may know exactly what the literary ambition is, before I can give my adhesion unreservedly to your (*b*), to which, on the whole, I do give it. It is absurd to set up as a goal of attainment, in school or college, the production of copy. Yet this perversity is perhaps inevitable, the market for copy is so active. Draining one's wits for copy is poor business. The legitimate business of the school is primarily storing the mind with forms of knowledge and imagination, and then, as the stimulus of occasion comes, the re-assembling and combining of these forms into original matter worth expressing with all care for correctness, and, so far as possible, with the elements of charm and grace.

"A literary ambition outrunning the mental supply is the cause of many of the weakest compositions. Hence the teacher has to be chary of solicitation for fine effects. If a pupil is not, and has not long been, a reader and an attentive listener, his mind remains sterile, and his composition must be set and formal; *his* best is to obey the rules of grammar and rhetoric. As I cannot segregate an original, inventing class from the plodders and docile performers of tasks, I cannot take my stand squarely on your (*b*); but must hover freely, with the privilege of alighting on either side of your line, almost as if it were not there."

(*n*) "Either extreme seems bad. I may be missing the point of the question, but I fail to see any justification for the existence of the two ideals as distinct. Few things, on the one hand, tend to become so dry, mechanical, and perfunctory as writing 'clearly and correctly about ordinary matters.' If the matter to be written about isn't to some appreciable extent a little out of the ordinary, a little out of the common run, a little worthy of attention because of some new phase to be noted, what difference does it make whether anything clear or correct be written about it or not? On the other hand, few things tend to become so dreary and remote, so trivial and sentimental, so empty of all reality, as 'the production of literature,' distinct from the ordinary matters of life, especially that 'production of literature' which is identified with the pumping up, or conjuring up, of 'literary thoughts' and the writing of them down 'with literary force and grace.' "

As to the question whether there should be any difference in the ideals of the teacher of composition in the elementary school, the secondary school, and the college, there is also divergence of opinion.

"Emphatically, no," says one. "The difference is one of degree, degree of maturity and degree of mastery of technique."

"The ideal should vary," says another; but the next opinion is: "Though the method may vary, the ideal is constant." This latter view is shared by a half-dozen others.

(*a*) "I draw no distinction between school and college. College students ought, of course, to write better than boys and girls in school. But the kind of writing to be asked of them is the same."

(*b*) "I should say that there should be difference only in degree between elementary, and secondary, and first-year college work. In college, I should devote the first or freshman year, two hours a week, to topic studies in 'visualization,' 'characterization,' 'treatment of moods,'—or what is attempted ordinarily under the heads of description and narration. The second year, I should devote the same amount of time to work in exposition, but in the form of practice in developing impressions, judgments, and potential or unexpressed ideas of every kind, the student going nowhere for his meanings, but making himself acquainted with what he really thinks, or means himself, in his own mind. The third year, I should set the student at studying classic models of English prose, and give the task, in many component topics, of clarifying and universalizing his own style. The fourth year, his work should be the expression of individual taste in both form and matter, using much comparison with the great masters (like Ruskin, Hawthorne, Stevenson, and even Hewlett and Hubbard, and Taine and De Amicis and others outside) of the personal or individual manner. The work should have, in each of the last two years, at least two class periods a week.

"The plan thus roughly outlined is the one, I may say, that we have followed here (at the University of Nebraska) for several years, and is one that seems to the seven teachers of college composition, in our department, very satisfactory. Argumentation is taught almost entirely in a department by itself."

But the reservation is made by some that "there isn't much difference between the '*ideals*' of the elementary school and the college; but there may well be considerable difference in *method*, simply because the college man has come to have a different kind of thought to express from that which he had when in the primary school. The method ought to be progressive, to match the expanding thought of the boy and man."

This view is variously presented, but the two following opinions are typical:

(*a*) "One doesn't teach a skater the grapevine twist in the first lesson; but the ideal of the beginner and the trained athlete is the same."

(*b*) "There should be no essential difference in the ideals of teaching composition at any stage of the student's course. The aim should be to teach him to use his mother-tongue clearly, correctly, and forcibly in treating subjects which he understands. With the student's advancement in knowledge and intellectual power, the subjects will, of course, assume a wider range. But at every stage simplicity and sincerity of utterance are worth far more, in my judgment, than all the literary or rhetorical tricks the student can be taught."

In the judgment of a decided majority there should, however, be a distinction drawn between the college and the preparatory school both in aims and in methods. Some, on the other hand, would not change the ideals or the methods except for the most advanced college classes, and some would make no concessions except to an advanced college class "made up of a very select list of picked men."

A mere summary can hardly do justice to the views expressed on this matter, and I therefore present as before a selection of the most characteristic opinions as phrased by those who hold them. We may note that emphasis is in general laid upon the importance of the early mastery of the mechanics of writing (even in such matters as the making up of manuscript), and the formation of habits of correct and clear expression. The last stage is then naturally the development and perfecting of technique so that the expression may be a spontaneous and accurate transcript of the thought. Writing produced at this stage may in favorable instances possess both force and grace and display genuine literary quality.

(*a*) "When a boy develops literary talents, they should be encouraged. This will ordinarily happen only at the later stages of a boy's educational career, and therefore the teacher will not need to alter his 'ideals' much except with advanced classes. I advocate a 'difference in ideals' not because some pupils are more 'advanced' in age, but because they are different in intellectual calibre."

(*b*) "My personal experience is that until a pupil reaches college he must work mainly for clearness and correctness; and scarcely more than one Freshman in fifty passes beyond this stage. Of course, as the boy advances from the elementary school, he can do each year a little more in the way of adding interest to his writing. Literary ideals may properly be considered in an advanced elective course."

(*c*) "Decidedly, yes. Consider the preposterous assumption—that teachers in elementary schools or teachers generally *could* teach the art of writing with literary force and grace in any considerable degree. They will probably go as far in that direction as their natural capacity leads them, and I should tremble for the result of a conscious attempt at anything more.

"We distinguish *between the advanced* classes in college, setting one apart for confessedly literary work and putting it into the hands of one who is competent in literary judgment."

(*d*) "The literary ideal must be in the background always until perhaps in the later of the latest stages of a pupil's training; but always present, and coming more and more to the front as the pupil goes on. I should not care to emphasize the literary aspects of composition till after the Freshman year in college, nor indeed to have a student think of his work as the production of literature till after that time; before that I should reckon it enough if the expression were always regarded and studied as the most appropriate expression of the thought.

That is I should wish the 'literary' ideal to be in the mind of the teacher, not that of the pupil; if the pupil's work does come to show literary promise, there will be plenty of time to inform him. In college classes after the Freshman year, the student may come to discover that the fit expression of worthy thought is literature, and may study it as literature, beginning with what is called the literature of thought, and ending with what is called the literature of feeling; always provided that he is not misled into thinking that as the result of his college training he will be a certified literary artist, that he is never allowed to forget that whatever taste and skill he may possess must be refined and perfected by years of effort."

(e) "The distinctions in the teaching of composition in the different stages of education rest finally on the ability of students to grasp greater masses of fact and to perceive more clearly and intimately the relations between them. Doubtless, from a technical point of view, correctness in grammatical rules and ordinary rhetorical precepts should have a comparatively large place in the early stages than the later; in these more general principles of composition and style may receive chief emphasis."

(f) "In the elementary school the teacher must surely have to aim chiefly at mere clearness and correctness; in the secondary school, some more conscious and definitie aim at the cultivation of 'taste' in composition (as well as in speech) should constitute a modification of the method of the elementary school; in the college the aim should be to set forth the whole truth of the matter, that the employment of language is an art. The practical and the artistic uses of the art may then be fully defined. No teacher will allow the fundamental principles of clearness and correctness to be neglected when striving to secure something in the way of 'force and grace.' The ultimate aim of the entire course should be the cultivation of *good taste*."

(g) "In the primary school the aim of the teacher should be *exclusively* to train the pupil to express his thoughts clearly and correctly. It will not often be the case that pupils of this grade will 'think literary thoughts' of any higher grade than the juvenile type, but such thoughts should be well expressed, if expressed at all; quite as much as 'ordinary' ones.

"When the pupil has reached the high-school grade he will in most cases begin to have 'literary thoughts'; generally not his own, but borrowed from his reading. It is important that he should be trained to express these thoughts *clearly* and *correctly*, if he uses them in his theme writing; as for the higher literary qualities of *force, harmony*, etc., I can see no reason why they should not have proper attention, but not at the expense of time needed for the other purpose.

"In the college I would have only literary composition. It seems to me supremely absurd to refuse to admit a pupil to college who commits errors in translation and grammar in his Latin or French and yet admit him without the ability to *read, write,* and *speak* the English language with clearness and correctness. The college should not be required to teach theme writing, with attention to such matters as punctuation, capitals, grammar, etc., any more than it should maintain a required elementary course in mathematics in order to assure itself that all the newcomers have mastered the multiplication table."

(*h*) "To all the subdivisions of this question I should be inclined to answer, yes. Premising that my inexperience with elementary and secondary schools may lead me to pronounce on the matter as I should perhaps not hold by in actual teaching therein, I would say: In the elementary school the pupil's interest, observing power, imagination, should be roused, and the subjects and exercises should have this in view, grammatical and minutely verbal matters being so incidental as not to check the observing and recording current of the pupil's mind. In secondary schools grammatical drill, choice of words, sentences, phrasing, and the like, should be the predominant matter, not on the score that these are best liked there, but because there is no other place and time so suitable to acquire them. We cannot always consult a pupil's mere likes and dislikes. In college I *have* to distinguish between beginning and advanced classes, partly because, to begin with, I have to bring considerable work left over from secondary schools up to date, and partly because it is inexpedient to enter upon the higher matters of rhetoric without making sure of the practical matters on which these are founded. For beginning classes I go over the elements of style—words, phrasing, figures, sentences, paragraphs, but in a way which the ordinary secondary school does not do, namely, as elements in literary work, and with the higher qualities of these recognized along with the practical. For advanced classes the more distinctively literary qualities come more to the front, and the finishing processes of the whole composition and of the literary types."

(*i*) "The too early attempt to produce literature stands directly in the way of clear and correct writing about ordinary matters. If the imagination of the elementary or secondary schoolboy is subjected to the forcing process, the results obtained are at the expense of observation, memory, and common sense. I should require of the pupil of the lower grades accurate relation of what he has seen, heard, read, or thought. If he be given to imaginative thinking and expression, I should not discourage him, in case he knew the difference between fact and fiction. If he be not so given, I should not encourage him to be a poet. The sooner we learn two things, the better for our much 'be-doctored' teaching of English: *First,* that we are paid by authorities of state and town to make not poets but citizens out of our pupils; *Second,* that all the poets the country may need will be furnished by Nature, cheaper and better without our artificial culture than with it.

"As to the distinction between classes in the university, it is based on a false assumption which also underlies the question of difference between elementary and secondary scholars. Since composition is the expression of individuality, the discrimination should be made not between beginning and advanced classes, but between practical and poetic individuals."

(*j*) "I would make the distinction, in a practical way. The beginning and required course in composition should afford the opportunity of testing the writing ability of members of the entering, or Freshman, class. Students who acquitted themselves creditably should not be further harassed. But no pains should be spared in developing, studying, and helping the pathological cases, wherever such cases were not absolutely hopeless. A beginning course extending over the entire four years of the college course might, in some instances, be deemed advisable. Advanced classes should, in my opinion, be elective.

"I would not advocate any invidious parting of the sheep from the goats. I would only raise this question: Is it not true that students who really need a good deal of special training in composition, and who often present cases interesting to study, are in too many instances allowed to escape uncured; whereas students who have run the gauntlet of the College Entrance Requirements in English with distinction, and in whom some zest for literature and composition has survived, are in too many instances kept on a diet of elementary husks, as if their previous training were something to be discredited?"

The third question is in a measure answered by the discussion of the two preceding questions. But a few words further may not be out of place. As regards the vague and somewhat pretentious phrase, "alien to the genius of the nation," the Pedagogical Section is unwilling to claim "veritable authorship." But the phrase, vague as it is, does suggest the practical question whether, in view of the sort of pupils to be found in the ordinary school, it is wise to emphasize the literary side of expression with a conscious aim at literary effect, and to organize the classes in composition into what may by courtesy be called associations of young American authors.

Having thus in a measure cleared the skirts of the Pedagogical Section, I may again give place to those whose opinions have been really asked for.

(*a*) "I think the last sentence in the quotation from the *Academy* is a good illustration of the inability of the writer to think clearly, and (in consequence) to express his thought clearly. In literary matters various nations have various *habits*, but I am at a loss to know what can be meant by the '*genius* of the nation,' expressed in its literature, any more than in its dress or its food and drink.

Genius, if my notion of the meaning of the word is right, belongs to the *individual,* and if he gets from his school training the power to express his thoughts clearly and correctly, his literary genius will probably be able to get along. But not one pupil in twenty will ever produce anything that can be called literature, while the mastery of a clear and correct expression of one's thoughts is of the highest value to all.

"Let me add that what I have said is not meant for the teacher of English Composition alone. In every recitation of the pupil, especially in translation, the teacher should use every means to train him in the clear and forcible use of his mother-tongue."

(*b*) "The writer in the *Academy* has not had in mind the fundamental facts, that language is a conventional institution, and its use an art. It never was contrary to the genius of any nation to use its language with 'literary' effect."

(*c*) "Taking literally the two statements quoted in the circular, I should agree with the former and disagree with the latter; that is, my answer to question three would be in the affirmative. But regarding the spirit of each statement, my answer would be, as I have indicated above, in the negative. Nothing is 'alien to the genius of this nation,' I believe, that seeks to develop in any individual, even in a schoolboy, some sense of the meaning and value of the ordinary matters of life, a sense which probably reaches its highest and most delicate development in the perception and appreciation of those values which we call literary values."

(*d*) "If to think clearly, to experience the appeal of beauty, to respond to high ideals, is 'alien to the genius of this nation,' why should we attempt to teach anything?

"The boy that, unaided, constructs a wheelbarrow is a 'maker,' a poet. The boy that, unaided, joins two sentences together is an author in embryo."

(*e*) "I do not see how the thing you mention is 'alien to the genius of this nation.' In fact, where can we draw the line, in anything above a business letter or agricultural report, in such way as to include the grammatical qualities and exclude 'force and grace'? If students do not come to see, in our schools and colleges, that literary force and grace are *practical,* serve a matter-of-fact purpose, as applied to their proper subjects, where can they come to see it? A college course is a culture course; if it isn't, then our country has none."

To some of these opinions are opposed the emphatic negatives of more than one of the best-known teachers of English in the country, and, significantly enough, of those men also who hold a recognized place among American men of letters. I cite first the view of the editor of one of the foremost American dailies that can point to a past with literary traditions:

"To teach the schoolboy to think literary thoughts is a sheer impossibility, and to tell him that he is undertaking veritable authorship is to lie to him unblushingly. I speak with feeling, because a considerable part of my life is given up to people who have far more ability than the average schoolboy, and who are laboring under the delusion that they are competent to undertake veritable authorship."

Says one of our leading men of letters: "Schoolboys can't think literary thoughts." To try to teach them to do so "is simply impossible. To pretend that they can, leads to sham." To lead them to suppose that in their themes they are undertaking veritable authorship, therefore, "seems very dangerous, because misleading."

More than one college teacher thinks that the attitude of veritable authorship is unwise because, as one puts the matter, "it is alien to the genius of the schoolboy, and to the principles of common sense. In this answer I accept the phrase 'literary force and grace,' at its intended value. I think boys can be taught to write with force and grace, but I think it is useless to try to teach them to write 'literary' prose or poetry."

Another briefly remarks: "It stands to reason that it is alien to the common sense of any nation to begin with *Chartreuse* instead of *soup*."

Equally emphatic are the two following:

(*a*) "It is not 'alien to the genius' of this nation, in *particular*, 'to think literary thoughts and write them down with literary force and grace'; it is akin to the genius of every nation. The *folk* will never have literary thoughts or literary expression.

"Our education is for large bodies of persons. The educated classes need some gift of expression, some training in the devices for securing clearness, force, and a moderate amount of use; above all, for securing order and method in what they write.

"How many of our college students, do you guess, have even this humble gift? Not one in ten, I should say. Why? Because school and college fail to convey the lesson that writing is part of the *business* of life, the genuine expression of what the writer really thinks and feels. Teachers and professors suffer their students to drift into the notion that writing is merely something that must be done for a 'pass'; get *through* and you are all right.

"But writing 'business' papers, whether in science, or in history, or in literature even, is not 'veritable authorship.' My conception of authorship is something far higher, something of an altogether different order. I am unable to define it, but I know it when it comes across my path.

"To teach 'authorship' to the ordinary mortal is mere waste of time upon the impossible. Going farther, I would say that we can't teach 'authorship,' even to the gifted mortal. We can teach him and his less favored brother how to outline his subject, how to frame respectable sentences and paragraphs. *There we must stop*. To attempt more is to do more harm than good. When one has learned from his teacher the ordinary routine of expression, one can only turn to the world at large, learn its wants, and try his hand at meeting them. Success in that is 'authorship,' whether in literature, in history, in philosophy, in science. Nothing else can be authorship."

(*b*) "The purpose of the schools, it seems to me, should be to prepare boys and girls, or young men and young women, for life; and life in this country is, in the main, eminently practical. It is true that it may be argued that the ability to 'think literary thoughts and to write them down with literary force and grace,' may not be unpractical, but the large majority of those whom we teach in the schools will not be called upon to do these things, and if they were, would not find that they have the ability to do them. Our chief purpose as teachers, then, I believe, should be to prepare students to meet the actual conditions which will confront them after they are out of college, and these are mainly practical.

"I may say in addition to the rather brief replies which I have given to the three questions, that my attitude toward this subject has almost completely changed in the ten or twelve years during which I have been engaged in teaching English composition. At first I felt strongly that it was the business of the teacher of composition to lead the young, or the older, to 'think literary thoughts and to write them down with literary force and grace,' and I expended all my energies to accomplish this end. My efforts were very satisfactory to me until I discovered that the people whom I had taught to write so easily and gracefully, and as it seemed to me effectively, were quite unable to express the ordinary ideas of life, either with clearness or force. I have gradually grown to believe that as they express their thoughts upon ordinary matters which every day concern them, as they work primarily for correctness and clearness, they are better prepared in time for real authorship, and it is because of this experience that I believe as I do."

After this presentation of representative opinions on the question suggested by the two quotations, there can be little doubt that conflicting ideals, both in aims and methods, are firmly held by many of the leading teachers of English throughout the country. More than one passage, however, in the contributions to this discussion would seem to show that in some cases the differences are not irreconcilable, for there is general agreement that the less attractive, formal side of the art must be thoroughly taught, as well as matters that are delightful and stimulating. It is probable, too, that all would urge the importance of sincere and natural expression from the beginning, and the avoidance of anything like posing, or whatever is characteristic of the literary prig. But, in the interests of educational theory and practice, it is to be hoped that the questions here raised will not be dropped, either here or elsewhere, until they have been discussed with the thoroughness that their importance demands.

The report was discussed by Professors H. E. Shepherd, E. E. Hale, F. N. Scott, E. H. Magill, and J. W. Bright.

Karl Young
"The Organization of a Course in Freshman English"
English Journal 4 (1915)

  (For biography of Young, see chap. 6, p. 477; for Scott, see above, p. 177.) This article charts, in abbreviated form, a dispute about composition programs between two very important figures in English studies, Karl Young (MLA president, 1940), representing the younger generation, and Fred Newton Scott (MLA president, 1907), representing the older. English Journal prints an "abstract" of Young's paper from the 1914 NCTE convention and a "digest" of Scott's response; the two representatives of great midwestern universities were debating the possibilities of the first-year writing course. Young, Shakespeare scholar and medievalist, coauthor of three composition readers, argues for what seems like a rigid, soulless course based on mass-production models, the standard composition program that Warner Taylor's survey shows had spread throughout the nation by the 1920s (see chap. 7, p. 545). Scott, always a champion of new thinking, argues for a broader conception of success in composition studies, the inclusion of a wider range of literature than just essays, and for an organic conception of thinking and writing. Though we can regret that we only have the sketchiest outline of a floor debate, these two English Journal pages provide a neat summary of competing schools of thought within two of America's most important composition programs.

THE PAPER MERELY DESCRIBES THE ACTUAL ORGANIZATION OF SUCH a course at the University of Wisconsin. The number of students is about eleven hundred. All students are subjected to an entrance test (see *Bulle-*

tin of the University of Wisconsin, No. 599). The instructional staff includes
all grades, from full professor to instructor. No theme-readers are employed. An instructor whose work is confined to this course teaches three
sections of twenty-five students each. Each section meets three times a
week, and each student writes about five hundred words a week. The
content of the course is indicated in a printed calendar. The work of the
first semester aims primarily at securing grammatical correctness and the
orderly arrangement of simple expositions. The work of the second semester is concerned primarily with the analysis of thought in substantial
essays, and with the writing of nine long expository themes dealing with
ideas. Supervision is accomplished through inspections by the chairman
of the course, and through conferences of instructors.

The following topics need investigation: 1. The introduction of oral
composition in the freshman course; 2. Supervision of the student's
writing in his third and fourth years; 3. Co-operation with other departments; 4. Relations with high-school teachers in regard to the efficiency
of high-school training in composition.

The following is a digest of the discussion of the subject by Fred N.
Scott, of the University of Michigan:

Success in teaching of English can be measured only by its ultimate
effects. If fifteen years later one's students have become leaders of men,
one may feel satisfied. Each teacher will have his own methods.

Referring to the thought that the older literature is becoming discredited, that it seems to be adapted to past forms of life, the speaker
observed that one may well ask whether human nature really changes.
The "conflict of life" as portrayed by Sophocles has not been surpassed.
Moreover, the older literature has been tested by time and hence it is
easier to use in teaching.

Freshman English is not bankrupt. The quality of work done now is
better than formerly. There are more people in the classes; hence more
mediocre ones.

The theory that ideas must come before expression, which has been
urged much of late in regard to courses in English composition, rests on
a false psychology. [Lane Cooper was one critic who used this terminol-
ogy. See chap. 4, p. 259.—ED.] Ideas and form seem to be born together. Any separation is alien to natural processes of thinking. When

idea comes before form the result is plagiarism; when form exists without the idea the result is delirium.

To urge that one can teach composition dealing with subjects like engineering, mathematics, and economics only when one knows these subjects as an expert is like declaring that one must not say, "It's a fine day," unless one has studied the law of storms. The teacher must take the student as he is and build up his personality.

4

The Attack on the Harvard Program, 1890–1917

THE HARVARD SYSTEM ALARMED MANY ENGLISH PRO-
fessors at other colleges. Here was America's oldest, most prestigious
university devoting the bulk of its English faculty's time to teaching
writing at all levels, assigning endless themes, and asking students to
write about what interested them. Chapter 3 demonstrated how elements of the Harvard program spread widely through American colleges
and universities. Chapter 4 shows how Harvard's program soon attracted
a good number of opponents who attacked it for a variety of reasons.
Some opponents were among the many literature professors who wanted
to devote class time to plays and poems, not themes. Others had a bent
for research and were wary of anything that would impinge on their
time, as reading themes surely did. (Harvard's Francis James Child was
almost lured away to Johns Hopkins in 1876 by the promise of not
reading any more student themes; Harvard kept him by freeing him
from theme grading and promising that he could devote full time to
literature.)

But there were many critics who claimed that the Harvard method of
pure composition teaching, without an "academic" subject matter, was
simply impossible, that it just wasn't effective enough to repay all the
time and energy spent on theme correcting. Some of these opponents
(William Lyon Phelps of Yale, for instance) thought that intelligent
students could pick up writing on their own or through other courses.
Many critics, however, claimed that writing needed a subject matter,
and the most appropriate one was English literature. The development of
an English literature-based composition course had begun with Thomas
Lounsbury's Yale course in 1870. According to Lounsbury's wife, "college professors from all parts of the country used to visit" his classes "to

see how he did it" (Cross 112). By 1900 such courses had become highly popular. The literature component varied widely, from great essays selected for their rhetorical effectiveness to poems and plays selected for their artistry. And a competing type of literature-based program, the ideas course, offered essays but stressed what instructors called their "thought value," that is, the structure of their arguments, their "ideas."

Opposed to these literature-based courses was a "pure" or "direct" composition course that emphasized the writer in his or her social relationships, what James Berlin terms a "rhetoric of public discourse" (*Rhetoric* 35–36), rather than the issues of style and correctness that came to dominate the Harvard program. This development persisted through the years 1875–1925, prominent mostly through the work of Fred Newton Scott, Joseph Villiers Denney of Ohio State, and Gertrude Buck of Vassar, all of whom argued for making theme assignments reflect students' personal experience. Another group of writing instructors wanted a wider range of materials; many taught from texts that included a mix of classics, newspaper and magazine journalism, and even student essays. Courses that employed such readings were much less likely to include literature for its own sake, nor did they emphasize the writer's desire for self expression. (See Young and Young, chap. 6, p. 477.)

The critics collected here are a highly varied lot; most refer to each other's work, but they came from quite different backgrounds and represented a great variety of approaches to composition. What united them was their search for an alternative to the Harvard system and, for most, a distaste for research and scholarship on the German model. Instead, some openly favored a competing (if somewhat outdated) university model, the English, which for many Americans held out the promise that a first rate university or collegiate education could still stress character formation instead of specialized scholarship. (Ironically, this infatuation with the traditional side of the British university took place at the very time when I. A. Richards was revolutionizing English studies at Cambridge University.)

This chapter includes thoughtful early-twentieth-century overviews of composition instruction by two opponents of the Harvard program, Gertrude Buck of Vassar writing in 1901 and Frank Aydelotte, then of MIT, writing in 1917. In between it supplies some of the criticism of the Harvard program along with critics' suggestions for improvement. Most of these attacks received no reply; Harvard at this time, 1910–1915, was scaling back its system, and the only senior faculty involved in composition were those with a special interest in collegiate as opposed to university education, teachers rather than researchers. When they passed from the scene, Harvard's great experiment in composition would be over, and all that remained would be a large first-year writing program staffed by part-time instructors and graduate fellows.

"Two Ways of Teaching English"
Century Magazine 51 (1896)

*ⅇ*ᴗ *This brief, anonymous article embodies an elite perspective that looks down both on preoccupation with a teaching methodology and on writing instruction through practice. The two erroneous ways of the title are: "exalting pedagogical method at the expense of the teacher's personality" and "placing mere training in composition superior to familiarity with good literature." The second is a direct attack on the Harvard method of theme teaching. This article's methods (and even its references) were commonplaces of the times, though this is an extreme example. Basically the author blames the poor state of writing in America on ineffective teaching methods in writing courses. The anonymous author's solution is to teach writing through literature in the secondary schools. William Lyon Phelps's piece below (287–91) uses some of the same arguments and supplies more information about the "experiment" referred to, the comparison of two sets of papers. This article was also the basis for the MLA's 1902 discussion of composition (see chap. 3, p. 202). (For a good bibliography of the debate about writing instruction in the popular press during the 1890s see Cmiel, p. 320, n. 10.)*

Tʜᴇʀᴇ ᴀʀᴇ ғᴇᴡ ʜᴀʀsʜᴇʀ ᴀɴᴅ ᴍᴏʀᴇ ᴍᴇʟᴀɴᴄʜᴏʟʏ ᴄᴏɴᴛʀᴀsᴛs observable at present than that between the training of French and of American youth in the knowledge of their respective literatures, and between the consequent ways of using language which the public men of the two countries display. In France boys are taught three things of which American school students are mainly ignorant: the political history of their country, the general outline of their literature, and the exact niceties of their vernacular. A Yale or Harvard freshman may know the history of Greece superficially, but he knows it better than the history of England or of the United States; his knowledge of Homer, Vergil, Plato, and Caesar may be unscholarly, but it is more trustworthy than his knowledge of Shakspere, Milton, and Swift; and whatever the result of his labors may show, he has spent far more time on his Greek and Latin sentences than on his English. Fortunately, public sentiment has become so thoroughly aroused on this subject that just now there is no more interesting educational question than the teaching of English. Recent reports show that the experts are all agreed on the diagnosis; as to the remedy we naturally find the customary divergence.

Two dangers loom up in the path of reform. First, that of exalting pedagogical method at the expense of the teacher's personality; second, that of placing mere training in composition superior to familiarity with good literature. The country is suffering at present from an acute attack of pedagogical psychology in its most malignant form; so that some zealous teachers spend more time on the study of method than on two things vastly more important—their specialty and human nature. Nothing is more vicious than to suppose that a man with a "psycho-pedagogical" method can teach either school or college students without a sympathetic and personal knowledge of his pupils. Much of the popular pedagogy of to-day is all moonshine, because the natural-born teacher (and there are many such) does not need so elaborate an apparatus, and the pedagogue who has no natural gift is deluded into thinking that this new-fangled machinery of soul-development is all that is required. There are really only two things the successful teacher needs to have— knowledge of his subject-matter and knowledge of his pupils. The first of these can be gained only by study, the second only by experience. The man who has never been a real child himself cannot effectively teach children; and he who does not know by experience the warm-hearted, exuberant gaiety of school and college boys cannot successfully teach them. Furthermore, the teacher who spends more time on the method of teaching literature than on literature itself is sure to come to grief. Greatest of all forces is the personality of the instructor: nothing in teaching is so effective as this; nothing is so instantly recognized and responded to by pupils; and nothing is more neglected by those who insist that teaching is a science rather than an art. After hearing a convention of very serious pedagogues discuss educational methods, in which they use all sorts of technical phraseology, one feels like applying Gladstone's cablegram, "Only common sense required."

The second danger which threatens the progress of reform is the supposition, very generally accepted in some high circles, that the pupil, in order to write good English, may profitably neglect literature, if only he steadily write compositions. We are told that the way to become a good writer is to write; this sounds plausible, like many other pretty sayings equally remote from fact. No one thinks that the way to become a good medical practitioner is to practise; that is the method of quacks. The best way, indeed, to become a good writer is to be born of the right sort of parents; this fundamental step having been unaccountably neglected by many children, the instructor has to do what he can with second- or third-class material. Now a wide reader is usually a correct writer; and he has reached the goal in the most delightful manner, without feeling the penalty of Adam. What teacher ever found in his classes a boy who knew his Bible, who enjoyed Shakspere, and who loved Scott, yet who, with this outfit, wrote illiterate compositions? This youth writes well principally because he has something to say, for reading maketh a full man; and he knows what correct writing is in the same way that he knows his friends—by intimate acquaintance. No amount of mere grammatical and rhetorical training, nor even of constant practice in the art of composition, can attain the result reached by the child who reads good books because he loves to read them. We would not take the extreme position taken by some, that all practice in theme-writing is time thrown away; but after a costly experience of the drudgery that composition work forces on teacher and pupil, we would say emphatically that there is no educational method at present that involves so enormous an outlay of time, energy, and money, with so correspondingly small a result. To neglect the teaching of literature for the teaching of composition, or to assert that the second is the more important, is like showing a hungry man how to work his jaws instead of giving him something to eat. In order to support this with evidence, let us take the experience of a specialist who investigated the question by reading many hundred sophomore compositions in two of our leading colleges, where the natural capacity and previous training of the students were fairly equal. In one college every freshman wrote themes steadily through the year, with an accompaniment of sound instruction in rhetorical principles; in the other college every freshman studied Shakspere, with absolutely no training in rhetoric and with no practice in composition. A comparison of the themes written in their sophomore year by these students showed that technically the two were fully on a par. That is weighty and most significant testimony.

If the teachers of English in secondary schools were people of real culture themselves, who both knew and loved literature, who tried to make it attractive to their pupils, and who were given a sufficient time-allotment to read a number of standard books with their classes, the composition question would largely take care of itself. Mere training in theme-writing can never take the place of the acquisition of ideas, and the boy who thinks interesting thoughts will usually write not only more attractively, but more correctly, than the one who has worked tread-mill fashion in sentence and paragraph architecture. The difference in the teacher's happiness, vitality, and consequent effectiveness is too obvious to mention.

Gertrude Buck
"Recent Tendencies in the Teaching of English Composition"
***Educational Review* 22 (1901)**

   Buck (1871–1922) graduated from the University of Michigan in 1894 and in 1898 was Fred Newton Scott's first rhetoric Ph.D. there; her dissertation was published in Scott's series Studies in Language and Literature. *Buck spent her career at Vassar, beginning in 1897 by specializing in composition and rhetoric, with critical and theoretical publications in the field as well as textbooks, which she wrote in collaboration with others, including Scott, Scott's sister Harriet, and Buck's Vassar colleague Elisabeth Woodbridge. Toward the end of her career she turned to literary topics but never lost her interest in connecting her teaching to its social and cultural context. Her last book,* The Social Criticism of Literature, *appeared in 1916.*

THE RECENT HISTORY OF ENGLISH COMPOSITION-TEACHING SEEMS at first glance made up of several distinct movements. Of these the revolt against the domination of the student's writing by formal rhetorical precepts was earliest and most conspicuous. Scarcely less marked, however, tho somewhat later in time, have been the tendencies to derive subjects for writing from the student's own experience, rather than from sources foreign to his knowledge or interest; to direct his writing toward some real audience; and, finally, to criticise his writing somewhat informally, in terms of the ultimate end of discourse, rather than by the direct application to it of prescriptive rules for composition.

Stated thus, no particular connection appears among these various movements. They are merely so many distinct efforts to better the teaching of English composition in our schools. Less superficially regarded, however, their common basis appears. Each aims at securing better writing from the student by furnishing more natural conditions for that writing. As early even as the time of Whately, "The cramped, meager, and feeble character of most of such essays, etc., as are avowedly composed according to the rules of any system"[1] of technical rhetoric, was noted, and the further observation made that "On the real occasions of after life (I mean when the object proposed is, not to fill up a sheet, a book, or an hour, but to communicate his thoughts to convince or persuade),—on these real occasions, he [the student] will find that he writes both better, and with more facility, than on the artificial occasion, as it may be called, of composing a declamation." From this dual discovery, so frequently made by the practical teacher of composition, the inference is plain. If the student writes both better and more easily when he has a real occasion for writing than when he composes an exercise to exemplify some rule for composition previously enjoined upon him, then let the teacher, so far as possible, replace this artificial situation by natural conditions for writing.

This general principle is rightly regarded as the foundation of our modern system of composition-teaching, as distinguished from the earlier teaching of formal rhetoric; but the practical problem, "How can natural conditions of writing be substituted in the schoolroom for artificial?" has found various answers. The first of these was inevitably negative; abolish all writing by rule.[2] Nowhere outside of composition classes does one write to conform with a certain rhetorical law. The condition is absurd. No wonder the student on whom it is imposed writes painfully and pretentiously; no wonder that continued exercises of this sort form "a habit of stringing together empty commonplaces and vapid declamations,—of multiplying words and spreading out the matter thin,—of composing in a stiff, artificial, and frigid manner."[3] No real literature, no genuine writing of any kind, was ever fashioned to the pattern of a rule. Let us, then, cast off the yoke of formal rhetoric, said the progressive teachers of an earlier decade. Let the student only write; the oftener the better. It is by writing that writing is learned. The process itself, if only it be normally conditioned, can work out its own perfection. And the first step toward securing normal conditions is to dispense with hampering rules.

Thus far the first reformers of the ancient régime. The difficulty in carrying out their program to its logical end was one quite inevitable at that stage in the development of the theory of composition-teaching. The deliberate setting of a rule as a guide for writing could indeed be avoided, but so soon as the student became aware that his composition was later to be criticised by this rule, the knowledge could not but condition to some extent his present writing. He was not yet wholly emancipated from the "artificial condition." And even the boldest advocates of the "composition-without-rules" theory hesitated to dispense with all criticism, since it was plain that in this case every act of writing (and these acts were by hypothesis to be as frequent as possible) must only cut more deeply the grooves of such bad habits as negligence or the false methods of the old system had already worn. The necessity for criticism, and the lack of any other method of criticism than that of testing the writing by accepted rhetorical canons, made it impossible, therefore, at this stage for the student to achieve perfect freedom from any thought of rules during the process of composition. A long step had, however, been taken toward the substitution of natural for artificial conditions in writing, and the next movement in this direction had become possible.

This next movement might easily have been foretold—so logically inevitable was it. After doing away with the artificial motive for writing, that of exemplifying certain rules of discourse, it became necessary to substitute a real motive. The first that suggested itself was naturally that which impels one to write on any "genuine occasion"—the motive of having something to say which another person wishes or needs to hear. The acceptance of this motive as essential to any normal process of communication both initiated and justified the movements in composition-teaching which immediately succeeded it; namely, the derivation of subjects for writing from the student's own experience and the direction of his writing toward a definite audience. Upon subjects remote from his own experience or interests the student had no natural impulse to write. We are often reminded that the average schoolboy has nothing to say to anybody about "Pereunt et imputantur," "The vice of ambition" or "Autumn thoughts."4 If left to himself, he would never voluntarily write a word on such a subject. Occasion would be wanting, since no observation or thought of his own presses for utterance, nor does any known interest on the part of another person in his ideas (if he had them) call forth their expression. Yet every schoolboy has interests, if one but knew them—interests which, however trivial they may be in the teacher's eyes, are for him and to his spiritual peers worth communicating. There is a real demand somewhere for the experiences which he is eager to impart. And until this supply and this demand are brought into relations with each other, there can be no genuine writing. That the teacher's function is that of the middleman in this process of communicating ideas is a conviction clearly implied in the doctrines that the student should write for a definite audience and upon a subject which interests both this audience and himself.5

These doctrines, tho comparatively so recent in origin, have already established themselves both in the practical teaching of composition and in the formulated theories thereof. Such opposition as they still encounter consists chiefly in the indication of certain perils into which the recent convert to them may often fall—that, for instance, of accounting subjects interesting to the student merely because they are not abstract or profound, or that of resting content with the mere naming of an audience, without regard to its interest in the writer's message or its actual relations to himself. These dangers, however, obviously spring not from the doctrines of the real audience and the real subject, but from the spirit of formalism and artificiality in writing against which those doctrines are explicitly directed. If the ultimate purpose of insisting on a real subject and a real audience be kept in view, namely, that of replacing an artificial by a genuine occasion for writing, no subject can be assigned to a student for any reason save that he has something he wishes to say about it, nor a reader designated who has no natural desire to know the thing that the writer wishes to say.

So far the outlines of this history have the perspective of a certain lapse of time, tho only of a few years. In proceeding, however, to the fourth of the recent tendencies under discussion, we confront a movement in itself appreciably more complicated, and as yet but half-conscious of its own direction or significance.

It will be remembered that the question of criticism had been left practically untouched by the previous movements to normalize the writing process of the student. Logically inconsistent as it was with these movements, the old method of criticism yet persisted for a time in the midst of them. The finished composition was estimated in terms of the formal rhetorical precepts from whose domination the writing act had but lately been freed. It soon became evident, however, that to say to the student "Write without a thought of the rules for unity, but I'll criticise your composition by them," was to demand of him the psychologically impossible. Under these circumstances he could not easily avoid thinking of the rules for unity and in effect writing to fulfill their requirements; the "artificial occasion" was restored, and the former sacrifice had become vain.

Nor did the case radically improve merely by reducing the number of rhetorical principles to which the student's writing must conform, by simplifying their phraseology or attuning it more kindly to the sensitive ear. Undoubtedly there is a real significance for the theory of composition-teaching in the practice of those professional critics who choose rather to say "Use short and simple sentences," than "Don't write such long and involved ones," and "This is a well-chosen word," than "That one is ill-chosen." Yet those who grant the palliative effect of this practice must yet recognize its failure to meet the main point of difficulty raised by the old method—the difficulty, once more, of the artificial occasion. The direct application to the student's composition of any rhetorical canon as such, however tactfully it may have been phrased, has invariably reached one result—that the student writes, consciously or unconsciously, to conform with this rule. This means, of course, that the end implied in the task assigned the student, that of sharing his own interesting experience with someone who wishes or needs to know it, has been displaced by another end, often quite unrelated to the first in the writer's mind, the end, namely, of fulfilling some injunction laid upon him by text-book, or teacher—to use figurative language, perhaps, or to alternate long with short sentences. The effect of such substitution may be briefly recalled.

In assigning a task in composition to the student, we have insisted, be it remembered, on a real occasion for his writing. He is not composing an essay to convince the teacher that he can observe all the laws of rhetoric which he has so far studied, but attempts to convey to the mind of a friend something which that friend is for some reason interested to know. If, therefore, it occurs to him at all to question his own performance of this task, he will naturally do so in terms of the end which he has proposed to himself. He will ask of himself, not "Are there enough figures of speech to satisfy the teacher?" "Have I written short sentences interspersed with long ones, as the text-book says to do?" "Did I make correct use of the method of obverse iteration?" but rather, "Have I told the thing so that Fred or Jim will know just how it happened?" "Will he see it as I did?" "Will he understand what I mean?" Even if thoroly indoctrinated with rhetorical formulae, the average student is conscious of no particular desire to "produce an effect of vivacity" on some unspecified and unimagined audience. He feels no insatiable longing to compose a paragraph which shall have unity, coherence, and proportion. Hence, when his work is estimated by these alien standards, he feels much as would any intelligent youth to whom, when making a kite, some insane elder should remark in passing—"That will never spin in the world." The reply, "Well, who wants it to? This isn't a top!" embodies emotions of mingled contempt, derision, and indignation no more acute than the unexpressed sensations of many a schoolboy reading the penciled criticisms on his returned theme.

But if the rhetorical standard be maintained by the teacher as the basis for criticism, that which the "real occasion" has suggested to the student's mind comes rapidly to be regarded by him as a mere pretense, and consequently to be ignored in his writing. His compositions are fashioned, so far as possible, with a view to sustaining the teacher's peculiar tests. Not that he sees any reason in them, but, being the teacher's, a due regard for marks constrains him. This perfunctory and external conformity is probably far from satisfying his task-master, who feels that the real occasion has here proved itself a failure; but surely this is not the student's fault. He is doing his best to fulfill all requirements, so far as he understands them, and the woodenly vacuous result should, he feels, be highly approved by his over-lord, for there is not a loose sentence in it!—or perhaps a mixed metaphor, if this chance to be the fault for which his last production fell under condemnation. Such are the cross-purposes inevitably consequent upon the attempt to pour the new wine of the genuine occasion into the old bottles of formal criticism.

Not finally convinced of the futility of this attempt, but keenly alive to the danger of allowing the rhetorical standard to coexist independently with the practical, and hence ultimately to dominate it in the student's mind, some ingenious teachers have undertaken to reconcile the two by translating the former into terms of the latter. Thus the student, altho holding in mind the injunction to use concrete words, shall yet understand that he is to do this, not finally because the text-book enjoins it, but because only by so doing can he succeed in flashing before the eyes of his reader the picture he himself has once seen.

There is no doubt that many of the accredited rhetorical precepts may be interpreted in this way, with reference to the normal writing process whence originally they were derived. And when this interpreta-tion has been successfully made, the printed rule forthwith ceases to be merely the arbitrary enactment of some unknown authority and gains for the student a real meaning in terms of the end which his writing seeks. He must, indeed, still write to conform with a certain requirement made by his text-book, but no longer with a requirement which is for him intellectually a *cul-de-sac*. It has now an outlet, leading him to a further end, that of the writing process itself. For the time, at least, conformity with the rhetorical law has taken its right position toward the ultimate end of communication, as a means thereto. In aiming at the means, the student's attention may be for an instant withdrawn from the final end of his spontaneous writing, namely, the communication of a certain content to the mind of another person, yet returns to it again thru the acknowl-edged relation of the means to this end.

This method of reconciling the proximate with the ultimate stan-dards for criticism assuredly marks an advance upon that crude system which allows mere conformity with rhetorical canons, as such, to seem to the student the end of his writing. Its difficulties are, however, consider-able. It requires at least a fair amount of psychological training, as well as native acuteness of mind, to perceive in all cases the exact relation between the somewhat abstract formulae of the text-book and the practi-cal aim of discourse; hence, some not unskillful teachers have abandoned the undertaking as impracticable. Furthermore, the critics of the method have not failed to point out its tendency to revert by imperceptible degrees to the more primitive type. Little by little, they assert, the rhetorical standard comes in the student's mind to take on, as before, an independent existence. Satisfied that it can be translated into terms of the ultimate end of the writing process, the student ceases thus to translate it except on explicit demand of the teacher. As a matter of fact he again writes to use concrete terms, instead of using concrete terms in order to write—that is, the real occasion has once more been displaced by the artificial.

Recognition of the failure of this method has perhaps closed the long list of attempts to tinker the old formal criticism into a practical consistency with the new theory of composition-teaching. Henceforth it became clearly evident that one of three courses must be followed: to turn back the previous movements to normalize the writing process, and restore the ancient order of composition-by-rules, in which case criticism-by-rules could logically be retained; or, rejecting formal criticism under all its disguises, and unable to conceive any other effective method, to discard all criticism, trusting to the normally conditioned writing process, unaided, to develop ultimately its highest efficiency; or, finally, to displace formal criticism by a method which should be both logically and practically consistent with the free and natural act of writing.

The first of these proposed courses has been mentioned only to exhaust the theoretic possibilities. While some few individuals may have solved the problem for themselves in this way, a general reversion to the old order has long been almost as inconceivable as the restoration of pre-laboratory methods in the teaching of natural science.

Nor has the second program met with general acceptance. So far as I am aware, there has been, even in these latter days, no visible tendency among teachers of composition to abolish entirely the article of criticism.[6] Against this last sacrifice for the freedom of the writing process practical considerations have always successfully protested. Granting that the normal act of writing has within itself the all-sufficient germ of its ultimate perfection, it is still maintained that such gradual, unassisted evolution requires a period of time far exceeding that set aside for the teaching of English in our schools or colleges; and further, that the entire hypothesis can very rarely be fulfilled, since, after the first year of a child's school life, composition has all but invariably become to him an artificial rule-regarding process, hence one has to deal not with the normal writing act which needs development only, but with an unnatural, perverted function which cannot develop rightly until it first has been restored to health.

Theoretically, also, criticism is commonly held essential to the highest efficiency of the writing act, however natural, even instinctive, we may allow that act in its origin to be. Without its bumps and falls— assuredly an objective criticism of its methods of locomotion—the child would hardly learn to walk. For psychology, as well as for ethics, it has become a truism that every intelligent act is in its freedom responsible—

not, indeed, to an arbitrary rule, externally imposed, but to the inner law of its own nature, as defined by the end it seeks to reach. From its success or failure in reaching this end arises that practical criticism thru which alone it gradually gains a higher and yet higher efficiency. Such criticism, then, is essential to the intelligent act of writing.

The third program[7] has thus been reached by successive rejections of the other two. Those teachers who have been forced to it, along this path or another, found its larger outlines already sketched for them. The genuine occasion for writing, like that for the child's walking, furnishes its own practical standard for criticism. Did I succeed in reproducing my experience exactly in my friend's mind? Did he receive from me the sensation I had previously felt? Did he see each event as it had passed before my eyes? Did he think my thought after me? Did he reach my conclusion as I had earlier reached it? Questions such as these furnish the starting point for all that new order of criticism which is held by its advocates to be both practically and theoretically consistent with genuine writing. The more objective and impersonal the answers given to these questions, the more likely is the criticism to be vital—the student's judgment of his own writing, not the teacher's externally imposed estimate of it. Hence the devices of some ingenious teachers[8] for returning directly to the writer, for comparison with the original experience, the experience which he has actually transmitted to the reader's mind. For instance, some outdoor scene is described to a friend skillful with the brush, whereupon he paints for the writer a sketch of that same scene as it flashed before his eyes while reading the description. Or, a fellow-student, taking the point of view of the reader addressed, gives back to the writer in other language, and possibly in further detail, a verbal account of the image transmitted to his consciousness. Thus the writer may know of a surety whether or not his communication reached home; and, more than this, often in the process of comparison the source of its failure or success becomes evident. Here we have, it is urged, the living germ of criticism. Not technically formulated, it yet serves to render the student vitally conscious of the adequacy or inadequacy of his communication to reach its end, with at least the grosser reasons therefor, while never for an instant deflecting his eyes from the thing he is saying and the person to whom he says it—those primary elements in the genuine occasion for writing.

That such criticism, altho at present but a rough-and-ready practical judgment of any piece of writing, such as the reader addressed by it could instantly give, is yet the original plasm of all the finer critical judgments, and hence capable of ultimate differentiation into them, is well maintained and certainly cannot at present be disproved. That it must finally yield a body of practical formulae for conveying a given content most directly or vividly under specified conditions is unquestionable. There is, however, no immediate cause for alarm in this prospect, even to the most uncompromising anti-formalist. So long as the student discovers in reaching the end certain means most effective for reaching it, these means never having been presented to his attention as ends in themselves, nor indeed having received undue emphasis by separation from the final aim of his writing,[9] the chances of his composing to rules are slight.

We have thus traced the evolution of the function of criticism in the teaching of English composition out of its early formalism and externality, thru many fruitless experiments, half-understood failures and unrecognized successes, into its present estate, of vital participation in the development of the act of writing. This transformation is clearly a corollary of the large movement whose various aspects have been successively discussed in this paper. The trend of every recent reform in composition-teaching has been toward a responsible freedom for the process of writing—a freedom from laws apparently arbitrary and externally imposed, a responsibility to the law of its own nature as a process of communication. Thus free and thus responsible, composition becomes for the first time a normal act, capable of development practically unlimited. The initial movement has been made toward teaching the student, in any genuine sense of the words, to write.

NOTES

1. Whately, *Elements of rhetoric*, Introduction.

2. Among the influential colleges, Harvard was perhaps the first to insist upon this doctrine.

3. Again from Whately. The Introduction contains many other passages equally pertinent to present conditions and problems.

4. That these particular subjects, and others similar to them, have actually been assigned to college preparatory students during the past year, by schools otherwise respectable, is a fact attested by documentary evidence in my possession.

5. These doctrines were first practically exemplified in Scott and Denney's *Composition-rhetoric*, and later, in Lewis's *First book in writing English*. A pamphlet by Mr. J. V. Denney, *Two problems in composition-teaching* (published by J. V. Sheehan, Ann Arbor, Mich.), expounds the principles with many concrete illustrations; and an

article in the *Technology review* (Massachusetts Institute of Technology), for October, 1899, by Mr. R. G. Valentine, on "Instruction in English at the Institute," reports them in active operation in the classroom. They have, perhaps, received their completest recognition and indorsement in Scott and Denney's recently issued *Elementary English composition,* in which the art of writing is consistently treated as a social function. [For Valentine, see chap 6, p. 458.—ED.]

6. In making this statement I do not ignore such recent declarations as those of Mr. Robert Herrick (in the pamphlet entitled *Methods of teaching rhetoric,* by Scott, Foresman & Co., Chicago), and at least one other writer, to the effect that when a pupil's writing is peculiarly anæmic and artificial, it is often desirable to omit criticism entirely for a time. The intention here is very evidently not to discard criticism altogether, but merely to postpone it until the writing-process has thereby gained a freedom and vigor which can defy its paralyzing effect. The question is not between criticism and no criticism, but solely as to the time when criticism will be most advantageous—or least injurious—to the student.

7. On the way to this program some have been deflected, in the blindness of their first reaction against the old formal methods, to that naïve expression of untutored personal preference sometimes dignified by the name of criticism. "I like that description," "That story somehow didn't appeal to me," are comments which, tho scornfully tabooed in the formalist's classroom, can yet be admitted as ultimate critical judgments only by those anti-conventional teachers who fail to recognize under this mask a standard at least equal in artificiality to that which they have once rightly repudiated. Such informal comments, tempting as they are to the protestant against rigid criticism by rules, must too frequently set before the student's mind a goal no less abnormal than mere conformity with some rhetorical law—the goal, namely, of approbation from a group of auditors to whom the writing is not actually addressed. A specious habit of writing "to the galleries"—briefly "rhetoric," in one of the most obnoxious senses of the term—must be the price for this kind of criticism, unless, indeed, the critic be invariably required to take the point of view of the person or persons actually addressed, and to trace his avowed pleasure or displeasure in the writing to an otherwise unformulated sense of its success or failure as an act of communication.

8. All emanating, I believe, from Professor F. N. Scott of the University of Michigan.

9. The description will be recognized as that of the laboratory, or inductive, or psychological method of composition-teaching, as it has variously been characterized.

Lane Cooper
"On the Teaching of Written Composition"
Education 30 (1910)

&. *Cooper (1875–1959), son of a professor of Greek, attended Rutgers (B.A., 1896), Yale (M.S., 1898), Berlin, and Leipzig*

(Ph.D., 1901). He taught English at Cornell from 1902 to 1943, publishing extensively in English and classics, including a widely used translation of Aristotle's Rhetoric. *(Nonetheless, he is* not *one of the "Cornell rhetoricians" Edward Corbett has memorialized; he remained in Cornell's English department, teaching mostly romantic literature.)*

Cooper's views were first delivered at the 1909 MLA convention. He argues strongly against required composition, drawing upon a range of classic English authors but ultimately resting his case upon the biblical precept that one can't make bricks without straw (Exod. 5.6–18). His attitude toward composition puts him against Harvard but not at all in Scott's camp; rather he is an exponent of the traditional liberal learning based on classical rhetoric that had preceded Harvard's innovations in composition. Cooper's choice of the year 1909 is significant; it marked Eliot's departure from Harvard and the growing dominance there of traditional values. (For Scott's reaction to Cooper's paper see Stewart, "Harvard's Influence.")

A PAPER READ BEFORE THE MODERN LANGUAGE ASSOCIATION OF AMERICA, DECEMBER 28, 1909.

The teaching of English composition is a large subject for consideration in a paper of necessity so brief as this. Properly amplified, the subject would involve some treatment of various other topics, among them the gradual decline of interest in the disciplines of Greek and Latin, which have been essential to the development of English style in the past; and the concomitant popular demand for a kind of education in the vernacular which shall directly liberate the utterance of the masses, rather than raise up leaders in scholarship whose paramount influence might elevate and sustain the standards of taste and good usage.

My purpose, however, is necessarily restricted, and very simple. It is my hope to direct the attention of teachers of English, particularly those who are concerned with classes in written composition, to certain underlying principles which ought to govern the practice of requiring themes or essays from the immature. Fundamental principles are seldom free from the danger of neglect. With reference to composition in the vernacular, the present seems to be a suitable occasion for reverting to such principles, since within the last two years or so a great and exemplary educational power in the East has been rediscovering one of them, and has at length concluded that the children of America should not be forced to make bricks without straw. In the academic year of 1907–1908 at Harvard University the number of undergraduates in courses primarily devoted to the writing of English was considerably larger than the number in courses primarily devoted to the study of English literature, the proportion being almost three to two. Since then, owing, as I understand, to measures designed by the Department of English, this disproportion has undergone a change, so that now there would appear to be a leaning toward courses whose first aim is the acquisition of knowledge, and the development of insight rather than expression. It is not my intention to make use of statistics, and I cite the preceding case, and the following, only in order to define a general impression, namely, that the tide has begun to drift away from courses in the daily theme and its like at the place from which many other institutions have ultimately borrowed such devices, though this drift may not as yet be perceptible everywhere else. For the present semester at a representative university in the Middle West, the number of students in courses mainly devoted to English composition, as against those in courses mainly devoted to the study of English literature, exclusive of graduate students, bears a proportion of about ten to seven. I have no desire to draw especial notice of the university in question, and have given the instance as presumably typical of a good many institutions.

To one who from the beginning could have watched the daily theme advance from its home in New England to a gradual conquest of the South and West—while Greek kept sailing ever farther into the north of Dame Democracy's opinion—the sight must have been attended with some misgivings. In the case of many teachers who, after years of experiment, persist—to use the words of Milton—in "forcing the empty wits of children to compose themes, verses, and orations, which are the acts of ripest judgment," a process which he compares to the wringing of blood from the nose, and "the plucking of untimely fruit,"[1] it may be that the only words to apply are those from Burns:—

> "One point must still be greatly dark,
> The moving *why* they do it."

To do a thing mainly because one hundred or one thousand others are engaged in the same pursuit, may be reasonable in a polity like that of Mr. Kipling's Bandar-log; it is not the sort of motive that ought to dominate the republic of American colleges and universities. Yet one may pertinently inquire whether some such external imitation of one institution by another in this country has not been the chief cause in forcing the jaded wits of partly trained instructors in English, sometimes known as "English slaves," to correct endless themes, essays, and orations, and allowing them to do little else, during what ought to be a most critical period of their growth, that is, during the period when the *docent* in a German university pursues the liberal investigations that shall shortly make him, within his field, a master of those who know. In a land like ours, which prides itself upon the development of efficiency, no harsher accusation could be brought against the daily theme than that it squanders the energy of the teacher. It causes him to spend an immoderate share of his time upon a mass of writing that has no intrinsic value, and easily leads him into the habit of regarding the details of outer form, rather than the substance of what he reads. "Here, therefore, is the first distemper of learning, when men study words and not matter." Is it true that if you take care of the teacher of English, his pupil will be taken care of? Whatever value may attach to this notion, daily themes and their like, once established in the curriculum, constitute a barrier to its acceptance. But let us turn to the pupil.

What, then, are the laws that should govern the kind and amount of writing which we may require from our undergraduates? In asking this question, we are to have in mind the needs of students of the first and second year, but the answer is applicable to a much larger circle of learners. By way of preliminary, one might inquire whether it is necessary that the art of written composition should be taught at all. The common belief that it is necessary may be too readily accepted. The wisest of all teachers, though He constantly referred to written tradition as a standard, and expected his hearers to be familiar with it, is not reported to have written more than once—and then in the sand. The wisest of the Greeks in the time of Pericles is represented by Plato at the end of the Phædrus as arguing to the uttermost against the art of written composition, except as a pastime for the old. Aside from his main contention, this argument of Socrates in favor of the spoken word offers no little support to the increasing number of those who maintain that our present courses in English composition should turn more and more upon the exercise of distinct utterance, that clear and well-formed speech is more intimately connected than writing itself with that precision of thought and feeling which is the basis of all good style. Yet it may be urged that Plato, the consummate artist in Greek prose, is himself an example with which to combat the argument against writing that he chooses to put into the mouth of a dramatic character. Even so, shall we, then, immediately rush away to the inference that it is desirable both for the individual and for the state that all persons, or all the persons in any group, should obtain an equal opportunity for self-expression, whether in writing or otherwise?

So far as concerns the individual, it is clear that the teacher, whether of English or any other subject, should prefer to make his pupil well-informed and happy, rather than enable him to advertise his wisdom and contentment. Even in a democracy it may now and then be true that silence is golden, and long, barren silence better than personal talk. As for the state, it is obvious that the commonwealth is benefited when the few who have a comprehension of its needs are allowed a hearing, and the many possess themselves in quiet; on some such basic thought rests Herbert Spencer's Philosophy of Composition. Nevertheless, among the platitudes that have escaped challenge is the current notion that every one should be taught to express himself when on his feet, since there is no telling how often, in the way of civic duty, the average man may need to address an audience. One may venture to think that an inordinate amount of precious time has been lavished in debate upon airy generalities by students who have never made a speech, or needed to make one, after turning their backs upon the academic rostrum; and the fact remains that the average man, either in civic or in private relations, always needs to know his business before he talks about it. A similar observation holds with reference to the excessive practice of written composition for its own sake. It sounds like a truism to say that to acquire, and to meditate upon what is acquired, are more essential than to express the result in writing. Yet this essential priority of insight over expression is not reflected in the large number of undergraduates throughout our country who engage in the writing of themes with little or no restriction of subjects, as compared with the number engaged in the systematic study of English literature under teachers who are supposed to have made this field, or part of it, their own.

It may be objected that such a disproportion exists only on the surface, and that the student's whole experience, including his activity at the time in other branches of the curriculum, should furnish him with material about which he can write the truth. But the experience of the under-classman is easily exhausted; and in the other subjects which he may be studying, his teachers are better fitted to gauge the precision of his statements than is the teacher of English. In any case, we can hardly avoid the admission that everywhere, and at all times, the truth is of more importance than any language into which it may happen to be translated.

May we not put the argument into a form like this? The main function of the vernacular, Talleyrand to the contrary notwithstanding, is the communication of truth. In a given case the importance of the function is measured by the importance of the truth to be conveyed. Since we may seldom take for granted that the immature student is in possession of a valuable truth, and since the first inquiry of the teacher should, therefore, be concerning the truth and accuracy of the pupil's communication, it follows that the teaching of expression can never safely be made the primary aim of any course. If a sense of values is, in the nature of things, primary, it will remain so in spite of a thousand courses that may be built upon some other hypothesis. If expression is a medium for imparting one's sense of values, if it is essentially a means to an end, we fall into the gravest possible error when we treat it as an end in itself.

Our main question, therefore, resolves itself precisely into this one of means and end; hence we must lay the emphasis where it is due, and no longer ask, "Can we teach such and such persons the art of composition?" Instead, we are bound to ask, "Can we use the practice of written composition as a means of imparting insight?" Obviously we can use it as a test for determining whether the pupil has gained an appreciation of any particular subject, and by successive tests can determine whether he continues to advance in his appreciation. We may perhaps use it with some frequency in order to note the increasing faithfulness of his observation within a definite province, more rarely in order to measure his ability to compare his observations and to draw inferences from them. Employed by a teacher who has such ends in view, the writing of English becomes an instrument of value for promoting a general education, which may be taken to mean a study of particular disciplines in the order of their importance and possibility. Employed for less serious, or mistaken, ends, written composition may be regarded as a pastime for the young, or as an injurious waste of time.

From these considerations we may pass to a few others, some of which may be implicit in what has gone before. The insight which it is the function of the teacher of English to impart is an insight, not into present-day theories of geology, or economics, or agriculture, or, in short, into much of the heterogeneous material that so often serves as a basis for studying the formal structure of exposition and the like; it is an insight into the best traditions of English literature and such other literatures as are inseparably connected with an understanding of the English. This, presumably, is the material into which the vision of the teacher himself has most deeply penetrated. If not, he ought to be teaching something else, or nothing. Let the teacher of writers, as well as the writer, observe the caution of Horace, and choose well his proper field. Some portion, or phase, of this subject which he loves is the thing about which he may ask his students to write; and not in helter-skelter fashion, as if it made no difference where one began, what one observed next, and so on, save as a question of formal order; but progressively, on the supposition that in the advance toward knowledge and understanding certain things, not formal, but substantial, necessarily precede others.

Further, the amount of writing demanded of the immature student should be relatively small. In the space of a term, how many teachers of English composition produce as much manuscript of an academic nature as they expect from individuals of the freshman or sophomore class? Are our courses in daily themes to any extent founded upon the educational theories of antiquity? We may imagine that by one channel or another they eventually go back to Quintilian. But what is their real connection with the familiar advice of Quintilian, so vigorously rendered by Ben Jonson, "No matter how slow the style be at first, so it be labored and accurate;" or with this, "So that the sum of all is, ready writing makes not good writing, but good writing brings on ready writing"? Or what relation have they to the Horatian counsel, not merely of filling the mind from the page Socratic before one commences writing, but, after one has written, of correcting, even to a tenth review? And the page Socratic itself in one case is said to have been seven times rewritten. Accordingly, from Plato, who remodeled the opening of the Republic these seven times, to Bacon, who revised the Instauratio Magna at least twelve times, and Manzoni, who would often recast a sentence a score of times, and then perhaps not print a word of it, and John Richard Green, who rewrote the first chapter of The Making of England ten times, there is a host of witnesses[2] crying out against the facile penmanship of five themes a week on five different subjects, or approximately one hundred and seventy-five in an academic year, from the empty wits of sophomores. To this number must be added six or eight "long themes." Could any course of reading be designed which at the end of the year preceding should make of the freshman a full man to the extent which such an exercise as this in the sophomore year demands?

In fact, the more one compares the current practice of theme-writing with traditional theory and the actual experience of good writers in the past, the less this practice seems to harmonize with either. Nor does it meet with the approval, so far as I can discover, of representative literary men in the present. Speaking at Oxford University some eleven years ago, Mr. Frederic Harrison delivered himself as follows:—

"I look with sorrow on the habit which has grown up in the university since my day (in the far-off fifties)—the habit of making a considerable part of the education of the place to turn on the art of serving up gobbets of prepared information in essays more or less smooth and correct—more or less successful imitations of the viands that are cooked for us daily in the press. I have heard that a student has been asked to write as many as seven essays in a week, a task which would exhaust the fertility of a Swift. The bare art of writing readable paragraphs in passable English is easy enough to master; one that steady practice and good coaching can teach the average man. But it is a poor art, which readily lends itself to harm. It leads the shallow ones to suppose themselves to be deep, the raw ones to fancy they are cultured, and it burdens the world with a deluge of facile commonplace. It is the business of a university to train the mind to think, and to impart solid knowledge, not to turn out nimble penmen who may earn a living as the clerks and salesmen of literature."[3]

And to much the same effect Lord Morley, speaking a decade earlier than Mr. Harrison:—

"I will even venture, with all respect to those who are teachers of literature, to doubt the excellence and utility of the practice of overmuch essay-writing and composition. I have very little faith in rules of style, though I have an unbounded faith in the virtue of cultivating direct and precise expression. But you must carry on the operation inside the mind, and not merely by practising literary deportment on paper. It is not everybody who can command the mighty rhythm of the greatest masters of human speech. But every one can make reasonably sure that he knows what he means, and whether he has found the right word. These are internal operations, and are not forwarded by writing for writing's sake. Everybody must be urgent for attention to expression, if that attention be exercised in the right way. It has been said a million times that the foundation of right expression in speech or writing is sincerity. That is as true now as it has ever been. Right expression is a part of character. As somebody has said, by learning to speak with precision, you learn to think with correctness; and the way to firm and vigorous speech lies through the cultivation of high and noble sentiments. So far as my observation has gone, men will do better if they seek precision by studying carefully and with an open mind and a vigilant eye the great models of writing, than by excessive practice of writing on their own account."[4]

Could one wish for a better defense than Lord Morley has given of the notion that the cultivation of the vernacular must go hand in hand with a systematic study of English literature, and of no models short of the best?

Now I am far from wishing to suggest that the battle which has been waged against the illiteracy of our freshmen and sophomores, and which has centered in the daily theme, has been totally without avail, though all of us must remember instances where a compulsory exercise in fluent writing has chiefly served to encourage shallowpates in shallow thinking and heedless expression. But where the battle has availed, this has resulted from the more or less random observance of this principle which has been enunciated, namely the priority of insight; for even where the teacher of composition at the outset announces his belief that the disease which shows itself in bad writing is bad thinking, he nevertheless is prone to spend the term, or the year, in warring against the symptoms. He lacks the courage of his convictions, and needs to restore his spirit with the passage in which Milton says: "True eloquence I find to be none but the serious and hearty love of truth."[5]

The whole question does, indeed, finally reduce itself to one of pedagogical faith, to a belief that the ideal will work—that it is the only thing that will work effectively. If we never ask the student to write for us save on the basis of something which we ourselves may properly be supposed to know; if the material is one concerning which his knowledge is made to grow throughout a considerable length of time; if we expect of every essay, paragraph, sentence, phrase and word which he writes that it shall tell the exact, if not the whole truth; if the subject-matter of his study be itself the truest and most inspiring that we can employ to fire his imagination and clarify his vision; if we observe all these conditions, will he altogether fail in acquiring the outward badge of education which is popularly demanded of the college graduate? Will he fail to express himself better as his personality becomes better worth expressing? If, for example, we took our cue from the Greeks, and restricted our training in the vernacular to the patient absorption of one or two supreme master-pieces, would not our students escape what Ruskin says such a practice enabled him to escape, "even in the foolishest times of youth," the writing of "entirely superficial or formal English"?[6] Nay, might they not thus appropriate a matter wherein, on occasion, they might with justice become right voluble? No teacher can deny it unless he is willing to pretend that insight and expression are separable, or that insight is subordinate. Yet the belief that they are inseparable, and that expression is subordinate, is not merely a matter of present-day common sense; it has received frequent enough vindication in the history of culture. But in closing we may content ourselves with one quotation, and that from the very practical man to whom, more than to any other one person in the history of Europe, the existence of modern culture is owing, that is, Charles the Great. In a plea for the study of letters, lest the knowledge of the art of writing vanish away, and hence the knowledge of how to interpret the Scriptures, he says to the abbots and bishops in the year 787:—

"While errors of speech are harmful, we all know that errors of thought are more harmful still. Therefore, we exhort you not merely not to neglect the study of letters, but to pursue it with diligence."[7]

NOTES

1. Tractate on Education. Throughout the following remarks I have kept in mind certain passages from Milton's Tractate, Wordsworth's sonnets entitled Personal Talk, and Bacon's Advancement of Learning.

2. On rewriting and other forms of painstaking in composition, see Horace, Ars Poetica, 289–294; Ben Jonson, Discoveries, ed. Castelain, pp. 34, 35, 84–86; Boswell's Life of Johnson, Oxford Edition, 2: 562; Rousseau, Confessions, Book 3 (in the translation published by Glaisher, pp. 86, 87); Gillman's Life of Coleridge, p. 63; Christabel, ed. E. H. Coleridge, p. 40; Journals of Dorothy Wordsworth, ed.

Knight, 1: 83 ff.; Letters of the Wordsworth Family, ed. Knight, 2: 312, 313, 470; Cooper, The Prose Poetry of Thomas De Quincey, p. 32; Letters of J. H. Newman, ed. Mozley, 2: 476, 477; Lucas, Life of Charles Lamb, 1: 335, 336; Nation, Nov. 9, 1905 (on Manzoni); Revue Politique et Littéraire, Feb. 22, 1890, p. 239; Faguet, Flaubert, pp. 145 ff.; William Allingham, A Diary, p. 334; W. P. Chalmers, R. L. Stevensons Stil, pp. 1–4; Life and Letters of Lafcadio Hearn, Elizabeth Bisland, pp. 132–135; Jowett, College Sermons, Preface.

3. On English Prose, in Tennyson, Ruskin, Mill, and other Literary Estimates.

4. Studies in Literature, pp. 222, 223.

5. "True eloquence I find to be none but the serious and hearty love of truth; and that whose mind soever is fully possessed with a fervent desire to know good things, and with the dearest charity to infuse the knowledge of them into others, when such a man would speak, his words (by what I can express), like so many nimble and airy servitors, trip about him at command, and, in well-ordered files, as he would wish, fall aptly into their own places."—*From the Apology for Smectymnuus.*

6. Ruskin, Praeterita, Chap. 1; cf. also Chap. II.

7. Comparetti, Vergil in the Middle Ages, pp. 96, 97.

Thomas Raynesford Lounsbury
"Compulsory Composition in Colleges"
Harper's Monthly 123 (1911)

   Lounsbury (1838–1915) graduated from Yale in 1859, spent time as a professional writer in New York, and served in the Civil War, seeing action at Gettysburg. After some teaching at private academies and as a tutor, he was appointed instructor in English at Yale's Sheffield Scientific School in 1870, where he remained until his retirement in 1908. He was famed for a wide variety of books on English language and literature.

Harvard's Adams Sherman Hill was a critic of language usage, an exponent of rhetoric, and an advocate of the direct teaching of composition. In contrast, Yale's Lounsbury was a scholar of language use, a philologist and linguist, and an advocate of teaching writing through literature. Here Lounsbury argues against learning to write, a wildly overstated position for him to take, since all during his career he was devoted to his own kind of writing course, one connected with literary studies, which he instituted in 1870 upon his arrival at Yale. In fact, he made his move to Yale contingent upon being permitted to teach such a course there (Cross 112). (For a description of the Sheffield Scientific School's composition course, see chap. 3, p. 161. For the context of Lounsbury's attack on "verbal critics" like Hill, see chap. 5 of Cmiel.)

THERE IS A PECULIAR SATISFACTION IN THE EXPRESSION OF NOVEL views with which everybody will agree. But little inferior is the satisfaction of expressing views with which nobody will agree. In this latter case exceptional keenness is added to the enjoyment when one recognizes that the sentiments set forth will meet not merely with dissent, but with unqualified condemnation from every right-thinking person: that these views will be fortunate indeed if they succeed in escaping the designation of diabolical. As a consequence, the utterer sinks so low in the estimation of the judicious that it becomes simply impossible for him to sink lower.

It is to a pleasure of this sort that I am about to treat myself by a discussion of that kind of theme-writing which goes with us under the name of college compositions. Along with it comes up for consideration the attitude of the public in regard to the desirability and importance of such compositions. The readiness I shall here exhibit in offering myself as a scapegoat to bear into the wilderness the iniquities of myself and my brethren may be taken as an apology, if it cannot be deemed an excuse, for the occasional record found here of personal experiences and the frequent employment of the pronoun of the first person.

It therefore seems right to say at the outset that there is one serious disadvantage under which I labor in discussing the subject. For about a quarter of a century a distinctly recognizable share of my time was spent in reading and correcting college themes. I have consequently had a good deal of experience in dealing with the questions to be considered. To the unthinking this may seem a help toward their proper treatment. On the contrary, it is a positive hindrance. There is nothing so certain to warp the conclusions of the pure intellect working on this subject as actual experience. Familiarity, either wearisome or disturbing, with details deprives the critical soul of the power of considering the various problems involved with full detachment from the notions and prejudices which these details beget. Accordingly more confidence is generally felt by the public, and invariably far more by the utterer himself, in the conclusions of him whose happy lot it has been to escape this drudgery. He can take a commanding view of the whole situation, unaffected by the intrusion of doubts which arise from the knowledge of discordant and disturbing fact. He can put forth dicta as to what ought and what ought not to be done, unembarrassed by beliefs born of experience in the classroom as to what can and what cannot be done.

There are those who will recall the fact that some forty years ago a great wave of educational reform swept over the land. Attention was directed to many subjects; but the one that concerns us here is English language and literature. It is to be borne in mind that at the time this agitation began there had never been any real requirement in the study of either, certainly no more than that which exists still in the two great English universities. Work of the sort now implied by it was then a novelty in American institutions of learning. The attention at present paid to English language and literature is not only modern, it is late modern. Knowledge of it as a requirement for entrance is even more modern. It was not until some years after the Civil War that the study of English literature was generally taken up in our higher institutions of learning. If provision chanced to be made for it anywhere previously, it was accidental, depending upon the desire or caprice of the instructor, not upon the policy adopted for instruction. A student could pass through most if not all of our leading colleges without being asked to read a single English book or to hear from any instructor the name of a single English author.

The first method taken to supply this assumed defect was to require the student not to make himself familiar with English literature itself, but with the contents of some text-book giving an account of it. This was the transition period. No more skilful device to kill interest in the subject was ever concocted. The unfortunate undergraduate was compelled to learn the titles of books which he had never read and never expected to read, written by authors of whose names he had frequently never heard before and in many cases would never hear of again. Long and dreary catalogues of dates and subjects, beggarly abstracts of the lives and writings of men of whom he knew little and for whom he cared less, was the sort of chaff which was served up as the food for the literary banquet provided. If there were latent in any soul a reprehensible desire to know something of literature itself, no more all-sufficient scheme could have been contrived to correct and repress any mischievous tendencies of the sort.

The result of the earlier neglect of the theoretically proper instruction, it may be remarked in passing, was not, after all, so bad as it might be inferred it would have been. In truth, the experience of the English universities, where the same indifference and even greater indifference in regard to this whole subject prevailed and probably still prevails, seems to indicate that there is more in the let-alone policy than most have been disposed to accord to it. Doubtless some persons missed an inspiration they would have received had this been a required study, just as others may have been saved from a corresponding aversion. But whatever reading of authors then took place was natural, because it was voluntary; whatever was taken into the mind was beneficial, because it was thoroughly assimilated. A haphazard system of education which has produced such men of letters as Longfellow, Hawthorne, Lowell, Bryant—to mention a few—may have something to say for itself when contrasted with a system which so far has not been successful in developing any persons to fill their places. But this is an altogether different story, which can wait its time. Our concern here is not with the study of English literature proper, but with an offshoot of it, which was then and even now is considered by large numbers to be the thing itself.

For the conception of the proper study of English literature, which was held by many and perhaps by most, during this point of agitation [c. 1870—ED.] was that it consisted mainly, if not entirely, in writing themes upon given subjects. With this the study of some text-book of rhetoric was to be conjoined. Theory and practice would thus happily go hand in hand. As an additional requirement, these themes were to be written frequently. They were also to be corrected with a care and thoroughness previously unknown. Such was the programme of the future. In the discussion of it the whole country engaged. So far as could be gathered from the newspapers, there was practical unanimity of view not merely as to the desirability of carrying it out, but as to the absolute necessity. There had been, we were told, shameful negligence in the past as regards this whole matter; there still continued to be shameful negligence in the present. It should be remedied at once. One thing in particular was imperatively demanded. Students must be taught to use their own language with purity and propriety. Not merely the best but the only way recognized to bring about this result was constant practice in writing by the student and constant criticism by the instructor of what was written.

The leading universities of the country were frequently reproached for their neglect of this all-important matter. They were told that in this particular they were far behind numerous other institutions which did not make their pretensions and possessed not a tithe of their resources. The newspapers poured forth comment and criticism in profusion from the never-exhausted cornucopia of editorial wisdom. Harvard University was for a time singled out for special attack. The decadence of its instruction in this particular was more than once regretfully or reproachfully pointed out. I remember a religious weekly—for some inexplicable reason they were in those days termed religious—censuring that university for its neglect of this subject. It was shamefully disregarding its duty of developing the budding literary genius of America by failing to require very frequent exercises in composition and to subject everything composed to the strictest examination and correction. In an article in another one of these so-called religious weeklies Harvard was not merely censured for its inaction in this particular, but another institution was held up to gaze as furnishing a standing reproach to it for its scandalous disregard of its duty. This, it may be said in passing, was a very excellent seminary for girls in Brooklyn [probably Packer Collegiate Institute— ED.]. In that, we were informed, each composition was carefully read over by the instructor in the presence of the writer. The former, after becoming fully gorged with the literary feast provided and thoroughly digesting it, proceeded to point out the errors committed in the concoction and mixture of the ingredients. "Go thou and do likewise," was the injunction implied and indeed almost directly asserted.

It was certainly consoling to learn from this inspired writer that there was balm in Brooklyn, if no longer in Boston. Provision had been made somewhere for budding native genius and for the training up of a body of great authors who were to illuminate the land. But the cheerfulness of this prospect did not mitigate the censure passed upon the university compared; its culpability was only the more vehemently insisted upon. It was in truth a hard time for professors in our older institutions of learning who were not impressed by this popular clamor, or, as I should prefer to call it, this popular cackle. No achievement in their legitimate field of activity saved them from attack. Professor Child, then the head of the English department in Harvard, had his duty constantly pointed out to him in the newspapers by graduates of the university—at least they termed themselves so. He was steadily called to account in language which implied reproach, when it did not convey censure. "What is the Boylston professor of Rhetoric and Oratory doing?" was, he told me, the burden of many a cry which found utterance in communications sent to the press of the neighboring city by men filled with anxiety, not to say anguish, for the literary future of the nation. They not infrequently contrasted him to his disadvantage with his predecessor.

I myself had been reading somewhere at the time an article in which this predecessor was authoritatively said to have raised the literary standard of all America. [Child's predecessor was Channing.—Ed.] Such a feat would naturally strike any one as a good deal of an achievement. Just placed in a somewhat similar position in another institution, I was anxious to learn how this result had been brought about. What was the proper course for me to take in order that I too might contribute what little I could toward the maintenance of this same literary standard, even though I could do nothing toward its further elevation? So I asked a number of questions as to the methods which had been followed, especially these two. Had any real effort been put forth to inspire the student with a taste for literature itself? Had he been asked or urged to read a single English classic author? To both these questions the answer was in the negative. Further inquiry showed that nothing had been undertaken outside of the old familiar methods. What had been done was very likely better done; but of itself it furnished no solution of the problem which presented itself to those who saw clearly the fallacy underlying the popular delusion on the subject.

That delusion, however, was then so prevalent and powerful that all our colleges were compelled to bow before the storm. Even the men who recognized clearly the fallaciousness of the views so clamorously proclaimed were forced to comply with the popular demand, if not to save themselves, to save the institution to which they belonged. If they failed to join in the chase started by this educational hue and cry, they were stigmatized as being behind the age—where, it may be added, it is often a very good place to be. Their attitude was declared to be one of culpable indifference to the progress of the race. If, however, they and the institutions with which they were connected would bend their energies to the performance of the work which their critics were good enough to lay out for them, we were assured that it would be a mere question of time, and indeed of comparatively short time, when every one would write good English, and some write English that was more than merely good. Consequently, unless all signs or rather all promises failed, we should in a quarter of a century behold the appearance of a body of great authors such as the country had never known before. If it be said that I am here setting up a standard which no men of sense ever pretended could be reached—though some pretended it who thought they were men of sense—I will modify the statement and say that we were to have a body of writers, every one of whom would know how to express himself clearly, would never use a word improperly, which never violate a rule of syntax, would never construct a sentence which could not endure the strictest grammatical scrutiny.

Assuredly these and similar glowing anticipations of the speedy coming of a spotless linguistic and literary millennium were then entertained and expressed. Forty years have gone by since the virtues of this panacea for our ills were loudly proclaimed. Ample time has accordingly been furnished to test its efficacy. By their fruits shall ye know them. No one is now likely to pretend that the results actually secured by the workings of this great regenerative experiment, faithfully carried on as it has been in some places even if slighted in others, correspond with the results predicted. Our heavens are not yet strown with literary stars of the first magnitude. If there is any method of producing great writers to order, the method from which so much was anticipated is manifestly not the one. To be sure, there are now many men who write excellently; but there is no increase in the proportional number of this body. Nor do these write better than their predecessors who did not enjoy their boasted advantages. It may be said that this result is no fault of the method adopted; but even were this to be conceded, it cannot be proclaimed as one of its successes.

In truth, to any thoughtful man who understood the nature of the problem presented, the experiment was foredoomed to failure. It rested throughout upon a series of false assumptions. I am by no means disposed to go so far as the historian of New England, John Gorham Palfrey, who, as I have been told, was wont to express the desire that an act of Congress should be passed forbidding on pain of death anyone under twenty-one years of age to write a sentence. Excess in one direction cannot be remedied by excess in the opposite. Still, none the less am I thoroughly convinced that altogether undue importance is attached to exercises in English composition, especially compulsory exercises; that the benefits to be derived from the general practice in schools is vastly overrated; that the criticism of themes, even when it is fully competent, is in the majority of cases of little value to the recipient; that in a large number of instances the criticism is and must ever be more or less incompetent; and that when the corrections which are made are made inefficiently and unintelligently, as in too often the case, the results reached are distinctly more harmful than helpful.

It is quite needless to say that such views are far from representing the opinion now prevailing. To that, in fact, they are utterly opposed. From hundreds of editorial and educational pulpits the duty of writing themes is constantly preached; furthermore, the duty of writing them frequently. It is not because there is any demand for the course of instruction, so earnestly recommended, on the part of a large proportion of those who are theoretically to be benefited by it. On the contrary, the average student loathes it. Instead of hungering and thirsting for this sort of intellectual nutriment, he has to have it forced down his throat. He is compelled to write whether he cares to write or not. In the majority of cases he does not care. The results follow which might naturally be expected. Not feeling its necessity or value, he not infrequently resorts to various devices to evade its requirements. Compositions are bought where they cannot be safely stolen. Here, as elsewhere in life, wealth enables its possessor to secure what his brains fail to supply. Hence the task of composition, while compulsory in theory, is to no small extent optional in practice. Even when sense of honor or lack of money or fear of consequences leads the student to reject extraneous aid and to produce something by his own unaided efforts, the work is, after all, done perfunctorily, for in it he has no real interest. The evils inevitably follow that wait upon perfunctory performance. In truth, were the object of these compulsory exercises to bring into being essays marked by slovenliness of diction, inaccuracy of statement, vapidity of thought, no better means could well have been devised to reach the end aimed at.

The belief in this method of developing literary ability rests in truth upon a series of fallacies. The fundamental one, underlying all the others, is that the art of expression is something which can be made a matter of direct instruction, just as arithmetic can be, or history, or chemistry, or any foreign tongue. There are things connected with it, or bearing upon it, of which this is undoubtedly true. There are certain results, largely mechanical in their nature, which can be achieved in the classroom. For the attainment of these the business of instruction can hardly be commenced too early or carried on too thoroughly. The child can be trained to master certain matters which are essential to all correct speaking and writing. He can be made to avoid, at any rate to recognize, certain common improprieties and vulgarities of expression. He can be taught the leading facts of declension and conjugation. He can be shown how to construct simple sentences which are not characterized by a virulent hostility to the ordinary rules of grammar. It is possible to go farther and make clear to the most immature mind how the arrangement of words in the sentence can cause or cure ambiguity of meaning. It is desirable also to impart a knowledge not of what grammar requires, but merely convention, such, for example, as the capitalization of words as practised in English. Again it is well for the pupil to learn some of the various systems of punctuation in vogue, if at the same time care be taken not to give him the conviction that the particular punctuation he is taught to use has been somehow divinely inspired.

All these things, however, are elementary. They can be learned and ought to be learned at a comparatively early age. That they are frequently not learned till late, and sometimes not at all, is unquestionably true. But this is largely so because the time and application which should have been devoted to the mastery of these elementary facts has been diverted to the more ambitious scheme of making the child set out to give expression to ideas before he has any ideas to express. The colleges throw upon the preparatory schools the responsibility for the inevitable failure to reach satisfactory results in these preliminary matters connected with composition, instead of placing it, where it belongs, upon their own preposterous expectations and requirements in another field.

For when we come to the communication of the results of investigation or the expression of thought we are entering upon a distinct field of intellectual activity. We are asking young and undeveloped minds to lay aside what is for them the natural occupation of acquiring knowledge, and to take up, on no matter how limited a scale, the rôle of producer and critic. A few may be fitted for this work; but necessarily at an early period of life such persons are very few. But were it conceded that this method was in itself good for all, two obstacles stand in the way of any success resulting from its universal adoption. One of these has already been indicated. No progress worth speaking of is ever made in any study where the learner himself is not interested in the subject. No one will pretend that under our present compulsory system interest in the writing of themes exists for the majority of students. As they have no desire to be taught, little heed is paid to the instruction given and to the corrections made, even when the work of examination and criticism has been done with peculiar excellence.

But just at this point the second practical difficulty shows itself. So far from the work of examination and criticism being performed with peculiar excellence, it is often performed with no excellence at all. To discharge this duty successfully requires, in addition to cultivated taste, a fullness of familiarity with our language and literature which it is out of the power of the average teacher to secure, even if he has the desire. Under the compulsory system now prevailing the task of reading and correcting themes is one of deadly dullness. Men who are really fitted to perform the work properly are exceedingly rare; and when found they will not persist in carrying on this most distasteful of occupations, unless compelled by necessity. It is consequently looked upon as merely a stepping-stone to something else.

We are indeed frequently assured by those who have been themselves careful never to try this sort of work that the state of mind just indicated is all wrong; that the reading and correcting of themes is one of the noblest occupations to which the human mind can devote itself. Occasionally men of letters have been found to express themselves as pained and shocked that the land does not swarm with instructors who are burning with eagerness to lead young and growing minds into the paths of pure and lofty expression, which these callow youth are supposed to be anxious to tread. Nothing more delightful could well be conceived than to round up this whole body of sorrowing souls and compel each and every one of them to prepare upon short notice essays upon subjects which they know nothing about and in which they have not the slightest interest; for this is the very thing which our institutions of learning are persistently asking, not of trained writers who are presumably possessed of some ideas of their own, but of raw and immature minds which are supplied with little knowledge and are but slightly addicted to reflection. These literary extollers of our present methods would rise up from the experiment wiser men, and probably a good deal sadder.

As a consequence of the condition of things just indicated, more and more does the business of correcting and criticizing themes tend steadily to fall into the hands of those who are incompetent to do anything much better, and therefore incompetent to do this well. They may be earnest and well-intentioned, but they have themselves little experience in the practice of composition and little knowledge of the best usage of which no one knows too much. Furthermore, they frequently have but slight familiarity with the literature upon which such usage is based. Even those who are free from this reproach are too rarely in the habit of noting the way in which the very authors express themselves whom they profess to admire and imitate. The practice of these they do not observe and follow. Instead they take as their guide some manual of usage which is peculiar in its class if it does not inculcate as many errors as it corrects.

The teaching of those who do not base their criticism of language upon the usage of the great writers of our literature has necessarily no value as a guide to propriety of expression. Worse than that, it is fairly sure to become to some extent a fountain of error. Though the words of such instructors are of no real authority, yet from the position of vantage they occupy they are enabled to impose upon the immature minds under them their crude and often erroneous conception of what is proper and improper in speech. They condemn what they have not sufficient knowledge of the historical development of the speech to understand. They naturally join in the relentless crusade which is carried on by the half-trained against the time-honored idioms of our tongue. The thoughtless and indifferent student usually is saved from the worst consequences of instruction of this sort by the habit he has formed of paying no heed to any instruction of all. Yet even the most careless is fairly certain to have lodged in his brain some one or two of the errors thus imparted, in spite of his untiring efforts not to learn anything. These in time come to serve him as his particular standard of good usage. They enable him to set up as the oracle of the fireside, on propriety of expression, and sometimes of the hamlet and of the editorial chair. All this diffusion of error is carried on under the guise of preserving the speech in its purity.

To write English with purity and propriety! In the eyes of those who derive their knowledge of good usage mainly from manuals which profess to set it forth, such a thing as expressing one's self with absolute correctness is hardly within the realm of possibility. The country swarms with educated prigs who are ready to prove to you that all the classic authors of our speech abound in errors, sometimes in gross errors. Not one of these authors, ancient or modern, has been able to produce anything in which some superior person, versed in the lore of the latest text-books on propriety of usage, is not able to point out numerous lapses from the pure and perfect diction which the critic is confident that he displays in his own utterance. Provender of this sort dished out in schools is naturally imparted to the rest of the community by the graduates of those schools as soon as they occupy the teacher's or editor's chair. Idioms and constructions employed unhesitatingly by every great master of our speech are as unhesitatingly condemned. Have we not been told again and again that *none* must never be used as the subject of a plural verb; that *whose* must never be used as a relative to an antecedent without life; that the superlative degree must never be employed in the comparison of two; that an objective case cannot properly follow a verb in the passive voice; that the dreadful neologism of *would better* with the infinitive should be substituted for *had better?* These and similar assaults upon correct and idiomatic diction, involving as they do ignorance of the language as well as of the literature, are regularly perpetrated under the pretense of maintaining the purity of the speech. The hapless victim of such instruction cannot take up a single classic author in our tongue without finding him doing the very things which he himself is told cannot be done with propriety. With these splendid failures before his eyes, what hope can the raw and untrained school-boy entertain of ever being able to write the language correctly?

It is fairly certain, indeed, that under our present system no small share of the instruction given in composition conveys as much error as truth. But let us assume for the sake of the argument that it is absolutely faultless; that the teacher himself is efficient; that the correction of mistakes or supposed mistakes is itself made correctly. Even then the result aimed at can never be reached in this way. The real object of all effort in this direction is or should be the attainment of positive excellence, whereas the main office of the instruction just described is to correct error. Its results are therefore almost entirely negative. The avoidance of error is unquestionably a good thing. No one is likely to deny its importance. But many will be found to deny its supreme importance. Yet this virtue, largely negative in its nature, is held up before the eyes of the public as the one thing all-essential. It is the misconception of the value to be derived from this sort of training in composition which has led to the beliefs now generally entertained and to the methods now generally pursued. The work which correction of error can do is humble work; but so far as it goes, if well done, it is good work. But it does not go far. It contributes practically nothing to that felicity of expression which it is the aim of the writer to attain, and but very little to his clearness. Furthermore, it is not the only way and hardly the best way to reach the result sought; for freedom from fault is itself fairly sure to come in time if positive excellence has once been secured.

There is an experience very far from being frequent, but still occasionally encountered by him who is intrusted with the duty of instruction in composition. Two themes come up for consideration which though treating of the same subject are marked by a peculiar contrast. One is deformed by errors of various sorts, by the use of locutions which are not permissible in correct speech, by constructions for which the resources of grammar would be tasked in order to find a satisfactory explanation. Yet in spite of these glaring faults the work done is somehow interesting. What is said is said with so much vivacity and occasional felicity that it attracts and holds the attention. Notwithstanding its linguistic lapses, it has fulfilled the first law of writing; it is readable.

The other is correct in the employment of words and in their arrangement. It is everything that it should be from the point of view of grammar and usage. Yet it is somehow so dull that it has upon the reader all the effect of an opiate. Its fairly aggressive tediousness, along with the impossibility of finding particular errors to cavil at, irritates the critic. Yet what is he to do? If he tells the brutal truth, he must say to the writer: I find no fault with your use of words or with the construction of your sentences or of your paragraphs; but the fact is you have contrived to take every particle of interest out of an interesting subject. Your essay is pervaded by an overpowering dullness which casts a burden upon the spirits beyond the justifiable limits of human endurance.

To this the hapless student may reply: I have given you all the information you asked for. You find no fault with the correctness of the way in which it has been conveyed. What more can I do; what more would you have me do? It is a perfectly just protest against the criticism received. No fair answer can be made to it under the conditions given. For we have reached here an ultimate fact. Nothing more can be said than that one piece with all its blunders is interesting because it is written in an interesting manner; the other, free as it is from grammatical or rhetorical errors, is dull beyond description because something is lacking, the want of which we feel but cannot exactly describe, at least in terms palatable to the writer. The difference between the two pieces is due to the presence in the one and to the absence in the other of a trace of that alchemical power of style which in its perfection can transmute the base matter of common thought and incident into the gold of literary achievement. Manifestly this is something which cannot be imparted by direct instruction. Wherever it comes from, it assuredly does not come from judicious criticism. It gets, indeed, little help from any criticism whether judicious or injudicious.

The question therefore at once presents itself, Upon what depends primarily the creation of that peculiar charm of expression which we call style? As obviously mere freedom from fault cannot impart it, how can it best be acquired, if it can be acquired at all? In seeking an answer to this question the great fundamental fact is to be kept in mind that ability to write is a growth, and that the rapidity and extent of this growth depend upon several agencies which the individual may not and usually does not employ with that particular end in view. One of these agencies, indeed, is practice; but at the outset practice is so far from being of highest importance that as compared with other agencies it is of but little. Clearness or effectiveness or felicity of expression can never be created by it, nor can they be developed by it satisfactorily unless the proper foundation has been previously laid. For the growth spoken of depends upon the development of mental power and of literary taste. The rapidity of the growth will naturally vary with the individual; but from the very nature of things it can in no wise be hurried. Accordingly we cannot trace its increase from day to day any more than we can trace the daily increase of a person's height. Only by a comparison of the achievement of the present with that of some period in the past can its progress be detected at all.

The confusion of thought which prevails upon this subject is due to confounding ability to write, which is a creative act, with ability to learn, which is merely an act of acquisition. The one is the result of agencies working directly to a particular end; the other the result of agencies most of which act indirectly. Hence increase in the acquisition of power of expression, depending as it does upon intellectual growth, differs radically from increase in the acquisition of knowledge. A man can assert very truly that on such or such a day he received information about certain facts; or that on such or such a day he mastered the meaning of some difficult passage in a great author, or that he deciphered some puzzling mathematical problem. What he cannot do is to assert that on such and such a day he became a learned man, or a wise man, or acquired a cultivated taste, or, what specially concerns us here, that he gained the ability to express himself clearly or effectively. All such things are the long result of time and of mental development. They can be recognized when they have come; rarely with certainty when they are coming.

So far as the art of expression is concerned, upon what does this intellectual growth depend? To any proper development of it two things may ordinarily be deemed necessary; to its highest development two things additional are indispensable. The first is the possession of knowledge. This can hardly be deemed an absolute essential. There are and doubtless will always continue to be cases where men write interestingly and even charmingly about matters of which they know little or nothing. Still there is a prejudice, which in the case of the beginner has to be reckoned with, in favor of a writer's having some degree of familiarity with what he is writing about before he attempts to impart information in regard to it. Men with reputations already established may venture to defy this feeling; but it cannot be slighted safely by him who has his reputation to make. It may be taken, indeed, as a general rule, that no one can write attractively any more than he can intelligently of matters with which he has only a limited acquaintance.

But while knowledge of a subject may produce something worth reading for its matter, it will not of itself make it readable. This fact has often been unhappily illustrated in the history of learning. Scholarship has become, in truth, so associated with dullness in the common mind that any treatise which makes interesting a subject ordinarily uninteresting begets the suspicion that its author must be superficial and inaccurate. There is apt to be doubt of if not actual disbelief in the trustworthiness of the writer's knowledge who does not bore his reader in the communication of it. This feeling has been largely fostered by the frequent inability of men of great learning to state lucidly what they know fully. The consequence is that they exhaust the reader even more than they exhaust the subject. The confusion in the author's mind is due to the knowledge he possesses having been ill-arranged and ill-digested. Naturally this condition finds its fitting counterpart in clumsiness of construction, in involved phrases, in sentences stuffed with parentheses, and paragraphs loaded with extraneous matter. So prevalent has this method of composition been with men of genuine learning that it has come largely to be regarded as a necessary accompaniment of learning itself. With many nothing contributes more to the acceptance of a writer as an authority than the impossibility of reading with pleasure what he says.

The existence of the belief indicated is mainly due to the neglect by men of learning of the second but far more important requisite which goes to constitute a good style. This is clearness of expression. Now upon what does this particular characteristic ultimately depend? Manifestly upon clearness of thinking. Where again does clearness of thinking come from? Almost entirely from the regular exercise and consequent growth of a man's own faculties. It is a result of an intellectual development which is the outcome of the efforts of the individual himself and never of the instruction given him by others. It can therefore never be imparted directly.

Fullness of knowledge and clearness of thinking are consequently the first two requisites which should be possessed by him who sets out to compose a work which has any reason for its existence. On the lower plane of intellectual achievement denoted by these characteristics it is possible for most of us to attain some degree of excellence, provided we are willing to put forth the requisite exertion. But when we come to the two other qualities which go to constitute the ideal style, an entirely different problem is presented. The first is the ability to write with effectiveness, to put forth one's ideas so as not merely to enlighten men, but to impress them, to influence their beliefs and acts. Higher even than that, though not infrequently conjoined with it, is that exquisiteness of diction, that indescribable charm of expression which we feel in the productions of great authors, but find it difficult if not impossible to analyze. Neither of these latter is it in the power of all of us to attain; in truth, it is in the power of but few. It depends upon the existence in the individual of an innate ability which education may develop but cannot itself create.

Knowledge of the subject, clearness of statement, power, and finally beauty of expression are accordingly the four constituent elements which enter into the composition of the perfect style. How can these qualities be best secured, assuming that it is possible for the individual to secure them? One way by which they cannot be acquired has been already pointed out— the correction of faults. Another allied delusion is that an effective agency to bring about such a result is the study of rhetoric. The denial of this must not be understood as denying the importance of that subject. It has a value of its own; but it has not the kind of value which is often mistakenly claimed for it. For as grammar is nothing but the generalization of the facts of utterance, so rhetoric is nothing but the generalization of the facts of style. In both cases the facts must be known before the generalizations can be appreciated or even understood. The child does not learn his language from his grammar. After he has learned it in other ways, grammar steps in and furnishes him a scientific analysis of what he has been doing. So rhetoric gives the student the names of the different styles and describes the particular characteristics which go to make up the one that is presumably perfect. But the perfect style itself it does not and cannot impart. Granted that the rules it gives are the best possible rules, it does not furnish the student with the power of applying them—the one thing, above all others, with which he as a writer is concerned. Skill and effectiveness and grace come from an entirely different quarter. Yet in this matter the most mistaken and sometimes the most ludicrous notions come up for notice. I call to mind a young man who before beginning his Commencement oration went carefully through the whole of Whately's treatise on rhetoric as a preparatory exercise, and was much astounded to discover, after finishing it, that he could write no better than he did before.

Let us lay aside another delusive notion. This is that institutions of learning have any monopoly of training in composition. All life, if it is worth living at all, contributes to ability in expression. To develop it in any marked degree, there needs, to be sure, innate capacity in the individual; but if that exist, the education of events is likely of itself to ripen it to its consummate flower of perfection. Why do men who have never had the advantage of any school training in composition so often express themselves with clearness, directness, and force? The answer is easy. They have had a special effective training of their own. They have been engaged in the conduct of vast business enterprises, or they have shouldered the burden of heavy responsibilities, or they have borne a part in the history of great events. To him who is fitted for it by nature, experiences of such a sort will in time impart to his utterance clearness, dignity, and force, though in early life he may never have set pen to paper, or if he did, may have been distinguished for the ineffectiveness of the work he was called upon to do. It is not probable that General Grant ever had much practice in writing in his youth. What little he did have, it is more than probable he did not profit by. But participation in a mighty struggle, the ceaseless pressure of arduous duties and wearing responsibilities furnished him an intellectual training which is was not in the power of the schools to impart. Hence when he came to write his autobiography, he wrote. it with a simplicity and consequent effectiveness which no mere drill in English could have wrought. Or take the more marked case of Lincoln. It is not likely that the direct instruction in composition he ever received took up much of his time, if indeed it took up any of it. But in his profession he found imposed upon him as a condition of success the necessity of clear thinking, with its usual accompaniment of clearness of expression. But the further education which produced the matchless simplicity and majesty of the brief Gettysburg oration was the outcome of the discipline of anxious days and sleepless nights, the never-ceasing pressure of the burden of care which waited upon the long agony of the Civil War. As a matter of fact, indeed, there is nothing like misery to improve the style.

But education of this sort reaches an exceedingly limited number. Such exceptional instances do not come under consideration in the case of the college student. Whatever ability in expression he acquires must be gained mainly through the agency of formal education. At once the question arises, What is the best way for him to procure that intellectual development which lies at the foundation not alone of the great style, but of that which is merely good? For the student there is one chief way and but one, though there are several subsidiary ones. This all-important one is the discipline of hard study. He who devotes himself to this faithfully and intelligently is taking the most efficacious method of strengthening his mind just as steady exercise strengthens his body. As a result it prepares him to perfect himself in clearness of expression, if not in power. He may not indeed have that end in view any more than the boy who takes proper nourishment and proper exercise does it with the conscious thought of contributing to the physical growth which is the result of it.

Accordingly this mental development, lying at the foundation of all good writing, while it can be gained in many ways, is gained best by the college student through the agency of the intelligent study which develops the muscles of the mind—if the expression be permissible—as physical development is gained by the exercise which develops the muscles of the body. But study, however faithfully and earnestly carried on, will never of itself produce skill in expression. It may furnish the student much knowledge; it may make him a vigorous and even profound thinker; but, unaided, it will do little toward making him a good writer. While it furnishes the best of foundations, the superstructure must owe its existence to another element. This element is the sense of style which is a result of the possession of literary taste. Hence comes up for consideration an even more important question. How can this taste be best imparted where it is not, how can it be best developed where it is, innate? The answer to this presents little difficulty.

The art of writing, like that of painting and sculpture, is an imitative art. Accordingly the culture and perception of beauty necessary to produce success in it are best and soonest acquired, not by the study of grammatical and rhetorical text-books, but by the imitation, conscious or unconscious, of some one or some number of those whom the race regards as its great literary representatives. Different minds, or minds in different grades of development, will exhibit preference for different authors. The choice is not a matter of moment, provided the one chosen is worthy and appeals to the chooser, not because the study of him is a duty, but because it is a delight. To become thoroughly conversant with the work of a great writer, to be influenced by his method of giving utterance to his ideas, to feel profoundly the power and beauty of his style, is worth more for the development of expression than the mastery of all the rhetorical rules that were ever invented. This has been the inspiration and salvation of numberless men who have never seen the inside of an institution of learning. He who of his own accord has sat reverently at the feet of the great masters of English literature need have no fear that their spirit will not inform, so far as in him lies, the spirit of their disciple. Connected with it, too, there is incidentally one further benefit. Constant familiarity with the language of authors of the first rank imparts in time that almost intuitive sense of what is right or wrong in usage which distinguishes the cultivated man of letters from the sciolist who bases his judgment upon what he has found in grammars and manuals.

If this point of view be correct, it follows that in the union of intellectual vigor which comes from hard and intelligent study and of cultivated taste begotten of familiarity with the great masterpieces of our literature lies for the college student his linguistic and literary salvation. But the clearness or power or beauty of expression thus gained is not the work of a day or a month or a year. It is not merely a growth, it is a slow growth. In this slow growth there is nothing which appeals to the men who have come to know by intuition just what can and what ought to be done in this matter. They demand immediate results. They want a short cut to the acquisition of ability in writing. They are the ones who are constantly clamoring for frequent practice in composition and for constant correction. A useful but subsidiary part of instruction has been exalted into one of paramount importance. Attention has been concentrated upon it, stress has been laid upon it to the neglect of things far more essential. An army of teachers has been assembled to carry it on, the unintelligent among them swearing by it, the intelligent swearing at it. One result has long been apparent. On no one subject of education has so great an amount of effort been put forth as on the teaching of English composition, with so little satisfactory to show for it. Every one recognizes the waste that has taken place in this expenditure of force; but the only way suggested to remedy the loss incurred is to go on expending still further effort with results for which there will be even less adequate return in the future than there has been in the past.

The belief in the capability of thus manufacturing good if not great writers to order is widely prevalent with the general public. Its attitude has affected the action of our highest institutions of learning. It has, in truth, brought about the following condition. A body of writings must be produced by all the undergraduates. These, many of whom are utterly uninterested in the general work or in the particular subject, must take the contract of filling the order. The faith of the average man in the benefit to be derived from this course of proceeding is of the kind that removes mountains. There is a prevailing belief in the whole country that it is absolutely essential to the intellectual salvation of every growing youth that he should write themes. No sooner does the child enter the primary school than this particular task looms before his eyes. It is, indeed, the one requirement from which he never escapes during the whole of his educational career. It follows him to the high school, it pursues him to the college. His own inclinations or tastes in the matter are not consulted at all. We have been called upon to bewail the woes of the supposedly hapless beings who are compelled to study Greek against their will. There are those who sorrow for him who has to learn Latin. But no voice is lifted up in behalf of the unfortunates who are asked not to master a distasteful subject, but to perform the infinitely harder task of writing, not because they have something to say, but because they have to say something.

For the great American community clings firmly to the faith that anybody and everybody can be taught to use the language with clearness and precision, to say nothing of effectiveness. Any failure to attain the result is imputed to wrong methods of instruction, any distrust of its feasibility to the stupidity or intellectual depravity of the doubter. The slightest display of skepticism encounters at once indignant protest. Our universities, it is said, pretend to send forth educated men. Can we assert that a man is really educated who is unable to express himself clearly, to say nothing of forcibly? Ought not at least so much as the former be demanded of every one bearing a degree? I should hope for the coming of the time when this will be so, just as I hope for the coming of the millennium; and I may venture to add my personal belief that the arrival of the two will be about simultaneous. Still, were we to concede that the result were as feasible as it is desirable, in seeking to reach it we persist in committing the fundamental error of going back-end foremost. For it has to be repeated again and again that clear thinking precedes clear writing and does not follow it. In this matter the result is demanded before the cause which produces it is in existence. It is enough to say that any system of instruction ever devised which succeeds in imparting to all those pursuing it clearness of ideas, will have solved the educational problem of the ages and have begun the intellectual regeneration of the race.

But if clearness of thinking cannot be attained universally, ought we not at least to demand correctness in the use of our speech? Are you in favor, it may be asked, of a system of instruction which will turn out annually a body of so-called educated men who are unable to express themselves with propriety, and as a result of their consciousness of this inability are deterred from presenting their ideas to the public at all? It might be sufficient to reply that it has never yet been settled what is meant by writing one's own language with propriety. On this very point the widest divergence of view prevails. But let it be conceded that here a reasonable degree of unanimity of opinion has been attained. Even in that case it must be confessed that universities the world over are not merely turning out men now who are incapable of using the language with perfect correctness, but they have been turning them out for centuries past, and are pretty sure to continue turning them out for centuries to come. To a mind not properly constituted, such as is my own, this inability of men to express themselves with propriety, if it contribute to taciturnity, is something to be contemplated with a chastened spirit of resignation. It is a benefit that has been produced and not a harm. There is but one way of keeping certain persons from writing wretchedly, and that is by keeping them from writing at all. Anything which brings about such a result is to be welcomed, not deplored. No fear need be felt that the men who have really anything of value to communicate to the world will not triumph over the difficulties of communicating it when the time comes, no matter how little has been the instruction in composition they received in early life, or how much they neglected such instruction as they received. But if they have nothing to say, why insist upon the desirability of their adding to the mass of new writing perpetually put forth which will never become old? Assuredly no fear need be entertained of any diminution in the supply, whatever schools or colleges do or fail to do. The mighty Mississippi of gabble will steadily continue to pour through the land, even if it be deprived of an inconceivable number of petty affluents which under existing methods are coaxed or compelled to contribute to its ever-swelling stream.

In fact, the notion that every man should seek to become a writer is a notion born of modern conditions. There is no more reason or necessity for it than there is for every man to become a mathematician or a musician or an architect or an engineer or a painter. But in the art of composition we demand of every student what no one expects or desires in the case of any of the other arts, whether liberal or useful. To love and appreciate music, for instance, is something more than a mere accomplishment. It brings to its possessor what is far higher than keen enjoyment. It tends, too, to exert a distinctly refining and elevating influence upon the nature. Still, we do not insist that he who has no ear for it should devote days and nights to its study, still less should torture his fellow-men by practising it. Mathematics, again, is a good thing. It resembles English composition, too, by being on a slight scale a necessary thing to know. We require enough of it to enable every one to transact the common business of life. Then if we are wise we let him go, if he has no inclination for it, and concentrate the work of instruction upon those to whom the subject is a pleasure. We recognize that men can lead happy, honored, and useful lives to whom sines, cosines, tangents, and hyperbolas remain little more than vague remembrances of a ghastly dream. In these and other like instances we go upon the assumption that if the student achieve any result worth striving for he must have genuine interest in the subject he pursues, to say nothing of genuine capacity for the pursuit. Wisely, therefore, we offer him the opportunity of instruction in it; but we do not insist upon its acceptance.

A university which should set out to make all its students musicians or mathematicians or architects or engineers or painters without taking into consideration their several tastes or capacities will deservedly incur both censure and ridicule. Yet this is exactly what all of them set out to do in the art of composition. Certain persons there are who both before and after graduation have no disposition to write. Why can they not be left undisturbed in this ideally desirable condition of voluntary abstention? The world is not suffering from a penury of manuscripts or of books. Here, therefore, individuality of choice comes properly into play. The elective system has been at times praised, and at times overpraised. Similarly it has been disapproved and undervalued. But if there be warrant for it on the score of reason, it ought to find its fullest and most satisfactory justification in the matter of English composition. Yet this is the one place where it is not tolerated at all. Even the great champion of the system [Eliot—ED.], who advocated the utmost liberty of choice in about everything else, drew the line here. He, too, insisted that upon this particular educational altar every student should be immolated as a victim.

The adoption of the elective system is far from implying the abandonment of the practice of composition. It means instead the fullest realization of its utility. The result would be not to have less instruction in it, but to have that instruction more advantageously applied. The excessive expenditure of force now put forth in carrying it on with the least good to the greatest number would then be employed where it would be of special benefit to those most needing it. Consider the actual conditions. In every institution of learning there is a large body of students who have not the slightest desire to write a line. Why should they be tempted or forced to discuss subjects about which they know little and care less? On the other hand, there is always a minority—sometimes a large minority—who do not have to be urged to this particular task, still less compelled. They take to it of their own accord. They would engage in it no matter what obstacles were placed in their path. They are anxious to be shown the best way to express themselves adequately, clearly, forcibly. They heed every correction, they listen to every hint and suggestion. They respond heartily and intelligently to the efforts of the teacher because their hearts are in the work. Are such men, eager to learn, treated with any favor under our present compulsory system? On the contrary, it works them gross injury. Instead of receiving the special attention they have a right to demand, they receive, as a matter of fact, just as much as is given to the heedless or hostile, and no more. Instead of the instruction being concentrated on those who would most profit by it, it is largely wasted in vain efforts to overcome the repugnance of the unwilling or to animate the torpid.

The adoption of the elective system would accordingly prevent the sacrifice in this matter of the interests of the earnest and eager to the supposed interests of the indifferent or the incompetent. But from it another and most important incidental advantage would result. The instruction given would steadily tend to become adequate. Even when it is so now, the one charged with it dislikes the toil of examination and correction because he knows that his labor will be largely thrown away. He knows that the student, detesting the task of writing, will pay little or no heed to the corrections made, beyond what is necessary to save himself from the consequences of neglect. The inevitable result has already been indicated. Competent teachers tend steadily more and more to drop out. But with the abolition of the compulsory system the character of the instruction would speedily be raised. For as there is no more disagreeable drudgery than to attempt to make men learn who are unfitted or unwilling to learn, so there is no more delightful occupation than to train those who are anxious and eager to learn. With only such as these to deal with, the teaching force would steadily become of a distinctly higher grade. Competent men, instead of being repelled from it as now, would be attracted to it.

So much for the theory that every student should be required to write themes. In so doing we have seen that we reverse the order of nature in attempting to make the expression of ideas precede their acquisition. The other fallacy to be considered is that these themes should be written with great frequency. Here the reversal of the order of nature is even more pronounced. Frequency of production necessarily involves rapidity of composition. In fact, this result has been sometimes held up as a most desirable end to be aimed at, if not the most desirable end. No worse ideal could well be placed before immature minds, no worse practice indulged in. The inevitable consequence of the best work produced under such conditions are essays which are hardly worth writing, still less worth reading, and not worth remembering at all. There is further involved in this proceeding something more than mere waste of time and effort. Far worse are the habits of mind engendered. The student falls into the way of discussing matters he knows little or nothing about. He gives expression to thoughts or so-called thoughts which are no result of reflection, but have either come to him on the spur of the moment or more usually have been borrowed from quarters to which he can gain easy and unsuspected access. He puts down the first ideas that come into his mind in the first words that come to hand. The evil effects of such intellectual habits are almost certain to characterize his work in later life; in fact, will surely characterize it unless corrected by severe study on other lines.

In this country, however, the public mind has been so long bedeviled by the belief that the one way to hasten the coming of the literary millennium we all desire is the frequent writing of themes and the constant correction of them, that it is just now hopeless to expect that this superstition, which stands in the way of all real progress, can be destroyed till the experiment breaks down from the weight of its successive failures. In the educational world there exists and always has existed the disposition to enforce a strict quarantine against the entrance of new ideas. Any practice, any belief connected with education dies hard. To many in consequence the doctrines here advanced will seem to tend to unsettle the very foundations upon which the whole system of instruction in our own speech is based. Yet novel as the views may be to many and shocking to some, they have been expressed in the past even more strongly. They have been expressed, too, by men whose opinions in matters pertaining to education still retain a good deal of repute, though, as might be expected, they fail to come up to the standard of the advanced thinkers of the present day.

One of these men is Bacon. In the second book of his treatise *On the Advancement of Learning* he spoke of the necessity of the re-examination of usages prevailing in education. One ancient and general error, derived from more obscure times, he found then prevalent in the universities. This was the early teaching of logic and rhetoric. On this point he expressed himself strongly. "Scholars in universities," he wrote, "come too soon and too unripe to logic and rhetoric, arts fitter for graduates than for children and novices. For these two, rightly taken, are the gravest of sciences, being the art of arts; the one for judgment, the other for ornament. And they be the rules and directions how to set forth and dispose matter; and therefore for minds empty and unfraught with matter, and which have not gathered that which Cicero calleth *sylva* and *supellex,* stuff and variety, . . . to begin with those arts, doth work but this effect, that the wisdom of those arts, which is great and universal, is almost made contemptible, and is degenerate into childish sophistry and ridiculous affectation. And further, the untimely learning of them hath drawn on by consequence the superficial and unprofitable teaching and writing of them as fittest indeed to the capacity of children."

Another one of the men of the past who advocated heretical views of a similar character was Milton. According to the scheme laid down in his tractate on Education the pupil was to go through a regular course of study, culminating in politics, church history, and theology—subjects which at that time engrossed the thoughts of all—and then take up the consideration of "those organic arts which enable men to discourse elegantly and according to the fittest style of lofty, mean, or lowly." This preliminary preparation was to be mastered before the student was himself in readiness to write. The view Milton took in this matter is so extreme that a phrase of it is worth italicizing. "From hence," he continued, "*and not till now,* will be the right season of forming them to be able writers and composers in every excellent matter, when they shall be thus fraught with an universal insight into things." This, it will be seen, does not differ essentially from the position, previously mentioned, of the historian Palfrey, though it is free from the drastic measure he recommended for maintaining it in its perfection. But Milton in his blindness could not foresee the results of the march of mind which has gone on under modern conditions. The arduous and protracted preparation which he prescribed for acquiring "universal insight into things" is no longer demanded. Art, science, statesmanship itself is now learned in short and easy lessons. Hence out of the mouths of babes and sucklings proceeds with us wisdom on every subject, nowhere more notably than on that of English composition.

Shortly after Lounsbury's article appeared, Wilbur Cross, head of composition at the Sheffield Scientific School, invited him to a staff dinner. As Cross recounts it,

I asked the men who had charge of English composition to describe, one by one, what they were doing. When he [Lounsbury—ED.] heard the full story, how for instance all the work in composition was related to the particular interest of each student, including even the fine arts, he threw up his hands and declared in his delightful formal manner that he was ready to take back all that he had ever said against the futility of teaching English composition. (Cross, *Connecticut Yankee* 128–29)

From this it is hard to tell precisely how ironical Lounsbury was being in taking back the criticism he wrote with such relish.

William Lyon Phelps
"English Composition"
in *Teaching in School and College* (1912)

    ❧ *Phelps (1865–1943) graduated from Yale in 1887,
went to Harvard where he taught writing after getting his M.A. (1891), and
returned to Yale for his Ph.D. (1891). Among his students were Stephen Vincent
Benét, Sinclair Lewis, Thornton Wilder, and nearly every Yale undergraduate
for forty years. He wrote many books of popular criticism, mostly on literature of
the nineteenth and twentieth centuries. He was by far Yale's most popular and
well-known English professor, a sort of counterpart to Harvard's C. T. Copeland.*

    *The "experiment" Phelps refers to (below, p. 289) seems to be the same one
mentioned in the* Century Magazine *article (above, p. 238), and some of
Phelps's language recalls that article as well.*

ON THE SUBJECT OF REQUIRED ENGLISH COMPOSITION, I AM A
stout, unabashed, and thorough sceptic. And although the majority is
still against me, I am in good company. Professor Child read and corrected themes at Harvard for about forty years: at the end of the time, it
was his fervent belief that not only was the work unprofitable to the
student, but that in many cases it was injurious. That it is always
injurious to the instructor, when it is intemperately indulged, is certain.
When I was an instructor at Harvard, I one day met Professor Child in
the yard. He stopped a moment and asked me what kind of work I was
doing. I said, "Reading themes." He put his hand affectionately on my
shoulder, and remarked with that wonderful smile of his, in which
kindness was mingled with the regret of forty years, "Don't spoil your
youth." Professor Wendell, who inherited the bondage under which his
predecessor groaned, has never really believed in the efficacy of the work.
Professor Lounsbury of Yale has given valuable and powerful testimony
against it.[1] Professor Cook and Professor Beers—two quite different
types of men—are in this point in absolute agreement. [A. S. Cook,
Yale professor (see chap. 3, p. 160). Henry A. Beers, one of Phelps's
teachers at Yale.—ED.]

    After spending a year in graduate study at Harvard, I was appointed
by President Eliot Instructor in English, an honour of which I have
always been proud. I observed a curious fact. Men who had been graduated from Harvard, had studied in the graduate school, had topped this

by some years of research in Europe were spending nine-tenths of their time doing what? Reading undergraduate required themes and correcting in red ink spelling, punctuation, and paragraphing. Why such mighty labour of preparation to perform work that could be done exactly as well by any young school-teacher? Some of the instructors were permitted to give one hour a week of teaching in English Literature, others did nothing but read themes. I read and marked over seven hundred themes a week—most of them were short themes, but some were not. Whenever I entered my room I was greeted by the huge pile of themes on the table, awaiting my attention. I read very few books the whole year—there was no time. I never went to bed before midnight. If I were sick for two or three days, a substitute had to be found, for it was only by steady daily reading that I could keep pace with the manuscripts pouring in like a flood, threatening to engulf me every day. I am very glad that I had this experience, for a variety of reasons: it brought me in relation with the Harvard English faculty, where I made friendships for life, and I cannot speak too highly of the kindness and encouragement shown to the beginner by these men. It brought me into remarkably close contact with one hundred and twenty Harvard seniors and juniors, whose daily themes I read. These young gentlemen practically kept a diary by this method, and told me frankly not only their experiences, but their thoughts. I also read freshman and sophomore required themes, and had an excellent opportunity to become acquainted with the mental states of the average Harvard undergraduate. And I learned what teaching English composition meant.

But with the highest respect and admiration for my colleagues, nothing on earth would have induced me to continue such brain-fagging toil another year. I do not know that I should have been invited to do so, for I accepted another situation without asking. The curious thing is, that I then believed in the efficacy of the system. I said to myself: "This is worse than coal-heaving. This is nerve-destroying, a torture to soul and body. But it is necessary. Someone must do it. Why not I? But not I any longer."

I entered upon my duties at Yale, and taught freshmen English Literature. These freshmen had passed no entrance examination in English, for Yale had not then adopted it. The next year I had the same students. I made them all write four or five rather long compositions during the year, in addition to and in connection with their classroom work in literature. When I took home the first batch, I said: "Now for trouble. These young men have never had instruction in English composition, and have never passed through the valuable drill in the freshman year given in other colleges." But, to my unspeakable amazement, their compositions were just as good technically as those written by Harvard sophomores! It was a tremendous surprise, for the writers were not, as a class, one whit more advanced mentally than their Harvard brothers.

Then in junior year, I required, as I do now, every student in a large lecture course to write a weekly theme. Indeed, for one who does not believe in required compositions, I of my own choice read a large number every year. But this is not so contradictory as it may seem, which will presently appear. I took one weekly batch, all of them, the few good, the few bad, and the many commonplace, up to Harvard, and submitted them to one of the Harvard professors who was immersed in the "system." He read them carefully, and told me they were exactly as good technically as those done by Harvard juniors.

Now unless the results of constant required themes are absolutely definite and satisfactory, it simply does not pay to require them; for the labour and expense involved in reading and correcting are prodigious, and grow every year like a corrupt pension bill. I know of nothing in the world that illustrates more beautifully the law of diminishing returns than required courses in composition. A class of students will never under any circumstances write five times as well by writing five themes as they will by writing one; but the reading and correcting of five themes require five times the effort on the part of the body of teachers. In those schools and colleges where the English departments believe in constant required compositions, they are constantly demanding more instructors, more time, and more money. Quite naturally. I read a very interesting report on the subject by that accomplished professor of English, Sophie Hart, of Wellesley. Here are some extracts: "The committee urges an increase in the time given to the reading and discussion of themes in class. . . . An increase in the rewriting of themes is also urged. . . . Students should, as they advance, be taught to expect to rewrite from 60 to 75 per cent of their themes. . . . The greatest need in college instruction in English, as in secondary schools, is a larger teaching staff. . . . Professor [James Morgan—ED.] Hart of Cornell strikes at the root of our difficulty in his communication to the committee: 'Our Cornell experience is that the most difficult thing to overcome is the lack of thought.

Many of our freshmen seem to believe that anything patched up in grammatical shape will pass for writing. . . . I urge school-teachers to train their scholars to *think;* especially to prepare outlines of compositions before writing the composition.' "

Art thou there, truepenny? Of course that is the real difficulty. They are forced to write before they have anything to say, and intelligent teachers are forced to read and correct this vain and empty stuff. If a student is well-read, familiar with good literature, and has opinions, his writing is usually technically adequate. I heard a college president say, "The way to learn to write is to write." But it is not true. A good physician or surgeon has not learned to practise by practising: that is the method of quacks. Years of instruction in knowledge and in principles must come first. I have known cases where a boy will write a required composition full of grammatical and rhetorical errors; then he will write a letter to his instructor, saying he is called home by illness in the family, and the letter is technically correct.

I once saw a hundred students, armed only with pencil and paper, shut up in a college classroom. The teacher sprung some subjects on them—"One Summer's Day" among others. No student could leave till he had finished his composition. Imagine the results! A man I know once remarked, "I want to write articles for the papers and magazines: the only trouble is, I find I have a paucity of words and ideas."

In the schools there must be some elementary instruction in writing: the simple principles can be taught, and themes written to illustrate spelling, sentence arrangement, punctuation, and paragraphing. Compositions on interesting contemporary subjects, or on subjects connected closely with the lessons in Literature can from time to time be required. A good plan is to have the class vote on a list of subjects.

In college, it is well to have critical writing accompany literary courses, especially in the last two years. This is true particularly of lecture courses in Literature, where the students should write, not a synopsis nor a description, but an honest opinion. And they should be encouraged to write truthfully, absolutely regardless of the world's valuation of a certain author. Let them say what they really think. Each theme should be a personal impression, a confession.

Then, although I absolutely disbelieve in the study of formal rhetoric, and also in courses in required composition, I believe that every college should furnish *elective* courses—as many as possible—for the benefit of those students who really wish to practise writing as a fine art, who wish to improve their literary style. These courses should be strictly limited in numbers, so that the teacher may have plenty of time for personal conference outside of the classroom with each pupil. This is much more valuable than the class meetings.

I am certain, however, that the best way to learn to write is to read, just as one learns good manners by associating with well-bred people. A student who loves good reading, who has a trained critical taste, will almost always write well, and is in a position to develop his style by practice, the reading and ideas having come in the proper order, first instead of last.

NOTE

1. *Harper's Magazine*, November, 1911. [The preceding essay—ED.]

Lane Cooper
"The Correction of Papers"*
English Journal 3 (1914)

ᘐ (See biography above, p. 251.) A conservative alternative for dealing with student writing, totally opposed to the assembly line approach coming to dominate American education, particularly in state universities. Cooper's elitist insistence on the character of the instructor, fully in keeping with his preference for classical values, would soon become impossible to maintain under the pressures of mass higher education, yet this ideal would persist in the minds of many twentieth-century professors, particularly at small liberal arts colleges.

One sign of Cooper's distance from the attitudes coming to dominate composition teaching is his manner of writing, with constant literary allusions and almost involuted, wandering sentences. Cooper's prose is very far from the plain style being taught to most of America's college students.

*An address delivered at the College Conference on English in the Central Atlantic States, Albany, November 29, 1913, slightly altered for the present form of publication.

IF THE GOOD WILL OF MY READERS MAY BE CAUGHT IN THE ANCIENT fashion, let me say at once that the following remarks are based upon eleven years' experience in the correction of papers, during which I have not consciously neglected the obligations arising from the nature of the work. In the course of a decade one is likely to scrutinize such obligations, and to search for the principles that underlie them.

The principles lie bare when we discover the real significance of our topic. What, then, does "the correction of papers" actually mean? Briefly, it means the correction, or straightening, or normalizing of one personality by another through the instrumentality of truth expressed in language. At least two personalities are concerned; and between A, the teacher, and B, the taught, lies the medium of the vernacular or some other tongue, representing a third element that needs consideration. A and B have each their rights as well as their duties, which require careful adjustment. They have also their relations to some larger group, of which they are individual members; as their studies involve the welfare of the national language, there are mutual obligations existing between them and C, the State; for it will hardly be denied that education is the chief affair of state, or that an ability to think, and to tell the truth, is the principal end of education.

In taking up the rights and duties of both teacher and pupil with reference to the national language, I shall advocate no hard-and-fast procedure for the classroom. We have had perhaps too much prescription of rules in the teaching of English, and too little discussion of first principles which the teacher may assimilate, and, when they have become a regulative force in his life, may instinctively apply in the varying circumstances of his profession. My aim is simply to encourage others in thinking about the fundamental obligations I have mentioned, and to suggest an ideal balance among them—something not in all respects within easy grasp, it may be, yet not, on the whole, so far beyond our reach that we cannot profitably strive to attain it. In order to suggest this ideal, it may be necessary to lay stress on certain elements in the problem of teaching English which are in danger of neglect—the rights of the State, for instance, in respect to the purity of the national language; and it may be useless to dwell at length upon those elements which commonly receive undue attention—as, for example, the claims of the mediocre to an education that is quite superficial.

Let us begin with the medium of utterance. First of all, it behooves us to remember that language, in its essence, is something spoken, and that speech lies closer to the personality we wish to correct than does writing. Hence the need of having the student read many of his exercises aloud, so that he may acquire the habit of uttering premeditated truth, may receive correction by word of mouth, and may reform a number of his thoughts and phrases with the living voice.

Now we cannot divorce language from the substance of which it is the expression. This substance, again, flows from the mind of the writer or speaker, but before that it has entered into his mind from sources without. In a sense, then, the correction of a theme or essay should begin with the sources of information, as it must end with the details of usage. Be this as it may, the first demand we make of language, whether spoken or written, is that it represent some portion of truth that deserves communication. Can we assume that the student in his last year of school, or in his first year at college, or indeed at any early stage, will have something worthy of utterance, if he is left to his own devices, or to chance, in his selection of subjects? So far as my experience with the undergraduate goes, we cannot safely assume it. We must know in advance that his mind has been filled, and we must know with what it has been filled; we must see to it that he has materials of thought, and that the materials are well in excess of all draughts we are likely to make upon them when we ask for written compositions. Emptiness of mind is a serious flaw in the writer of a theme, and needs correction. We must see to all this because the first and sharpest of censures must be uttered when the student undertakes to write upon a subject of which he knows nothing. In the study of the vernacular, so close as this is to the soul of the learner, it is perilous to dally with the truth. We dare not let our pupils infer from our treatment of their compositions that the truth can ever be a secondary matter, or that substance is of less account than the way one manipulates it.

The truth of the individual thoughts is the first consideration. Next in importance comes their sequence. Here is a topic which our present generation is not likely to forget, much attention being paid to it in our manuals of composition. Yet there is something more to be said about it. Not only must we expect a sequence in the matter which a student on a given day exhibits in his theme; but there is an order, by no means superficial, which the immature pupil cannot be expected to provide in his work—which nevertheless must be forthcoming—namely, a substantial order in the tasks that are assigned from week to week and from month to month in a course of systematic study. An essential progress in the thinking of the student must be assured. How can this be brought about? The following is one suggestion. Let the teacher of English restrict the subject-matter of his courses to the field he is supposed to know. Within this field let him select a body of material that is interesting to him, and at the same time is not beyond the capacity of his class. In preparing to teach his chosen material, let him meditate long upon the point where he must begin if he is to attain his object, and longer yet upon this object, that is, upon the precise end he wishes to reach with his group of learners by the close of the year. Let the writing of his students deal with successive parts of that material, and let the correction of papers, like any other educational device, be at all times subservient to the end he has in view, namely, to convert unfed, unorganized, unsensitive minds into minds that are well-nourished, orderly, and sensitive. Otherwise he may wage an unceasing strife with the external symptoms of illiteracy, and never touch the inner seat of weakness and disease.

But we are verging on the duties of the teacher. What, in general, may we demand of the personality that is engaged in correcting others through the medium of the vernacular? First, the teacher must have had the right sort of personality to begin with; this affords the only guaranty that he will have sought out and received the right sort of training before he enters upon his profession. It is almost indispensable that he come from a family where good books are read and a good custom is observed in speaking. It is absolutely indispensable that from early youth he shall have been a reader of the best things. He must be so familiar with the masterpieces of literature that he has a standard of good sense and good English within him. He must be a well of English undefiled. Late-learners may have their use in the teaching of other subjects; they will not do for English. Mere conscious rules, acquired when one has reached maturity, will never take the place of a correct habit; they cannot rectify a vicious tendency in one's mode of utterance, they cannot change one's mental disposition.

Yet the only proper complement of natural aptitude and correct habit is adequate professional training:

> To me nor art without rich gifts of mind,
> Nor yet mere genius rude and unrefined,

> Seems equal to the task. They each require
> The aid of each, and must as friends conspire.

Our guardians of usage must have some such education as the poets and orators who have enriched, refined, and established the English tongue. Upon this great topic I may not enlarge. Suffice it to say that a candidate for the teaching of English in the preparatory school should have a thorough grounding in Latin (if possible also in Greek), a substantial knowledge of all the ancient literary masterpieces—of the Latin mainly at first hand, and of the Greek at least through translations. In addition to the Bachelor's degree he should have a year of special work in the theory of poetry, reaching back from Shelley and Sidney to Aristotle, and accompanied by judicious reading in the chief English poets; in Old and Middle English, so that he may see the modern literature in due perspective, and may be able to consult a historical dictionary of the language with intelligence; and perhaps in the development of prose, beginning with Cicero and Quintilian and coming down to Burke and Newman. Quintilian, at all events, should not be omitted, as the very best advice on composition and the correction of errors is to be found in him. The prospective teacher of English in the college or university should have something more. He should have the literary insight and human sympathy that come from a full three years of special preparation under competent guidance.

In any case, the corrector of personalities has a right, nay, a duty— his primary right, and his essential duty—to live, and to live abundantly. Nothing could be worse than a teacher of English who is half-dead or half-alive, from whatever cause. A half-trained instructor may be deemed to be only half-alive. But suppose he has the natural endowment and the acquired training that the teacher needs; one requisite to the continuance of his life is leisure for study. Not only that, but he must have the strength and the inspiration as well, and also the incentive. In reinforcing what has just been said, let us mention a few things a university instructor in English ought not to be. He ought not to be untrained in any branch that is essential to an understanding of the English language and literature. He ought not to be a person who affects to despise scholarship. He ought not to be lacking in ambition, or on any score unworthy or hopeless of advancement in his profession. Furthermore, he ought not to be overburdened, stultified, or disheartened with the reading of excessive amounts of uninspiring manuscript. There must not be an overplus of uninteresting sentences and paragraphs in the sumtotal of what he reads, but the reverse: he must have more hours for Chaucer, Spenser, Shakespeare, and Milton than for Freshman themes; otherwise he will begin to die—to die at the top, so to speak. It is his right and duty to be a vital influence in the lives he is supposed to be shaping. The personalities intrusted to him he may shape for better or for worse. It is hardly conceivable that he will not modify them at all. Yet if there are three possibilities, only one of them is tolerable. He must not leave his timber as it is, he must not warp it more, he must straighten it; and this requires ever-renewed vitality.

And what of the timber? What are the rights and duties of the personalities to be corrected? I shall not speak of what is patent, that is, of obligations that spontaneously suggest themselves on a superficial consideration, as the right of the pupil to the best kind of correction. No teaching could be too good for our land of promise, with the civilization here to be developed. This is obvious. When we penetrate deeper, we note, first of all, that not every person has the same right to an education in the vernacular. An idiot, for example, has not the same right as a genius, nor in general have those who are below the average in capacity or attainments the same right as those who are above it. Doubtless every one in a sense has a claim to instruction in English, but the point is that some have a better claim, or a claim to more of it, than others. Who are these? Clearly, as has been suggested, they who have the greater capacity. It is a law of nature that to those who have shall be given. In our teaching we may well observe the tendencies of nature, following her laws, and aiding her in the accomplishment of her purposes. It is said that "Whom the Lord loveth, He chasteneth." An easy application of the text may be made to the teaching of English composition.

Moreover, they who show promise have a right not to be herded in classes so large as to be unmanageable, where the individual is lost, and where the teacher, instead of being lifted up and drawing young men after him, must descend to their level, and appeal to the spirit, not of a social group, but of a mob. Extremes should be avoided. Large portions of time should not be lavished on the correction of single individuals or knots of two or three, unless these persons are extraordinarily gifted or exceedingly well-trained. On the other hand, an hour devoted to a class of ten or twelve is likely to produce results more potent and lasting than will three hours a week devoted to a class of thirty. Accordingly, with a given complement of instructors, and a given number of hours for English in the curriculum, it is better to divide our forty-five or thirty students into sections of fifteen or ten, so as to teach them properly when we teach at all. It has been my experience that Freshmen and Sophomores will study more, and will prepare better compositions, when they must read their work aloud before a dozen of their fellows whom they have come to know as individuals, and in the presence of a teacher whom they know in an intimate way, than under any other external conditions. Assuming that the student of English is worthy of his teaching, he has a right, not only to the best kind of teacher, but also to the best educational conditions.

Another right of the student may be stated thus. We must not require him to read books too rapidly, or to compose too many themes. How many teachers of English have a clear conscience as to their demands on either score? And who shall guard those guardians if they lack a conscience? Better a little reading carefully done, and a little writing based upon adequate thought and reading, than much hasty work of any sort. "No matter how slow the style be at first," says Ben Jonson, "so it be labored and accurate." Connected with his right to an opportunity for thought, and to leisure for the slow and often painful business of expression, is the just and proper claim of the student to some adequate form of publication or utterance. It is unfair to ask him to write week after week, and month after month, without a single chance to produce his best in the hearing of his fellows. In general, when they are not thus presented, let him take charge of his own papers, since he is the one who is most interested in them. It is bad for the teacher to stupefy himself with them in private, and the morality of throwing them into the waste-basket is doubtful. Worse still is an unseen public of one, an assistant, not the teacher, who comes into no personal contact with the pupil, and whose humanity touches the soul of the writer of a theme only through hieroglyphics on its margin.

Finally, if a youth has a right to any teaching whatsoever, he has a right to sympathetic treatment from the person who corrects him. The impulse to correct, which is natural, and is very strong in some teachers, is good only when, like other natural impulses, it is properly regulated. Doubtless we are all acquainted with pedantic men who cannot bridle their tongues when another tongue has made a slip, or withhold their censure if another's pen has gone astray. I am far from arguing against rigorous correction at intervals; but the wise and sympathetic teacher is likely to suppress something like five out of six impulses to chastise a fault, keeping ever in mind the advice of Ben Jonson, who says: "There is a time to be given all things for maturity, and that even your country husbandman can teach, who to a young plant will not put the pruning-knife, because it seems to fear the iron, as not able to admit the scar. No more would I tell a green writer all his faults, lest I should make him grieve and faint, and at last despair. For nothing doth more hurt than to make him so afraid of all things as he can endeavor nothing."

As to the duties of the pupil little need be said. He must try to tell the truth, and to express it distinctly, in speech as well as in writing. He must learn to be self-critical, so that he may correct himself. This will be accomplished when he is taught to respect the rights of others in the subject he is studying or explaining. His audience has a right to a clear and orderly exposition, and to correct usage. The word he employs must correspond to the object he has in mind, and must mean the same thing to others as to him. Hence it must accord with the meaning in the dictionary. I plead for a generous use of the dictionary in the teaching of English.

Let us pass to the rights and duties of the State. With reference to the vernacular its main duty is no secret. It must provide and encourage able and well-trained teachers, according them ample means of subsistence and a degree of honor not far short of the highest. On this head we may give ear to the words of Milton as they are quoted by Lord Morley for a similar purpose:

Whoever in a state knows how wisely to form the manners of men, and to rule them at home and in war with excellent institutes, him in the first place, above others, I should esteem worthy of all honor. But next to him the man who strives to establish in maxims and rules the method and habit of speaking and writing received from a good age of the nation, and, as it were, to fortify the same round with a kind of wall, the daring to overleap which let a law only short of that of Romulus be used to prevent. . . . The one, as I believe, supplies noble courage and intrepid counsels against an enemy invading the territory. The other takes to himself the task of extirpating and defeating, by means of a learned detective police of ears, and a light band of good authors, that barbarism which makes inroads upon the minds of men, and is a destructive intestine enemy of genius. Nor is it to be considered of small consequence what language, pure or corrupt, a people has, or what is their customary degree of propriety in speaking it. . . . For, let the words of a country be in part unhandsome and offensive in themselves, in part debased by wear and wrongly uttered; and what do they declare but, by no light indication, that the inhabitants of that country are an indolent, idly-yawning race, with minds already long prepared for any amount of servility? On the other hand, we have never heard that any empire, any state, did not at least flourish in a middling degree as long as its own liking and care for its language lasted. [1]

So much for Milton's letter to Bonmattei, with the warning it contains for our own generation and the application we may make of it to the duties of the State. Turning now to the question of rights, one may argue as follows. The State demands an education in the vernacular which shall do the greatest good to the greatest number; this does not necessarily mean conferring an equal benefit upon every individual. Under certain circumstances it might signify the careful education of a few because of the preponderant influence to be exercised upon the language by a relatively small body of persons, such as poets, orators, clergymen, editors, and teachers; a small body, that is, as compared with the population as a whole. If we consider, not the present generation alone, but future generations also, as concerned in our present system of education, we may admit that thoroughly training a few persons of great capacity is of greater advantage to the State that a superficial or ostensible culture of many. Accordingly, my remarks on the correction of papers turn out to be a plea for cherishing the more gifted among our students who show promise of becoming influential in maintaining the purity of the English language. It is, above all, a plea for safeguarding the interests of those who may become teachers of English. Such a plea is never untimely; it cannot be urged too often. The rights of the average student are in no peril, save as they are involved in the rights of neglected potential leaders; and the claims of those who are below the average will not in this humanitarian age go unnoticed. The poor, and their champions, we have always with us.

NOTE

1. Morley, *Studies in Literature*, pp. 223, 224.

Frank Aydelotte
"The History of English as a College Subject in the
United States"
in *The Oxford Stamp and Other Essays: Articles from
the Educational Creed of an American Oxonian* (1917)

❧ *Aydelotte (1880–1956) graduated from Indiana University, taught in a normal school, then took an M.A. at Harvard, where he taught composition under C. T. Copeland. His experience of composition turned him against the Harvard system, and when called back to Indiana he proceeded to reform the composition program there. His articles on turning composition into a course in thinking earned him a position as professor in the MIT writing program; the first-year English course, under Aydelotte's shaping, provided culture to an engineering college. Having been at Oxford as a Rhodes Scholar, Aydelotte remained an ardent advocate for the values of the English higher educational system rather than the German. Aydelotte's connections to the Guggenheim Foundation enabled him to influence funding decisions for scholarship in English; he was also the originator of the college honors program as president of Swarthmore, 1921–39, and headed the Institute for Advanced Study at Princeton.*

This essay and the one following contain, in largely altered form, material first put together by me for the section on English in Dr. C. R. Mann's report on Engineering Education for the Carnegie Foundation for the Advancement of Teaching. My thanks are due to Dr. Mann and to the Foundation for their kindness in allowing me to use this material in advance of their publication of it.

THERE IS A WIDE-SPREAD FEELING IN THE COUNTRY, IN COLLEGES and technical schools alike, that our work in English does not produce the values that it ought. Our college and technical-school graduates are condemned in various quarters as being unable to write and speak their mother-tongue, although the men who agree in that condemnation would perhaps disagree violently in their conception of what is good writing and speaking. In the same way English work is pronounced a failure because it does not produce the love of good reading, although there is the widest variety of opinion as to what constitutes good reading and why men should love it. This prevalent confusion of points of view in the critics is reflected by an equal confusion in the efforts of those who are undertaking to improve instruction in English. An extraordinary number of experiments are being tried, and the record of the results, in articles and text-books, is staggering in its bulk. The greater number of these experiments, like the criticisms which they answer, are concerned with matters of detail. The result is the invention of ingenious pedagogical tricks for doing this thing or that, which have their value, but which do not go to the heart of the matter.

This discussion, for better or for worse, follows a much simpler line. It is an attempt to determine, from the history of English as a college subject in this country, whether there is not something in the attitude with which we approach the subject, literature and composition alike, which is at the root of all our difficulties.

I

Our methods of treating English are a double inheritance from rhetoric and from the classics, and it seems pretty clear that the ineffectiveness of our study of English is due to precisely those methods which caused the study of rhetoric and of the classics in this country to decline. This will be evident if we look more closely at the two elements of this legacy. From 1800 to 1850, such study of English literature and composition as there was in our colleges was conducted by the professor of rhetoric. It was only after 1850, or rather after the Civil War, that English literature began rapidly to displace the classics, and it was during the last thirty years of the century that our present methods of dealing with it were evolved.

The first standard texts on rhetoric were those of Blair, Campbell, and Whateley. Hugh Blair's *Lectures on Rhetoric* were first published in 1783, just after he had resigned his professorship of Rhetoric and Belles-Lettres in the University of Edinburgh. The lectures had been read for twenty-four years in the University, and they were enormously popular.[1] They had, the author alleges, been quoted in print from students' notes before they were published. They form a learned disquisition on the philosophy of style, the character of the beautiful and the sublime, the nature of language, and the virtues and defects incident to different species of writing. They are diffuse, copious, erudite, fastidious in style, instinct with classical culture, and written from the point of view of the literary standards of the eighteenth century. They contain a great many just observations and a great many more elegant platitudes. They formed a storehouse of opinions which students apparently learned up. A favorite way of editing them was to append to each chapter analyses and sets of questions. For instance, these questions in Mill's edition (1844), at the end of the fifth chapter, on "Beauty and Other Pleasures of Taste":

"Why was it necessary to treat of sublimity at some length?

"Why will it not be necessary to discuss, so particularly, all the other pleasures that arise from taste?

"Why are several observations made on beauty?

"Beauty, next to sublimity, affording the highest pleasure to the imagination, what is the nature of the emotion which it raises?"

These four questions, out of the fifty or sixty on this chapter, will be sufficient to make clear to any discriminating teacher the nature of the emotions which such work would raise in the breast of the pupil, and the nature of the illumination which it would give him.

Campbell's *Philosophy of Rhetoric,* 1776, printed and written a little earlier than Blair's, is a book of much the same character. Campbell was principal of Marischal College, Aberdeen, and was a friend of Blair's: his canons of taste are the same. Both Blair and Campbell, in true eighteenth-century fashion, make "correctness" their ideal. Both censure many details of the works of the best authors whom they use as illustrations. The tone of this censure is curiously like the red-inked comments of their present-day descendants on the more modest productions of undergraduates. The ideal of correctness of the eighteenth century was an impossible and a sterile ideal; it strove for a correctness which never existed on sea or land. It was an attempt to cultivate taste by a negative process. And the same thing is true of the standards of many a present-day teacher of English composition.

Archbishop Whateley's *Elements of Logic,* 1826, and *Elements of Rhetoric,* 1828, expanded from articles which he contributed to the *Encyclopedia Metropolitana* some years before, vied with Blair and Campbell in popularity in American colleges during the first half of the nineteenth century. Whateley was at Oriel College, Oxford, in the days of Copleston, Davison, and Newman. His work contains more sound sense perhaps than Blair's or Campbell's, and tends somewhat more to a practical point of view. Rhetoric to Whateley is less a philosophy and more a practical art, always in danger of degenerating into a collection of juggler's tricks; he discusses the danger of putting these tricks into the possession of the wicked, who may use them to deceive. His conclusion is, however, that publicity will guard the public against this danger, a wide-spread knowledge of the art being the surest protection against the illegitimate practice of it.

These three texts were in well-nigh universal use in American colleges and universities before 1850. The classes recited from their textbooks the principles of style and of criticism,[2] and from four to eight times a year each student produced a theme or an oration. Apparently not much writing was required in college outside these formal set theses, except where essays were written or speeches prepared for literary and debating societies. So far as instruction went, the undergraduates had immense quantities of principle and very little practice. The lack of formal practice may have been a good thing on the whole, as leaving less danger of the undergraduate's forming habits of stilted self-conscious writing; as it was they grew up apparently pretty unscathed by rhetoric to learn to express themselves naturally in their literary societies and in personal letters. When we look back with admiration at the elegance with which our grandfathers wrote, we are inclined perhaps to give too much credit to the formal instruction they received and too little to their flourishing literary societies.

In 1854 G. P. Quackenbos (author of *First Lessons in Composition,* 1851, of which it is said 40,000 copies were sold) supplemented these classic works with his *Advanced Course of Composition and Rhetoric.* It is a compendious treatise, including in its five parts a history of the language, a guide to punctuation, a rhetoric, a section on composition or invention, and one on prosody. It presents all the old abstractions about the beauties of language in condensed textbook form, together with an immense number of more seemingly practical facts and rules. It contains many more suggestions for exercises than the earlier books, but these are of that artificial nature apparently inevitable in works devoted to the study of words rather than matter. For instance:

"A DESCRIPTIVE LETTER—*Dated Niagara Falls.*

I. Acknowledge receipt of a friend's letter, and offer to give an account of a summer tour which you are supposed to have taken.

II. Preparations for leaving home.

III. Incidents on the way to Niagara.

IV. General remarks on the pleasures, fatigues, and advantages of travelling.

V. Description of the Falls and the surrounding places.

VI. Comparisons with any other scene.

VII. Emotions awakened by sublime scenery.

VIII. General remarks about returning, and the anticipated pleasure of rejoining friends."

That exercise and the five hundred and sixty-five others of its like in the *Advanced Course* were destined to point the way for rhetoric for a generation. The subject became, as in this book, more practical in a sense, but at the same time more artificial. In addition to the exposition of abstract principles of style, it became the rule to provide concrete exercises for showing the working of these principles in action; only the fact was ignored that men do not write to illustrate principles of style, and that whatever is written for that purpose, even if successful, is useless for any other.

During the fifties and sixties, the number of manuals slowly increased, and during the seventies they increased very rapidly. The names of Bascom, Day, Haven, J. S. Hart, Bain, Hunt, Hill, Genung, and Wendell are a kind of history of the subject. We need not attempt the difficult and delicate task of commenting on the character and merits of these books one by one. In general the later treatises are shorter, abler, more sound and sensible, and more practical than the earlier ones. They eliminate the effusive piety, the shaky linguistic theories, and the girls'-finishing-school exercises of books like that of Quackenbos. But they are constantly concerned with the form of thought rather than the substance, and hence the tendency toward artificiality in their results with the average beginner.

Whateley says, in the preface to his work, that while those who have already formed their style may not find his book of any particular interest or value, he hopes that it will prove of worth to those who have yet to develop the power of writing. He might more reasonably have hoped the opposite. While abstract principles of style are worth little and mean little to the beginner, they are both interesting and instructive to the practiced writer, and that remark will be found true of the whole series of books here considered. They contain sound sense, elegant and discerning thought, and fine and lofty ideals of the art of writing, but all these have been practically wasted on the thousands of elementary students who have been drilled in their precepts as a means of learning to write.

In this discussion I have omitted works on logic, like Whateley's and Thomson's, which were often, especially in the earlier half of the century, studied in rhetoric classes. The two subjects, rhetoric and logic, were very properly linked together. They are similar in attitude and aim; and the *formal* study of them is equally interesting to the practiced thinker and equally futile in the case of the elementary student.

While the impression given above of the divorce of rhetoric from thought is substantially correct, it is nevertheless true that now and then a textbook attempted to take the opposite line. T. W. Hunt's *Principles of Written Discourse,* 1884, is a remarkable example of this. It opens with an outline history (rather meager, it is true) of the rise and fall of rhetoric as a study, and points out clearly the tendency, which has existed from the days of the Sophists until now, to make it a study of words rather than of meanings. He sets for himself the task of again uniting form and content. The book is a valiant, if not quite successful, effort to resist the traditional organization of rhetorical ideas. But the main current flowed on in its old channel.

Alexander Bain, from 1860 to 1880 Professor of Logic and English at the University of Aberdeen, and author of an *English Composition and Rhetoric,* first published in 1866, which was a good deal used in American colleges, was extremely clear and outspoken in recommending this divorce of writing from thinking to which the whole study of English composition tended. In the preface to the 1871 edition of the *Composition and Rhetoric,* he explains clearly his theory of the negative function of composition teaching,—pruning, correcting, disciplining the student's use of words. He doubts the value of original themes or essays as a training in composition: too much attention may be diverted to the matter. "The writing of Themes," he says, "involves the burden of finding matter as well as language; and belongs rather to classes in scientific or other departments, than to a class in English composition. The matter should in some way or other be supplied, and the pupil disciplined in giving it expression." He suggests, as a better exercise than themes, improving imperfect passages in old authors, converting poetry into prose, abridging and summarizing longer passages or expanding brief sketches.[3]

In his little book *On Teaching English*, 1887, Bain develops this idea at greater length. "Care and correctness" are the things for the composition instructor to teach. All mixed exercises, involving attention both to matter and form, or even to various qualities of style at one time, are bad. The only possible justification of themes is because "we can find so little to do in expression proper, that we need to add to the work by throwing in a lesson of knowledge or of thought."[4] That possibility he indignantly repudiates. He would organize and simplify the whole subject of composition beyond anything that has been attained so far, taking up one principle at a time, mastering it, and passing on to the next. The idea that a man's style is the expression of the whole man he implicitly denies. In this, as in all other subjects, he is distinctly opposed to reaping where he has not sown. He would deal with no ideas in the rhetoric class except those proceeding from the rhetoric teacher and the text-book. "A learner should not be asked even to show off what he can do outside the teaching of the class. . . . If you depart ever so little from the principle of testing pupils on your own teaching, and on nothing beyond, you open the door for any amount of abuse."[5]

This is perhaps the frankest statement in the latter half of the nineteenth century of that belief in the separation of writing from thinking which has always been the danger of English composition. I do not mean to imply that Bain's extreme views were very widely accepted. A review of the book in the *Academy*, in 1887, criticizes it severely on just these grounds, but Bain makes only an extreme statement of the position which was implied in the current methods then and is to-day.

Since 1890 composition teaching has advanced rapidly from theory to practice. But the practice is really based on the old theory. Textbooks on writing have been less and less used or have become more and more useful manuals of information needed by writers (advice on hard points of grammar, punctuation, usage, and arrangement of material, more or less like the indispensable "style books" issued by publishing houses), but the themes have continued to be written for the sake of practice rather than for the sake of saying something. Students are advised to *write, write, write*, when the advice they need is *think, think, think*. The required themes have increased in length and frequency until many undergraduates are compelled to produce in one course in a year an amount of writing which, if it were really to say anything, would tax the strength and fertility of most professional men of letters, even though they gave all their time to the work. This tendency has reached its climax in the daily theme. When the instructor requires an essay from each student every day he must of necessity be lenient as regards thought. Such work encourages glibness and facility and wordiness rather than sincerity and brevity and care. It tends inevitably to put the emphasis on words rather than on matter, and to divorce writing from thinking. Professor Phelps, of Yale, argues from his own experience that our undergraduates write quite as well without this stupendous amount of drudgery, and the author of this paper would go so far as to say that the results are better.

II

The study of rhetoric, with its eighteenth-century standards of correctness in form and its eighteenth-century tendency to minimize the importance of the idea, its belief that

> True wit is nature to advantage dress'd;
> What oft was thought, but ne'er so well express'd,

was indirectly an inheritance from the Renaissance study of the classics. The influence of the study of the classics is more directly visible however in the teaching of English literature. The old professor of rhetoric was likely to be professor of *belles-lettres* as well, but his use of literature was mostly as an illustration of rhetorical effects. The classics were primarily the material for purely literary study. After the middle of the past century, English literature began gradually to displace the classics, during the sixties it became a full-fledged college subject, and in the seventies courses in English literature began to take on their present form.

English literature did not displace the classics without vigorous opposition. The common objection was that English was too easy; reading straight along what could be readily understood without the aid of grammar or dictionary was considered to be of very little value educationally, or, even if valuable, was something which the student might do as well by himself as with a teacher. In self-defense teachers of English felt called upon to prove that their subject was difficult, and to make it difficult in order to substantiate their proof, in both of which efforts they amply succeeded. The middle of the century was a period of great advance in English scholarship, and the newly heaped-up stores of knowledge were freely drawn upon to lend body and substance to the teaching of English literature. Old English was a ready resource; if not quite so hard and not quite so ancient as Latin, it was still both hard and old. The fact that the value of Old English literature was infinitesimal as compared with that of Latin or Greek was ignored. Old English (or Anglo-Saxon as it was generally called) was advocated as the logical study with which to begin the English course and constituted in some colleges the work of the freshman year. In many places during the seventies and eighties, English literature later than Shakespeare or Milton was rarely studied. It was an age of productive scholarship in English studies as in science, and in both fields scholars taught what they were most interested in, emphasizing contributions to knowledge above the use of knowledge for the purposes of education. Now and then a scholar like Child achieved both ends, but such men were rare.

There is no lack of evidence that the study of English literature was modeled closely on the study of the classics: all the educational writers of the time say so, and the college catalogues confirm it. For example, the following quotation from the catalogue of Columbia College in 1860. In the section devoted to Philosophy and English Literature, we are told that, "The latter half of the year is devoted to the critical study of an English classic, *treated in the same manner as an ancient classic is treated by a Professor of Ancient Languages, etc.*"

Another example of the influence of the classical method on the study of English literature is a little book by F. A. March, who, in 1857, became professor of the English Language and Comparative Philology at Lafayette College. It is his *Method of Philological Study of the English Language,* 1865. The book is an imitation, as the author states in his preface, of a *Method of Classical Study,* 1861, by Samuel H. Taylor, Principal of Phillips Academy, Andover. Dr. Taylor's book prints a few short passages of Greek and Latin—five fables from the *Latin Reader,* a chapter from *Nepos,* a section of one of Cicero's orations, twenty-three lines from the *Aeneid,* a chapter of the *Anabasis,* and thirty-two lines of the *Iliad*—with questions. The book is like the Variorum Shakespeare or the work on Magic which Merlin read,

> every page having an ample marge,
> And every marge enclosing in the midst
> A square of text that looks a little blot . . .
> And every margin scribbled, crost, and cramm'd

With comment, densest condensation, hard
To mind and eye,

except that in place of comment we have questions,—a few on subject-
matter, and hundreds on every detail of the construction and grammatical form of every word. March's book is an exactly similar treatment of a
few short passages from Bunyan, Milton, Shakespeare, Spenser, and
Chaucer. The total amount of the reading is insignificant; hardly enough
is given from each author to make a connected impression or to offer the
slightest difficulty to the understanding, but the questions are "hard to
mind and eye." They demand of the young pupil first an immense
number of facts about the life of the author and the literary history and
sources of the work under discussion. Following this comes a series
which involves a minute grammatical analysis of the selection sentence
by sentence and the parsing of words, with special attention to the
difficult forms of the verb. The first questions would not be unprofitable
for a graduate class which had read and understood the work in question:
the second part would not be unprofitable drill for a class in grammar.
But in no real sense is either a literary exercise.

Our copiously annotated school texts and the traditional method of
using them are another expression of this point of view. A great deal of
literary study became a study of notes rather than of texts, and the story
is universal of the undergraduate who, not having time in preparation for
an examination to read both text and notes, chose the latter to his profit.
In classics the emphasis had somehow got shifted from literature to
language, from literary training to grammatical discipline (a fact which
has had more influence perhaps than any other in their decline), and this
became true of the study of English literature. The whole matter was of
course one of emphasis and degree: in any reading the student must
understand the words before he can understand the meaning. And the
more closely he reads, the more widely he grasps the significance of
allusions, the more richly he understands the meaning of words and how
they came to have their meanings, the more keenly he tastes the fine
flavor of the language of an author, and the more truly he understands
what the author is trying to say. But this last is the important thing, all
else is subservient to it, and this fact the student must also see or he will
never see the true meaning of his work. Too much of the literary study of
the last generation never got to literature.

If this historical account and my interpretation of it are sound, it would seem that the root of our troubles in English is that we have inherited an attitude toward the subject which has led us, both in literature and composition, to emphasize technique rather than thought. As a result, our courses in English literature have tended to stress the history of literature, the "evolution" of literary forms, the language, rather than the thought of the authors studied. It has often been said that every student of literature should be also either a historian or a philosopher. In this country we have tended to divorce literature from philosophy and from history, except for that unreal kind of history which we call the history of literature. The result is to leave our instruction thin, lacking in grip on human problems, in a very real sense of the word unliterary.

In like manner our instruction in composition has inherited from the study of rhetoric its preoccupation with form rather than content. We still tend to think it better for the student to write on easy subjects, which will not demand much thought, in order that he may put all his attention on the words he is using. We ask him to deal not so much with ideas as with "forms of discourse." We grade him not on what he says, but on how he says it.

It is of course to be admitted that we all know teachers whose work is an exception to this; no statement of a tendency can be true of every particular; but the foregoing pages describe with substantial accuracy the prevailing temper of our English work, both in colleges and technical schools. And that temper accounts for its ineffectiveness. This external point of view has been often enough denounced in our own literature. "The chief vices of education," says Ruskin, in his lecture on "Art and Morals," "have arisen from the one great fallacy of supposing that noble language is a communicable trick of grammar and accent, instead of simply the careful expression of right thought." Our study of English has labored too much under that fallacy; it has fallen into what Bacon calls "the first distemper of learning, when men study words and not matter."

NOTES

[1]The Boston Public Library contains what seem to be sixteen separate editions and twenty-four "abridgements," and yet lacks some editions, notably the first. [I have retained Aydelotte's idiosyncratic spelling "Whateley" throughout his essay. —Ed.]

²"The Sophomores recited twice a week from Campbell's Rhetoric, during the First Term."—*Catalogue of Harvard College*, 1850.
³Bain, *English Composition and Rhetoric*, 1871, Preface, p. 6.
⁴Bain, *On Teaching English*, p. 26.
⁵Bain, *On Teaching English*, p. 27.

Bliss Perry
And Gladly Teach (1935)

   Perry (1860–1954) graduated from Williams and taught rhetoric there. He studied in Germany, taught English at Princeton, edited the Atlantic Monthly, *and taught English at Harvard from 1907 to 1930. As an outsider who came to Harvard rather late in his career, Perry viewed the system of compulsory composition with fresh eyes—and condemned it.*

ANOTHER THING THAT PUZZLED ME AT HARVARD WAS THE PERSIStent faith, among undergraduates and many teachers, in the value of courses in Composition. This tradition went back to the days when John Quincy Adams held the Boylston Professorship of Rhetoric and Oratory, a chair subsequently filled by 'Ned' Channing, Child, and A. S. Hill. Surely these men, followed by such expert teachers of composition as Briggs, Wendell, Copeland, [Briggs and Copeland also held the Boylston Professorship—ED.] and the rest, could not have labored in vain! Although it was known that Child and Wendell, toward the end, had grown sceptical of the value of 'themes,' there was a comfortable creed that the graduates of Harvard wrote better than the graduates of other colleges. I kept to myself the dreadful secret that in ten years of reading manuscript for the *Atlantic* I had never observed that Harvard men wrote any better than Yale man or Bowdoin men or men like Howells and Aldrich and John Burroughs who had never gone to college at all! It seemed to me that writing was a highly personal craft, to be perfected only after long practice, and that it made little difference where or how the practitioner learned the rudiments of his trade. Many years afterward, I admired Professor Grandgent's courage in declaring his fear that Harvard students 'write rather poorly, and speak worse.'¹ Having been myself in youth an enthusiastic teacher of English composition, and in middle age infected somewhat with Wendell's scepticism as to its unique worth as a college study, I may be allowed to unburden myself of some truisms:

(1) The mechanics of English composition can be taught. They are taught well in hundreds of schools, and may if necessary be imparted to such college students as have failed to receive proper instruction. Beyond this field of mechanical correctness lies the domain of literary art, and art in writing is mainly a matter of self-discipline, although the practitioner may be helped by expert criticism. (2) We expect too much, however, from the teachers of English in American colleges. They have had to shoulder a great part of that burden of accurate training in the mother tongue which was formerly carried by means of daily drill in translating Greek and Latin. Year after year in the Harvard Graduate School, I used to notice that the best writers were the Canadians who had kept up their classics. No boy well trained in Latin or Greek composition ever found difficulty in expressing himself clearly in English. It was hoped that drill in the modern languages would ultimately supply the discipline once given by the classics, but thus far the results are disappointing. (3) Undergraduates with literary ambitions should have the opportunity for writing verse, prose, drama, fiction—any literary form they prefer— under competent instruction. This individual instruction is, however, very costly, both in time and money, and it should be limited to students of special promise. Even from these youths one should not expect imme- diate triumphs. One cannot make bricks without straw [Cooper used the same biblical reference above, p. 253—ED.] or a work of art without materials, and very few undergraduates have read enough, experienced enough, pondered enough, to have even the raw material for a literary masterpiece.

NOTE

¹S. E. Morison, *Development of Harvard University, 1869–1929*, p. 104.
[Grandgent wrote the chapter on the modern languages in Morison's book.—ED.]

5

Textbooks for a New Discipline

THE OLD COLLEGIATE CURRICULUM MADE INSTRUC-
tors dependent upon textbooks in ways we find hard to conceive. College
catalogues often listed the books to be covered: they *were* the course.
Most often, students dealt with a text by committing its main points to
memory. Class sessions were mostly recitations which tested how much
of the text the students had memorized or absorbed. The teacher sat in
front with a class chart open and called on the students one by one to
"recite," that is, to tell what was in the text. A typical question would
be, "What was Macauley's method of composition?" (Cross 64). If the
student knew what the book had said, the teacher wrote down a good
mark; if the student didn't, the teacher entered a bad mark. There was
no discussion, no questioning of the book or teacher. Lecture courses
were rare, and usually reserved for seniors. (In 1870 the term "lecture"
implied that the instructor was giving students the benefit of wisdom
that was not yet in book form; the notion of lecturing on matter that was
already published was ludicrous, since instructors had in the recitation a
proven method of inculcating book learning.)

The German model challenged this traditional approach to a collegiate education. For the new university the ideal teacher was an independent scholar and researcher who would make use of up-to-date
teaching configurations like the lecture and the seminar, and new
teaching techniques and equipment, like the quiz and the blackboard.
As composition grew, however, more and more of its teaching was done
by instructors and teaching assistants who were new to the classroom,
untrained in the discipline, and in many cases only a page or two ahead
of the class. The composition text in such hands dominated the class-
room in a very different way; it was not just meant to be mastered by

students, but was to teach the instructor as well (Connors, "Textbooks" 189–90).

When modern composition began around 1875 professors imported some key textbooks from overseas. Soon, however, texts were created by the very people who were instituting the discipline at Harvard. And Harvard's prestige helped the spread of its approach to composition. The half century 1875–1925 witnessed a significant evolution in textbooks. In 1875 there was no college reader, no college book of exercises, just Blair, Campbell, Whately, and their followers, authors of treatiselike books explaining the subject of rhetoric. Most of these authors spent little time on grammar or mechanics, which presumably had been mastered in preparatory school. They combined lengthy discussions of style (with illustrations taken from Greek, Latin, and English classics) and literary effects, along with detailed discussions of principles behind rhetoric, with special attention to organization and arrangement.

Harvard's new program introduced Abbott's *How to Write Well,* a brief book of exercises written for the use of English schoolboys in their translations from Latin and Greek. A. S. Hill later wrote his own extremely popular text, *Principles of Rhetoric,* for the Harvard course; a lengthy, demanding book, it provided a sort of up-to-date version of the eighteenth-century treatises (1st ed., 1878; 2nd ed., 1895). In many colleges the 1870s and 1880s saw a gradual displacement of classical rhetorical treatises and the gradual introduction of easier, more accommodating texts. This change was slower at Harvard, where Hill's demanding text (see below, p. 320) remained supreme in basic courses; in fact, English A had almost the same description and used the same text from 1878 to 1914. Change was faster elsewhere, where composition was not so entrenched, and students were perhaps not so well prepared. A dramatic change came with two books of the 1890s, Wendell's *English Composition,* the first book with genuine flair and style, and especially Scott and Denney's *Paragraph-Writing,* a textbook with a radically slimmed down purview of a writing course and the first of the big sellers to include actual topics for compositions. Connors ("Personal Writing Assignments") supplies an excellent overview of the development of theme topics within textbooks. At first there was a gap between the discussion of the general compositional issues at hand (descriptions, introductions, etc.) and the actual compositions themselves. Presumably the instructor was expected to assign compositions which required the students to think up topics on their own. Over the years, topics for composition gradually began appearing in textbooks. With Scott and Denney, however, we are in the world of total domination by a text that provides topics by the thousand. (A notable feature of the Harvard program was its refusal to supply these topics; students had to develop them on their own, thus preserving, in however truncated form, the traditional practice of invention.)

The modern composition reader evolved at this time, born from a pedagogical mix of imitation and modeling. Robert Louis Stevenson's theory of composition, enunciated in his essay "A College Magazine" (1873), urged the beginning writer to be a "sedulous ape" and imitate the masters. Many teachers preferred the looser notion of modeling, which was not as strict or as rigid as the imitation. By the 1880s instructors began assigning readings to students, first from some of the standard, highly popular collections of essays, speeches, and stories meant for general readers or in use in secondary schools, and then by the 1890s in college composition textbooks assembled for use in class, with or without the series of introductory remarks, questions on the reading, and topics for writing that we now know by the wonderfully old-fashioned term "apparatus." (Imitation, of course, had been recommended as far back as Quintilian, and students knew it well from Latin classes.) And around this time the popular genre of the handbook developed. The term itself had been around for a long time, but the new handbook provided a brief compendium of rules and precepts, arranged for easy access, to aid the college writer. It soon became enormously popular as a supplement to readers and to rhetorics, which were much fuller books than the early handbooks (see Connors, "Handbooks").

By 1910 every modern type of college text and guide had appeared except the workbook, and it existed in the high schools (and was perhaps thought too low level for college classrooms). During the forty-year stretch from 1870 to 1910, one of the most intensive periods of change American higher education has ever seen, students proceeded from elaborately written, dense treatises on rhetoric, some of them like Blair and Whately classics of the field, to Woolley's *Handbook of Composition* and endless collections of essays as models for writing. The new books were easier, more up to date, less imposing, more practical, and much more attractive. In fact, the earlier treatises were perfectly adapted to a recitation-based pedagogy that demanded mastery of their subject matter but did not assign very many themes; the new books were practical survival guides meant for students who had to produce plenty of simple, brief themes in a fast-paced intensive writing course.

Edwin A. Abbott
How to Write Clearly: Rules and Exercises on English Composition (1875)

❧ Abbott (1838–1926), a Cambridge graduate, became headmaster of the City of London School in 1865. He was a reformer of Latin pronunciation, teaching methods, science education, and the curriculum, being among the first to introduce English literature and philology. He is now best known for his science fiction novel Flatland *(1884). How to Write Clearly was originally intended for high-school-age English students (the word "pupil" appears throughout, a sign of its youthful intended audience) but was quickly adopted by American colleges when they began composition course work. It was used extensively at Harvard and at the University of Michigan before Scott arrived, and Genung admired it (see chap. 3, p. 150).*

This American edition is a reprint of the tenth English printing of Abbott's widely used 1872 text. Though Abbott's preface speaks of the book's simplicity and brevity, it is really one of the oddest and most complicated textbooks in this collection. The rules below on "clearness and force" (318) seem totally arbitrary, the instructions to the exercises (319) are extraordinarily complicated, and the prose style of the exercise sentences reads like a poor translation from the Latin.

PREFACE.

Almost every English boy can be taught to write clearly, so far at least as clearness depends upon the arrangement of words. Force, elegance, and variety of style are more difficult to teach, and far more difficult to learn; but clear writing can be reduced to rules. To teach the art of writing clearly is the main object of these Rules and Exercises.

Ambiguity may arise, not only from bad arrangement, but also from other causes—from the misuse of single words, and from confused thought. These causes are not removable by definite rules, and therefore, though not neglected, are not prominently considered in this book. My object rather is to point out some few continually recurring causes of ambiguity, and to suggest definite remedies in each case. Speeches in Parliament, newspaper narratives and articles, and, above all, resolutions at public meetings, furnish abundant instances of obscurity arising from the monotonous neglect of some dozen simple rules.

The art of writing forcibly is, of course, a valuable acquisition— almost as valuable as the art of writing clearly. But forcible expression is not, like clear expression, a mere question of mechanism and of the manipulation of words; it is a much higher power, and implies much more.

The rules are stated as briefly as possible, and are intended not so much for use by themselves as for reference while the pupil is working at the exercises. Consequently, there is no attempt to prove the rules by accumulations of examples. The few examples that are given, are given not to prove, but to illustrate the rules. The exercises are intended to be written out and revised, as exercises usually are; but they may also be used for *vivâ voce* instruction. The books being shut, the pupils, with their written exercises before them, may be questioned as to the reasons for the several alterations they have made. Experienced teachers will not require any explanation of the arrangement or rather non-arrangement of the exercises. They have been purposely mixed together unclassified to prevent the pupil from relying upon anything but his own common sense and industry, to show him what is the fault in each case, and how it is to be amended. Besides references to the rules, notes are attached to each sentence, so that the exercises ought not to present any difficulty to a painstaking boy of twelve or thirteen, provided he has first been fairly trained in English grammar.

The "Continuous Extracts" present rather more difficulty, and are intended for boys somewhat older than those for whom the Exercises are intended. The attempt to modernize, and clarify, so to speak, the style of Burnet, Clarendon, and Bishop Butler, may appear ambitious, and per- haps requires some explanation. My object has, of course, not been to *improve upon* the style of these authors, but to show how their meaning might be expressed more clearly in modern English. The charm of the style is necessarily lost, but if the loss is recognized both by teacher and pupil, there is nothing, in my opinion, to counterbalance the obvious utility of such exercises. Professor Bain speaks to the same effect: "For an English exercise, the matter should in some way or other be supplied, and the pupil disciplined in giving it expression. I know of no better method than to prescribe passages containing good matter, but in some respects imperfectly worded, to be amended according to the laws and the proprieties of style. Our older writers might be extensively, though not exclusively, drawn upon for this purpose."

INDEX OF RULES.

I. Clearness and Force.

Words.

1. Use words in their proper sense.
2. Avoid exaggerations.
3. Avoid useless circumlocution and "fine writing."
4. Be careful in the use of "not . . . and," "any," "but," "only," "not . . . or," "that."
4*a*. Be careful in the use of ambiguous words, *e.g.* "certain."
5. Be careful in the use of "he," "it," "they," "these," &c.
6. Report a speech in the First Person, where necessary to avoid ambiguity.
6*a*. Use the Third Person where the exact words of the speaker are not intended to be given.
6*b*. Omission of "that" in a speech in the Third Person.
7. When you use a Participle implying "when," "while," "though," or "that," show clearly by the context what is implied.
8. When using the Relative Pronoun, use "who" or "which," if the meaning is "and he" or "and it," "for he" or "for it." In other cases use "that," if euphony allows. Exceptions.
9. Do not use "and which" for "which."
10. Equivalents for the Relative: (*a*) Participle or Adjective; (*b*) Infinitive; (*c*) "Whereby," "whereto," &c.; (*d*) "If a man;" (*e*) "And he," "and this," &c.; (*f*) "what;" (*g*) omission of Relative.
10*a*'. Repeat the Antecedent before the Relative, where the non-repetition causes any ambiguity. See 38.
11. Use particular for general terms. Avoid abstract Nouns.
11*a*. Avoid Verbal Nouns were Verbs can be used.
12. Use particular persons instead of a class.
13. Use metaphor instead of literal statement.
14. Do not confuse metaphor.
14*a*. Do not mix metaphor with literal statement.
14*b*. Do not use poetic metaphor to illustrate a prosaic subject.

. . . .

EXERCISES

For an explanation of the manner in which these Exercises are intended to be used, see the Preface.

A number in brackets by itself, or followed by a letter, e.g. (43), (40 *a*), *refers to the Rules.*

Letters by themselves *in brackets,* e.g. (*b*), *refer to the explanations or hints appended to each sentence.*

N.B.—(10 *a*) *refers to the first section of Rule* (10); (10 *a'*) *to the Rule following Rule* (10).

1. "Pleasure and excitement had more atttractions for him *than* (*a*) (36) (37 *a*) *his friend,* and the two companions became estranged (15 *a*) *gradually.*"

   (*a*) Write (1) "than for his friend," or (2) "than had his friend," "had more attractions than his friend."

2. "(*a*) He soon grew tired of solitude even in that beautiful scenery, (36) the pleasures of the retirement (8) *which* he had once pined for, and (36) leisure which he could use to no good purpose, (*a*) (30) *being* (15) *restless by nature.*"

   (*a*) This sentence naturally stops at "purpose." Also "being restless" seems (wrongly) to give the reason why "leisure" could not be employed. Begin "Restless by nature . . ."

3. "The opponents of the Government are naturally, and not (*a*) (40 *a*) *without justification,* elated at the failure of the bold attempt to return two supporters of the Government at the recent election, (*b*) (10 *a'*) *which* is certainly to be regretted."

   (*a*) "unjustifiably." (*b*) Write, for "which," either (1) "an attempt that &c.," or (2) "a failure that &c."

4. "Carelessness in the Admiralty departments has co-operated with Nature to weaken the moral power of a Government that particularly needs to be thought efficient in (*a*) (5) *this respect,* (*b*) (29) *to* counterbalance a general distrust of its excessive *desire* (*c*) (47 *a*) *to please everybody* in Foreign Affairs."

   (*a*) Write "the Navy." (*b*) Instead of "to" write "in order to," so as to distinguish the different infinitives. (*c*) "obsequiousness."

5. "(*a*) He was sometimes supported by Austria, who, oddly enough, appears under Count Beust to have been more friendly to Italy *than* (37 *a*) *France,* (30) *in this line of action.*"

   (*a*) Begin with "In this line of action." Why? (*b*) Write "than was France" or "than France was."

6. "There was something so startling in (*a*) (5) *this* assertion, (*a*) (4) *that* the discoveries of previous investigators were to be (*b*) (47 *a*) *treated as though they had never been made,* and (4) *that one who had not yet* (47 *a*) *attained the age of manhood* had superseded the grey-headed philosophers (8) *who* had for centuries patiently sought after the truth, (4) *that* (*a*) (5) *it* naturally provoked derision."

(*a*) "This," "that," and "it," cause a little perplexity. Write "The startling assertion that the discoveries. . . ." (*b*) "ignored." (*c*) "a mere youth," "a mere stripling."

7. "One of the recommendations (*on which very* (*a*) (26) (47, *a*) *much depended*) of the Commission was that a council in each province should establish smaller councils, each to have the oversight of a small district, and (*b*) (37) report to a central council on the state of Education in (*c*) (5) it."

(*a*) Write "cardinal recommendations." Derive "cardinal." (*b*) Write, either (1) "and should report," or (2) "and to report." (*c*) Write "in its province," or "district."

8. "At this (*a*) (1) *period* an (*b*) (11) *event* (*c*) (1) *transpired* that destroyed the last hopes of peace. The king fell from his horse and died two hours after the fall (*d*) (30), *which was occasioned by his horse's stumbling on a mole-hill, while he was on his return from reviewing his soldiers.*"

(*a*) What is a "period"? (*b*) Express the particular kind of event ("accident"). (*c*) What is the meaning of "transpired"? (*d*) Transpose thus: "While the king was on his return . . . his horse . . . ; the king fell and &c." The cause should precede the effect.

9. "He determined (*c*) on selling all his estates, and, as soon as this was done (40 *a*), *to* (*c*) *quit* the country, (*a*) (33) believing that his honour demanded this sacrifice and (40) (40 *a*) *in* (*b*) *the* hope of satisfying his creditors."

(*a*) Begin with "Believing that &c." (*b*) "hoping thereby to satisfy &c." (*c*) "to sell" or "on quitting."

10. "He read patiently on, Leading Articles, Foreign Correspondence, Money Article and all; (*a*) (43) during which his father fell asleep, and he (*b*) went in search for his sister."

Point out the absurdity of "during which" applied to the last part of the sentence. (*a*) "Meanwhile." (*b*) Insert "then."

Adams Sherman Hill
The Principles of Rhetoric and Their Application
(1878)

&⬝ *Hill's was the first American text to be widely adopted in the new composition courses that were springing up in colleges. It is the first of what Albert Kitzhaber has termed the "big four," the most influential of the new textbooks in late-nineteenth-century composition studies. The others, whose books are excerpted below, are Genung, Wendell, and the team of Scott and Denney. (For background on Hill see chap. 2, p. 45.)*

INTRODUCTION.

For the purposes of this treatise, Rhetoric may be defined as the art of efficient communication by language. It is not one of several arts out of which a choice may be made; it is *the* art to the principles of which, consciously or unconsciously, a good writer or speaker must conform.

It is an *art,* not a science: for it neither observes, nor discovers, nor classifies; but it shows how to convey from one mind to another the results of observation, discovery, or classification; it uses knowledge, not as knowledge, but as power.

Logic simply teaches the right use of reason, and may be practised by the solitary inhabitant of a desert island; but Rhetoric, being the art of *communication* by language, implies the presence, in fact or in imagination, of at least two persons,—the speaker or the writer, and the person spoken to or written to. Aristotle makes the very essence of Rhetoric to lie in the distinct recognition of a hearer. Hence, its rules are not absolute, like those of logic, but relative to the character and circumstances of those addressed; for though truth is one, and correct reasoning must always be correct, the ways of communicating truth are many.

Being the art of communication by *language,* Rhetoric applies to any subject-matter that can be treated in words, but has no subject-matter peculiar to itself. It does not undertake to furnish a person with something to say; but it does undertake to tell him how best to say that with which he has provided himself. "Style," says Coleridge, "is the art of conveying the meaning appropriately and with perspicuity, whatever that meaning may be;" but some meaning there must be: for, "in order to form a good style, the primary rule and condition is, not to attempt to express ourselves in language before we thoroughly know our own meaning."

Part I. of this treatise discusses and illustrates the general principles which apply to written or spoken discourse of every kind. Part II. deals with those principles which apply, exclusively or especially, to Narrative

or to Argumentative Composition,—the two kinds of prose writing
which seem to require separate treatment.

. . . .

PART I

COMPOSITION IN GENERAL.

Book I

Grammatical Purity.

Chapter I
Good Use.

Importance
of correct
expression.

Grammar, in the widest sense of the word, though readily distinguishable from Rhetoric, is its basis. He who has mastered the mechanics of language has a great advantage over one who cannot express himself
correctly, as a painter whose pencil rarely errs has a great advantage over
one who cannot draw correctly. To know the proper use of one's native
tongue is no merit; not to know it is a positive demerit,—a demerit the
greater in the case of one who has enjoyed the advantages of education.
Yet, not even eminent speakers or writers, not even those who readily
detect similar faults in others, are themselves free from errors in
grammar,—such, at least, as may be committed, through inadvertence,
in the hurry of speech or of composition. "A distinguished British
scholar of the last century said he had known but three of his countrymen
who spoke their native language with uniform grammatical accuracy;
and the observation of most persons widely acquainted with English and
American society confirms the general truth implied in this declara-
tion."[1] "It makes us blush to add." says De Quincey,[2] "that even grammar is so little of a perfect attainment amongst us, that, with two or
three exceptions (one being Shakspere, whom some affect to consider as
belonging to a semi-barbarous age), we have never seen the writer,
through a circuit of prodigious reading,[3] who has not sometimes violated
the accidence or the syntax of English grammar."

Grammatical
purity defined.

Correctness (or Purity) is, then, the first requisite of discourse,
whether spoken or written. Whatever is addressed to English-speaking
people should be in the English tongue. With a few exceptions, to be
hereafter noted, it should (1) contain none but English words, phrases,
and idioms; (2) these words, phrases, and idioms should be combined

according to the English fashion; and (3) they should be used in the English meaning.

What, now, determines whether a given expression is English?

Evidently, the answer to this question is not to be sought in inquiries concerning the origin, the history, or the fundamental characteristics of the language. However interesting in themselves, however successfully prosecuted, such investigations are foreign to a study which has to do, not with words as they have been, or might have been, or may be, but with words as they are; not with the English of yesterday or to-morrow, still less with a theorist's ideal English, but with the English of to-day. *False tests of good English.*

In the English of to-day, one word is not preferred to another because it is derived from this or from that source; the present meaning of a word is not fixed by its etymology, nor its inflection by the inflection of other words with which it is commonly classed, nor its spelling by what some writers are pleased to call "reason."

Arithmetic (from the Greek), *flour* (from the Latin), *mutton* (from the French), *gas* (a term invented by a chemist)[4], are as good words as *sheep, meal,* or *fire.* In its proper place, *manufacture* is as good as *handiwork, purple* as *red, prairie* as *meadow, magnificent* as *great, murmur* as *buzz, have* as *be, oval* as *egg, convention* as *meeting.*

Though a vast majority of nouns form the plural in *s,* the plural of *ox* is still *oxen,* and that of *mouse* is still *mice;* though we may no longer say that "a bee *stang* John," we may say that "the bells *rang;*" though *its* has been used only three centuries, it is as much a part of the language as *his* and *her,* and one can only smile at a recent writer's hostility to this "unlucky, new-fangled word."[5]

"There is," says Landor, "a fastidiousness in the use of language that indicates an atrophy of mind. We must take words as the world presents them to us, without looking at the root. If we grubbed under this and laid it bare, we should leave no room for our thoughts to lie evenly, and every expression would be constrained and crampt. We should scarcely find a metaphor in the purest author that is not false or imperfect, nor could we imagine one ourselves that would not be stiff and frigid. Take now, for instance, a phrase in common use. *You are rather late.* Can any thing seem plainer? Yet *rather,* as you know, meant originally *earlier,* being the comparative of *rathe:* the 'rathe primrose' of the poet recalls it. We cannot say, *You are sooner late;* but who is so troublesome and silly as to question the propriety of saying, *You are rather late?* We likewise say, *bad orthography* and *false orthography:* how can there be false or bad *right-spelling?*"[6]

The fastidiousness that objects to well-established words because their appearance "proclaims their vile and despicable origin;"[7] or to well-understood phrases, because they "contain some word that is never used except as a part of the phrase;"[7] or to idiomatic expressions, because, "when analyzed grammatically, they include a solecism,"[7] or because they were "originally the spawn, partly of ignorance and partly of affectation,"[7]—the fastidiousness, in short, that would sacrifice to the proprieties of language the very expressions that give life to our daily speech and vigor to the best writing, deserves no gentler treatment than Landor gives the etymologists.

Pell-mell, topsy-turvy, helter-skelter, hurly-burly, hocus-pocus, hodge-podge, harum-scarum, namby-pamby, willy-nilly, shilly-shally, higgledy-piggledy, dilly-dally, hurry-scurry, carry their meaning instantaneously to every mind.[8]

Though the italicized words in "by *dint* of," "as *lief,*" "to and *fro,*" "not a *whit,*" "*kith* and kin," "might and *main,*" "*hue* and cry," "*pro* and *con,*" "*spick* and *span* new," are unused except in the phrases quoted, the phrases are universally understood, and there is no more reason for challenging the words composing them than there is for challenging a syllable in a word.

Would God, whether or no, never so good, whereabouts, many a, to dance atten-dance, to scrape acquaintance, whether easy to parse or not, are easy to understand, are facts in language. *Currying favor* may at once defy grammatical analysis and smell of the stable; but what other expression sums up the low arts by which a toady seeks to ingratiate himself?

In the use of language, there is only one sound principle of judgment. If to be understood is, as it should be, a writer's first object, his language must be such as his readers understand, and understand as he understands it. If, being a scholar, he uses Latinisms or Gallicisms known only to scholars like himself; if, being a physician or a lawyer, he uses legal or medical cant; or if, living in Yorkshire or in Arkansas, he writes in the dialect of Yorkshire or in that of Arkansas;—his work, even if not partially unintelligible, will be distasteful to the general public. If he is so fond of antiquity as to prefer a word that has not been in good use since the twelfth or the seventeenth century to one only fifty years old but in good use to-day, he is in danger of being shelved with his adopted contemporaries; if, on the other hand, he is so greedy of novelty as to snatch at the words of a season, of which few survive the occasion that gave them birth, his work is likely to be as ephemeral as they. By avoiding vulgarity and pedantry alike, a writer, while commending himself to the best class of readers, loses nothing in the estimation of others; for those who do not speak or write pure English themselves understand it, when spoken or written by others, but rarely understand more than one variety of impure English.

The reasons, in short, which prevent an English author from publishing a treatise in Greek, Celtic, or French, or in a dialect peculiar to a place or a class, prohibit him from employing any expression not familiar to the great body of cultivated men in English-speaking countries, and not sanctioned by *good use,*—that is, by *reputable, national,* and *present* use: reputable as opposed to vulgar or affected; national as opposed to foreign, local or professional; present as opposed to obsolete or transient.

Good use defined.

. . . .

Chapter II.
Method.

It is not enough that a narrative should move; it should move *forward.* There should be *method*[9] in it—that is, *progressive transition.* Important as method is in every kind of composition, it is not always essential to success. A philosopher may contribute detached sayings (aphorisms) to the general stock of wisdom, an essayist may be charming as he rambles in pleasant fields of thought and gossips with his readers; and even a composition mainly intended to persuade the persons addressed may, to accomplish some incidental purpose, leave the main line of argument for a moment; but a narrative is defective, as a narrative, in so far as it does not go right on from the beginning to the end.

A prolix writer, creep though he may, creeps in the right direction; a "word-painter," though he may detain his readers while he is "doing" a sunset or a heroine, detains them at the road-side; but a story-teller who runs this way and that, who is reminded of something which is entirely aside from his narrative, but which happened at about the same time or near the same place, and who returns to his subject as if by accident, is perhaps the most vexatious of all who try to communicate by language with their fellow-beings.

A methodical habit of mind constitutes the most important difference between a well-educated and an uncultivated man.

The superiority of the educated man is due to the unpremeditated and evidently habitual *arrangement* of his words, grounded on the habit of foreseeing, in each integral part, or (more plainly) in every sentence, the whole that he then intends to communicate. However irregular and desultory his talk, there is *method* in the fragments.

"Listen, on the other hand, to an ignorant man, though perhaps shrewd and able in his particular calling; whether he be describing or relating. We immediately perceive that his memory alone is called into action; and that the objects and events recur in the narration in the same order, and with the same accompaniments, however accidental or impertinent, as they had first occurred to the narrator. The necessity of taking breath, the efforts of recollection, and the abrupt rectification of its failures, produce all his pauses; and with exception of the '*and then,*' the '*and there,*' and the still less significant '*and so,*' they constitute likewise all his connections."[10]

Coleridge goes on to contrast the narration given by Hamlet to Horatio of his voyage to England (Hamlet, act v. scene ii.) with the Clown's evidence (Measure for Measure, act ii. scene i.), the talk of the Nurse (Romeo and Juliet, act i. scene iii.; act ii. scene vi.), and Mrs. Quickly's relation of the circumstances of Sir John Falstaff's debt to her (Henry IV. part ii. act ii. scene i.).

An example may be taken from Webster's speech in the White murder case. Here the narration not only serves as a methodical statement of (supposed) facts, but also paves the way for the argument;—

"The circumstances now clearly in evidence spread out the whole scene before us. Deep sleep had fallen on the destined victim, and on all beneath his roof. A healthful old man, to whom sleep was sweet, the first sound slumbers of the night held him in their soft but strong embrace. The assassin enters, through the window already prepared, into an unoccupied apartment. With noiseless foot he paces the lonely hall, half-lighted by the moon; he winds up the ascent of the stairs, and reaches the door of the chamber. Of this, he moves the lock, by soft and continued pressure, till it turns on its hinges without noise; and he enters, and beholds his victim before him. The room is uncommonly open to the admission of light. The face of the innocent sleeper is turned from the murderer, and the beams of the moon, resting on the gray locks of his aged temple, show him where to strike. The fatal blow is given! and the victim passes, without a struggle or a motion, from the repose of sleep to the repose of death! It is the assassin's purpose to make sure work; and he plies the dagger, though it is obvious that life has been destroyed by the blow of the bludgeon. He even raises the aged arm, that he may not fail in his aim at the heart, and replaces it again over the wounds of the poniard! To finish the picture, he explores the wrist for the pulse! He feels for it, and ascertains that it beats no longer! It is accomplished. The deed is done. He retreats, retraces his steps to the window, passes out through it as he came in, and escapes. He has done the murder. No eye has seen him, no ear has heard him. The secret is his own, and it is safe!"[11]

The main cause of this difference between the products of an undisciplined and those of a cultivated mind lies in the absence from the one and the presence in the other of a leading thought, a central idea, around which facts group themselves in accordance with their relative value and pertinence. This leading thought gives Unity to that which would otherwise be a meaningless Variety. Without *movement* a narrative can have no life; without *method* its life will be to little purpose.

NOTE

1. George P. Marsh: Lectures on the English Language, lect. v.
2. Essay on Style.
3. Query as to the position of this clause.
4. Von Helmont, a Fleming (born in 1577).
5. T. L. Kington Oliphant: The Sources of Standard English, p. 309. (1873.)
6. Walter Savage Landor: Works, vol. iv. p. 165.
7. George Campbell: The Philosophy of Rhetoric, book ii. chap. ii. (1750.)
8. See Irving's "Legend of Sleepy Hollow," Browning's "Hervé Riel," and various passages in Burke.
9. Μέθοδος, from μετά, after, and ὁδός, a road or way.
10. Coleridge: The Friend, sect. ii. essay iv.
11. Webster: Works, vol. vi. p. 53.

John Franklin Genung
The Practical Elements of Rhetoric, with Illustrative Examples (1885)

≥⊸ *The second of the "big four," Genung's book was adopted by at least eighteen Eastern colleges during the decade 1890–1900, more than any single competing text. Genung spent his entire career at Amherst; his program is described in chapter 3, which also gives a brief biography.*

FOLLOWING THE SUGGESTION OF THE TITLE, A WORD MAY BE SAID, by way of preface, concerning the scope and character of this book.

The author has aimed to give the practical elements of rhetoric; and the standard adopted as practical, in connection with any element, is its capability of being employed in actual composition. This standard has led him to exclude extended philosophizing on principles and usages, and to give brief, yet it is hoped sufficiently clear, results. Nor has he felt it practical to discuss such subjects as wit and humor and pathos, because these depend mostly on principles that cannot be imparted by a text-book.

The examples are merely illustrative, that is to say, in barely sufficient number to elucidate the principles given, but not intended for practice. Opportunity for practice is to be supplied by an accompanying handbook of exercises.

> *"For Fact, well-trusted, reasons and persuades,*
> *Is gnomic, cutting, or ironical,*
> *Draws tears, or is a tocsin to arouse—*
> *Can hold all figures of the orator*
> *In one plain sentence; has her pauses too—*
> *Eloquent silence at the chasm abrupt*
> *Where knowledge ceases."*
>
> —GEORGE ELIOT.

INTRODUCTORY.

I.

Definition of Rhetoric.—Rhetoric is the art of making discourse effective in the accomplishment of an end.

Rhetoric, here called an art, is sometimes defined as a science. Both of these designations are true; they merely regard the subject in two different aspects. Science is systematized knowledge; if then the laws and principles of discourse are exhibited in an orderly system, they appear in the character of a science. Art is knowledge made efficient by skill: if then rhetorical laws and principles are applied in the actual construction of discourse, they become the working rules of an art.

According to its predominant character as an art or as a science, rhetoric may be regarded as of two kinds: constructive rhetoric, which is concerned with the production of discourse; and critical rhetoric, which traces the laws of discourse through the study of works of literature. The present manual, having principally in view the practical ends of constructive rhetoric, starts from the definition which views rhetoric as an art.

The word discourse, as here used, is a general term, denoting any coherent literary production, whether spoken or written.

The end sought in discourse may be, to convey information, as in essays, treatises, history, fiction; to convince of some truth, as in argumentative discourse; or to persuade to some course of action, as in oratory. As means to such ends, the writer may employ plain, or impassioned, or imaginative expression; may seek to rivet attention by energetic terms, or to please the taste by elegant language; but always these devices are subordinated to some object beyond the production's form. Whatever truly makes for the writer's purpose, whether regular or irregular, belongs legitimately to the resources of rhetoric; whatever makes against it is not rhetorical, because it is not artistic.

What is excluded.—By the foregoing definition, poetry is excluded from the domain of rhetoric, or at least comes only partly within it. So far as includes grammatical correctness, accuracy in the use of words and figures, and logical consistency in the thought, poetry must obey the same laws as prose; and so for the two many of the elements of expression coincide. But while prose seeks, by skill in language and thought, to accomplish some end, poetry (considered as a manner of expression) has no end outside of itself. It may incidentally instruct, or convince, or persuade; but primarily it is the spontaneous language of the feelings, and seeks only to obey the emotion that gives it birth. Being governed by emotion, its language is more highly wrought than that of prose. It is full of imagery and picturesque terms; it seeks beautiful forms for form's sake; and ordinarily it has a regular measured rhythm. Such poetical devices, so far as they seek not adaptedness to an end but mere perfection in themselves, are governed by laws apart from the province of rhetoric.

On what Rhetoric is founded.—Rhetoric is mainly founded on two sciences, logic and grammar. "Now it is by the sense that rhetoric holds of logic, and by the expression that she holds of grammar."—*Dr. Campbell.*

Grammar investigates the uses of words, and the structure of phrases and sentences, with a view to ascertaining what are the facts of the language; and when these are presented so as to show what is correct in expression, its end is accomplished. Rhetoric, also, employs the facts of the language to secure grammatical correctness; but this only because discourse cannot be effectual without it. Nor does rhetoric stop with mere correctness of expression. Having an end to accomplish beyond simple utterance, it must seek also clearness, or beauty, or force of style, according as these qualities may best serve to instruct or convince or persuade. Further, while the science of grammar extends only as far as the sentence, rhetoric discusses also the structure of paragraphs and larger sections, and so on through the various details of an entire discourse.

Logic investigates the laws of thought, with a view to ascertaining its exact and consistent sequences; and, like grammar, it is satisfied with discovering and presenting facts. Rhetoric, also, must observe the laws of thought, because the ends of discourse fail if these are transgressed; but this it does only as its hidden beginning. What it has found by logical processes to be true, it seeks to make luminous, or attractive, or cogent, or persuasive, in order to gain men's attention and influence them.

Thus the laws of thought combine with the laws of expression to make up what Dr. Campbell calls the soul and the body of discourse.

II.

Value of Rhetoric as an art.—Art in expression is exactly analogous to art in painting, or music, or handicraft. No one becomes really eminent in these pursuits without first possessing some natural aptitude for them; and just so true genius for expression must be to some extent born in a man, and some indeed cannot hope to attain eminence as writers. There is in the highest literary work a grace and freedom that cannot be imparted by rules. But though all cannot become great writers, all can at least learn to express their thought directly and without ambiguity; nor is there any excuse on the score of nature for crudeness and inaccuracy in speech.

Again, just as in these other arts one does not think of stopping with mere inborn aptitude, but develops and disciplines all his powers by precept and training; so in the art of expression one needs by faithful study and practice to get beyond the point where he only *happens* to write well, and attain that conscious power over language and thought which gives him precision and grace in adapting means to ends, and fine discrimination in choosing among his resources. This is rhetorical art, and this assured power is its value.

Sources of failure.—"All fatal faults," says Ruskin, "in art that might have been otherwise good, arise from one or other of these three things: either from the pretence to feel what we do not; the indolence in exercises necessary to obtain the power of expressing the truth; or the presumptuous insistence upon, and indulgence in, our own powers and delights, and with no care or wish that they should be useful to other people, so only they be admired by them."

This, written primarily with reference to painting, applies with equal fitness to the literary art; and the order in which the faults are named corresponds well to the frequency of their occurrence.

First and commonest, insincerity. By this is not meant that writers intentionally make pretence of feeling what they do not. None the less truly, however, they may fall into insincerity and unreality, by unconsidered use of conventionalisms, stock expressions, outworn figures, and the like. Young writers especially are liable to employ such ready-made expressions without stopping to think how much or how little they mean; and thus they commit themselves to what does not represent their real thought.—Secondly, indolence in necessary exercises. This fault is the special temptation of those to whom composition comes easy; they think their cleverness will obviate the necessity of discipline. But it is to be remembered that this art, like every other, has its technicalities, which it is disastrous to neglect or undervalue.—Lastly, rhetorical vanity. This comes from being so taken with literary rules and devices as to rate form before thought; and it manifests itself in mannerisms, affectations, tricks of style, and the like. It is to be remembered that rhetoric does not exist for itself, but only as the handmaid of the truth which it seeks to make living in the minds and hearts of men.

Initial difficulties of the art of Rhetoric.—These are just such as occur in the beginning of every art: the difficulty of making skilled achievement take the place of crude untrained effort. To submit one's work in composition to rules is to regulate the free creative impulse by critical processes; and this, until the writer gets used to it, is apt to check and chill the flow of thought. Beginning thus, the work of composing is too self-conscious; and the art of the discourse, at the best, is too apparent. But such a self-conscious stage in the writer's experience cannot well be avoided; it is simply a sign that the art is not fully mastered. Sooner or later rhetorical rules must be learned, either from precept or from experience; for they are not arbitrarily invented, as something that a writer may disregard, but discovered and formulated from confessedly good usage, as principles that *must* be observed. The question then is, whether the writer will learn without rules, by blundering experience, or take what the approved usage of others has found to be best. And there is no doubt of the proper answer. The true way is to submit to rhetorical laws and methods; and though in the beginning these may be obtrusive and tyrannical, by diligent practice they will become second nature.

The crowning excellence of skilled writing as all acknowledge, is naturalness. But such an achievement, wherein everything seems in its right place and degree, we call also artistic. Art at its highest and nature at its truest are one. The result seems ideally free from pains and effort; this, however, not because art is not present, but because the art is so perfect as to have concealed its processes.

III.

Province and distribution of Rhetoric.—The principles included in the art of rhetoric group themselves naturally into two great divisions; the first comprising what relates to expression, the second what relates to the thought. Under the first division are discussed what may be called the mechanical principles of composition: how to use words and figures, and how to build them together into sentences and paragraphs. Under the second division are discussed the logical features of discourse: how to work out a line of thought, from its central theme through its plan to its final amplified form; and how to arrange and modify it for the requirements of the various kinds of discourse.

Barrett Wendell
English Composition, Eight Lectures Given at the Lowell Institute (1891)

𝕫 *(For biography see chap. 2, p. 127.) Based on a series of lectures delivered in 1890,* English Composition *seems very different from most other texts on the subject. If Hill's* Principles of Rhetoric *reads like a scholarly disquisition, then Wendell's book, true to its origins, reads like the lectures of a clever professor intent on reaching a wide audience.*

This book helped make Wendell famous; its highly readable style made it valued by many who never used it in a college classroom. The Baltimore social work pioneer Mary E. Richmond provides an example. Her biographer writes:

In the effort to improve her style in writing, she studied attentively such books as *English Composition* by Barrett Wendell, professor of English at Harvard, her copy of which is full of marked passages. Some of his suggestions regarding the occurrence of long and short, loose and periodic sentences in English prose excited her curiosity, and we find her, about 1895, making a rather elaborate search, counting and listing examples from selected authors from the sixteenth to the nineteenth centuries. She sent her tables to Professor Wendell, and received from him an amazed and grateful reply. (Richmond, *The Long View* 144)

THE ELEMENTS AND THE QUALITIES OF STYLE.

During the past ten years I have been chiefly occupied in teaching, to undergraduates of Harvard College, the principles of English Composition. In the course of that time I have been asked a great many questions concerning the art, mostly by friends who found themselves writing for publication. Widely different as these inquiries have naturally been, they have possessed in common one trait sufficiently marked to place them, in my memory, in a single group: almost without exception, they have concerned themselves with matters of detail. Is this word or that admissible? Why, in a piece of writing I once published, did I permit myself to use the apparently commercial phrase "at any rate"? Are not words of Saxon origin invariably preferable to all others? Should sentences be long or short? These random memories are sufficient examples of many hundreds of inquiries.

They have in common, as I have just said, the trait of concerning themselves almost wholly with matters of detail. They have too another trait: generally, if not invariably, they involve a tacit assumption that any given case must be either right or wrong.

These two traits—the one indicative of rather surprising ignorance of the nature of the matter in hand, the other of a profound error—are what has prompted me to prepare this book. Year by year I have seen more and more clearly that although the work of a teacher or a technical critic of style concerns itself largely with the correction of erratic detail, the really important thing for one who would grasp the subject to master is not a matter of detail at all, but a very simple body of general principles under which details readily group themselves. I have seen too that although a small part of the corrections and criticisms I have had to make are concerned with matters of positive error, by far the greater, and incalculably the more important part are concerned with what I may call matters of discretion. The question is not whether a given word or sentence is eternally right or wrong; but rather how accurately it expresses what the writer has to say,—whether the language we use may not afford a different and perhaps a better means of phrasing his idea.

The truth is that in rhetoric, as distinguished from grammar, by far the greater part of the questions that arise concern not right or wrong, but better or worse; and that the way to know what is better or worse in any given case is not to load your memory with bewilderingly innumerable rules, but firmly to grasp a very few simple, elastic general principles. Consciously or not, these principles, I believe, are observed by thoroughly effective writers. Of course, nothing but long and patient practice can make anybody certain of writing, or of practising any art, well. Of course too if the principles I state be, as I believe them, fundamental, whoever practises much cannot help in some degree observing them; but the experience of ten years' teaching leads me more and more to the belief that a knowledge of the principles is a very great help in practice.

I may best begin, I think, by stating these principles as briefly and as generally as I can. Then I shall try to show how they apply to the more important specific cases that present themselves to writers. Each case, I think, presents them in a somewhat new light. Certainly, without considering them in various aspects we can hardly appreciate their full scope. First of all, it will be convenient to fix a term which shall express the whole subject under consideration. I know of none more precise than Style. A good deal of usage, to be sure, and rather good usage too, gives color to the general impression that *style* means *good style,* just as *criticism* is often taken to mean *unfavorable criticism,* or *manners* to mean *civil behavior.* Very excellent authorities sometimes declare that a given writer has style, and another none; only a little while ago, I heard a decidedly careful talker congratulate himself on having at last discovered, in this closing decade of the nineteenth century, a correspondent who, in spite of our thickening environment of newspapers and telegrams, wrote letters that possessed style. I dwell on this common meaning of the word *style* for two reasons: in the first place, clearly to define the sense in which I mean not to use the word; in the second place, to emphasize the fact, which we shall find to be highly important, that in the present state of the English language hardly any word not unintelligibly technical can be trusted to express a precise meaning without the aid of definition. *Style,* as I shall use the term, means simply the expression of thought or emotion in written words; it applies equally to an epic, a sermon, a love-letter, an invitation to an evening party.

This definition brings us face to face with an obvious trait which the art we are considering shares with all the other arts of expression,— painting, sculpture, architecture, music, and indeed those humbler arts, not commonly recognized as fine, where the workman conceives some-thing not yet in existence (a machine, a flower-pot, a sauce) and pro-ceeds, by collaboration of brain and hand, to give it material existence. Thought and emotion, the substance of what style expresses, are things so common, so incessant in earthly experience, that we trouble ourselves to consider them as little as we bother our heads about the marvels of sunrise, of the growth of flowers or men, of the mystery of sin or death, when they do not happen to touch our pockets or our affections. But for all that they are with us from morning till night, and not seldom from night till morning,—for all that together they make up the total sum of what to most of us is a very commonplace affair, our earthly existence,— thought and emotion, when we stop to consider them, are the most fascinatingly marvellous facts that human beings can contemplate. They are real beyond all other realities. What things are, no man can ever know; analyzed by astronomy, the material universe vanishes in infinite systems of spheres revolving about one another throughout infinitely extended regions of space, in obedience to law that may be recognized, but not comprehended; analyzed by physics, this same material universe vanishes again in infinitely small systems of molecules bound together by the same mysterious forces that govern the stellar universe. The more we study the more we learn that neither the heavens nor the very paper on which I write these words are what they seem, and that what they really are is far beyond the perception of any faculty which the history of the human race can lead us rationally to hope for even in our most remote posterity. But what we think of all these marvels, the forms in which they present themselves to us, we know as we know nothing else. Our whole lives, from the day when our eyes first open to the sunlight, are constant series of thoughts, sometimes seemingly springing from within ourselves, often seeming to come from without ourselves, through the medium of those senses that in careless moods we are apt to think so comprehensive. To each and all of us, the final reality of life is the thought, which, with the endless surge of emotion,—now tempestuous, again almost imperceptible,—makes up conscious existence.

Final realities though they be, however, thought and emotion are essentially things that in our habitual thoughtlessness we are apt to call unreal. As we know them, they are immaterial. No systems can measure their extent or their bulk; and though they are in some degree conditioned by time, it is so slightly that we may almost say—as in a single instant our thought ranges from primeval nebulae to cosmic death and celestial eternity—they are free from time-limit, as well as from the limits of space. Real at once, then, and unreal, or better, real and intangible, real yet immaterial, each of us who will stop to think must find the thought and the emotion that together make that fresh marvel,—himself. Each of us, I say purposely; for there is one more thing that we must remember here. Like one another as we seem, like one another as the courses of our lives may look, there are no two human beings who tread quite the same road from the cradle to the grave. No one of us in any group has come from quite the same origin as any other; no two, be they twin brothers or husband and wife, can go thence by quite the same path. The laws of space and of time forbid; unspeakably more the still more mysterious laws of thought forbid that any two of us should know and feel just the same experience in this world. If two or three of us, habitually together, suddenly utter the same word, we are surprised. The thought and emotion of every living being, then, is an immaterial reality, eternally different from every other in the universe; and this is the reality that style must express.

And style, we remember, must express this reality in written words; and written words are things as tangible, as material, as the thought and emotion behind them is immaterial, evanescent, elusive. The task of the writer, then, is a far more subtle and wonderful thing than we are apt to think it: nothing less than to create a material body, that all men may see, for an eternally immaterial reality that only through this imperfect symbol can ever reveal itself to any but the one human being who knows it he knows not how.

. . . .

And here we come to what has appeared to me the fault of almost every textbook of Rhetoric I have examined. These books consist chiefly of directions as to how one who would write should set about composing. Many of these directions are extremely sensible, many very suggestive. But in every case these directions are appallingly numerous. It took me some years to discern that all which have so far come to my notice could be grouped under one of three very simple heads, each of which might be phrased as a simple proposition. Various as they are, all these directions concern either what may be included in a given composition (a sentence, a paragraph, or a whole); or what I may call the outline, or perhaps better, the mass of the composition,—in other words, where the chief parts may most conveniently be placed; or finally, the internal arrangement of the composition in detail. In brief, I may phrase these three principles of composition as follows: (1) Every composition should group itself about one central idea; (2) The chief parts of every composition should be so placed as readily to catch the eye; (3) Finally, the relation of each part of a composition to its neighbors should be unmistakable. The first of these principles may conveniently be named the principle of Unity; the second, the principle of Mass; the third, the principle of Coherence. They are important enough to deserve examination in detail.

I have said that all compositions should have unity,—in other words, that every composition should group itself about one central idea. The very terms in which I have phrased this principle suggest at once the chief fact that I have tried to keep before you in the earlier part of this chapter,—that words are after all nothing but arbitrary symbols standing for ideas. So really, when we come to consider the substance of any composition, we may better concern ourselves rather with what the words stand for than with the visible symbols themselves. If we once know what ideas we wish to group together, the task of finding words for them is immensely simplified; on the other hand, if in the act of composition—an act which is generally rather hasty—we have grouped together a number of words, the question of whether we shall leave them together, or strike out some, or add some, is generally to be settled by considering not what visible forms our composition has associated, but what ideas. Now, the principles on which we may properly group ideas together are as various as anything well can be. In the first place, as we have just seen, there are various kinds of compositions,—sentences, paragraphs, and those larger kinds which for convenience I have grouped under the single head of wholes. Obviously there is in good style some reason why the unity of the sentence should be more limited than that of the paragraph, and the unity of the paragraph than that of the whole. Yet, as our purposes in composing vary, we may perfectly well devote to a single subject—George Eliot, for example—a book, a chapter, a paragraph, or a sentence. Any decently written life of George Eliot—Mr. Cross's [John Walter Cross, *George Eliot's Life as related in her letters and journals* (1885).—ED.], let us say—has unity, in that it groups itself about one central idea; namely, the notable writer in question. Any history of English fiction in the nineteenth century—to be sure, I do not at this moment recall one worth mentioning—would probably contain a chapter about George Eliot which would possess unity for precisely the same reason. So, in a general account of contemporary English literature, we should be rather surprised not to find at least a paragraph devoted to George Eliot, and this paragraph would have unity for precisely the same reason that caused us to recognize it in the imaginary chapter, or in Mr. Cross's book. And a very short article—a leader in a newspaper, for example—which should deal with modern novels in general would be more than apt to contain at least a sentence about George Eliot, of which the unity would be demonstrable in exactly the same way. In other words, the question of scale—in many aspects important—has very little to do with the question of unity. The question of unity is whether for our purposes the ideas we have grouped together may rationally be so grouped; if we can show that they may, we are safe. Analogies are often helpful: we may liken the grouping of ideas in compositions to the grouping of facts in statistics. A group of statistics, such as the director of the Harvard gymnasium calls anthropometic, may concern a single individual; again, a genealogy concerns, as the case may be, a family, or a group of families related by blood or marriage; a local history, such as we have hundreds of in New England, properly concerns a considerable number of families who have lived at different times under the same political conditions; a State or a national census concerns the entire population of State or nation, and groups it too in any number of different ways. But each of these things has a unity of its own; and to a certain degree each larger group contains each smaller one. Here, I think, is the chief thing to keep in mind: just as the sentence is a group of words, the paragraph is a group of sentences, and the whole a group of paragraphs. We should take care that each group has, for our purpose, a unity of its own; and that the unity of each larger group is of a kind that may properly be resolved into the smaller unities of which it is composed.

In considering the question of unity, then, we consider rather what

.the words stand for than the visible words themselves. In considering the second principle of composition,—the principle of Mass,—I conceive the case to be different. Style, you will remember, I defined as the expression of thought and emotion in written words. Written words we saw to be visible material symbols of that immaterial reality, thought and emotion, which makes up our conscious lives. What distinguishes written words from spoken, literature from the colloquial language that precedes it, is that written words address themselves to the eye and spoken words to the ear. Though this fundamental physical fact has been neglected by the makers of textbooks, I know few more important. The principle of Mass, you will remember,—the principle which governs the outward form of every composition,—is that the chief parts of every composition should be so placed as readily to catch the eye. Now, what catches the eye is obviously not the immaterial idea a word stands for, but the material symbol of the idea,—the actual black marks to which good use has in course of time come to attach such subtle and varied significance. In these groups of visible marks that compose style certain parts are more conspicuous than others. Broadly speaking, the most readily visible parts of a given composition are the beginning and the end. Run your eye over a printed page; you will find it arrested by every period, more still by every one of those breaks which mark the division of paragraphs. Compare a book not broken into chapters—Defoe's "Plague" for example—with a book in which the chapters are carefully distinguished; and you will feel, on a conveniently large scale, the extreme mechanical inconvenience of the former arrangement. On the other hand, compare the ordinary version of the Bible—broken into verses whose separation is based chiefly on the fact that each by itself will make a tolerable text—with the Revised Version, in most respects so deplorably inferior as literature: in the former case, it is mechanically hard, unless somebody is reading aloud to you, to make out which break is important, which not; in the latter case, the task is mechanically easy. Or again, remark a fact that is becoming in my literary studies comically general: familiar quotations from celebrated books are almost always to be found at the beginning or the end. "Music hath charms" are the opening words of Congreve's "Mourning Bride." Don Quixote fights with the windmill very early in the first volume; he dies with the remark that there are no birds in last year's nests near the end of the last. Until I read "Don Quixote" through, a few years ago, these two incidents were the chief ones concerning him which general reading and talking had fixed in my mind. Now, the fact that, for better or worse, human readers notice the beginning and the end of compositions a good deal more readily than the parts that come between is the fact on which the principle of Mass is based. A writer who is careful so to mass his compositions as to put in places that catch the eye words which stand for ideas that he wants us to keep in mind, will find his work surprisingly more effective than that of a perhaps cleverer man who puts down his words in the order in which they occur to him.

The principle of Unity, we have seen, concerns itself chiefly with the immaterial ideas for which the material written words stand; the principle of Mass chiefly with the written words themselves; the third principle of composition—the principle of Coherence—concerns itself, I think, about equally with both. I phrased it, you will remember, in the words that the relation of every part of a composition to its neighbors should be unmistakable. In a given composition, for example, no word should appear without apparent reason for being there,—in other words, no incongruous idea should destroy the impression of unity. Again, to put the matter differently, no written word should be so placed that we cannot see at a glance how its presence affects the words about it. Sometimes coherence is a question of the actual order of words; sometimes, as in the clause I am at this moment writing, of constructions; sometimes, as in the clause I write now, it demands a pretty careful use of those convenient parts of speech to which we give the name "connectives." In that last clause, for example, the pronoun *it,* referring to the word *coherence,* which was the subject of the first clause in the sentence, made possible the change of construction from "it is a question of" this or that to "it demands" this or that. But perhaps the most important thing to remember about this last principle of composition is its name. Coherence is a much more felicitous name than Unity or Mass. To "cohere" means to "stick together." A style that sticks together is coherent; a style whose parts hang loose is not.

We find, then, an answer to the first question we proposed a little while ago: if there were no such troublesome thing as good use to interfere with the free exercise of our ingenuity, we might clearly put together our compositions in contented obedience to the principles of Unity, Mass, and Coherence. It remains for us to inquire how far the action of these principles is hampered in practice by good use.

Perhaps the simplest way of answering this inquiry is to study an example of style frequently cited in the textbooks. Among the various facts which have conspired to give unfavorable fame to the Emperor Nero is the general belief that he killed his mother. In English we state this belief in these words: Nero killed Agrippina. If asked to parse this sentence, we say that *Nero* is in the nominative case because it is the subject of the verb *killed;* and that *Agrippina* is in the objective case—or the accusative—because it is the object of the verb. But if Agrippina had been the slayer and Nero the slain, Agrippina nominative and Nero objective, the word *Agrippina* would still remain *Agrippina;* the word *Nero* still *Nero.* In English the only way to change the meaning would be to change the order of words and to say, "Agrippina killed Nero." In Latin, on the other hand, the accusative case is different in form from the nominative; the original sentence would be, "Nero interfecit Agrippinam." That convenient final *m* does Agrippina's business; the three words may be arranged in any order we please. But if we wished to say that Agrippina killed Nero, we should have to alter the form of both names, and say "Neronem interfecit Agrippina." In this single example we can see as plainly as we need, I think, the chief way in which good use interferes with the free operation of the principles of composition. The English language has fewer inflections than almost any other known to the civilized world; that is, each word has fewer distinct forms to indicate its relations to the words about it. All nouns have possessives and plurals; all verbs have slightly different forms for the present and the past tense; but this is about all. In English, then, the relation of word to word is expressed not by the forms of the words, but generally by their order; and any wide departure from the normal order of a sentence—in brief, subject, verb, object—is apt to alter or to destroy the meaning. "Nero interfecit Agrippinam," "Agrippinam interfecit Nero," "Nero Agrippinam interfecit," all mean exactly the same thing; the difference in mass alters the emphasis, that is all. "Nero killed Agrippina," on the other hand, means one thing; "Agrippina killed Nero," means another; and what "Nero Agrippina killed" may mean, nobody without a knowledge of the facts can possibly decide.

What is true of this simplest of sentences is true in a general way of any sentence in the English language. Good use has settled that the meaning of one great class of compositions in English—namely, of sentences—shall be indicated in general, not by the forms of the words which compose them, but by the order. Except within firmly defined limits, we cannot alter the order of words in English without violating good use; and in no language can we violate good use without grave and often fatal injury to our meaning. "Nero Agrippina killed," to revert to our example, is as completely ambiguous as any three words can be. While, on the one hand, then, we who use uninflected English are free from the disturbing array of grammatical rules and exceptions which so bothers us in Latin or in German, we are far less free than Romans or Germans to apply the principles of composition to the composing of sentences. The principle of Unity, to be sure, we may generally observe pretty carefully; but the principle of Mass is immensely interfered with by the fact that it is the order of words in a sentence that in general gives the sentence meaning; and so to a less degree is the principle of Coherence.

When we turn to the larger kinds of composition, however, we find the case different. As a matter of fact, the sentence is the only kind of composition that inevitably appears in spoken discourse. Until words are joined together, composed in sentences, there is, of course, no such thing as intelligible communication. The moment they are so joined, the organism of spoken language is complete. Paragraphs, on the other hand, do not appear in spoken discourse at all. And though, of course, in serious compositions the organic structure of the whole ought to be almost as palpable to hearers as to readers, the fact remains that in by far the greater part of oral discourse—the conversation, the chat, the bustle of daily life—there are no wholes at all. In other words, then, while oral usage—actual speech—is what the sentence is based on, the paragraph and the whole composition are based on written usage, which is commonly a great deal more thoughtful.

What is more, while the sentence is as old as language itself, the whole composition is hardly older than literature, and the modern paragraph is considerably younger than the art of printing. It follows, then, and a very slight study of the facts will prove the conclusion, that while in sentences good use very seriously interferes with the operation of the principles of composition, it interferes very little with their operation in paragraphs and in compositions of a larger kind. In other words, we are free to arrange sentences in paragraphs, and paragraphs in chapters, and chapters in books, pretty much as we think fit.

We are now, I think, in a position to sum up in a very few words the theory of style which I shall try to present to you. Style, you will remember, I defined as the expression of thought and feeling in written words. Modern style—the style we read and write to-day—I believe to be the result of a constant though generally unconscious struggle between good use and the principles of composition. In words, of course good use is absolute; in sentences, though it relaxes its authority, it remains very powerful; in paragraphs its authority becomes very feeble; in whole compositions, it may roughly be said to coincide with the principles.

In the chapters that follow, I purpose first to examine as carefully as may be the outward and visible body of style. It is made up of what I may call four elements,—the prime element Words, composed in Sentences, composed in Paragraphs, composed in Whole Compositions. Each of these elements I shall examine in detail, inquiring first how far it is affected by the paramount authority of good use, and then how within the limits of good use it may be made, by means of the principles of composition or otherwise, to assume various forms and to perform various offices. Then, when we have studied the visible body of style, its material elements, as carefully as we can, I shall turn to the three qualities, Clearness, Force, and Elegance, and try to determine what it is in the elements by which each of them may be secured or lost.

A dull business this seems to many, yet after ten years' study I do not find it dull at all. I find it, rather, constantly more stimulating; and this because I grow more and more aware how in its essence this matter of composition is as far from a dull and lifeless business as earthly matters can be; how he who scribbles a dozen words, just as truly as he who writes an epic, performs—all unknowing—one of those feats that tell us why men have believed that God made man in His image. For he who scrawls ribaldry, just as truly as he who writes for all time, does that most wonderful of things,—gives a material body to some reality which till that moment was immaterial, executes, all unconscious of the power for which divine is none too grand a word, a lasting act of creative imagination.

Fred Newton Scott and Joseph Villiers Denney
Paragraph-Writing (1893)

ᘒ *(For background on Scott, see chap. 3, p. 177.) Denney (1862–1935) received his B.A. from the University of Michigan in 1885 and studied extensively abroad. He taught at Ohio State from 1891 to 1933. The last of the big four to appear,* Paragraph-Writing *is very different from other texts of its time; it focused entirely upon the paragraph as a unit of discourse, a somewhat radical notion at the time. This book was not adopted widely in the East; its greatest sales were in the Midwest and West, where more conservative Eastern standards did not hold sway (Kitzhaber; Wozniak). It looks and feels more modern than most texts of its time.*

PREFACE.

The principles embodied in this work were developed and put in practice by its authors at the University of Michigan several years ago. When the nature of the classroom work and its results became known, there were many inquiries from teachers in preparatory schools and colleges in regard to the methods employed. In response to these inquiries a small pamphlet (now out of print) was published and circulated. The present work, while in a limited sense a revision of that pamphlet, is virtually another book. In the earlier work the aim was to suggest a useful exercise in writing English. This book goes farther. Its aim is to make the paragraph the basis of a method of composition, to present all the important facts of rhetoric in their application to the paragraph. Since the point of view which is assumed is in some respects novel, a few words of explanation will not be out of place.

Learning to write well in one's own language means in large part learning to give unity and coherence to one's ideas. It means learning to construct units of discourse which have order and symmetry and coherence of parts. It means learning theoretically how such units are made, and practically how to put them together; and further, if they turn out badly the first time, how to take them apart and put them together again in another and better order. The making and re-making of such units is in general terms the task of all who produce written discourse.

The task of the teacher of those who produce written discourse, it follows, is in great part setting students to construct such units, explaining the principles upon which the units are made, arousing a sense that they *are* units and not mere heaps or nebulous masses, and (*hoc opus, hic labor est*) correcting departures from unity, order, and coherence when such departures occur.

Work of this kind on the part of writer or of teacher presupposes a unit of discourse. Of these units there are three,—the sentence, the paragraph, and the essay or whole composition. Which of these three is best adapted, psychologically and pedagogically, to the end proposed? The sentence may be rejected at the outset as at once too simple and too fragmentary. Practice in the composing of disconnected sentences is not of much service to students of composition. This remark applies to the lower as well as to the higher grades.[1] Moreover, as Professor Barrett Wendell has pointed out (*English Composition* 117), the sentence is properly a subject of revision, not of prevision,—good sentences are produced by criticising them after they are written rather than by planning them beforehand. Putting the sentence aside, then, what shall be said of the paragraph and the essay? Of the two the essay is theoretically the more proper unit of discourse. But is it always so in practice? Is it not true that for students at a certain stage of their progress the essay is too complex and too cumbersome to be appreciated as a whole? Aristotle long ago laid down the psychological principle which should govern the selection of a structural unit: "As for the limit fixt by the nature of the case, the greatest consistent with simultaneous comprehension is always the best." If students who have written essays for years have with all their labor developed but a feeble sense for structural unity, may the reason not lie in the fact that the unit of discourse employed has been so large and so complex that it could not be grasped with a single effort of the mind?

If there is a measure of truth in what has here been urged, it would appear that for certain periods in the student's development the paragraph, as an example of structural unity, offers peculiar advantages. The nature of these advantages has already been suggested. They are, in brief, as follows: The paragraph, being in its method practically identical with the essay, exemplifies identical principles of structure. It exemplifies these principles in small and convenient compass so that they are easily appreciable by the beginner. Further, while the writing of the paragraph exercises the student in the same elements of structure which would be brought to his attention were he drilled in the writing of essays, he can write more paragraphs than he can write essays in the same length of time; hence the character of the work may be made for him more varied, progressive, and interesting. If the paragraph thus suits the needs of the student, it has even greater advantages from the point of view of the teacher. The bugbear of the teacher of Rhetoric is the correcting of essays. When the compositions are long and crude and errors abound, the burden sometimes becomes almost intolerable. In many cases it is a necessary burden and must be borne with patience, but this is not always so. Since the student within the limits of the paragraph makes the same errors which he commits in the writing of longer compositions, in the greater part of the course the written work may profitably be shortened from essays to paragraphs. Paragraph-writing has the further advantage that, if necessary, the composition may be re-written from beginning to end, and, most important of all, when completed is not too long for the teacher to read and criticize in the presence of the class.

Finally, the paragraph furnishes a natural introduction to work of a more difficult character. When the time comes for the writing of essays, the transition from the smaller unit to its larger analogue is made with facility. Upon this point we cannot do better than to quote the words of Professor Bain:—

Adapting an old homely maxim, we may say, Look to the Paragraphs, and the Discourse will look to itself, for, although a discourse as a whole has a method or plan suited to its nature, yet the confining of each paragraph to a distinct topic avoids some of the worst faults of Composition; besides which, he that fully comprehends the method of a paragraph will also comprehend the method of an entire work.—Bain: *Composition and Rhetoric,* I. § 178.

This book is an attempt to embody in a manual the ideas which have just been advanced,—to utilize this convenient element of discourse, this half-way house between the sentence and the essay, as a basis for a method of English composition. In Part I., following the natural order of treatment, the nature and laws of the paragraph are presented; the isolated paragraph, its structure and function, are discussed: and finally, considerable space is devoted to related paragraphs, that is, those which are combined into essays. Part II. is a chapter on the theory of the paragraph intended for teachers and advanced students. In Part III. will be found copious materials for class-room work,—selected paragraphs, suggestions to teachers, lists of subjects for compositions (about two thousand in all), and helpful references of many kinds.

. . . .

Introductory.

(a) Definition of the Paragraph.

A paragraph is a unit of discourse developing a single idea. It consists of a group or series of sentences closely related to one another and to the thought expressed by the whole group or series. Devoted, like the sentence, to the development of one topic, a good paragraph is also, like a good essay, a complete treatment in itself.

The following paragraphs illustrate this close relation of sentences:—

I willingly concede all that you say against fashionable society as a whole. It is, as you say, frivolous, bent on amusement, incapable of attention sufficiently prolonged to grasp any serious subject, and liable both to confusion and inaccuracy in the ideas which it hastily forms or easily receives. You do right, assuredly, not to let it waste your most valuable hours, but I believe also that you do wrong in keeping out of it altogether.

The society which seems so frivolous in masses contains individual members who, if you knew them better, would be able and willing to render you the most efficient intellectual help, and you miss this help by restricting yourself exclusively to books. Nothing can replace the conversation of living men and women; not even the richest literature can replace it.—Hamerton: *The Intellectual Life,* Part IX. Letter V.

(b) Classes of Paragraphs.

A paragraph may be studied as constituting with other paragraphs a complete essay, or, it may be regarded by itself as a separate and complete composition in miniature.

(1) THE RELATED PARAGRAPH.

Paragraphs of the first class we will call *related* paragraphs since they are closely related to each other and to the essay of which they are the constituent units. Successive related paragraphs, as portions of a larger whole, treat in turn the topics into which, according to the general plan of the production, the subject naturally divides itself. If the subject of the essay requires but a brief treatment and the plan includes but two or three main headings, a single paragraph may suffice for each. Of a more extensive production, involving carefully planned divisions and subdivisions in the outline, each sub-topic may require a separate paragraph for its adequate treatment.

(2) THE ISOLATED PARAGRAPH.

A large class of subjects, however, admit of complete treatment in single paragraphs. Such are simple in their nature; for example, incidents, brief descriptions of persons and of places, terse comments upon current events, and short discussions on isolated phases of political and social questions. A single paragraph, which in itself gives an adequate treatment of any subject or of a single phase of any subject, we will call an *isolated* paragraph.

Both classes of paragraphs are units of discourse, though in slightly different senses. An isolated paragraph, standing by itself and existing for itself is an independent unit, whereas related paragraphs, existing as portions of a larger whole, are dependent or subordinate units.

The quotation from Hamerton, on page [347, above—ED.], illustrates related paragraphs, treating two phases of a single idea. The topic in the outline treated by the first of these paragraphs is, "Society is frivolous as a whole"; that treated by the second is, "But society contains individuals who are not frivolous." These paragraphs are so closely related, in thought, that each is necessary to the other; but each represents a distinct phase of the thought.

. . . .

Narrow each of the following general subjects to an available working theme, and then give to each an appropriate title:—

1. Algebra.	11. Prison Reform.
2. Literature.	12. Commerce.
3. Law.	13. The Arts.
4. Travel.	14. Longfellow.
5. High Schools.	15. Talking Machines.
6. Athletics.	16. Public Libraries.
7. Science.	17. City Governments.
8. Manual Training.	18. English.
9. Newspapers.	19. Letter-Writing.
10. The Jury System.	20. Protective Tariff.

. . . .

APPENDIX C.

I.

(*a*) Ten-Minute Themes in Exposition and Argument.

The exercises provided in Appendix A 12 demand deeper subjects of a character requiring time for preparation and reading on the part of the student. As a corrective for the bookishness that will often appear in the paragraphs written outside the class, it will be well for the student to write frequently, in the class-room, paragraphs on simple familiar subjects. The time for writing should be limited to ten or fifteen minutes, at the expiration of which, members of the class should be called upon, at random, to read what they have written, the class and instructor joining in the criticism. This exercise may be continued advantageously throughout the course. Constant practice in writing under pressure produces rapidity, facility, naturalness, and individuality of expression. At first it will be well to allow each student to select his own subject and to determine what he will say about it, before coming to the class. Later, the exercise should be wholly impromptu. Subjects of immediate local interest about which the student community is talking and thinking at the time are especially valuable for this impromptu work. Subjects which have come up during the week in the history and literature classes may also be utilized in this work. The following are printed merely to show the range and character of subjects that may be employed in this connection. They are necessarily general in character, whereas the actual subjects given should be specific. The instructor will be able to supplement this list with other subjects of more immediate interest and better adapted to the grade and attainments of his class. A choice of subjects should, if possible, be offered at all times.

1. Why do many dislike the study of rhetoric?
2. Advantages of literary societies.
3. Proper observance of Sunday by students.
4. Manners in the class-room.
5. Advantages of the work in manual training.
6. What does the school most need? Reasons.
7. How may a student best divide his time?
8. Some of the uses of writing frequently.
9. Why we lost the last ball-game.
10. Why I like or dislike the last book I read.
11. A defense of Shylock.
12. Arguments against long examinations.

. . . .

(b) Other Sources of Themes.

The work which the class may be doing in other branches of study will frequently suggest numerous themes for impromptus. Thus, if the composition class is also working in English history, themes like the following may occasionally be given:—

1. Life of our ancestors in Germany.
2. How our ancestors punished crime.
3. Roman influences in England.
4. A description of the Conqueror's reforms.
5. Wat Tyler's Rebellion.
6. The scene at Runnymede.
7. The work of the Star-chamber.
8. The story of Mary, Queen of Scots.
9. Jack Cade's Rebellion.
10. Story of Thomas à Becket.
11. Richard and the princes.
12. The Royal Oak.
13. The Spanish Armada.

Thus, too, if the composition class is also doing work in reading and studying English authors or American authors, themes in abundance may be chosen in the direct line of their work. To illustrate, a class studying Longfellow, and reading some of his poems, might properly be given themes like the following:—

1. Longfellow at Bowdoin and at Harvard.
2. The great sorrow of Longfellow's life.
3. How Edgar A. Poe regarded Longfellow.
4. A description of Longfellow's home.
5. The story of the children's armchair.
6. Longfellow's friends.
7. The main points of Morituri Salutamus.
8. Longfellow's travels.
9. The story of Evangeline.
10. The story of Miles Standish.
11. The story of one of the Tales of a Wayside Inn.
12. Longfellow's ideas of slavery.
13. A scene from Hiawatha.

(c) Practice in Outlining Themes.

Set down in brief the points you would mention if writing on the following topics. Re-arrange the points under a few main heads, distinguishing principal from subordinate points. Account for the order in which you have re-arranged the points.

DESCRIPTIONS.

1. A bridge. 2. The human hand. 3. A landscape. 4. A ball-game. 5. A portrait. 6. A room. 7. A face. 8. A statue. 9. A flower. 10. A church. 11. A foot-race. 12. A city. 13. A busy street. 14. A building. 15. A riot. 16. A field of corn. 17. A skating scene. 18. A fire. 19. A workshop. 20. A country village. 21. A flour mill. 22. A gypsy woman. 23. A book agent. 24. A wanderer. 25. A lawyer's office.

NARRATIVES.

1. An eventful day. 2. A horseback ride. 3. Learning to swim. 4. Sitting for a picture. 5. Earliest recollections. 6. A beggar's story. 7. Story of the Prisoner of Chillon. 8. Story of Burns's life. 9. A visit to Bunker Hill Monument. 10. Story of Goldsmith's life. 11. Story of Rasselas, Prince of Abyssinia. 12. Early life of John Milton. 13. Story of Joan of Arc. 14. The Regicides. 15. The Charter Oak. 16. Paul Revere's ride.

ARGUMENT.

1. Military schools should be encouraged. 2. Thackeray had no sympathy for the poor. 3. A large standing army is desirable in this country. 4. Our sea-coast defenses should be increased. 5. The assassination of Julius Caesar was justifiable. 6. Intercollegiate athletic contests should be abolished. 7. The execution of Mary, Queen of Scots, was justifiable. 8. There should be an educational qualification for voting. 9. Church property should be taxed like other property. 10. The Governor of Ohio should have the veto power. 11. The treatment of Roger Williams was unjustifiable. 12. Mohammedanism has been a benefit to the world. 13. Foreign missions are not so important as home missions. 14. The Sandwich Islands should be annexed to the United States. 15. Grant's administration was a failure. 16. The civil service reform law should be extended to apply to more classes of officials. 17. The Indian has not been treated justly. 18. Protection by bounties is cheaper than protection by tariff. 19. The war of the United States against Mexico was unjustifiable. 20. England's occupation of Egypt is right. 21. Strikes are inexpedient. 22. English is likely to become the language of the world. 23. Capital punishment for murder is justifiable. 24. Party spirit is beneficial. 25.

Prohibition is rightfully made a national issue. 26. Trusts and trade combinations are an evil. 27. Education should be compulsory. 28. Fortunes should be limited by law.

2.

Ten-Minute Themes in Narration and Description.

Subjects for ten-minute impromptus in narration and description are found in abundance. The writing of such paragraphs constitutes the greater part of the work of newspaper men, and, indeed, of almost all writing, and a large amount of such practice should be given. The list appended will suggest the class of subjects suitable for this work. Others of more local interest should be provided.

1. A description of a sleigh-ride.
2. A report of the last lecture I heard.
3. How I spent the holidays.
4. The coasting party.
5. A description of the ball-game.
6. Antics of a fountain-pen.
7. The new building.
8. Views from my window.
9. The room in which we recite.
10. The reading-room.
11. A day camping.
12. My experience at fishing.
13. A personal adventure.
14. Loss of a trunk.
15. A visit to an art-gallery.
16. A visit to a machine-shop.
17. Below the falls at Niagara.
18. A report of the last concert.
19. An historical incident.
20. A story from General Grant's life.
21. A letter describing my school-life.
22. A report of last Sunday's sermon.

NOTE

1. A series of experiments conducted by Miss H. M. Scott, Principal of the Detroit Training School for Teachers (Report of the Detroit Normal Training School

for 1893), show that children even in the lowest grades comprehend a paragraph-group, or 'sequence' of sentences, more readily than sentences taken separately. They learn to read more easily and rapidly by the 'paragraph method' than by the sentence method. [Harriet Scott was F. N. Scott's sister.—ED.]

Luella Clay Carson
Compilation of Standard Rules and Regulations Used by the English Department of the University of Oregon (1898)

Carson (1856–1943) attended but did not graduate from the University of Oregon and did additional study at Harvard and Columbia. She taught rhetoric and literature at the University of Oregon from 1888 to 1909, serving also as dean of women. She left to become president of Mills College (1909–1914). Later she was a teacher and administrator at a number of colleges in the Midwest. She and her Oregon colleague Ida Bel Roe collaborated on Public School Libraries for All the Grades *(1903)*.

Carson's book illustrates how the modern handbook evolved from a college's list of rules. Carson compiled her list in 1898; she revised it in 1903, and in 1907 it appeared as Handbook of English Composition: A Compilation of Standard Rules and Usage *(Harvard's copy of this edition was owned by George Lyman Kittredge); the last edition appeared in 1919. Though plenty of composition texts had used the word "Handbook" in their titles, Carson's seems to be the first college handbook organized around a numbered list of rules. The most famous examples of this type are Woolley's* Handbook *(1907), the* Harbrace College Handbook *(1935), and of course,* Strunk and White.

PREFACE.

The following rules and regulations have been compiled from standard authors for the use of classes in the English department in the University of Oregon. It is hoped that they may also be valuable to students in other departments. They have been, in the main, taken from standard authors in the English library of the University. Among the works consulted were Bigelow's Hand-book of punctuation; the grammars of West, Whitney, Waxwell and Carpenter; the rhetorics of Genung, A. S. Hill, Carpenter, Williams, Scott and Denney, Bain, Wendell and McElroy.

I am indebted to Miss Ida Bel Roe, assistant in the English department, for compiling many of these rules. Blank pages and spaces are left so that students may insert other rules and illustrations.

The purpose in making this little pamphlet is to put into the hands of students, in convenient form, a few suggestions and standard rules for the making of good English prose.

LUELLA CLAY CARSON.

CONTENTS.

Capitalization.

General Rules for Capitals.

The following words shall begin with capitals:—

1. The first word after a period; and usually after the interrogation point and the exclamation point.

2. The first word of every line of poetry.

3. The first word of an exact quotation in a direct form; as, He said, "There will be war."

4. The first word of every direct question; as, He said, "Who will go?"

5. The pronoun I and the interjection O.

6. Proper nouns.

7. Adjectives derived from proper nouns, unless, by long usage, they have lost all association with the nouns from which they are derived; as, Christian.

8. The words *street, river, mountain,* etc., when they are used in connection with proper names; as, Columbia River.

9. The words *north, south, east* and *west,* whenever they refer to parts of the country, and not simply to points of the compass.

10. Names of the days of the week and the months of the year, but not the seasons.

11. Words denoting family relations, such as *father,* when they are used with the proper name of the person or without a possessive pronoun; as, Uncle John.

12. Titles of honor or office whenever they are used in a formal way, or in connection with a proper name; as, General Grant.

13. Divine names; as, God, the Supreme Being.

· · · · · · · ·

Special Symbols

1. Apostrophe.

The apostrophe is used in the following instances:—

1. To mark the elision of a syllable in poetry or in familiar dialogue; also the elision of letters in a word.

2. To denote the elision of the century in dates; as, '98.

3. To denote the plural of figures and letters; as, p's and q's.

· · · · · · · ·

Form.

1. General.

1. Have good material: good quality of paper, black ink and good pen. (Spencerian bank-pen or Spencerian counting-house pen recommended; stub pen is not desirable.)

2. All writing should be in clear, legible hand with no flourishes and show care and accuracy in spelling and punctuation.

3. Write on but one side of the paper.

4. Number all pages in the upper right hand corner.

5. All paragraphs should be indented about one inch from the margin.

6. After each sentence a space of about an inch should be left before the beginning of the next sentence.

7. Be exact in making the different points of punctuation.

8. Write subject, name, class, division and date on outside cover.

. . . .

Style.

1. Vocabulary.

1. Endeavor to enlarge your *vocabulary* to at least three thousand words, so as to have some richness of diction.

2. Good Use.

1. Get knowledge of the principles of *good use* as codified in standard dictionaries, grammars and rhetorics and as exemplified by reputable writers and speakers so as to be able to recognize and to write good prose.

2. Words are well chosen when they are authorized by *present, national* and *reputable* use.

   A. A word very old or comparatively new or a word derived from any source, if generally understood in our own time, is in *present* use.

   B. A word understood, and understood in the same sense, in every part of the same country, and among all classes of equal intelligence is in *national* use.

   C. A word which is used by speakers and writers of established reputation is in *reputable* use.

D. Violations of the rule for good use are called *Barbarisms* and *Improprieties*.

   a. A *Barbarism* is a word unauthorized by either present, reputable or national usage. It may be an *obsolete* word, a word too *new* to have a recognized place, a *foreign* word or a *slang* word.

   b. An *Impropriety* is an authorized word used in an improper place; as, The gas was *sightless*. (Used for *invisible*.)

3. Words are *well arranged* and *well connected* when they follow the laws of grammatical and rhetorical usage.

   A. Violations of grammatical laws are *Solecisms*.

      a. A *solecism* is a faulty construction.

   B. Violations of rhetorical laws may be called *"Irregularities."*

      a. An *"Irregularity"* is a departure from the natural order of English words and is justifiable only when used for greater force or for some definite purpose; as, *Now* is the accepted time.

4. A. S. Hill classifies three of these errors as follows: There are three offences against the usage of the English Language:

   A. *Barbarisms,* words not English.

   B. *Solecisms,* constructions not English.

   C. *Improprieties,* words or phrases used in a sense not English.

   To these may be added the fourth offence:

   D. *Irregularities,* words or phrases used in an arrangement not English.

Recommendations.

It is recommended that each student own and use throughout his course, a *dictionary*, a *book of synonyms*, a *grammar* and a *rhetoric*. (Campbell's "Handbook of Synonyms and Prepositions" will be found very valuable.) Among standard grammars those of West and Whitney and among standard rhetorics those of Genung, Carpenter and A. S. Hill are valuable.

Edwin Campbell Woolley
Handbook of Composition (1907)

&❧ *Woolley (1878–1916) received his B.A. from Chicago in 1898 and his Ph.D. from Columbia in 1901. He spent his entire college teaching career at the University of Wisconsin.*

This is the handbook that made the genre famous; the slim 239-page book covered exactly 350 rules, everything from the standards of usage to the placement of stamps on an envelope. Though small print and thin paper allowed the publisher to keep the book slim, its length and detail alone might have overwhelmed some. It could be that in 1918 Cornell's William Strunk Jr. was moved to write his famous "little book" of rules in reaction to Woolley's inclusiveness.

PREFACE

This manual is designed for two uses. It may be used, first, by students of composition for reference, at the direction of the instructor, in case of errors in themes. Second, it may be used for independent reference by persons who have writing of any kind to do and who want occasional information on matters of good usage, grammar, spelling, punctuation, paragraphing, manuscript-arrangement, or letter-writing.

The aim of the book is not scientific, but practical. The purpose is to make clear the rules in regard to which many people make mistakes. No material has been put into the book for the sake of formal completeness. Many statements that would be essential to a treatise designed to exhaust the subjects here discussed (a treatise, for instance, on grammar, or composition-structure, or punctuation) have been omitted because they concern matters about which the persons who may use the book do not need to be told. In the knowledge and the observance of the rules fixed by good usage and suggested by common sense for the expression of thoughts in English and the representation of them on paper, there are many widely prevalent deficiencies, some natural enough, some very odd, but all shared by many people. The purpose of this manual is simply to help correct some of these deficiencies.

Some of the rules in this book, making no mention of exceptions, modifications, or allowable alternatives, may perhaps be charged with being dogmatic. They *are* dogmatic—purposely so. Suppose a youth, astray and confused in a maze of city streets, asks the way to a certain place. If one enumerates to him the several possible routes, with comments and admonitions and cautions about each, he will probably continue astray and confused. If one sends him peremptorily on one route, not mentioning permissible deviations or equally good alternative ways, the chance is much greater that he will reach his destination. Likewise, the erring composer of anarchic discourse can best be set right by concise and simple directions. This is one reason for the stringency of some of the rules. There is another reason; let me use another parable in explaining it. A student of piano-playing is held rigidly, during the early period of his study, to certain rules of finger movement. Those rules are sometimes varied or ignored by musicians. But the student, in order to progress in the art, must for a certain time treat the rules as stringent and invariable; the variations and exceptions are studied only at a later stage of his progress. So, in acquiring skill in the art of composition, it is necessary for most students to observe rigidly and invariably rules to which masters of the art make exceptions. . . .

I. THE COMPOSITION OF DISCOURSE

The Standard of Good Usage

Good usage defined

1. English discourse employing words generally approved by good usage, and employing them in the senses and in the grammatical functions and combinations generally approved by good usage, is called good English. English discourse employing words not generally approved by good usage, or employing words in senses and in grammatical functions and combinations not generally approved by good usage, is called bad English. By *good usage* is meant the usage generally observed in the writings of the best English authors and in the speech of well-educated people.

Mistaken standards:

2. Regarding questions of good or bad English, there are several common errors:

Colloquial usage

(*a*) The supposition that an expression current in common conversation is thereby proved to be good English. If currency in common conversation were a valid test, such expressions as "ain't," "I says," "them fellows," "he laid down," "you hadn't ought," and "has went" would be good English.

Limited usage

(*b*) The supposition that the usage of a number of well-educated persons with whom one is acquainted proves whether or not an expression is good English. It should be remembered that (as the foregoing definition of *good usage* implies) the true standard is the usage in which the *majority* of well-educated people, including the writers of undisputed literary merit, agree; not the usage of a relatively small number of well-educated persons. Some well-educated people say "he don't" and "proven"; but these expressions are none the less bad English, for the majority of well-educated people, including the writers of good literature, reject them.

(*c*) The supposition that an expression current in the newspapers is thereby proved to be good English. Our newspapers are almost universally characterized by provincial and vulgar diction. (There are a few honorable exceptions.) An expression like "Rev. Clifford has proven himself a hustler" is no more justified by the wide currency of similar expressions in the newspapers than "has went" is justified by wide currency in conversation. General newspaper usage has nothing whatever to do with good English usage. (Cf. Rule 16 and the note to Rule 129.) *Newspaper usage*

(*d*) The supposition that the employment of an expression by recent writers of popular fiction proves that the expression is good English. A writer does not, merely by being popular, take rank among the best English authors; such rank can be taken only upon the general judgment of scholars and critics, as well as of the reading public, and only after that judgment has endured a sufficient length of time to become established. The student will do well to rely for indications of what is good usage, not on recent writers, about whose literary rank he may make mistakes, but on authors of whose high rank he is sure,—such authors as Addison, Irving, Burke, Macaulay, De Quincey, Mill, Matthew Arnold, Ruskin, Emerson, Holmes, Dickens, Thackeray, George Eliot, Hawthorne, Poe, Stevenson. But, in consulting even such authors as these, he should beware of another common error regarding good usage; *viz.,* — *The usage of recent fiction*

(*e*) The supposition that a single instance of the use of a word by one of the best English authors proves the word to be good English. A word must be shown to be in *general* use among such authors, in order to be proved good English. The word "vim" can be found in the works of Stevenson, but it is nevertheless bad English. *Isolated instances not decisive*

3. From the foregoing considerations it follows that in order to know by direct evidence what is good and what is bad English, one must have a wide acquaintance with English literature and a wide—in fact, an international—acquaintance with people of the best education. Lacking such acquaintance, one must look to trustworthy books on grammar, rhetoric, composition, and other subjects involving discussion of good usage, and to good dictionaries. *Means of learning good usage*

Inclusion
of a word
in a dictionary
is not
decisive

NOTE.—Regarding the use of a dictionary for determining questions of good or bad English, a mistaken idea is often held,—*viz.*, the supposition that the inclusion of a word in a dictionary proves the word to be good English. In consulting a dictionary for the standing of a word, one ought to observe, not merely whether the word is in the dictionary, but whether, being there, it is marked Obsolete, Slang, Low, Vulgar, Local, or Colloquial. If it is so marked, it is either bad English or English not in good literary standing.

. . . .

Newspaper
mannerisms:

16. Obvious effort to decorate one's style with striking phraseology is a hackneyed newspaper mannerism (cf. Rule 2 *c*). This effort appears particularly in the following objectionable practices:

Nicknames of
States and
cities

(*a*) The tediously habitual designation of States and cities by their nicknames (*e.g.*, "the Buckeye State," "the Sunflower State," "the Gopher State," "the Cream City," etc.). This practice becomes especially objectionable when the nickname is obtruded, as it often is, at a place where no name at all is needed; *e.g.*,

> Vulgar: He arrived in Boston yesterday. Many citizens *of the Hub* were gathered to meet him.
> Right: He arrived in Boston yesterday. Many citizens were gathered to meet him.

Current
newspaper
rhetoric

(*b*) The regular employment of miscellaneous current verbal ornaments, such as "fatal affray," "fistic encounter," "struggling mass of humanity," "scantily attired," "knights of the pen" (for *reporters*), "the officiating clergyman," "tied the knot," "pachyderm" (for *elephant*), "equines" (for *horses*), "canines" (for *dogs*), "felines" (for *cats*), etc.

Straining
for novelty of
phrase

(*c*) Obtrusive straining for novelty of phrase.

> Vulgar: The football warriors of the Badger State will play the Windy City's squad of pigskin-chasers this afternoon.
> Right: The Wisconsin football team will play the Chicago team this afternoon.
> Vulgar: The guests spent the evening in doing the "light fantastic" act.
> Right: The guests spent the evening in dancing.

Genuine and
counterfeit
humor

NOTE.—The jocular purpose with which the above-mentioned mannerisms are often practiced furnishes no justification of them. Hackneyed and tawdry English, whatever its purpose, is still hackneyed and tawdry. In condemning the jocular use of these forms of expression, good taste does not condemn humorous writing; it condemns the crude and obvious counterfeiting of humor. A comic account of a football game or of an evening party is commendable if the humor is genuine and entertaining; but in saying "squad of pigskin-chasers" for *football team*, "did the light fantastic act" for *danced*, "the Hub" for *Boston*, or "Indefatigable knights of the pen dogged his steps as far as his hostlery" for *Reporters followed him to his hotel*,—in such language there is only a dull pretense of humor.

Affectation

17. Do not use high-flown language for plain things.

High-flown language

Bad: To keep the horse healthy you must be careful of his environment.
Right: To keep the horse healthy you must be careful of his stable.

NOTE.—Showy language, like showy dress, is in bad taste. The essence of artistic language, as of everything artistic, is not abundant ornament but appropriateness. Straining for high-sounding expressions to replace plain English makes a style weak and crude. Call a leg a leg, not a limb; call a book a book, not an effort; call a letter a letter, not a kind favor; call socks socks, not hose; call a house a house, not a residence; say "I went to bed," not "I retired"; "I got up," not "I arose."

Plain English

18. In prose avoid the use of words suited only to poetry, such as *dwelt, oft, oftentimes, ofttimes, morn, amid, 'mid, 'midst, o'er, 'neath, 'tis, 'twas.*

Poetic diction

. . . .

Structure of Sentences

Some Fundamental Errors

24. Subordinate sentence-elements should not be capitalized and punctuated like independent sentences.

Subordinate elements mistaken for sentences

A. Wrong: It offers a course for those who wish to study painting. At the same time affording opportunity for literary study.
Right: It offers a course to those who wish to study painting, at the same time affording opportunity for literary study.

B. Wrong: Among her suitors were two she favored most. One a college student, the other a capitalist.
Right: Among her suitors were two she favored most; one a college student, the other a capitalist.

C. Wrong: The care of oil lamps requires every day some untidy and disagreeable labor. While electric lights give the housekeeper no trouble.

Right: The care of oil lamps requires every day some untidy and disagreeable labor, while electric lights give the housekeeper no trouble.

Elements without syntax

25. Do not use a word, phrase, or clause without proper grammatical construction.

Bad: The resonator responds in a manner analogous to that *which* one tuning fork responds to another.

Right: The resonator responds in a manner analogous to that *in which* one tuning fork responds to another.

Bad: That's all I want, is a chance to test it thoroughly. ["Is" has no subject.]

Right: That's all I want—a chance to test it thoroughly; [or] All I want is a chance to test it thoroughly.

Wrong: There were some people whom I could not tell whether they were English or American. ["Whom" has no construction.]

Right: There were some people about whom I could not tell whether they were English or American.

Sentences or sentence-elements left uncompleted

26. Do not begin a grammatical construction and leave it unfinished.

Bad: The fact that I had never before studied at home, I was at a loss what to do with vacant periods. [The noun "fact" with its appositive modifier "that . . . home" is left without any construction.]

Right: The fact that I had never before studied at home made me feel at a loss as to what to do with vacant periods.

Bad: The story tells how a young German, who, having settled in Dakota, returns to Wisconsin and there marries an old schoolmate. [The clause beginning "how a young German" is left unfinished; "German" (modified by the clause "who . . . schoolmate") has no construction.]

Right: The story tells how a young German, having settled in Dakota, returns to Wisconsin and marries an old schoolmate.

Wrong: Any man who could accomplish that task, the whole world would think he was a hero. ["Man," with its modifier "who . . . task," is left without any construction.]

Right: Any man who could accomplish that task the whole world would regard as a hero.

Sentence as subject or predicate complement

27. The use of a sentence (except a quoted sentence) as the subject of *is* or *was* is a crudity.

Crude: I was detained by business is the reason I am late.

Right: I was detained by business; that is the reason I am late.

A similar fault is the use of a sentence (except a quoted sentence) as a predicate substantive after *is* or *was*. This fault may be corrected by changing the sentence to a substantive clause.

> Crude: The difference between them is De Quincey is humorous and Macaulay is grave.
> Right: The difference between them is that De Quincey is humorous and Macaulay is grave.

28. Do not use a *when* or *where* clause in place of a predicate noun; use a noun with modifiers.

When *or*
where
clause for
predicate
noun

> Bad: Intoxication is when the brain is affected by the action of certain drugs.
> Right: Intoxication is a state of the brain, caused by the action of certain drugs.

. . . .

Structure of Larger Units of Discourse

Unity of a Composition

134. A composition should treat a single subject and should treat it throughout according to a self-consistent method.

The general
principle

The following composition is an example of the violation of unity by failure to hold to one subject:

OUR TRIP UP SPRUCE CREEK

While I was in Port Orange, Mr. Doty, the proprietor of the hotel there, took some of his guests five miles up Spruce Creek on a launch. It was the third of February. As the boat steamed up the creek, we stood on the deck, some of us taking pictures and others shooting at alligators with revolvers. The alligators are of all sizes. Sometimes you will see one seven or eight feet long, lying on the bank in the sunshine. As the boat goes past, he slides into the water and swims away with only his head above the water. When we have gone a little farther, we see another alligator about four feet long, with ten or twelve little ones crawling over her back.

When the launch has gone about five miles, it stops at the wharf of an orange grove. Here the passengers are allowed to take all the oranges they want. After they have walked about the grove for a while, they have a picnic dinner, and then start back.

The writer of the foregoing composition keeps to his subject—a trip which he took up Spruce Creek on February 3—for only three sentences. After the third sentence he shifts to a different subject—the Spruce Creek trips in general—and throughout the rest of the composition forgets all about "our trip." Unity may be given to this composition (*a*) by making it entirely a narrative, dealing with the trip of February 3; or (*b*) by making it, throughout, a general discussion of the Spruce Creek picnics provided by Mr. Doty.

. . . .

Organization of a Composition

The general principle   140. In order that a composition be effective, it must not merely contain good thoughts or interesting statements; it must be a well-organized whole. It can not be a well-organized whole if the writer puts down thoughts or statements at haphazard, just as they occur to him. To get good organization, a writer must proceed by a definite plan; that is, he must, before he begins to write, or at least before he puts the composition into its final form, decide on a few topics, and on each topic write a passage, constituting a unit of the whole composition. Unless this plan of organization is followed, the composition is likely to be a mere collection of pieces—not a well-made whole. The pieces may be individually good, but the composition is poor. As in warfare a band of men, though strong and brave individually, is collectively weak if it is not well organized; so a speech, a report, an editorial, an essay, any composition, though its parts may be forcible or clever, is weak as a whole if it is not well organized.

For example, an essay on Denver consists of a short paragraph on each of the following topics:

1. Location.
2. History.
3. Local pride.
4. Water supply (derived from mountain snow).
5. Capitol and United States mint.
6. Museums.
7. Principal businesses.
8. Dwelling houses (none built of wood).
9. Schools.

10. Wealth of citizens.
11. The city as a health resort.
12. Churches.
13. Strange spectacle of men skating in winter in their shirtsleeves.

This production, however interesting its material, is as far from being a good composition as two wheels, a diamond frame, a chain, and a pair of handle bars, all piled in a heap, are from being a good bicycle. It is a series of haphazard remarks not organized into a whole. There is no reason for most of the parts' standing where they are—no reason, *e.g.*, for discussing public buildings after the water supply, or skaters' costumes after churches. The material of this essay may be organized into a whole by the method shown in the following outline. The numbers within the brackets refer to parts of the preceding outline.

I. History. [2]
II. Location and climate. [Put 1 and 13 here—13 as an illustration of the statements about the climate.]
III. Especially striking peculiarities of the city.
   1. Evidences of its being a health resort. [11]
   2. Absence of wooden buildings. [8]
   3. Public buildings. [5]
   4. Water supply. [4]
   5. Most striking of all,—local pride. [3]
IV. Conditions of the people's life.
   1. Economic: Principal occupations. General wealth. [7 and 10]
   2. Educational and moral: Schools, museums, churches. [9, 6, and 12]

141. Material belonging to one part of an essay should not be placed carelessly in another part. *Passages misplaced*

In the following paragraph, the italicized sentence is evidently misplaced:

The physical training department of our college is very good and is constantly improving. *A good gymnasium for the women is greatly needed, to replace the present unsatisfactory make-shift.* As I am more acquainted with the work of the girls, I shall confine myself to the physical training provided for them.

The italicized sentence does not belong in this introductory part, but in a subsequent part,—*viz.,* that which discusses the equipment for the girls' exercise.

. . . .

Sundry Mechanical Directions

Ink

339. The ink used in letter writing should be of no other color than black.

Writing-paper:
Four-page sheets
Flat sheets

340. Letter-paper consisting of sheets so folded that each sheet is like a little book of four pages, is suitable for all letters,—commercial, professional, or social; and for the letters of private individuals, as distinguished from those of public officials and those of business firms, it is, on the whole, preferable to writing-paper in flat sheets. The use of the latter kind is best confined to business or professional correspondence. Writing-paper that is ruled, or limp and flimsy in texture, or conspicuous because of unusual color, should be used for no letters whatever—except in case of emergency.

Margin at top
Margin at left
Legibility

341. The writing should not be crowded close to the top of any page, but should begin an inch or two below. For the sake of neat and attractive appearance, it is best to keep a blank margin at least half an inch wide at the left side of every page. Rules 165–177 and 183–187 should be observed in letters as well as in other manuscripts.

Order of pages:
Flat sheets

342. When flat sheets of paper are used, it is usually best that only one side of each sheet be written on. If both sides are written on, the reader is slightly inconvenienced in holding and turning the sheets as he reads.

Four-page sheets

343. When four-page sheets are used, all four pages may be written on. The letter should be so written that a person reading the first page has at his left the fold, and at his right the coinciding edges opposite the fold. If the substance of the letter occupies less than two pages of the sheet the first and third pages may be written on and the second be left blank. If the substance of the letter occupies more than two pages, it is best, both on the ground of good usage and on that of the reader's convenience, that the pages be written on in their natural order,—*viz.,* 1, 2, 3, 4; not in the order 1, 3, 2, 4 or 1, 4, 2, 3. On the same grounds, it is best that the lines of writing on all the pages be at right angles to the fold, not parallel with the fold.

Folding and enclosing:
Four-page sheets

344. A letter written on a four-page sheet should be enclosed in an envelope of the same material and of such shape and size that the letter will fit into it when folded with one horizontal crease through the center.

The letter should be so folded that the upper and the lower halves of page 1 face each other; or, in other words, so that the horizontal crease will appear as a groove on pages 1 and 3, and as a ridge on pages 2 and 4. The letter should be so placed in the envelope that the horizontal crease is at the bottom of the envelope, and the two coinciding halves of the vertical crease originally dividing the sheet are at the left hand of a person looking at the sealed side of the envelope.

. . . .

347. The foregoing rules in regard to the manner of folding letters and inserting them in envelopes are merely detailed applications of the simple rule of courtesy: Fold and enclose the letter in such a way that the receiver will be able, with the least possible effort, to get it right side up in his hand, ready to read. A few experiments will show that if any of the directions in Rules 344–346, above, are disregarded in the folding and enclosing of a letter, the addressee, on taking the letter from the envelope and unfolding it in the natural way, will find it with the first page turned from him or with the writing upside down. *The fundamental principle underlying Rules 344–346*

. . . .

350. The postage stamp should be attached in the upper right-hand corner. It should be right side up, and its edges should be parallel to the edges of the envelope. A postage stamp upside down or affixed in a haphazard fashion raises against the sender of the letter a suspicion of slovenliness. *The postage stamp*

. . . .

Exercises for Breaking Certain Bad Habits in Writing and Speaking

Exercises chiefly in Grammar

I. See *Lay* in the Glossary. Write three sentences containing present indicative forms of the verb *lie* (in the sense of *recline*), three containing the present participle, three containing past tense forms, and three containing perfect tense forms. Write three sentences containing present indicative forms of the verb *lay,* three containing the present participle, three containing past tense forms, and three containing perfect tense forms. *Lay* and *lie*

Lay and
lie

II. See *Lay* in the Glossary. Write the following sentences, filling each blank with some form of the verb *lie* or some form of the verb *lay:* 1. The logs are _____ing where they fell. 2. Yesterday I _____ it on the grass. 3. I will _____ down and rest. 4. They _____ still and said nothing. 5. Inmates are not allowed to _____ in bed after six o'clock. 6. They let the torpedo _____ on the railroad. 7. I have _____ all his things in readiness. 8. The scythe _____ in the rain so long that it got rusty. 9. _____ing quietly in the grass, he watched. 10. Have they _____ their wet hats on the parlor table? 11. Coming from Florida, I was surprised to find the snow still _____ing on the ground.

Raise and
rise

III. See *Raise* in the Glossary. Write three sentences containing present indicative forms of the verb *rise,* three containing the present participle, three containing past tense forms. Write three sentences containing present indicative forms of the verb *raise,* three containing the present participle, three containing past tense forms, and three containing perfect tense forms.

Raise and
rise

IV. See *Raise* in the Glossary. Write the following sentences, filling each blank with some form of the verb *raise* or some form of the verb *rise:* 1. Don't be embarrassed; _____ up and speak. 2. A man suddenly _____ up and interrupted. 3. I will _____ up and deny it publicly. 4. Slowly the load yielded to the upward force; and little by little it _____ until it reached the desired point. 5. It was too late; the balloon had already _____ ten feet. 6. Has the river _____ at all during the night?

Set and
sit

V. See *Set* in the Glossary. Write three sentences containing present indicative forms of the verb *set,* three containing the present participle, three containing past tense forms, and three containing perfect tense forms. Write three sentences containing present indicative forms of the verb *sit,* three containing the present participle, three containing past tense forms, and three containing perfect tense forms.

Set and
sit

VI. See *Set* in the Glossary. Write the following sentences, filling each blank with some form of the verb *set* or some form of the verb *sit:* 1. The ink-well doesn't _____ level. 2. I enjoy _____ in the dark. 3. How long we had _____ there I do not know. 4. He brought the little girl in his arms and _____ her in a chair by the fire.

VII. Comment on the use of *set* in each of the following sentences, correcting all errors: 1. Around the table set four chairs. 2. She left the umbrella setting against the chair. 3. You have set a hard task. 4. He saw the pie setting on the doorstep. 5. With the spirit level, he made the table set exactly horizontal. 6. Did you notice the order in which the cups were set? 7. Ready; get set; go. 8. The bluffs appear to set back some distance from the shore.

Set

VIII. See *Lay, Raise,* and *Set* in the Glossary. Write a short story about a balloon ascension, using the words *lie, lying, lay, lain, laying, laid, rise, rising, rose, risen, raise, raising, raised, sit, sitting, sat, set,* and *setting.*

Lay, lie, raise, rise, set, and *sit*

IX. Remember the principal parts of *do* and *see.*

Done and *seen*

I do	I did	I have done
I see	I saw	I have seen

Write five sentences each containing past tense forms of the verbs *do* and *see,* and five sentences each containing *done* and *seen* properly used.

Write the following sentences, filling the blanks with *did* or *saw:* 1. I _____ the damage that the fire _____ 2. There we _____ a magician, who _____ some tricks. 3. I _____ my duty and I _____ it. 4. He _____ the work with his own hands; I _____ him do it. 5. She _____ that it would do harm, and so she _____ all she could to stop it.

X. Remember the principal parts of *write, rise, ride,* and *drive:*

Write, rise, ride, drive

I write	I wrote	I have written
I rise	I rose	I have risen
I ride	I rode	I have ridden
I drive	I drove	I have driven

Write sentences containing perfect tense forms and past-perfect tense forms of *write, rise, ride,* and *drive.*

XI. Remember the principal parts of the verb *run:*

Run misused for *ran*

I run	I ran	I have run

Write five sentences containing the verb *run* in the past tense, and five containing the form *run,* properly used.

Began,   XII. Notice the relation between the past tense and the perfect tense
sang,   of the following verbs:
sprang,
rang,   I began   I have begun
drank,   I sang   I have sung
ran,   I sprang   I have sprung
swam   I rang   I have rung
                                 I drank   I have drunk
                                 I ran   I have run
                                 I swam   I have swum

Write sentences containing perfect tense forms and past-perfect tense
forms of the foregoing verbs.

Six Modern Readers, 1907–1915

THESE SIX ARE EARLY readers for college composition; like many books
of their time, they are all organized around a controlling idea. The
earliest, Cooper's *Theories of Style,* looks more like a collection of literary
criticism; only when one reads the preface does it becomes clear that it is
intended for upper-level composition. Berkeley's looks like a thoroughly
modern reader. Directed at first- or second-year composition: it includes
a full "apparatus," questions for study and topics for further writing, and
it contains student examples as models to be emulated. (Berkeley taught
at Wisconsin with Foerster and his collaborator Karl Young, whom she
married in 1911. She and Young wrote the second edition of her book in
1914.) Steeves and Ristine's book is a collection of essays on closely
linked modern topics which serve as models of writing and spurs to
thinking about the issues raised. The editors thank their Columbia
colleague John Erskine, a powerful influence on this type of course work
in composition programs. The two Wisconsin *Essays for College Men*
maintain a narrower focus—education—forcing students to examine
their own college experience in light of some prominent educational
statements of the era. It is possible to think of this type of reader—and
the subsequent composition course—as propaganda, or acculturation,
for a new generation of college students, most of whom come from
backgrounds that did not include higher education. They aim, in the
words of Maurice Garland Fulton, author of another popular textbook, to
make students "good college citizens" (Fulton, *College* x). The readings

introduce students to the "official" side of college, with the implicit understanding that they are to be read straight. The arguments and thoughts in these essays are to be mastered, not criticized or wrestled with, even though at this very time many scholars and critics (e.g., Charles Beard and Joel Spingarn at Columbia, Randolph Bourne in the *New Republic*) were doing just that. From the looks of these and many other texts of the time, it seems that teachers assumed that first-year students were not ready for reading and writing that were truly critical.

The connections among some of these authors appear in acknowledgments, and correspondence files also contain evidence of united efforts. For instance, in 1913 Norman Foerster wrote to Frank Aydelotte:

> Your name and your convictions are by this time familiar to our entire teaching staff in freshman English, and our plans for next year have been made in such wise that we shall devote the whole second semester to exposition, using one or more complete books—Carlyle and Hazlitt or Newman and Thoreau—as a basis for class discussion and theme writing. You may also be interested to hear, if no one has told you, that two Columbia instructors, Steeves and another [Ristine], are publishing a 500-page book of long and solid selections with the title "Representative Essays in Modern Thought," and that their prospectus lays great emphasis on "Cultivation of Ideas." And various things point to the fact that throughout the country substance is to be stressed, rather than "artistic" fluency or accuracy of detail. (Blanshard 111)

And this to Aydelotte from Roosevelt P. Walker:

> Professor Phelps of Yale has referred me to you as a person who can render valuable help in an attempt we are making at the University of Arkansas to make the work of our English department more effective. (Blanshard 111)

There was, not surprisingly, a network of like-minded thinkers and writers who supported each other's ideas and helped to restructure the composition course along new lines.

Lane Cooper
Theories of Style: With Especial Reference to Prose Composition (1907)

    (See chap. 4, p. 251, for biography.) This is one of the first anthologies claiming to be specifically designed for college composition course

work. It is an interesting mix of Cooper's heavily romantic theory of literary composition joined to a sense of style based on classical sources. In 1952 Cornell University Press reprinted this book with only minor changes as The Art of the Writer.

PREFACE

This volume, the editor imagines, may prove serviceable to teachers of English in more than one way.

From its origin—and apart from the style of the editor's translations—it may be regarded first of all as a body of literary models to be used in illustration of some good handbook on English prose composition, by classes in what is technically known as Exposition, *i.e.* written explanation. The editor's conception of such a volume of models arose partly from his belief—which needs no discussion here—that of the three generally recognized Forms of Prose Writing, namely, Description, Narration, and Exposition, only Exposition can be advantageously taught as a practical art by the average instructor in English to the average class; partly from his objection to certain books of "standard" selections, which professed rhetoricians have seen fit to compile for similar purposes of illustration in the classroom. In his opinion these compilations suffer from one fairly obvious defect.

As a rule, they seem to lack a fundamental principle which every teacher of thinking and writing is supposed to demand of every book, and to inculcate in the mind of every pupil. They seem lacking in unity. The several selections in a typical volume, if they happen to be complete in themselves, and if they are really taken from *standard* authors, have otherwise a purely formal bond of similarity: they are merely samples of one or other of the three kinds of writing that comprise all literature. Diversity of authorship, of course, is inevitable in an anthology. Whether the *substance* of any book employed in the teaching of composition should be so heterogeneous as of itself to produce no definite and lasting impression on the plastic mind, merits serious consideration. Perhaps it is a question to be decided by experience. So far as the writer's observation goes, the typical book of illustrative excerpts, drawn from many authors, and dealing with widely diverse topics, is not a ready instrument for coördinating the processes of the average undergraduate brain. Hurrying, within the space of a college term, from some popular

account of a glacier through eighteen other disconnected and often fragmentary discussions, and ending, let us say, with a chapter from Darwin's *Descent of Man,* the student of such a collection will hardly observe
along the route much more of the method of exposition than can be
totally dissociated from a well-earned grasp of any one subject.

In brief, the present volume owes its origin to a conviction that the
link between substance and form, between knowledge and expression,
ought never to be broken; and that before an underclassman is urged to
write a composition, he ought to begin systematic thinking in a field
where his teacher is qualified to judge of his manner of discussion,
through a critical acquaintance with the matter discussed. A specialist in
English need not be thoroughly versed in Darwinism; he can scarcely be
expected to show much familiarity with the theory of glacial action; he
may properly be supposed to know something about the mechanism of
style, and to have made some study of the evolution of types in literature. Hence arose in my mind the idea of an orderly collection of essays
on style, with especial reference to prose composition; a body of expository writing, for the most part by masters of expression, at once illustrating and reiterating the salient principles of the text-book[1] which it may
accompany; a group of stimulating and, on the whole, mutually corroborative selections, representing not too many literary types for easy comprehension of their structure, and printed as far as possible without
curtailment.

The material of the volume has been chosen, however, with a view to
possible applications other than the one just outlined, though not, it is
hoped, inconsistent with it. For example, aside from the question of
models for practical criticism and imitation, the selections offer some
opportunity for a purely theoretical investigation of at least two closely
allied literary species, the *essay* and the *address* on *style.* Facilities for the
study of specific types in prose are as yet not too abundant. In addition to
its use in the classroom, the volume may likewise serve as a work of
outside reference, since, although it makes no pretence to inclusiveness,
it aims to bring together a considerable number of historic utterances on
style, not all of which are very accessible elsewhere. By supplying an
adequate historic background for the more recent treatises, it has, I
think, a substantial advantage over text-books of composition and rhetoric that ignore, or underrate, the debt of English style to the Greek and
Latin classics.

In the actual employment of material like this, every teacher, of course, will pursue to a certain extent his own method, in accordance with his personal leanings and the constitution of his classes. In general,—even with not very advanced students,—the writer inclines to a practice somewhat as follows. Some text-book having afforded a preliminary knowledge of the main forms of prose composition, at a given meeting let the class be ready to discuss the substance and the form of one of the earlier selections, say that from Wackernagel, with sufficient free play of opinion; each individual, however, basing his share in the discussion upon a thorough written analysis of the whole selection. In the case of immature students these analyses would afterward be subject to the instructor's private supervision. At the next meeting let each member of the class be prepared with a paper—also accompanied by an outline—expanding some special topic in that selection, or elaborating some point raised in the discussion. When one has read, the others should feel encouraged to question and comment. The instructor may or may not pass final judgment on a paper. He is a moderator, whose function is to stimulate his class to mental self-activity, and quietly to mould it into a living, intelligent, social unit. This function he can best perform with groups of not more than fifteen pupils—preferably of ten or twelve; and, if he has tact, with much younger minds than are usually drilled in anything approaching a "seminary" course. Each student should preserve his own papers, properly revised, for special conference from time to time with the instructor. The net amount of writing expected of an underclassman per week should be far less than is customary in some of the "theme" courses at our American universities; the amount of time spent in the preparation and revision of any one theme, far greater. The student who cannot be sufficiently interested in his English to plan a composition twice, and to rewrite it thrice, should not, under ordinary circumstances, hope to master even the rudiments of plain exposition.

Save for the introductory translation from Wackernagel, the order of the selections is roughly chronological; but it need not be followed. The excerpt from Aristotle might be read before that from Plato. Lewes or Thoreau might be kept until the close of the term. Manifestly, Wackernagel, Aristotle, Plato, and Longinus are inserted as standards by which to measure the remaining authors, and should be taken up before Swift, Buffon, and the rest.

In the process of comparing one selection with another, students should cultivate the habit of marginal cross-reference; for the various authors may be made, so to speak, to annotate and reënforce one another on essential points. A few parallels are indicated in the Notes: enough, it is hoped, to suggest to a reader the possibility of his discovering many more by himself. A complete critical apparatus has not been attempted, the editor having desired throughout to suppress adventitious matter, so as to include a greater number of masterpieces, and thus to increase the general field of comparison. However, he hopes that the remarks preceding and following the several selections will be of some utility to students or to teachers.

In the introductory notes teachers will not overlook certain references that would enable classes inadequately furnished with copies of this book, but near a good library, to find many of the selections in a variety of sources.

As a general introduction to the volume, the editor offers, not, of course, his own theory of style—nobody would want that—but a theory, or the skeleton thereof, by an established modern authority, Wackernagel, with whom the editor feels himself essentially in agreement. The Introduction, then, amounts merely to an extra selection taken out of chronological order, and placed for the sake of prominence at the beginning. . . .

NOTE

1. For example, Professor J. M. Hart's *Essentials of Prose Composition*, Philadelphia, 1902.

CONTENTS

378   THE ORIGINS OF COMPOSITION STUDIES

Frances Campbell Berkeley
A College Course in Writing from Models (1910)

੧ढ *Berkeley received her Ph.D. from Wisconsin in 1911,
with a dissertation published as* Mary Sidney, Countess of Pembroke *(1912).
She taught at Wisconsin and married her Wisconsin colleague and teacher Karl
Young in 1911, after which she left the profession. In 1954, after Young's death,
she published* The Berkeleys of Barn Elms, *a genealogical work. A second
edition of the textbook,* Frances Berkeley Young and Karl Young, Freshman
English: A Manual, *appeared in 1914. (See chap. 6, p. 477 for selections.)*

PREFACE

The order of selections in the following volume is recommended as a
practicable one for a class to follow consecutively. The editor has particularly striven for a sequence in selections and exercises which should
represent the normal, logical growth in comprehension and facility of the
average Freshman or Sophomore. Under nearly every type of exercise,
however, alternative "models" have been offered, in order to provide
greater breadth of choice to students of varying tastes and capacities.

In printing the selections, the punctuation and spelling of the original texts have been almost invariably retained. Changes have been made only when they seemed absolutely necessary, either for greater intelligibility to students, or for the correction of obvious errors.

For permission to reprint various copyrighted selections, my acknowledgments are made.

I am indebted to Mr. Carl H. Ruenzel, Wisconsin, 1912, for the use of his themes on *The Fireless Cooker* and *How to Curve a Baseball.*

I have been fundamentally aided by the criticism and advice of Professor W. T. Brewster, and the late Professor G. R. Carpenter, of Columbia University. To the members of the Department of English at the University of Wisconsin I am also greatly indebted for valuable suggestions, in particular to Professor W. B. Cairns, and Professor W. G. Bleyer. My chief acknowledgments are due, however, to Professor J. W. Cunliffe and Professor F. G. Hubbard, without whose counsel and assistance the completion of this volume would have been impossible.

F. C. B.

CONTENTS

INTRODUCTION

The present volume of prose selections urges, as its best excuse for being, the conviction of the editor that it is founded on a principle psychologically and pedagogically sound. Although this principle, in the abstract, has been recognized by teachers, and although it has been delightfully expounded and advocated by Robert Louis Stevenson, it has not, so far as I am aware, had a sufficiently wide nor definite application to the study of writing among undergraduates.

It is my own firm belief that no student ever yet learned to write by means of studying rules and abstract principles from a text-book on rhetoric. After a fairly long experience with the endeavors of Freshmen and Sophomores, I feel absolutely sure that, to these long-suffering youngsters, "unity, mass, coherence," and all their works remain "miching mallecho" [*Hamlet* 3.2.135—ED.] to the end of the chapter. Still another objection to this sort of teaching, besides its abstractness, and consequent unintelligibility to the undergraduate mind, is that such teaching is mainly destructive. A freshman, for instance, is obliged to learn, for a recitation, chapter five of So-and-so's book, on the particular question of "Diction and Usage," or—say—on "Style." He memorizes ten or a dozen minute prohibited points. All of these things he is told never to do,—many of them he never does do, anyhow. The actual writing required of him, at the same time, may be an entirely irrelevant sort of thing, in which no connection between theory and practice is either contemplated or achieved by the instructor. It is little wonder that we fail to "get results," or that rhetoric is considered "dry," and "Freshman English" "a stupid bore." We all, indeed, feel the inadequacy of much of our present system, with its abundant destructive and its scanty constructive elements. Who has not been more than once confronted, after class, with a flushed and puzzled face, and disconcerted by the innocent, yet searching plaint: "If I only knew what to do to improve my writing, I would try to do it!"

To this practical question, then,—"What must I do to improve my writing?"—the following exercises are offered as an attempt at a constructive answer. They are based on the proposition that we learn to write as the result of a very subtle, and, for the most part, unconscious process of absorption and imitation. It is a truism to say that, other things being equal, the man who has read widely, who is saturated with literary prose, will be the man who will *unconsciously* write well. In what other way, on the whole, can we account for the prose style of Macaulay, of Hazlitt, of J. S. Mill, of Lamb? And, strangely enough, although rhetorical principles seem to be hopelessly recondite to most undergraduates, nearly every Freshman, even, has the power of imitating a definite form or effect once it is shown him, squarely. He may do it in a queer, clumsy way, perhaps often unconsciously, but—he does it! The teaching of abstract prohibitive rules has, of course, its function,—the function of pruning the too-carelessly growing, or over-luxuriant, foliage. But such teaching can never ultimately succeed in vivifying the germ and fostering the growing plant.

The average instructor of Freshmen, in English composition, is confronted with a difficult problem. To him are entrusted a more or less heterogeneous company of young people, whom he is to have charge of for only a limited period. In this limited period, he is expected to "get results," and, before the year is over, to reduce fifty or more variously imperfect "preparations" to some sort of uniform power of achievement. Few of these Freshmen have had an adequate home or school training. It then becomes the instructor's duty to produce, in eight or nine months, some tithe of the effect that should have been produced in the past, by long years of unconscious absorption.

To meet this need, the ideal Freshman course in writing would represent as much and as varied reading as might be crowded into the time, with a sufficient amount of reading aloud, from week to week, in order that the student's ear as well as his eye may be trained. Writing in the course would be equally constant and, at least in part, based upon or adapted from the reading. The discussions of rules and theory would be confined, as far as possible, to text criticism on themes and to conferences. This last might easily be done with the aid, for reference, of so orderly and useful a compendium of rules, for example, as Dr. E. C. Woolley's *Handbook of Composition*. (D. C. Heath, 1907). In such a course, the work of the class room would be entirely constructive, entirely concerned with the actual expression of ideas in the writing of people who write effectively, and with the immediate assimilation of all these modes and suggestions into the actual practice of the student.

It is far from my intention to seem ignorant of the already well-nigh universal practice of "studying models," after one fashion or another, in the teaching of composition. The following exercises claim originality, indeed, only in the adaptation of such "models" to a more definite and immediate end,—to give the student, along with his subject, an example of how some one else has written upon a subject largely, if not entirely similar in type. Even these extracts are, so to speak, hardly original, since many of them have already been "selected" by previous editors. If the book has any merit of choice, it lies rather in what has been excluded than in what has been included. It might be added that I have myself tried nearly all of these exercises, with satisfactory results.

The "adapted subjects" and the "suggestions" are intended to be suggestive rather than definitive. Every class will have to have its subjects modified, or more closely adapted to local conditions.

It is recommended that the exercises be used as a basis for at least half of the writing, and for a good deal of the class work in a Freshman course in composition. The extracts from the *American Commonwealth,* for example, should be carefully studied in class for several recitations before the students do any writing whatever. Then the first or the second exercise might be assigned as a theme to be prepared outside, and the third exercise be given as an impromptu. The adapted writing should be interspersed systematically with optional writing,—that is, with themes written from subjects of the student's own choosing, and without assistance from the instructor.

The remaining work of the course would consist of "outside reading," to be very carefully done and reported on, at regular intervals. These reading reports might be either written or oral. Four whole books for the year would not be too much to require. One of the following combinations, for example, would be sure to profit our hypothetical "average Freshman."

A

1. Huxley's *Essays* (selected).
2. Ruskin: *The Crown of Wild Olive*, or *The Seven Lamps of Architecture*.
3. Stevenson: *An Inland Voyage*, or *Travels with a Donkey*.
4. Any good novel, or volume of short stories.

B

1. John Burroughs' *Essays* (selected).
2. Stevenson: *Memories and Portraits* or *Virginibus Puerisque*.
3. One of Lafcadio Hearn's books of travel.
4. Some short stories by Kipling.

Yet every class will of course have to have a different treatment in the matter of outside reading. It is an advantage to have a whole section reading the same books, however, as this makes general class discussion practicable.

A word is perhaps needed to explain, or to justify, the absence of any models for Argumentation. As this book, however, has grown out of an elementary course in which there was no time for the study of argument, it has seemed inexpedient to add, arbitrarily, exercises in a kind of writing which is usually postponed until the later years of a college course.

My great indebtedness, finally, must be acknowledged to such collections as "*Modern English Prose*," by Professors G. R. Carpenter and W. T. Brewster, and "*Studies in Structure and Style*," by Professor Brewster. By Miss Gertrude Buck's two books, also,—"*Narrative Writing*" and "*Expository Writing*,"—I have been assisted fundamentally, if not in a way that may be specifically acknowledged. I likewise owe much, indirectly, to "*Materials for the Study of Rhetoric and Composition*," by Professor Fred N. Scott, published at Ann Arbor for use in the University of Michigan.

Harrison Ross Steeves and Frank Humphrey Ristine, Editors
Representative Essays in Modern Thought: A Basis for Composition (1913)

   ❧ *Steeves (1881–1981) spent his entire academic career at Columbia (B.A., 1903; M.A., 1904; Ph.D., 1913; English department faculty, 1905–1949). His publications include many editions of literary works and* The Teaching of Literature *(with Charles Carpenter Fries and James Holly Hanford, 1926). He justified his approach in this collection in his 1912 article, "The Cultivation of Ideas in the College Writing Course," which appeared in* Educational Review. *In it he asks, "How can we relieve the study of rhetoric from its depressing formalism?" (45). He seeks a middle ground: "One group of teachers favors subjects from the common experience of the writer. Another group recognizes the force of the argument of departmental convenience and kills two birds with one stone by basing the course on literary selections" (45). Neither, Steeves claims, will work well.*

Ristine (1884–1958) studied at Wabash College (B.A., 1905), Columbia (M.A., 1907; Ph.D., 1910), and Oxford and Heidelberg. He taught at Wabash, Columbia, and from 1915 to 1952 at Hamilton College, becoming dean of the college, 1932–39, and dean of the faculty, 1939–42.

PREFACE

In presenting this volume to teachers of English composition, the editors realize that it can hardly fail to suffer from the suspicion of novelty which confronts new publications in a conservative educational field. It is hoped, however, that initial distrust of the book because of its novelty will not outlive a fair trial of the methods and materials which it offers. This hope is based upon successful experiment with much of the substance of the volume among students as varied and as cosmopolitan as the undergraduates in Columbia College, and upon the generous and often enthusiastic support that the underlying idea has received from prominent educators throughout the country who have had occasion to pass judgment upon its value.

In the preparation of the collection for classroom use we have prefixed to each essay a brief introductory note intended to give relevant biographical facts and to assist the student to an understanding of the design of the work. In addition, where suggestions as to other material of direct bearing upon the subject under discussion seemed to us to be of value for collateral reading, we have included references to such writings. Some of the authors' footnotes to the essays have been omitted as foreign to the purpose of the book, and others have been supplied wherever the text seemed to require elucidation or interpretation. Our principle has been, however, to restrict the formal teaching apparatus of the volume to the general introduction, and to encumber the selections themselves with the minimum of annotation. In the printing of the essays we have followed accurately the original forms, retaining sub-titles and numbered divisions where these were essential to the logical arrangement of the essay.

This volume includes substantially the essays which, when we first discussed the plan of publication, we chose tentatively as the most available for our purpose. That what seemed to us the ideal plan should be brought to completion with scarcely a modification is for us a matter for special gratitude, since any effort to reproduce on an extensive scale writings still in copyright must be conditioned largely upon the generosity of publishers. Our thanks for publishing privileges, therefore, are emphatically more than formal. We have been enabled to use copyright material through the kindness of Mr. Henry James, Jr., Dr. Dole, Mr. Mallock, Professor Hobhouse, Professor Clark, President Hadley, and Mr. Harrison; and by the permission of Messrs. D. Appleton and Company, Henry Holt and Company, Longmans, Green, and Company, John Murray, The Macmillan Company, the American Association for International Conciliation, the *Fortnightly Review,* the *Harvard Theological Review,* and the *Atlantic Monthly.* We desire also to express our acknowledgments to Viscount Morley and Dr. Alfred Russel Wallace, and to Macmillan and Company (London), the *Popular Science Monthly,* the *Contemporary Review,* and the Edinburgh Co-operative Printing Company Limited.

The task of selecting the essays and preparing the collection for publication has been materially lightened by the friendly coöperation of a number of our colleagues who have interested themselves in the undertaking. We are under special obligation to Professor John Erskine, to whom in large measure the credit for the educational program must be given, and who has aided our work with many helpful suggestions. Others to whom we have been indebted for advice and active interest are Professor Frederick J. E. Woodbridge, Professor Herbert G. Lord, Professor Ashley H. Thorndike, Professor Robert A. Harper, Professor Monroe Smith, Mr. Frederick P. Keppel, Dean of Columbia College, Professor Joseph V. Denney, of Ohio State University, Dr. Carl Van Doren, Mr. John J. Coss, and Dr. Ernest Stagg Whitin.

H. R. S.
F. H. R.

CONTENTS

Norman Foerster, Frederick A. Manchester, and Karl Young
Essays for College Men (1913)

🦚 *Foerster (1887–1972) studied at Harvard (B.A., 1910), where he was influenced greatly by Irving Babbitt, and at Wisconsin (M.A., 1912). He taught at Wisconsin (1911–14), North Carolina (1914–30), Iowa, where he directed the school of letters and was instrumental in establishing the creative writing doctoral program (1930–44), and Duke (1948–51). He was eminent both as an interpreter of American literature and a conservative critic of American higher education. His writing and literature textbooks were prominent landmarks from 1920 well into the 1950s.*

Manchester and Young (see chap. 6, p. 477 for biography) were Foerster's Wisconsin colleagues and fellow composition instructors.

CONTENTS

Norman Foerster, Frederick A. Manchester, and
Karl Young
Essays for College Men, Second Series (1915)

CONTENTS

Maurice Garland Fulton
Expository Writing (1912)

&⬥ *Fulton was born in 1877 and attended the University of Mississippi (Ph.B., 1898; M.A., 1901). He studied in Fred Newton Scott's rhetoric program at Michigan but did not take a degree. He taught at a variety of colleges and universities: Mississippi (1900–01), Michigan (1901–03; 1904–05), Illinois (1903–04), Centre College in Kentucky (1905–09), Davidson College (1909–19, where he wrote* Expository Writing*), and Indiana (1919–22). He settled at the Junior College of New Mexico Military Institute from 1922 until his retirement in 1948. Among his many publications was another composition text,* College Life: Its Conditions and Problems *(1914), a focused five-hundred-page anthology of "writings of college presidents and other educators."*

In contrast to the most popular texts of the late nineteenth century, Fulton concentrated on one mode of discourse, expository writing, and focused quite explicitly on writing of a scientific (as opposed to a literary) cast. But the table of contents reveals that what Fulton advertised as scientific prose was of a decidedly belletristic type: Wallace, James, Huxley, Spencer, Mill, Wells, Darwin, Tyndall, Shaler. Composition was, after all, taught by English teachers.

PREFACE

In preparing this book of selections illustrative of some of the various phases of expository writing, for use either in the general Freshman course in English composition or in a special course in exposition to be taken in the Sophomore or Junior year, I have had in mind certain definite aims, the principal of which are the following: First, to make definite and systematic application of the method of learning to write through the examination and imitation of good models. Second, to centre attention upon exposition since it is the kind of writing that is most directly serviceable in practical life and that most readily exemplifies the essential qualities of effective composition—accuracy, logicalness, and economy of presentation. Third, to draw the selections chiefly from the field of scientific writing because of the intrinsic interest of such subject-matter to young persons. Fourth to have the selections of such length that the analysis of them will afford a "severe logical setting-up exercise." As some of the aims I have briefly named above may be new—though they are not untested—I may be pardoned for setting them forth somewhat more fully and pointing out the ways in which this book embodies them.

The study of composition by the method of analysis and imitation is both psychologically and pedagogically sound. To obtain principles of effective writing, not by conning from the pages of a text-book ready-made rules and philosophizings upon principles of structure and style, but through one's own self-effort in the examination and study of the actual expression of ideas in the writing of those who have written successfully, is to add interest and effectiveness to the study of composition. To the careful analysis of models of good writing must be added the imitation of their principles of structure and style in the student's own practice upon subjects similar in method and type. The quantity of writing may with advantage be decreased in the interest of the careful study of models, for it is questionable whether our present methods of teaching composition in the colleges do not tend to set a quantitative rather than a qualitative standard for the work in composition.

This book aims to give material for conducting a course in composition by this method of analysis and imitation. No attempt has been made to teach systematic rhetoric. The purpose has been the simple one of opening in a practical way the student's eyes to some of the major problems of writing. In order to make the analysis of the selections adequate and definite, study questions have been included. These questions attempt to challenge the student's curiosity, to set a problem before him for solution, to rouse thought and set it going, rather than to give information. The sets of questions are of differing degrees of fullness, but are never designedly exhaustive or restrictive. They should be increased or decreased, or otherwise modified as the instructor sees fit. Nor is the order of the selections to be rigidly observed. To give system to the book as a whole and to avoid repetitions, each set of questions has been confined to a single principle or set of principles, and while this fact gives to the book a sequence and progression corresponding somewhat to the growth in comprehension and facility to be expected of the average student, such arrangement is not intended as a fetter upon the teacher. The exercises following the questions are intended to afford material for practice in composition. The subjects chosen for these exercises are intended to be merely suggestive, and should be freely changed or adapted to meet the interests and proficiency of a particular class.

The selections in this volume are broadly illustrative of expository types and methods. In Part I exposition is taken as the norm for the general principles of composition relating to the whole composition, the paragraph, the sentence, and the word. Students who are well grounded in these matters may be allowed to omit this part of the book, or to pass over it rapidly as a review. With Part II begins the study of expository methods. Examples of definition have been placed first; these are followed by selections showing the complementary process of classification and division. The remaining selections illustrate such matters as the statement of the problem involved in a piece of investigation, the straightforward and complete exposition of a single definite topic, the skilful treatment of material demanding special adaptation to audience or reader, methods of handling large and complex masses of details, the treatment of subject-matter involving unusual difficulties and requiring special devices of illustration, and finally the use of descriptive and narrative methods for purposes of exposition.

The selection of material from the field of science rather than from that of literature in the narrower sense, perhaps requires a few words of explanation. Undeniably writing of fact makes more of an appeal to the average young person than writing of literature. It is interesting in itself to the student, because he is essentially in the popular science age. Moreover, it emphasizes more strongly than other kinds of writing accuracy, directness, conciseness, power of system and organization, sense of logical relationships, and the student more easily perceives these qualities in the direct expression that characterizes scientific writing than in the suggestiveness and indirectness of artistic expression. In still another way the study of scientific literature may be made of most helpful service to the student. It may be made a means of introducing him to certain procedures of scientific method as well as to the adequate and convincing presentation of scientific results.

The selections presented are complete articles, chapters, or other large component parts of books, rather than excerpts of a few paragraphs, in order that the study of them may afford training in the power to think straight, which is so little a part of the rising generation. It is the duty of the modern college not to truckle to this weakness, but to cure it. In few ways can the strengthening and developing of the thinking power be more readily secured than by the careful analysis of expository selections. Hence the selections in this book are of greater length than is usual in similar volumes.

I cannot send this book forth without some expression of my obligations to those who have helped in its equipment. It owes much to the copyrighted material it contains, and although due acknowledgments for permission to reprint are scattered through its pages, it is a pleasure here to record in a general way my grateful appreciation of these generous permissions. It would be impossible and unprofitable to name all the works on composition and rhetoric I have consulted. Through class-room use I am especially familiar with Scott and Denney's *Paragraph-Writing* and *Composition-Rhetoric,* Baldwin's *A College Manual of Rhetoric* and *Composition, Oral and Written,* Canby's *English Composition in Theory and Practice,* Genung's *Practical Elements of Rhetoric* and *Working Principles of Rhetoric,* and I have no doubt that I have borrowed more of their ideas than is anywhere formally acknowledged. Earle's *The Theory and Practice of Technical Writing*—a book that parallels in a theoretical way the studies in this book—came to hand while I was reading this book in proof, and I have been able to avail myself to some extent of suggestions from it.

I would also express my indebtedness to Mr. Royal A. Abbott of the Commercial High School, Brooklyn, for valuable assistance. Several years ago, when I began the preparation of a book similar in some respects to this one, I invited Mr. Abbott, then a colleague in the department of rhetoric at the University of Michigan, to collaborate with me. [Abbott and Fulton had written *Manual of Exercises in Composition* in 1905.—ED.] Our paths soon after diverged, and I have finished the book, so modifying and enlarging the original plan, however, that it is practically an independent book. Mr. Abbott suggested several of the selections and prepared the questions accompanying Stevenson's *Apology for Idlers,* Morgan's *Definition of Instinctive Behavior,* Ely's *Types of Monopolies,* George's *Progress and Poverty,* and Tyndall's *Scope and Limits of Scientific Materialism.*

M. G. F.

TABLE OF CONTENTS

INTRODUCTION

PART I

SELECTIONS ILLUSTRATING GENERAL PRINCIPLES OF
COMPOSITION IN THEIR RELATION TO EXPOSITION

THE EXPOSITION AS AN ORGANIC STRUCTURE

ADAPTATION TO THE READER

LAWS OF PARAGRAPH-MAKING

INTRODUCTION

I
The Nature of Exposition

The search for a satisfying definition of exposition soon reveals that books on composition and rhetoric give definitions of varying degrees of comprehensiveness. One writer will designate it broadly as "the explanation of ideas";[1] another, as "the art of stating facts clearly, so that the reader will understand them";[2] a third, as "the succinct and orderly setting forth of some piece of knowledge."[3] Other writers will define it more specifically as "the fixing of meaning by generalization, that is, the exhibiting of objects, material or spiritual, as conceived and organized in thought,"[4] or as "the kind of discourse in which the writer's aim is to make others see the meaning of some idea as clearly as he himself sees it; its subject matter is general ideas, laws, or principles, not (as in description and narration) particular things."[5] Although any one of these definitions is more or less adequate, we may attempt to come to a clearer understanding of the nature of exposition by ascertaining the characteristics that distinguish it as a form of composition from the other kinds of writing—description, narrative, and argument. The particular characteristics of exposition will be discussed under the three heads of subject-matter, purpose, and mood.

The Subject-Matter of Exposition

Broadly speaking, the material of all writing is experience. In experience two aspects or elements may be observed, corresponding to whether our knowledge is confined to bare acquaintance with externals, or whether it embraces an understanding of the meaning of a given experience. The first of these elements may be called the element of *fact*. This is the concrete element, knowledge of which is derived through the sense-organs. The second element may be called the element of *meaning*. This is the abstract element, to knowledge of which we ascend by rallying our wits, and beginning to notice, to analyze, to think, until finally the mind shapes for itself an interpretation of the meaning or significance of the experience.

In reality, given experiences do not belong rigidly under either of these aspects. They have been spoken of as distinct and distinguishable elements mainly for convenience, and in order to accentuate their presence. As a matter of fact, they are constantly merged and are not separable. If, for instance, we look at a building, we not only receive impressions of external appearance, such as size, shape, color, and the like, but simultaneously we begin an interpretation of these experiences. We begin to think of the nature, or the significance, or the function of the building—more or less vaguely at first, it may be, but with gradually increasing definiteness. In short, by mental processes we come to some generalization about it.

The writer, however, is able more or less completely to separate these two elements in his writing. He may simply show the appearance of some object or the details of an event with little or no regard to their significance, or he may merely explain an operation or process or idea, disregarding the concrete element in it. This being the case, we are able to divide writing into two large classes. There is first that which concerns itself with the outer world of scenes and happenings. There is secondly that which deals with the inner world of thoughts and the relations of thoughts. To the first of these classes evidently belong description with its endeavor to show the appearance of the individual object, and narrative with its aim of recounting the details and particulars of some transaction or event. To the second class belong exposition and argument. It is not needful in this connection to dwell upon the differences between exposition and argument; more to the point for the present purpose is their likeness in having for their subject-matter, not, as in the case of description and narrative, particular things, but general ideas or abstract qualities. In the words of Professor Genung, "We are to remember that in exposition we are dealing not with an object whose parts and peculiarities are displayed in space before us, as in description; nor with an event, whose incidents succeed each other in time, as narration; but with a man-made concept, whose aspects and divisions are discerned by the laws of thought and association that exist in human minds."[6]

There are, however, some cases where exposition deals with the concrete and the individual. If one should carefully examine a typewriter, and then write out a full description of its parts—keyboard, type-bars, carriage, platen, ribbon, index, etc.—giving the form and position of each and even the material of which it is made, or if one should visit a great newspaper building, and afterwards write an account of the printing of the paper from the writing of the news to the delivery of the printed sheet to the delivery wagons, would he, in the one case, be writing a description, in the other, a narrative? In both of these two examples, we have the concrete and individual subject-matter characteristic of description and narrative, but evidently, in neither case is the writer dealing merely with the element of fact in his subject-matter. While he may not seem to get very far away from the element of fact in either instance, nevertheless, in the case of a typewriter, his endeavor is not so much to induce in the mind of the reader a picture of the typewriter and its parts as to explain its mechanism and its use; and in the case of the visit to the newspaper building, the writer's purpose is not to relate interestingly the happening of his visit, but to explain the process of making a newspaper. Such portrayal of the concrete, although loosely called description or narrative, is more exactly designated as exposition. Nor are such portrayals simply narrative or description converted into exposition by single occurrences or objects of a similar kind becoming blended into a composite—what is commonly called generalized narrative or description. They are rather instances in which the general class, the type, is presented as an individual, and the individual is made to serve as a type.

Instances such as have just been described of exposition presenting the type through the individual are, however, exceptions rather than the rule. It still remains true that the most commonly found subject-matter of exposition is the abstract and the general. These abstractions and generalizations are divisible into two classes—terms and propositions. "An object to be expounded expresses either an idea or the relation between ideas. Hence its form is either a term or a proposition. Though exposition may be applied to any object—an object described, or an event narrated, as well as an object of thought—yet in its state as a concept or generalization, the object must be reduced to one of these forms; it must either name an idea, or make an assertion in regard to it."[7] That is, exposition may take a term like *psychology, nature, erosion, art,* or *culture,* and seek to set forth clearly what it is, what are its essential qualities, how much it includes, what it excludes, how it differs from other similar ideas, into what kinds it is divided. Or, exposition may take a general proposition, such as "Natural phenomena are uniform," or "Education is beneficial in all the pursuits of life," or "Honesty is the best policy," or "The area of a triangle is equal to half the product of the base and the perpendicular," and, without assuming the truth or falsity of the proposition, endeavor to give an explication of it—elucidating the words of the original statement, suggesting what is implied in the idea expressed, hinting at its relationship to other ideas, and possibly indicating its application.

The Purpose of Exposition

Exposition is further distinguished from other kinds of composition by its purpose. Another broad twofold grouping of writing according to the writer's purpose is given in De Quincey's well-known division of literature. "In the great social organ," says he in his *Essay on Pope,* "which we may collectively call literature, there may be distinguished two separate offices that may blend and often do so. . . . There is, first, the literature of knowledge, and, secondly, the literature of power. The function of the first is to teach, the function of the second to move." De Quincey further points out that the first kind of writing appeals to the intellect, the second to the emotions and the imagination. Writing that appeals to the intellect may be said to have as its general purpose *instruction;* while writing that stirs the emotions and the imagination has as its general purpose *entertainment.* Entertainment is primarily the aim of narration and description; instruction is the main purpose of argument and exposition.

It frequently happens that we must determine whether or not a given piece of writing is exposition from a careful consideration of the purpose of the writer. As we have seen, exposition sometimes deals with the particular and the concrete, and the classification of such expositions is oftentimes a matter of doubt. Among the selections in the latter part of this book is one describing the surface of the moon. This clearly deals with a particular object. Another of these selections tells the life history of a salmon. It also appears to deal with an individual member of the species. Although we might be inclined to classify the one selection as description and the other as narrative, we should find upon more careful consideration of the purpose of the writers that indubitably they were using the specific and concrete in order to show its significance or to set forth some generalization in regard to it. In the selection, *The Surface of the Moon,* the purpose of the writer is not to stimulate our imagination to form mental pictures of the surface of the moon, but to explain clearly to the understanding certain facts in regard to this satellite. In the case of the selection entitled *The Story of a Salmon,* the purpose of the writer is not simply to tell a story about a salmon, but rather to elucidate the development and the habits of this species of fish, the story form being chosen because of the greater interest. Despite such seeming exceptions, it still remains true that the purpose of exposition is to show the essence, the underlying principle, the general law to the understanding.

The Mood of Expository Writing

There is still a third distinction of great importance between exposition and the other forms of writing. The various subjects of experience may be treated in two ways. We may consider them as at rest, as fixed in space, as spread out before us like a map—in short, as static. Or we may regard them as living, growing, developing—in short, as dynamic. This difference may be made clearer by taking as an example a tree and supposing it the subject of our writing. We may regard the tree as fixed in space so that in our writing we may pass from point to point or take it up a part at a time. This is to treat the tree statically. Or we may think of the tree as growing, developing; we may be interested chiefly in showing its stages of growth, and the like. This is to write about the tree dynamically.

From the difference between static and dynamic treatment, we may distinguish again two large divisions of writing. The dynamic mode is characteristic of narrative and argument. In narrative we either show the individual object as growing and developing, or we display a given event as a succession of particulars and details having movement. In argument the procedure is likewise essentially dynamic. The conclusion we wish the reader to accept is made to come into being in the course of the argument—to grow, so to speak, from its elements—the facts and principles with which we start. The static mode is characteristic of description and exposition. In description, we treat the object we are writing about as spread out before us while we pass from point to point in our examination. In exposition, the subject-matter—the general truth underlying an idea or group of ideas—is, so to speak, spread out before the mind and a map made of it. It is carefully bounded by the process known technically as definition, it is separated into its parts by division; finally each part of the idea is set before the reader with adequate development. Such a conception of a static view of the idea to be expounded is, as Professor Gardiner has pointed out in his *The Forms of Prose Literature,* inherent in the signification of the terms we employ to designate this form of writing. "The natural figure of speech which you use is this figure of *seeing.* It is a noticeable fact, moreover, that the words which have to do with explanation spring from just this same sense of a clear and lucid view of the subject. *Exposition* is a setting forth, as one arranges cards in a game of solitaire; *explanation* is a making plain or smoothing out; *perspicuous* springs from the figure of 'seeing through.' These etymological facts have deep suggestiveness for anybody who is going to make explanations."[8]

From this static treatment of its material comes the typical mood of exposition. It appears that we instinctively care more for living than for dead things, for motion than for rest, for evolution than for arrested development, and from this perhaps springs the general fact that a dynamic treatment invites the author to greater or less display in his writing of his feelings. Whether the explanation hazarded for this fact be true or not, it seems to be generally true of both the forms of writing that have typically the dynamic mode of treatment—narrative and argument—that they are more or less subjective in mood. On the other hand, the static mode of treatment is essentially dispassionate and unbiassed. This objective and uncontroversial tone is eminently characteristic of both description and exposition.

Although expository writing is characterized by impartiality of treatment, we must not understand this as implying that "exposition must be bare, cold, impersonal. Bare, cold, impersonal it may be, indeed, and still worthy; as in a text-book of physics; but it need not be, and in such expository essays as most of us write, it should not be. For a listless reader will not take pains to understand; and, on the other side, the significance of a subject will be the more readily found by the writer for whom that significance has some real interest. So, in detail, the abundance of example and illustrations which makes Macaulay's essays popular is a direct means of clearness. Else the same means would not be so freely used by Huxley also, and by Tyndall, and proverbially by the most effective teachers and preachers. In this and in other ways the transpiring of the writer's personality makes the exposition better. The only caution necessary is not to forget the prime object which is to reach significant generalizations and to reach them clearly."[9]

Summary

Concluding what has been said about the nature of exposition, we may succinctly define exposition as *that kind of writing which has as its primary function the impartial unfolding of any phenomenon, hypothesis or generalization to the understanding of the reader.*

II
Kinds of Exposition

Since the motive common to all exposition is the desire to explain something to the reader, it is evident that this form of writing is not only of exceeding great practical value, but is very extended in its range of subjects. As we have seen, without exposition we might know and communicate to others the particulars of our experience; but the meaning of those particulars, the general principles that underlie them, could not be definitely set forth. From the small matters of daily life and experience, up to handing on the torch of knowledge from one generation to the next, and so making progress and civilization possible, exposition is everywhere called into use.

According to method and purpose, two kinds of expository writing may be distinguished, which we may call, for want of more exact designations, *scientific* exposition, and *familiar* exposition. In scientific exposition, the writer selects a subject within his powers, states it clearly and accurately, gathers material by careful thinking and reading, and develops it into a serious, thorough, and sustained piece of explanation. The writings of Macaulay, Huxley, Bryce, Tyndall, Mill, Spencer, Newman, are examples of this type of exposition showing its severity of method and careful accuracy.

Familiar exposition, on the other hand, is generally looser in structure and aims to give the personal impressions of the writer, his whims and fancies, in a manner resembling the easy confidential tone of conversation. The subjects chosen are usually of a light character, and an original point of view is not infrequently presented. The essays of Charles Lamb, Steele, Addison, Thackeray, and Stevenson are illustrations of this type of exposition. It was this looser type of exposition which first gave vogue to the term *essay,* but the development of this form of literature has been so markedly away from a subjective, personal, and leisurely discussion towards an objective, concentrated, and unemotional method, that when we hear the word *essay* to-day we think rather of the scientific exposition than the familiar.

NOTES

1. Mitchill and Carpenter's *Exposition in Class-room Practice*, p. 1.
2. Canby's *English Composition in Theory and Practice*, p. 1.
3. Baldwin's *A College Manual of Rhetoric*, p. 40.
4. Genung's *Working Principles of Rhetoric*, p. 554.
5. Scott and Denney's *Composition-Rhetoric*, p. 302.
6. *Practical Elements of Rhetoric*, p. 386.
7. Genung's *Practical Elements of Rhetoric*, p. 386.
8. *The Forms of Prose Literature*, p. 27.
9. Baldwin's *A College Manual of Rhetoric*, p. 38.

William Strunk Jr.
The Elements of Style (1918)

ॐ *Strunk (1869–1946) received his B.A. from Cincinnati in 1890 and spent a year teaching math at the Rose Polytechnic Institute in Terre Haute (1890–91). He then moved to Cornell, where he received his Ph.D. (1896) and spent the rest of his career teaching English and journalism. Strunk's "little book" has become perhaps the most widely read work by any American professor of English.*

Strunk published his forty-three-page book on his own and used it in his composition classes. As his student E. B. White noted, it was idiosyncratic in its arrangement and particularly in its special rules. The book was resurrected not once but twice: first in 1935, when Harcourt Brace published a greatly changed version by Strunk and Edward A. Tenney, and second in 1959, when White revised it, adding his brilliant introduction (which had appeared as a 1957 New Yorker sketch). With the exception of that introduction and the superb concluding essay on style, White's changes, as he himself notes, are quite modest. I have printed the opening pages so readers may compare the two books; I have also printed Strunk's section on paragraphs, which White dropped.

CONTENTS

I. INTRODUCTORY

This book is intended for use in English courses in which the practice of composition is combined with the study of literature. It aims to give in brief space the principal requirements of plain English style. It aims to lighten the task of instructor and student by concentrating attention (in Chapters II and III) on a few essentials, the rules of usage and principles of composition most commonly violated. The numbers of the sections may be used as references in correcting manuscript.

The book covers only a small portion of the field of English style, but the experience of its writer has been that once past the essentials, students profit most by individual instruction based on the problems of their own work, and that each instructor has his own body of theory, which he prefers to that offered by any textbook.

The writer's colleagues in the Department of English in Cornell University have greatly helped him in the preparation of his manuscript. Mr. George McLane Wood has kindly consented to the inclusion under Rule 11 of some material from his *Suggestions to Authors*.

The following books are recommended for reference or further study: in connection with Chapters II and IV, F. Howard Collins, *Author and Printer* (Henry Frowde); Chicago University Press, *Manual of Style;* T. L. De Vinne, *Correct Composition* (The Century Company); Horace Hart, *Rules for Compositors and Printers* (Oxford University Press); George McLane Wood, *Extracts from the Style-Book of the Government Printing Office* (United States Geological Survey); in connection with Chapters III and V, Sir Arthur Quiller-Couch, *The Art of Writing* (Putnams), especially the chapter, Interlude on Jargon; George McLane Wood, *Suggestions to Authors* (United States Geological Survey); John Leslie Hall, *English Usage* (Scott, Foresman and Co.); James P. Kelley, *Workmanship in Words* (Little, Brown and Co.).

It is an old observation that the best writers sometimes disregard the rules of rhetoric. When they do so, however, the reader will usually find in the sentence some compensating merit, attained at the cost of the violation. Unless he is certain of doing as well, he will probably do best to follow the rules. After he has learned, by their guidance, to write plain English adequate for everyday uses, let him look, for the secrets of style, to the study of the masters of literature.

II. ELEMENTARY RULES OF USAGE

1. **Form the possessive singular of nouns with 's.**

Follow this rule whatever the final consonant. Thus write,

> Charles's friend
> Burns's poems
> the witch's malice

This is the usage of United States Government Printing Office and of the Oxford University Press.

Exceptions are the possessives of ancient proper names in *-es* and *-is*, the possessive *Jesus'*, and such forms as *for conscience' sake, for righteousness' sake.* But such forms as *Achilles' heel, Moses' laws, Isis' temple* are commonly replaced by

> the heel of Achilles
> the laws of Moses
> the temple of Isis

The pronominal possessives *hers, its, theirs, yours,* and *oneself* have no apostrophe.

2. In a series of three or more terms with a single conjunction, use a comma after each term except the last.

Thus write,

> red, white, and blue
> honest, energetic, but headstrong
> He opened the letter, read it, and made a note of its
> contents.

This is also the usage of the Government Printing Office and of the Oxford University Press.

In the names of business firms that last comma is omitted, as

> Brown, Shipley and Company

The abbreviation *etc.,* even if only a single term comes before it, is always preceded by a comma.

3. Enclose parenthetic expressions between commas.

The best way to see a country, unless you are pressed for time, is to travel on foot.

This rule is difficult to apply; it is frequently hard to decide whether a single word, such as *however,* or a brief phrase, is or is not parenthetic. If the interruption to the flow of the sentence is but slight, the writer may safely omit the commas. But whether the interruption be slight or considerable, he must never omit one comma and leave the other. Such punctuation as

Marjorie's husband, Colonel Nelson paid us a visit yesterday,

or

My brother you will be pleased to hear, is now in perfect health,

is indefensible.

Non-restrictive relative clauses are, in accordance with this rule, set off by commas.

The audience, which had at first been indifferent, became more and more interested.

Similar clauses introduced by *where* and *when* are similarly punctuated.

In 1769, when Napoleon was born, Corsica had but recently been acquired by France.

Nether Stowey, where Coleridge wrote *The Rime of the Ancient Mariner,* is a few miles from Bridgewater.

In these sentences the clauses introduced by *which, when,* and *where* are non-restrictive; they do not limit the application of the words on which they depend, but add, parenthetically, statements supplementing those in the principal clauses. Each sentence is a combination of two statements which might have been made independently.

The audience was at first indifferent. Later it became more and more interested.

Napoleon was born in 1769. At that time Corsica had but recently been acquired by France.

Coleridge wrote *The Rime of the Ancient Mariner* at Nether Stowey. Nether Stowey is only a few miles from Bridgewater.

Restrictive relative clauses are not set off by commas.

The candidate who best meets these requirements will obtain the place.

In this sentence the relative clause restricts the application of the word *candidate* to a single person. Unlike those above, the sentence cannot be split into two independent statements.

The abbreviations *etc.* and *jr.* are always preceded by a comma, and except at the end of a sentence, followed by one.

Similar in principle to the enclosing of parenthetic expressions between commas is the setting off by commas of phrases or dependent clauses preceding or following the main clause of a sentence. The sentences quoted in this section and under Rules 4, 5, 6, 7, 16, and 18 should afford sufficient guidance.

If a parenthetic expression is preceded by a conjunction, place the first comma before the conjunction, not after it.

He saw us coming, and unaware that we had learned of his treachery, greeted us with a smile.

4. Place a comma before *and* or *but* introducing an independent clause.

The early records of the city have disappeared, and the story of its first years can no longer be reconstructed.

The situation is perilous, but there is still one chance of escape.

Sentences of this type, isolated from their context, may seem to be in need of rewriting. As they make complete sense when the comma is reached, the second clause has the appearance of an after-thought. Further, *and* is the least specific of connectives. Used between independent clauses, it indicates only that a relation exists between them without defining that relation. In the example above, the relation is that of cause and result.

. . . .

III. ELEMENTARY PRINCIPLES OF
COMPOSITION

9. Make the paragraph the unit of composition: one paragraph to each topic.

If the subject on which you are writing is of slight extent, or if you intend to treat it very briefly, there may be no need of subdividing it into topics. Thus a brief description, a brief summary of a literary work, a brief account of a single incident, a narrative merely outlining an action, the setting forth of a single idea, any one of these is best written in a single paragraph. After the paragraph has been written, it should be examined to see whether subdivision will not improve it.

Ordinarily, however, a subject requires subdivision into topics, each of which should be made the subject of a paragraph. The object of treating each topic in a paragraph by itself is, of course, to aid the reader. The beginning of each paragraph is a signal to him that a new step in the development of the subject has been reached.

The extent of subdivision will vary with the length of the composition. For example, a short notice of a book or poem might consist of a single paragraph. One slightly longer might consist of two paragraphs:

A. Account of the work.
B. Critical discussion.

A report on a poem, written for a class in literature, might consist of seven paragraphs:

A. Facts of composition and publication.
B. Kind of poem; metrical form.
C. Subject.
D. Treatment of subject.
E. For what chiefly remarkable.
F. Wherein characteristic of the writer.
G. Relationship to other works.

The contents of paragraphs C and D would vary with the poem. Usually, paragraph C would indicate the actual or imagined circumstances of the poem (the situation), if these call for explanation, and would then state the subject and outline its development. If the poem is a narrative in the third person throughout, paragraph C need contain no more than a concise summary of the action. Paragraph D would indicate the leading ideas and show how they are made prominent, or would indicate what points in the narrative are chiefly emphasized.

A novel might be discussed under the heads:

A. Setting.
B. Plot.
C. Characters.
D. Purpose.

A historical event might be discussed under the heads:

A. What led up to the event.
B. Account of the event.
C. What the event led up to.

In treating either of these last two subjects, the writer would probably find it necessary to subdivide one or more of the topics here given.

As a rule, single sentences should not be written or printed as paragraphs. An exception may be made of sentences of transition, indicating
the relation between the parts of an exposition or argument.

In dialogue, each speech, even if only a single word, is a paragraph
by itself; that is, a new paragraph begins with each change of speaker.
The application of this rule, when dialogue and narrative are combined,
is best learned from examples in well-printed works of fiction.

**10. As a rule, begin each paragraph with a topic sentence; end it in
conformity with the beginning.**

Again, the object is to aid the reader. The practice here recommended enables him to discover the purpose of each paragraph as he
begins to read it, and to retain this purpose in mind as he ends it. For
this reason, the most generally useful kind of paragraph, particularly in
exposition and argument, is that in which

(a) the topic sentence comes at or near the beginning;
(b) the succeeding sentences explain or establish or develop the statement
    made in the topic sentence; and
(c) the final sentence either emphasizes the thought of the topic sentence or
    states some important consequence.

Ending with a digression, or with an unimportant detail, is particularly to be avoided.

If the paragraph forms part of a larger composition, its relation to what
precedes, or its function as a part of the whole, may need to be expressed.
This can sometimes be done by a mere word or phrase (*again; therefore; for
the same reason*) in the topic sentence. Sometimes, however, it is expedient
to precede the topic sentence by one or more sentences of introduction or
transition. If more than one such sentence is required, it is generally better
to set apart the transitional sentences as a separate paragraph.

According to the writer's purpose, he may, as indicated above, relate the body of the paragraph to the topic sentence in one or more of several different ways. He may make the meaning of the topic sentence clearer by restating it in other forms, by defining its terms, by denying the converse, by giving illustrations or specific instances; he may establish it by proofs; or he may develop it by showing its implications and consequences. In a long paragraph, he may carry out several of these processes.

¹Now, to be properly enjoyed, a walking tour should be gone upon alone. ²If you go in a company, or even in pairs, it is no longer a walking tour in anything but name; it is something else and more in the nature of a picnic. ³A walking tour should be gone upon alone, because freedom is of the essence; because you should be able to stop and go on, and follow this way or that, as the freak takes you; and because you must have your own pace, and neither trot alongside a champion walker, nor mince in time with a girl. ⁴And you must be open to all impressions and let your thoughts take colour from what you see. ⁵You should be as a pipe for any wind to play upon. ⁶"I cannot see the wit," says Hazlitt, "of walking and talking at the same time. ⁷When I am in the country, I wish to vegetate like the country," which is the gist of all that can be said upon the matter. ⁸There should be no cackle of voices at your elbow, to jar on the meditative silence of the morning. ⁹And so long as a man is reasoning he cannot surrender himself to that fine intoxication that comes of much motion in the open air, that begins in a sort of dazzle and sluggishness of the brain, and ends in a peace that passes comprehension.—Stevenson, *Walking Tours.*

¹Topic sentence. ²The meaning made clearer by denial of the contrary. ³The topic sentence repeated, in abridged form, and supported by three reasons; the meaning of the third ("you must have your own pace") made clearer by denying the converse. ⁴A fourth reason, stated in two forms. ⁵The same reason, stated in still another form. ⁶⁻⁷The same reason as stated by Hazlitt. ⁸Repetition, in paraphrase, of the quotation from Hazlitt. ⁹Final statement of the fourth reason, in language amplified and heightened to form a strong conclusion.

¹It was chiefly in the eighteenth century that a very different conception of history grew up. ²Historians then came to believe that their task was not so much to paint a picture as to solve a problem; to explain or illustrate the successive phases of national growth, prosperity, and adversity. ³The history of morals, of industry, of intellect, and of art; the changes that take place in manners or beliefs; the dominant ideas that prevailed in successive periods; the rise, fall, and modification of political constitutions; in a word, all the conditions of national well-being became the subjects of their works. ⁴They sought rather to write a history of peoples than a history of kings. ⁵They looked

especially in history for the chain of causes and effects. [6]They undertook to study in the past the physiology of nations, and hoped by applying the experimental method on a large scale to deduce some lessons of real value about the conditions on which the welfare of society mainly depend.—Lecky, *The Political Value of History.*

[1]Topic sentence. [2]The meaning of the topic sentence made clearer; the new conception of history defined. [3]The definition expanded. [4]The definition explained by contrast. [5]The definition supplemented: another element in the new conception of history. [6]Conclusion: an important consequence of the new conception of history.

In narration and description the paragraph sometimes begins with a concise, comprehensive statement serving to hold together the details that follow.

> The breeze served us admirably.
> The campaign opened with a series of reverses.
> The next ten or twelve pages were filled with a curious set of entries.

But this device, if too often used, would become a mannerism. More commonly the opening sentence simply indicates by its subject with what the paragraph is to be principally concerned.

> At length I thought I might return towards the stockade.
> He picked up the heavy lamp from the table and began to explore.
> Another flight of steps, and they emerged on the roof.

The brief paragraphs of animated narrative, however, are often without even this semblance of a topic sentence. The break between them serves the purpose of a rhetorical pause, throwing into prominence some detail of the action.

Norman Foerster and John Marcellus Steadman Jr.
Sentences and Thinking: A Practice Book in Sentence Making (1914)

Steadman (1889–1945) studied at Wofford College (B.A., 1909; M.A., 1912), North Carolina, and Chicago (Ph.D., 1916). He taught at Emory from 1916 to 1942, publishing textbooks with Foerster and, in 1930, Spelling for Everyday Use. *(For more on Foerster see above, p. 390 and Brereton, "Composition" 47–51.) Connors quite rightly regards this the first modern rhetoric ("Rise" 451); its first edition appeared in 1914 and its last in 1951. Foerster completely breaks with the past distinctions between thought and expression. He unites the two, producing an organic conception of the writing process that foreshadows elements of the New Criticism.*

PREFACE

SENTENCES AND THINKING IS A TEXTBOOK FOR THE FIRST TERM OF Freshman English. Although it could be used as a review of fundamentals at the end of the high school course, it is designed primarily for the college freshman, who can scarcely be said to have mastered fundamentals in composition, but who nevertheless tends to regard himself as sufficiently acquainted with unity, coherence, and emphasis. It is true that the large rhetorics are also designed for the college freshman; but too often they are obsessed with the sacred need of comprehensiveness, or adhere to the language and modes of thought of the old mechanical rhetoric. The authors of this little book, instead of seeking comprehensiveness, have sought absolute essentials; instead of following tradition blindly, have worked out a new approach to Freshman rhetoric—the substance being old, of course, but the mode of presentation, it is hoped, fresh and attractive because it is philosophical in a simple way. When the freshman comes to college, he is prepared to exchange his excellent high school conviction "that authority is the soundest basis of belief" for the equally excellent college conviction that blind faith is "the one unpardonable sin" and independent inquiry into the nature of things the prerequisite to all progress. We have asked the freshman, not to master "rules," but to think out the reasons behind the rules in terms of the psychology of the human mind.

Chapter I, "Sentences and Punctuation," deals with the appalling blunders in sentence construction that abound during the first month of the course. Chapter II, "Sentences and Thinking," the core of the book, is a connected, constructive account of the principles of subordination, parallelism, emphasis, etc. A third chapter, on "Summary Sentences," offers material for training in the construction of sentences through a special kind of paragraph analysis. Finally, "A List of Common Errors" will enable the instructor, if he so desires, to use the book, not in addition to the usual rhetoric during the first few months of the course, but in place of it throughout the year.

CONTENTS

CHAPTER II
SENTENCES AND THINKING

1. **Subordination.** A sentence, we have seen, is a group of words expressing a complete thought. A complete thought may contain any number of constituent thoughts.

When a sentence contains only one thought, it is a *simple sentence;* for example:

The man stands in the doorway.

We usually think, so to speak, in simple sentences,—our thoughts coming, not in bundles, but successively and singly. The following might represent a train of thought:

The man stands in a doorway. He is tall. Perhaps the doorway is low. His figure is shadowy. His clothes are dark. The house is dark within. One cannot distinguish the man's features.

Obviously, that would be a hopelessly monotonous and ineffective way of expressing oneself on paper, no matter how accurately it represents our undirected thinking. The first step that one naturally takes in endeavoring to avoid this jerky, incoherent manner of writing is the binding together of closely related ideas, tying them in bundles. So one writes:

The man is tall, or else the doorway is low. His clothes are dark, and the house is dark within. Etc.

In each of these two sentences, we have united two ideas by using a coördinating conjunction that expresses the relation of the constituent thoughts to each other,—*or* expressing alternation, *and* addition. The result in each case is a *compound sentence:* it presents a complete thought composed of two independent constituent thoughts.

Frequently,—in telling a story, for instance,—we express our thoughts in the form of compound sentences containing a large number of constituent thoughts. Thus:

The street was bare, and not a soul was visible, and the horse and buggy went crashing on, and then we saw a child just round the curve. It seemed doomed, and we were frantic with horror, but suddenly we saw a man in a dark doorway, but we didn't recognize him, and he blocked the way, and he turned out to be our friend Martin.

Here are two compound sentences, one containing four, the other six, constituent thoughts. Each is a correct sentence, because the result in each case is one complete thought—first, the runaway horse was about to crush to death a child, and second, the child was unexpectedly saved by our friend Martin. But although these compound sentences are correct, they are only a little less monotonous and ineffective than that insufferable string of brief simple sentences with which we began.

Why is this so? We have bound our thoughts in bundles, so that they might be regarded as orderly groups, but the result is still crude. What more can be done?

The difficulty is that our bundles are like piles of logs of the same girth, neatly placed side by side and on top of each other, and capable of the addition of as many more of the same size as one cares to put on the pile. Adding a few logs to our second pile, we get this result:

It stood there looking at a bright pebble, and *it didn't move at all,* and *it seemed doomed,* and *we were filled with horror,* and *some of us turned pale as death,* but *suddenly we saw a man in a dark doorway,* and *he had doubtless been there right along,* but *we hadn't noticed him before,* and *he came out like a flash,* and *he blocked the way,* and *it was Martin.* (The principal clauses have been italicized.)

Now, we do not want piles of dead logs, but living trees. Our sentences should not be built mechanically; they should grow, as organisms grow. The tree might well be taken as the symbol of a skillfully constructed sentence.

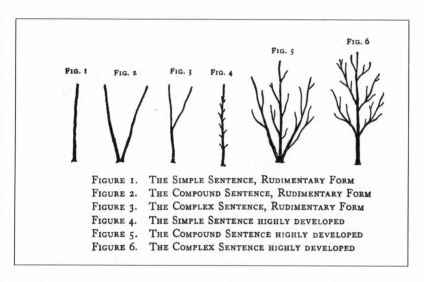

FIG. 5

FIG. 6

FIG. 1   FIG. 2   FIG. 3   FIG. 4

FIGURE 1.   THE SIMPLE SENTENCE, RUDIMENTARY FORM
FIGURE 2.   THE COMPOUND SENTENCE, RUDIMENTARY FORM
FIGURE 3.   THE COMPLEX SENTENCE, RUDIMENTARY FORM
FIGURE 4.   THE SIMPLE SENTENCE HIGHLY DEVELOPED
FIGURE 5.   THE COMPOUND SENTENCE HIGHLY DEVELOPED
FIGURE 6.   THE COMPLEX SENTENCE HIGHLY DEVELOPED

A sentence may contain, like the sentence above, many constituent thoughts, but of these thoughts perhaps one will stand out as the main thought (the trunk), which divides into several subordinate thoughts (large branches), which again divide into subordinate thoughts (small branches), etc. Our sentence, if rewritten on this principle, might read as follows:

Standing there looking at a pebble, quite motionless, and apparently doomed, *the child filled us with* such *horror* that some of us turned pale as death; but *suddenly we saw a man in a dark doorway,* whom we hadn't noticed before (though he had doubtless been there right along) and who, coming out like a flash, blocked the way—*it was Martin!* (The principal clauses have been italicized.)

Here instead of eleven independent thoughts, we have three:

(1) The child filled us with horror.
(2) Suddenly we saw a man in a dark doorway.
(3) It was Martin.

All of the other thoughts are subordinate:

to (1): (*a*) Standing there looking at a pebble.
(*b*) Quite motionless.
(*c*) Apparently doomed.
(*d*) Such that some of us turned pale as death.
to (2): (*a*) Whom we hadn't noticed before.
(*b*) Though he had doubtless been there right along.
(*c*) Coming out like a flash.
(*d*) Who blocked the way.
to (3): None.

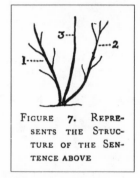

FIGURE 7. REPRE-
SENTS THE STRUC-
TURE OF THE SEN-
TENCE ABOVE

In general, the skillful writer is he who composes his sentences so that they abound in subordination,—in dependent constituent thoughts,— who in each group of thoughts infallibly picks out the most important for expression in the main clause or clauses and puts the subordinate thoughts in subordinate clauses and phrases.

How shall we find the important thoughts? This question confronts even the most experienced writer. We have, let us say, a thought to express that is composed of a number of constituent thoughts; we are aware of the fact that some are more important than others—that is almost bound to be the case; but how shall we find the chief among them, the trunk? There are but two methods: first, we may experiment, by writing our thoughts in various ways, till we succeed in putting emphasis on the chief among them (when the sentence perfectly expresses our thought we may be quite certain that the emphasis is properly

distributed); or, second, we may reflect, i.e., experiment mentally, reviewing the constituent parts of the whole thought until we see them so
clearly that the subordinate ideas fall into the background and the most
important idea or ideas stand forth luminously.

How shall we express the subordinate thoughts? To express the most
important thoughts is fairly easy—we have but to keep them in the
foreground of the mind as we write the sentence, and they will find
expression without much concern on our part. To express the subordinate
thoughts, however, is not so easy. They are not so vivid in our minds,—
they are remote and blurred, like the background of a landscape,—and
they demand skill in phrasing on account of the large number of relationships that may exist between a subordinate clause and a principal
clause,—time, condition, cause, purpose, result, concession, relativity,
comparison, means, reference, consecutiveness, correlation, adversity,—
relations that are to be expressed by the appropriate connective or by the
use of a special construction. If, for example, the relation be condition,
we might combine these two thoughts—

It rains
I will not go

—either by the use of a connective:

If it rains, I will not go;

or by the use of a special construction:

Should it rain, I would not go.

CHAPTER III
SUMMARY SENTENCES

The most profitable practice in the principles of subordination, parallelism, and emphasis will be found in the writing of summary sentences.
The summary sentence, as the term is here used, is a sentence which
expresses all the essential thought of a paragraph. Such a sentence is not
ordinarily used in actual writing, though it sometimes occurs at the end
of a long or difficult passage, and though the topic sentence is sometimes
a virtual summary sentence.

Generally, the topic sentence is inadequate as a summary of the thought of the paragraph, for the reason that it merely *points to* the subject treated, without indicating precisely *how* it is treated. It is often no more than the label on a bottle; the summary sentence, on the other hand, is always a distillation of the contents.

How should one set about the writing of a summary sentence? Given a paragraph, more or less misunderstood by a hasty reader; wanted, a single, deft sentence that shall embody the thought of the paragraph: obviously, the thing cannot be done in a moment. Although the practiced writer of summary sentences may sometimes compose his sentence by merely reflecting on the substance of the paragraph, the novice will probably find it necessary to go through a rather exacting analysis. A short paragraph from the War Message will afford an example.

We have no quarrel with the German people. We have no feeling toward them but one of sympathy and friendship. It was not upon their impulse that their Government acted in entering this war. It was not with their previous knowledge or approval. It was a war determined upon as wars used to be determined upon in the old, unhappy days, when peoples were nowhere consulted by their rulers and wars were provoked and waged in the interest of dynasties or of little groups of ambitious men who were accustomed to use their fellowmen as pawns and tools.

1.   **What does the paragraph mean?** It goes without saying that one must know exactly what the thought is before one is in a position to express it in a sentence. The paragraph above happens to be a very simple one, so that its meaning will be clear on a second reading if it is not clear on the first. Often, however, certain difficulties must be overcome: (*a*) unusual words, (*b*) words used in unusual senses, (*c*) tangled or obscure sentences, (*d*) allusions. A good dictionary is an indispensable part of our equipment.

2.   **What is the topic sentence?** Now that we know what the paragraph means, we are prepared to begin to express its meaning. Let us choose, as a convenient skeleton for our summary sentence, the topic sentence. If the topic sentence is found to express all the important thought of the paragraph, we shall need to modify it very little; but ordinarily it will serve only as a starting-point. The topic sentence in our paragraph is the first sentence:

We have no quarrel with the German people.

3.   **What additions to and subtractions from the topic sentence are to be made?** We can see at a glance that our topic sentence does not

express all the important meaning of the paragraph. "We have no quarrel with the German people"—is that all that President Wilson is saying? By no means. After repeating the idea in the second sentence, he goes on, in the third and succeeding sentences, to explain *why* we have no quarrel with the German people. The topic sentence indicates *what he is talking about,* but *what he is saying* is another matter. The fact that the war was begun without the German people's knowledge or approval must be got into our summary sentence. It must be added; apparently there is nothing, in this case, to subtract. Let us add it then:

> We have no quarrel with the German people, and this is the case because the German Government began the war without their knowledge or approval.

4. **Can the sentence be made periodic?** Since one thought in the paragraph is likely to be of more importance than all other thoughts, we shall rarely be able to accept a summary sentence that is cast in the mould of a compound sentence. We shall need a simple or a complex sentence, preferably periodic in structure. That means putting first our subordinate matter: "and this is the case because" etc. Reserving our main clause to the end, then, we may get some such result as this:

> Because the German Government began the war without their knowledge or approval, we have no quarrel with the German people.

Or, better:

> Because the Government began the war without the knowledge or approval of the German people, with them we have no quarrel.

5. **Can the phrasing of the sentence be condensed?** There is always danger that a summary sentence will be cumbersomely long and involved. What we are seeking is the briefest, neatest form compatible with comprehensiveness. In the sentence above, no further condensation is necessary; several words have already been omitted—the first sentence numbering twenty-five words, the last one twenty-one.

6. **Have we a connective?** Have we repeated one of the pivotal words or phrases of the preceding summary sentence, or used a suitable pronoun, or added a conjunction? In this case, the link is the word *Government,* which would occur in a good summary sentence of the preceding paragraph of the War Message. If possible, link every summary sentence to the preceding summary sentence by the use of some sign of transition in the thought.

If these suggestions are faithfully followed, the student will not only learn to write acceptable summary sentences, but will strengthen his command of the principles of sentence and paragraph construction.

Exercise XXII

Write summary sentences for the following paragraphs, taking care to observe the six points treated above:

Now, there are some clear objects for choice here in college, for real choice, for discreet choice. I will mention only two. In the first place, choose those studies—there is a great range of them here—which will, through your interest in them, develop your working power. You know that it is only through work that you can achieve anything, either in college or in the world. Choose those studies on which you can work intensely with pleasure, with real satisfaction and happiness. That is the true guide to a wise choice. Choose that intellectual pursuit which will develop within you the power to do enthusiastic work, an internal motive power, not an external compulsion. Then, choose an ennobling companionship. You will find out in five minutes that this man stirs you to do good, that man to evil. Shun the latter; cling to the former. Choose companionship rightly; choose your whole surroundings so that they shall lift you up and not drag you down. Make these two choices wisely, and be faithful in labor, and you will succeed in college and in after life. (*Charles W. Eliot.*)

The entry of Charles the Second into Whitehall marked a deep and lasting change in the temper of the English people. With it modern England began. The influences which had up to this time molded our history, the theological influence of the Reformation, the monarchical influence of the new kingship, the feudal influence of the Middle Ages, the yet earlier influence of tradition and custom, suddenly lost power over the minds of men. From the moment of the Restoration we find ourselves all at once among the great currents of thought and activity which have gone on widening and deepening from that time to this. The England around us becomes our own England, an England whose chief forces are industry and science, the love of popular freedom and of law, an England which presses steadily forward to a larger social justice and equality, and which tends more and more to bring every custom and tradition, religious, intellectual, and political, to the test of pure reason. Between modern thought, on some at least of its more important sides, and the thought of men before the Restoration there is a great gulf fixed. A political thinker in the present day would find it equally hard to discuss any point of statesmanship with Lord Burleigh or with Oliver Cromwell. He would find no point of contact between their ideas of national life or national welfare, their conception of government or the ends of government, their mode of regarding economical and social questions, and his own. But no gulf of this sort parts us from the men who followed the Restoration. From that time to this, whatever differences there may have been as to practical conclusions drawn from them, there has been a substantial agreement as to the grounds of our political, our social, our intellectual and religious life. Paley would have found no difficulty in understanding Tillotson: Newton and Sir Humphry Davy could have talked without a sense of severance. There would have been nothing to hinder a perfectly clear discussion on government or law between John Locke and Jeremy Bentham. (*Green.*)

The vast scale of things here, the extent of your country, your numbers, the rapidity of your increase, strike the imagination, and are a common topic for admiring remark. Our great orator, Mr. Bright, is never weary of telling us how many acres of land you have at your disposal, how many bushels of grain you produce, how many millions you are, how many more millions you will be presently, and what a capital thing this is for you. Now, though I do not always agree with Mr. Bright, I find myself agreeing with him here. I think your numbers afford a very real and important ground for satisfaction.

Not that your great numbers, or indeed great numbers of men anywhere, are likely to be all good, or even to have the majority good. "The majority are bad," said one of the wise men of Greece; but he was a pagan. Much to the same effect, however, is the famous sentence of the New Testament: "Many are called, few chosen." This appears a hard saying; frequent are the endeavours to elude it, to attenuate its severity. But turn it how you will, manipulate it as you will, the few, as Cardinal Newman well says, can never mean the many. Perhaps you will say that the majority *is,* sometimes, good; that its impulses are good generally, and its action is good occasionally. Yes, but it lacks principle, it lacks persistence; if to-day its good impulses prevail, they succumb to-morrow; sometimes it goes right, but it is very apt to go wrong. Even a popular orator, or a popular journalist, will hardly say that the multitude may be trusted to have its judgment generally just, and its action generally virtuous. It may be better, it is better, that the body of the people, with all its faults, should act for itself, and control its own affairs, than that it should be set aside as ignorant and incapable, and have its affairs managed for it by a so-called superior class, possessing property and intelligence. Property and intelligence cannot be trusted to show a sound majority themselves; the exercise of power by the people tends to educate the people. But still, the world being what it is, we must surely expect the aims and doings of the majority of men to be at present very faulty, and this in a numerous community no less than in a small one. So much we must certainly, I think, concede to the sages and to the saints. (*Arnold.*)

The failure of the melting pot, far from closing the great American democratic experiment, means that it has only just begun. Whatever American nationalism turns out to be, we see already that it will have a color richer and more exciting than our ideal has hitherto encompassed. In a world which has dreamed of internationalism, we find that we have all unawares been building up the first international nation. The voices which have cried for a tight and jealous nationalism of the European pattern are failing. From that ideal, however valiantly and disinterestedly it has been set for us, time and tendency have moved us further and further away. What we have achieved has been rather a cosmopolitan federation of national colonies, of foreign cultures, from whom the sting of devastating competition has been removed. America is already the world-federation in miniature, the continent where for the first time in history has been achieved that miracle of hope, the peaceful living side by side, with character substantially preserved, of the most heterogeneous peoples under the sun. Nowhere else has such contiguity been anything but the breeder of misery. Here, notwithstanding our tragic failures of adjustment, the outlines are already too clear not to give us a new vision and a new orientation of the American mind in the world. (*Randolph Bourne.*)

Why, then, do we hesitate to swell our words to meet our needs? It is a nonsense question. There is no reason. We are simply lazy; too lazy to make ourselves comfortable. We let our vocabularies be limited, and get along rawly without the refinements of human intercourse, without refinements in our own thoughts; for thoughts are almost as dependent on words as words on thoughts. For example, all exasperations we lump together as "aggravating," not considering whether they may not rather be displeasing, annoying, offensive, disgusting, irritating, or even maddening; and without observing too, that in our reckless usage we have burned up a word which might be convenient when we should need to mark some shading of the word "increase." Like the bad cook, we seize the frying pan whenever we need to fry, broil, roast, or stew, and then we wonder why all our dishes taste alike while in the next house the food is appetizing. It is all unnecessary. Enlarge the vocabulary. Let any one who wants to see himself grow, resolve to adopt two new words each week. It will not be long before the endless and enchanting variety of the world will begin to reflect itself in his speech, and in his mind as well. I know that when we use a word for the first time we are startled, as if a firecracker went off in our neighborhood. We look about hastily to see if any one has noticed. But finding that no one has, we may be emboldened. A word used three times slips off the tongue with entire naturalness. Then it is ours forever, and with it some phase of life which had been lacking hitherto. For each word presents its own point of view, discloses a special aspect of things, reports some little importance not otherwise conveyed, and so contributes its small emancipation to our tied-up minds and tongues. (*G. H. Palmer.*)

Freshmen and Life[1]

This is the freshman's hour. Day by day during the past week entering classes have been asked by presidents and deans to consider why they have come to college and to remember that student days are but a preparation for after-life. Books for their special benefit also come out at this season. One by a professor mindful of a first year at college wasted lies at hand. It contains the usual admonition to young men to bear in mind that life is earnest, to maintain steadfastness of purpose, and to cling to the ideals of one's childhood. With its exalted purpose no one will quarrel. In America as elsewhere the number of freshmen who idle, or fall into grievous follies, through lack of timely warning, is large; and only by serious, straightforward talk can they be raised to their better selves.

Yet it is a question whether such advice does not misplace the emphasis. Neither in the comments just cited nor in the various addresses of college presidents which the book includes, are the possibilities of the essential freedom of collegiate existence sufficiently stressed. This freedom is what undoubtedly most impresses the freshman, be he by nature a loafer or serious minded; for the moment it is the central fact of his life. Issuing from the discipline of home or boarding school, he finds himself in an atmosphere in which he seems to be master of his destiny. The resultant zest might wisely be taken by educators as a starting-point. In a negative sense it *is* so taken. That is, men are cautioned not to fancy that this is really freedom, and with such a lead it is easy to point out that no moments of life are detached from the thread of our being, that what we do to-day helps to shape our attitude years hence. Now, not all freshmen are weak, by any means; yet appeal is not made to the imagination of the strong as it should be. To them the hearty if raucous tone of a famous professor, now dead, would have a welcome sound. He used to urge certain young gentlemen to have experience. "It will cost you dear, but have it." The goodness of his own life forbade one to read into his words permission to do unworthy acts. Out of the strong cometh forth sweetness. If colleges are to maintain their distinction, the note must be struck by exceptional men, and the great opportunities of these should not be slighted by preoccupation with saving the unfit from hardships. Democracy in education need lead to no such extreme.

The democratic spirit has given to the accepted phrase "preparation for life" a meaning too strict. It is not necessary that all freshmen should be made to see the precise connection between college and the world at large. Colleges by splendid traditions have amply justified themselves, and the important point for entering students to understand is the opportunity for intellectual expansion which lies before them. The magic of pure speculation is something which even a boy, if rightly handled, can distinctly feel. From signifying preparation for life in a very general way, the college has too often, in the minds of educators, come to mean life itself, in the conventional sense. This it legitimately is not. What have the problems of pure mathematics to do with "real life"? Yet it would be a pity if mathematicians, sensitive over the clamorings of efficiency sharpers, should entirely forego their labors on infinity for nearer examples drawn from our everlasting shops and factories.

In some way the freshman must be made to think of college not only as a preparation for life, but also as being much detached from life. Properly used, college should be analogous to a journey to Europe taken for the purpose of better understanding America. Conditions in the two spheres greatly differ, but neither distorts eternal values. The point could be the more easily enforced because of the attitude in which even the freshman ordinarily presents himself. Emancipated for the moment he really is, as he imagines, and in a sense is free to shape the world unto his desire. The trust which at the outset many a boy places in the efficacy of thought as taught by his masters is pathetic when contrasted with the little that is done to foster it. In this country this disillusioning comes much sooner than in Europe. Take men fresh from Oxford. Almost invariably they show great self-assurance in applying their book-learning to life. Amusing they may appear to hardened worldlings, yet they testify to a wholesome state of instruction. From reading the accepted authorities and from discussing these as though they were still matters of live importance, they emerge with the "jump," as they suppose, on their less educated fellows. And it is indeed significant that Oxford, which in so many ways stands aloof from the world of the immediate present, yet contrives to prepare her sons almost at once to undertake pressing duties of the realm. Oxford men pride themselves upon having dwelt while at college in regions somewhat magical. It would be well if this magical element in college education were not neglected by presidents and deans at opening time. This it is, we fancy, which a rightminded freshman vaguely feels, and calls freedom; the pity is that too often he is not encouraged to convert his yearnings into a freedom of the noblest sort.

NOTE

1. A *Nation* editorial; reprinted with the kind permission of the *Nation*.

John Matthews Manly and Edith Rickert
The Writing of English (1919)

≈▶ *Manly (1865–1940) studied at Furman (M.A., 1883) and Harvard (Ph.D., 1890; dissertation with George Lyman Kittredge). He taught at Brown, then in 1898 became the first English department head at the newly formed University of Chicago, where he remained until 1933. He published extensively on Chaucer and became MLA president in 1920. (For more on Manly see Brereton, "Composition" 43–47.)*

Rickert (1871–1938) graduated from Vassar in 1891 and taught there from 1897 to 1900 (with Gertrude Buck) while completing her Ph.D. at Chicago in 1899. She moved to England, where she wrote five novels and some modernizations of medieval works. Eventually she returned to Chicago, where she began collaborating with Manly on a series of textbooks and anthologies. In 1924 she became associate professor of English at Chicago, teaching courses in Chaucer and contemporary literature.

The eminent Chaucer scholars Manly and Rickert produced a series of composition texts in the years 1919–29, most of them imbued with a belief in success that seems to anticipate Dale Carnegie. In their preface Manly and Rickert provide a rare depiction of remedial students actually succeeding at college work. At a time when colleges were being swamped by hordes of new learners, hardly any professor mentioned this vast new constituency except to complain about the presence of unprepared students, but Manly and Rickert prove an exception.

PREFACE

Our primary purpose in this book is to awaken in the student the desire for self-expression through the written and spoken word. Without this desire all teaching is futile; and with it learning is inevitable. With the student in an attitude of confidence in the worth of his own thinking and of eagerness to learn the methods by which it can be conveyed to others in words, the problem of teaching the use of English reduces to the balancing of constructive practice over against the corrective drill necessary to eradicate the bad habits due to foreign birth, defective training, or indifference.

The methods here presented have grown out of experiment at the University of Chicago with sections of freshmen who, being below the standard for entrance, were required to take additional training before they could be admitted to the regular freshman course in English. By the kind of practice and study developed in this book the following results were obtained with a hundred students:

1. Approximately one-third were brought up to the freshman standard.
2. Approximately one-third were permitted to take a supplementary half-course and given credit for freshman English.
3. Approximately one-third were given freshman credit without delay or further training.

In brief, two-thirds of the class accomplished what had before been done by a very small percentage.

This improvement in results was due not merely to the student's changed attitude toward writing but also to his acquired sense of responsibility in the corrective drill work. He was shown how errors in form can be eliminated; and if, after fair trial, he did not begin to take an active part in his own salvation in this respect, his work was ruthlessly rejected on this basis alone. With such an understanding, most of the papers soon showed a steady and rapid gain in the use of English; and with the freeing of energy from the continual consideration of mechanics, a decided improvement in the thought expressed and in the technique of expression. To see the stirring of interesting and original lines of thought in students supposedly dull or indifferent was no less gratifying than to read almost faultless English written by Russians, Poles, Lithuanians, Chinese, Japanese, and young people of many other nationalities, whose work in the beginning was almost unintelligible.

Of the many unorthodox features in the treatment of various subjects it is perhaps unnecessary to speak: they should be their own warrant. One point only in the general structure of the book does not at once appear, and needs a word of explanation. Remembering that the term "freshman" does not connote a fixed standard of attainment, we have tried to plan the work outlined so that it can be adapted to the needs of students in various stages of proficiency. By the average student the Appendix should be used only for reference during the writing and correcting of papers; but by the poor student it should be made the subject of continual study and drill outside the classroom, with emphasis placed according to individual needs. It can be used to advantage by several students working together. In the constructive part of the book more exercises have been provided than any class could do; but these are purposely of many types to meet the experience and powers of different students. Again, by classes that need to spend much time on the preliminary and outside drill work whole chapters in Part III may be omitted or relegated to the sophomore year without in any way interfering with the integrity of the course. It is hoped that this flexibility of plan may be accounted among the merits of the book.

To the teacher overburdened with dead weight of daily themes we hope that our methods may be of special use. We try continually to suggest ways in which by stimulating the student to take a more active part in the coöperative work of education the teacher's energies may be conserved for that constructive criticism in which the finest elements of personality are indispensable.

To Dr. Charles Manly and Mrs. Hellen Manly Patrick are due thanks for invaluable assistance in the reading of manuscript and proof, and in the preparation of the Index.

J. M. M.
E. R.

CHAPTER I
WRITING AND READING

Do you like to write? Probably not. What have you tried to write? Probably "themes."

The "theme" is a literary form invented by teachers of rhetoric for the education of students in the art of writing. It does not exist outside the world of school and college. No editor ever accepted a "theme." No "theme" was ever delivered from a rostrum, or spoken at a dinner, or bound between the covers of a book in the hope that it might live for centuries. In a word, a "theme" is first and last a product of "composition"—a laborious putting together of ideas, without audience and without purpose, hated alike by student and by instructor. Its sole use is to exemplify the principles of rhetoric. But rhetoric belongs to the past as much as the toga and the snuffbox; it is an extinct art, the art of cultivating style according to the mannerisms of a vanished age.

Forget that you ever wrote a "theme," and ask yourself now: "Should I like to write?" Of course you would—if you could. And you can. You have had, and you will have, some experiences that will not be repeated exactly in any other life—that no one else can express exactly as you would express them. And the art of expressing what you have experienced, what you think, what you feel, and what you believe, can be learned.

If you stop to consider the matter, you will realize that self-expression is one of the laws of life; you do express yourself day after day, whether you will or not. Hence, the more quickly you learn that successful self-expression is the source of one of the greatest pleasures in life, the more readily will you be able to turn your energy in the right direction, and the more fun will you get out of the process. The kind of delight that comes through self-expression of the body, through the play of the muscles in running or hurdling, through the play of muscles and mind together in football or baseball or tennis or golf, comes also through the exercise of the mind alone in talk or in writing.

Remember always throughout this course, that you have something to say—something peculiar to yourself that should be contributed to the sum of the world's experience, something that cannot be contributed by anyone but yourself. It may be much or it may be little: with that you are not concerned at present; your business now is to find out how to say it; how to clear away the obstacles that clog self-expression; how to give your mind free swing; and how to get all the fun there is in the process.

The initial problems in learning to write are: How can you get at this store of material hidden within you? and how can you know when you have found it? Your experience, however interesting, is as yet very limited. How can you tell which phases of it deserve expression, and which are mere commonplace? The quickest way to answer this question is by reading. Reading will tell you which phases of experience have been commonly treated and which have been neglected. Moreover, as you read you will be surprised to find that very often the features of your life which seem to you peculiarly interesting are exactly those that are commonly—and even cheaply—written about, while those which you have passed over as not worth attention may be aspects of life that other people too have passed over; they may therefore be fresh and well worth writing about. For instance, within the last twenty-five years we have had two writers, Joseph Conrad and John Masefield, writing of the sea as it has never been written of before. Both have been sailors; and both have utilized their experience as viewed through the medium of their temperaments in a way undreamed of before. Again, within the last ten years we have had Algernon Blackwood, using his imagination to apply psychology to the study of the supernatural, and so developing a field peculiar to himself. Still again, H. G. Wells, who began his career as a clerk and continued as a teacher of science, has found in both these phases of his experience a mine of literary wealth; and Arnold Bennett, born and educated in the dreariest, most unpicturesque, apparently least inspiring, part of England, has seen in the very prosiness of the Five Towns untouched material, and has given this an enduring place in literature. In your imagination there may lie the basis of fantasies as yet unexpressed; or in your experience, aspects of life that have not as yet been adequately treated. As you read you will find that until recently the one phase of life most exploited in literature was the romantic love of youth; this was the basis of nearly all novels and of most short stories; its presence was demanded for either primary or secondary interest in the drama; and it was the chief source of inspiration for the lyric. But within the last thirty years all sorts of other subjects have been opened up. To-day the writer's difficulty is, not that he is restricted by literary convention in his choice of material, but that he is so absolutely unrestricted that he may be in doubt where to make his choice. He is, to be sure, conditioned in two ways: To do the best work, he must keep within the bounds of his own temperament and experience; and he should as far as possible avoid phases of life already written about, unless he can present them under some new aspect.

With these conditions in mind, you are ready to ask yourself: What have I to write about? Let us put the question more concretely: Have you lived, for instance, in a little mining town in the West? Such a little town, with its saloons and automatics and flannel-shirted hero, stares at us every month from the pages of popular magazines. But perhaps your little mining town is dry, perhaps there has not been a shooting fray in it for ten years, and all the young men go to Bible class on Sunday. Well, here is something new: let us have it. Is New York your home? The magazines tell you that New York is parceled out among a score of writers: the Italian quarter, the Jewish quarter, the Syrian quarter, the boarding-houses, Wall Street. What is there left? The suburbs? Surely not; and yet have you ever seen a story of just your kind of street and just the kind of people that you know? If not, here is your opportunity.

You have read about sailors, fishermen, farmers, detectives, Italian fruit-peddlers, Jewish clothes-merchants, commercial travelers, financiers, salesmen and saleswomen, doctors, clergymen, heiresses and men about town, but have you often read a thrilling romance of a filing clerk? How about the heroism of a telephone collector? the humors of a street-car conductor? The seeing eye will find material in the street car, in the department store, in the dentist's waiting room, in college halls, on a lonely country road—anywhere and everywhere. And the seeing eye is cultivated by a perpetual process of comparing life as it is with life as it is portrayed in literature and in art. In other words, to get material to write about, you must cultivate alertness to the nature and value of your own life-experience, and to the nature and value of all forms of life with which you come into contact; but this you can never do with any degree of success unless you at the same time learn how to read.

You may say that you know how to read. It is almost certain that you do not. If by reading you mean that you can run your eye over a page, and, barring a word here and there, get the general drift of the sense, you may perhaps qualify as able to read. If you are set the task of interpreting fully every phrase in an article by a thoughtful writer, the chances are that you will fail. When only a small part of a writer's meaning has passed from his mind to yours, you can hardly be said to have read what he has written. On the other hand, no one can get out of written words all that was put into them. What was written out of one man's experience must be interpreted by another's experience; and as no two people ever have exactly the same experience—no two people are exactly alike—it follows that no interpretation is ever entirely what the writer had in mind. The ratio between what goes into a book and what comes out of it varies in two ways. Granted the same reader, he will take only to the limit of his capacity from any book set before him: he may get almost all from a book that contains but little, a good share of a book that contains much, but very little of a book that is far beyond the range of his experience. Granted the same book, one reader will barely skim its surface, another will gain a fair idea of the gist of it, a third will almost relive it with the author.

The main point is that this varying ratio depends upon the amount of life-experience that goes into the writing of a book and the amount of life-experience that goes into the reading of it. For as writing is the expression of life, so reading is vicarious living—living by proxy, reliving in imagination what the author has lived before he was able to write it. Hence, we grow *up to* books, grow *into* them, and grow *out of* them. Our growing experience of life may be measured by the books that we read; and conversely, as we cannot have all experience in our own lives, books are necessarily one of the most fruitful sources of growth in experience.

This is true, however, only of what may be called vitalized reading—reading, not with the eyes alone, nor with the mind alone, but with the stored experiences of life, with the emotions that it has brought, with the attitudes toward men and things and ideas that it has given—in a word, with imagination. To read with imagination, you must be, in the first place, active; in the second place, sensitive, and, because you are sensitive, receptive. Instead, however, of being merely passively receptive of the stream of ideas and images and sensations flowing from the work you are reading, you must be alert to take all that it has to give, and to re-create this in terms of your own experience. Thus by making it a part of your imaginative experience, you widen your actual experience, you enrich your life, and you increase the flexibility and vital power of your mind.

In order, then, to tap the sources of your imagination, you must learn to experience in two ways: first, through life itself, not so much by seeking experiences different from those that naturally come your way, as by becoming aware of the value of those that belong naturally to your life; and second, through learning to absorb and transmute the life that is in books, beginning with those that stand nearest to your stage of development. In the process of reading you will turn more and more to those writers who have a larger mastery of life, and who, by their skill in expressing the wisdom and beauty that they have made their own, can admit you, when you are ready, to some share in that mastery.

Assignment

Read slowly the following extract from G. H. Palmer's *Self-cultivation in English:*

"But the very fact that literary endowment is immediately recognized and eagerly envied has induced a strange illusion in regard to it. It is supposed to be something mysterious, innate in him who possesses it, and quite out of the reach of him who has it not. The very contrary is the fact. No human employment is more free and calculable than the winning of language. Undoubtedly there are natural aptitudes for it, as there are for farming, seamanship, or being a good husband. But nowhere is straight work more effective. Persistence, care, discriminating observation, ingenuity, refusal to lose heart,—traits which in every other occupation tend toward excellence,—tend toward it here with special security."

Does Mr. Palmer mean that anyone can learn to write well? How?

6

Writing the Essay

In almost every account of composition studies the students are silent, a fine irony in light of the enormous amounts of discourse they have elicited as well as produced. This chapter contains two separate parts: pamphlets, exams, and textbooks that tell students how to write their compositions, and examples from the professional literature of the compositions themselves, some in the students' own handwriting, and a few with the instructors' markings.

The half century this volume covers involved a dramatic shift in the kinds of prose students produced. Originally, in the college of 1860, writing most often involved planning and composing a speech that would be memorized and delivered orally. Some speak nostalgically of this kind of composition; it signified a genuine connection to the affairs of the nation, and provided a direct link to the two-thousand-year tradition of the classics (Miller, *Textual Carnivals* 59–63). To be sure, it often involved no truly original thinking, just the manipulation of the commonplaces of rhetoric and some attention to the niceties of style. The eclipse of the old rhetoric is neatly symbolized by an afternoon at Gettysburg, Pennsylvania, when the noted orator Edward Everett, trained at Harvard and in Germany, spoke glowingly for two hours, and the unschooled Abraham Lincoln spoke for only three minutes. Lincoln's Gettysburg Address, every bit as much a work of rhetoric as Everett's speech and filled with echoes of the high rhetorical style, marked a new departure in simplicity, dignity, and plainspokenness. It heralded a change that was to be accomplished slowly over the next generation (Wills; Cmiel).

The new kind of writing required by composition courses, class assignments, and final examinations was not a speech but an essay.

437

Writing became more of a one-way process: the teacher did the assigning, the student did nothing but respond in writing. Gone was the public testing in front of the class, the speech or disputation for all to hear and judge. The new university's concept of discourse gradually narrowed writing to a private interchange, much more like the kind of writing students had done in the lower schools, with topics set by the teachers. By the end of the century, college communication was almost exclusively written for the teacher's eyes, and a large part of the teacher's role was to point out the errors. In this sense the college English teacher had taken on more and more of the classics teacher's traditional role of error correcting, of being the college gatekeeper and enforcer.

The new university also extended its instruction in the writer's role to such mundane subjects as letters. The amount of space that texts, particularly handbooks, devoted to letter writing and to the etiquette and format of personal as well as business letters indicated the presence of a new type of student, one who needed to be taught how to format a letter and where to place the stamp. The composition course had come a long way since 1875.

This was not the only path colleges could have taken; other conceptions of writing did not require the instructor to set narrowly focused assignments or to examine them for blunders. Lab reports in the sciences, for instance, were records of observations and discoveries. Instructors assigned them and often looked them over carefully, but the criteria for success were subject-based. The same applied to field notes in geology or to research papers in history or philosophy; the writing mattered as it did in the real world, as part of the discovery and transmission of information, and operated in a well-defined structure of apprenticeship. For composition courses, on the other hand, where the aim was to inculcate an art, the relationship was radically different, schoolmaster to pupil. To be sure, college teachers often took on a schoolmaster role when they taught subjects like languages, mathematics, or introductory sciences. But those courses also had the structure of an academic discipline to sustain them; students were being introduced, no matter how uncomfortably, to a subject. But composition had no subject; nothing lay behind it; the class was all there was to it. To most instructors it was a skill, similar to, though more private than, athletic prowess, rather than an academic subject.

The apprentice-master relationship was not followed in composition work because writing teachers were not representatives of some overarching subject, did not connect themselves with a discipline, and in many cases were not even writers themselves. Thus writing in itself was free-floating, and attempts were soon made to link it to one of the fastest-growing academic disciplines, English literature. As the century neared its end, composition commonly became a course in writing about English literature, either in the form of classic essays or as a straight literature course with written assignments graded for the quality of the writing.

Examinations from Adams Sherman Hill's English A for the Academic Year 1887–88

ʒ❧ *(For Hill's career, see chap. 2, p. 45.) These three examinations were printed in a pamphlet sold to Harvard students; the first part contained a twenty-three-page summary of Hill's 1878* Principles of Rhetoric. *Like the "pony" used in Latin or Greek class which provided word-for-word translations, this pamphlet was a shortcut for students, who could save themselves the labor of reading Hill's whole text. The examinations, printed at the end so students could tell what was coming, tested knowledge of the book but also asked students to display knowledge from other course work in school and college. Harvard's copy of the pamphlet was owned by Hill himself.*

[One-hour examination, Dec., 1887.]

Make your answers thorough, and pay attention to form as well as to substance.

The following sentences are from Freshman compositions. Discuss such questions of English usage as they suggest, and correct all the errors that you find in them—supposing yourself obliged to make clear to the authors the value of your corrections.

1. We got back just in time to wash and get ready for dinner, which was quickly finished although much was eaten.
2. The little insecure steamboat of Fulton is now transplanted by the massive Cunarder.
3. Deformed, small, delicate, living in continual pain, Nature had

compensated him in a degree for his infirmities by granting him "the precious jewel" of poetic genius.

4. Cambridge did vote no licence and we will see whether it will "save the boys" or not. I think it will do the opposite.

5. Unless you have authority over some one it would be very impolite to say he shall or you shall. In speaking of yourself it is entirely proper as then you have control over yourself.

[Three-hour examination, Mid-Year, 1888.]

Pay attention to form as well as to substance. Make your answers thorough and illustrate them by examples wherever you can.

I.

Write in a short essay on one of the following subjects:—

1. Conciseness as an Element of Strength.
2. The Test of a Metaphor.
3. How Metaphors affect the Growth of Language.
4. The Relation of Clearness to Precision.
5. The Relation of Elegance to Force.

II.

Discuss such questions of English usage as the following sentences suggest:—

1. It was told you before, that Prudence bid the boys, that if at any time they would, they should ask her some questions that might be profitable, and she would say something to them.

2. It sets before your eyes the absent object as perfectly and more delightfully than nature.

3. So in the shape that Horace presents himself to us in his satires we see nothing at the first view which deserves our attention.

4. In May the Directory for Public Worship was again proceeded with, but only to bring on to the carpet the long-dreaded discussion as to the Lord's Supper, on which any approach to agreement was hopeless.

5. Hence it is, that one afternoon last summer four boys, myself among the number, and two guides found ourselves upon the sides of Mt. Marcy.

6. He did his utmost to keep as private as possible such discoveries of the supposed plot as were communicated to him, the intention of which his perspicuity soon canvassed.

III.

Discuss the rhetorical qualities of the following passages:—

1. Tuesday morning an hour-examination in English A was held, and the freshmen labored over a paper containing three sentences for recasting, a good many finding mistakes where there were none and passing over the treacherous pitfalls without finding them out.

2.   One spirit animating old and young,
   A gipsy fire we kindled on the shore
   Of the fair Isle with birch-trees fringed—and there,
   Merrily seated in a ring, partook
   The beverage drawn from China's fragrant herb.

3. Herein [in a collection of local proverbs] I have neglected such narrow and restrictive Proverbs as never travelled beyond the smoke of the chimneys of that town wherein they were made.

4. A noble author would not be pursued too close by a translator. We lose his spirit, when we think to take his body. The grosser part remains with us, but the soul is flown away, in some noble expression, or some delicate turn of words, or thought.

5.   The Soul's dark cottage battered and decayed,
   Lets in new light through chinks that Time has made;
   Stronger by weakness—wiser men become,
   As they draw near to their eternal home.

IV.

Give your opinion of the literary worth of either 1 or 2.

The following heads may help you in the arrangement of your criticism:—

(*a*) Accuracy.
(*b*) Clearness.
(*c*) Force.
(*d*) Elegance.
(*e*) General Remarks.

1. For, after all, a translator is to make his author appear as charming as possibly he can, provided he maintains his character, and makes him not unlike himself. Translation is a kind of drawing after the life: where every one will acknowledge there is a double sort of likeness, a good one and a bad. It is one thing to draw the outlines true, the features like, the proportions exact, the colouring itself perhaps tolerable; and another thing to make all these graceful, by the posture, the shadowings, and chiefly by the spirit which animates the whole. I cannot, without some indignation, look on an ill copy of an excellent original. Much less can I behold with patience Virgil, Homer, and some others, whose beauties I have been endeavouring all my life to imitate, so abused, as I may say, to their faces, by a botching interpreter. What English readers unacquainted with Greek or Latin, will believe me, or any other man, when we commend those authors, and confess we derive all that is pardonable in us from their fountains, if they take those to be the same poets, whom our Ogilbys have translated? But I dare assure them, that a good poet is no more like himself in a dull translation, than his carcass would be to his living body. There are many who understand Greek and Latin, and yet are ignorant of their mother tongue. The proprieties and delicacies of the English are known to few: it is impossible even for a good wit to understand and practise them, without the help of a liberal education, long reading, and digesting of those few good authors we have amongst us, the knowledge of men and manners, the freedom of habitudes and conversation with the best of company of both sexes; and, in short, without wearing off the rust, which he contracted while he was laying in a stock of learning. Thus difficult it is to understand the purity of English, and critically to discern not only good writers from bad, and a proper style from a corrupt, but also to distinguish that which is pure in a good author, from that which is vicious and corrupt in him. And for want of all these requisites, or the greatest part of them, most of our ingenious young men take up some cry'd-up English poet for their model, adore him, and imitate him, as they think, without knowing

wherein he is defective, where he is boyish and trifling, wherein either his thoughts, or the turn of both is unharmonious. Thus it appears necessary, that a man should be a nice critic in his mother-tongue, before he attempts to translate a foreign language. Neither is it sufficient that he be able to judge of words and style; but he must be a master of them too: he must perfectly understand his author's tongue, and absolutely command his own. So that, to be a thorough translator, he must be a thorough poet.

2. So, then, we have the three ranks: the man who perceives rightly, because he does not feel, and to whom the primrose is very accurately the primrose, because he does not love it. Then, secondly, the man who perceives wrongly, because he feels, and to whom the primrose is any-thing else than a primrose: a star, or a sun, or a fairy's shield, or a forsaken maiden. And then, lastly, there is the man who perceives rightly in spite of his feelings, and to whom the primrose is for ever nothing else than itself—a little flower, apprehended in the very plain and leafy fact of it, whatever and how many soever the associations and passions may be, that crowd around it. And, in general, these three classes may be rated in comparative order, as the men who are not poets at all, and the poets of the second order, and the poets of the first; only however great a man may be, there are always some subjects which *ought* to throw him off his balance; some, by which his poor human capacity of thought should be conquered, and brought into the inaccurate and vague state of perception, so that the language of the highest inspiration be-comes broken, obscure, and wild in metaphor, resembling that of the weaker man, overborne by weaker things.

And thus, in full, there are four classes: the men who feel nothing, and therefore see truly; the men who feel strongly, think weakly, and see untruly (second order of poets); the men who feel strongly, think strongly, and see truly (first order of poets); and the men who, strong as human creatures can be, are yet submitted to influences stronger than they, and see in a sort untruly, because what they see is inconceivably above them. This last is the usual condition of prophetic inspiration.

[Three-hour examination. Final. 1888.]

Make your answers thorough, and illustrate them by examples wherever you can.

I.

Write a short essay on one of the following subjects:—

1. Uncle Toby.
2. Burke's Attitude toward the American Colonies.
3. Webster's Style.
4. One of Miss Austen's Characters.
5. Scott's Boyhood.
6. Scott's Leading Characteristic as a Writer.
7. Scott's Heroines.
8. Hawthorne's Style.

II.

1. Name the authors that we have studied this year, with the dates (as nearly as you can remember them) of birth, death, and publication of principal works.
2. Who wrote (*a*) The Blithedale Romance? (*b*) The Monastery? (*c*) Northanger Abbey? (*d*) The Vanity of Human Wishes? (*e*) The Citizen of the World? (*f*) Dolph Heyliger? (*g*) The Traveller?
3. Name Miss Austen's Novels.
4. What keeps Johnson's fame alive?
5. [*Take either* (*a*) *or* (*b*).]
(*a*) What are the merits and the demerits of Irving as a historian?
(*b*) What are the main characteristics of Webster's speeches?

III.

Discuss the idea expressed in the following sentence:—

"Words, like men, have nervous prostration from overwork: they lose for a time their efficiency, their vitality; they cannot do their work, and they need rest."

IV.

In the light of what you have learned from text-book and from lectures, discuss the substance of the following passage:—

"It is a wrong done to good taste to hold up this *item* kind of description any longer as deserving any other credit than that of a good memory. It is a mere bill of parcels, a *post-mortem* inventory of nature, where imagination is not merely not called for, but would be out of place. Why, a recipe in the cookery-book is as much like a good dinner as this kind of stuff is like true word-painting. The poet with a real eye in his head does not give us everything, but only the *best* of everything. He selects, he combines, or else gives what is characteristic only; while the false style of which I have been speaking seems to be as glad to get a pack of impertinences on its shoulders as Christian in the Pilgrim's Progress was to be rid of his. One strong verse that can hold itself upright (as the French critic Rivarol said of Dante) with the bare help of substantive and verb, is worth acres of this dead cord-wood piled stick on stick, a boundless continuity of dryness. I would rather have written that half stanza of Longfellow's in the 'Wreck of the Hesperus,' of the 'billow that swept her crew like icicles from her deck,' than all Gawain Douglas's tedious enumeration of meteorological phenomena put together. A real landscape is never tiresome; it never presents itself to us as a disjointed succession of isolated particulars; we take it in with one sweep of the eye—its light, its shadow, its melting gradations of distance: we do not say it is this, it is that, and the other; and we may be sure that if a description in poetry is tiresome there is a grievous mistake somewhere. All the pictorial adjectives in the dictionary will not bring it a hair's-breadth nearer to truth and nature."

V.

1. Define Exposition.
2. Explain the relation of Induction to Deduction.
3. Distinguish between the Argument from Sign and the Argument from Example.

VI.

Criticise the following paragraph thoroughly and temperately, pointing out such merits and such faults as you see, and treating the work as if it were a theme and you the examiner. After giving it both detailed and general criticism, rewrite it with special attention to accuracy, clearness, and brevity:—

"The freshmen have so far this year shown themselves so thoroughly alive and enthusiastic over the interests of their teams that it would be truly a shame should they not support their nine heartily when they play Yale next Saturday. A book has already been placed at Leavitt & Peirce's for the signatures of those intending to make the trip, and nothing should deter every freshman who can possibly go to do so. The encouragement infused into a team by the presence and cheering of a large number of their class-mates is a potent factor of success, and it would be a pity, indeed, if the freshmen here could not muster as large a delegation to go to New Haven as their rivals brought to Cambridge last Saturday. Besides the duty which devolves upon every member of Ninety-one to support his team to the best of his ability, the game at Yale is one of those land-marks in the history of every freshman class, the retrospect of which is always pleasant. If the nine win, nothing will surpass the joy of those who witnessed the victory and by their presence and encouragement helped keep Yale 'off the fence'; if defeat be their fate, the complimentary dinner tendered all the Harvard men after the game will purge their melancholy."

Barrett Wendell
"Note for Teachers"
in *English Composition, Eight Lectures Given at the Lowell Institute* (1894)

🐌 *(For Wendell's career, see chap. 2, p. 127.) This four-page "how-to" guide addressed to teachers aims at turning Wendell's book, which originated as a series of lectures, into a workable college text. Interesting is the emphasis upon group work. This was almost a necessity, given the large number of themes any instructor had to grade each week. The course Wendell describes is English B, a required sophomore composition course.*

USING WENDELL'S ENGLISH COMPOSITION.

Inquiries concerning the use of this book in teaching lead me to add this statement of how I have used it at Harvard College.

In the course where I regularly use it as a text-book, compositions, called *themes,* of from five hundred to a thousand words, are written every fortnight. On the introductory chapter, which I direct the class to read at once, I do not formally examine the students at all; but I expect them to have read it intelligently before writing the first theme. Between the first theme and the second, I direct them to read the chapter on Words, the suggestions in which they are advised particularly to consider in writing the second theme. When this theme is handed in, each student takes the theme of a fellow-student and devotes an hour to making, in the class-room, a written analysis of its vocabulary. In this work he is guided by the following plan, sketched on a blackboard:

WORDS: 1. Grammatical Purity: *a.* Barbarism.
  b. Impropriety.
2. Kinds of Words: *a.* Latin or Saxon.
  b. Long or short.
  c. General or specific.
  d. Figurative or literal, etc.
3. Number of Words.
4. Denotation and Connotation.

At the close of the hour each criticism is folded within the theme it deals with, and both documents are handed in together.

By this means several ends are generally attained. The student, aware of the test to which his work will be exposed, is apt practically to apply, in his own writing, the rhetorical matter contained in the chapter under consideration; he thus learns, half insensibly, to consider the subject not as an abstract one, but rather as a body of practical advice concerning artistic conduct. In categorically criticising the theme of somebody else, he is compelled at once intelligently to master the theory of the chapter under consideration, and to display his knowledge of it in an orderly way. And if he criticises well—which proves the case rather oftener than one would expect—he greatly lightens the task of the instructor who has finally to criticise the theme in question.

Between the second theme and the third, I direct the class similarly to master the chapter on Sentences, their knowledge of which is similarly tested by the following plan:

SENTENCES: 1. Grammatical Purity: Solecism.
2. Kinds of Sentences: *a.* Long or short.
  b. Periodic or loose, etc.

3. Principles of Composition: *a.* Unity.
                                b. Mass.
                                c. Coherence.
4. Denotation and Connotation.

With the next theme, their knowledge of the chapter on Paragraphs is similarly tested thus:

PARAGRAPHS: I. Summarize the theme you criticise, paragraph by paragraph.
             II. 1. Kinds of Paragraphs.
                 2. Principles of Composition.
                 3. Denotation and Connotation.

With the next theme, their knowledge of the chapter on Whole Compositions is tested thus:

WHOLE COMPOSITION: I. Summarize, paragraph by paragraph.
                    II. 1. Principles of Composition.
                        2. Denotation and Connotation.

Having thus accustomed students to analyzing the Elements of Style, I proceed in the following three themes similarly to call their attention to the Qualities of Style. After studying the chapter on Clearness, they are directed to analyze one another's themes by the following plan:

I. ELEMENTS OF STYLE.
   1. Words.
   2. Sentences.
   3. Paragraphs.
   4. Whole Composition.
II. QUALITY OF STYLE.
   1. Clearness.

In similar manner I test their knowledge of the two remaining chapters—the chapters on Force and on Elegance.

For the rest of the year, they are regularly required every fortnight to make a complete analysis of one another's themes. The complete scheme of criticism is as follows:

I. ELEMENTS OF STYLE.
   1. Words.
   2. Sentences.
   3. Paragraphs.
   4. Whole Composition.
II. QUALITIES OF STYLE.
   1. Clearness.
   2. Force.
   3. Elegance.
III. GENERAL REMARKS.

In every case, each student is generally expected to make some comment under each head. Repeated use of this scheme certainly fixes the book in their minds to a rather surprising degree.

I may add that I have for years been accustomed, in reading themes, to make a hasty categorical analysis of every theme I read. The pages of my note-book are divided thus:

NAME OF STUDENT:

	Theme I.	Theme II.	Theme III., etc.
Title of theme .... Mark			
Words .... Sentences .... Paragraphs .... Whole Compositions ...			
Clearness .... Force .... Elegance			
Remarks			

When one has sixty or seventy themes to read every week, each single analysis must of course be hasty. If several separate analyses, however, made at considerable intervals, and necessarily in various moods and under various conditions, prove to have much in common, they result in a valid basis for generalizations about the style of the individual they concern. The experience of more than ten years confirms my belief that this method of keeping pupils in hand is efficient.

James Morgan Hart
A Handbook of English Composition (1895)

Hart (1839–1916) was trained as a lawyer in Germany and wrote a well-known book on German universities. He spent his career at Cornell and Cincinnati and served as the MLA president in 1895.

Chapter 13 of Hart's writing textbook provides the student with a step-by-step overview of the actual production process of a college essay. Hart breaks the essay down into four separate parts (Formulating the Subject, Working Plan, The First Draught, Revision), deplores separate introductions and conclusions in brief six-hundred-word essays, and calls for an open notion of composition: "to embody the knowledge, views, and feelings of a young writer upon a subject within the range of school and college life or study." Interestingly, in 1891 ("Cornell Course") Hart had argued for confining composition topics to literature. He had either changed his mind, or his publishers insisted on his enlarging his purview.

PREPARING A COMPOSITION.

120. The term Composition may be applied to any piece of writing, whether long or short, whether complicated or simple. Thus any one of the independent paragraphs quoted in Chapter III. is no less a composition than Carlyle's *Frederick the Great,* a work in several volumes, each volume divided into books, chapters, sections, and paragraphs.

In the present chapter, however, the term Composition is employed in the usual high-school and college sense, to denote a piece of writing which may vary in length from 600 words to 1500 or 2000 words, and which is to embody the knowledge, views, and feelings of a young writer upon a subject within the range of school and college life or study.

Whether the writing be actually called a composition, or an essay, does not matter. Neither does it matter, for the present chapter, whether the subject be chosen by the writer or assigned to him by the teacher.

Assuming that the scholar has got his subject and has thought it over in a general way, how shall we direct him to write out his thoughts in a composition?

FORMULATING THE SUBJECT.

121. The first direction is this:

Formulate your subject in a complete and clearly-worded sentence, before you begin to write.

Every subject is elastic: not only may it be treated briefly or at length, but it may also be treated under one or another of numerous aspects. The writer, then, before writing, should first determine the particular aspect. *E.g.,* the subject in general may be:

Camping in the Adirondacks.

The writer is supposed to have passed some weeks in the region.

1. He may narrate the more striking incidents of his trip, from the time he entered the region until he left it.

2. He may give in detail the incidents of a single day in the woods, as a sample of his tent-life in general.

3. He may describe the prominent features of lakes and rivers, woods and mountains.

4. He may mention the peculiarities of fishing or of hunting in the Adirondacks.

5. He may discuss the gain to body and mind from such a trip. Or, the social features of such close companionship.

From the above, and other similar aspects which may suggest themselves, the writer should select that one which suits him best, as the one upon which to concentrate his thinking powers, and should formulate it in a sentence. Thus:

In this composition I am going to describe the lakes, woods, etc. in the Adirondacks.

A sentence of this sort, written down, will be the writer's guide throughout his work, will be his working formula. He need not insert it in his composition; still less need he take it for the title. But the sentence, the *formula,* he should have constantly before his eye and his mind.

In a composition of more than usual length, say of 2500 or 3000 words, the writer might combine all, or most, of the above-mentioned aspects. He should, in that case, draw up his formula more carefully, somewhat in this fashion:

> I am going to narrate a three weeks' trip in the Adirondacks, telling where I went, describing some of the scenery, giving in detail the incidents of one day as a sample of the life, and stating facts enough to justify the conclusion that the trip has done me good.

Here the description would be subordinate to the narrative, and the two together would lead up to the conclusion.

Instead of narration or description, the subject may be in exposition; *e.g.:*

The University Extension Movement.

Here the writer may treat:

1. The impulse to the movement, and its history: when and where it started, who started it; what methods were first employed; what changes introduced in methods and subjects.

2. Difference between England and the United States; advantages of England.

3. Actual operation of the movement in the city in which the writer resides.

4. Character of the persons engaged in giving and receiving instruction.

5. Possible effect of the movement upon high schools and colleges.

In a long composition these several aspects might be combined. Thus:

> I shall mention what gave rise to the movement, the persons who began it, their methods, the changes introduced, the spread of the movement to America, and the present outlook here.

It is quite possible that the above formulation might not suit any one writer. It is not offered here as a model, but only as a suggestion. Nevertheless *some such formula* should be clearly present to the writer before he begins to write.

WORKING PLAN.

122. The directions for a working plan are these:

1. Having formulated your subject, think out the details or items, jotting down each one on a separate slip of paper. This jotting down need not always be in the form of a complete sentence; usually a catch-word will be enough; *e.g.,* for a composition upon the Adirondacks:

> Difficult crossing _____ stream; heavy rains.
> Thick moss on trees at _____ .
> Mysterious noises in woods after sunset.
> Curious outline of _____ mountain.
> Big catch of trout, Saturday.
> M. [the guide] making coffee and roasting potatoes.

For a composition upon University Extension:

> Heard _____ lecture on ancient Greek life; lantern slides, buildings and costumes.
> How many miles must _____ travel to deliver his lectures; easier in England?
> Difference between hearing _____ lecture on Virgil, and reading Virgil in school.

2. Having thus jotted down recollections and ideas, read over the slips and sort them into groups, putting into one group those slips which naturally go together. *Each group will constitute a paragraph,* the separate jottings being the items of the paragraph; see § 7, 3. Then *formulate the substance of each paragraph into a sentence,* like the formula for the whole composition, § 121.

3. After all the paragraphs are formulated, prepare a *Working Plan,* by writing at the top of a sheet of paper the formula of the whole composition, and below, in succession, the formula of each paragraph, in the order which—after careful reflection—seems best.

Remember that in Narration and Description the formula of a paragraph is not necessarily the Topic-Sentence. Not even in Exposition is it always such a sentence. But in Exposition it would at least suggest one. (See §§ 11, 12.)

This process of formulating the subject, then jotting down numerous items, grouping these into paragraphs, formulating each paragraph, and lastly drawing up a working plan, is necessarily slow. Certainly the first attempt will cost time and effort. But with every fresh composition the task will become lighter, until—after the fourth or fifth composition— the young writer perceives that he is acquiring a certain skill in formulating and outlining.

But, whether slow or rapid, the process is the only sure means of curing the chronic fault of school and college composition, the lack of unity, order, coherence, and proportion. Every teacher of English knows that the ordinary composition, even if correct in grammar and diction, is rambling. The writer does not start off promptly, he is diffuse where he ought to be concise, or meagre where he ought to amplify, he omits necessary statements, and ends with a limp. All these evils can be traced back to one source: the writer has undertaken to compose without a plan. The cure, therefore, will consist in training him to form a plan. One feature, especially, of good writing can be brought out with the aid of a good working plan, namely, Proportion. The writer, we may assume, is about to describe the lakes, rivers, woods, and mountains of the Adirondacks, in a composition of 600 words. Shall he treat all four parts of the subject alike, giving to each 150 words? Or may he, by grouping together the lakes and rivers, reduce the number of parts to three, and give to each 200 words? Or may he introduce another variation, by giving 150 words to the mountains and 250 to the woods? Such questions can be answered only by the writer himself, and his answer will depend upon the range of his personal knowledge and the bent of his personal tastes. But, in any case, it is his duty to raise the questions and to answer them. And he should answer them arithmetically:

> Given so many hundred words for a whole composition in four, six, eight, nine paragraphs, how may words shall I apportion to each separate paragraph, according to my estimate of its relative importance?

THE FIRST DRAUGHT.

123. Having prepared his working plan, the scholar is now to fill out his first draught. Here the following suggestions may be of service:

1. Use ruled paper, the lines pretty far apart. Also leave an ample margin, perhaps of two or two and a half inches. This will give space for corrections and insertions.

2. Before beginning a paragraph, read over the items which make up its substance. Having these fresh in mind, write out the paragraph rapidly. At least, do not linger over words and phrases, but be satisfied with putting your thoughts in tolerably coherent shape. Your present aim is to compose the paragraph as a whole, rather than to perfect each clause and sentence. It is a safe method to plan deliberately (§ 122); to write rapidly, with *impetus* (§ 123); to review with minute care (§ 124).

REVISION.

124. When the whole composition is rough-draughted, *lay it aside for a day or two, if possible.* An intermission, if only of a single day, enables the writer to approach the task of revision in the proper mood. While writing is a creative act, implying energy, concentration, warmth, not to say enthusiasm, revision, on the contrary, is *critical,* and calls for coolness and circumspection. The writer is to revise his work in a judicial spirit, approving or rejecting his own words and phrases as impartially as if he were judging the work of another person.

In revising each paragraph, try to employ the Echo, § 8; Connectives, § 9; Repeated Structure, § 10; Topic-Sentence, §§ 11–13. Also try the Paragraph-Echo, § 17.

In revising sentences, scrutinize sharply every *and* and *but,* §§ 90, 91; careless writers use them twice as often as they should. Also scrutinize the Historical Present, § 97. Pay especial attention to Stability of Structure, § 93. Bear in mind that the striking places in the sentence are the beginning and the end, especially the end. Hence the exhortation:

End with words that deserve distinction.[1]

In general, guard against redundancy. If the working plan has been carefully prepared, according to § 122, there ought not to be any marked redundancy of matter. But redundancy of expression is a common vice. Old or young, experienced or inexperienced, we are all given to using too many words. Hence the constant duty of learning to condense. But, since condensation cannot be taught by rule, each clause and sentence must be reduced in its own way.

The following device, if employed with caution, may be helpful. In rough-draughting (§ 123), use more words than you are entitled to; *e.g.*, if the number of words allowed for the whole composition is 600, use 800, or perhaps even 900. But use them, of course, with the conscious effort to avoid redundancy, *i.e.*, try to say with them as much as possible. Then, in revising, you will know that there are 200 words, or 300, which must be eliminated. This will be a definite object.

In revising, scrutinize every adjective and adverb, to make sure that it truly adds something to the expression. Also weigh every two terms coupled by *and,* to see if one or the other may not be rejected. The word *very* is usually superfluous. Especially acquire the art of weeding out phrases and clauses (see § 94).

· · · · · · · ·

INTRODUCTION AND CONCLUSION.

125. It is not easy to lay down precise rules for the employment of paragraphs of Introduction and Conclusion.

Are they always necessary? The ordinary text-book of rhetoric seems to teach that they are. Thus:

> Every theme, when complete, consists of three parts—the Introduction, the Discussion, and the Conclusion.[2]

Another term for the Discussion is the Body of the discourse.

There are grave objections to the doctrine as thus put. The whole theory of Introduction and Conclusion, in fact, is applicable to the preparing of orations, public discourses, essays, books, and other matter for print, rather than to the writing of school and college compositions. (See §§ 20, 21, 206.)

In a paper of 600 or 800 or even 1000 words there is little or no room for a formal beginning and ending. The scholar will do better to content himself with his working plan, first draught, and revision, securing thereby the advantages of simplicity and directness.

· · · · · · · ·

In the preceding paper I have made some general observations on the Christmas festivities of England, and am tempted to illustrate them by some anecdotes of a Christmas passed in the country; in perusing which I would most courteously invite my reader to lay aside the austerity of wisdom, and to put on that genuine holiday spirit which is tolerant of folly and anxious only for amusement.—IRVING: *The Stage-Coach*.

The Conclusion should be a summing-up and application. Thus Irving ends his Christmas descriptions with two paragraphs. In the first he answers the supposed objection:

"To what purpose is all this; how is the world to be made wiser by this talk?"

with the assertion that his object is not to instruct, but to please. This goes back directly to the paragraph of introduction, quoted above. Then comes the final paragraph:

What, after all, is the mite of wisdom that I could throw into the mass of knowledge; or how am I sure that my sagest deductions may be safe guides for the opinions of others? But in writing to amuse, if I fail, the only evil is my own disappointment. If, however, I can, by any lucky chance, in these days of evil, rub out one wrinkle from the brow of care, or beguile the heavy heart of one moment of sorrow; if I can now and then penetrate through the gathering film of misanthropy, prompt a benevolent view of human nature, and make my reader more in good-humor with his fellow-beings and himself, surely, surely I shall not then have written entirely in vain.—IRVING: *The Christmas Dinner*.

From Irving, as a representative author not too far above the reach of the ordinary student, one lesson at least can be learned, namely, to make introductions and conclusions direct, specific, *to the point*. But, since the young writer is too apt to turn them into a mere exhibition of glittering generalities and commonplace, we are perfectly justified in saying to him: If you cannot make them as they should be, *omit them altogether*.

126. Link-Paragraph.—The nature of this is discussed and illustrated in §18. In a short composition there is scarcely room for one. But in a composition of some length, *e.g.,* one that seems to require an introduction and a conclusion, such a paragraph may be a desirable feature. By means of it the writer can sum up the details of description or of narration before passing to a different part of the subject. It is especially useful in exposition and in argument, as a means of summing up phenomena pointing to a common cause, or causes operating toward a common result. In addition to the quotations in §18, the following deserves careful study. In it Burke sums up the six causes or *sources* of the peculiar spirit of liberty in America, sketching briefly that spirit in its

outward manifestations. The first sentence of the succeeding paragraph is also given here, to exhibit Burke's manner of passing to a fresh aspect of his subject:

> Then, sir, from these six capital sources: of Descent; of Form of Government; of Religion in the Northern Provinces; of Manners in the Southern; of Education; of the Remoteness of Situation from the First Mover of Government; from all these causes a fierce Spirit of Liberty has grown up. It has grown with the growth of the people in your Colonies, and increased with the increase of their wealth; a Spirit that, unhappily meeting with an exercise of Power in England, which, however, lawful, is not reconcileable to any ideas of Liberty, much less with theirs, has kindled this flame that is ready to consume us.
>
> I do not mean to commend either the Spirit in this excess, or the moral causes which produce it, etc.—BURKE: *Conciliation*, p. 134.

NOTE

1. Wendell, *English Composition*, p. 103.

2. Williams, *Composition and Rhetoric*, p. 271; see also D. J. Hill, *Elements of Rhetoric and Composition*, p. 16. On the other hand, see the caustic remarks of Wendell, *English Composition*, p. 167, upon the impulse "to preface something in particular by at least a paragraph of nothing in particular, bearing to the real matter in hand a relation not more inherently intimate than that of the tuning of violins to a symphony."

Robert Grosvenor Valentine
"On Criticism of Themes by Students"
Technology Review 2 (1901)

ଛକ *A former instructor in the Harvard program, Valentine taught at MIT from 1896 to 1899 and from 1901 to 1902, where he developed the interactive classroom model he recounts in this article. (Gertrude Buck praises Valentine's program in "Recent Trends in the Teaching of English Composition," chap. 4, p. 241.) When Frank Aydelotte arrived at MIT, he established a completely different, much more ideas-based writing curriculum. (For an account of Valentine's years at MIT see Russell 109–17.)*

This article demonstrates some innovative notions about group work. Valentine reprints some student themes with corrections and reactions by classmates.

THE THEMES PRINTED HERE ARE PRECISE COPIES OF THEMES written by Freshmen at the Massachusetts Institute of Technology. Some of these themes will give the reader too low an idea of the abilities of the Institute Freshmen. To present fair specimens of the work in English composition is not the aim of this paper. The object is to tell of a plan, tried last year, of which the chief characteristic is that criticism of themes is done largely by the students.

The details of methods used must be spoken of to some extent in order to make clear the principles on which the work rests. In applying these principles, each teacher will of course have his own scheme.

The student takes home the theme of another, and writes his criticism upon it in red ink. This work counts as half of his work for the week; his own theme, as the other half. His mark is, therefore, the sum of the parts of two fifties. As the next step, both the writer of the theme and the critic study it with the instructor in a consultation of from five to twenty minutes. The records are so kept that, when a man comes for consultation, he talks over all his own themes and also his criticism of other themes. Thus, in the end, the student both gives and receives criticism which is careful and full, and of which the inaccuracies are pointed out by the instructor. Relieved of drudgery, the instructor is enabled to put his whole force on whatever is each student's most vital need.

This method succeeds better with some classes than with others. Classes, like individuals, are sociable, retiring, light-headed, dull, bright, capable of working well only in leading-strings or capable of themselves hacking their way to power. Different as classes are, the work here explained should be useful to them all in the hands of a first-class teacher, and probably, if his method be right, in those of a poor one. Under this system a poor teacher may possibly become less of a drag; for, if the method is capable of living, it has its life firmly seated within itself, and the teacher becomes, like the manager of one department of a corporation, potentially greater for good, but with less power to do harm.

To the student the immediate results of this work form a sure foundation for the best use of his abilities, both while he is an undergraduate and when he enters upon his profession. At the end of a lecture, writer and critic have been seen, in the class-room or on the stairs or steps, in attitudes of discussion that at a bound put English composition into the realm of vital affairs. What spectacles and arguments take place among the lodgings is unknown; but it can hardly be doubted that much good is done there, too, since the discussions noticed, though often energetic, are anything but incoherent. Last year several students did such effective work in criticism, and the help they were able to give was so gladly received by their fellows that they were equivalent to an addition to the instructing force, with full pay, in benefit to themselves. As the work progresses, the qualities developed in the student are precisely those which will be most valuable to him in his work in the world. He becomes wide-eyed in seeing faults, workmanlike in the correction of them, sportsmanlike, hitting hard, and giving and demanding fair play. All this he learns to do with dignity and courtesy.

One of the methods for starting this work is to have the writer of the theme, before he begins to write, make a brief character sketch of some person to whom the theme is to be written. In such cases it becomes the critic's duty to put himself into the mental attitude of this reader. To make the work of more meaning to the men, several devices have been used. Sometimes students hand in requests for themes on subjects about which they wish to know. The instructor then reads these requests to the class, and such men as think they can give the information wanted volunteer to try. Often they make the acquaintance of the questioners, and the work is thus made so much the more telling. Again, the subjects and titles of themes handed in are read to the class, and the themes are distributed for criticism, as far as possible, to the men who desire them.

The following theme illustrates some of the points already mentioned, and will make the remaining remarks more clear. The corrections which the student makes on the body of the theme are given here in the wide margin. His comment is printed at the end of the theme across the whole page.

TROUT FISHING IN A BROOK IN THE WOODS

ADDRESSED TO A FISHERMAN WHO THINKS IT TOO MUCH TROUBLE TO SIT
ON A WHARF OR IN A BOAT AND WAIT FOR FISH TO COME TO HIS LINE

This sentence might very well have been omitted. It is not directly connected with the subject.

*great numbers

Fishing for trout in a brook which runs through a dense woods, is a rather difficult task, but it is in such brooks that trout are found in greatest quantities,* and this is what a true fisherman wants rather than an easy time.

Reconstruct for emphasis.

Going along in a thick woods, without carrying anything, is hard enough; but when a person has to drag a long pole and line with him, it becomes doubly difficult.

I don't understand this operation.

*to weave his line

*vines (probably)

*bushes. Finally he again gets, etc.

*casts; then he must again go through the place, where he can, . . . with some safety. (at end for emphasis)

*Often a fish bites and does not get hooked. When this happens

2nd paragraph
*these difficulties which he

*a man who fishes in a brook has to endure other annoyances. He gets (1) his face etc. he gets (2) . . . his . . . his and (3) he has his face etc.

Why do you change your person from the indefinite 3rd to the 2nd, from "one" and "he" to "you"? (on this page)

*though exciting, unpleasant.

"Trout fishing in a brook

It is hard enough to get along in a thick woods without carrying anything, but with a long pole and a line attached to its end, it is very troublesome.

Sometimes to go as short a distance as ten feet along the edge of a brook in the woods, one has to drop the butt end of his pole, wind the line around the point, and then weave * it through a perfect net work of small trees, viands, * and bushes * until he gets to an open space large enough to again allow him to take his pole at its proper end. At this point he has to unwind his line, sometimes to make but one or two casts, * and then again repeat the trouble of getting to another place where he can with some safety cast his line again.

* Often times a fish will bite and not get hooked, and when such cases happen a long time is spent in getting the line unfastened from limbs of trees which project directly over the stream.

Besides the * difficulties one has in making his way along the edges of a brook in the woods, there * are many annoyances to be put up with, such as getting your face into the webs of large spiders, getting your face and hands scratched, and fine needles and small sticks down your back by way of your collar.

All these trials, with an occasional tumble into the water from trying to lean too far over the bank, go to make trout fishing * come under the head of sport.

is unpleasant," is the general
thought of your theme. Why
not end with this thought.
Your last six words "side-
track" the purpose of the
theme.
  According to your last sentence, you do not consider fishing in open water a sport. Is
that so?

As a whole, the theme has unity because it is all about fishing. But that
organised unity, which makes a theme forceful, is lacking. There are a number
of thoughts, but they seem all thrown together.
  Your sentences are, positively too long. You have exactly 13 thoughts and
you should have that many sentences. You have only 8.
  Then you have 7 Paragraphs for 8 sentences. This is evidently too many.
Two are sufficient for your theme.
  Put *one* thought in a sentence and form paragraphs!!!

To make the student feel that his criticisms and comments upon
themes can be really of value is no easy task. His perfectly natural
scepticism in this respect is an almost insurmountable barrier. It is
crossed, however, as he comes to recognize what it means for him to see
another student's work. In this light he writes both his criticisms and his
own themes. The rubbish and undue confidences so often written to
instructors in English prove that instructors have often been held by the
college man to be in nature something between a god and a waste-paper
basket. This is an animal for which no student can mistake his fellow.
Before another student he becomes humanly conscious of the real nature
of the demands upon him and of his own shortcomings. At precisely this
moment he begins to improve. Work that "would do" for the more
abstract instructor he is ashamed to hand to his concrete classmate. His
writing gains in arrangement and neatness. He becomes more simple and
direct in his statements. His themes grow to mean something to the men
they are written for. His criticisms do likewise, and so steadily win his
own respect and care.
  These advantages to a composition are much the same as those of
electric lighting and efficient police to a city. Above these is a further and
constructive advantage. A college man soon finds that his fellows will

not care about him unless he makes himself cared for. It is necessary for him to win himself friends. If he does not come out of himself, he will be left alone; and, since he can hardly escape his fighting nature, he will struggle with phantoms. To help him to know the real men around him is one of the powers of English composition, and one which the writer of this paper believes can be made of great advantage to composition itself. When the student graduates, the reports he will write, the arguments he will make, will depend for their success not only on his scientific training, but on his knowledge of men and on the training he has had in expressing himself to men. Under the plan here outlined the student has brought home to him the importance of this training.

A CONTINUOUS DEMAND

*When going in to bat in a game etc.	* Starting to play a game of baseball, one steps to the plate with his bat, and faces the pitcher * and right here, at the beginning, he must start * in to forget everything else and concentrate his whole mind on his * game. From the time the pitcher begins his preliminary motions until the ball reaches him, he must fasten his eyes * right on the ball, to find out, as nearly as he can, just when and how near * it will come to him. It may come straight, and as swiftly as a rifle bullet, or it may be a deceptive slow curve,* it may come right over the plate, or it may come high, low, out, or in. In any case * he must be ready, just as it reaches the plate, to either let it go by, or hit it in such a way as to send it to exactly * the right place. This he can do only by fixing his whole attention directly on the ball.
*pitcher. Right here etc.	
*begin	
*the	
*give the closest attention, in order to find out etc.	
*the ball	
*curve;	
*case,	
*to send it exactly to the right place. He can only do this by etc.	
	He gets a hit, or a base on balls,

*diminish his attention

*This sentence has three or four ideas in it. Two sentences are made by cutting it in two.

*advantage. He must be ready to utilize any opportunity

*a base

*Besides all this,

*should

*keep

*in order to take in every

*time. It may etc.

*liner; *go

   *Omit away

*judge

*and start for that place

This sentence is nearly a repetition of the main idea and is practically repeated in the beginning of the next paragraph.

*At all times he must keep in mind etc.

perhaps, and advances from the plate to the bases, but he can by no means let up * on his direct concentration of mind on the game. He must watch every motion of the pitcher and be ready, if the latter tries to catch him, to get back to his base instantly. * Besides this, he must watch the batter carefully, so that he may cooperate with him to the greatest advantage, be ready * to take advantage of any opportunity to steal his * base and be prepared, in case of any kind of a hit or emergency, to act immediately and in the best way. *For all of this it is absolutely necessary that he follow * the ball closely and centre * his mind right on the play.

His side gets out, and he goes into the field, and here, still, he must put the whole energy of his mind into the game, so * that as to take in every detail of the play. The ball is likely to be hit in his direction at any time *; it may be a fly, a ground ball, or a swift "liner": it may move * some distance in back of him, away * in front of him, or off to one side. At the crack of the bat he must decide * just where it will come, and be off to * that place instantly. To do this it is obvious that he must have his whole attention fastened on the game.

All through the game, therefore, he must devote to the play the entire strength of his mind. He must be wide awake to everything that is going on in the game. * He must at all times keep in mind every detail of the situation and be prepared for any emergency that may arise. His thoughts cannot wander away for an instant; in fact, he must shut everything else from his mind, and * as it were bury himself in his game.

* . . . bury himself in the

This theme is a theme of exposition. It tells just how a player has to concentrate his mind on the different parts of a ball game; at bat, on the bases, and in the field. It is perfectly logical that there should be four paragraphs in this theme. The first paragraph speaks of the player at bat, the next on the bases, the third in the field, and the fourth of the game in general. These are four distinct phases and each calls for a new paragraph.

The idea, and especially the expression of "Concentration of mind" is brought in a little too frequently and gets a little monotonous unless varied somewhat. There is also a little too much slang of the game; such expressions as "fasten his eye on the ball," etc.

. . . .

THE RECOVERY OF BY-PRODUCTS OF
THE BLAST FURNACE

The by-products of the blast furnace are about the same as those of the gas works, * but * the * conditions are much different. In the gas works a ton of coal produces about 10,000 cubic feet of gas which carried with it the products to be recovered. In the blast furnace a ton of coal produces from 130,000 * to 180,000 * cubic feet of gas with about the same amount of recoverable matter scattered through it. A group of blast furnaces each consuming about 1000 tons of coal per week will produce an enormous amount of gas. * Thus it appears that very much larger recovering apparatus would be required for the blast furnace gases than would be required for the gas of an ordinary gas

*. *Omit but. *The condition in which these by-products of the blast furnace is obtained is much different from the condition of the by-products of the gas works.

*Do not use figures.

*This has nothing to do with the subject therefore omit.

*Theme begins here.

*Omit but. It

*This is where your theme should begin, all that you have written thus far has nothing to do with the recovery of the by-products of the blast furnace.

Intended to say theme begins on preceding page.

*, *for

*are.

*place of them. *New Paragraph

*. *Omit and This tank.

*Do you mean sucked through the tar or do you mean forced through the tar?

*which is *gases (tar?)

*are

*Omit and. At

*from this washer at intervals and are conducted into a stor-

plant. * The gases from the blast furnaces have been used for many years for heating the air blast and also as fuel under the boilers, * but * it * has been only in comparatively recent years that a more extended use has been made, and valuable products extracted from them. * These products are ammonia and coal tar. The ammonia is generally converted into ammonium sulphate * as * this is the most convenient and salable form of ammonia.

The apparatus required for the recovery of these products generally consists of a preliminary washer for the gases, an atmospheric condensor, and scrubbers. In some places the scrubbers are done away with and two or more washers * used in their * stead.* * The preliminary washer consists of a large boiler-shaped tank with sloping bottom, * and * * is partly filled with tar. Through this tar the hot gases from the furnaces are drawn, * with the result that the water * in the tar * is partly evaporated and the gases * somewhat cooled, and * at * the same time the particles of tar and of dirt in the gases are caught and precipitated to the bottom of the tank. The heavier tars are drawn off * at intervals into a storage tank. The atmo-

age tank.

*up

* There

*in order

*I should like to know
how the gases pass from one
pipe to another; do they pass
up one pipe and then down
the next pipe etc.?

*Do these boards project
from the sides of the tank or
how are they set on edge?

*(into what?)

*How can water be
pumped from the last tank to
the next. I think you mean the
water is pumped from one tank
to the next tank, but you should
use a word which expresses
what you have in mind. *first
*tank *. *Omit so that. As
the result of the water flowing
through a number of tanks

Do you mean liquids if so

spheric condensors consist of a large
number of pipes set * vertically and far
enough apart to allow a free circulation
of air between them. These pipes are
from forty to fifty feet in height with a
diameter of one and a half to two and a
half feet, * and * are generally about
two hundred in number. The pipes are
placed in rows and arranged so that the
gas passes through everyone of them.
They are arranged however so that any
row of pipes may be cut out of the circuit * to be cleaned or repaired. At the
bottom of each row of pipes is a long
tank to receive the lighter tars and ammonia liquors which have condensed in
the pipes. *

The scrubbers are huge iron tanks
from fifty to one hundred feet in height
and ten to twenty-five feet in diameter.

These are filled with boards * set on
edge and placed very near together. This

thoroughly breaks up the gas * and allows full contact with the water which
continually runs over these boards. The
water * from the last * tank is pumped

to the next * and so on * so that * the
liquids * are somewhat condensed when
they leave the scrubbers. The gases are
thoroughly washed in these scrubbers

what liquids? Do you not
mean gases?

*pieces of

*Where has this fact been
shown? Never heard of it.

Answer (See Banerman's
"Metallurgy of Iron" p. 267
and the account of some experiments on the value of blast furnace gas as a producer of power
in the Engineering Magazines
of 1898 and others.)

*What has this to do with
the subject?

*This has absolutely nothing
to do with the recovery of the

and the remaining tar and ammonia removed. The gas now passes on to the
receiver.

Let us see the effect of this different *
apparatus on the gas. The gas comes from
the blast furnace at a temperature of
$400°-600°$ F, it enters the preliminary
washer where the gas is cooled to some
extent and much of the heavier tars and
dirt is removed. It then passes on to the
atmospheric condensors which, in hot
weather, are cooled by sprays of cold water. Here the gas is cooled to $70°$, or
lower, and the lighter tars and moisture
contained in the gas is condensed. The
scrubber removes the remaining ammonia and tar. The gas is now ready to be
used for heating the air blast, for burning under boilers, or to be used in gas
engines. The non purified gases from
the furnaces cannot be used in the gas
engines on account of the tar and also
moisture which is present, and, * as it
has been shown that in the gas engine
only 94.2 cubic feet of gas is required to
produce one horse power, while by burning under boilers 794 cubic feet are required, it will be seen that in this one
case a large saving has been

made.*

The tar is separated from the ammonia
liquors by gravitation. The tar is placed
in a still and oils of different grades are
produced.* These have small values as
illuminants except when used in a

by-products of the blast furnace.

*too vague.

*You should not assume
that the reader knows how the
sulphuric acid acts on the ammonia.

*. Each

lucigen or other blast lamp, but they are
good heat producers. The pitch which is
left behind is in demand for making
briquettes, and is used for asphalting
and roofing. The ammonia liquors are
placed in a suitable * still and the ammonia vapors are passed through sulphuric
acid.* This ammonium sulphate in addition to its value in chemistry is a valuable fertilizer.

From these furnaces all the fuel required by the iron works outside of that
consumed in the furnace itself is produced,* each * ton of coal produces
twenty-two or twenty-six pounds of ammonium sulphate, one hundred pounds
of pitch and about twenty gallons of oil.
The cost of one of these plants is considerable but the profits are large.

The main fault with this theme is that you did not stick to your subject.
You should begin your theme with "the gases from" on page one, and end with
"the scrubbers remove the remaining ammonia and tar" on page four. Of course
it is interesting to know what the purified gas is used for, but unless you change
you title to :—"The recovery of the by-products of the blast furnace and some of
their uses;" you must omit the uses of the by-products. You are careless in your
use of words; for instance the word "last" at the top of page three, you do not
mean the "last tank" and so should not use the word "last." Most of your
sentences contain but one idea. This is very good. But there are a few sentences
which have more than one idea, for instance the long sentence at the bottom of
page two beginning with:—"Through this tar, etc." This sentence should be
broken up into at least two sentences one beginning with "Through this tar,"
the other "At the same time." The last page of your theme seems as though it
were written simply to fill up space. It is better to write four pages than to write
five and give the impression that the fifth page is only written to make the
theme five pages long. In many places you leave the subject very vague, for
instance you say at the bottom of page three "the gas breaks up." You should tell
how and into what it breaks up. In writing this theme you should tell a great
deal more about how the tars are separated and how the oils are produced. For

these two products are of much more importance than the gas. You confine yourself too much to the purifying of the gas and not enough to the other by-products.

It would be impossible to give here themes to illustrate or to prove all the statements made in this paper; nor is it needful. One point alone is essential. For the plan proposed to be of use it must have adequate foundation in the critical abilities of the students. The results shown above seem to prove that, at least in the classes in which it has been tried, the work has this foundation. The method has proved excellent in its direct bearing upon the teaching of composition, and perhaps its indirect effects may be more valuable still in bringing into closer relation the student's work in the class-room and his experiences in daily life.

University of Illinois
"Outline of Rhetoric 1" (1907)

ᣚ *This four-page pamphlet provides first-semester composition students with the bare bones of the course requirements, stated in a bureaucratic manner. This kind of booklet illustrates the kind of mass production model that first-year composition followed at large midwestern universities. Interestingly, the reading list includes Le Baron Russell Briggs's collection* School, College and Character, *a book perpetuating an Eastern, elitist approach to the character-building qualities of postsecondary education. The juxtaposition of the rule booklet, Briggs's book, and* Walden, *reveals more than a little inconsistency at the heart of the Illinois program. No doubt books like Briggs's, as well as Fulton's* College Life, *were chosen to introduce young people to the traditional ideals of higher education, ideals which were not always part of the cultural heritage of the first-generation college students flocking to large public universities.*

This advertising notice was originally printed on the pamphlet's back cover:

HOSPITAL ASSOCIATION

Fifty cents a semester pays your hospital bill in case of sickness. You should see the new students' ward. It is as attractive as a private room. Join now while you have the money. The fee may be paid at the Business Office; or to Dean Kollock, Professor Baker, or Dean Clark.

THE TEXT BOOK

Fulton's Composition and Rhetoric.
Recitations on Wednesday or Thursday.

THE READING

October, Briggs' School, College and Character.
November, Macaulay, History of England, Chapter III.
December, A novel or a volume of short stories.
January, Parkman's Oregon Trail, or Thoreau's Walden, or any other approved book containing description.

THE THEMES

Two short themes a week of about two pages will be required, due on the first and third meeting of the class.

A long theme of about six pages will be due on October 18 or 19, November 15 or 16, December 13 or 14, and January 17 or 18. A careful plan for each long theme will be required one week before the theme itself, and will count for one short theme.

THE QUIZES

A one hour quiz will be given near the middle of November and one near the middle of January.

A FEW DIRECTIONS

1. All themes should be on theme paper and written in ink.
2. Leave a margin of one and one-half inches on the left side of the paper.
3. Write the title on the first line, and leave the second line blank, beginning the body of the theme on the third line.
4. Fold the theme lengthwise through the middle from right to left, with the single edge on the right. Endorse on the first three lines as follows:

Rhetoric 1 A,
John J. Jones
September 20, 1907

5. Themes not properly endorsed, and themes in which there is bad spelling, will not be given a grade higher than C.

6. Do not use abbreviations in endorsement.

University of Minnesota
"Instructions to Students in Rhetoric 1–2" (1913)

&❧ *This pamphlet, distributed to all composition students at one of the largest state universities, sets the tone by admonishing on its cover, "Read carefully. Paste in your text-book or note-book." This pamphlet supplies the official rules and regulations for a heavily administered course. (Minnesota had separated rhetoric from English since the 1890s, running composition as part of a distinct program for which the English department took no responsibility.)*

PREPARATION OF MANUSCRIPT

1. Manuscript which is illegible, slovenly, or carelessly prepared will not be read.

2. Write with dark ink; use standard rhetoric paper; write on one side of the sheet only.

3. Do not fold or crumple the sheets, or pin them together, or turn down the corners.

4. Indent for a paragraph at least one inch. Do not leave a blank space at the end of a sentence except at the close of a paragraph.

5. Put the title on the first line of the first page only. Leave one ruled line blank before beginning the theme.

6. Write your name, file number, theme number, and the page number in the upper right hand corner of each page of your manuscript. On pages other than the first, initials may be substituted for the name. Use Arabic numerals for all notations.

The following is a model for the form in which themes should appear:

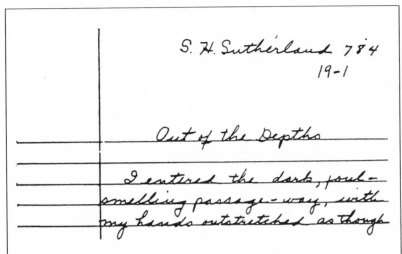

S. H. Sutherland 784
19-1

Out of the Depths

I entered the dark, foul-
smelling passage-way, with
my hands outstretched as though

Explanation: 784 indicates the number of the student's file in the theme room; 19 the number of the theme; 1 the number of the page. The next pages of the same theme would be numbered 19-2, 19-3, etc.

GRADES

A student's grade is based upon his class work and examinations. Four grades, A, B, C, and D, are given for work done satisfactorily. Work not done satisfactorily is marked E (condition), or F (failure). Work of a satisfactory character but not finished is marked I (incomplete).

An "incomplete" must be removed within one month after the opening of the following semester; otherwise it becomes a "condition." A "condition," if not removed before the opening of the corresponding semester of the following year, becomes a "failure." A "condition" in rhetoric incurred because of unsatisfactory theme work will not be removed merely by examination. The student will be required to do additional writing sufficient to show that he has overcome his deficiency.

A "failure" in Rhetoric 1 or 2 must be removed by pursuing the work again in class the next time the course is offered.

A grade of F will be given to a theme or essay for any one of the following offenses:

1. Misspelling[1] of three or more words such as those given in Mac-Cracken's *Manual of Good English,* VI, 108 (p. 233).
2. Two sentences with violent changes of construction: Mac-Cracken, II, 53, IC (p. 109); II, 61 (p. 125).
3. Two instances of faulty reference: MacCracken, II, 19 (p. 69); II, 62 (p. 126).
4. Two dangling modifiers: MacCracken, II, 37 (p. 92); 38 (p. 95).
5. Two errors in agreement: MacCracken, II, 30 (p. 78).
6. Two instances of failure to separate the clause of a compound sentence by any mark of punctuation: MacCracken, IV, 76 (p. 177).
7. One incomplete sentence: MacCracken, 11, 56, 2 (p. 118).
8. Two instances of sentences run together: MacCracken, IV, 76, Note (p. 178).
9. A noticeable number of improprieties or barbarisms.
10. A marked lack of unity in sentence, paragraph, or whole composition.
11. A marked lack of coherence in sentence, paragraph, or whole composition.
12. Any combination, equally serious, of such faults.

If a theme which receives a grade of F would have deserved, except for technical faults, a grade of A, B, or C, it may be given a double grade. In determining the mark of the student for the semester, only the higher of the two grades will be considered, provided the grade of F has ceased to appear. Any student, however, whose themes are repeatedly given the grade of F will receive a mark of F for the semester.

REVISION

1. A passing grade will not be given to any student at the end of a semester unless all assigned themes have been properly revised and are on file, arranged in numerical order.
2. Return revised themes to the instructor within one week.
3. Do not remove themes from the theme room without the permission of the theme clerk.
4. Make all corrections, however slight. Use *red ink* for corrections.

5. Do not erase the instructor's correction signs; write over them when necessary.

6. Draw a line through any word, phrase, or sentence that is not to be retained. Parentheses do not indicate omission.

7. Do not rewrite the theme unless directed to do so. Should it be necessary to rewrite, *return the original* with the rewritten copy, marking the latter in red ink beneath the theme number "Rewritten."

8. Revise carefully and intelligently. The grade for the semester will be based upon both the revised work and the original copy.

MARKS USED IN CRITICISM

amb.—Ambiguous.

ant.—Antecedent needs attention.

awk. or K—Awkward expression.

bal.—Balance in construction lacking.

C or cap.—Error in capitalization.

cf.—Compare two expressions underlined.

cl.—Not clear.

cnst.—Construction faulty.

coh.—Coherence of sentence, paragraph, or theme faulty.

con.—Connection lacking.

cond.—Condense.

D—Consult dictionary.

dic.—Poor diction.

emph.—Emphasis of sentence, paragraph, or theme faulty.

Eng.—Not good English.

exp.—Expand.

fig.—Error in use of figurative language.

gr.—Ungrammatical.

inv.—Involved.

kp.—Out of keeping with style of essay.

l. c.—Lower case. Do not capitalize.

MS—Careless manuscript.

p.—Punctuation.

phr.—Poor phrasing.

ref.—Reference uncertain.

rep.—Repetition.

sp.—Spelling.

tense seq.—Sequence of tenses.
tr.—Transpose words indicated.
trans.—Transition faulty.
trite.—Hackneyed or commonplace expression.
U—Unity of sentence, paragraph, or theme faulty.
V—Vague.
wk.—Weak.
δ—Omit.
?—Truth or accuracy questionable.
1, 2, 3, 4, etc.—Rearrange in conformity with numbers.
X or ! !—Error obvious.
∧—Word or words omitted.
¶—Paragraph.
No ¶—Do not paragraph.
‖ *cnst.*—Parallel construction.

PLAGIARISM

The themes assigned, unless it is explicitly stated that they are exercises in selection or reorganization, are to be the original work of the student. Whenever he has occasion to use the language of another, even if only a single phrase, he should indicate the fact by quotation marks. The borrowing of ideas from another should be indicated by marginal or footnote references to the original. Failure to observe these rules scrupulously will be regarded as cheating; and the offense will be reported to the Student Council.

LATE THEMES

A theme is late, if, for any reason, it is not handed in at the beginning of the hour for which it is assigned. A late theme will be excused only when the student gives satisfactory evidence of his inability to present it on time. Except in cases of extended illness, all late themes must be made up within two days.

. . . .

NOTE

1. The following simplified spellings are permissible: altho, catalog, decalog, demagog, pedagog, program, prolog, tho, thoro, thorofare.

Frances Berkeley Young and Karl Young
Freshman English: A Manual (1914)

This is the thoroughly revised version of Frances Campbell Berkeley, A College Course in Writing from Models *(1910).* Freshman English *provides an extended analysis of the process of writing a college theme; it encourages strong expressions of opinion and personal writing, and prints student essays in first-draft-revision form in their text. Young (1879–1943) received his B.A. from Michigan (1901) and Ph.D. from Harvard (1907). An eminent scholar, he became MLA president in 1940.*

THE PLANNING AND WRITING OF THEMES

It is now generally agreed that skill in written expression is attained only by practice. In most of our schools and colleges, therefore, students are given a generous amount of this necessary drill through the device of written themes. In order that this drill may be really profitable to the student, he should understand, at the outset, what themes really are, and how he is to go about the writing of them.

Many a Freshman, no doubt, has, at one time or another, been driven to the conclusion that theme-writing is merely a device for exposing the grammatical errors of a bungling student to the ruthless correction of an expert instructor. This conclusion results naturally enough from the circumstance,—almost inevitable,—that the greater proportion of correction marks on themes at the opening of a course in Freshman English have to do with elementary errors of grammar and usage. This rigorous attention to elementary faults, moreover, must continue unabated in any good course in composition, until such faults finally disappear altogether. It is true, then, that the themes of Freshmen must be frankly used as exercises in grammar, until the writing of Freshmen finally becomes grammatical.

Freshman themes, however, are far from being mere exercises in grammar. They are, as a matter of fact, primarily expressions of thought. Every student should begin promptly to regard his writing,—and to have it regarded,—as the sincere and thoughtful expression of his own observation and opinion. The fundamental value of any theme lies not in its grammatical correctness,—important as that may be,—but in the thought communicated. A frank and living opinion, even though it be distorted by bad grammar, has more real worth than an idle platitude presented in faultless style. In order to be valuable the thought need not be profound, or novel, or even convincing; the one requirement is that it be sincere and accurate. If the student expresses honestly and precisely what he thinks and sees, he may be sure of the reader's real respect, and he may fairly regard himself as a "real author."

In his role of "real author," then, the student enjoys the utmost freedom in range of observation and in variety of opinion. At the same time, he binds himself to follow the processes through which all successful prose writing has been produced.

When we survey the work of successful writers, and try to discover the secret of their success, we find that they all agree in this fundamental practice: they all follow a *plan*. Although the charm of the finished masterpiece may withdraw our attention from the fundamental design of the work, we may be sure that such a design exists, and that by seeking we may find it. As we analyse the masterpiece, we see clearly that the writer knew what he was about before he began to write: he had his precise subject clearly in mind, he had summoned forth his observations and reflections upon the subject, and he had arranged his ideas in some sort of logical order. In learning to write effectively, then, every one must submit to three logical processes or stages of thought:

1. Finding the special subject.
2. Analysing the special subject.
3. Arranging the divisions of the special subject logically and effectively.

Let us now consider each of these logical steps.

The Planning of Themes

1. Finding the Special Subject

Finding something to write about ought not to be a painful process, for the minds of all of us are teeming with opinions, prejudices, preferences, memories, incidents, and designs. Daily life abounds in matters about which anybody might write naturally and enthusiastically. The student's real difficulty, then, is not in finding things to write about, but in making the scope of the proposed subject fit the limits within which the subject must be treated. If, for example, a student is asked to write a theme of 300 words, he obviously should not try to discuss such a subject as *History*, for the number of ideas included in that term is far too large to be treated within the limits of 300 words. *My Reasons for Disliking the Study of History*, however, might be very interestingly developed even within so small a compass. It appears, then, that one must not be content with selecting a general subject for discussion, but must decide what particular part of the subject may be treated on a scale appropriate to the limitations imposed. This logical procedure we have called *Finding the special subject*.

2. *Analysing the Special Subject*

Assuming that I have found a special subject about which I have some definite ideas, I may next proceed to an analysis of what I propose to say. As I ponder upon the subject *My Reasons for Disliking the Study of History*, for example, the following definite observations occur to me:

1. The events of remote ages are uninteresting to me.
2. Our instructor in history is not a genial person.
3. Manual training and similar practical studies should be encouraged in the modern high school.
4. I cannot remember a long series of detailed facts.
5. It is not pleasant to sit still for an hour listening to the glib recitations of one or two "grinds."
6. The courses in history are not properly correlated with the other elements in the curriculum.
7. The disputes of popes and kings have nothing to do with modern life in America.
8. Our text-book in history is wretchedly printed, and is hard to understand.

In scrutinizing this list of reasons we must first ask these questions: Are all of these observations worth making? Is each of them really vital to me, the writer? Have I really something to say on each of the points mentioned? In response to such questions the writer will probably confess that on No. 6 he has, as a matter of fact, nothing to say, and that he inserted this conventional observation merely because he once heard the teacher say something of the sort, or because it sounded impressive. Under these circumstances, then, No. 6 must certainly be dropped.

Another test that the list must withstand is embodied in the following questions: Do all of these observations apply strictly to the precise subject in hand? Do any of them suggest irrelevant digressions? Are any of them "off the track"? Certainly No. 3 cannot withstand this test, for although the proposition is worth discussing for its own sake, it does not present a direct reason for disliking the study of history. It appears, then, that No. 3 also must be rejected.

A further challenge appears in the following questions: Is each of these reasons important enough to stand by itself? May not two or more of the less important reasons be grouped as a single substantial reason? Although writers might disagree as to the precise relative importance of this point or that, one may fairly suggest that whereas Nos. 1, 4, and 7 may be regarded as essential reasons, Nos. 2, 5, and 8 have to do only with superficial details. It may be, then, that Nos. 2, 5, and 8 should be combined into a single substantial observation, or subordinated to some unobtrusive position, or omitted altogether.

And now arises a final query, as to whether the reason placed first ought really to come first, and whether the remaining reasons follow in a sensible and effective order. This query leads to a consideration of the third logical step in the planning of a theme.

3. Arranging the Divisions of the Special Subject Logically and Effectively

Every one has observed that the order in which a succession of ideas arises casually in the mind is not inevitably the logical order. Ideas commonly occur to us at random, suggested often by mere whimsical associations. It should be remembered, moreover, that an arrangement which is intelligible to the writer, who knows all about his subject, may not be intelligible to the reader, who may possess no information in advance. In arranging his ideas, then, the writer must always take the point of view of the reader, and must follow such an order as will unfold the thought gradually and clearly. What this order shall be in a particular case must, of course, be determined by the nature of the subject in hand, and by the sort of reader to be addressed. A man who had never seen an explosion engine, for example, could not understand the working of such an engine until he had first been enlightened as to its parts and construction.

Quite as important as the order in which ideas are to be arranged, is the manner in which they are to be subordinated one to another. It has been suggested above that our several ideas upon a given subject are not, usually, of equal importance. Whereas one idea may be fundamental in the discussion, another may concern only a superficial detail. Our ideas, then, must be grouped not only in such a way that the order may be intelligible, but also in a manner that will clearly indicate their just relations to one another.

In order to apply these simple principles, let us consider a student's outline for a theme:

THE GAME OF TENNIS

I. Playing the game.
1. Counting.
2. Special points of skill.
II. The court.
1. Shape and dimensions.
2. Kind of turf.
3. Boundary lines.
III. The equipment.
1. Racquet.
2. Balls.
IV. The net.
1. Material.
2. Dimensions.

This plan clearly violates both of the general principles discussed above. In the first place, the order of ideas is not such as to be intelligible to the uninformed reader. The writer would launch us into the actual playing of the game before explaining to us the material equipment. In the second place, the outline gives an entirely false impression as to the relative importance of the several ideas. The two chief points seem really to be (1) the equipment, and (2) the playing of the game. Upon the basis of these two points the outline may be revised into the following:

I. The equipment.
1. The court.
a. Kind of turf.
b. Dimensions and lines.
c. The net.
2. Racquets and balls.

II. The playing of the game.
  1. The process of play.
  2. The method of scoring.
  3. Special points of skill.

This outline is more logical and satisfactory than the first one because it places like matters under the same heading,—*e.g.*, turf, net, racquets, and balls, under equipment,—and because it explains the equipment *before* it introduces the actual process of play.

Reverting now to our proposed theme of 300 words on the subject *My Reasons for Disliking the Study of History*, we find that the eight observations which we formulated by analysis may be reduced and subordinated into some such outline as the following:

I. The subject-matter of history is not interesting to me, for
  1. I am not interested in the struggles of popes and kings in remote ages.
  2. I cannot remember a long series of detailed facts.
II. The subject is not presented in an attractive manner, for
  1. The instructor is not a genial person.
  2. The text-book is inadequate.
  3. The recitations are monopolized by one or two "grinds."

On the basis of this outline one might readily proceed with the writing of an orderly theme, which would consist, presumably, of two substantial paragraphs.

These, then, are the simple but fundamental processes involved in expressing one's thoughts in writing. The student must first learn to reduce his subject to a scope appropriate to the conditions under which he is writing. He must then discover the definite ideas which should be taken up under this limitation of the subject. Finally, he must arrange his ideas in an intelligible and logical order. Upon the completion of these processes he is ready to write.

The Writing of Themes

In a Freshman course in English students are, as a rule, asked to write "short" themes frequently, and "long" themes at stated and less frequent intervals. The value of short themes at the outset of a course is obvious: (1) they are easy to plan; (2) they furnish an admirable basis for practice in grammatical accuracy, correct sentence construction, and appropriate diction,—in short, for all the elementary problems of written expression. We may begin, therefore, by a survey of the technique of the short theme. Let us take a subject for a short theme, analyse and outline it, and then study themes actually written by students on this subject.

Short Themes

We may suppose that a class of Freshmen have been asked to explain the chief differences that they have observed between a student's experience in the high school and his experience in college. The subject may be phrased as *The Chief Differences that I Observe between High School and College*. Upon this subject such ideas as the following come readily to mind:

(1) College life is pleasanter than high school life, because at college one's life is much freer, both for study and for recreation.

(2) College work is harder than high school work, because in college one's work is less closely supervised, and one has fewer mechanical aids in being diligent.

(3) The methods of teaching in the two places are very different, for in the high school the work is based largely on a few definite text-books, whereas college work is often based upon elaborate lectures, and upon a formidable list of books of reference.

(4) College life is lonelier than high school life, for during the high school years one lives at home, and one knows everybody in town, whereas at college one lives in a dreary boarding-house, and one is bewildered by the enormous number of strangers.

This brief enumeration of ideas is, of course, far from exhaustive. The number of aspects in which the high school and the college may be compared is, as a matter of fact, unlimited, and any alert observer would wish to add to the suggestions made above. To some persons, moreover, certain of these suggestions may seem positively erroneous. The normal writer, then, after analysing the subject, would extend, eliminate, and recombine his ideas, until, upon the basis of a firm outline, he should begin actually to write.

Without narrowing the subject further, let us see what four different students actually wrote upon the proposed subject. Their preliminary outlines are, unfortunately, not available. From their themes, indeed, we may be driven to the conclusion that these students used no outlines at all!

THEME I

In the High School at home all the students were supposed to begin work at nine o'clock; at this hour the attendance for the morning session was taken, and the students were expected to be present even if they had no classes before noon. The afternoon session began at one-thirty o'clock and closed at four.

5   All the studying was done in one main room, and all the classes were conducted in one building. In the main room, a desk was assigned to each student, in which he kept his books and at which he studied.

At college, the individual instructors take the attendance, so that if a student has no classes in the morning he may remain at home. The regular University exercises commence at eight o'clock and continue until twelve; they begin at one-thirty and stop at five-thirty in the afternoon.

10   Sometimes the students have first a class, then a free hour. Most of the studying is done at home, during these free study periods. The classes in different branches of work are conducted in different buildings. The students keep their books at home, and are given desks or lockers only in those buildings where such an arrangement is necessary. The Freshman in college in confused by this lack of a study-room, and it takes him two or three months, usually, to become accustomed to the change.

15

Ignoring, for the present, the vocabulary and the sentence-structure in this theme, let us criticise it merely as to (1) subject-matter and (2) plan.

(1) As a whole the subject-matter is dull. The aspects of student-life chosen for discussion are the mere material surroundings and the external machinery. All matters of real human interest are omitted, and of the broad difference in method between high school and university instruction no mention is made.

(2) Since this writer has divided his theme into four paragraphs, we may assume that he has in mind some four topics. Let us see what they are:

1. Periods of attendance in the high school.
2. Study and recitations in the high school.
3. Periods of attendance at college.
4. Study and recitations at college.

Certainly the four paragraphs cannot be justified. A possible re-arrangement is suggested by the following outline:

I. High School Work.
  1. Periods of attendance.
  2. Study and recitation.
II. College Work.
  1. Periods of attendance.
  2. Study and recitation.

From such a plan we might expect two clearly differentiated paragraphs: one dealing with the high school, the other, with the college. A second student writes as follows:

THEME II

(1) At college the student is allowed many more liberties than he is at high school. (2) At college he is not kept in an assembly or study-room when he is not attending classes, but is permitted to go home and study or work when he pleases. (3) In the high school, on the contrary, he is boxed up in a study-hall and is placed under the immediate control of the teacher in charge. (4) If a man possesses a normal amount of ability at high school, he is the man of the hour, the genius whose uplifting influence permeates every corner of its life, and the man who represents it in all contests with other institutions, whether such contests are mental or physical, athletic or oratorical. (5) At college, the same man finds that he is but one little drop in an ocean of his fellow men. (6) In the high school, a student is under the direct control of a teacher, and in a certain sense is dependent upon that teacher; whereas in college a student is taught to become independent and to shift for himself. (7) In other words, the boy becomes a man, gains confidence in himself, and learns his first lesson in fighting the battle of life.

As far as its content is concerned, this theme is, perhaps, a little better than the preceding one. The writer shows a more fundamental interest in his subject, and he has a larger vocabulary than his predecessor. As to structure, however, the theme is hopelessly chaotic. The material here jumbled into one paragraph should be arranged in two paragraphs, on the following topics:

  1. The relative freedom of college and of high school.
  2. The relative intensity of competition in college and in the high school.

In the rewritten version, sentences 1, 2, 3, 6, 7 would be arranged in paragraph 1, in the order named. Sentences 4 and 5 partly embody the idea of paragraph 2. A transition sentence and a topic-sentence for paragraph 2 should be formulated, in addition, and a sentence in conclusion would be desirable. The student's revision in this case resulted in the following:

THEME II (REVISED)

1. At college the student is allowed many more liberties than he is in the high school. 2. At college he is not kept in an assembly or study-room when he is not attending classes, but is permitted to go home and study or work when he pleases. 3. In the high school, on the contrary, he is boxed up in a study-hall and
5 is placed under the immediate control of the teacher in charge. 4. In the high school, a student is under the personal direction of a teacher, and is, in a certain sense dependent upon that teacher; whereas in college, a student is taught to become independent and to shift for himself. 5. In other words, the boy becomes a man, gains confidence in himself, and learns his first lesson in fighting
10 the battle of life.

6. But this difference,—the restrictions of high school as compared with the freedom of college,—is not the only difference. 7. The high school student learns to consider himself a much more clever and important person than the college student usually has any opportunity to do. 8. If a man, in high school,
15 possesses a normal amount of ability, he is the man of the hour, the genius whose uplifting influence permeates every corner of its life, and the man who represents it in all contests—mental or physical, athletic or oratorical—with other institutions. 9. At college, the same man finds that he is but one little drop in an ocean of his fellow men. 10. The first lesson to be learned, then, by the high
20 school student newly arrived at college, is the lesson of humility.

Although the revised theme still contains faults of awkward expression,—such as the repetition involved in the third and fourth sentences,—the improvement in general structure is obvious.

A third theme approaches the subject in still a different manner:

THEME III

Although high schools and colleges are alike in one way, that is, their object is to teach theory more than practice, their methods and aims are quite different. The high school compels a young person to study certain subjects in which he is very little interested. This, of course, is only to train the mind to quick
5 thought, and to find out in what a person is interested. College, however, offers

any course that one takes a liking to. Here he can prepare for his life-work, or at least broaden his mind until he finds out what he is intended for. A college does not compel a person to study,—it is taken for granted that he comes here to study.

The difference most easily seen is that of the college life. In high school one lives at home and is more dependent on his parents than he thinks, until he leaves. College does more to develop a man by putting him on his own responsibility and bringing him in contact with others, than by the course of study. This does not mean that the studies are of minor importance. They broaden the mind and prepare one for something else later; but they do not cultivate that spirit of independence and self-confidence which is absolutely necessary if one is to succeed.

In this theme, likewise, we find a gain in the interest and solidity of the thought. The writer touches upon more than one significant matter which might be, with profit, further developed. In structure also this theme improves upon the two that precede it, in that it shows two fairly well differentiated paragraphs. The substance of the paragraphs may be indicated as follows:

1. Intellectual differences between high school and college.
2. Social differences between high school and college.

This theme might be greatly improved, however, by an attempt to make the internal structure of each paragraph more striking. The topic-sentence of the second paragraph, for example, could be stated with greater definiteness:

(Original) The difference most easily seen is that of the college life.
(Revised) The most obvious difference, however, between high school and college life appears in the relatively greater freedom allowed to college students in their social relations.

The second version of the sentence shows clearly that more words were needed to express the idea which introduces the second paragraph, and this criticism is applicable to the whole theme,—more words are needed to express the thought adequately.

The fourth theme stands as follows:

THEME IV

The principal points of difference between the high school and the college are in the method of teaching, and in the life and environment of the student. In the high school, the teacher watches the development of his or her pupil much more closely than the instructor at college does. This is much more true of

5　instructors at large colleges, however, than it is of those at smaller colleges. In preparing a lesson, the high school pupil takes any difficulty encountered to his teacher for explanation. The college student either works at this difficulty until he has mastered it himself, or else omits that part of the preparation. Thus a more intimate relationship is found between the high school teacher and his
10　pupils than between the college instructor and his pupils. The college student is thrown upon his own resources a great deal more than is the high school student.

　　The life and environment of the college student are vastly different from those of the high school student. In most cases the former is living away from
15　home, whereas the latter is usually living at home. Naturally the temptations of the college student are much greater than those of the high school student.

In thought, this theme is, as far as it goes, clear and solid. The proposed organization of the theme is admirable. The two ideas discussed are wisely chosen, and are clearly announced at the outset:

1. Differences in method of teaching.
2. Differences in social surroundings.

The theme might fairly have been called good, had not the writer grown weary or pressed for time before he finished thinking out his second paragraph. The fault of this theme, then, is at once simple and fundamental: the thought is incomplete.

What, then, are the conclusions to be drawn from our brief survey of these four short themes?

1. In subject-matter, themes must be sincere and must arise from first-hand observation and opinion.
2. The expression of the thought must be thorough. If an idea is announced, it must be developed.
3. Themes must have a definite and well thought out organization. Each idea that the writer intends to advance must be grouped with those to which it is most closely related.
4. As far as possible, themes must *show* this organization. Paragraphs must have clear opening or topic-sentences; and the transition from one paragraph to another must be at once evident and smooth.

Long Themes

Many a student, no doubt, has felt terror upon encountering the term "long theme," and has shrunk from undertaking the task that these forbidding words usually suggest. As a matter of fact, however, this dread rests upon no real foundation. If the student imagines that he knows nothing sufficiently important to write about, he has been misled, for any matter upon which he has a thoughtful opinion, or concerning which he can find out something definite and fairly detailed, or which seriously and practically concerns his own life, is worth communicating to some one else.

As subjects for long themes the following two types will be found particularly useful: (1) matters of one's own subjective life and experience, and (2) matters of opinion based upon fact. The first type of subject will require no study or research, but a great deal of reflection; the second will entail a certain amount of inquiry. . . .

Summary:
The essentials of clear exposition, then, are:

1. Accurate limiting and defining of one's subject.
2. Clear-cut analysis of the subject into its logical divisions.
3. Arrangement of divisions in a logical order.
4. Careful attention to devices for transition from one division of the exposition to another.
5. Careful attention to emphasis and proportion in the arrangement of the subject-matter.

. . . .

THE FIRELESS COOKER

The fireless cooker is the most modern device for saving fuel and trouble in cooking. The principle upon which it is based is the non-conductivity of heat of some substances, such as dry hay, mineral wool, and excelsior. When a heated liquid or solid is enveloped in one of these substances the time required for the heat to escape is greatly lengthened, and the process of cooking continues for a 5 long time, even though the source of heat is withdrawn. There is, moreover, no danger from burning or boiling over.

The fireless cooker is such a simple device that it can be made by the prospective user with little trouble and a great saving. The cooker, as made in the home, consists of an outer wooden box which contains a good-sized metal 10 pail, the box being made large enough to allow for at least five inches of packing with one of the above-named substances on all sides of the pail except the top. Into the metal pail a dish containing the substance to be cooked is placed, and

the pail is provided with a tight-fitting cover. To insure against the escape of
15 heat from the top of the pail, a cushion of the same substance as that used for the
packing is provided. This cushion is about four inches thick and is of the same
size as the interior of the box, so that it fits snugly on all sides. The cover of the
box is hinged on one side, and when the cover is raised the cushion can be
removed and food can be put into or taken out of the pail at will. The outer pail
20 is usually partly filled with boiling water when food is to be cooked in it; this
water retains its high temperature until fresh air is allowed to reach it when the
cover of the box and pail is removed. The food is cooked in the usual way for a
short time before being put into the pail. The heating of the boiling water and
that imparted to the food before putting it into the cooker are sufficient to
25 prepare the dish, and the food is now left in the cooker until it is thoroughly
done. — A STUDENT'S THEME.

· · · · · · · ·

HOW TO THROW A CURVE WITH A BASEBALL

The average American boy who becomes interested in baseball has always
the ultimate intention of becoming a pitcher. Knowing that in order to be a real
pitcher, he must be able to curve the ball in every way known to baseball, he sets
out to master the curves which are easiest to throw. I will try to tell the reader
5 how the most simple curve, known as the out-curve, is thrown by a right-
handed pitcher. This curve is called the out-curve because it curves out from a
right-handed batter.

The ball is grasped in the right hand and is held mainly by the thumb and
two first fingers, the third finger resting lightly against the sphere and helping
10 to support it, while the fourth or little finger does not come into contact with
the ball at all. When the ball is to be delivered, the arm is brought around with
a sweeping over-handed or under-handed motion, and the ball is allowed to
leave the hand just before the swing is completed. When the ball leaves the
hand, it is allowed to roll over the inner surface of the first finger, the thumb
15 being used to start the ball in this direction. By rolling the ball over the index
finger in this manner and by giving the hand an outward turn when the ball
leaves it, the player makes the ball spin on a vertical axis, and this spinning
causes the ball to curve in the desired direction.

The curve may be thrown as a sweeping curve or as a quick-breaking one. A
20 sweeping curve is one that curves slowly from the time it leaves the pitcher's
hand until it strikes some resistance, while a quick-breaking curve goes straight
until it comes to within two or three feet of the plate and then suddenly shoots
out and away from the batter. The latter curve is the more deceptive of the two,
and is caused to break so quickly by snapping the wrist back just before the ball

is allowed to leave the hand. Speed is not required to throw the sweeping out- 25
curve, so that any boy can learn to deliver it, but a medium amount of speed is
required to throw the quick-breaking one. Hence the latter curve is rarely seen
among the younger set of baseball enthusiasts, who have not acquired the speed
necessary to throw this ball.—A STUDENT'S THEME.

Adapted Subjects

Machines and apparatus:

A fountain pen.	A milking machine.
An electric door-bell.	A cash register.
A telephone transmitter.	The weather flags.
A type-writer.	A piece of laboratory apparatus.
The turbine wheel.	A racing shell.
A camera.	A street sprinkler.
A coffee-percolator.	A "penny-in-the-slot" machine.
A silage cutter.	A cream separator.

The Burroughs Adding Machine.

Processes:

How to paddle a canoe.	How a boat goes through a lock.
The lariat and its uses.	Two modes of high jumping.
How to manage an auto-mobile.	Sailing a boat.
	Throwing the hammer.
Harnessing a horse.	Making a stroke in golf.
Calling up a telephone number.	How to tell time.
	The Lawford stroke, in tennis.

Learning to sew on a sewing machine.
The Leschetizky method of piano practice.
The crawl and the trudgen strokes in swimming.
The jack-knife dive.

Thirteen Themes from Franklin William Scott and Jacob Zeitlin
College Readings in English Prose (1914)

ᔟ *Scott and Zeitlin both illustrate the connections that link
so many in the early-twentieth-century composition community. Scott (1877–
1950) received all of his degrees from the University of Illinois (B.A., 1901;
M.A., 1910; Ph.D., 1912) and taught there in 1901–03 and 1905–25,*

serving as chair of English in 1924–25 and heading journalism from 1905 to 1918 and from 1921 to 1925. He published Composition for College Students *with J. M. Thomas and Frederick A. Manchester (first edition 1923; fourth and last edition, 1947). Scott left Illinois to become an editor at D. C. Heath from 1925 to 1946, where he revised Woolley's* Handbook of Composition, *beginning in 1927 and continuing through the 1948 edition.*

Zeitlin (1883–1937) was born in Russia and arrived in America in 1892. He attended Columbia (B.A., 1904; M.A., 1905; Ph.D., 1908) and taught at Illinois from 1907 to 1937. Among his publications are his Columbia dissertation, The Accusative with the Infinitive *(1908); a translation of Montaigne (1934); and with others,* Life and Letters of Stuart Sherman *(1929), a tribute to his former colleague. Sherman, Irving Babbitt's student and Norman Foerster's friend at Harvard, had left Illinois to edit the* New York Herald Tribune *book review. Along with William Lyon Phelps and John Erskine, Sherman is a key figure in Joan Rubin's* The Making of Middlebrow Culture.

In addition to many familiar names from the composition canon (Woodrow Wilson, Newman, James Bryce, Huxley, Hazlitt, Stevenson, William James, Ruskin) this popular six-hundred-page anthology included some frankly journalistic prose (a description from Popular Mechanics*), some imaginative literature (Poe, Dickens, Conrad, Arnold Bennett), and in a fifty-page appendix, twenty-six student themes.*

Scott and Zeitlin's College Readings in English Prose *went through four editions, the last in 1936; the student papers did not appear in the 1926 or 1936 editions. The essays should be regarded as heavily edited models to emulate, not as a representative sampling.*

THE MANUFACTURE OF MALLEABLE IRON

The vast majority of iron castings made to-day are of either malleable or gray iron. We intend in this paper to concern ourselves only with the former; but a brief comparison—or rather contrast—of its qualities with those of gray iron will be of great assistance towards the comprehension of the subject.

Malleable iron, then, differs from gray iron both in its physical properties and in its chemical composition. It is softer and less brittle, and can be beaten out like lead—though, needless to say, to a very much less degree. It is also stronger under tension and better able to resist a jarring shock. These qualities make it in every way the superior metal; it is, indeed, kept from supplanting gray iron entirely only by the fact that it is approximately twice as expensive.

The constituent elements in the chemical composition of the two irons are identical; for the analytical chemist a slight difference in the form or proportions of these elements alone distinguishes malleable from gray iron. Each contains about ninety-six per cent of pure iron, mixed or combined with varying proportions of carbon, silicon, sulphur, phosphorus, and manganese. The soft and pliable nature of malleable iron is chiefly due to the state of the free carbon it contains. This is amorphous rather than graphitic; in other words, it is scattered evenly and minutely divided throughout the mass, not segregated in flakes, as in gray iron. The fact that sulphur and phosphorus are present in far smaller quantities also adds considerably to its strength, as those two elements always tend to make the metal more brittle.

Such are the qualities of malleable iron. The processes involved in its manufacture are, essentially, two. In the first place, the material is prepared in the form of white iron—the hardest and most brittle form of iron known; in the second place, this white iron is converted by a special heat treatment into the finished malleable product.

We are first concerned with the making of the white iron. For this, pig iron and scrap iron in almost equal proportions provide the material. The pig used consists of malleable Bessemer—an ordinary pig iron containing less sulphur and phosphorus than the "foundry pig" used in the manufacture of gray iron—or, preferably, of charcoal pig, which has been melted with charcoal in place of coke as fuel. The superiority of the latter is due to the practically negligible amount of sulphur it contains. Of the scrap iron used, three-fourths consists usually of "sprue," as it is called. This comprises the waste iron left over from the previous day, the metal from the channels in the moulds through which it ran to form the castings, the shop "sweepings," etc. The remaining fourth is made up of equal amounts of malleable scrap—worn out malleable iron castings, and steel scrap—old steel rails and the like.

This material is melted up either in a cupola or an air furnace. The former is a vast hollow cylinder in which the fuel (coke) and the metal are placed in alternate layers. The iron is thus melted in direct contact with the fuel—an arrangement by no means desirable, as the metal invariably absorbs a certain amount of sulphur from the coke.

The air furnace is a decidedly better arrangement. It comprises a fire-box, in which a huge fire is kept up with good gas-coal as fuel, and a melting hearth containing the material to be melted. The hearth is separated from the fire-box by a low wall, over which the flame is driven by a forced draught. When the material has been melted down in such a furnace and run out into the moulds, it is in the form of white iron, and the first process in the manufacture of the malleable casting is completed.

White iron is almost as hard and brittle as glass, but its nature is entirely changed by the simple heat treatment known as annealing. The castings are tightly packed with iron oxide in cylindrical pots of about two feet in depth and diameter—much as one would pack crockery with straw in a barrel,—the chief object being to keep them from warping at the high temperature to which they are soon to be subjected. They are next placed in huge ovens and slowly heated to about 1600° F., then gradually allowed to cool down. They stay in the ovens altogether between four and five days.

The physical alteration which has taken place in the properties of the metal is evident, but the reasons for the chemical change which takes place at the same time have not yet been definitely discovered. That the carbon, which in the white iron had been chemically combined with the metal as iron carbide, is separated out and distributed through the mass in a free amorphous form mechanically mixed with it, is an indisputable fact. Chemists, however, are not yet agreed as to why the simple heat treatment should produce such a result. Certain it is that the hard, brittle metal first obtained has been converted into the soft, strong, and durable product described in the opening paragraphs.

From this brief description it will be evident that the manufacture of malleable iron is an operation both complicated and expensive, owing to the double process involved. At the same time, however, it should be quite clear that the superior quality of the metal obtained more than repays the difficulties of its manufacture.

HOW A ROSEBUD UNCLOSES

Did you ever watch a rosebud unclose? If not, you have missed one of nature's wonderful processes. Take a bud of the crimson cochet variety just as it begins to unfold. I warn you beforehand that to watch this transition from bud to rose will require much patience. Nature requires patience first of all from those who would learn her secrets. For three hours you can see no difference in the bud; seemingly it is absolutely idle. You will perhaps perceive, at the end of that time, that the bud is larger, especially in girth, and that the color is several shades darker. These changes have gone on within the bud. The little inner petals have awakened and are sleepily stretching themselves, and by their quickened life are sending through the veins of the delicate outer petals a flood of deeper color. Now, almost imperceptibly at first, the outer leaves begin to unclose. Watch closely. A tremor seems to run through the outermost petal; then suddenly it falls a little from its fellows. A second or two later another quivers and falls away, and then another, until finally the first four courses are leaning back. Now the movement begins again from within. The little petals at the centre begin to push out. The first perfume is exhaled. Those little petals push farther and farther until the petals of the fifth course touch those of the fourth; then the movement ceases. The bud is a full-blown rose.

STRAWBERRY PICKING

As the sun rises over the dewy, glistening field, the manager, a short businesslike man with a quick eye and a quicker step, comes out of the shed with the bosses. To these bosses he assigns spaces of about twenty rows each. The duty of this functionary is to watch the pickers in his territory, keep them on their own rows, see that they pick the berries properly and do not mash those on the edges of the rows nor leave any which would be too ripe for the next picking, which occurs the second day after. His place is about as agreeable as that of a baseball umpire. When the bosses are allotted their positions, the signal is given and the pickers, one to each row, merrily set to work. The cool dew wets hands and arms and trousers or skirts as, on their knees, the pickers rapidly turn the leaves this way and that, searching for the luscious low-lying fruit. The girls, their hands and arms covered with the legs of old stockings, race and talk with their neighbors; old men stoop painfully over their work; the women cast frequent anxious glances toward the shed where the crying babies have been left. The snap of the berries as they are pulled from the vines keeps up a continuous patter, like rain falling on still water.

Soon the carriers of the swifter pickers are filled and they start down between the rows (no boss would let a picker cross a row) for the shed, and the work of the packing department begins. Each picker, as he comes in with his six quarts passes the ticket woman, who gives him his ticket, a cardboard, crediting him with the proper number of quarts. If the boxes are not full she "docks" him, that is, gives him a ticket for only four or five quarts, as the case demands. After he secures his ticket he passes on down the shed, takes the boxes from the carrier and puts them on the bench, refills with empties and returns to the patch. It is while he is disposing of his berries that he meets the *czar* of the whole business. This man is the shed boss. It is this same man with the quick eye who *sizes up* each picker and his berries as they pour in in a constant stream. Here he takes out a green berry, and with a meaning look shows it to the picker; there he punches off a long stem and tells the culprit to be careful in the future; he fairly *jumps* on to the awkward fellow with telltale stains upon his knees, and scolds the girl with like stains upon her lips. He dumps the boxes of a suspicious looking tramp to see that they are honestly filled, and if found otherwise, he points to the fence, telling him to "git, and git quick!" From no one does he brook an answer.

Behind the bench upon which the pickers place their berries stand the packers,—women who take the quarts from the bench, place them in the cases and dress the tops. The work requires neatness and despatch, for with four hundred pickers working as fast as possible, a short delay in the shed would cause a confusion entirely demoralizing. From the packers the cases go to the mailers, and from the mailers to the marker, a man who brands each case with its destination and sender. The berries, now ready for the shipment, are hauled away to the train. Since the pay depends entirely on the amount picked, and the work must be stopped and the berries shipped by the middle of the afternoon, dinner is a rather neglected function except with the children about the shed and those worn out with work and heat. When the work is finished or the time is up, the pickers are called in, and the final rush for tickets tests the skill and patience of the woman who dispenses them. Some have boxes partly filled, others have picked unripe berries in their efforts to make out even quarts, and all want full pay for the ragged results.

The confusion ends at last, the pickers straggle away, talking of their successes and aspirations. The rosy girl in the sunbonnet takes her tickets from the pocket at her breast and compares them with the checks of him in the hickory hat, with the curious result that the gallant youth spends his surplus with her at the ice cream festival that night; the tired woman, with hair unkempt, lugs home her crying baby and does her household work; the young men repair to the store for a game of horseshoe; the tramps to the same place for bread and coffee; the shed hands, bosses, and owner rattle homeward in the empty wagons, and the day's picking is done.

THE COLLEGE GIRL'S VOCABULARY

The influence of environment seems to leave nothing untouched; it sets the direction not only of one's thought and habit of life, but determines in large measure one's manner of speech. Girls that spend several consecutive years in a preparatory school and in college become so accustomed to surrounding conditions that unconsciously they develop a vocabulary typically different from that of other people. To a person who has been away from college for some time and who has mingled with other than college girls, this difference is decidedly noticeable.

It is not a question of slang, as one might hastily suggest, but simply of the abuse or misapplication of perfectly good, legitimate words. In our language, as in many other things American, the prevailing character is extravagance. Any adjective that makes the trifles of conversation appear interesting or exciting is not only permissible, but imperative. The most commonplace remark is splashed with the high color of adventure; and an incident is scarcely worth listening to if it is not "the most exciting thing you ever heard in your life"—the last three words uttered with an inflection gradually rising to a shriek on "life." Naturally, the speaker "nearly died" under the stress of it all.

"Exciting" and "killing," however, are mild descriptives. To obtain a ready listener, events must be "thrilling." Girls are "thrilled" at seeing each other after a short absence; they are "thrilled" at the idea of a cut, of a good mark; and above all things, they are "thrilled" at a "spread." In regard to a tennis appointment I overheard a sophomore say to an unsophisticated freshman, "Oh, I am so thrilled at the idea of playing with you." "I don't know why you should be," said the freshman, "for I'm not at all a good player." "Oh, yes, but don't you see, if *I* win I should be thrilled with triumph, and if *you* win I should be thrilled with eagerness to play better." To keep up an existence of thrills steadily for several years must be very hard on the system. This life surely requires strong nerves!

"Weird" and "ghastly" both are words often dragged from their proper surroundings into broad daylight, but, fortunately, not as yet with such frequency and boldness as the world "wonderful." This adjective is perhaps the most abused in the college vocabulary. Of course when one thinks about it, everything in the universe is really wonderful; nevertheless some things are incomparably more amazing than others, and if we describe mere nothings as "wonderful," how can we express the really vital *somethings?* Twenty times a day we hear, "Oh, we had the most *wonderful* time at Katherine's last night!" and "Really, it was perfectly wonderful ice-cream." Surrounded by such intemperate absurdities, is it strange that any attempt adequately to express genuine wonder is almost hopeless? It is as baffling as to try drawing music from a useless worn-out instrument.

The result of all this extravagance is ruin to our vocabulary. Strong words are deliberately stolen from their places and are used to express trifling nonsense. When we need these words, they are no longer at hand, and in our weakness we shrink into silence rather than venture terms that have no meaning. Not only is our expression weakened but our mental poise is threatened. The constant use of highly exciting language tends to keep one in a state of nervous agitation, of irritability. During the student period, when perhaps mental composure is most needed, it is least encouraged.

FUZZY: THE IDEA MAN

Under an obscure "Obituary" yesterday's paper published this notice:—

"Lorenzo F. Woodward, 42, single, County Hospital, alcoholic heart failure."

Many of the deceased man's friends who glanced ignorantly over "Lorenzo F. Woodward" would have gazed through tears at that announcement had it read "Fuzzy Woodward." And had it stated that Fuzzy was a newspaper man it would have been unnecessary to state that the cause of his death was alcohol; for his avocation was news-gathering. With his love of liquor, however, this journalist had combined a talent for "the news game" that might have developed into a genius for literature had not alcohol enfeebled his hand and pinched his heart and gnarled his brain.

Some years ago there ambled into the "local room" of our daily newspaper a lean, lank, loose-jointed man with greenish gray eyes. Several clean-cut wrinkles creased his face, which bore a look of premature age. The little, old face started out from under a shock of yellow curls. The awkward figure shuffled toward the city editor:

"Need a man? I'm ready for work."

The editor, after many procrastinations, finally hired this persistent applicant, one of those many journalistic victims of the *wanderlust*. And a week later this same Lorenzo Fuzzy Woodward had a regular staff job on the *Leader*.

It was there that I began to know him. He seldom mentioned his early years, of which we knew nothing. Evidently he had been once an omnivorous reader, for he was well versed in learning of various sorts. The Ptolemaic astronomical theories, Xenophon's *Anabasis,* Euclid's problems were topics intimate and dear to him. I remember one instance in particular which showed his knowledge and luck. It was his night "on the desk," while the city editor was taking a vacation. The reporter assigned to write up a famous mathematician's lecture on "The Theory of Functions" had failed to return to the office. At a late hour—after all hope of his return had fled—Fuzzy began to fabricate a report of the lecture. He audaciously concocted a resounding effusion and hurried it out to the linotypes. He thought no more about it until two days later the editor received a letter from the mathematical lecturer thanking and congratulating the paper for the intelligent and accurate manner in which the *Leader* had reported his address.

It was on account of such marvellous luck and skill that seven months later Fuzzy became the *Leader's* Idea Man. He would do anything for a "good story." Profligate, reckless, unscrupulous, he never considered the means, but ever the end. He was a successful "yellow journalist" of the deepest dye. And as such he was recognized by West, who found in Fuzzy another keen-edged tool to use at his infamous craft of chiselling out morbid details upon which to build the framework of yellow news.

Some months after Fuzzy took up his duties as Idea Man, he had occasion to display this talent for "yellow journalism" in a way characteristic of all his work. Basing his story on some unusual event, he had to fill a two-column space on the front page of every morning's paper. Not the slightest spark of news had appeared to kindle his explosive imagination on this particular night. Everything was dry politics. The clock ticked, the printers scurried more and more rapidly, the heavy iron "forms" banged louder and louder. Fuzzy sat down in the corner of the room. Two columns to fill with—what? His eyes stared a ghastly gray at the inkstand, which they did not see. He gnawed his lower lip. At twenty minutes past the hour, the dull roar of the huge steel presses, grinding out the first feature section, began to throb through the walls. Fuzzy twitched. His greenish eyes swept from ceiling to wall—to floor—to paper—ah, there! He paused a moment, then eagerly examined a despatch from a country correspondent:

"Jonesboro—William Jenkins, prominent Tutt County farmer, killed yesterday by kick from his old mule, while ploughing in field, near town."

A clumsy account of details followed. Fuzzy began to write furiously. He was there when I left the office. The titanic presses devouring bundles of paper, screaming from below, in muffled groans for "more copy!"; Fuzzy scribbled speedily over a farmer's death notice. All the way home I wondered what possible interest he could see in that despatch. The next morning I looked to see Fuzzy's space occupied by an account of some political convention. I was disappointed. His space was filled by his own story. It was his—all his; no one else could have done it. His headline read:—

THE OLD FLAME REKINDLED!

Prominent Tutt County Farmer Killed While Ploughing With Former Fire Horse—Animal Ran Wild On Hearing Distant Alarm Bell

Below that he had treated the death as a minor incident, despite the fact—perhaps—that he has mercilessly doubled the grief of some bereaved family; but—what of it?—he had "scooped 'em on a good story." For the article Fuzzy received a personal letter from Mr. West, with a check for twenty-five dollars for "the correspondent who knows how to nose out news when he smells it." Every detail of how the old blood in the horse had called him back to the strenuous life was depicted in such a graphic style as to bring every false fact home to the reader's heart.

Several nights after this episode occurred, Fuzzy staggered into the office. He was drunk, disgustingly drunk. "Demon Rum"—as he jokingly called it—had him again. He wouldn't stay at his desk that night.

And the next morning his chair was empty and his little two-column space was profaned by a pagan hand. Even now, perhaps, a despondent managing editor and a discouraged circulation manager are halfway hoping for Fuzzy's return. But the little obituary notice, brief as it is, will tell an old, old story to the friends who had warned him long ago that some night he would be unable to survive the tremens. A martyr to the nervous strain of Yellow Journalism, Fuzzy has faked his last story. And when yesterday I read the unceremonious announcement of his death, I could not help thinking what a story he could have written about his own obituary notice.

. . . .

THE FEAR OF PEW

Why is it that I dread and hate David Pew? The very name is ghastly. Wickedness, craftiness, bloodiness, power, and the devil himself seem bound up in it. I cannot think of him without a shudder and whenever I recall his "vice-like grip" and the "tap-tap-tapping of his stick," the blood rushes in little whirls through my breast.

Stevenson doubles the horridness and supernaturalness of Pew by making him blind. Blindness itself carries a tragic, fearsome atmosphere with it. The blind are both pitied aand held in awe, because we imagine that they live in a world different from ours, a world of black, heavy shadows and dark, whirling winds, and that they are, to some extent, of this world of phantoms. It is uncanny to see a blind man do a seeing man's work and ghostlike when he hears sound to which we are deaf. To know that when a blind man touches us a stream of information, which seems out of all proportion, rushes up to his brain, to know that he marks every tremor and inflection of our tones is to have for him a respect tinged with fear. But invest a hateful villain with these unusual powers, as Stevenson has invested David Pew with them, and we have an infernal spirit whose very image makes the feverish sweat burst out at the temples.

. . . .

OUR MILITARY UNPREPAREDNESS

If the Mexican situation has done nothing more, it has, at least, shown our military weakness and opened our eyes to the necessity of increasing our military forces. There is little probability that this Mexican fracas will develop into a great war, but nevertheless military commanders are in a quandary as to what they would do if war should be declared. They have under their command only 18,000 trained United States army men. As at least 250,000 volunteers would be needed in any struggle large enough to be called a war, we can to some extent realize the great problem of drilling these men in the simple military movements in a short space of time. Undrilled men are almost worthless in a battle field. In substance, we do not have a sufficient standing army to defend ourselves or uphold the dignity and honor of the United States. Increasing the state militia or National Guards would alleviate conditions.

As long as there are separate nations, so long will there be need of force, need of armies to enforce peace. David Starr Jordan, in advocating disarmament, has made the assumption that the spirit of struggle and warfare has disappeared in this twentieth century. Although tempered by the study of the humanistic and sociological sides of life, this spirit of war is yet burning in the breasts of men to-day. Therefore, to reiterate, it is our duty as one of the foremost nations of the world to represent a bulwark of military strength to enforce peace, especially on this side of the Atlantic.

. . . .

OF THE IMPORTANCE ATTACHED TO ATHLETIC SPORTS

Among the deplorable failings of the present day, none is more astonishing than the rapidly increasing tendency to set hopelessly false values upon the institutions and customs peculiar to the period. The absurd importance attached to athletic sports forms one of the most striking instances of this modern hallucination.

The original object of athletic sports, and the only excuse for their existence to-day, is found in the undoubted necessity for supplementing mental exertion with physical exercise. At the present time, however, the intellect seems to be generally subordinated to physical strength. There is an alarmingly large number of men who condescend to recognize intellect only as a useful assistant in bodily recreation—as a means of devising clever plays in foot-ball and base-ball, or as a profitable adjunct to muscular proficiency in the running of races.

The athlete, again, is the recipient of a lamentable amount of popular favor. The individuals of a college athletic team are known by sight to almost every member of the undergraduate body. Yet how many of the most brilliant scholars in the institution are similarly recognized? The result is that athletic disctinction has become infinitely more highly prized than scholastic distinction—a state of affairs that would be laughable were it not so woefully serious.

Vast sums of money that might do infinite good are annually squandered on "spectacular sport"—a phrase, by the way, in its essence amusingly paradoxical. Rome in her most decadent days cannot have lavished more on trivial amusement than is now spent on the unedifying exhibitions daily thronged by the patrons of so-called sport. Intellectual refinement is everywhere neglected, and sport cultivated with idolatrous reverence. By the average citizen of the United States, the name Wagner is instantly associated with the person of a popular baseball player. Another man, of widely different fame, may have borne the name before, but the thoughts of the modern concern themselves with the field of sport alone.

Such is the state of affairs to-day; very similar was it at Rome fifteen centuries ago. The fall of Rome is a matter of history.—What will be the result here?

. . . .

PITTSBURGH BY NIGHT

It was on a balmy evening in April that we climbed a steep hill in the outskirts of Pittsburgh to view the lights of the city. The moon hung low, red-faced, and dull through the all-enveloping veil of smoke. Down below, away in all directions, were the lights,—steady yellow lights, winking green and red ones, millions of them. They pierced the dark surface of the stately Alleghany as it wove its course among them. Brightly illumined steamers, gliding up and down the river, shattered these placid reflections, leaving golden or parti-colored ripples in their wake. Now and then a dark tug swept the valley with its great searchlight or shot its white shaft into the smoky starless sky, while from over the hills to the south, where the great blast furnaces stood, a lurid light leapt quivering over the horizon and cast a livid glow over all the sky. The flame rose high for a moment, then died quickly away, leaving murky darkness save for the smoldering embers low in the south. Soon it rose again, more ominous than before, till it seemed to merge all in a vast glowing crucible of light.

THE SONG OF THE VACUUM-CLEANER

The song of the river is peaceful and soothing; the song of the bird is cheering and inspiring; but the song of the vacuum-cleaner can scarcely be described in such specific terms. House-cleaning time! What visions of rugs strewing the dusty grass; furniture promiscuously littering the front porch, the back porch, and, indeed, the entire yard; women scuttling back and forth, frantically waving dusters and mops in all directions; and, above all these sounds, the steady drone of the untiring vacuum-cleaner buzzing in the ear like a determined monster bee, bent on subordinating all other sounds in nature to its own disturbance. It groans, as if discouraged at the amount of work before it, yet labors on, stopping now and again with an asthmatic wheeze to get its breath, and then once more taking up its persistent buzzing. There is a brief interval of silence while it is being moved from one room to another. But just as the grateful hush begins to be noticed, the demon of cleanliness starts again on his old theme—buzz, buzz, groan, wheeze; buzz, buzz, groan, wheeze. And so the monotonous song drones on through the day until the last bit of work is done. Then the machine abruptly emits a final wheeze, buzzes an instant, and stops.

THE DESERT

Stretching to the east of Calcha, the heaped sands of the desert gleam red in the sun. The trail, a faint mark in the sand, crawls along painfully, here and there turning aside to avoid a cactus and finally disappearing among the sand wastes, away, away in the distance. At the base of the rounded hills, so far away that they seem a part of the sky, there floats a cloud of white dust slowly moving. Here and there the dust devils dance their mystic dance to the music of the drifting sand. To the right a clump of yuccas flanked by greasewood and mesquit, flaunt their spikes of white bells. Wonderful colors, from deep purple to lilac and gold, as the light shines on the sands, gleam and disappear and gleam again. And always the sun shines burning out of an empty sky.

. . . .

MADEMOISELLE FIFI

Hastily scanning all the faces, dear old Mrs. Rogers glanced about the cozy parlor. When she finally saw Mademoiselle Fifi, as the men called her, her eyes lit with interest, and she leaned forward the more closely to examine the girl. Fifi's eyes held her attention: a hazel green they seemed (though some insisted that they were black), with queer, dancing lights; large, but shallow withal, their beauty strangely marred by the curiously scant lashes, and eyebrows of a light brown color. Her eyes narrowed—maliciously, Mrs. Rogers thought—as she smilingly greeted another girl, then slowly dilated as she turned again to her companion and listened gravely to his inane chatter. Her nose was small and flippantly tilted. Her skin, just tinged with pink, was marvellously clear and smooth, save where a few, faint lines of discontent crossed the low, broad forehead. Her hair was auburn, silken rather than heavy, and fell loosely about her tiny ears. "But," thought Mrs. Rogers, "the girl's mouth will show her real character." The lips were thin and tightly compressed, and of a vivid scarlet. Danger and malice lurked at the corners and in the sharp chin. "A coquette," Mrs. Rogers said to herself, and sighed.

. . . .

TONY

For more than an hour Tony had perched saucily on the Major's big roll-top desk, waiting for that officer to finish his government report. It was far past time for their afternoon frolic, but Tony was patient, for the Major's feats with pen, paper, and ink had never ceased to be fascinating to the little gray monkey. It was an absurdly intricate thing, this monthly report to headquarters, for governing this small island in the tropics was very much of a problem. But at last the accounts were all balanced, and the hundredth disquieting symptom duly tabulated. Tony blinked owlishly as the Major neatly folded the closely written sheets and placed them under a weight; and his little eyes eagerly followed his master's every movement as he carefully destroyed the loose copies lying about. Then the last sheet was torn in pieces and consigned to the waste-basket. Tony leaped from his perch and the frolic began.

For a time the ball flew merrily to and fro. Tony dashed madly about, his shrill chatter and staccato bark mingling strangely with the Major's laughing banter. They were indeed good chums. Then, just when the game was at its height, some thoughtless person called the Major away. Tony plainly resented such desertion. Five minutes he beguiled by rather aimlessly rolling the ball about, and then climbed to his perch on top of the desk and sulked. That is how he happened to spy the open inkwell. Fifteen minutes later the Major burst into the room. He had suddenly remembered Tony—and the report lying loose on his desk. With inky paws the little gray monkey was slowly and delightedly tearing the tenth sheet in long strips, which he dropped one by one into the wastebasket below. "Tony, you rascal!" yelled the Major in a fury. The little fellow had never heard that voice before. Like a flash he leaped to the low partition and turned bewildered eyes to the angry officer just as he hurled the inkwell. It struck the partition near the top. The dark contents showering Tony set him aquiver with rage and fright. With a shrill scream he leaped through the window, scuttled shrieking across the clearing, and disappeared in the jungle.

Many months later one of the lieutenants returned from a scouting expedition with the story of a strangely spotted ape which had followed him several miles through the jungle, scolding shrilly and shying sticks and stones. But no one else at the Post ever again saw Tony.

Ten 1891 Harvard First-Year Composition Essays
from Charles Francis Adams, Edwin Lawrence
Godkin, and Josiah Quincy
Report of the Committee on Composition and Rhetoric
(1892)

& *The report quotes Professor Adams Sherman Hill to the effect that these essays were significantly better than average, since most students had already written on the topic and received corrected papers from their instructors. These ten including four in facsimile were used as examples of the worst.*

NO. 8

My Preparation in English

I am happy to state that I succeeded in passing the English examination.

I received my training in English at the _____ School, where we wrote about one composition a week.

The subjects of these compositions varied; sometimes we wrote about the books we had read in our English work, sometimes on a subject chosen by the instructor, and now and then on a topic selected by ourselves.

On the average we spent about three quarters of an hour a week on compositions, sometimes but not often more. The relative time devoted to English was small. In comparison with the amount of work we were expected to do, the time given was very short.

NO. 19

Preparatory Work in English Composition

The last four years I have spent at the _____ High School _____ preparing for college. As the name of the school indicates, much time is devoted to English. But of course composition makes up only one part of the many into which English is divided. As I remember it, we had a composition about every six weeks during the first year. The subject were generally taken from some book we had been reading. Scott's "Ivanhoe," Franklin's "Autobiography" come to my mind as some of the books we read. An hour every week was the time usually given to the whole subject of composition. This was about a fifth of the time given to such studies as French or Algebra.

During the second year we had compositions every three weeks. The whole time devoted to composition was one hour a week. For two weeks we read parts of Macaulay and selections from Irving's "Sketch Book" and then wrote the third week. After the compositions had been corrected, we were obliged to hand in a revised copy. We also studied Hill's Rhetoric one hour a week. These two hours a week constituted as much time as we gave to Geometry or Drawing, but about two thirds of the time we gave to French.

The third year we did not have, as a class, so much composition as in the previous two years. One composition,—we dignified them by the name of essays then,—every two months was the average. The subjects were historical, since the English and History were taught by one man. This was only about one tenth of the time devoted some subjects. I, however, prepared some "essays" to deliver in the school exhibitions. One subject I remember was "The advantages of a scientific education over a collegiate." A fellow-student had just the opposite. My presence here shows how well he acquited himself, though. I believe he is now at a scientific school. I also read a number of books from standard authors in order to try for an essay prize. The character of this theme makes it needless to say that I did not get it.

The fourth year work was directly preparatory to Harvard college. We read the prescribed books and wrote compositions every two weeks, on various subjects connected with these books. We studied Strang's "Exercises in False Syntax." Two hours a week, about two-thirds of the time given to the generality of studies, was the amount of time devoted to English composition as a whole. After this preparation I expected to pass in English and I did.

NO. 27

My Preparation in English Composition

For three years our class devoted one hour a week to written composition, and, during the last year, two hours more a week to Strang's Exercises and Professor Hill's Rhetoric, which we studied through Improprieties.

Our subjects were taken from the required reading, with only one exception that I remember. Our teacher let us go to the game at Springfield last November, and when we came back to school Monday, we were required to write about what we had seen.

We had written criticism on our work in the symbols used at college. At the end of the composition we were told our principal faults and we corrected the paper on that day, and gave it back. If it was not properly corrected, our mark was lowered.

We had English three hours a week, which is as long a time as we devoted to anything but Greek. We spent three hours a week on Homer and two on Herodotus, during a portion of the year.

We spent some time on the Rhetoric, and studied it carefully, using the Century dictionary to look up Barbarisms such as Gerrymander. In the examination I wrote on Irving's "Adventure of the Mason," and passed.

NO. 31

My Preparation in English Composition

I took the full four years Classical course at _____ Academy. I remember writing four or five essays. One was on the "Story of

Marmion", and the rest were all on subjects taken from Rob Roy. These were all written when I was taking the English of the middle year. These essays were all about four pages in length. They were corrected by the Professor and returned to me. I have them in my possession now and anyone who desires may see them.

I should say that the total amount of time I spent in the practice of composition writing during my four years course was not less than eight nor more than twelve hours. The *relative* time spent in English Composition to that of my other studies was, I should say, in the ratio of this twelve hours work to four years work in the rest of the course. The ratio of hours would be about one in English Composition to five hundred in other branches.

I *passed* in English on my entrance examinations for Harvard.

NO. 36

My Preparation for English A

My first really specific preparation for the Harvard examinations began in the fall of 1889 when I entered _____ School. Before that time I had had continual practice in composition writing, preparing generally two compositions per month. At _____ my work was, for the first year, to read the books which were prescribed by Harvard College for entrance examinations, and then to write a criticism or a summary of each book. This gave me about one composition per month to prepare. The following year, I read the books which I had already read (the first year I did not complete the list) and the others also, treating them in the same way, as regards composition-writing, as I did the first year. Last year also, I studied Professor Hill's Rhetoric, and I had practice in correcting mistakes in English sentences. The time spent upon English by my class was on average two hours per week, excluding time spent upon extra reading, to be done outside in whatever time we had to devote to it. On comparing time spent upon English with time spent upon my other studies, I find that the proportion varies with different studies from one third to one half. But English was not slighted, by any means, for every paper we wrote from Latin or Greek or French or German, every recitation we made, all our conversation, at least that part of it where the instructors could hear and correct all our writing of any kind,—all these things were brought as much as possible under the sway

No. 4 p 129

My Preparation in English Composition

I received my preparatory education at ___ Academy. There was not much attention given to English there, being behind the times in English, and compulsory church and chapel. In three years at ___ I wrote four compositions. I chose my subjects from ten or a dozen furnished by the teacher. I remember two "John Hampden" & "The search for truth." The relative time spent on English composition was even less as special attention is given to Greek at Latin in that institution which I believe is considered the best in the country.

5

of good English. And it was always impressed upon us to try and make our conversation & writing as correct as possible, at the same time not sacrificing plainness, smoothness & interests.

I passed my entrance examination in English.

NO. 42

My preparation in English

I passed the entrance examinations in English in June 1891. In preparation for the examination we were required to write a written exercise

No-10-p-133.

My Preparation in English.
I am a regular student of
Harvard University, and passed
my admission examination in
English
I graduated from the
Latin School last June. At that
school they do not give nearly
as much study to English, as to
Greek or Latin, I think the
proportion is about as one is to
twelve, for they are supposed to
have English, one school hour a week,
but very often that hours is taken
for something else.
I should say the number of
written exercises, were about four
or five a year for the first four
years, and about twelve for the last
year. The subjects, were generally
upon some portions of the books that
were required by the College to be
read .   13

each month of the school year. The first year we were in school we had, of course, very little knowledge of Composition, so easy subjects were given us to write upon, so that our essays were usually in the form of narrative or stories about such things as, "A Summers Experience," or "A Fishing Excursion," or "A Sleigh-ride." The second year we were in school we wrote about the same general class of subjects but our compo-

No.17 p.134..

My Preparation in English Composition

During the first three years of my career in the High School, where I prepared my self for this (University, I recieved no knowledge in the art of writing; but at the begining of my last year in that school the rule was made compelling each scholar to write a composition evry month, the subject of which could be chosen by the scholar from four subjects given out by the teacher which would sometimes require a knowledge of some author and at others a good imagination. The teacher would correct these compositions out of the class and then read them at the next recitation at the same time calling attention to the pupils errors.

This is the extent of my preparation in english composition nevertheless I passed the entrance examination to this (University successfully.   26

sitions were longer and fuller in descriptions and details. Sometimes fanciful objects were chosen in writing which imagination only and not experience could assist, such as "A Trip to Mars" or "Journey to the North Pole."

No 39. p 14 8

My Preparation in English.

I was asked to spend one hour a week at home, writing a composition. The subject of this was given out by the teacher. During the recitation hour, which took place once a week. I wrote on topics taken from the book which I was reading.

The subjects for home work were on such thing as Electric Cars and etc.

The time and work devoted to the English Class did not compare with the attention shown to the others requirements nor the proportion of one to five.

Although not being very well prepared I managed to pass my examination in English.

67

In our third school year we changed the class of our subjects and made them deeper and harder to write about. Very often they were lives of famous characters we had read about in our studies of the classics, for instance, Cicero or Cyrus. Some of them were essays on the books we had read in our preparation or were comparisons of style of two of the authors with which we were familiar.

In our last year we had quite a wide range of choice for our subjects. In this year we had to write only one composition each term, but we had to memorize these and deliver them as "orations" to the whole school. Of course, the style of writing had to be entirely different for pieces which were to be spoken than for mere essays.

Our subjects were made still harder and deeper this year. We were advised to choose classical subjects, such as "Achilles in his Tent," "The Influence of Homer on the Greek Life," ect.

We spent, on the average, about four hours a month on our Composition, or about an hour a week. There were nine months in the school year.

About one-twentieth or one twenty-fifth of our entire work was spent on our Composition. Persons who could write with readiness without taking much time for it would spend about one-fortieth of their work on English Composition.

Eight Harvard Themes from C. T. Copeland and H. M. Rideout
Freshman English and Theme-Correcting in Harvard College (1901)

ᐦ᠍ *Copeland (1860–1952) graduated from Harvard in 1882 and became a book and theater reviewer for Boston newspapers. In 1893 he was hired to teach writing at Harvard, where he became an institution. His famous course was a continuation of Wendell's English 12, which he taught from 1905 to 1928, holding conferences at which he listened to each student read his paper aloud and dictated corrections and evaluations. Copeland was famous for his public readings; his favorite pieces were collected in* The Copeland Reader *(1926).*

Rideout (1877–1927) graduated from Harvard in 1899 and taught there for five years while editing English literary works. He resigned in 1904 to travel and write novels. He published many books with Far Eastern locales.

Some of the following essays are collected in two versions, original and revised. The book included actual instructors' marks to demonstrate how Harvard faculty marked essays.

SPECIMEN THEME I

SPECIMEN THEME I. REWRITTEN VERSION

The day was clear, as few of the days in Cambridge appear to be. We took advantage of the weather and set out for that Mecca of all visitors to Boston—Bunker Hill.

Our first experience in the subway was rather enjoyable because it was something entirely new.

When we had reached the Monument, we sat down for a few moments, to rest. My friend who had been sick, feeling unable to attempt the journey, remained below, while I began the tedious ascent. The winding stairway, on which I counted two hundred and ninety-four steps, seemed interminable, but at last I gained the summit.

As the sun was bright, I was able to obtain a few snap-shots of the city below with my camera, which I, for a wonder, had not forgotten to take. During the descent, weird sounds echoed and reëchoed through the hollow center of the Monument. They sounded to me as though the ghosts of the heroes of the battle, in whose memory the Pile was erected, were resenting the intrusion of the sight-seers.

After signing the register I went forth to join the throng which greets new-comers to Boston with: "Have you been to Bunker Hill yet? Well, you really must visit it before you leave town."

SPECIMEN THEME 2

Verb?   A little girl of about eight years, a poodle, and a doll. This was the party that entered a Harvard Square car a little above Harvard Bridge. The little girl sat down with the poodle under one arm, and the doll under the other, and smiled at the other occupants of the car. She seemed *p.*   to mean, "I'm a pretty big girl to be travelling all alone, don't you think ∧   so." The car rolled on until it reached Holyoke St∧. Here the little girl *p.*   with her two darlings, calmly and proudly arose, passed down the aisle, jumped off the car, and walked slowly down the street, pausing every *Ease?*   now and then to admonish her doll, which was <u>exceedingly refractory</u>.

Loose.

SPECIMEN THEME 2. REWRITTEN VERSION

A little girl of about eight years, a poodle, and a doll made up the party which entered a Harvard Square car the other day. With a smile at the other occupants of the car, she sat down with the poodle under one arm, and the doll under the other. She probably wished to say, "I'm a pretty big girl to be travelling all alone, don't you think so?" The car rolled on until it reached Holyoke Street, where the child calmly and proudly rose and left the car. As she walked slowly down Holyoke Street, I could see her pause every now and then to admonish her doll, which was evidently in very poor temper.

SPECIMEN THEME 3

Conversation.

The art of intelligent conversation is far more important than the art of writing, for the reason that for every time we write a letter, we converse with someone a hundred times.

We should therefore do everything in our power to develop our vocabulary and to improve our style. For this purpose let us not be afraid of using new words, merely because they sound a trifle forced at the first attempt; let us not be afraid of employing a spirited or even an audacious style of speech; but let us like Patrick Henry plunge into the midst of a sentence and trust in God to pull us through.

Only in this way can an intelligent, spirited interesting flow of language be developed; for as the well-worn proverb "nothing ventured, nothing have" applies here as elsewhere. Unless we break away from the fetters of a hackneyed worn-out vocabulary, and stilted conventional sentences, we can never hope to become brilliant conversationlists.

SPECIMEN THEME 3. REWRITTEN VERSION

Conversation

The art of conversation is far more important than the art of writing, for the reason that we are apt to talk with some one many times oftener than we write a letter, or otherwise express our thoughts in writing.

We should therefore do everything in our power to develop our vocabulary, and to improve our style. For this purpose, let us not be afraid of using new words, merely because at the first attempt they sound a trifle forced; let us not be afraid of employing a spirited or even an audacious style of speech. But let us rather, like Patrick Henry, plunge into the midst of a sentence and trust in God to pull us through.

Only in this way can an intelligent, spirited, interesting, flow of language be developed; for here, as elsewhere, the well-worn proverb, "nothing venture, nothing have," may be advantageously applied. Unless we enlarge and improve our threadbare, and all too incomplete vocabulary, and change our stilted conventional sentences into something more fluent, we can never hope to become brilliant, or even interesting conversationalists.

SPECIMEN THEME 8. REWRITTEN VERSION

A Day on the Charles River

We started from Riverview, Waltham, early one morning last summer, to paddle as far up the river as we could and return that day. Our party consisted of only three, my sister, a friend of ours, and me. I had never been in a canoe before, but as there were two to paddle, I only pushed straight ahead and let the other fellow steer. The day promised to be perfect, there were no clouds and just enough breeze to make things comfortable.

Along the lower part of the river there was nothing new; it was just as I had often seen it. I soon got the 'hang' of paddling, and we made good time till we came near Newton Lower Falls. As the river was narrower and not so deep there, the current was quite strong. A little further on the river divided. We started up the branch to the right, since it seemed to be the deeper, but we had not gone far when the canoe

SPECIMEN THEME 4

R.
Too many "and's".

There were groups of fellows standing about in a circle. Every now and
then the observer from his distant
stand could see different members
of the various groups gesticulate to
each other; and they appeared to
be explaining the attempt of some
person to grasp a swinging body
that was suspended in the centre
of the group on a rope. The observer
drew nearer and he could hear the
remarks and see the gesticulations
which showed how this one should
have done, and explained why that
one had succeeded or failed.
      The observer had drawn his con-
clusions and made up his mind
that the onlookers belonged to
the 'varsity squad, but this illusion was soon dispelled. The
cry of "Freshman squad this way!"
drew nearly all the onlookers
away, and the observer changed
his conclusion as to how the
foot-ball dummy should be
tackled.

Too impersonal

p.

p. + cap.

K.

SPECIMENT THEME 5

Use fewer words.

A maple tree stands close by. Its foliage is green yellow and red. With every puff of wind the leaves rustle, then some let go their slender hold, and down to the ground the come fluttering where they dance around in little chours bands happy that there days of a life well spent are almost over! Every night and every morning I see that the leaves on the tree grow fewer, that the green one are losing their green hue to a greenish yellow, and that the yellow ones become still more yellow. As they turn from green to yellow their little stems lose their firm hold [they had] and when fully ripe drop. Soon all will be gone. The leaves of the trees show that winter is coming on and they form a blanket for the earth to cover the tender grass and roots beneath them from the cold snow.

rubbed on the bottom. We were, however, near enough to the island to step out on it. This was the beginning of a long carry past two or three dams. Crossing the island and the other branch of the river, we were soon out on the highway. After a hard carry we at last reached the water and continued our way up the river. This part of the river was rather shallow, and full of large rocks rising above the surface of the water.

In a few minutes we were at Newton Upper Falls, where there were two dams. The short distance between them is, perhaps, the most beautiful part of the river, though a great part of its beauty is due to the high arch of Echo Bridge. A mile or so beyond this, the river became broad and deep, flowing through a wide tract of meadow. By this time it was noon, or at least time to eat something. Right opposite us on the shore there was a little hummock covered with pine trees. We made for that, and were soon comfortably seated under the trees eating potato-salad, sandwiches, and stuffed eggs.

After we had rested, we started towards home. The return was a repetition of the journey up, except that the order of things was reversed. When we arrived at the upper falls, we noticed a bluish haze on the western horizon, and by the time we reached the lower falls, the sky was covered with great banks of clouds blowing by at a lively rate. We made the last and longest carry in a hurry, but in our haste we put the canoe in the water before it was deep enough. By this time it had darkened, and the wind began to blow and tear through the trees as if trying to keep pace with the clouds above. After struggling and shoving for almost five minutes, we reached deeper water. A little way ahead there was a private boat-house which had a covered porch, the only shelter in sight. Just before we reached the float there was a great flash of lightning, followed immediately by a sharp crack, and then by a deep roll of thunder. This seemed to have shattered the clouds, for it began to pour as I never saw it pour before. When we recovered from the blow of the lightning we found the canoe was fast on a rock. My sister, who had been rather nervous during all this fun, now gave a terrible groan, for she thought we were lost. A final shove sent the canoe off the rock and up to the float, so that we were soon under cover.

After the downpour had lasted for about half an hour, it settled into a steady rain. We waited over an hour to see if it would not stop, but as it did not, and as it was getting late, we decided to go on in the rain. We fellows gave our coats, collars and ties, and caps to my sister to

SPECIMEN THEME 9

THE SALZKAMMERGUT

~~The sight that greeted us~~ [that July morning] was   R.
very pleasant.   Looking from our window ↙ I could
see the sun ~~with all its rays~~ clearing the mist that   R.
hung over the hills.   Overhead was the clear, blue
sky, with a white, fleecy cloud rapidly scudding   Trite.
over it.   The fresh, bracing air, the cheerful sun, the
sweet-smelling grass heavy with dew, (all the splen-   Too much.
dours of the morning) tended to make everyone in
our party feel happy.   Even the bird singing on the
tree, and the curly-headed shepherd boy slowly   p.
driving along his flocks, seemed to be suffused with   p.   ? ?
the warmth and brightness of the sun on that day.
    As we stepped into our carriage and drove to the   Quite a
salt-mines we| passed many fields with the fresh mown   trick !
hay in large stacks, and in the gentle breeze the   p.
pleasant odor drifted upwards.   The farmers drove   Trite.
past on their large, rumbling wagons bound for the
market, which was already filled with a mass of| Pt. of view
venders disposing of their wares. | lost.
    At last we arrived at the mines and we soon had   p.
slipped on the rubber suits and caps they provide
for you there, each [with a lantern in his hand ready   ?
for the fray.   A funny looking set we were.   The   K.
ladies with large bloomers and bulky coats and the| p.
gentlemen looking just as awkward. | Vb.

101

keep dry with herself under all the pillows, shawls, and things we had.
Although we had to go thus for about four miles through a steady rain,
it was not cold, and the canoe seemed to go easily through the darkness. I am sure I enjoyed it as much as, if not more than, the dry part
of our journey.

SPECIMEN THEME 9. REWRITTEN VERSION

The Salzkammergut

Looking from our window, that July morning, I could see the sun clearing the mist that hung over the hills. Overhead was the clear, blue sky with a white cloud rapidly scudding over it. The fresh, bracing air, the cheerful sun, the sweet-smelling grass heavy with dew tended to make everyone in our party feel happy. Even the bird singing on the tree, and the curly-headed shepherd boy slowly driving along his flocks, seemed to be affected by the brightness of the sun on that day.

After stepping into our carriage we drove to the salt-mines, and on the way we passed many fields with the fresh mown hay in large stacks, and in the breeze the pleasant odor drifted upwards. At last we arrived at the mines, and we soon had slipped on the rubber suits and caps they provide. A funny looking set we were. The ladies were resplendent in large bloomers and bulky coats, and the gentlemen looked just as awkward.

The guide now led the way into a narrow tunnel. We walked a long distance until we came to a large space. The air was biting and cold, the atmosphere was damp, and not a ray of light penetrated the darkness except that which came from our flickering lanterns; nevertheless the excitement and interest drove away all feeling of depression and cold. The walls of this large vault were white and looked like crystal. The guide told us that this was rock salt in the form in which the miners found it.

At the end of the vault was a thing they call a "Rutchbalm." This is simply a log carefully planed and put on an incline at an angle of 45°. It has ropes for people to hold on to if necessary. The guide seats himself at the head, and the party follows. Then they are pushed off and slide down the pole. I shall never forget the sensation of this mad ride. The velocity is increased the nearer one gets to the bottom, and though the whole thing takes only a few seconds, it seemed to last an hour. There we were sliding down a frail piece of wood into a bottomless depth.

At the bottom of this infernal machine we came to a large, salt lake, the sides of which were surrounded with innumerable lanterns. The air tastes salty down there, and everything is soaking wet. We stepped into a boat and were rowed across. This lake is one hundred feet long and three feet deep. It is of pure salt water which comes from the mine. We next came to another "Rutchbalm." Descending this, we reached the place where the mine had been worked, for the stones were strewn about and huge piles of rock nearly covered the place. In one corner stood a large square block made completely of salt from the mine, and bearing the inscription, "Glück Aůf," the miners' expression for "Good Luck." Now another tunnel opened before us, and we were on our way back. But we were to return with more speed. Soon a little car appeared, with a bench in the middle, on which we all seated ourselves. Before we knew it we had shot out of the tunnel into daylight again. I felt dazed and absolutely hot compared to my sensations in the tunnel. We then had our pictures taken in our miners' costume, and started homewards.

SPECIMEN THEME 10. REWRITTEN VERSION

A Morning in Tarrytown Harbor

"Get up, old man! it's four o'clock," was spoken so close to my ear as to make it seem as though some one had shouted into it, and as I slowly opened my eyes, I saw our captain's face bending over me. At first I was half-dazed, and did not comprehend the meaning of his words. Suddenly, like a flash, and by the aid of another poke in my ribs, I realized that it was my watch, and scurried out to relieve the captain.

After a few whispered instructions the captain retired to the cabin, and left me to keep the lookout. Although it was August, the damp chilly air penetrated me through and through. A dense fog had settled all round us, and I could distinguish only those objects immediately near the boat. It was very lonely and quiet; hardly a breeze stirred. In fact, the air was filled with a fishy smell which made the atmosphere almost stifling. Occasionally I heard the mournful howl of a dog which was rendered all the more woeful and greatly magnified by the heavy atmosphere. And now, wonders of all wonders! The captain was snoring. It was no common snoring, either. He had a peculiar way of whistling whenever he exhaled, and at each exhalation the tone was of a little higher pitch than the previous one—a sort of "music of the spheres."

Just as I was thinking of spheres a large, fiery orb peeped up on the horizon. It grew larger and larger, and rose so quickly that it seemed as if I could see it move. The mist began to scatter before its warning rays as if by magic. Now the curtain of fog raised and revealed to me the beautiful valleys of Sleepy Hollow, with its fields of ripening grain. The heavy dew on the grain shone and glistened in the morning sun. From a cottage near the shore rose small curls of gray smoke which were wafted away into oblivion, and there were signs of life and activity near by.

At the sight of this activity I concluded that it must be nearly breakfast time, and called the crew. After much yawning, and some "cussing," the other "Three men in a boat" came out on deck, and helped in the preparations for breakfast. Our larder was so well filled with canned meats and preserves, cookies, bread, and in fact, all the necessary food supplies, that it was not much work to prepare a meal. For breakfast, however, we always made coffee, and now our troubles began. By some unknown accident the coffee-pot had fallen overboard the day before, and no doubt was now being used by the mermaids. But the genius of four Yankee boys was equal to the occasion. We determined to have peaches for breakfast and use the empty can for a coffee-pot. Never was coffee more delicious.

While we were eating, a glorious breeze sprang up, and, moreover, it was down the river. The tide, also, was going out. Now for a sail! The waves danced round the boat; white-caps were omnipresent. Our nerves tingled with delight as we hurried about to make ready for the start. Hurrah! we're off! The sails caught the breeze, and the small craft bounded over the waves as if she too were glad to be released from her moorings.

A University of Wisconsin First-Year Student Essay from Edwin C. Woolley
"Admission to Freshman English in the University"
English Journal 3 (1914)

& *Written in 1912, this theme was printed as an example of what a remedial student's writing was like. In his* English Journal *article Woolley cited the Wisconsin catalogue's statement: "No student will be . . . permitted to pursue the Freshman English Course whose work shows serious weakness in spelling, punctuation, grammar, sentence-construction, or division into paragraphs" (239). And to pin down precisely what Wisconsin meant,*

Woolley quoted the University's bulletin "Requirements for Admission to the Freshman English Course":

When we say that a certain amount of proficiency is necessary, we mean a certain amount of proficiency in the rudiments of writing. Students whose writing is devoid of interest, originality, or any other literary merit, are qualified if their writing is satisfactory as to the rudiments.

THE KIND OF BOOKS I LIKE

I am not much of a hand at reading books, by this I mean reading novels. When I do read a novel I like to get ahold of a good one, not one by Chambers because I think if a person reads one of Chambers books he knows what the main theme of all his books are, but I think if a person reads one of Wrights or Porters stores he is always wishing to read any others by these two authors because he know that each one of the books written by the last two men will always have a different theme, anyway that is the way I think it is. I dont very often read a novel, but one in a while I will pick one up and read it, because is kind of give me a change but when I do read one I want one which deals with the happier thoughts in life and not one which makes a joke out of life as some of the authors do of the present day. I for myself would much rather read some of the older books than start to read the trash written in over half of the books of the present day, which are written to sell and not to stay in the list of great writers.

Two Anonymous Themes Presented as Samples of Proficient First-Year College Writing (1912)

❧ *These were the final two samples in the scale of student writing quality developed by Milo Burdette Hillegas (1872–1961). Hillegas (B.A., Rochester; Ph.D., Columbia) served as Vermont's commissioner of education, 1916–20, then as a professor at Teachers College, 1920–37. He developed his scale as a way of making reliable comparative judgments of student writing. These rather innocuous looking themes were quite important; they were used as "range finders" for determining excellence on the Hillegas scale. (Within a decade the first "objective" tests of English composition would be in use, and rating scales such as this would lose their influence.)*

WRITTEN BY A BOY IN THE FRESHMAN CLASS IN COLLEGE.

Venus of Melos.

In looking at this statue we think, not of wisdom, or power, or force, but just of beauty. She stands resting the weight of her body on one foot, and advancing the other (left) with knee bent. The posture causes the figure to sway slightly to one side, describing a fine curved line. The lower limbs are draped but the upper part of the body is uncovered. (The unfortunate loss of the statue's arms prevents a positive knowledge of its original attitude.) The eyes are partly closed, having something of a dreamy languor. The nose is perfectly cut, the mouth and chin are moulded in adorable curves. Yet to say that every feature is of faultless perfection is but cold praise. No analysis can convey the sense of her peerless beauty.

WRITTEN BY A BOY IN THE FRESHMAN CLASS IN COLLEGE.

A Foreigner's Tribute to Joan of Arc.

Joan of Arc, worn out by the suffering that was thrust upon her, nevertheless appeared with a brave mien before the Bishop of Beauvais. She knew, had always known that she must die when her mission was fulfilled and death held no terrors for her. To all the bishop's questions she answered firmly and without hesitation. The bishop failed to confuse her and at last condemned her to death for heresy, bidding her recant if she would live. She refused and was lead to prison, from there to death.

While the flames were writhing around her she bade the old bishop who stood by her to move away or he would be injured. Her last thought was of others and De Quincy says, that recant was no more in her mind than on her lips. She died as she lived, with a prayer on her lips and listening to the voices that had whispered to her so often.

The heroism of Joan of Arc was wonderful. We do not know what form her great patriotism took or how far it really led her. She spoke of hearing voices and of seeing visions. We only know that she resolved to save her country, knowing though she did so, it would cost her her life. Yet she never hesitated. She was uneducated save for the lessons taught her by nature. Yet she led armies and crowned the dauphin, king of France. She was only a girl, yet she could silence a great bishop by words that came from her heart and from her faith. She was only a woman, yet she could die as bravely as any martyr who had gone before.

Six University of California Placement Essays from Howard Eugene Potter
Abilities and Disabilities in the Use of English Found in the Written Compositions of Entering Freshmen at the Univesity of California (1922)

ᐓ *Berkeley's famous first-year writing course, Subject A, enrolled the bulk of entering students in this era. Of the five hundred papers he collected, Potter printed only these six, including none he judged among the very weakest. The six papers are presented in Potter's order: two weaker papers first, two judged to fall in the middle, one from the top quarter, and one of the five best. All are over 500 words; the best is the longest (and most literary): 733 words.*

WHY I CAME TO COLLEGE

All my life I have wanted to go to college. Even as a very small child, I thought it a great many times. A person attending college was something very wonderful to me.

As I grew older, the desire became greater and greater, but I did not think my wish would ever come true. My parents were as anxious as myself, for me to secure a college education.

It was one month after my graduation from high school, that the great unexpected happened. A large oil company struck oil on my father's farm. We were then quite wealthy, if not enormously rich.

I then entered college without the slightest hesitation. It was wonderful to me to think that I did not have to lose even a year.

My reasons for coming to college are, I suppose, quite like that of many other people. I think college broadens the minds of every one who attends, it makes no difference which part of the college you go to, or what subject you specialize in. They all have the same effect in that one respect.

I came to college to get all I possibly could out of it. The time to learn is when you are young. The mind, at this time, grasps learning immediately. Of course no one is hardly ever too old to go to college. I believe in people going to college at almost any age, if they had not the chance when they were young. At every university, one sees a great number of older people.

The course one takes now at the colleges are so thorough, that it is the fault of the student if they don't get a great amount of good from them. There are so many, many courses now. A student may find any one subject that they wish to pursue during life. There is no reason for ignorant men and women of this generation. The colleges are so wonderfully equipped with everything up-to-date, that the work is not a drudge. It really cannot help but be interesting.

Aside from the learning you receive, there is another important matter. This is the association with the other students. This is one of the greatest reasons why I came to college. There is something in the school life that is laking in anything else As life goes on, one never finds anything like it again. Your association with your classmates broadens your mind and teaches consideration of others. A person who does not attend college certainly misses something in life which can never be made up.

As I want to specialize in music, I think college is the very best place to obtain the best instruction. The teachers are always of the best. I'm sure that I will find a great deal of pleasure in all my classes. I came to get everything I could out of the course. I think music is a wonderful study. It is becoming to be chassed a real worth while subject. A few years ago, many thought that only the idle and pleasure loving people studied music. It is now considered necessary to the world.

A student should not come to college just alone for the social life. It counts a great deal, but one must not have all play and no work.

There is till another reason which I must mention. That is concerning the associations of the students with the teachers in college. These instructors are most always fine, clean men and women. Their morals are unexcelled, and they are persons of great personality. They have spent the greater part of their life in study. The faculty may influence the students a very great deal, and I condier this one an especially good reason for attending college.

WHY I GO TO CHURCH

There are two reasons why I go to church. The first is because my training has included, that I attend church every Sunday. As soon as I could go myself, I was sent to Sunday School. Thus my religious training was started very early in life. My parents believed that all should attend church as soon as they could go and understand the sermon. If you were too young to stay to the morning service, you at least had to go to Sunday School.

Force of habit, has a good deal to do whether you go, or do not go to church. If you were brought up to believe that it was the only thing to do, you would of course go to church every Sunday morning. You do not question; one only performs their righteous duty in attending the religious ceremony on Sunday.

Then again, if your training was such that all who went to church, were the only people who did things correctly; you would go because you thought it your duty. Of course there were people who didn't go to church and were not heathenish, still they could not think right or they would at least go to church, to show that their souls were right. That was practically what I was taught to believe.

Until I was about twelve I went to church, because I had to. My parents sent me off every Sunday morning to Sunday School, then they followed by coming later to the morning service. Of course I enjoyed my Sunday School class, that I was in, I liked the girls and my teacher. Going to church was something to look forward to. I started to go, because my parents saw fit to do so and then I went because I wanted to.

My second reason, although it follows the first; is really the reason why I attend church. Not only do I go to the service in the morning but also the service in the evening; because I wish to go.

Aside from the religion that the church teaches; it is the one of the greatest social centers of the community. The church gives you something in the way of amusement that you can not get in the moving picture show or the dance hall.

The church realized the value of good clean wholesome sports and most churches are fostering and trying to get the community interested. The church tries not only to bring the people together on Sunday for the good of their souls; but also during the week for amusements and recreation; which when come right down to it help and foster the growth of your mind.

I will have to confess that I go to church now more on account of the social field it has open for young people. Boys and girl realize that they may get all the fun they want and good times right in the church. The church is one way in bringing boys and girls together for a good time. That is why I go to church now, because I know I can have a good time and will meet the kind of boys and girls that my parents would care to have me know.

I go to Church now because I enjoy the boys and girls that go, and I like the amusement and recreation that the church offers. I also enjoy working in the church; there are many opportunities open for those who care for that sort of work. I care for that kind of work so that is why I now go to church.

THE GREATEST ADVENTURE OF MY LIFE

The person who has never felt the inexplicable thrill of a daring adventure, has missed one of the greatest joys of his life. Some people write their adventures in books, others hold them jealously in their hearts; but if you, are interested I shall tell you of my greatest adventure.

The day dawned clear, but cold on that famous peak, overlooking the entire Yosemite Valley, Glacier Point. I had enjoyed an early breakfast with the rush and roar of the falls in my ears, and a lightness of heart caused by the, altitude. A party of friends suggested that I accompany them in a "hike" to the valley. I refused pleading that a head ache was the cause of my refusal. I thought, surely, they would go without me, but, no, stay they would, and to make matters worse, suggested that we have a sort of child's party, and play games. Not wishing to appear cross I consented to play.

Running to a little knoll, quite near the world-famous "Overhanging Rock", we started the silly list of childish games. "Ring-a-round-a-rosy" was first, "London Bridges" second, "Beef-steak" third, and so on until both the time, and ourselves were nearly spent.

We seated ourselves on the flat rocks close by, and laughing, out-of-breath, and warm, tried to think of more games. It was not long before someone suggested "Blind Man's Bluff"; and it took still less time to have me nominated and elected as "blind man".

A large white handkerchief was produced and tied, about my eyes in such a fashion, that I could see nothing. My friends grouped themselves in a circle, and it was my business to touch one, and then guess his name. I failed several times. Then I felt the presence of one near me, whom I thought I knew, so I started in pursuit. Stumbling over pebbles and boulders, I followed the elusive being before me. On, on I went, while my companions shouted with glee! On, on I continued, but came no nearer my goal.

The laughter of my friends gradually died away and someone shouted:—

"Quick, stop her!"

Two strong hands grasped my shoulders stopping me, suddenly. I pulled the cloth from my eyes. For a brief moment, I had no idea of where I was standing. That was for, a brief moment only, the whole horrible truth dawned on me as soon as my eyes became accustomed to the light of the sun! I was standing within, an, arm's length of the outer edge of "Over-hanging Rock." Three thousand feet below lay the valley. Two more steps meant Oblivion.

The entire situation would have been grotesque, and grim, were it not for the fact that I had been following an Airdale pup, belonging to one of the girls! The poor creature sat at my feet, snilling [This seems to be Potter's transcription error for the handwritten "sniffing."—ED.] the end of my dress.

I was at the end of my adventure, and, above all things else to be grateful for,—safe!

THE VALUE OF INTERCOLLEGIATE ATHLETICS

During the past five years their has been a great deal of comment on the relative merits of Intercollegiate Athletics. A day does not pass without one hearing some bit of criticism on the value of athletics.—This discussion has been brought about by the wonderful strides competitive athletics have taken on the last year. Some people argue, that too much time is being devoted to them and not enough to the business of obtaining an education, that will fit you for the business world, and not the baseball diamond or football gridiron. Having participated in athletics in high school I am strong personally, for competitive athletics, whether they be Intercollegiate or otherwise.

The value of Intercollegiate athletics lies in the fact that it develops

friendly rivalry between colleges, as well as broadening the scope of acquaintances between the members of the oppossing teams. Some of the
most brilliant men in the country, during their college day's, were members of the teams of their Alma Mater. They made friends with their
opponents and widened their acquaintances. The greatest thing outside of
the actual value of the college course, is the amount of friends one makes
while at college. Here in the different colleges, you meet men who will
amount to something in the business world, after their college days are
over; and who are more fitted to meet, than men who have fought for the
honor of their Alma Mater When a big game is held, it is more like a re-
union than anything else. You hear the different students from each college, kidding each other about the respective merits of their team. Thus,
the two colleges are brought together, as a unit, and democracy prevails.

Intercollegiate Athletics are also a great advertisement for the various
Universities. Thousands of dollars are saved annually by a university,
because it is not necessary to advertise on a large scale, due to the free
publicity obtained thru competive athletics.

Many students would not go out for athletics if it were't for the fact
that they desired to represent their college in competition. By going out
for the Varsity they develop physically, as well as mentally. They learn to
take hard knocks, and to be mentally alert. If they do not make the
team, they will be disappointed, quite naturally, but they will have
gained strength weight, and endurance, which they will need when they
get older. Many a fellow, who was weake physically, before taking up
athletics, has turned out to be robust and energetic.

People who say athletics district the students from getting an education are mistaken because, if a student wishes to participate in Intercollegiate Athletics, he must, first of all, maintain a good grade of work. If he
fails he is barred from competition, which is a sad blow to any athlete.

In conclusion, I might say that I hope the same standard of Intercollegiate Athletics will be maintained, and that the few criticizers of this
system, will see where they have made their mistake.

WHY I PREFER A BUICK TO ANY OTHER MAKE OF
AUTOMOBILE

The choice of an automobile depends primarily upon the purse of the
prospective purchaser. There are three classes of automobiles to be consid-

ered: the high priced, medium priced, and the cheap cars. Each has its advantages and disadvantages. Cheap cars are not easy riding. Expensive ones are easy enough to ride in but their cost is prohibitive to the majority. The medium priced car strikes the happy medium: and decreases the disadvantages of each of the extremes while yet partaking of the advantages of each of them.

At present, the price ranges of the medium class is from fourteen hundred to twenty five hundred dollars in the six and eight-cylinder models; and from one thousand to two thousand dollars in the four-cylinder types. In this category are included such cars as the Essex, the Reo, The Buick, the Oldsmobile, and the Hupmobile.

Out of this selection, I have chosen the Buick. Probably the choice was purely personal and not founded upon scientific comparison. All of the cars mentioned in the preceding paragraph are excellent. It seemed to me, however, that the Buick is just a trifle more reliable, a little sturdier in construction, and possibly longer-lived than the rest. From observation, I have learned that the Buick stands the test of rough usages: that it is always ready to respond; and that it will give excellent service from six or eight years covering, perhaps, from one to two hundred thousand miles.

Mechanically, the Buick has a great advantage in construction. The valve-inhead motor was originated by the Buick and has been copied recently by many other manufacturers. But the Buick engineers have had the longer experience and have been able to add refinements to that feature that the other motor cars do not possess. The valve-in-head motor is designed to give the maximum power to the transmission of the car. Formerly, a considerable part of the force of the explosion was lost in the valve chamber. This has now been practically eliminated and, in the Buick especially, all the power is used to send the car forward.

This device tends to lessen the cost of operating the machine to some extent. A Buick will run almost twenty miles on one gallon of gasoline, which is about the average of much cheaper and rougher riding machines.

The Buick is constructed to ride easy. The springs are resilient and the upholstery is springy and comfortable.

I believe that in the Buick one gets practically all of the advantages of riding-comfort that one finds in the expensive makes. And with that ease one gets the great advantage of the cheaper car—low maintenance costs. It does not cost much to run a Buick; its sturdy construction prevents the necessity of frequent repairs; its longevity reduces the immense cost of replacement that many automobile owners encounter every second or third year; and added to all of those advantages, it is as nicely finished and good-looking as the best.

All these considerations, it seems to me, lead inevitably to the choice of a Buick. For one who desires a car that is not expensive or troublesome, but instead is comfortable, durable, sturdy, and long lived, I recommend the purchase of a Buick. There are, I grant, finer cars; and there are cheaper ones. But in this car one finds the golden mean—a maximum of good points and a minimum of faults—the epitome of automobile construction of this day.

THE BEST POEM I KNOW

After the freedom, vigor, and realism of modern poetry, with its insistence on life as it seems and as it is, and its flat, stultified spirituality, one reads "Crossing the Bar" by Lord Tennyson and the feeling is akin to that of a traveller emerging from the arid wastes of Arizona and New Mexico into California.

Perhaps the new poets touch so little on the subject of death, because the Great War made it too terrible a reality for them. However it is always a favorite theme in poetry. Browning's

> "Fear Death? To feel the mist in my breath
>   The fog in my throat?
> Not I! I was always a fighter;
>   And one fight more, the best and the last."

As in true Browning style. However, his closing lines:

> "Oh Thou Soul of my Soul
>   I shall clasp thee to my breast
> And with God be the rest.",—

has so much more feeling for Elizabeth Barret Browning than for God, its appeal can hardly be universal.

Bryant's "Thanatopsis"—that remarkable expression for a young man of nineteen comes next to mind. He wrote it at an age when most young poets are essentially pagan and it stands a pagan poem. If one can read Christianity into these lines:

"So live, that when thy time comes to join that unnum-
　　bered throng which moves to its appointed end,
Thou go, not like the quarry slave,
　　Scourged to his dungeon,
But sustained and soothed by an unfaltering trust
　　Approach they grave
Like one who wraps the drapery of his couch about him
And lies down to pleasant dreams."

then Christianity is much more distant, cold and elusive than it has
seemed to me.

Now, Tennyson wrote his poem at the completion of a life ripened
with years of depth and richness. One can see and hear him reading aloud
to Queen Victoria the rhythmic stanzas of "Crossing the Bar." Each had a
glimpse of the life beyond, because each was so near to it. Perhaps this
explains its spirituality, which is felt life that of a hymn. Only John
Henry Newman in his "Dream of Gerontius" shows such depths of
religious feeling. As in the latter poem, only one thing matters,—the
relation of a soul departed to its Maker,

"Jsu, Mari, I am dying
And Thou has called me"—

which opens one is indeed the key-note of both. This God one is to meet
is no shadowy figure, nor stern Jehovah, but a personal God. Nowhere
does Tennyson call him Friend, Father, or Savior, but there is complete
understanding in the lines:

"I hope to meet my Pilot Face to Face
When I have crossed the bar."

The imagery of the piece is conventional. Since the days of Homer
and Hesiod, bards have sung of man, the ship sailing the ocean of life or
of death. Yet the depiction of a vessel tugging and straining at the bar,
before making bigger waters, may well suggest the soul released from
the ties of life about to enter the sea of Eternity.

The setting is sunset, through the peace of twilight and into dark is
fine.

"Sunset and evening star
　　And one clear call for me
And may there be no moaning of farewell
　　When I put out to sea."

"For though from out our bourn of Time and Place
  The tide may bear me far
I hope to see my Pilot Face to Face
  When I have crossed the bar."

This is poetry as Milton said it should be: simple, sensuous and passionate.

The imagery of Amy Lowell, of H. D. or of Robert Frost is exquisite and the magnificent lines of Rupert Brooks still echo from Mediterranean waters, and one feels the spell of "Vers Libre", without consenting at all that to be conventional is to be "unknown and unkist." "Crossing the Bar" is conventional in theme, in imagery, and in melody, yet where can we look today for such simple dignity, such fine normality of feeling, and such spirituality? It is a poem singularly free from straining after effect; nowhere does love of the unusual mar its lines. Spenser might have signed his name to it for it recalls the richness of the Elizabethan painter-poet. Yet its greatest power is in its suggestion,—and upon this basis, I rank it among the best poems I know—high as this rating may seem.

Seven Purdue Papers from Herbert LeSourd Creek and James Hugh McKee
"The Preparation in English of Purdue Freshmen"
Purdue Studies in Higher Education 5 (1926)

¿&⸱ *Creek studied at Butler College and took his doctorate at the University of Illinois in 1910. He taught at Illinois from 1908 to 1920 and served as professor and chair at Purdue from 1920 to 1949. He wrote* A Handbook of Modern Writing *with H. M. Baldwin and J. H. McKee (1930) and* The Literature of Business *with Alta Gwinn Saunders (5th ed., 1946).*

These papers, written in 1924 and 1925, were collected as part of an ongoing survey of entering students' English abilities. The authors state that the first three papers were written by students found "unprepared for college composition."

My dear Mr. _____,

Well I have found college life a great adventure. I learn and see many things every day. I found out that I didn't know anything about traveling.

School and I are getting along alright on everything except English, and I found that I had many things to learn yet, for fact I don't believe I knew hardly anything. But if I keep on learning you can probable tell the difference when I come home.

This is one great place here there are all kinds of sports played but it take a lot of work to stay here and expect to play.

I do more work in one night than I did in a month at high school and it telling on me, for I lost three pound since I came.

Well this is all my spare time so will close. Answer.

Yours Truly

WHERE I SHOULD MOST LIKE TO TRAVEL

My only desire for traveling is to travel in the oriental countries. It has been my ambition for several years to visit China, Japan, and most of the U. S. Government's Islands in the Pacific ocean.

Some reason for wanting to visit China and Japan are; because they are old countries. I want to learn their character their habits of farming as to compared with that in the United States. I have often heard how density populated those two countries were. It would seem a mystery to me to live in so thickly populated country. After living in the United States where you can go to the country every summer to spent your vacation along the beautiful creeks and rivers. While I have learned it is altogether different in the oriental countries. I love to learn how the people in other countries live as well as in my own country.

Another place where I would like to spend considerable amount of time and that is in the Hawaii Island. I have so many beautiful pictures from there which I am very proud of.

I have several friends who have traveled through the Hawaii Island and they have often informed me. To travel too the Hawaii Island and make a special study of structure of those Islands, especially the beautiful scenery. Which is considered the beauty spot of the world.

WHAT THANKSGIVING IS

Thanksgiving is a day of grace and rememberance. At the beginning of winter the Pillgrams landed at Plymouth Rock on the last Thursday of November in 1620. They were homeless, foodless and almost clotheless. Due to like of protection from weather and like of food, about half of the number died during the winter.

Their were some of the choice men and women of the day represented
in the colony. Men and women that had power of forseeing and laboring
to advantages for the well fare of the colony. The colony as a whole
prayed each day for savior. Friendly Indians brought them food each day.
The colony agreed to give a "big" feast in honor of their deceased,
friendly Indians and survivors of the colony. They had wild turkey,
sauces, berries and breads.

From that day on it has been a custom of American men to treat their
families and guests with a feast of delicious foods; in remembrance of the
landing of the Pilgrams.

THE SUPERIORITY OF THE FORD

The Ford, comparatively speaking, is far superior to all other makes of
automobiles. Of course this question can be studied from several different view points but nevertheless the Ford in my estimation far surpasses
all other makes of cars. The Ford is the least complicated of any car
made. Its engine is very simple in construction, for it is built so that
every part will come off by the loosening of a few bolts & taps. As a
matter of fact the Ford Car is so simple that it is sometimes said that it is
possible to buy parts in every 5 & 10c store and every cross roads store in
the country.

The Ford is very simple in opperation and also very easy to learn to
opperate. There are no gears to shift, only the using of a pedal starts and
stops it at a minutes notice. One of the very important parts of the
starting of a Ford is the fact that the starting is due to the clamping of
bands arrond a revolving cylinder, and thus doing away with the old
toothed gears which would only mesh under certain conditions and were
always in danger of having two or three teeth knocked out at each shift of
gears.

The Ford car is not a speedy car but it will take you and bring you
back.

Recently there have been several new changes in the Ford which have
added greatly to its appearance and which have caused it to be a very
attractive and pleasing to the eye.

Baloon tires have been a great addition to this car and now it is a rich
mans car as well as a poor mans.

So suming up all these things and the multitude of others which I have not mentioned; if the Ford is not superior, why do rich men drive a Ford while their chauffier rides around with the cook, in the rich mans Packard.

. . . .

CLASSIFICATION OF STUDENTS

There are many classes of students who come to a University. Some for pleasure, others for hard and solid work. The purpose of going to college is to prepare a person for his future.

The person with too much money does not appreciate what he has and he does not know what the lower class has to contend with. The rich student have everything furnished them to make their life enjoyable while here. They are given an auto and are privileged to do as they please.

The class who has enough to make them comfortable are better off, because they don't run around because they are working for their future. This class person is more willing to work and study. When some one does a person of this class a favor he is never forgotten and this person will do anything for the assistant.

There is the poor class who come to college and haven't sufficient money to give them the things which are needed to make them healthy and able to stand the grind of school work.

In college all men are equal to the rights of the school and the person makes himself by the aid of professors. The person may make high grades in college but he must have the getup about him, after he is out of college, to make a success.

There are classes of students according to their ability to learn. There is the class who can learn quickly. They are generally students who have been aided by their parents in former years. It is an aid to children to have their parents converse with them and explain to them the things they don't understand.

The dull student has often times had something holding him back. Sickness or some physical defect may cause it and again it may be himself. He may not work hard on his subjects.

HOME SICKNESS

I consider home sickness to be one of the most desperate kind of sickness; in which any one can experience. A person, who becomes over taken by this unfortunate disease, is one to be much sympathized with by other people, who have had experienced such in their previous lives.

That person who is inflicted with such has a feeling that every thing is working against them and they become down-cast and appear that they have no friends. It is true also, they loose interest in practically everything and in many instances cease to eat and sleep. I must confess by having already experienced this kind of sickness that it is the most remorseful and discouraging thing that ever befell me in my life. It can be suppressed and over come by friends and participating and showing those who are afflicted with such the absurdity of such a thing. It is true their thoughts must be kept away from home affairs and other things of interest must be substituted until the person has broken away from such a habit.

IMPORTANCE OF ENGLISH COMPOSITION

English composition is, without question, one of the most fundamental subjects in our schools. There is no study that so thoroughly permeates the work of all other subjects and that is so essential to their successful understanding. From one viewpoint every recitation is a language recitation and has to do with English composition work in some way or the other. English composition affords an opportunity by which the student may be able to express his ideas in a logical and grammatical way.

The teacher, therefore, who does not take cognance of the language used in all the various recitations and try to bring it to a high standard of excellence will find the work of his regular English composition exercises barren and very deficient. He must remember that the recitation periods of the day afford a constant field for applying in actual use the lessons learned in the English composition exercises. If, for example, the teacher emphasizes the correct use of certain verbs or pronouns in the composition lesson, and then allows the pupils to disregard this knowledge in the language used in the history or geography lesson the next period, it would be better not to teach the language facts at all, for such self contradiction makes the language and composition work a mere failure.

Again, the importance of language and English composition exercises must be admitted when we realize how closely they are identified with the thinking process. Most of the ineffective work of the past has been due to such failures on the part of teachers to understand this fact.

They must understand that English composition teaches the student to know and to use correctly these "signs of ideas," and that leads him to develop new thoughts and creates a desire of the student to give the best expression to all his writings. I consider this to be paramount and of the greatest importance in developing good expression and logical thinking in the high schools of our Nation.

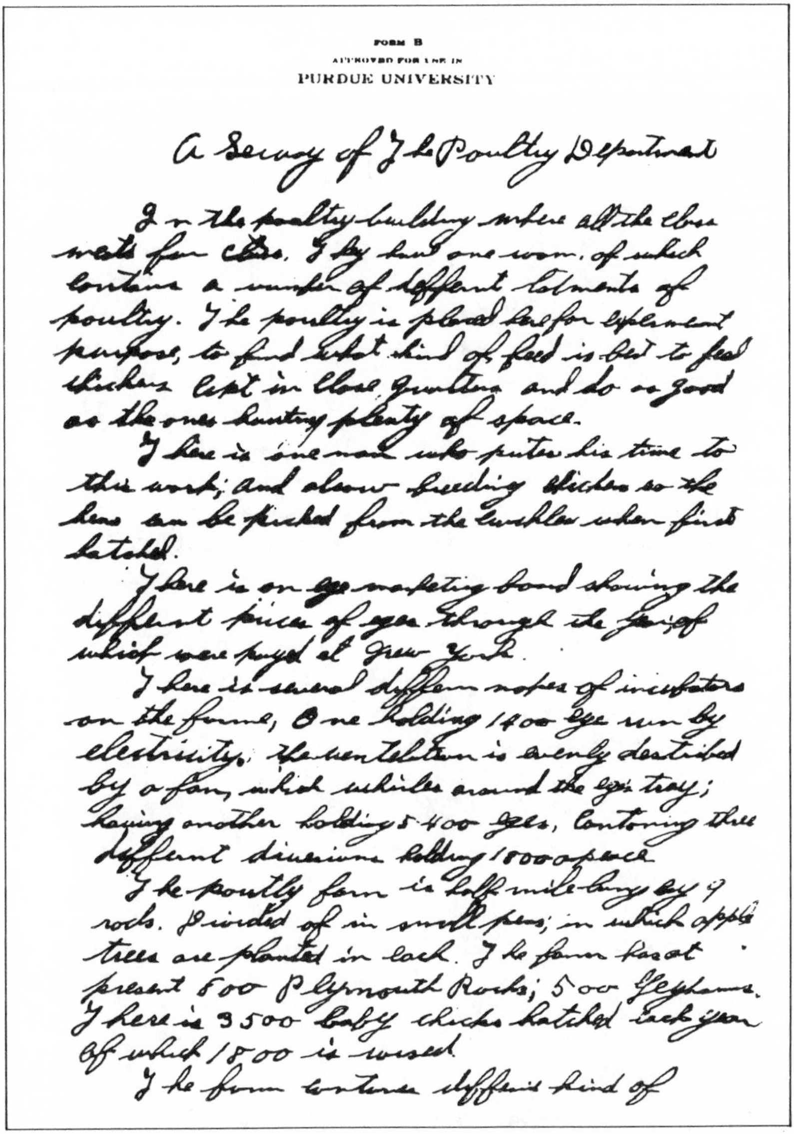

FORM B
APPROVED FOR USE IN
PURDUE UNIVERSITY

A Servey of The Poultry Depatment

In the poultry building where all the class waits for class. They had one room, of which contains a number of differnt lotments of poultry. The poultry is placed here for explament purpose, to find what kind of feed is best to feed chickens kept in close quarters and do as good as the ones having plenty of space.

There is one man who putes his time to this work; and also breeding chicken so the hens can be picked from the chickens when first hatched.

There is an egg marketing board showing the different prices of eggs through the year of which were payed at New York.

There is several differnt makes of incubators on the farm, One holding 1400 eggs run by electricity. The ventelation is evenly destributed by a fan, which whirles around the egg tray; having another holding 5400 eggs, contaning three different divisions holding 1800 apeace.

The poultry farm is half mile long by 4 rods. Divided of in small pens; in which apple trees are planted in each. The farm has at present 600 Plymouth Rocks; 500 Leghorns. There is 3500 baby chicks hatched each year of which 1800 is raised.

The farm contains differnt kind of

Plate II: This is a reproduction of a page from a theme of a student who is clearly unable to do college work in English. He is a graduate of a high school of 50 students: his grade in English as reported by the high school was 81.

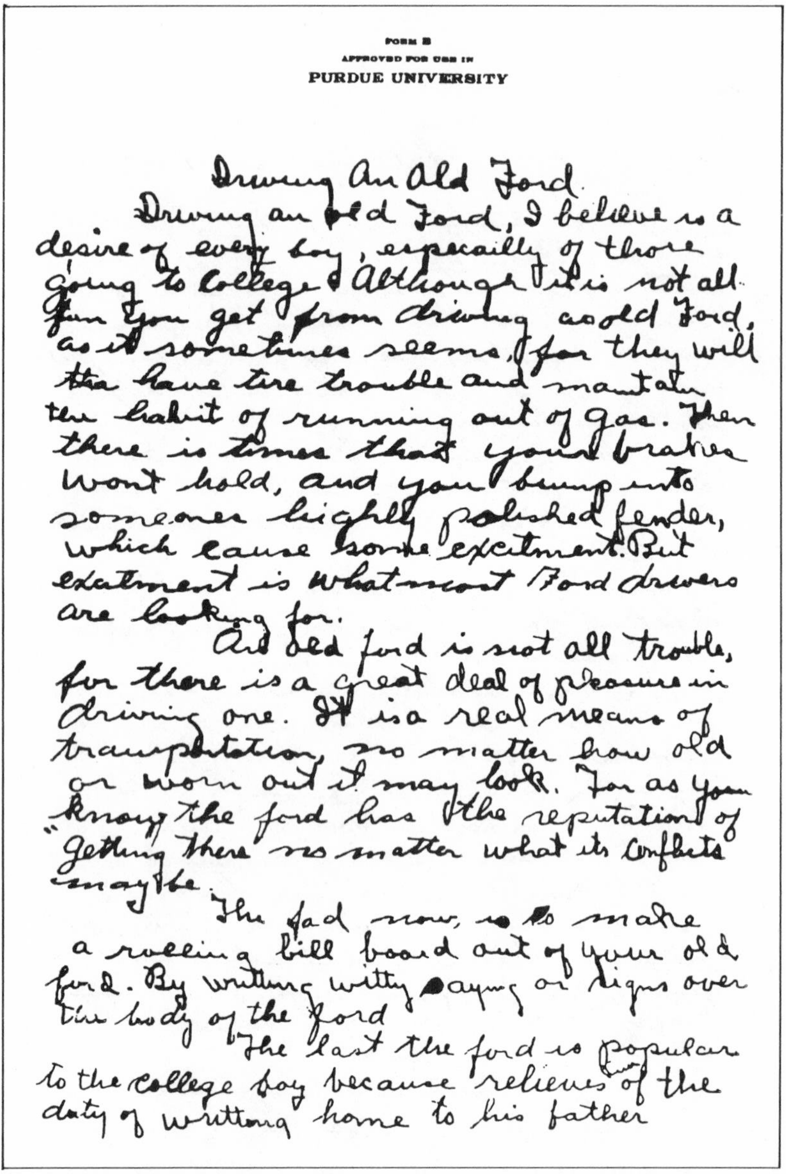

FORM B
APPROVED FOR USE IN
PURDUE UNIVERSITY

Driving An Old Ford.

Driving an old Ford, I believe is a desire of every boy, especially of those going to college. Although it is not all fun you get from driving a old Ford, as it sometimes seems, for they will the have tire trouble and maintain the habit of running out of gas. Then there is times that your brakes wont hold, and you bump into someone's highly polished fender, which cause some excitment. But excitment is what most Ford drivers are looking for.

And a old ford is not all trouble, for there is a great deal of pleasure in driving one. It is a real means of transportation, no matter how old or worn out it may look. For as you know the ford has the reputation of getting there no matter what its conflicts may be.

The fad now, is to make a rolling bill board out of your old ford. By writing witty sayings or signs over the body of the ford

The last the ford is popular to the college boy because relieves of the duty of writting home to his father

Plate III: The page above reproduces part of a theme written by a boy who showed some interest in his subject but whose work was so full of errors that the instructor had trouble in finding room to mark them. This boy came from a high school of about 800 students.

7

Conclusion

A FITTING END TO THIS VOLUME IS WARNER TAYLOR'S comprehensive survey of first-year English at the end of the 1920s. Drawing upon questionnaires returned from 232 colleges and universities, Taylor compiled a detailed picture of composition as it passed its first half century.

Warner Taylor
A National Survey of Conditions in Freshman English
(1929)

෨ *Taylor (1880–1958) studied at Columbia (B.A., 1903; M.A., 1905) and taught English there, 1907–11, moving to Wisconsin in 1911 and becoming professor in 1927. He published a writing text (*Freshman Themes, *with F. A. Manchester, 1918), a scholarly monograph (*A Study of the Prose Style of Samuel Johnson, *1918), and edited two essay anthologies. He states that when he started teaching at Wisconsin, "every member of the department save one . . . had at least one section of Freshman English. It was a policy of the department. To-day I am the only person instructing in the regular course" (below, p. 556). From full participation at one great university, Harvard, in 1875, to almost no participation at another great university, Wisconsin, we see the extent of a half century of change.*

FRESHMAN ENGLISH

The following report on Freshman English procedure in the United States is based on an extensive survey begun in November, 1927, and concluded in July, 1928. Three hundred questionnaires were sent to colleges or universities, with enrollments of five hundred students or more, located in all parts of the country and representative of all types.

The percentage of returns was far higher than anticipated: Two hundred thirty two replies were received, or 77.3%. Seven came from Canadian institutions, but it seemed wiser to omit them from the general report since their practices differed somewhat radically from those in the United States. (I shall summarize their tendencies briefly later.)

The summary that follows represents the results from two hundred twenty-five institutions that marshall among them more than one hundred thousand Freshmen. Practically without a single exception every major college or university in the country co-operated. To all those who did, gratitude is due,—especially, perhaps, to such universities as were moved by a spirit of courtesy rather than by any expectation of being enlightened through the findings. And further expression of gratitude is owing such chairmen of Freshman English or heads of departments as submitted reports transcending the bounds of the questions asked and entering into many fields of general interest.

There is unquestionably, if not a spirit of unrest over Freshman English throughout the country, at least a spirit of inquiry. And there may well be. No other course is so universal, no other enlists so much sustained effort. Furthermore, aside from some changes wrought by the older, endowed institutions of the East, the course stands fundamentally as it was a decade and more ago. More colleges are using placement tests for sectionizing students today, fewer are using standard rhetorics; but at bottom traditional practices persevere. The East alone is modifying the time-tried Rhetoric-Handbook formula; the Middle-West, the West, and the South tend to retain it. Each section is serving its special interests and meeting its obligations as they fall due. The gates of the older Atlantic seaboard institutions have partly closed: Only students of proved fitness penetrate beyond their registrars. Their endowments render them independent and put them beyond the reach of relative illiterates. The great tax-supported universities beyond New York and Pennsylvania and south of the Mason-Dixon line must, through their very nature, prove unquestioning hosts. The survey I am presenting bears out this difference clearly. It should always be remembered, however, that this divergence of method is due not necessarily to the greater vision or liberalism or forward looking of Eastern educators but to a very practical adaptation of means to end.

. . . .

I. THE CONTENT OF THE COURSE

A—The Rhetoric-Handbook-Essay Volume Situation

The catalog of Harvard College for 1874–75 offers among the prescribed studies a course in rhetoric for Sophomores under Professor A. S. Hill. The texts designated were Campbell's "Philosophy of Rhetoric," first published in 1762, Whately's "Rhetoric" of 1828, and Herbert Spencer's "Philosophy of Style." Campbell and Whately together with Blair, whose "Rhetoric" was issued in 1783, were the dominant rhetoricians of the period when Latin and Greek were basic in our colleges. Their rhetorics still stressed heavily the logic and elocution associated with the three liberal arts of the mediaeval trivium. With a difference, of course, in that the rules governing correct and elegant composition had found practical emergence. Professor John Bascom, of Williams College, in his "Philosophy of Rhetoric," 1865, was in large part their legatee. The first of the modern rhetorics was that of Professor A. S. Hill in 1878, a volume followed eight years later by Professor J. F. Genung's "The Working Principles of Rhetoric." [Taylor is most likely referring to *The Practical Elements of Rhetoric* (1885). *Working Principles* appeared in 1900.—ED.] The vitality of these texts is proved by their continued use, diminished almost to the vanishing point, and haphazard, but persistent.

The scores of rhetorics issued during the past forty years have in the main been the product of an informed and pragmatic pedagogy that has discarded the lofty and somewhat nebulous theories of the earlier schoolmen and has faced squarely the seeming needs of institutions serving a democracy in which, during these two decades, the number of undergraduates has increased ten fold. It may be, however, that the current rhetoric has tended to make a science of an art.

At present there are signs of rebellion against the dominance of the rhetoric. It still holds its sway in the Middle-West, West, and South, but the older East is discarding it. And this general dissatisfaction is not to be wondered at, for the situation has changed in several ways,—in two particularly. Little attention was paid in high schools and academies before 1870 to the formal study of the writing of the English language, nor did the colleges exact evidence of preparation in the mother tongue. In 1865 for the first time we find English required for entrance to Harvard when the modest statement, "Candidates will also be examined in reading English aloud" was appended to the list of entrance examinations. But for many years past the secondary schools have stressed English,—the excellent private schools of the East and elsewhere with marked success, the public high schools of remote communities with something like failure. Each type of school has succeeded in terms of its teaching personnel and the cultural heritage of its community. But at least a national effort has been made to train secondary students to write with decency. Insofar as this has met with success there has been a decreasing need for administering formal rhetorical principles in the colleges.

The second agent has already been mentioned, the power of student selection possessed largely by endowed institutions. Granted the ability to reject the relatively unprepared, a college may start its Freshmen at a point beyond the simpler rules of rhetoric. The East is in that position today and is exercising its right of choice unremittingly. The 'omnibus' institutions of the rest of the country tend to provide for the better qualified students by sectioning through placement tests and other examinations, and, with their upper group students, to substitute other material for the rhetoric.

The Handbook is still in high favor everywhere, though less beloved in the East where there is a tendency to use it more for mere reference than is evidenced elsewhere. It was in 1907 that Mr. Woolley published the first comprehensive Handbook; since then, as all of us who teach know, there have been many worthy rivals. Its use even in the most aristocratic seat of learning is easily justified: So many of the things that all of us ought to know, and which so few of us do know thoroughly, are indexed and calendared with logical nicety. It will be a long time before the Handbook is history.

The volume of selected essays has found almost as wide favor as the Handbook. Its use even in the East is fairly widespread. It was about twenty years ago that essay volumes began to appear with regularity. And so popular has the form become that practically every text book publishing house has two or three on the college market. When these collections first appeared, it was the convention to draw their material from the works of the great dead. Arnold, Huxley, Macaulay, Newman, were among those who contributed most. I suppose few students of a generation ago will forget Arnold's *Sweetness and Light*. I won't for one. Nor was I grateful for it. These prose anthologies were derived from the classics and, in that they paraded some of the least compelling essays of the masters, they passed into memory without regret. Their passing was speeded, it seems to me, by the fact of the weight and greyness of the essays they selected. Happily all the prose classics are not heavy and colorless. Wisely chosen, perhaps the work of the masters could still engage young America.

Today another story. Many of the present volumes requisition the current magazines for their material, finding much virtue in essays so fresh that they have scarcely been blotted. The trend seems to be in favor of compilations presenting discussion essays, essays that offer challenges to the student mind, that start his thinking apparatus. The content is of chief concern with them. Whether such volumes offer mental discipline and have the power to arouse a sense of appreciation for thought memorably and permanently expressed, is, I suppose, a controversial question. Certainly they are easier to administer. It's another battle of the books with ancients unsaddled.

The facts of the Rhetoric-Handbook-Essay Volume situation can best be presented through tables. I trust that those I offer will be intelligible.

Table I

THE RHETORIC-HANDBOOK-ESSAY VOLUME SITUATION BY
REGIONS AND TYPES OF INSTITUTIONS[1]

	Rhetoric		Handbook		Essay Volume	
	Percentage Students Using	Percentage Institutions Using	Percentage Students Using	Percentage Institutions Using	Percentage Students Using	Percentage Institutions Using
MIDDLE-WEST (79)[2]	69	73	97	96	86	84
(35715)[3]						
STATE UNIVERSITIES (12)	86	82	98	100[4]	86	90
(16500)						
OTHER INSTITUTIONS (67)	55	71	96	95	86	83
(19215)						
EAST (61)	30	40	62	58	56	67
(25717)						
STATE UNIVERSITIES (4)	42	50	84	75	71	75
(1740)						
COEDUCATIONAL (15)	47	60	97	93	46	73
(6847)						

	Rhetoric		Handbook		Essay Volume	
	Percentage Students Using	Percentage Institutions Using	Percentage Students Using	Percentage Institutions Using	Percentage Students Using	Percentage Institutions Using
MEN'S (25)	20	33	44	48	41	50
(12305)						
WOMEN'S (17)	26	31	58	41	83	80
(4825)						
SOUTH (34)	57	60	94	90	94	88
(11055)						
STATE UNIVERSITIES (8)	50	59	100	100	100	100
(4600)						
COEDUCATIONAL (15)	44	46	81	78	84	79
(3360)						
MEN'S (5)	73	86	100	100	91	86
(1130)						
WOMEN'S (6)	87	75	100	100	100	100
(1965)						
WEST (30)	62	65	92	87	95	87
(17170)						
STATE UNIVERSITIES (13)	60	54	93	100[4]	97	92
(10280)						
OTHER INSTITUTIONS (17)	66	75	89	76	91	83
(6890)						
TECHNICAL SCHOOLS (21)	61	57	89	86	82	76
(10500)						
ALL INSTITUTIONS (225)	55	59	86	83	81	80
(100157)						

1. *The Technical Schools are regionally placed as follows: Middle West 4, East 5, South 4, West 8.*
2. *Refers to number of institutions summarized.*
3. *Refers to number of students summarized.*
4. *One institution makes use of Handbook optional with instructors. My assumption was that at least 50% used it.*

Note. All tables in this report are corrected to make requisite allowance for 'blank' and equivocal replies. Tables II, III, and IV present the same matter from different points of view.

Table II

THE RHETORIC-HANDBOOK-ESSAY VOLUME SITUATION BY TYPES OF INSTITUTIONS IRRESPECTIVE OF GEOGRAPHICAL LOCATION[1]

	Rhetoric		Handbook		Essay Volume	
	Percentage Students Using	Percentage Institutions Using	Percentage Students Using	Percentage Institutions Using	Percentage Students Using	Percentage Institutions Using
STATE UNIVERSITIES (37) (33120)	70	63	97	97	90	92
COEDUCATIONAL (107)[2] (34002)	50	62	91	91	78	81
MEN'S (32) (14440)	31	48	53	59	56	56
WOMEN'S (28) (8045)	52	50	72	61	86	81
ALL INSTITUTIONS (225)[3] (101157)	55	59	86	83	81	80

Table III

STATE UNIVERSITIES (37) (33120)	70	63	97	97	90	92
ALL OTHER INSTITUTIONS (188) (67037)	48	56	81	76	75	74

Table IV

EASTERN INSTITUTIONS (61)[4] (25717)	30	40	62	58	56	67
ALL OTHERS (164) (74440)	65	67	95	93	91	34

1. The Technical Schools are entered appropriately according to their classification as coeducational or not.
2. Coeducational—exclusive of state universities.
3. Including technical schools.
4. Not including the five technical schools.

. . . .

B—Literature in Freshman English

It was often difficult to determine, and very naturally, from the questionnaires I received, the extent to which literature is taught in Freshman

English courses. At best literature is an elusive term. There is little question about the matter with the drama, or lyric and epic poetry, forms of literary expression not ordinarily the staples of the first year course. But what of the omnipresent essay or of the short story? Both are literature, of course, if their quality be high enough. The trouble lies in the use made of them. If they are studied from a rhetorical standpoint, dissected for unity, emphasis, and coherence,—if, to put it differently, they are employed as models and stimuli for themes, they become a means to an end and lose their significance as pure literature. So for that matter may Milton's *Lycidas;* at least it did for me. Some who answered my queries on the presence of literature in the Freshman course puzzled me—and this was inevitable—by their replies. When in the following tables I state that literature forms part of the curriculum, I have in mind such an approach to letters as, say, a survey or a literary types course would present.

Table VII
INSTITUTIONS COMBINING RHETORIC AND LITERATURE

	No. With Combination Rhet. and Lit.	Percentage	Proportion of Literature					To a Degre
			25%	33%	50%	66%	100%	
State Universities (37)	13	35						
Middle-West (12)	2	16						2
East (4)	4	100	1	2				1
South (8)	3	43	1	1				1
West (13)	3	23	1	1				1
Older Eastern Institutions								
Men's (20)	14	70	1	3	1	2		7
Women's (7)	5	71				1		4
All Other Institutions[1]								
Middle-West (71)	17	24	1		4	2	2	8
East (35)	25	71		4	7		3	11
South (30)	15	50	2	8	2			3
West (25)	6	24	1	2	1		1	1

1. Includes technical schools.
It will be observed from the above that, according to my interpretation of the answers I received, there are only 9 out of 225 institutions giving only literature to Freshmen.

The appended table shows the number of colleges and universities concerning themselves only with rhetoric during the Freshman year.

Table VIII

TABLE OF FRESHMAN 'RHETORIC' COURSES

Middle-West (83)	65	78%
East (66)	23	35%
South (38)	18	47%
West (38)	28	74%
Middle West and West (121)		73% straight rhetoric courses
East and South (104)		39% straight rhetoric courses

C—The Status of Argumentation, Narrative, and Description

Argumentation, without question, is taught less frequently than it was even a decade ago. It has lost ground with the wane in popularity of college debating. Doubtless the increasing attention given to the study of collections of essays has been a factor. Perhaps this wide use of essay anthologies, demanding more of the calendar temporally, is as responsible as anything else. It may merely be, however, that the Freshman course in its development away from classic procedure has turned naturally from the polemical traditions of earlier years.

Personally I was surprised to find that narration was as little in favor as argumentation. It is an age of fiction, but apparently the study of short stories and novels is generally reserved for courses in literature. And yet, in such courses, although the novel is usually taken up, the short story is not. I had presupposed before facing the facts that the latter was in definite favor. With description the case appears different. One assuming that the form offered merely a fitting introduction to the study of narration will be surprised at the evidence seemingly tending to establish it as an independent type. The following table represents the situation with reasonable accuracy.

Table IX

INSTITUTIONS NOT STUDYING ARGUMENTATION, NARRATIVE, DESCRIPTION[1]

	No Argumentation[3] Number	Percentage	Blank or Questionable	No Narrative[3] Number	Percentage	Blank or Questionable	No Description[3] Number	Percentage	Blank or Questionable
MIDDLE WEST (83)[4]									
Large[2] (34)	17	65%	(8)	21	75%	(3)	3	11%	(6)
Small (49)	20	44%	(4)	36	75%	(4)	4	8%	(1)

	No Argumentation[3] Number	Percentage	Blank or Questionable	No Narrative[3] Number	Percentage	Blank or Questionable	No Description[3] Number	Percentage	Blank or Questionable
EAST (66)[4]									
Large (33)	18	64%	(5)	15	60%	(8)	8	32%	(8)
Small (33)	15	54%	(5)	19	70%	(9)	9	33%	(4)
SOUTH (38)[4]									
Large (21)	7	41%	(4)	12	75%	(2)	2	12%	(5)
Small (17)	4	30%	(2)	11	85%	(2)	2	15%	(4)
WEST (38)[4]									
Large (28)	11	52%	(7)	15	62%	(3)	3	12%	(4)
Small (10)	3	37%	(2)	4	50%	(1)	1	12%	(2)

1. Technical Schools included.
2. By 'large' is meant an institution with 300 or more Freshmen.
3. The numbers and percentages are expressed after due deductions for blank and equivocal returns.
4. Totals before deductions.

. . . .

2. CLASSIFICATION OF STUDENTS

A—Sub-Freshman English, Advanced Freshman English, and Sectioning

There is a strongly growing tendency in the country to assign students to such divisions of Freshman English as will be most suited to their training and capacity. The argument I have heard most often against the practice contends that the draining off of talent from a class leaves a dead-level sediment difficult of stirring up emotionally and mentally; that bright students serve to stimulate dull. But pedagogically the 'ayes' seem to have it: Well prepared and intelligent Freshmen can advance faster and master a more exacting program with greater profit to themselves. The larger institutions, of course, find it simpler to classify than the smaller; the latter have fewer students from whom to select graded divisions and a narrower choice of recitation hours. Many of those who answered my questionnaire had much to say on the matter. There appears to be general dissatisfaction with classes of varied accomplishment.

The usual method of divisioning is by standard placement tests, the use of which seems to be growing; by grammar tests and theme writing; or by a combination of both. At Wisconsin we have four themes written, two impromptu, two prepared, on which we base our sectioning. An elaborate placement test, given during Freshman week, is used to check the theme results and may, in border-line cases, be the determining element in assigning a student to his proper group. With us there are four groups, designated as A, B, C, D. The A group, that of the advanced Freshman sections, comprises 4% of the class, the B group 60%, the C group 30%, and the D group—Sub-Freshman English, for which no credit is given,—6%. The A group is in large part given over to literature; the B group uses no rhetoric and has literary leanings in its handling of the essays, the short stories, and the novel.

Table XI

SUB-FRESHMAN ENGLISH, ADVANCED FRESHMAN ENGLISH, AND OTHER MEANS OF CLASSIFICATION[1]

Institutions with both 'Sub' and 'Adv.' Number	Percentage	Institutions with 'Sub' and not 'Adv.' Number	Percentage	Institutions with 'Adv.' and not 'Sub.' Number	Percentage	Institutions Classifying in other ways Number	Percentage	Institutions not Classifying Number	Percentage
56	26%	30	14%	24	11%	32	15%	74	35%

1. Four 'blank' entries are subtracted from the total of 225 and the 9 (4%) indicating literature only.

· · · · · · · ·

C—Teachers of Professional Rank in Freshman English

Almost everyone is in theory committed to the principle that Freshmen deserve the best, and regrets that the theory should have so little in common with the condition. The institutional budget, in effect a practical ways-and-means committee, stands between the theory and the fact. Treasuries are usually shallow and copper-lined; "Jupiter is poor." And, waiving that, there is often a settled disinclination among older teachers of English, finally entrenched in literature, to do any more of the hard work a writing course entails. I once heard this prejudice expressed in homely Anglo-Saxon by a full professor in a departmental meeting. "No man," he said, "wants to read themes after he has reached forty."—But mutely arraigned against these hostile forces stand the Freshmen. One of the most enlightened comments I received was the following: "Our practice is to put the best men at our disposal in the Freshman course. We should prefer to put a fresh graduate on a senior course." This came from one of the older endowed colleges of the East with ivy on its walls.

When I came to Wisconsin eighteen years ago, every member of the department save one, who had never taught in the course, had at least one section of Freshman English. It was a policy of the department. To-day I am the only person instructing in the regular course. (The four advanced sections, however, are given by assistant professors.) I represent 1.2% of the total instruction,—less than that, really, because my experimental section is ordinarily smaller than the average. During eighteen years, then, professorial participation has shrunk from almost 100% to a negligible figure. But the situation is worse than that. As soon as an instructor gains experience and shows promise, he is drafted to serve other interests, notably those of the advanced courses, the heavy enrollment in which demands competent tutors and readers. The Wisconsin situation is duplicated time and again by other state institutions of the country. Whatever of salvation is found in it is due to the eager loyalty and ungrudging service of the Freshman staffs as constituted.

Table XVI
Proportion of Teachers of Professional Rank in Freshman English[1]

STATE UNIVERSITIES

Middle West	(9)	Average	17%
East	(3)	Average	58%
South	(8)	Average	38%
West	(13)	Average	52%

Note: Wisconsin, Minnesota, Ohio State, and Iowa average 6.7%

EAST (Selected groups)

(Harvard, Yale, Princeton, Columbia average	23%
(Dartmouth, Amherst, Wesleyan, Williams average	66%
(Wellesley, Vassar, Smith, Mt. Holyoke average	65%

1. The percentages presented do not mean the proportion of instruction given, but the percentage of the professorial staff teaching at least one section.

Note: Although I have tried to be accurate in this table, in view of the rough estimating implied in some of the returns, the findings are probably indicative rather than accurate.

D—The Teaching Load

A glance at the table that follows is enough to fill a person with dismay. The average number of Freshman rhetoric students for which an instructor is responsible in the ninety institutions responding intelligibly is 93. It was not very uncommon to find that teaching hours, even where heavy Freshman English demands were made, ran to thirteen or fourteen per week. The most humane situation exists among the older endowed colleges and universities of the East. (See table). At Wisconsin the average is 80. This condition is largely due to restricted budgets. The upper courses, conducted, naturally, by higher-ups, courses often-times with narrow enrollments, are costly to administer; Freshman English can go through its paces with cheap labor and mass production. It would be enlightening if chairmen of the first-year course would obtain from the business managers of their institutions the comparative unit cost per student as between Freshman English and any other course in the curriculums. It would almost seem as if Freshman rhetoric in many places was regarded as a necessary evil; as if, too, the *status quo* was traditionally fixed.

I should say that relatively few places force their instructors to teach Freshman English exclusively. Most of them round out the teaching schedules with quiz or tutorial sections in the elementary, prescribed courses in literature. It is well that it should be so. Those of us who have taught many types of subjects will, I am certain, admit that no one of them demands such an expenditure of nervous force as the Freshman course.

Table XVII
TEACHING LOAD

1. These figures were carefully compiled: they are, however, more indicative than accurate.

2. Colleges employing readers were not included.

3. Colleges giving only literature, and colleges combining literature and rhetoric were not included.

4. It is noteworthy that, however heavy the teaching load, weekly writing requirements did not vary between institutions apportioning few students to an instructor and those apportioning many.

(*continued*)

Table XVII, continued

	Number Replying Definitely	Average Students per semester
LARGER INSTITUTIONS¹	60	94
Middle West	15	88
East	22	91
South	7	108
West	16	101
SMALLER INSTITUTIONS²	30	91
Middle West	12	99
East	11	87
South	5	88
West	2	84
STATE UNIVERSITIES	27	95
Middle West	8	88
East	4	107
South	6	99
West	9	93

EAST (17)—average 73
Older, Endowed Women's Colleges (10) average 69
Older, Endowed Men's Colleges (7) average 78

Note: 1. Institutions with 300 or more Freshmen (60 definite returns)
2. Institutions with fewer than 300 Freshmen (30 definite returns)

E—Percentage of Freshman English Taught By Women

The accompanying table is purely informational. A glance at it will establish the fact, long known to be true whether certified by statistics or not, that the East and South prefer to have their men taught by men, their women by women; and that the Middle West and West, the regions dedicated to co-education, are committed to no such policies. Incidentally, there are very few institutions in the latter sections that do not admit men and women students impartially. Perhaps the differing attitudes can best be shown if we take parallel situations, say those inherent in the co-educational technical schools in the four sections of the country—2 in the Middle West, 3 in the East, 2 in the South, and 4 in the West. (I am omitting men's schools of which there are 2 in each region, and one woman's school in the West. These men's schools everywhere are taught entirely by men; the one woman's 75% by women.) The Middle West and West combined are 43% taught by women, the East and South 2%, one institution having 8% of the instruction given by a woman, the others none.

Several of those who answered the question, "What percentage, if any, of your instruction is given by women?" used blunt pens and bore down hard when they entered "None whatever!," "Absolutely none!" Which showed a state of mind. I sometimes think, however, that of the two, man or woman, the latter has to be the stronger to secure a contested position. Certainly talented women can bring many special endowments to Freshman English.

Table XVIII

PERCENTAGE OF FRESHMAN ENGLISH TAUGHT BY WOMEN[1]

MIDDLE WEST (83)			SOUTH (38)		
Large ins'ts (34)	44%		MEN'S (9)		
Small ins'ts (49)	37%	40%	Large ins'ts (4)	0%	
			Small ins'ts (5)	0%	0%
EAST (66)					
MEN'S (27)			WOMEN'S		
Large inst'ts (17)	0%[2]		Large ins'ts (3)	88%	
Small ins'ts (10)	0%	0%	Small ins'ts (3)	100%	94%
WOMEN'S (17)			COEDUCATIONAL		
Large ins'ts (4)	79%		Large ins'ts (16)	27%	
Small ins'ts (13)	75%	76%	Small ins'ts (7)	48%	33%
COEDUCATIONAL (22)			WEST (38)		
Large ins'ts (13)	25%		Large ins'ts (28)	48%	
Small ins'ts (9)	25%	25%	Small ins'ts (10)	40%	46%
MIDDLE WEST AND WEST					
Large and small (121)	42%				

(continued)

Table XVIII, continued

EAST AND SOUTH (104)	29%	
MEN'S		
Large and small (36)	0%	
WOMEN'S		
Large and small (23)	80%	
COEDUCATIONAL		
Large and small (45)	30%	
STATE UNIVERSITIES		
Middle West and West (24) (Enrollment 26004)		49%[3]
East and South (12) (Enrollment 6890)		22%

1. Includes all American institutions replying to this query—216.
2. One institution stated that less than 10% of its teaching was given by women. I did not take account of this.
3. One State University did not answer question.

F—Readers in Freshman English

I suppose every teacher would admit that ideally an instructor should read his own themes. For a piece of written work is a part of him who wrote it and is to be interpreted in terms of the individual. I think personally that it is entirely possible to judge a theme in the absolute, given the standard imposed, though I know there are many who insist that product cannot be divorced from personality. Certainly living knowledge of a writer informs judgment. And yet there are necessitous situations calling for the aid of reader assistants. A composition teacher can read the work of a limited number of students; when the limit is exceeded, unless the theme schedule be reduced, he must call in outside aid. And he would be the first to admit the imperfection of the system that forced him from a close supervision over what his students were doing. Several teachers who replied to the query regarding the use of readers at their institutions answered with a 'no' in indignant italics. They were sitting in the seats of the fortunate.

Table XIX

READERS IN FRESHMAN ENGLISH

	To small extent	33%	50%	75%	100%	As needed	For drill and mechanics	Minus drill and mechanics
MIDDLE WEST (83)								
Large institutions (34)	3	1	0	0	2	0	4—10 = 30%	18%
Small institutions (49)	4	0	4	2	4	6	3—23 = 48%	42%
EAST (66)								
Large institutions (33)	2	2	0	0	1	1	0—6 = 20%	20%
Small institutions (33)	3	2	3	0	0	0	2—10 = 30%	27%
SOUTH (38)								
Large institutions (21)	1	2	0	1	1	2	1—8 = 38%	33%
Small institutions (17)	1	1	3	1	0	0	0—6 = 35%	35%
WEST (38)								
Large institutions (28)	2	1	2	2	0	2	0—8 = 29%	29%
Small institutions (10)	0	2	1	0	0	0	0—3 = 33%	33%

All sections with drill and mechanics subtracted—
Large institutions—24%
Small institutions—35%

G—Teaching Assistants in Freshman English

I suppose one may, in general, classify assistants under two categories: Those who are merely readers, seniors, extra-departmental aids,—anyone not under regular appointment whose function is to relieve busy teachers from the theme-reading load; and those who are official, part-time members of a staff and who conduct classes of their own in the Freshman course. The former are agents of relief; the latter are ordinarily students taking graduate work, in conjunction with their teaching, thus serving two masters both of whom are often strangers to them when the fall semester opens. The first group is likely to be associated with the small college, the second with the large. For the small institution has no graduate school. As a matter of fact it draws to a relatively slight degree on readers or assistants, only 18% of the instruction and reading being done by assistants as against 47% in the places of heavy enrollment. The graduate-student teacher has apparently come to stay. Universities find him useful. Not only does he bring youthful eagerness and a spirit of ready cooperation to his new profession, but he adds to the numbers in the graduate schools—a condition wholly acceptable to those responsible for the creation of Masters of Arts and Doctors. There is, of course, potential danger in the situation: it's a question of sane balance in the composition of a staff. Chairmen of departments who put the needs of Freshman English first will see to it that there is a ponderable nucleus of experienced instructors on the first-year corps. Any large university can gracefully absorb a certain percentage of novitiate teachers; but the determination of the danger point is a matter for informed deliberation.

Table XX
Teaching Assistants in Freshman English[1]

	Yes	Rarely, to small extent	No	Percent using assistants	
MIDDLE WEST (83)					
Large institutions (34)	10	6	17	48	
Small institutions (49)	0	5	39	11	27%
EAST (66)					
Large institutions (33)	6	4	17	37	
Small institutions (33)	5	2	21	25	31%
SOUTH (38)					
Large institutions (21)	3	6	12	43	
Small institutions (17)	4	0	9	31	38%
WEST (38)					
Large institutions (28)	9	7	11	59	
Small institutions (10)	1	0	6	14	50%
	38	30	132	34%	

All large institutions—47%
All small institutions—18%

1. Subtractions were made for 'blank' entries and for institutions having only literature.

Bibliography

PRIMARY SOURCES: BOOKS

Abbott, Edwin A. *How to Write Clearly: Rules and Exercises on English Composition.* Boston: Roberts Brothers, 1875.

Abstract of Hill's Rhetoric: English A in Harvard College. Cambridge: William H. Wheeler, Printer and Publishers, 1888.

Adams, Charles Francis. *Three Phi Beta Kappa Addresses.* Boston: Houghton Mifflin, 1907.

———. *An Autobiography, with a Memorial Address Delivered November 17, 1915 by Henry Cabot Lodge.* Boston: Massachusetts Historical Society, 1916. Reprint, New York: Russell and Russell, 1968.

Adams, Charles Francis, Edwin Lawrence Godkin, and George R. Nutter, *Report of the Committee on Composition and Rhetoric.* Cambridge: Harvard University, 1895.

———. *Report of the Committee on Composition and Rhetoric.* Cambridge: Harvard University, 1896.

———. *Report of the Committee on Composition and Rhetoric.* Cambridge: Harvard University, 1897.

Adams, Charles Francis, Edwin Lawrence Godkin, and Josiah Quincy, *Report of the Committee on Composition and Rhetoric.* Cambridge: Harvard University, 1892.

Aydelotte, Frank. *The Oxford Stamp and Other Essays: Articles from the Educational Creed of an American Oxonian.* New York: Oxford University Press, 1917.

———. *College English: A Manual for the Study of English Literature and Composition.* New York: Oxford University Press, 1913.

Babbitt, Irving. *Literature and the American College: Essays in Defense of the Humanities.* Boston: Houghton Mifflin, 1908.

Baker, George Pierce. *Specimens of Argumentation.* New York: Henry Holt and Co., 1893.

Baldwin, Charles Sears. *A College Manual of Rhetoric.* New York: Longmans, Green, 1917.

————. *College Composition*. New York: Longmans, Green, 1902.

Bates, Arlo. *Talks on Writing English, First Series*. Boston: Houghton Mifflin, 1896. 2nd series, 1901.

Berkeley, Frances Campbell. *A College Course in Writing from Models*. New York: Henry Holt and Co., 1910. (See also Young, p. 567.)

Brewster, William Tenney. *Studies in Structure and Style (Based on Seven Modern English Essays)*. With an introduction by George Rice Carpenter. New York: Macmillan, 1896.

Brown, Rollo Walter. *Dean Briggs*. New York: Harper and Brothers, 1926.

————. *Harvard Yard in the Golden Age*. New York: Current Books, 1948.

————. *How the French Boy Learns to Write: A Study in the Teaching of the Mother Tongue*. Cambridge: Harvard University Press, 1915.

Buck, Gertrude. *A Course in Argumentative Writing*. New York: Henry Holt and Co., 1899.

————. *The Metaphor: A Study in the Psychology of Rhetoric*. Contributions to Rhetorical Theory no. 9. Ann Arbor: Inland Press, 1899.

Buck, Gertrude, and Elisabeth Woodbridge. *A Course in Expository Writing*. New York: Henry Holt and Co., 1899.

Buck, Gertrude, and Elisabeth Woodbridge Morris. *A Course in Narrative Writing*. New York: Henry Holt and Co., 1906.

Carson, Luella Clay. *Compiliation of Standard Rules and Regulations Used by the English Department of the University of Oregon*. Eugene, Ore.: University of Oregon Press, 1898.

————. *Handbook of English Composition: A Compilation of Standard Rules and Usage*. 3rd ed. Yonkers-On-Hudson, N.Y.: World Book Co., 1907.

Channing, Edward Tyrrel. *Lectures Read to the Seniors in Harvard College*. 1856. Reprint, edited by Dorothy I. Anderson and Waldo W. Braden. Carbondale: Southern Illinois University Press, 1968.

Cook, Albert Stanburrough. *The Higher Study of English*. Boston: Houghton Mifflin, 1906.

Cooper, Lane. *Theories of Style: With Especial Reference to Prose Composition*. New York: Macmillan, 1907. Reprinted as *The Art of the Writer*. Ithaca: Cornell University Press, 1952.

————. *Two Views of Education*. New Haven: Yale University Press, 1922.

Copeland, Charles Townsend. *The Copeland Reader: An Anthology of English Poetry and Prose*. New York: Charles Scribner's Sons, 1926.

Copeland, Charles Townsend, and H. M. Rideout. *Freshman English and Theme-Correcting in Harvard College*. New York: Silver, Burdett, 1901.

Cross, Wilbur L. *Connecticut Yankee: An Autobiography*. New Haven: Yale University Press, 1943.

Curl, Mervin James. *Expository Writing*. Boston: Houghton Mifflin, 1919.

Du Bois, W.E.B. *Autobiography of W.E.B. Du Bois: A Soliloquy on Viewing My Life from the Last Decade of Its First Century.* New York: International Publishers, 1968.

Erskine, John. *My Life as a Teacher.* Philadelphia: J. B. Lippincott and Co., 1948.

Erskine, John, and Helen Erskine. *Written English: A Guide to the Rules of Composition.* New York: The Century Co., 1910. Revised edition, 1914.

Foerster, Norman. *Outlines and Summaries: A Handbook for the Analysis of Expository Essays.* New York: Henry Holt and Co., 1915.

Foerster, Norman, and John Marcellus Steadman Jr. *Sentences and Thinking: A Practice Book in Sentence Making.* Boston: Houghton Mifflin, 1914.

————. *Sentences and Thinking: A Handbook of Composition and Revision.* 2nd ed. Boston: Houghton Mifflin, 1923.

————. *Writing and Thinking.* (3rd ed. of *Sentences and Thinking.*) Boston: Houghton Mifflin, 1931. 4th ed., 1941. 5th ed., revised by James B. McMillan, 1952.

Foerster, Norman, Frederick A. Manchester, and Karl Young. *Essays for College Men.* New York: Henry Holt and Co., 1913. 2nd Series, 1915.

Fulton, Maurice Garland. *Expository Writing.* New York: Macmillan, 1912.

————. *College Life: Its Conditions and Problems.* New York: Macmillan, 1914.

Genung, John Franklin. *Handbook of Rhetorical Analysis: Studies in Style and Invention.* Boston: Ginn and Co., 1888.

————. *Outlines of Rhetoric; embodied in rules, illustrative examples and a progressive course of prose composition.* Boston: Ginn and Co., 1893.

————. *The Practical Elements of Rhetoric, with Illustrative Examples.* Amherst: Press of J. E. Williams, 1885.

————. *The Study of Rhetoric in the College Course.* Boston: D. C. Heath, 1887.

————. *The Working Principles of Rhetoric.* Boston: Ginn and Co., 1900.

Hart, James Morgan. *A Handbook of English Composition.* Philadelphia: Eldredge and Brother, 1895.

Hill, Adams Sherman. *Beginnings of Rhetoric and Composition, Including Practical Exercises in English.* New York: American Book Co., 1902.

————. *The Foundations of Rhetoric.* New York: Harper and Brothers, 1892.

————. *Our English.* New York: Harper and Brothers, 1889.

————. *The Principles of Rhetoric and Their Application.* New York: Harper and Brothers, 1878. 2nd ed., 1895.

Hofstadter, Richard, and Wilson Smith, eds., *American Higher Education: A Documentary History.* 2 vols. Chicago: University of Chicago Press, 1961.

Howe, Mark A. DeWolfe. *Barrett Wendell and His Letters.* Boston: Atlantic Monthly Press, 1924.

Hunt, Theodore W. *The Principles of Written Discourse.* New York: A. C. Armstrong and Son, 1884.

Lomer, Gerhard R., and Margaret Ashmun. *The Study and Practice of Writing English.* Boston: Houghton Mifflin, 1914.

Manly, John Matthews, and Edith Rickert. *The Writing of English.* New York: Henry Holt and Co., 1919.

Mead, William Edward. *Elementary Composition and Rhetoric.* Boston: Leach, Shewell, and Sanborn, 1894.

Nason, Arthur Huntington. *Efficient Composition: A College Rhetoric.* New York: New York University Press, 1917.

Northup, Clark Sutherland, Martin Wright Sampson, William Strunk, Jr., and Frank Thilly, eds. *Studies in Language and Literature in Celebration of the Seventieth Birthday of James Morgan Hart, November 2, 1909.* New York: Henry Holt and Co., 1910.

Patee, Fred N. *Tradition and Jazz.* New York: Century Co., 1925.

Payne, William Morton, ed. *English in American Universities, by Professors in the English Departments of Twenty Representative Institutions.* Boston: D. C. Heath, 1895.

Pearson, Henry G. *Freshman Composition.* With an introduction by Arlo Bates. Boston: D. C. Heath, 1897.

Perry, Bliss. *And Gladly Teach.* Boston: Houghton Mifflin, 1935.

Phelps, William Lyon. *Teaching in School and College.* New York: Macmillan, 1912.

Potter, Howard Eugene. *Abilities and Disabilities in the Use of English Found in the Written Compositions of Entering Freshmen at the University of California.* University of California, Bureau of Research in Education Study no. 12. Berkeley and Los Angeles: University of California, 1922.

Richmond, Mary E. *The Long View: Papers and Addresses.* Edited by Joanna C. Colcord and Ruth Z. S. Mann. New York: Russell Sage Foundation, 1930.

Scott, Franklin William, and Jacob Zeitlin. *College Readings in English Prose.* New York: Macmillan, 1914.

Scott, Fred Newton. *The Standard of American Speech and Other Papers.* Boston: Allyn and Bacon, 1926.

Scott, Fred Newton, and Joseph Villiers Denney. *Composition-Literature.* Boston: Allyn and Bacon, 1903.

———. *The New Composition-Rhetoric.* Boston: Allyn and Bacon, 1911.

———. *Paragraph-Writing.* Boston: Allyn and Bacon, 1893.

Sherman, Lucius Adelno. *Analytics of Literature: A Manual for the Objective Study of English Prose and Poetry.* Boston: Ginn and Co., 1893.

Slosson, Edwin Emery. *Great American Universities.* New York: Macmillan, 1910.

Steeves, Harrison Ross, and Frank Humphrey Ristine, eds. *Representative Essays in Modern Thought: A Basis for Composition.* New York: American Book Co., 1913.

Strunk, William, Jr. *The Elements of Style*. Ithaca, N.Y.: privately printed, 1918.

Taylor, Warner. *A National Survey of Conditions in Freshman English*. University of Wisconsin Bureau of Educational Research Bulletin no. 11. Madison: University of Wisconsin, 1929.

Twenty Years of School and College English. Cambridge: Harvard University, 1896.

Wendell, Barrett. *English Composition, Eight Lectures Given at the Lowell Institute*. New York: Charles Scribner's Sons, 1891. Reprint, 1894.

Woolley, Edwin Campbell. *Handbook of Composition*. Boston: D. C. Heath, 1907.

Young, Frances Berkeley, and Karl Young, *Freshman English: A Manual*. New York: Henry Holt and Co., 1914. (See also Berkeley, p. 564.)

PRIMARY SOURCES: ARTICLES AND CHAPTERS

Adams, Charles Francis. "Preparatory School Education: The Classics and Written English." *Harvard Graduates Magazine* 1 (January 1893): 177–89.

Aydelotte, Frank. "English As Training in Thought." *Educational Review* 43 (April 1912): 354–77.

Briggs, Le Baron Russell. "The Harvard Admission Examination in English." *The Academy* (1888). Reprinted in *Twenty Years of School and College English*. Cambridge: Harvard University, 1896.

———. "The Correction of Bad English as a Requirement for Admission to Harvard College." *The Academy* (1890). Reprinted in *Twenty Years of School and College English*. Cambridge: Harvard University, 1896.

Buck, Gertrude. "Recent Tendencies in the Teaching of English Composition." *Educational Review* 22 (November 1901): 371–82.

———. "What Does Rhetoric Mean?" *Educational Review* 22 (September 1901): 197–200.

Cook, Albert Stanburrough. "The Teaching of English." *Atlantic Monthly* 87 (1901): 710–22. Reprinted in *The Higher Study of English*. Boston: Houghton Mifflin, 1906: 37–70.

Cooper, Lane. "On the Teaching of Written Composition." *Education* 30 (March 1910): 421–30. Reprinted in *Two Views of Education*. New Haven: Yale University Press, 1922: 72–87.

———. "The Correction of Papers." *English Journal* 3 (May 1914): 290–98. Reprinted in *Two Views of Education*. New Haven: Yale University Press, 1922: 88–104.

Creek, Herbert LeSourd, and James Hugh McKee. "The Preparation in English of Purdue Freshmen." *Purdue Studies in Higher Education* 5. Lafayette, Ind.: Purdue University Bureau of Educational Reference, 1926.

Dodd, William G. "Some Objects and Problems in Teaching English." *Bulletin of the Florida State College for Women* 7 (December 1914): 1–17.

Eliot, Charles William. "The New Education." *Atlantic Monthly* 23 (1869): 203–20; 358–67.

Gardiner, J. B. "Training in Illiteracy." *School Review* 17 (1909): 623–30.

Garnett, James M. "English in the Preparatory Schools." Read before the Virginia Association for the Advancement of Higher Education at White Sulfur Springs, West Virginia, July 9th, 1890. Pamphlet, n.d.

Godkin, Edwin Lawrence. "Rhetorical Training." *The Nation* 20 (4 March 1875): 145–46.

Goodwin, W. W. "The Root of the Evil." *Harvard Graduates Magazine* 1 (January 1893): 189–93.

Gurney, E. W. "Report of Dean of Faculty." In *Forty-Fifth Annual Report of the President of Harvard College, 1869–70.* Cambridge: Harvard University Press, 1871.

Hart, James Morgan. "Cornell Course in Rhetoric and English Philology." *The Academy* (1891): 181–93.

Hill, Adams Sherman. "An Answer to the Cry for More English" (1879). Reprinted in *Twenty Years of School and College English.* Cambridge: Harvard University, 1896.

Hillegas, Milo Burdette. "Scale for the Measurement of Quality in English Composition by Young People." *Teachers College Record* 13 (1912). Reprint, New York: Teachers College, 1913.

Hurlbut, Byron S. "College Requirements in English." *The Academy* (1892). Reprinted in *Twenty Years of School and College English.* Cambridge: Harvard University, 1896.

———. "The Preparatory Work in English as Seen by a Harvard Examiner." *The Academy* (1891). Reprinted in *Twenty Years of School and College English.* Cambridge: Harvard University, 1896.

"Instructions to Students in Rhetoric 1–2." Minneapolis: University of Minnesota Department of Rhetoric and Public Speaking, 1913.

Lounsbury, Thomas Raynesford. "Compulsory Composition in Colleges." *Harper's Monthly* 123 (1911): 866–80.

Mead, William Edward. "Report of the Pedagogical Section: The Graduate Study of Rhetoric." *PMLA* 16 (1901): xix–xxxii.

———. "Report of the Pedagogical Section: The Undergraduate Study of English Composition." *PMLA* 17 (1902): x–xxiv.

———. "Report of the Pedagogical Section: The Undergraduate Study of English Composition." *PMLA* 18 (1903): viii–xxiii.

O'Neill, J. M. "The National Association." *Quarterly Journal of Public Speaking* 1 (1915): 51–58.

569

bibliography

"Outline of Rhetoric 1." Champaign, Ill.: University of Illinois, 1907.

Scott, Fred Newton. "College-Entrance Requirements in English." *School Review* 9 (1901): 365–78.

———. "What the West Wants in Preparatory Education." *School Review* 17 (1909): 10–20.

Steeves, Harrison Ross. "The Cultivation of Ideas in the College Writing Course." *Educational Review* 44 (June 1912): 45–54.

Stevenson, Robert Louis. "A College Magazine" (1873). Reprinted in *The Travels and Essays of Robert Louis Stevenson*. New York: Charles Scribner's Sons, 1900. Vol. 13; 211–22.

"Two Ways of Teaching English." *Century Magazine* 51 (1896): 793–94.

Valentine, Robert Grosvenor. "On Criticism of Themes by Students." *Technology Review* 2 (1901): 459–78.

Woolley, Edwin Campbell. "Admission to Freshman English in the University." *English Journal* 3 (1914): 238–44.

Young, Karl. "The Organization of a Course in Freshman English." *English Journal* 4 (1915): 63–64.

SECONDARY SOURCES: BOOKS

Adams, James Donald. *Copey of Harvard: A Biography of Charles Townsend Copeland*. Boston: Houghton Mifflin, 1960.

Applebee, Arthur N. *Tradition and Reform in the Teaching of English: A History*. Urbana, Ill.: National Council of Teachers of English, 1974.

Berlin, James A. *Rhetoric and Reality: Writing Instruction in American Colleges, 1900–1985*. Carbondale: Southern Illinois University Press, 1987.

———. *Writing Instruction in Nineteenth-Century American Colleges*. Carbondale: Southern Illinois University Press, 1984.

Blanshard, Frances. *Frank Aydelotte of Swarthmore*. Edited by Brand Blanshard. Middletown, Conn.: Wesleyan University Press, 1970.

Brereton, John, ed. *Traditions of Inquiry*. New York: Oxford University Press, 1985.

Campbell, JoAnn Louise. *Gertrude Buck and the Celebration of Community: A History of Writing Instruction at Vassar College*. Ph.D. dissertation, University of Texas at Austin, 1989.

Cmiel, Kenneth. *Democratic Eloquence: The Fight Over Popular Speech in Nineteenth-Century America*. New York: William Morrow and Co., 1990.

Cremin, Lawrence. *American Education: The Metropolitan Experience*. New York: Harper and Row, 1988.

Crowley, Sharon. *The Methodical Memory: Invention in Current-Traditional Rhetoric*. Carbondale: Southern Illinois University Press, 1990.

The Department of English at Indiana University Bloomington, 1868–1970. Bloomington: Indiana University, 1974.

Diehl, Carl. *Americans and German Scholarship, 1770–1870.* New Haven: Yale University Press, 1978.

Gere, Anne Ruggles. *Writing Groups: History, Theory, and Implications.* Carbondale: Southern Illinois University Press, 1987.

Graff, Gerald. *Professing Literature: An Institutional History.* Chicago: University of Chicago Press, 1987.

Graff, Gerald, and Michael Warner, eds. *The Origins of Literary Studies in America, a Documentary Anthology.* New York and London: Routledge, 1989.

Hook, Julius Nicholas. *A Long Way Together: A Personal View of NCTE's First Sixty-Seven Years.* Urbana: National Council of Teachers of English, 1979.

Horner, Winifred Bryan, ed. *The Present State of Scholarship in Historical and Contemporary Rhetoric.* Revised edition. Columbia, Mo.: University of Missouri Press, 1990.

Johnson, Loaz. *The Administrative Function of English in the University of California: The Evolution of the Examination in Subject A.* University of California Publications in Education, vol. 7, no. 4. Berkeley and Los Angeles: University of California Press, 1941.

Johnson, Nan. *Nineteenth-Century Rhetoric in North America.* Carbondale: Southern Illinois University Press, 1991.

Kitzhaber, Albert R. *Rhetoric in American Colleges, 1850–1900.* Dallas: Southern Methodist University Press, 1990.

Kliebard, Herbert M. *The Struggle for the American Curriculum, 1893–1958.* New York and London: Routledge, 1989.

Krug, Edward August. *The Shaping of the American High School.* 2 vols. Madison: University of Wisconsin Press, 1969–72.

Martin, Theodora Penny. *The Sound of Our Own Voices: Women's Study Clubs, 1860–1910.* Boston: Beacon Press, 1987.

Miller, Susan. *Rescuing the Subject: A Critical Introduction to Rhetoric and the Writer.* Carbondale: Southern Illinois University Press, 1989.

———. *Textual Carnivals: The Politics of Composition.* Carbondale: Southern Illinois University Press, 1991.

Morison, Samuel Eliot. *The Development of Harvard University Since the Inauguration of President Eliot, 1869–1929.* Cambridge: Harvard University Press, 1930.

Morris, Elizabeth Woodbridge, ed. *Miss Wylie of Vassar.* New Haven: Yale University Press, 1934.

Murphy, James J., ed. *The Rhetorical Tradition and Modern Writing.* New York: The Modern Language Association of America, 1982.

North, Stephen M. *The Making of Knowledge in Composition: Portrait of an Emerging Field.* Upper Montclair, N.J.: Boynton/Cook Publishers, 1987.

Ohmann, Richard. *English in America: A Radical View of the Profession.* New York: Oxford University Press, 1976.

———. *Politics of Letters.* Middletown, Conn.: Wesleyan University Press, 1987.

Rampersad, Arnold. *The Art and Imagination of W.E.B. Du Bois.* Cambridge: Harvard University Press, 1976.

Rubin, Joan Shelley. *The Making of Middlebrow Culture.* Chapel Hill: University of North Carolina Press, 1992.

Rudolph, Frederick. *The American College and University: A History.* New York: Knopf, 1962.

———. *Curriculum: A History of the American Undergraduate Course of Study Since 1636.* San Francisco: Jossey-Bass Publishers, 1977.

Russell, David R. *Writing in the Academic Disciplines, 1870–1990: A Curricular History.* Carbondale: Southern Illinois University Press, 1991.

Seager, Allan. *The Glass House: The Life of Theodore Roethke.* New York: McGraw-Hill, 1968.

Simmons, Lovie Sue. *A Critique of the Stereotype of Current-Traditional Rhetoric: Invention in Writing Instruction at Harvard, 1875–1900.* Ph.D. dissertation, University of Texas at Austin, 1991.

Trachsel, Mary. *Institutionalizing Literacy: The Historical Role of College Entrance Examinations in English.* Carbondale: Southern Illinois University Press, 1992.

Veysey, Laurence R. *The Emergence of the American University.* Chicago: University of Chicago Press, 1965.

Weir, Vickie E. *Revisioning Traditions Through Rhetoric: Studies in Gertrude Buck's Social Theory of Discourse.* Ph.D. dissertation, Texas Christian University, 1989.

Wozniak, John Michael. *English Composition in Eastern Colleges, 1850–1940.* Washington, D.C.: University Press of America, 1978.

SECONDARY SOURCES: ARTICLES AND CHAPTERS

Berlin, James. "Revisionary History: The Dialectical Method." *Pre/Text* 8 (1987): 47–61.

Brereton, John. "Composition and English Departments, 1900–1925." In *Audits of Meaning: A Festschrift in Honor of Ann E. Berthoff.* Edited by Louise Z. Smith. Portsmouth, N.H.: Boynton/Cook Publishers, 1988: 41–54.

Campbell, JoAnn. "Controlling Voices: The Legacy of English A at Radcliffe College 1883–1917." *College Composition and Communication* 43 (1992), 472–85.

Connors, Robert J. "Grammar in American College Composition: An Historical Overview." In *The Territory of Language: Linguistics, Stylistics, and the Teach-*

ing of Composition. Edited by Donald A. McQuade. Carbondale: Southern Illinois University Press, 1986: 3–22.

———. "Handbooks: History of a Genre." *Rhetoric Society Quarterly* 13 (1983): 87–98.

———. "Mechanical Correctness as a Focus in Composition Instruction." *College Composition and Communication* 36 (1985): 61–72.

———. "Overwork/Underpay: Labor and Status of Composition Teachers Since 1880." *Rhetoric Review* 9 (1990): 108–25.

———. "Personal Writing Assignments." *College Composition and Communication* 38 (1987): 166–83.

———. "Rhetoric in the Modern University: The Creation of an Underclass." In *The Politics of Writing Instruction: Postsecondary.* Edited by Richard H. Bullock and John Trimbur. Portsmouth, N.H.: Boynton/Cook Publishers, 1991: 55–84.

———. "The Rhetoric of Mechanical Correctness." In *Only Connect: Uniting Reading and Writing.* Edited by Thomas Newkirk. Upper Montclair, N.J.: Boynton/Cook Publishers, 1986: 27–58. (This is an enlarged version of "Mechanical Correctness as a Focus in Composition Instruction," above.)

———. "The Rise and Fall of the Modes of Discourse." *College Composition and Communication* 32 (1981): 444–55.

———. "The Rise of Technical Writing Instruction in America." *Journal of Technical Writing and Communication* 12 (1982): 329–51.

———. "Textbooks and the Evolution of the Discipline." *College Composition and Communication* 37 (1986): 178–94.

———. "Writing the History of Our Discipline." In *An Introduction to Composition Studies.* Edited by Erika Lindemann and Gary Tate. New York: Oxford University Press, 1991: 49–71.

Corbett, Edward P. J. "The Cornell School of Rhetoric." *Rhetoric Review* 4 (1985): 4–14.

Douglas, Wallace. "Accidental Institution: On the Origin of Modern Language Study," In *Criticism in the University.* Edited by Gerald Graff and Reginald Gibbons. Evanston: Northwestern University Press, 1985: 35–61.

———. "Barrett Wendell," In *Traditions of Inquiry.* Edited by John Brereton. New York: Oxford University Press, 1985: 3–25.

———. "Barrett Wandell and the Contradictions of Composition." *Arizona English Bulletin* 16 (February 1974), 182–90.

———. "Rhetoric for the Meritocracy." In *English in America: A Radical View of the Profession.* Edited by Richard Ohmann. New York: Oxford University Press, 1976: 97–132.

Gere, Anne Ruggles. "Kitchen Tables and Rented Rooms: The Extracurriculum of Composition." *College Composition and Communication* 45 (1994), 75–92.

Hall, David. "The Victorian Connection." In *Victorian America*. Edited by Daniel Walker Howe. Philadelphia: University of Pennsylvania Press, 1976: 81–94.

Halloran, Michael. "Rhetoric in the American College Curriculum: The Decline of Public Discourse." *Pre/Text* 3 (1982): 245–69.

Hollis, Karyn. "Liberating Voices: Autobiographical Writing at the Bryn Mawr Summer School for Women Workers, 1921–38." *College Composition and Communication* 45 (1994), 31–60.

Jolliffe, David A. "The Moral Subject in College Composition: A Conceptual Framework and the Case of Harvard, 1865–1900." *College English* 51 (1989): 163–73.

Lindemann, Erika. "Student Writing at the University of North Carolina, 1800–1860." Paper presented at annual meeting of the Conference on College Composition and Communication, San Diego, April 1993.

Miller, Thomas P. "Where Did College English Studies Come From?" *Rhetoric Review* 9 (Fall 1990): 50–68.

Moran, Michael. "Frank Aydelotte, Social Criticism, and Freshman English." *Notes on Teaching English* 18 (May 1991): 13–19.

Newkirk, Thomas. "Barrett Wendell's Theory of Discourse." *Rhetoric Review* 19 (1991): 20–30.

Parker, William Riley. "Where Do English Departments Come From?" *College English* 28 (1967): 339–51. Reprinted in *The Writing Teacher's Sourcebook*. Edited by Gary Tate and Edward P. J. Corbett. 2nd ed. New York: Oxford University Press, 1988: 3–15.

Ried, Paul E. "Francis J. Child: The Fourth Boylston Professor of Rhetoric and Oratory." *Quarterly Journal of Speech* 55 (1969): 268–75.

Reid, Ronald F. "The Boylston Professorship of Rhetoric and Oratory, 1806–1904: A Case Study in Changing Concepts of Rhetoric and Pedagogy." *Quarterly Journal of Speech* 45 (1959): 239–57.

Schilb, John. "Differences, Displacements, and Disruptions: Toward Revisionary Histories of Rhetoric." *Pre/Text* 8 (1987): 29–44.

Sollors, Werner. "A Critique of Pure Pluralism." In *Reconstructing American Literary History*. Edited by Sacvan Bercovitch. Cambridge: Harvard University Press, 1986: 250–79.,

Stewart, Donald. "The Status of Composition and Rhetoric in American Colleges, 1880–1902: An MLA Perspective." *College English* 47 (1975): 734–46.

———. "Fred Newton Scott," In *Traditions of Inquiry*. Edited by John Brereton. New York: Oxford University Press, 1985: 26–49.

———. "Harvard's Influence on English Studies: Perceptions from Three Universities in the Early Twentieth Century." *College Composition and Communication* 43 (1992), 455–71.

————. "The Nineteenth Century," In *The Present State of Scholarship in Historical and Contemporary Rhetoric.* Edited by Winifred Bryan Horner. Revised edition, Columbia, Mo.: University of Missouri Press, 1990: 151–70.

————. "Rediscovering Fred Newton Scott." *College English* 40 (1979): 539–47.

————. "Two Model Teachers and the Harvardization of English Departments." In *The Rhetorical Tradition and Modern Writing.* Edited by James J. Murphy. New York: The Modern Language Association of America, 1982.

Turner, James. "Secularization and Sacralization: Speculations on Some Religious Origins of the Secular Humanities Curriculum, 1850–1900." In *The Secularization of the Academy.* Edited by George M. Marsden, and Bradley J. Longfield. New York: Oxford University Press, 1992: 74–106.

Veysey, Laurence R. "Stability and Experiment in the American College Curriculum." In *Content and Context.* Edited by Carl Kaysen. New York: McGraw Hill, 1973: 1–63.

————. "The Plural Organized Worlds of the Humanities." In *The Organization of Knowledge in Modern America, 1860–1920.* Edited by Alexandra Oleson and John Voss. Baltimore: Johns Hopkins University Press, 1979: 51–106.

Vitanza, Victor. " 'Notes' Towards Historiographies of Rhetorics: Or the Rhetorics of the Histories of Rhetorics: Traditional, Revisionary, and Sub/Versive." *PrelText* 8 (1987): 63–125.

Index

This index lists people and institutions. Boldface indicates a quoted passage.

PITTSBURGH SERIES IN COMPOSITION, LITERACY, AND CULTURE

David Bartholomae and
Jean Ferguson Carr, Editors

Academic Discourse and Critical Consciousness
Patricia Bizzell

Between Languages and Cultures: Translation and Cross-Cultural Texts
Anuradha Dingwaney and Carol Maier, Editors

Eating on the Street: Teaching Literacy in a Multicultural Society
David Schaafsma

The Emperor's New Clothes: Literature, Literacy, and the Ideology of
Style
Kathryn T. Flannery

Feminine Principles and Women's Experience in American
Composition and Rhetoric
Louise Wetherbee Phelps and Janet Emig, Editors

Fragments of Rationality: Postmodernity and the Subject of
Composition
Lester Faigley

The Insistence of the Letter
Bill Green, Editor

Knowledge, Culture, and Power: International Perspectives on Literacy
as Policy and Practice
Peter Freebody and Anthony R. Welch, Editors

Literacy Online: The Promise (and Peril) of Reading and Writing with
Computers
Myron C. Tuman, Editor

The Origins of Composition Studies in the American College, 1875–
1925: A Documentary History
John C. Brereton

The Powers of Literacy: A Genre Approach to Teaching Writing
Bill Cope and Mary Kalantzis, Editors

Pre/Text: The First Decade
Victor Vitanza, Editor

Word Perfect: Literacy in the Computer Age
Myron C. Tuman

Writing Science: Literacy and Discursive Power
M.A.K. Halliday and J.R. Martin